Rereading America

Cultural Contexts for
Critical Thinking and Writing

Rereading America

Cultural Contexts for Critical Thinking and Writing

Edited by

Gary Colombo
UNIVERSITY OF CALIFORNIA, LOS ANGELES
Robert Cullen
SAN JOSE STATE UNIVERSITY
Bonnie Lisle
UNIVERSITY OF CALIFORNIA, LOS ANGELES

A Bedford Book

St. Martin's Press · New York

For Bedford Books

Publisher: Charles H. Christensen
Associate Publisher: Joan E. Feinberg
Managing Editor: Elizabeth M. Schaaf
Developmental Editor: Ellen Darion
Production Editor: Mary Lou Wilshaw
Copyeditor: Deborah Fogel
Text Design: Daniel Earl Thaxton
Cover Design: Hannus Design Associates

Library of Congress Catalog Card Number: 88–70429

Copyright © 1989 by St. Martin's Press, Inc.

Manufactured in the United States of America.

3   2   1
j   i   h

For information, write: St. Martin's Press, Inc.
175 Fifth Avenue, New York, NY 10010

Editorial Offices: Bedford Books of St. Martin's Press
29 Winchester Street, Boston, MA 02116

ISBN: 0–312–00846–5

Acknowledgments
Paula Gunn Allen, "Where I Come from Is Like This." From *The Sacred Hoop: Recovering the Feminine in American Indian Traditions,* by Paula Gunn Allen. Copyright © 1986 by Paula Gunn Allen. Reprinted by permission of Beacon Press.

Acknowledgments and copyrights are continued at the back of the book on pages 661–665, which constitute an extension of the copyright page.

Preface for Instructors

What's Different About This Reader

Designed for freshman writing classes, *Rereading America* anthologizes a diverse set of selections on a single theme: personal and cultural identity in a pluralistic society. The idea of pluralism in the United States brings together 76 readings on a broad range of topics — social justice, cultural assimilation, feminism, family, education, work, television — topics that raise controversial issues meaningful to college students of all races and backgrounds. We've drawn these readings from many sources, both within the academy and outside of it; the selections are both cross-cultural and cross-curricular, and therefore represent an unusual variety of voices, styles, and subjects.

The readings in this text speak directly to students' experiences and concerns. Every eighteen-year-old has had some brush with prejudice, and most have something to say about the changing family or the stereotypes they see on television. The issues raised here help students link their personal experiences with broader cultural perspectives and lead students to analyze, or "read," the cultural forces that have shaped and continue to shape their lives. And these readings allow us to show students that they are not academic outsiders — that they do have knowledge, assumptions, and intellectual frameworks that give them authority within academic culture. Connecting personal knowledge and academic discourse helps students see that they are able to think, speak, and write academically and that they don't have to absorb passively what the "experts" say.

At the heart of this collection is our dedication first to a unified book — not just a disconnected series of chapters — and second to broad ethnic representation among its authors. We propose here a coherent curriculum in which women and minority writers are central, not peripheral, and one which revolves around thought-provoking readings. These writers do not shy away from issues like racism and gay parenthood; indeed, many of the selections question comfortable views of the world. Nor do we condescend to students by relying primarily on simple, straightforward narratives. We've included some quite challenging readings, because we've found that underprepared as well as advanced writers can master difficult materials, given sufficient context and incentive.

Critical Thinking in the Classroom

Although many composition instructors agree that it's important to teach students how to write academic prose, methods differ widely. Most popular strategies focus on getting students to *sound* like academics by teaching appropriate style, tone, and language (current-traditional rhetoric, sentence combining) or by training them to shape ideas into academic *form* (rhetorical modes, cross-curricular models). We don't reject these approaches; we've found them valuable, even essential. But they address only the surface of student writing.

The more difficult problem, the one *Rereading America* addresses, is that students often haven't developed the habits of mind necessary for academic inquiry. These habits include the ability to imagine and value points of view different from their own — then to strengthen, refine, enlarge, or reshape their ideas in light of those other perspectives. They include openness to new ideas combined with a skepticism that demands testing those ideas against previous experience, reading, and belief. They include a desire to see things whole and to integrate specific knowledge into larger frameworks. In more traditional terms, these intellectual habits mean the ability to synthesize, analyze, evaluate, and argue — to engage ideas actively and write substantively about them. This is what we mean by critical thinking, and this, we think, is what we must foster in our students.

The central question, then, is how to engage students in real intellectual activity. We don't believe that serious thought arises primarily from following formulas, whether these are grammatical rules, rhetorical models, or prescribed steps for "creative" problem-solving. Intellectual growth demands questions, not answers. Students won't learn to think critically if they approach their education as a matter of imitation or the mechnical application of rules.

Ironically, while college demands critical thinking, the structure and methods of traditional schooling often work against it. Few courses in high school or college ask students to approach education as a dialogue of ideas. The teacher-centered classroom encourages students to look to instructors for the "right answer," not for conversation and debate. And while this may promote a narrow kind of learning — the kind needed to follow directions and reproduce information on an exam — it does little to promote the rich interplay of ideas that nurtures critical inquiry.

The fragmented curriculum of most schools also inhibits dialogue. The knowledge students acquire in a history class is segregated from the reading they encounter in English or the experiments they perform in chemistry. Few courses ask students to connect what they learn in class with the social, political, and cultural realities around them, and fewer still try to link these realities to students' personal expriences. Even textbooks tend to reinforce a simplified, sterilized view of learning: Presenting information in the flat monotone of objectivity, they convey the false impression that knowledge is static, not continually recreated through tension, struggle, and debate. No wonder, then, that for many students the experience of school becomes academic in the worst sense — an empty exercise or cynical game played for grades, not a way to make sense of the world.

For those students, *Rereading America* can make a difference. This text is designed to help students become active in and responsible for their own education — that is, to become "authors" in the truest sense of the word. We encourage students to acknowledge and assume responsibility for their *authority* as people with the power to shape, not merely absorb, knowledge. This means cultivating the ability to ask difficult questions, and the self-confidence to reject easy answers — two fundamental goals of *Rereading America*.

The Structure

Rereading America organizes readings into eight unified chapters:

American Dreams
Justice for All: The Problem of Equality
One Nation or Many? Immigration and Assimilation
Women: The Emerging Majority
The Changing Family
Grading American Education
Making a Living: How Work Shapes the Worker
Television and the Consumption of Images

Because chapters are thematically linked — each connecting to the central concerns of pluralism and identity in the United States — readings from different chapters speak to the same issue. This abundance of interrelated material encourages students to explore connections, even between apparently disparate disciplines and styles. It allows them to build on what they've learned from week to week, providing the continuity they need to make their thinking and writing increasingly well-informed and complex.

The Selections

Our selections, you'll notice, diverge sharply from those of conventional composition texts. You won't find many of the essayists so often featured in those readers; indeed, many of our writers will be new to you. Is "Para Teresa," Inéz Hernández's English/Spanish poem about an elementary school confrontation, great literature? You decide. We do know that it engages Spanish-speaking students, that it interests students usually put off by poetry, and that it provokes discussion about responses to cultural domination.

We've deliberately chosen provocative and controversial readings in order to stimulate classroom debate. For students, developing a point of view and an argument that they have a real stake in defending is an important step toward critical thinking. But we have not tried to "balance" pro and con arguments so that students are encouraged — ever so predictably — to see both sides and find truth always in the middle. The issues here quickly get more complicated than that. While some of the readings are classic texts, we've included more strongly dissenting views than mainstream opinions. These minority views are meant to challenge the messages that many years of education, television, and other forms of socialization have inculcated in us all.

Our selections come from a wide variety of sources: professional books and journals from many disciplines, popular magazines, college textbooks, autobiographies, oral histories, and diverse literary genres, including poetry, fiction, and drama. In addition, different types of discourse and different academic disciplines meet here on equal terms. Theoretical essays, for example, provide analytic frameworks for personal narratives, interviews, and imaginative literature. The anthology's rhetorical diversity fosters flexible reading and writing skills. And by putting a rock lyric or other noncanonical text next to a traditional scholarly essay, we invite students to question what the academy recognizes as "legitimate" discourse, what it does not recognize, and why.

The Editorial Apparatus

Rereading America offers a wealth of specific suggestions for class discussions, critical thinking activities, and writing assignments. We believe strongly in the generative power of collaborative work, and have included many exercises that lend themselves to small group activity. The *prereading exercises* that introduce each chapter encourage students to reflect on what they already know about the subject before they begin reading the essays; our purpose here is to make them conscious of the critical perspectives that they bring to their reading. The *questions following each selection* ask students to consider the piece carefully in several contexts: by itself, in relation to other readings in the book, and in relation to sources of knowledge outside the anthology (including library research, personal experience, interviews, observation, and so forth). *Further Connections*, a small number of elaborate questions which appear after the book's last chapter, ask students to draw upon many readings to address very complex, wide-ranging issues. Finally, a glossary of frequently used terms concludes the book. The accompanying manual, *Resources for Teaching Rereading America: Cultural Contexts for Critical Thinking and Writing*, provides detailed advice about ways to make the most of both the readings and the questions; it also offers further ideas for discussion, class activities, and writing assignments. Whatever the specific instructions, the overall challenge is to let the text speak to students and simultaneously to engage their intelligence, emotions, and experience so that they can speak back.

Acknowledgments

A collaborative effort in practice as well as in theory, this book reflects the labor, insight, and dedication of many friends and colleagues. We owe considerable gratitude to the students, instructors, and staff of UCLA's Freshman Summer Program for inspiring much of the pedagogy and content of this book, and for testing many of the readings and assignments found here. We've also benefited from the sound advice and enthusiasm of the following colleagues, whose thoughtful suggestions helped refine and reshape our first conception of this reader: Geoffrey Chase, Miami University; Mary Ann Cooley, University of Houston; Gretchen Flescher, Gustavus Adolphus College; Carl Friedlander, Los Angeles Community College; Susan Simons, Community College of Denver; Jon Christian Suggs, John Jay College of Criminal Justice; Linda Woodson, University of Texas, San Antonio; and our good friend, Malcolm Kiniry, Rutgers University, Newark. We owe many thanks to Charles Christensen and Ellen Darion of Bedford Books, who gave us the freedom and encouragement to break new ground, and who helped us think critically when our own energies flagged. At Bedford, we also wish to thank Mary Lou Wilshaw and Elizabeth Schaaf for steering the book through production. Finally, Elena Barcia, Liz Silver, and Roy Weitz deserve special thanks for their sound editorial advice, good humor, and love — all undiminished by the three years they've lived with this project.

Contents

1

American Dreams   1

LAND OF FREEDOM AND OPPORTUNITY

"We hold these truths to be self-evident, that all men are created equal, that they are endowed by their Creator with certain un-alienable Rights, that among these are Life, Liberty and the pursuit of Happiness."

"We have no princes, for whom we toil, starve, and bleed: we are the most perfect society now existing in the world. Here man is free as he ought to be."

"O, let America be America again —
The land that never has been yet —
And yet must be — the land where *every* man is free."

THE FRONTIER

"That restless, nervous energy; that dominant individualism, working

2

Justice for All: *The Problem of Equality*   84

3

One Nation or Many? *Immigration and Assimilation*   191

5

The Changing Family

to you. She will finally say in a flat voice: How wonderful, gee, you really send me."

CHALLENGING THE TRADITIONAL CLASSROOM

7

Making a Living: *How Work Shapes the Worker*

CONSUMERISM AND TV CULTURE

Introduction for Students

Reading and Rereading

This is an unconventional book and thus requires an unconventional introduction. We've designed *Rereading America* to put you, the student, at the center of your writing course — to use the knowledge and experience you bring with you to help you take responsibility for your own development as a critical thinker and writer. To get the most out of this book, you'll need to know how it works. Let's begin with the title.

What does it mean to "read" something besides a book — especially something as complicated and unwieldy as a nation? And why *re*reading? In a nutshell, reading a nation, or culture, means looking thoughtfully and inquisitively rather than passively at the society around you, examining the culture which has shaped and continues to shape your dreams, your values, your very identity. It means rethinking ideas — like what constitutes a family — that are so ingrained they seldom receive conscious attention. And it's *re*reading or *re*thinking because most of us, whether we like it or not, have absorbed "readings" of America from countless sources: advertisements, movies, politicians, teachers, parents, . . . even textbooks. These versions of what America stands for too often present a simplified image — one more mythical than real. We'll introduce you to voices and views that challenge such familiar but limited "readings" of our culture.

Here's an example of the kind of rereading we're talking about. Take another look at the book's title. When you read the word "America," what portion of the world do you visualize? Most U.S. citizens picture the fifty states; a few might include Puerto Rico or American Samoa on their mental maps. In truth, however, America consists of *all* the countries in North, South, and Central America; so a citizen of Canada, Mexico, Guatemala, or Brazil can rightly claim to be as American as we are. Thus, the way most of us read even the word "America" is quite limited. Critical reading — critical thinking — requires an adjustment of perspective, a wider context, and a recognition of alternative points of view. It also requires courage — the courage it takes to challenge habitual ways of thinking, to question ideas and values you've always accepted as given.

Identity and Diversity

Why, then, have we used the word America in our title, when all of the selections in the book focus on life in the United States? We've chosen this problematic term because we want you to begin your rereading precisely here, with the most basic question of American identity. Our title reflects this question, because the title seems like a logical place to start in a book that asks you to think critically about who you are. Our theme — individual identity in a pluralistic society — places the question of what it means to be an American at the heart of the text.

The first four chapters will help you investigate the American experiment from a variety of critical perspectives. The first chapter, "American Dreams," centers on the ideology of individualism as embodied in the myth of the frontier and the rags-to-riches ethic of success. In the next three chapters ("Justice for All: The Problem of Equality," "One Nation or Many? Immigration and Assimilation," and "Women: the Emerging Majority"), you'll examine three groups whose histories call into question the ideals of individualism and fair play that dominate our culture. The experiences of these three groups — ethnic minorities, immigrants, and women — offer a critical perspective for rethinking our notions about American identity.

The second half of the book focuses on major cultural forces that shape our lives and our sense of self: "The Changing Family," "Grading American Education," "Making a Living: How Work Shapes the Worker," "Television and the Consumption of Images." Selections in these pivotal chapters will help you appreciate the impact these cultural forces have had on your values and thinking. You'll read, for example, about the myth of family perfection, the "hidden curriculum" of America's schools, and the power of TV advertising. As you become increasingly aware of these influences, we hope you'll begin to take a more active role in defining your own values, voices, and ways of seeing.

Our commitment to diversity shows up clearly in the range of authors whose works you'll read. Many of the writers you'll encounter in these pages are professional scholars: historians, psychologists, sociologists, anthropologists. But we've also tried to feature authors who offer other, unique perspectives on the American experience. Working through the chapters, you'll hear the voices of steelworkers, convicts, feminists, and farmers; activists, mechanics, executives, lesbians, and gays — each speaking of a different facet of life in America, each adding to the complexity of what it means to be an American. And while it's impossible to represent every ethnic group in the United States, we've tried to highlight authors who reflect our rich cultural diversity. We hope that as you encounter these strong, often conflicting perspectives, they'll stimulate you to ask critical questions about the selections themselves and about your own ideas and assumptions.

Discovering Your Own Authority

The world of college may seem foreign at first; many first-year students experience a kind of culture shock in making the transition from high school. Besides changes in your personal life, like being away from home or being financially independent, you most likely face academic adjustments. College typically imposes fewer rules than high school, but it also makes greater demands: one professor may ask you to read a book a week, and another may test you on material you've never covered in class. Your previous experience as a student may suddenly seem irrelevant: you end up taking subjects you've barely heard of before; your history professor says she doesn't care whether or not you remember all the dates as long as you can synthesize everything you've read for your term paper; your perfect five-paragraph essay fails to impress your English professor, who calls it "mechanical and dull."

What do college instructors want? Generally, they expect students to be both open and skeptical. Learning to think and write well is never as simple as memorizing a few definitions or becoming acquainted with the vocabulary and conventions of a particular academic field. Indeed, the most powerful thinkers continually test the limits of convention, question rules, and break established patterns of thought. But you can do this only by first recognizing your own knowledge and authority, and by discovering the power and validity of your own voice.

Feeling like an authority can be pretty difficult in an unfamiliar environment, but in fact, you already have plenty of information and experience to draw on. You have knowledge, assumptions, and ideas you can bring to a discussion of family relationships, prejudice, or the meaning of work — knowledge that comes from direct personal experience or the cultural values you've absorbed from the media, school, and other sources. *Rereading America* takes advantage of all you know about living in the United States — an immense amount — and provides contexts for interpreting and building on that knowledge. We invite you to test the validity of new ideas against your own experience; at the same time, we hope that the academic perspectives you find here will enable you to think critically about ideas you've always taken for granted. The intention, in both cases, is to broaden your understanding of your own identity within our common culture.

You may wonder what all this has to do with writing. We believe that in order to be a serious writer, you need to be a serious thinker — to ask yourself hard questions about the world around you. Writing gives you the opportunity to crystallize your best ideas, bringing an order, complexity, and development to your thinking that you rarely achieve in reading or discussion.

The Power of Dialogue

Good thinking, like good writing and good reading, is an intensely social activity. Thinking, reading, and writing are all forms of relationship — when you read, you enter into dialogue with an author about the subject at hand; when you write, you address an imaginary reader, testing your ideas against probable responses, reservations, and arguments. Thus, you can't become an author — an accomplished writer — simply by declaring your right to speak or by criticizing as an act of principle: Real authority comes when you enter into the discipline of an active exchange of opinions and interpretations. Critical thinking, then, is always a matter of dialogue and debate — discovering relationships between apparently unrelated ideas, finding parallels between your own experiences and the ideas you read about, exploring points of agreement and conflict between yourself and your listener.

We've designed the readings and questions in this text to encourage you to make just these kinds of connections. You'll notice, for example, that we often ask you to divide into small groups to discuss readings, and we frequently suggest that you take part in group projects that require you to collaborate with your classmates. We're convinced that the only way you can learn critical reading, thinking, and writing is by actively engaging others in a critical intellectual exchange. So we've built into the text as many opportunities as possible for debate, critical listening, and discussion.

The questions that follow each selection should guide you in critical thinking. Like the readings, they're intended to get you started, not to set limits; we strongly recommend that you also devise your own questions and pursue them, either individually or in study groups. You'll find that our questions divide into three categories; here's what to expect from each:

Those labeled "Engaging the Text" focus on the individual selection they follow. They're designed to highlight important issues in the reading, to help you begin questioning and evaluating what you've read, and sometimes to remind you to consider the author's choices of language, structure, evidence, or style.

The questions labeled "Exploring Connections" will lead you from the selection you've just finished to one or more other readings within this book. It's hard to make sparks fly from just one stone; if you think hard about these connecting questions, though, you'll see some real collisions of ideas and perspectives, not just polite and predictable "differences of opinion."

The final questions for each reading, "Extending the Critical Context," invite you to extend your thinking beyond the book — to your family, your community, your college, the media, or to the more traditional research environment, the library. The emphasis here is on creating new knowledge by applying ideas from this book to the world around you, and by testing these ideas in your world. Remember, the readings are just a starting point for discussion: You have access to a wealth of other perspectives and ideas among your family, friends, and classmates; in your college library; in your personal experience; and in your own imagination. We urge you to consult them all as you grapple with the perspectives you encounter in this text.

Rereading America

Cultural Contexts for
Critical Thinking and Writing

1

American Dreams

Familiar notions are often those least examined, and for many Americans the idea of an "American Dream" surely fits that category. All around us, references to the American Dream abound, in contexts ranging from politics to advertising. Americans aren't the only people who dream, of course, but America has always had the reputation as a country where dreams seemed especially likely to come true: people *did* find more religious freedom here than in the Old World, an Illinois rail-splitter *did* become President, and some penniless immigrants *did* build up thriving businesses. In this chapter we look at two of the main embodiments of the American Dream and at some of the complexities of history, society, and psychology that give the dream its power but make it at the same time so elusive.

The first section of the chapter, Land of Freedom and Opportunity, contains three statements about America's potential — two dating back to the nation's birth, the third more recent. The Declaration of Independence, besides heralding the foundation of the country, articulates a philosophy of freedom and justice — basic American dreams to which many readings in this chapter, and indeed this book, refer. J. Hector St. Jean de Crèvecoeur's "What Is an American?" argues that the unique conditions of frontier life gave birth to a new kind of man, one he admires almost without reservation; to Crèvecoeur, nearly anything seems possible. In contrast, "Let America Be America Again," by poet Langston Hughes, looks back at American dreams quite critically, but does hold on to a dream for the future.

The next section, The Frontier, will help you examine one important

American dream in more detail. If the Declaration of Independence and the Constitution established the political structure of the United States, the frontier gave the new country its energy, its character, and — for more than a hundred years — its future. Frederick Jackson Turner, in an address penned in 1893, offers a classic definition of American character and American society based on the role of the frontier. Next, Jane Kramer's "Cowboy" examines the frontier myth as it haunts a modern cowboy and would-be hero. Rounding out and complicating this section, Louise Erdrich's "Dear John Wayne" reviews the conquest of the West from a Native American's point of view.

The concluding section, Individualism and Success, examines two dominant themes in American life. Robert Bellah's "The Paradox of Individualism" briefly notes this issue's prominence in American literature and then articulates a central paradox; he argues that Americans want complete freedom *and* want to fit into society at the same time. Next, John Gwaltney's interview with Charlie Sabatier, an injured Vietnam vet and crusader for social justice, provides a forum for a strong non-conformist voice. Andrew Carnegie's "The Gospel of Wealth," written by a man who amassed a huge fortune, outlines fascinating assumptions about the road to monetary success and the duties of those who achieve it. The interview with Stephen Cruz adds the perspective of a minority member who succeeds in a predominantly Anglo setting. While Carnegie and Cruz are scarcely frontiersmen, we believe that the definition of success clearly echoes the themes of the earlier readings. The same questions of values — of individual vs. society, of independence vs. conformity — still apply.

Before Reading . . .

Working in groups or on your own, create a list of American heroes. (You may look at film and TV characters, historical figures, or contemporary leaders in business, government, entertainment, or other fields.) Next list the specific qualities or accomplishments that make these people heroic. As you work through the chapter, analyze your list, compare it to classmates' lists, test it against our authors' claims about American heroes and ideals, and test their claims against your list.

LAND OF FREEDOM AND OPPORTUNITY

The Declaration of Independence
THOMAS JEFFERSON

Drafted by Thomas Jefferson (1743–1826) when he was only thirty-three years old, the Declaration of Independence was meant to announce and defend the colonies' decision to throw off British rule. But since its adoption by the Second Continental Congress on July 4, 1776, it has come to mean much more: its vision of the purpose of government and its insistence upon the fundamental equality of the governed have inspired democratic reforms for the past two hundred years — from the Bill of Rights to Civil Rights. Conceived as a revolutionary manifesto, the Declaration has become a preamble to the American Dream.

As third President of the United States (1801–1809), Thomas Jefferson promoted westward expansion in the form of the Louisiana Purchase and the Lewis and Clark Expedition. In addition to his political career he was a scientist, architect, city planner (Washington, D.C.), and founder of the University of Virginia; his writings fill fifty-two volumes.

THE UNANIMOUS DECLARATION of the thirteen united STATES OF AMERICA.

When in the Course of human events, it becomes necessary for one 1 people to dissolve the political bands which have connected them with another, and to assume among the powers of the earth, the separate and equal station to which the Laws of Nature and of Nature's God entitle them, a decent respect to the opinions of mankind requires that they should declare the causes which impel them to the separation. —— We hold these truths to be self-evident, that all men are created equal, that they are endowed by their Creator with certain unalienable Rights, that among these are Life, Liberty and the pursuit of Happiness.

— That to secure these rights, Governments are instituted among Men, deriving their just powers from the consent of the governed. — That whenever any Form of Government becomes destructive of these ends, it is the Right of the People to alter or to abolish it, and to institute new Government, laying its foundation on such principles and organizing its powers in such form, as to them shall seem most likely to effect their Safety and Happiness. Prudence, indeed, will dictate that Governments long established should not be changed for light and transient causes; and accordingly all experience hath shewn, that mankind are more disposed to suffer, while evils are sufferable, than to right themselves by abolishing the forms to which they are accustomed. But when a long train of abuses and usurpations, pursuing invariably the same Object[1] evinces a design to reduce them under absolute Despotism, it is their right, it is their duty, to throw off such Government, and to provide new Guards for their future security. — Such has been the patient sufferance of these Colonies; and such is now the necessity which constrains them to alter their former Systems of Government. The history of the present King of Great Britain is a history of repeated injuries and usurpations, all having in direct object the establishment of an absolute Tyranny over these States. To prove this, let Facts be submitted to a candid world. —— He has refused his Assent to Laws, the most wholesome and necessary for the public good. —— He has forbidden his Governors to pass Laws of immediate and pressing importance, unless suspended in their operation till his Assent should be obtained; and when so suspended, he has utterly neglected to attend to them. —— He has refused to pass other Laws for the accommodation of large districts of people, unless those people would relinquish the right of Representation in the Legislature, a right inestimable to them and formidable to tyrants only. —— He has called together legislative bodies at places unusual, uncomfortable, and distant from the depository of their public Records, for the sole purpose of fatiguing them into compliance with his measures. —— He has dissolved Representative Houses repeatedly, for opposing with manly firmness his invasions on the rights of the people. —— He has refused for a long time, after such dissolutions, to cause others to be elected; whereby the Legislative powers, incapable of Annihilation, have returned to the People at large for their exercise; the State remaining in the mean time exposed to all the dangers of invasion from without, and convulsions within. —— He has endeavoured to prevent the population of these States; for that purpose obstructing the Laws for Naturalization of Foreigners; refusing to pass others to encourage their migrations

[1] *Object:* goal, purpose.

hither, and raising the conditions of new Appropriations of Lands. ——
He has obstructed the Administration of Justice, by refusing his Assent
to Laws for establishing Judiciary powers. —— He has made Judges
dependent on his Will alone, for the tenure of their offices, and the
amount and payment of their salaries. —— He has erected a multitude
of New Offices, and sent hither swarms of Officers to harass our people,
and eat out their substance. —— He has kept among us, in times of
peace, Standing Armies without the Consent of our legislatures. ——
He has affected to render the Military independent of and superior to
the Civil power. —— He has combined with others to subject us to a
jurisdiction foreign to our constitution, and unacknowledged by our laws;
giving his Assent to their Acts of pretended Legislation: — For Quartering
large bodies of armed troops among us: — For protecting them, by a
mock Trial, from punishment for any Murders which they should commit
on the Inhabitants of these States: — For cutting off our Trade with all
parts of the world: — For imposing Taxes on us without our Consent:
— For depriving us in many cases, of the benefits of Trial by Jury: —
For transporting us beyond Seas to be tried for pretended offences: —
For abolishing the free System of English Laws in a neighbouring Province,
establishing therein an Arbitrary government, and enlarging its Boundaries
so as to render it at once an example and fit instrument for introducing
the same absolute rule into these Colonies: — For taking away our
Charters, abolishing our most valuable Laws, and altering fundamentally
the Forms of our Governments: — For suspending our own Legislatures,
and declaring themselves invested with power to legislate for us in all
cases whatsoever. — He has abdicated Government here, by declaring
us out of his Protection and waging War against us: — He has plundered
our seas, ravaged our Coasts, burnt our towns, and destroyed the lives
of our people. — He is at this time transporting large Armies of foreign
Mercenaries to compleat the works of death, desolation and tyranny,
already begun with circumstances of Cruelty & Perfidy scarcely paralleled
in the most barbarous ages, and totally unworthy the Head of a civilized
nation. — He has constrained our fellow Citizens taken Captive on the
high Seas to bear Arms against their Country, to become the executioners
of their friends and Brethren, or to fall themselves by their Hands. —
He has excited domestic insurrections amongst us, and has endeavoured
to bring on the inhabitants of our frontiers, the merciless Indian Savages,
whose known rule of warfare, is an undistinguished destruction of all
ages, sexes and conditions. In every stage of these Oppressions We have
Petitioned for Redress in the most humble terms: Our repeated Petitions
have been answered only by repeated injury. A Prince, whose character
is thus marked by every act which may define a Tyrant, is unfit to be

the ruler of a free people. Nor have We been wanting in attentions to our British brethren. We have warned them from time to time of attempts by their legislature to extend an unwarrantable jurisdiction over us. We have reminded them of the circumstances of our emigration and settlement here. We have appealed to their native justice and magnanimity, and we have conjured them by the ties of our common kindred to disavow these usurpations, which would inevitably interrupt our connections and correspondence. They too have been deaf to the voice of justice and of consanguinity. We must, therefore, acquiesce in the necessity, which denounces our Separation, and hold them, as we hold the rest of mankind, Enemies in War, in Peace Friends.

WE, THEREFORE, the Representatives of the UNITED STATES OF AMERICA, in General Congress Assembled, appealing to the Supreme Judge of the world for the rectitude of our intentions, do, in the Name and by Authority of the good People of these Colonies, solemnly publish and declare, That these United Colonies are, and of Right ought to be FREE AND INDEPENDENT STATES; that they are Absolved from all Allegiance to the British Crown, and that all political connection between them and the State of Great Britain, is and ought to be totally dissolved; and that as Free and Independent States, they have full Power to levy War, conclude Peace, contract Alliances, establish Commerce, and to do all other Acts and Things which Independent States may of right do. —— And for the support of this Declaration, with a firm reliance on the protection of divine Providence, we mutually pledge to each other our Lives, our Fortunes and our sacred Honor.

Engaging the Text

1. PARAPHRASE the opening of the Declaration, up to the phrase "former systems of Government." Are the truths named here "self-evident"?

2. Outline the essential structure of the Declaration in three to five lines. What structure of argument is revealed here?

3. What attitudes toward women and Native Americans does the Declaration reveal?

4. How would you characterize the VOICE of this document? Read some of it aloud. What is its TONE, and how is that tone created, specifically?

Extending the Critical Context

1. Using a history text or other sources, research one or more of the claims made against the "present King of Great Britain." Write a brief summary of what you've learned and share it with classmates.

What Is an American?

J. HECTOR ST. JEAN DE CRÈVECOEUR

Jean Hector St. Jean de Crèvecoeur's Letters from an American Farmer *represents one of the earliest and most optimistic assessments of the American character. A French immigrant who became a diplomat as well as a farmer and writer, Crèvecoeur (1731–1813) contrasts the freedom, equality and opportunity that abound in the new land to the rigid class structure of Europe. His vision of a classless, melting-pot society where anyone could attain success through honesty and hard work fired the imaginations of many European readers. However, reality didn't always measure up to the* Letters' *promise: one group of nearly five hundred French families, inspired to emigrate by Crèvecoeur's book, found only fever and starvation in America; few of them survived. This passage evokes many of the dreams that still shape our national consciousness and reminds us how dramatically different the American experiment once seemed.*

I wish I could be acquainted with the feelings and thoughts which 1
must agitate the heart and present themselves to the mind of an enlightened
Englishman, when he first lands on this continent. He must greatly
rejoice that he lived at a time to see this fair country discovered and
settled; he must necessarily feel a share of national pride, when he views
the chain of settlements which embellishes these extended shores. When
he says to himself, this is the work of my countrymen, who, when
convulsed by factions, afflicted by a variety of miseries and wants, restless
and impatient, took refuge here. They brought along with them their
national genius, to which they principally owe what liberty they enjoy,
and what substance they possess. Here he sees the industry of his native
country displayed in a new manner, and traces in their works the embryos
of all the arts, sciences, and ingenuity which flourish in Europe. Here
he beholds fair cities, substantial villages, extensive fields, an immense
country filled with decent houses, good roads, orchards, meadows, and
bridges, where an hundred years ago all was wild, woody and uncultivated!
What a train of pleasing ideas this fair spectacle must suggest; it is a
prospect which must inspire a good citizen with the most heartfelt pleasure.
The difficulty consists in the manner of viewing so extensive a scene.
He is arrived on a new continent; a modern society offers itself to his

contemplation, different from what he had hitherto seen. It is not composed, as in Europe, of great lords who possess every thing, and of a herd of people who have nothing. Here are no aristocratical families, no courts, no kings, no bishops, no ecclesiastical dominion, no invisible power giving to a few a very visible one; no great manufacturers employing thousands, no great refinements of luxury. The rich and the poor are not so far removed from each other as they are in Europe. Some few towns excepted, we are all tillers of the earth, from Nova Scotia to West Florida. We are a people of cultivators, scattered over an immense territory, communicating with each other by means of good roads and navigable rivers, united by the silken bands of mild government, all respecting the laws, without dreading their power, because they are equitable. We are all animated with the spirit of an industry which is unfettered and unrestrained, because each person works for himself. If he travels through our rural districts he views not the hostile castle, and the haughty mansion, contrasted with the clay-built hut and miserable cabin, where cattle and men help to keep each other warm, and dwell in meanness, smoke, and indigence. A pleasing uniformity of decent competence appears throughout our habitations. The meanest of our log-houses is a dry and comfortable habitation. Lawyer or merchant are the fairest titles our towns afford; that of a farmer is the only appellation of the rural inhabitants of our country. It must take some time ere he can reconcile himself to our dictionary; which is but short in words of dignity, and names of honour. There, on a Sunday, he sees a congregation of respectable farmers and their wives, all clad in neat homespun,[1] well mounted, or riding in their own humble waggons. There is not among them an esquire, saving the unlettered magistrate. There he sees a parson as simple as his flock, a farmer who does not riot on the labour of others. We have no princes, for whom we toil, starve, and bleed: we are the most perfect society now existing in the world. Here man is free as he ought to be; nor is this pleasing equality so transitory as many others are. Many ages will not see the shores of our great lakes replenished with inland nations, nor the unknown bounds of North America entirely peopled. Who can tell how far it extends? Who can tell the millions of men whom it will feed and contain? for no European foot has as yet travelled half the extent of this mighty continent! . . .

In this great American asylum, the poor of Europe have by some   2
means met together, and in consequence of various causes; to what purpose should they ask one another what countrymen they are? Alas,

[1]*homespun:* clothes made of fabric "spun" or manufactured at home, as opposed to imported British cloth.

two thirds of them had no country. Can a wretch who wanders about, who works and starves, whose life is a continual scene of sore affliction or pinching penury; can that man call England or any other kingdom his country? A country that had no bread for him, whose fields procured him no harvest, who met with nothing but the frowns of the rich, the severity of the laws, with jails and punishments; who owned not a single foot of the extensive surface of this planet? No! urged by a variety of motives, here they came. Every thing has tended to regenerate them; new laws, a new mode of living, a new social system; here they are become men: in Europe they were as so many useless plants, wanting vegetative mould,[2] and refreshing showers; they withered, and were mowed down by want, hunger, and war; but now by the power of transplantation, like all other plants they have taken root and flourished! Formerly they were not numbered in any civil lists of their country, except in those of the poor; here they rank as citizens. By what invisible power has this surprising metamorphosis been performed? By that of the laws and that of their industry. The laws, the indulgent laws, protect them as they arrive, stamping on them the symbol of adoption; they receive ample rewards for their labours; these accumulated rewards procure them lands; those lands confer on them the title of freemen,[3] and to that title every benefit is affixed which men can possibly require. This is the great operation daily performed by our laws. From whence proceed these laws? From our government. Whence the government? It is derived from the original genius and strong desire of the people ratified and confirmed by the crown. This is the great chain which links us all. . . .

What attachment can a poor European emigrant have for a country 3 where he had nothing? The knowledge of the language, the love of a few kindred as poor as himself, were the only cords that tied him: his country is now that which gives him land, bread, protection, and consequence: *Ubi panis ibi patria*,[4] is the motto of all emigrants. What then is the American, this new man? He is either an European, or the descendant of an European, hence that strange mixture of blood, which you will find in no other country. I could point out to you a family whose grandfather was an Englishman, whose wife was Dutch, whose son married a French woman, and whose present four sons have now four wives of different nations. *He* is an American, who leaving behind him all his ancient prejudices and manners, receives new ones from the new mode of life

[2]*wanting vegetative mould:* lacking nourishing soil.
[3]*freemen:* citizens with full civic and political rights.
[4]*Ubi panis . . . :* [Latin] "Where there is bread, there is our country."

he has embraced, the new government he obeys, and the new rank he holds. He becomes an American by being received in the broad lap of our great *Alma Mater*.[5] Here individuals of all nations are melted into a new race of men, whose labours and posterity will one day cause great changes in the world. Americans are the western pilgrims, who are carrying along with them that great mass of arts, sciences, vigour, and industry which began long since in the east; they will finish the great circle. The Americans were once scattered all over Europe; here they are incorporated into one of the finest systems of population which has ever appeared, and which will hereafter become distinct by the power of the different climates they inhabit. The American ought therefore to love this country much better than that wherein either he or his forefathers were born. Here the rewards of his industry follow with equal steps the progress of his labour; his labour is founded on the basis of nature, *self-interest;* can it want a stronger allurement? Wives and children, who before in vain demanded of him a morsel of bread, now, fat and frolicsome, gladly help their father to clear those fields whence exuberant crops are to arise to feed and to clothe them all; without any part being claimed, either by a despotic prince, a rich abbot, or a mighty lord. Here religion demands but little of him; a small voluntary salary to the minister, and gratitude to God; can he refuse these? The American is a new man, who acts upon new principles; he must therefore entertain new ideas, and form new opinions. From involuntary idleness, servile dependence, penury, and useless labour, he has passed to toils of a very different nature, rewarded by ample subsistence. — This is an American. . . .

Men are like plants; the goodness and flavour of the fruit proceeds 4 from the peculiar soil and exposition[6] in which they grow. We are nothing but what we derive from the air we breathe, the climate we inhabit, the government we obey, the system of religion we profess, and the nature of our employment. Here you will find but few crimes; these have acquired as yet no root among us. I wish I were able to trace all my ideas; if my ignorance prevents me from describing them properly, I hope I shall be able to delineate a few of the outlines, which are all I propose.

Those who live near the sea, feed more on fish than on flesh, and 5 often encounter that boisterous element. This renders them more bold and enterprising; this leads them to neglect the confined occupations of the land. They see and converse with a variety of people; their intercourse

[5]*Alma Mater:* [Latin] "fostering mother." Now used exclusively to refer to the school one attended.
[6]*exposition:* exposure to the sun.

with mankind becomes extensive. The sea inspires them with a love of traffic, a desire of transporting produce from one place to another; and leads them to a variety of resources which supply the place of labour. Those who inhabit the middle settlements, by far the most numerous, must be very different; the simple cultivation of the earth purifies them, but the indulgences of the government, the soft remonstrances of religion, the rank of independent freeholders, must necessarily inspire them with sentiments, very little known in Europe among people of the same class. What do I say? Europe has no such class of men; the early knowledge they acquire, the early bargains they make, give them a great degree of sagacity. As freemen they will be litigious; pride and obstinacy are often the cause of law suits; the nature of our laws and governments may be another. As citizens it is easy to imagine, that they will carefully read the newspapers, enter into every political disquisition, freely blame or censure governors and others. As farmers they will be careful and anxious to get as much as they can, because what they get is their own. As northern men they will love the chearful cup. As Christians, religion curbs them not in their opinions; the general indulgence leaves every one to think for themselves in spiritual matters; the laws inspect our actions, our thoughts are left to God. Industry, good living, selfishness, litigiousness, country politics, the pride of freemen, religious indifference, are their characteristics. If you recede still farther from the sea, you will come into more modern settlements; they exhibit the same strong lineaments, in a ruder appearance. Religion seems to have still less influence, and their manners are less improved.

Now we arrive near the great woods, near the last inhabited districts; 6 there men seem to be placed still farther beyond the reach of government, which in some measure leaves them to themselves. How can it pervade every corner; as they were driven there by misfortunes, necessity of beginnings, desire of acquiring large tracks of land, idleness, frequent want of œconomy, ancient debts; the re-union of such people does not afford a very pleasing spectacle. When discord, want of unity and friendship; when either drunkenness or idleness prevail in such remote districts; contention, inactivity, and wretchedness must ensue. There are not the same remedies to these evils as in a long established community. The few magistrates they have, are in general little better than the rest; they are often in a perfect state of war; that of man against man, sometimes decided by blows, sometimes by means of the law; that of man against every wild inhabitant of these venerable woods, of which they are come to dispossess them. There men appear to be no better than carnivorous animals of a superior rank, living on the flesh of wild animals when they can catch them, and when they are not able, they subsist on grain. He who would wish to see America in its proper light, and have a true idea of its feeble beginnings and barbarous rudiments, must visit our extended line of frontiers where the last settlers dwell, and where he may see the first labours of settlement, the mode of clearing the earth, in all their different appearances; where men are wholly left dependent on their native tempers, and on the spur of uncertain industry, which often fails when not sanctified by the efficacy of a few moral rules. There, remote from the power of example, and check of shame, many families exhibit the most hideous parts of our society. They are a kind of forlorn hope, preceding by ten or twelve years the most respectable army of veterans which come after them. In that space, prosperity will polish some, vice and the law will drive off the rest, who uniting again with others like themselves will recede still farther; making room for more industrious people, who will finish their improvements, convert the loghouse into a convenient habitation, and rejoicing that the first heavy labours are finished, will change in a few years that hitherto barbarous country into a fine fertile, well regulated district. Such is our progress, such is the march of the Europeans toward the interior parts of this continent. In all societies there are offcasts; this impure part serves as our precursors or pioneers; my father himself was one of that class, but he came upon honest principles, and was therefore one of the few who held fast; by good conduct and temperance, he transmitted to me his fair inheritance, when not above one in fourteen of his contemporaries had the same good fortune.

Forty years ago this smiling country was thus inhabited; it is now 7 purged, a general decency of manners prevails throughout, and such has been the fate of our best countries. . . .

But to return to our back settlers. I must tell you, that there is 8 something in the proximity of the woods, which is very singular. It is with men as it is with the plants and animals that grow and live in the forest; they are entirely different from those that live in the plains. I will candidly tell you all my thoughts but you are not to expect that I shall advance any reasons. By living in or near the woods, their actions are regulated by the wildness of the neighbourhood. The deer often come to eat their grain, the wolves to destroy their sheep, the bears to kill their hogs, the foxes to catch their poultry. This surrounding hostility, immediately puts the gun into their hands; they watch these animals, they kill some; and thus by defending their property, they soon become professed hunters; this is the progress; once hunters, farewell to the plough. The chase renders them ferocious, gloomy, and unsociable; a hunter wants no neighbour, he rather hates them, because he dreads the competition. In a little time their success in the woods makes them neglect their tillage. They trust to the natural fecundity of the earth, and therefore do little; carelessness in fencing, often exposes what little they sow to destruction; they are not at home to watch; in order therefore to make up the deficiency, they go oftener to the woods. That new mode of life brings along with it a new set of manners, which I cannot easily describe. These new manners being grafted on the old stock, produce a strange sort of lawless profligacy, the impressions of which are indelible. The manners of the Indian natives are respectable, compared with this European medley. Their wives and children live in sloth and inactivity; and having no proper pursuits, you may judge what education the latter receive. Their tender minds have nothing else to contemplate but the example of their parents; like them they grow up a mongrel breed, half civilized, half savage, except nature stamps on them some constitutional propensities. That rich, that voluptuous sentiment is gone that struck them so forcibly; the possession of their freeholds no longer conveys to their minds the same pleasure and pride. To all these reasons you must add, their lonely situation, and you cannot imagine what an effect on manners the great distances they live from each other has! . . .

There is no wonder that this country has so many charms, and presents 9 to Europeans so many temptations to remain in it. A traveller in Europe becomes a stranger as soon as he quits his own kingdom; but it is otherwise here. We know, properly speaking, no strangers; this is every person's country; the variety of our soils, situations, climates, governments, and produce, hath something which must please every body. No sooner does an European arrive, no matter of what condition, than his eyes are opened upon the fair prospect; he hears his language spoke, he retraces many of his own country manners, he perpetually hears the names of families and towns with which he is acquainted; he sees happiness and prosperity in all places disseminated; he meets with hospitality, kindness, and plenty every where; he beholds hardly any poor, he seldom hears of punishments and executions; and he wonders at the elegance of our towns, those miracles of industry and freedom. He cannot admire enough our rural districts, our convenient roads, good taverns, and our many accommodations; he involuntarily loves a country where every thing is so lovely. When in England, he was a mere Englishman; here he stands on a larger portion of the globe, not less than its fourth part, and may see the productions of the north, in iron and naval stores; the provisions of Ireland, the grain of Egypt, the indigo, the rice of China. He does not find, as in Europe, a crouded society, where every place is over-stocked; he does not feel that perpetual collision of parties, that difficulty of beginning, that contention which oversets so many. There is room for every body in America; has he any particular talent, or industry? he exerts it in order to procure a livelihood, and it succeeds. Is he a merchant? the avenues of trade are infinite; is he eminent in any respect? he will be employed and respected. Does he love a country life? pleasant farms present themselves; he may purchase what he wants, and thereby become an American farmer. Is he a labourer, sober and industrious? he need not go many miles, nor receive many informations before he will be hired, well fed at the table of his employer, and paid four or five times more than he can get in Europe. Does he want uncultivated lands? thousands of acres present themselves, which he may purchase cheap. Whatever be his talents or inclinations, if they are moderate, he may satisfy them. I do not mean that every one who comes will grow rich in a little time; no, but he may procure an easy, decent maintenance, by his industry. Instead of starving he will be fed, instead of being idle he will have employment; and these are riches enough for such men as come over here. The rich stay in Europe, it is only the middling and the poor that emigrate. Would you wish to travel in independent idleness, from north to south, you will find easy access, and the most chearful reception at every house; society without ostentation, good cheer without pride, and every decent diversion which the country affords, with little ex- pence. It is no wonder that the European who has lived here a few years, is desirous to remain; Europe with all its pomp, is not to be com- pared to this continent, for men of middle stations, or labourers. . . .

This great continent must in time absorb the poorest part of Europe; . . . 10 and this will happen in proportion as it becomes better known; and as war, taxation, oppression, and misery increase there. The Hebrides[7] appear to be fit only for the residence of malefactors, and it would be much better to send felons there than either to Virginia or Maryland. What a strange compliment has our mother country paid to two of the finest provinces in America! England has entertained in that respect very mistaken ideas; what was intended as a punishment, is become the good fortune of several; many of those who have been transported as felons, are now rich, and strangers to the stings of those wants that urged them to violations of the law: they are become industrious, exemplary, and useful citizens. The English government should purchase the most northern and barren of those islands; it should send over to us the honest, primitive Hebrideans, settle them here on good lands, as a reward for their virtue and ancient poverty; and replace them with a colony of her wicked sons. The severity of the climate, the inclemency of the seasons, the sterility of the soil, the tempestuousness of the sea, would afflict and punish enough. Could there be found a spot better adapted to retaliate the

[7]*Hebrides:* islands west of Scotland.

injury it had received by their crimes? Some of those islands might be considered as the hell of Great Britain, where all evil spirits should be sent. Two essential ends would be answered by this simple operation. The good people, by emigration, would be rendered happier; the bad ones would be placed where they ought to be. In a few years the dread of being sent to that wintry region would have a much stronger effect, than that of transportation. — This is no place for punishment; were I a poor hopeless, breadless Englishman, and not restrained by the power of shame, I should be very thankful for the passage. It is of very little importance how, and in what manner an indigent man arrives; for if he is but sober, honest, and industrious, he has nothing more to ask of heaven. Let him go to work, he will have opportunities enough to earn a comfortable support, and even the means of procuring some land; which ought to be the utmost wish of every person who has health and hands to work. I knew a man who came to this country, in the literal sense of the expression, stark naked; I think he was a Frenchman, and a sailor on board an English man of war. Being discontented, he had stripped himself and swam ashore; where finding clothes and friends, he settled afterwards at Maraneck, in the county of Chester, in the province of New-York: he married and left a good farm to each of his sons. I knew another person who was but twelve years old when he was taken on the frontiers of Canada, by the Indians; at his arrival at Albany he was purchased by a gentleman, who generously bound him apprentice to a taylor. He lived to the age of ninety, and left behind him a fine estate and a numerous family, all well settled; many of them I am acquainted with. — Where is then the industrious European who ought to despair?

After a foreigner from any part of Europe is arrived, and become a 11 citizen; let him devoutly listen to the voice of our great parent, which says to him, "Welcome to my shores, distressed European; bless the hour in which thou didst see my verdant fields, my fair navigable rivers, and my green mountains! — If thou wilt work, I have bread for thee; if thou wilt be honest, sober, and industrious, I have greater rewards to confer on thee — ease and independence. I will give thee fields to feed and cloath thee; a comfortable fire-side to sit by, and tell thy children by what means thou hast prospered; and a decent bed to repose on. I shall endow thee beside with the immunities of a freeman. If thou wilt carefully educate thy children, teach them gratitude to God, and reverence to that government, that philanthropic government, which has collected here so many men and made them happy, I will also provide for thy progeny; and to every good man this ought to be the most holy, the most powerful, the most earnest wish he can possibly form, as well as the most consolatory prospect when he dies. Go thou and work and till; thou shalt prosper, provided thou be just, grateful and industrious."

Engaging the Text

1. Compare and contrast Crèvecoeur's views of life in Europe, in settled American regions, and on the American frontier.

2. According to Crèvecoeur, what is necessary for an individual's success in America? To what extent do you think this is true today? Which other of Crèvecoeur's observations about America hold true today? Which no longer apply, and when did they become outdated?

3. Crèvecoeur seems to believe strongly in the importance of one's environment or circumstances in shaping CHARACTER, behavior, and values. Summarize his way of thinking and illustrate it with one or two particular instances from his writing. Do you find his reasoning persuasive?

4. "Men are like plants: the goodness and flavor of the fruit proceeds from the peculiar soil. . . ." What is Crèvecoeur saying through this IMAGE? What are the implications of comparing men to plants? Try to frame this idea using another SIMILE to see if your choice of image affects the meaning conveyed.

Exploring Connections

1. What features of Crèvecoeur's STYLE seem unfamiliar? Working in groups, compare the PROSE here to that of the Declaration of Independence, which was written during the same historical period. Which of the differences you see can be explained by the different purposes of the two authors? What stylistic features do they share?

2. Read Milton Gordon's essay on models of ASSIMILATION (Chapter Three, "One Nation or Many?"). Which model does Crèvecoeur assume will be the norm in the United States?

Extending the Critical Context

1. "Translate" a paragraph of Crèvecoeur into modern English *or* describe your neighborhood or campus in Crèvecoeur's style. Read these passages aloud in class.

2. Try your hand at writing your own view of "What Is an American?" If you want, you can restrict your subject to a particular region (i.e., "What Is a Midwesterner?" or "What Is a New Yorker?") After sharing your work with the class, discuss the validity of your observations: Is it really possible to classify people in this manner? How accurate do you think Crèvecoeur's characterization is?

Let America Be America Again

LANGSTON HUGHES

Langston Hughes, writing one hundred fifty years after Crèvecoeur published his utopian view of American life, reminds us in this poem that not all Americans have enjoyed the freedom and opportunity associated with the American Dream. [James] Langston Hughes (1902–1967) was a major figure in the Harlem Renaissance — a flowering of black artists, musicians, and writers in New York in the 1920s. His poems, often examining the experiences of blacks in American cities, use the rhythms of jazz, spirituals, and blues.

Let America be America again.
Let it be the dream it used to be.
Let it be the pioneer on the plain
Seeking a home where he himself is free.

(America never was America to me.)   5

Let America be the dream the dreamers dreamed —
Let it be that great strong land of love
Where never kings connive nor tyrants scheme
That any man be crushed by one above.

(It never was America to me.)   10

O, let my land be a land where Liberty
Is crowned with no false patriotic wreath,
But opportunity is real, and life is free,
Equality is in the air we breathe.

(There's never been equality for me,   15
Nor freedom in this "homeland of the free.")

Say who are you that mumbles in the dark?
And who are you that draws your veil across the stars?

I am the poor white, fooled and pushed apart,
I am the red man driven from the land.   20
I am the refugee clutching the hope I seek —
But finding only the same old stupid plan

Of dog eat dog, of mighty crush the weak.
I am the Negro, "problem" to you all.
I am the people, humble, hungry, mean —   25
Hungry yet today despite the dream.
Beaten yet today — O, Pioneers!
I am the man who never got ahead,
The poorest worker bartered through the years.
Yet I'm the one who dreamt our basic dream   30
In that Old World while still a serf of kings,
Who dreamt a dream so strong, so brave, so true,
That even yet its mighty daring sings
In every brick and stone, in every furrow turned
That's made America the land it has become.   35
O, I'm the man who sailed those early seas
In search of what I meant to be my home —
For I'm the one who left dark Ireland's shore,
And Poland's plain, and England's grassy lea,
And torn from Black Africa's strand I came   40
To build a "homeland of the free."

The free?
Who said the free? Not me?
Surely not me? The millions on relief today?
The millions who have nothing for our pay   45
For all the dreams we've dreamed
And all the songs we've sung
And all the hopes we've held
And all the flags we've hung,
The millions who have nothing for our pay —   50
Except the dream we keep alive today.

O, let America be America again —
The land that never has been yet —
And yet must be — the land where *every* man is free.
The land that's mine — the poor man's, Indian's, Negro's, ME —   55
Who made America,
Whose sweat and blood, whose faith and pain,
Whose hand at the foundry, whose plow in the rain,
Must bring back our mighty dream again.

   O, yes,   60
   I say it plain,
   America never was America to me,

And yet I swear this oath —
America will be!

Engaging the Text

1. Explain the two senses of the word "America" as Hughes uses it in the title and REFRAIN of the poem.

2. According to Hughes, who must rebuild the dream and why?

3. Why does Hughes reaffirm the dream of an ideal America in the face of so much evidence to the contrary?

4. Explain the IRONY of lines 40–41 ("And torn from Black Africa's strand I came/To build a 'homeland of the free.'")

5. Examine the way Hughes uses line length, repetition, STANZA breaks, typography, and indentation to call attention to particular lines of the poem. Why does he emphasize these passages?

Exploring Connections

1. How would Hughes respond to Crèvecoeur's appraisal of America?

Extending the Critical Context

1. Working in groups, "stage" a reading of the poem, using multiple speakers. Consider carefully how to divide up the lines for the most effective presentation. After the readings, discuss the choices made by the different groups in the class.

2. Working in pairs or in groups, write PROSE descriptions of the two versions of America Hughes evokes. Read these aloud and discuss which description more nearly matches your own view of the United States.

THE FRONTIER

The Significance of the Frontier in American History[1]

FREDERICK JACKSON TURNER

In a speech at the 1893 World Columbian Exhibition in Chicago, Frederick Jackson Turner first proposed his "frontier thesis" — a theory that became a milestone in American historical analysis. Where previous historians had emphasized the influence of Europe on U.S. development, Turner (1861–1932) argued that the western frontier had been the primary force in shaping American history and national character. Turner had been impressed by Crèvecoeur's description of how the "primitive" West quickly transformed European immigrants into American frontiersmen. He also drew on the writings of Franklin and Jefferson, who had seen the western territories as a safety valve drawing malcontents and unemployed workers away from the more populous East. Turner published widely and taught history for many years at the University of Wisconsin and at Harvard.

In a recent bulletin of the Superintendent of the Census for 1890 appear these significant words: "Up to and including 1880 the country had a frontier of settlement, but at present the unsettled area has been so broken into by isolated bodies of settlement that there can hardly be said to be a frontier line. In the discussion of its extent, its westward movement, etc., it can not therefore, any longer have a place in the census reports." This brief official statement marks the closing of a great historic movement. Up to our own day American history has been in a

1

[1]*Note:* The text of Turner's essay is reprinted from *Annual Report for 1893*, American Historical Association, pp. 199–227. Turner's own punctuation and capitalization, except in a few instances, have been retained. The subheadings are those of the original essay. [Editor's note]

large degree the history of the colonization of the Great West. The existence of an area of free land, its continuous recession, and the advance of American settlement westward, explain American development.

Behind institutions, behind constitutional forms and modifications, lie the vital forces that call these organs into life and shape them to meet changing conditions. The peculiarity of American institutions is, the fact that they have been compelled to adapt themselves to the changes of an expanding people — to the changes involved in crossing a continent, in winning a wilderness, and in developing at each area of this progress out of the primitive economic and political conditions of the frontier into the complexity of city life. Said Calhoun[2] in 1817, "We are great, and rapidly — I was about to say fearfully — growing!" So saying, he touched the distinguishing feature of American life. All peoples show development. . . . In the case of most nations, however, the development has occurred in a limited area; and if the nation has expanded, it has met other growing peoples whom it has conquered. But in the case of the United States we have a different phenomenon. Limiting our attention to the Atlantic coast, we have the familiar phenomenon of the evolution of institutions in a limited area, such as the rise of representative government; the differentiation of simple colonial governments into complex organs; the progress from primitive industrial society, without division of labor, up to manufacturing civilization. But we have in addition to this a recurrence of the process of evolution in each western area reached in the process of expansion. Thus American development has exhibited not merely advance along a single line, but a return to primitive conditions on a continually advancing frontier line, and a new development for that area. American social development has been continually beginning over again on the frontier. This perennial rebirth, this fluidity of American life, this expansion westward with its new opportunities, its continuous touch with the simplicity of primitive society, furnish the forces dominating American character. The true point of view in the history of this nation is not the Atlantic coast, it is the great West. Even the slavery struggle, which is made so exclusive an object of attention by writers like Prof. von Holst,[3] occupies its important place in American history because of its relation to westward expansion.

In this advance, the frontier is the outer edge of the wave — the

[2]*Calhoun:* John Calhoun (1782–1850), statesman and vice-president of the United States (1825–1832).

[3]*Prof. von Holst:* Hermann Eduard von Holst (1841–1904), author of a seven-volume history of the United States and ardent supporter of the Union during and after the Civil War.

meeting point between savagery and civilization. Much has been written about the frontier from the point of view of border warfare and the chase, but as a field for the serious study of the economist and the historian it has been neglected.

The American frontier is sharply distinguished from the European 4 frontier — a fortified boundary line running through dense populations. The most significant thing about the American frontier is, that it lies at the hither edge of free land. In the census reports it is treated as the margin of that settlement which has a density of two or more to the square mile. The term is an elastic one, and for our purposes does not need sharp definition. We shall consider the whole frontier belt, including the Indian country and the outer margin of the "settled area" of the census reports. This paper will make no attempt to treat the subject exhaustively; its aim is simply to call attention to the frontier as a fertile field for investigation, and to suggest some of the problems which arise in connection with it.

In the settlement of America we have to observe how European life 5 entered the continent, and how America modified and developed that life and reacted on Europe. Our early history is the study of European germs developing in an American environment. Too exclusive attention has been paid by institutional students to the Germanic origins, too little to the American factors. The frontier is the line of most rapid and effective Americanization. The wilderness masters the colonist. It finds him a European in dress, industries, tools, modes of travel, and thought. It takes him from the railroad car and puts him in the birch canoe. It strips off the garments of civilization and arrays him in the hunting shirt and the moccasin. It puts him in the log cabin of the Cherokee and Iroquois and runs an Indian palisade[4] around him. Before long he has gone to planting Indian corn and plowing with a sharp stick; he shouts the war cry and takes the scalp in orthodox Indian fashion. In short, at the frontier the environment is at first too strong for the man. He must accept the conditions which it furnishes, or perish, and so he fits himself into the Indian clearings and follows the Indian trails. Little by little he transforms the wilderness, but the outcome is not the old Europe, not simply the development of Germanic germs, any more than the first phenomenon was a case of reversion to the Germanic mark. The fact is, that here is a new product that is American. At first, the frontier was the Atlantic coast. It was the frontier of Europe in a very real sense. Moving westward,

[4]*palisade:* defensive fence made of large pointed stakes.

the frontier became more and more American. As successive terminal moraines result from successive glaciations, so each frontier leaves its traces behind it, and when it becomes a settled area the region still partakes of the frontier characteristics. Thus the advance of the frontier has meant a steady movement away from the influence of Europe, a steady growth of independence on American lines. And to study this advance, the men who grew up under these conditions, and the political, economic, and social results of it, is to study the really American part of our history.

Composite Nationality

First, we note that the frontier promoted the formation of a composite 6 nationality for the American people. The coast was preponderantly English, but the later tides of continental immigration flowed across to the free lands. This was the case from the early colonial days. The Scotch-Irish and the Palatine[5] Germans, or "Pennsylvania Dutch," furnished the dominant element in the stock of the colonial frontier. With these peoples were also the freed indented servants, or redemptioners, who at the expiration of their time of service passed to the frontier. Governor Spottswood of Virginia writes in 1717, "The inhabitants of our frontiers are composed generally of such as have been transported hither as servants, and, being out of their time, settle themselves where land is to be taken up and that will produce the necessarys of life with little labour." Very generally these redemptioners were of non-English stock. In the crucible of the frontier the immigrants were Americanized, liberated, and fused into a mixed race, English in neither nationality nor characteristics. The process has gone on from the early days to our own. Burke[6] and other writers in the middle of the eighteenth century believed that Pennsylvania was "threatened with the danger of being wholly foreign in language, manners, and perhaps even inclinations." The German and Scotch-Irish elements in the frontier of the South were only less great. In the middle of the present century the German element in Wisconsin was already so considerable that leading publicists looked to the creation of a German state out of the commonwealth by concentrating their colonization. Such examples teach us to beware of misinterpreting the fact that there is a common English speech in America into a belief that the stock is also English.

[5]*Palatine:* from the Palatinate, a region of Germany west of the Rhine.
[6]*Burke:* Edmund Burke (1729–1797), British statesman and political writer, most famous for his conservative masterpiece, *Reflections on the Revolution in France*.

Intellectual Traits

From the conditions of frontier life came intellectual traits of profound 7
importance. The works of travelers along each frontier from colonial days
onward describe certain common traits, and these traits have, while
softening down, still persisted as survivals in the place of their origin,
even when a higher social organization succeeded. The result is that to
the frontier the American intellect owes its striking characteristics. That
coarseness and strength combined with acuteness and inquisitiveness;
that practical, inventive turn of mind, quick to find expedients; that
masterful grasp of material things, lacking in the artistic but powerful
to effect great ends; that restless, nervous energy; that dominant individualism, working for good and for evil, and withal that buoyancy and
exuberance which comes with freedom — these are traits of the frontier,
or traits called out elsewhere because of the existence of the frontier.
Since the days when the fleet of Columbus sailed into the waters of the
New World, America has been another name for opportunity, and the
people of the United States have taken their tone from the incessant
expansion which has not only been open but has even been forced upon
them. He would be a rash prophet who should assert that the expansive
character of American life has now entirely ceased. Movement has been
its dominant fact, and, unless this training has no effect upon a people,
the American energy will continually demand a wider field for its exercise.
But never again will such gifts of free land offer themselves. For a
moment, at the frontier, the bonds of custom are broken and unrestraint
is triumphant. There is not *tabula rasa*.[7] The stubborn American environment is there with its imperious summons to accept its conditions;
the inherited ways of doing things are also there; and yet, in spite of
environment, and in spite of custom, each frontier did indeed furnish
a new field of opportunity, a gate of escape from the bondage of the
past; and freshness, and confidence, and scorn of older society, impatience
of its restraints and its ideas, and indifference to its lessons, have accompanied the frontier. What the Mediterranean Sea was to the Greeks,
breaking the bond of custom, offering new experiences, calling out new
institutions and activities, that, and more, the ever retreating frontier
has been to the United States directly, and to the nations of Europe
more remotely. And now, four centuries from the discovery of America,
at the end of a hundred years of life under the Constitution, the frontier
has gone, and with its going has closed the first period of American
history.

[7]*tabula rasa:* [Latin] literally, a blank slate, with an allusion to the philosophy of John
Locke, who used the term to describe the mind at birth.

Engaging the Text

1. Turner argues that the frontier has left an indelible impression on the American CHARACTER. Explain this position, giving examples of how American consciousness was shaped by the frontier.
2. What kinds of METAPHORS does Turner use to describe westward expansion and migration? What is their effect? Are they appropriate?

Exploring Connections

1. Compare Turner's view of frontier Americans to Crèvecoeur's earlier in this chapter.
2. Read Milton Gordon's models of ASSIMILATION in Chapter Three, "One Nation or Many?" Which model does Turner stress in his "composite nationality" section? Can you spot any differences between Gordon's and Turner's views of this model?
3. Consult the *Harvard Encyclopedia of American Ethnic Groups* or other historical sources to investigate the role of minority peoples in settling frontier areas of the United States. Summarize your findings for the class. You may wish to limit yourself to a particular time period, minority group, and area.

Extending the Critical Context

1. Examine popular culture (TV shows, movies, music, magazines, advertising, etc.), political speeches, and other contemporary phenomena for traces of the dream of the frontier that are still with us. How does the dream of the frontier function in such contexts today? What does it tell us about ourselves, our past, or the messages it is associated with?
2. Assuming that Turner's "frontier thesis" is true, what changes in the American character or American history would you expect to occur after the closing of the frontier in 1890? Has any of these changes occurred?

Cowboy

JANE KRAMER

The cowboy is perhaps the most famous embodiment of the myth of the rough-and-ready American frontiersman. Certainly it has proven one of the most enduring and influential incarnations of the American ideal of individualism. In The Last Cowboy, *Jane Kramer offers a close look at this vanishing breed. This excerpt, an example of what has come to be known as "the new journalism," is the nonfictional account of the experiences of Henry Blanton, modern cowboy and ranch manager, who works a corporate-owned spread in the Texas panhandle. Modeling himself on cowboy heroes in the movies, Henry Blanton struggles to maintain ideals and a way of life that may exist only in his fantasies.*

Jane Kramer (b. 1938) has won numerous awards for her intimate profiles of people living on the margins of society. She writes biographical studies that seek to break down the barriers between sociology and journalism, information and entertainment.

Henry Blanton turned forty on an April day when the first warm winds   1
of spring crossed the Texas Panhandle and the diamondback rattlers, fresh and venomous from their winter sleep, came slipping out from under the cap rock of the Canadian River breaks. It was a day full of treachery and promise, the kind of day that Henry would have expected for the showdown in a good Western. Henry was particular about Westerns. When he was a boy and hired out in the summer — for fifty cents a day and the privilege of keeping a local rancher's thirsty cows from ambling downriver from their summer pasture — he saved his pay in a rusty tin bank shaped like a bull and planned a winter's worth of Westerns at Amarillo's movie houses. At night, summers, with the covers pulled tight above his head, Henry braved the moaning ghosts who rode the river breeze past the old stone line camp where he slept alone — and the way he did it was by fixing his thoughts on calm, courageous movie cowboys. He never summoned up the image of his father, who once had been as fine a cowboy as any man in the Panhandle, or the image of his Grandaddy Abel, who had made the long cattle drive to Wyoming back when Indians were still marauding and a rustler with a long rope would as often as not shoot a trail boss who rode out looking for his strays. Henry, deep in his bedroll, shoring up courage against the river's dead, called on John Wayne, Gary Cooper, and Glenn Ford. Especially Glenn Ford. He was convinced then that for "expressin' right," as he put it, there had never been a cowboy to equal Glenn Ford — and he was still convinced of this at forty.

"Expressin' right" was important to the man I call Henry Blanton. It   2
was a gift that he had lost, and he did not know why and was ashamed of himself anyway for wondering, since part of expressing right as a cowboy had to do with the kind of quiet certainty that sustained a man when times were bad. Henry believed that other men might talk to

themselves too much, like women, or fret and complain, but a proper cowboy did not. When he watched a Western now, on the big television console he had bought on credit the day the electric lines reached his house on the Willow Ranch, it was less for pleasure or amusement, or even courage, than to find a key to the composure that eluded him. Henry never doubted his abilities as a cowboy. He was the foreman of ninety thousand acres, and he ran them well, considering that he had to take his orders from a rancher who had moved to Eaton Square, in London, and that those orders came to him through a college-boy ranch manager who knew more about juggling account books than raising cattle and was so terrified of cows anyway that he did most of his managing from the driver's seat of a locked, air-conditioned Buick. Henry was a good rider and a fine roper. He could pull a calf with considerable skill, and when he had to he could cut a dogie from the belly of its dying mother. He could account for every one of the twenty-two hundred cows in his charge as if they were his own. He knew which cows delivered strong, healthy calves each spring, which cows needed help calving, which ones tended to miss a year or deliver stillborn. He knew by instinct when a fence was down or a pole had rotted. He could put his ear to the pump pipe of a windmill well that was drawing poorly and tell in minutes whether the checks were broken or the water, three hundred and fifty feet underground, was drying up. He had all those skills, but somehow he was not the sort of cowboy who inspired admiration or respect.

People regarded Henry with exasperation or indulgence. There was something unsettled about his character — something that made him restless and a little out of control. He could not quite manage that economy of gesture and person which was appropriate in a cowboy. Some frustration drove him to a kind of inept excess. He drank too much in town, and worked with a bottle of bourbon in his Ford pickup truck and another bottle in his saddlebag. His stunts were famous — people still talked about the time Henry and his brother, Tom, backed a wild mare into a Pampa funeral parlor — but lately they had turned ugly and immodest. He was hard on his wife, Betsy, and neighbors had begun to remark that he was getting hard on his animals, too. He moved his cows a little too fast for their placidity, drove his yearlings a little too fast for their daily gain. When he worked cattle these days, he was apt to forget to keep his knife sharpened. Sometimes, dehorning, he sawed too deep into a calf's horns, and the creature's lowing turned mad with pain.

Henry had lived on ranches where his camp was thirty or forty miles from a paved road; ranches where Betsy had to cart water from a spring to do the dishes or wash her babies' diapers; ranches where even the best cowboy was worth no more to his boss than a hundred and fifty dollars a month in wages, a shack for a home, and the meat from steers that were too scrawny to send to auction. He did not like to complain about his life now, in a neat prefabricated house with electricity and a telephone and running water — a house with a highway only twelve miles away down a negotiable dirt road. But a rancher could trust his foreman with ninety thousand or nine hundred thousand acres and still regard him as a kind of overgrown boy who was best protected from himself by a stern paternal hand guiding him through a life's indenture.

The movies Henry loved had told him that a good cowboy was a hero. 5 They had told him that a cowboy lived by codes, not rules — codes of calm, solitude, and honor — and that a cowboy had a special arrangement with nature and, with his horse under him and the range spread out around him, knew a truth and a freedom and a satisfaction that ordinary men did not. Even the circuit preacher who came to town every second Sunday claimed that, while no one was really free, a man on a horse surely had a head start in the business of grace over Communists and New Yorkers and all the other sinners who lived by malice and greed. But the movies were changing — they were full of despair lately. The preacher himself had started making money giving I.Q. tests to the Baptists on his route for a rich Bible college that was running a study called God and Intellect. And Henry, turning forty, had little to show for his life as a cowboy except a hand-tooled saddle and a few horses. Betsy had baked a cake, but she was not speaking to him that birthday morning. His daughter Melinda, washing for school, had used up all the hot water. Henry began his forty-first year with a hangover and an icy shower, and, pulling on his boots, he brooded about the future. The West was full of fences and feedyards now. It was crowded with calf traders and futures brokers, college boys who didn't know a Hereford from an Angus, and ranchers who commuted from London or the South of France — and, whatever the movies once promised, there was not much chance, in a showdown, for a hero on a horse.

The road to Henry Blanton's house began as a narrow, rutted cowpath 6 off a highway north of the town of Canadian, and the only thing that distinguished it from a hundred other cowpaths off that stretch of highway was the big, rusty Willow Ranch brand that swayed, suspended, from an arch above the ranch gate. The brand made a fine target for the high-school boys from town who liked to cruise the highway nights in their fathers' pickups, taking potshots. Henry had to keep a standing order with the local blacksmith for a new brand every other year, but all in all he took the damage philosophically. Everyone he knew owned guns and rifles, and liked to use them. Henry himself carried a .30–30 Winchester slung across the gun rack on his Ford pickup. He believed that hiding weapons was low and cowardly — that a man's right to arm himself against villainy was something sacred, and came straight from God. Lately, of course, there was not much villainy of the sort that Henry and his neighbors could take on with a rifle or a six-gun. They heard a lot about the criminals down in Amarillo, but Amarillo was almost a hundred and fifty miles away, and out in the country people had to content themselves with shooting rattlers and coyotes. The only criminals they were apt to meet were a few fast-talking cattle dealers who specialized in swindling widows and were always safely across the state line anyway by the time people started looking for them.

The land on either side of the Willow gate was flat, irrigated land, 7 planted in wheat for winter grazing, and by April it was almost ready for harvesting. The path ran straight between those precious wheat fields, following a line of wire fence that carried a mean dose of electric current. But once the grassland started, the path began to dip and curve. It followed a fence here, circled a patch of burned-out mesquite there, and veered off toward a windmill somewhere else. The land turned vivid and surprising then. Old, gnarled cactus, tall as trees, sprouted delicate, obscene caps of yellow flowers. Tiny white blossoms sprinkled themselves like spun sugar over the fanning spikes of giant yucca plants. The short blue-grama grass of the pastures, moist and green for a month before the summer sun began to cure it, made strange patches on the clay soil. And cows blocked the path at every turning. They stood motionless in the mud while their calves suckled — stubborn, melancholy creatures, staring out over the scrubby land as if it puzzled and repelled them. For miles, the only sign of human life was an old bunkhouse where Henry's three Mexican hands lived, along with a simple drifter named Jerome, who had wandered onto the ranch a couple of years ago, and who cooked for the Mexicans now and did their wash in exchange for a share of the bunkhouse food, a bed, and the Mexicans' reluctant company. But the road wound on and on, tracing enormous curves across the pastures. Twelve miles in from the highway, it dipped behind a little rise shaded by hackberry trees and cottonwoods, and there it trailed off into a footpath to the Blantons' front door.

Henry's camp was the ranch headquarters. Henry could stand at his 8 door and look across a dirt courtyard to a sheet-metal barn the size of an airplane hangar which held nearly all the supplies he needed to run the Willow. Over the nine years that Henry had worked the ranch, the barn had grown by sections. Just last year, sixty feet had been added, but Henry had seen to it that the things that pleased him most as a cowboy were still within sight of his courtyard. The little hill, with its grove of hackberries and cottonwoods. The shabby, solitary willow by the well. The pasture where his horses grazed. The wooden pens, off the barn, where the milk cows and the dogies[1] fed from troughs, and where Melinda, at fourteen, scrubbed and curried and adored her new roan, Sugar. The old chuck wagon that Abel Blanton once used on roundups — Henry had rescued it for twenty dollars and a promise to haul it home when the Caliche Ranch, where his grandfather had worked for thirty years, was sold to an Eastern conglomerate. By now, all the paraphernalia of modern ranching was well hidden behind the barn, out of sight of the house and the courtyard. Henry worked there when he had to — when he and his hands were branding the little calves that arrived regularly, in truckloads, from farms in Mississippi and Louisiana. Henry had improvised a kind of outdoor assembly line behind the barn. It was a line of ramps and chutes and sprayers ending up at one of the huge iron clamps that cowboys refer to tenderly as "calf cradles" and that can flatten a struggling calf with the turn of a handle and tip it onto its side for the ordeal of castration, branding, and dehorning. The cradle at the Willow was only two years old, but thousands of head of the mangy southern calves — Mississipps or Okies, the cowboys called them — that Henry's rancher bought and grazed for quick profit had already been run through it. It was foul with a crust of blood and feces which no spring rain could wash away.

Sometimes, toward evening, Betsy climbed onto a rail of one of the rough pine cattle chutes, with her copy of *Woman's Day* and a glass of sweet iced tea, to watch the sunset. There was a fine view west, from the chutes, to the Canadian breaks, and Betsy had always loved that moment just before the sun dropped, when the cliffs lit up like a jagged slash of fire on the horizon. But she could never persuade Henry to sit and watch with her. *His* favorite place for sitting was the driver's seat of his Granddaddy Abel's chuck wagon, which he kept parked under the willow tree. Henry had restored the wagon and was proud of it. The job had taken the better part of three days and nights, with Henry living out of his pickup in a pasture on the Caliche Ranch, but he had been determined. By the time Betsy got worried and sent a state trooper out to find him, he had mended the rotting boards with scraps of barn siding, painted the chuck box, realigned the wheels, and was heading

[1] *dogies:* calves.

home. The trooper found him easily — driving up the highway with the ancient wagon rattling along behind his pickup and a pint of bourbon in his hand. There was a brief bad moment between them after the trooper suggested taking Henry into town for a breath test. Henry had to explain that he was hauling his granddaddy's chuck wagon home to the family, where it belonged, so that no son-of-a-bitch corporation college boys would ever get the opportunity to pretty it up like a dude-ranch buggy and show it off to their Wall Street friends on hunting-season picnics. Then, of course, the state trooper repented. He even joined Henry in the pickup for some reminiscing. They knew each other well enough for that — they were old antagonists, in the way that cowboys and lawmen were meant to be antagonists, and between them they could count up eight serious confrontations over fights and stunts. But, sitting together in the Ford pickup on the hot, dusty day that Henry brought his grandfather's chuck wagon home, they shared a momentary truce, mourning the West that was supposed to be — mourning, even, their old, useless animosity.

After that, Henry did his best to introduce the chuck wagon to the   10 Willow. Once, for a spring roundup, he fitted the wagon out with pots and pans, a water keg, and bedrolls, and ordered one of his Mexican hands to practice making sourdough biscuits and coleslaw and rhubarb pie from Betsy's "Chuck Wagon Cookbook." He wanted his hands and all the neighbors who would be helping on the roundup to sleep out under the stars, the way cowboys used to do in Abel Blanton's time. And everybody did sleep out — the first night. Henry brought his harmonica, and Tom — who always neighbored for his brother, despite the fact that their ranchers had not spoken since a lawsuit over some gas-drilling rights five years earlier — brought his guitar. The men sang and drank and enjoyed their pie and managed to put away an entire side of spit-roasted grass-fed beef. They had a splendid time, in fact, until the wind blew up and the bugs, attracted by the campfires and the cooking smells, started coming. By morning, they were grumpy and exhausted. And by late afternoon, after roping and branding some three hundred frisky calves, they had all mumbled apologies and were leading their horses to their horse trailers and heading home to hot baths, kitchen dinners, and dry beds. Henry spent that night in a pasture with the woeful Mexican cook, who served him another fine chuck-wagon supper and then went off to eat alone, because Henry did not really approve of breaking bread with wetbacks. Henry still brought the wagon out to roundups, but by now the gesture was more ceremonial than practical, and he always hauled it home after supper. Summers, the local cowboys' children borrowed it for serving hot dogs and Dr Pepper at their Peewee Rodeo, but mostly it stayed put under the willow, where Henry could sit and daydream in the morning while he waited for his hands.

Henry was up at six most spring and summer mornings — in winter, when the days were short, he got up at five — and on school days he helped Melinda with the barn chores, which were hard for her to manage by herself, now that her three older sisters were grown and gone. While Betsy was in the kitchen grilling the bacon and eggs and making coffee, they fed the milk cows and groomed the horses. Sometimes Melinda would lead the horses out to the small pasture off the courtyard. More often lately Henry did it for her, stopping on his way back to breakfast to fill his pickup at the gas tank by the last barn door and to switch off the two-way radio that Lester Hill, the Willow ranch manager, had insisted on installing in the truck a couple of years ago. The radio, set to a base station at Lester's house, shamed Henry. He kept it on when he was touring the ranch alone or doing the chores at headquarters, but when he imagined Lester, mornings, loafing in pajamas by the swimming pool of his fancy new house on the edge of town, the picture convinced him that no ranch manager would ever get the chance to challenge his authority when he was with his hands.

Henry valued his authority. He hurried through breakfast so that he could always greet his men with the day's orders looking relaxed and confident. He liked to sit on the wagon, waiting, with his scratch pad in his hand and a pencil behind his ear, and he made it a point to be properly dressed for the morning's work in his black boots, a pair of clean black jeans, and his old black hat and jacket. Henry liked wearing black. The Virginian, he had heard, wore black, and so had Gary Cooper in the movie "High Noon," and now Henry wore it with a kind of innocent pride, as if the color carried respect and a hero's stern, elegant qualities. Once, Betsy discovered him at the bathroom mirror dressed in his black gear, his eyes narrowed and his right hand poised over an imaginary holster. She teased him about it then — at least, until he got so mad that he stayed out half the night in town drinking — but a few weeks later she took a snapshot of him in that same gear and sent it to the Philip Morris company, with a note saying that in her opinion Henry Blanton was much more impressive as a cowboy than the people they used to advertise their Marlboro cigarettes. Henry was, in fact, a handsome man. He was tall and rugged, and ranch life had seasoned the smooth, round face that grinned, embarrassed, in the tinted wedding picture that Betsy kept on the upright piano in her parlor. There was a fine-lined, weathered look about Henry at forty. Too much bourbon and beer had put a gut on him, but his gray eyes were clear and quick most days, and often humorous, and his sandy hair had got thick and wiry as it grayed — a little rumpled and overgrown, because he hated haircuts, though never long enough to cause comment in a cowboy bar. He had a fine, solemn swagger. Saturday nights at the country-and-Western dance in Pampa, he thumped around the floor, serious and sweating, and the women liked to watch him — there was something boyish and charming about his grave self-consciousness. When he was younger, he used to laugh and bow and shake hands with everybody after a good polka. Now, more often than not, he blinked and looked around, suddenly embarrassed, and his laugh was loud and nervous, and made the women who had been watching him uncomfortable.

Betsy attributed the change in Henry to disappointment and drinking. 13 She did not really approve of drinking. She did not want liquor in her house — none of the cowboys' wives she knew did — and even Henry agreed that there was something a little indecent about a bottle of bourbon on display in a Christian living room. Henry drank with guile — the guile of a schoolboy waiting to be caught and punished. It gave an edge to his pleasure, and turned his evasions of the household rules into an artful and immensely satisfying pastime. Besides the bottles in his pickup and his saddlebag, he kept a fifth of Jim Beam hidden behind some old cereal boxes on the top shelf of a kitchen cabinet and another stashed underneath the chuck-wagon seat. He liked to have a drink in the mornings with his white cowhands, but he was careful never to bring the wagon bottle out until his daughter and his wife were gone.

Usually, Melinda left first, careening down the cowpath in an old 14 ranch jeep that Henry had overhauled years earlier to get his daughters to the Willow gate, where the school bus stopped at seven-thirty and, again, late in the afternoon. Then Betsy followed in the family Chevrolet. Betsy worked as an invoice clerk in a grain-sorghum dealer's warehouse thirty miles down the highway. Given the condition of the cowpath and the Panhandle weather, she had to spend some two and a half hours every day commuting, and in spring and summer, with tornado warnings out so often, there were nights when she had to stay in town and sleep at a cousin's house. The drive tired her, and the job had begun to bore her, but she kept working, because the family depended on the money that she made. She liked to say that the ranch took care of everything they needed except a decent income. The ranch provided their house, paid their electric bill, and kept their freezer full of beef. Two ranch steers went to Henry every year — he chose them himself, when they were coming off winter wheat, and then he turned them back to pasture, because, like most cowboys, he preferred the lean, sinewy meat of a range-fat steer to the rich, marbled meat of an animal fattened in a feedyard.

Still, Henry made only seven hundred dollars a month running the 15 Willow, and most of that went out on payday just for bills and taxes. His monthly pickup allowance from the ranch gave him two hundred dollars more, but his pickup costs, for gas and bank payments, came to three hundred, and he had to add fifty dollars to meet the loan for the family car. Every winter, too, the pickup needed new tires, and they cost more than three hundred dollars. Then, there was the expense of keeping horses. The price of a colt, in a private deal, was over two hundred dollars, while a two-year-old quarter horse with some training could cost as much as seven hundred. A good saddle for that horse was another seven hundred lately; the bridle to go with it cost a hundred more, and the price of a nylon rope for roping and dragging calves was up to twenty dollars. And Henry was expected to provide the horses that he rode and to carry his own gear and saddle, just as he was expected to own the pickup that he drove. Every rancher he had ever worked for had made the assumption that cowboys took better care of their own property than somebody else's, and Henry agreed — in practice, if not in principle, his own assumption being that ranch gear was bound to be shoddy and unsafe and that ranch horses were untrustworthy. He had heard of a ranch hand down near Amarillo who had ridden out one day with a ranch bridle and suffered the rest of his life for it. The bridle was old and worn, but none of the cowboys on the ranch knew that the bit had snapped once and been welded. It snapped again that day, and the hand was thrown and trampled. Now, fourteen years and as many operations later, he was still paralyzed.

Henry had ordered his last saddle from the Stockman's Saddle Shop, 16 in Amarillo, as a kind of compensation when Betsy started working, five years ago. His monthly pay then was only five hundred and fifty dollars, and there was never enough money to buy the groceries, keep the girls in school clothes, settle Henry's debts at the package store,[2] and meet Betsy's Christmas Club payments at the bank. All four Blanton girls were still at home then. They wanted their own horses, and Betsy thought it would be nice if they had music lessons with the new piano teacher over in Perryton — the one who had been doing so well on the concert stage in Oklahoma City until she happened to start a conversation with a handsome cowboy in front of a statue at the National Cowboy Hall of Fame and abandoned her career for a ranch wife's life. As Betsy

[2] *package store:* liquor store.

saw the problem, she had no choice but to take a job, and she took the first one that she was offered. Henry shouted a lot about it, and then he sulked, and finally he left the ranch one morning in the middle of work and drove straight to the sorghum dealer's office. He had been thinking, he said later, about his brother Tom, whose wife, Lisa Lou, had got herself a job in a bakery, and how humiliating it was for Tom to have to stay in the kitchen cooking lunch for everybody when he and the other hands at the Circle Y Ranch were working cattle near his camp. Henry told Betsy's boss that a cowboy's wife had her duty to her husband and to the ranch that paid him. He was eloquent. A foreman's house, he said, was a kind of command post, and a foreman's wife was like a general — well, maybe not a general but the general's secretary — whose job it was to stay at that post taking messages, relaying messages, keeping track of everybody on the ranch, sending help in an emergency. He talked about the time that winter that he had had a flat tire far from home, in a freezing and remote pasture. He said that he might have died waiting out there in the cold all night if Betsy had not been home to miss him — to call the hands from their supper and tell them where to search. But the sorghum dealer was stubborn. Betsy could type and knew some shorthand, and she looked to him, he said, like a respectable woman — not like one of those town women, with their false eyelashes and skimpy skirts, who thought of a job as the free use of somebody else's telephone. Eventually, he and Henry arrived at a compromise: Betsy would work most days, but whenever Henry was working cattle at headquarters she would stay home and cook the hands a proper branding lunch.

The arrangement was fine with Betsy, whose only interest in a job 17 anyway had been the money she would earn. That year, she gave the girls their horses, arranged for their music lessons, and bought herself a velvet pants suit with a lacy blouse for the Christmas holidays, and now, after two raises, she was making three dollars and sixty-five cents an hour and could afford a standing Saturday appointment with the hairdresser in Pampa. Still, Betsy was looking tired lately. All the cowboys' wives said so. She looked as if her life had hurt her and worn her out. Years ago, when Henry began to court her, she was the prettiest girl in her class at the district high school — a slender girl with wide blue eyes and a dimpled smile and wavy yellow hair that flipped in the wind when she went riding and was the envy of her friends. Now there was a tension — a kind of tightness — about her. Her face had hardened under the bright, careful pouf of hair that her hairdresser said was just the thing for softening the features of tall, thin women. She was getting sallow, the way people who spend their youth outdoors turn sallow when they are shut up in closed cars and offices. And there was an anxious, bewildered look in her blue eyes when she left the house mornings and passed her husband at the chuck wagon, his black boot tapping on the spot where she suspected that his bourbon was hidden. There was something shy and tentative about those morning partings. If Henry watched the Chevrolet disappear down the cowpath and started thinking about a wife who had to go to work and shame her husband, he was apt to be edgy and dispirited by supper. He would eat too fast then, and retreat to the parlor with a copy of *TV Guide*, looking for a Western to watch on television. But if he spent the day with his head full of dreams and schemes about the future, he sat down to supper exuberant and overwrought, and then he was ready for a night in town — just like one of his Granddaddy Abel's hands on the first payday after four months out on a spring roundup.

On the evening of his fortieth birthday, Henry picked Tom up at the Circle Y Ranch and the brothers drove to Pampa. Henry was in a celebrating mood, because he had just made a birthday resolution. "It's like this, Tom," he said after they had driven in silence for half an hour, passing Henry's pickup bottle back and forth. "Here I'm getting a certain age, and I find I ain't accumulated nothing. I find . . ." 18

Tom nodded. 19

"I mean, it was different with Daddy," Henry said. "Those old men like Daddy — they turned forty and they was just glad if they had a job. But nowadays, you turn forty — you figure you got ten, fifteen years left to really do something." Henry thought for a while. "So that's what I'm figuring to do," he said finally. "Do something." 20

"Shoot, Henry, we're just peons, you and me," Tom said. Tom was known for his way of putting things. He was nearly thirty-seven, but he was still all bones and joints and bashful blushes, like a boy, and when he talked, with his Adam's apple jumping around above his T-shirt collar, even his brother half expected that his voice would crack. 21

"Peons," Tom repeated. It was his favorite word for himself, and he liked to stretch it out in a long drawl — "peeeeons." But the fact was that Tom had been thinking about doing something, too. He had just bought an old jukebox for twenty-five dollars, and he was planning to fix it up, sell it, and, with his profit, buy two old jukeboxes, and then four, until he had bought and sold his way to a used-jukebox fortune. 22

When he and Henry got to town, Henry bought the first round in honor of Tom's jukebox, and Tom the next in honor of Henry's birthday resolution. They drank their bourbon and swapped stories about their 23 best stunts. Tom played his guitar. Henry sang his favorite gospel song — "Love Lifted Me" — to anybody who would listen. And they agreed that the West was still a fine, promising place for a cowboy. They had such a good time celebrating, in fact, that when they left the bar they drove straight to a package store, with the idea of continuing in a pasture on the way home. An hour later, Henry appeared at the kitchen door of a big adobe house near Canadian, where a young ranching couple by the name of Robinson lived. His left eye was swollen shut, and he was holding Tom, who was barely conscious, in his arms.

Henry often ended up at Bay and John Robinson's house when he 24 got into trouble. His own rancher didn't bother to keep a house in the Panhandle any longer, and Tom worked for an oilman whose wife did not like cowboys coming to her house. But the Robinsons were known to be in residence — a condition that had less to do with their living on their ranch than with a kind of patron's jurisdiction. Henry admired John Robinson because John was the nearest thing he knew to the old cattle barons in the movies that he liked so much — someone on the order of, say, John Wayne in "McClintock." John Robinson was just a boy, really, who had come home from studying Greek in Cambridge, Massachusetts, to take over the family ranch from an ailing father. But John understood his duty to the whole mythic enterprise of the West, and that meant he could be counted on to shield a cowboy, speak up for a cowboy, and use his extraordinary influence, as the owner of a piece of property the size of a French province, to settle a problem quickly and quietly for a cowboy, calling on his armamentarium of doctors, lawyers, friendly policemen, and obliging judges, so that a cowboy in trouble was spared the humiliation and confusion of accounting for himself. John had taken Henry on, the way a mama cow takes on a dogie, because Henry was without a rancher of his own in residence to stand up to a sheriff or an angry wife and say, "My cowboy, right or wrong" — even when that cowboy had been in the kind of fight that left his little brother with knife slashes on his back and the skin of his right hand in shreds from plunging through the glass door of a package store.

Henry waited outside the Robinsons' kitchen, with a light spring rain 25 pattering on his black hat, until Bay Robinson looked up from the table, where she was writing out the morning's marketing list, and noticed him. Bay had been raised in Dallas, and she wore long dresses and perfume and huge pale-purple sunglasses around her house, and kept her red hair straight and shiny, like a schoolgirl's. When John first brought her to his ranch, the cowboys figured that she was one of those fluffy, fragile city girls whom ranchers' sons were fond of marrying, but

Bay turned out to be a natural cowman's wife. The look that she gave Henry at the kitchen door was shrewd and maternal and amused. She helped him deposit Tom in a chair at the table, poured two drinks from a bottle of wine on the counter, and left for her library to start making phone calls. Henry sat and waited for her in the kitchen, turning his wet hat over and over in his hands and staring down at the designs on Bay's fancy Spanish floor tiles, trying to avoid the stares of the children, who came running in from their bedrooms to see what was going on. Tom, who was beginning to revive, hung his head, stuffed his tattered hand discreetly in his jacket pocket, and began hiccupping.

"Oh, no," Tom told the children. "Ain't nothing wrong with old Tom here. Just the drizzles. The drizzles plus the hiccups." 26

"Come on, Tom, you been up to something," Bay said, coming back in and sitting down between the brothers. She had already called her husband, who was in Oklahoma buying a supermarket chain, as well as their lawyer, their ranch manager, and one of John's business partners with clout at police headquarters. And by the time the men drove out from town for a kitchen conference she had managed to coax a look at Tom's hand, send him down the hall to change into one of John's shirts, scrub the trail of blood off her floor tiles, and produce a platter of barbecued ribs for her visitors. 27

Henry did not talk to the three men who came to help him. He acknowledged them with a nod, and followed their hurried conversation about police and doctors less by listening than by a kind of furtive appraisal of the scene itself. He accepted an ice pack for his swollen eye, and with his other eye he watched the men, in their immaculately faded jeans and expensive Western shirts, talk about "Tom's troubles" while Tom himself sat patiently beside them, smiling bashfully and trying to eat his barbecued ribs with his left hand. From time to time, the men looked over at Henry, about to ask a question, but something about the way he stared back at them made them stop short. John's lawyer and the partner from town had been cultivating fine mustaches. They had let their hair grow long, nearly to their shoulders, and hair like that was a strong subject among Panhandle cowboys. When youngsters with long hair hitchhiked across the Panhandle in the summer on their way to communes in New Mexico, a lot of cowboys took it as a duty to pick those youngsters up, drive them off onto a lonely cowpath, and remove their hair with a razor or a knife. Henry himself had taken a few hippie scalps, as he put it. He had a lot of contempt for the people he called hippies, and now he counted John Robinson's lawyer and partner among them. Actually, he had never talked with any real hippies except a couple of ranchers' sons and the Pampa and Amarillo boys who drifted into 28 town every now and then to pick up a few days' work at the local feedyard. But he associated hippies and their long hair with some insidious Eastern effeminacy that had infected the moral landscape of the West and left a man like him nearly helpless in his outrage. Tonight in the package store, when two long-haired strangers dressed in boots and hats and flashy Western suits took their time comparing bourbons, Henry had nudged Tom, and the two of them had taken up an old familiar litany.

"Seems like we're getting a lot of hats in this here store, Tom," Henry had started off politely. 29

"Yup, Henry, I'd say four hats — counting us, of course." Tom spoke so sweetly, and his smile was so shy and friendly, that one of the strangers smiled back. 30

"And how many hands, do you suppose, Tom?" Henry had asked him. 31

"Well, shoot, Henry, seems to me it takes more than a hat to make a hand." 32

"Now, Tom, I do believe you got a point there," Henry had said. Then he motioned toward the strangers. "I imagine our two new friends over here might just want to take them hats off." 33

No one had moved then except the clerk, who backed away from the counter. 34

"Second thought, Tom," Henry went on, "let's you and me be real nice and give these boys a hand taking off them hats." 35

The fight was over quickly. One of the strangers swung at Henry with a bottle. Henry kicked him back across the counter. Then the other stranger flicked open a switchblade knife, and Tom went wild. He charged blindly, leaping and kicking and butting, and the strangers fled. They took off down the street on a pair of orange motorcycles while Tom crashed through the glass door in pursuit and the clerk cried into his telephone, pleading with the lady on his party line to interrupt her nightly conversation with her married daughter so that he could call the police. Henry ran out of the store to get Tom off the sidewalk and start the pickup, but Tom was already feeling sorry about the blood and the broken bottles, and he wanted to go back in and apologize. He wanted to explain to the clerk that no one pulled a knife on Henry Blanton while Henry's little brother Tom was around. Henry had to drag him to the pickup, kicking and shouting, but finally they made their getaway. For a while, they cruised the highway, discussing what to do. There was no point in taking Tom to the hospital, where someone was sure to recognize the knife wounds on his back and report the fight to police headquarters. Then, too, Tom was modest. He would rather bleed to death than get undressed in front of a nurse, and, in fact, the last time a fight put him in the hospital he had made a fuss and insisted on 36 sleeping in his hat and boots. There was no point in taking Tom home, either, until he was cleaned up and had a good story ready. So, a few miles past Canadian, with Tom getting weaker, Henry had turned in at the gate of the Robinsons' house. In a week or two, when Tom's hand healed, the fight tonight might enter Henry's repertoire of stories — he might brag about it then, embellishing some, until it made a dazzling stunt. But tonight Henry just sat, silent, in Bay Robinson's kitchen, looking as if he had done his duty to his brother and did not know why, suddenly, his duty seemed so humiliating to him. He waited while the men made their phone calls and Bay, setting a pan of water and some peroxide on the kitchen table, went to work cleaning Tom's hand. But when Bay noticed fresh blood seeping through the back of her husband's shirt and tried to talk Tom into taking the shirt off and letting her clean his back, too, Henry spoke up for the first time and said, "I wouldn't insist, Ma'am, if I was you."

Henry left them. He simply stood up and announced that it was time   37
he and Tom were heading home.

Bay helped him steer Tom to the door. "Come on now, Henry," she   38
whispered. "What were you boys up to?"

"Just celebrating, Ma'am," Henry said.   39

Engaging the Text

1. How do westerns affect Henry Blanton's view of himself? How does his life differ from the lives of movie cowboys?

2. Kramer attributes Blanton's erratic behavior to frustration; what specific sources of frustration does her NARRATIVE suggest?

3. Why does Henry Blanton's "duty" seem humiliating to him at the end of "Cowboy"? Why did he provoke the fight in the package store?

4. Describe Blanton from the POINT OF VIEW of his wife, Betsy, or one of the Mexican ranch hands who works for him.

5. Overall, what seems to be Kramer's attitude toward Henry Blanton? Does she want you to feel sympathetic toward Henry? On what do you base your response? To what extent do you share her attitude?

Exploring Connections

1. How has the West changed since Grandpa Abel's day? How would Frederick Jackson Turner (p. 20) account for these changes? What reasons not covered by Turner's THESIS might account for these changes?

Extending the Critical Context

1. If Henry Blanton were a real-life friend of yours, what advice would you give him to help him better his situation?

2. Assuming that you've just been hired as a staff writer by a large Hollywood studio, how would you rewrite Henry Blanton's story to make it "more positive" or "more heroic" for the movies? Sketch out, in writing, one or two scenes to show your strategy at work.

3. As a literary journalist, Jane Kramer consciously departs from conventional journalistic STYLE. Compare the style of this passage to that of a newspaper or news magazine. What differences do you find in focus, descriptive and FIGURATIVE LANGUAGE, sentences and paragraph structure, and organization of the story? Working in pairs or small groups, rewrite the account of Henry and Tom's "stunt" as a news item. Read these aloud and discuss what the story gains or loses by this treatment.

Dear John Wayne

LOUISE ERDRICH

Most stories of the American frontier neglect the perspective of the peoples who were displaced by the westward expansion of the United States. This contemporary poem, about a group of Native Americans watching a John Wayne movie at a drive-in, questions some of the assumptions about frontier history and heroism found in earlier readings. Louise Erdrich (b. 1954) is of mixed German-American and Chippewa descent. She has published a volume of poetry, many short stories, and two novels, Love Medicine *(1984) and* The Beet Queen *(1986). The former won the National Book Critics Circle Award for fiction.*

August and the drive-in picture is packed.
We lounge on the hood of the Pontiac
surrounded by the slow-burning spirals they sell
at the window, to vanquish the hordes of mosquitoes.
Nothing works. They break through the smoke-screen for blood.   5

Always the look-out spots the Indians first,
spread north to south, barring progress.
The Sioux, or Cheyenne, or some bunch
in spectacular columns, arranged like SAC missiles,
their feathers bristling in the meaningful sunset.   10

The drum breaks. There will be no parlance.
Only the arrows whining, a death-cloud of nerves
swarming down on the settlers
who die beautifully, tumbling like dust weeds
into the history that brought us all here   15
together: this wide screen beneath the sign of the bear.

The sky fills, acres of blue squint and eye
that the crowd cheers. His face moves over us,
a thick cloud of vengeance, pitted
like the land that was once flesh. Each rut,   20
each scar makes a promise: *It is
not over, this fight, not as long as you resist.*

Everything we see belongs to us.
A few laughing Indians fall over the hood
slipping in the hot spilled butter.   25
The eye sees a lot, John, but the heart is so blind.
How will you know what you own?
He smiles, a horizon of teeth
the credits reel over, and then the white fields
again blowing in the true-to-life dark.   30
The dark films over everything.
We get into the car
scratching our mosquito bites, speechless and small
as people are when the movie is done.
We are back in ourselves.   35

How can we help but keep hearing his voice,
the flip side of the sound-track, still playing:
Come on, boys, we've got them
where we want them, drunk, running.
They will give us what we want, what we need: 40
The heart is a strange wood inside of everything
we see, burning, doubling, splitting out of its skin.

Engaging the Text

1. Identify which lines refer to actions and CHARACTERS in the movie and which lines describe what's going on at the drive-in. What parallels or contrasts does Erdrich draw between the movie and the people watching it?

2. Does the SPEAKER of the poem change? If so, where do the changes occur and how can you tell?

3. This poem is filled with details that suggest meanings beyond the simple DENOTATION of the things themselves. What do you make of the way Erdrich emphasizes the mosquitoes that attack for blood, the "SAC missiles," the "meaningful sunset," the "sign of the bear," the "land that was once flesh"? What do these details say about the history of Native Americans?

4. Whose POINT OF VIEW does the line "The Sioux, or Cheyenne, or some bunch" reflect? What unspoken assumptions does it reveal?

5. Why do the Indians laugh in STANZA 5? Why, at the end of the stanza, does the speaker say, "We are back in ourselves"?

6. What do you make of the poem's enigmatic concluding METAPHOR? How does the poem as a whole illustrate the heart "burning, doubling, splitting"?

Exploring Connections

1. How does the poem call into question the view of the frontier offered by Frederick Jackson Turner earlier in this chapter?

Extending the Critical Context

1. The heroes of movie westerns had a tremendous impact on Henry Blanton's IMAGE of himself as he grew up (Blanton is Jane Kramer's "hero" in the previous selection, "Cowboy.") In light of Erdrich's poem, speculate about the kind of impact they might have on a Native American child.

INDIVIDUALISM AND SUCCESS

The Paradox of Individualism
ROBERT N. BELLAH, RICHARD MADSEN,
WILLIAM M. SULLIVAN, ANN SWIDLER,
AND STEVEN M. TIPTON

"The Paradox of Individualism" offers carefully articulated insights into a huge, potentially confusing issue: the relationship of the individual American to American society itself. As the authors explain, this relationship is problematic because while Americans value freedom and independence, we also hunger for acceptance and identification with a larger group or community. The passage offered here is excerpted from Habits of the Heart: Individualism and Commitment in American Life, *an influential study of American social values which first appeared in 1985.* Habits of the Heart *was the result of sociological research involving more than two hundred subjects in American communities between 1979 and 1984.*

Individualism lies at the very core of American culture. . . . We 1
believe in the dignity, indeed the sacredness, of the individual. Anything
that would violate our right to think for ourselves, judge for ourselves,
make our own decisions, live our lives as we see fit, is not only morally
wrong, it is sacrilegious. Our highest and noblest aspirations, not only
for ourselves, but for those we care about, for our society and for the
world, are closely linked to our individualism. Yet . . . some of our
deepest problems both as individuals and as a society are also closely
linked to our individualism. We do not argue that Americans should
abandon individualism — that would mean for us to abandon our deepest
identity. But individualism has come to mean so many things and to
contain such contradictions and paradoxes that even to defend it requires
that we analyze it critically, that we consider especially those tendencies
that would destroy it from within.

Mythic Individualism

A deep and continuing theme in American literature is the hero who   2
must leave society, alone or with one or a few others, in order to realize
the moral good in the wilderness, at sea, or on the margins of settled
society. Sometimes the withdrawal involves a contribution to society, as
in James Fenimore Cooper's *The Deerslayer*. Sometimes the new marginal
community realizes ethical ends impossible in the larger society, as in
the interracial harmony between Huckleberry Finn and Jim. Sometimes
the flight from society is simply mad and ends in general disaster, as in
Moby Dick. When it is not in and through society but in flight from it
that the good is to be realized, as in the case of Melville's Ahab, the
line between ethical heroism and madness vanishes, and the destructive
potentiality of a completely asocial individualism is revealed.

America is also the inventor of that most mythic individual hero, the   3
cowboy, who again and again saves a society he can never completely
fit into. The cowboy has a special talent — he can shoot straighter and
faster than other men — and a special sense of justice. But these characteristics make him so unique that he can never fully belong to society.
His destiny is to defend society without ever really joining it. He rides
off alone into the sunset like Shane, or like the Lone Ranger moves on
accompanied only by his Indian companion. But the cowboy's importance
is not that he is isolated or antisocial. Rather, his significance lies in his
unique, individual virtue and special skill and it is because of those
qualities that society needs and welcomes him. Shane, after all, starts
as a real outsider, but ends up with the gratitude of the community and
the love of a woman and a boy. And while the Lone Ranger never settles
down and marries the local schoolteacher, he always leaves with the
affection and gratitude of the people he has helped. It is as if the myth
says you can be a truly good person, worthy of admiration and love,
only if you resist fully joining the group. But sometimes the tension
leads to an irreparable break. Will Kane, the hero of *High Noon*, abandoned
by the cowardly townspeople, saves them from an unrestrained killer,
but then throws his sheriff's badge in the dust and goes off into the
desert with his bride. One is left wondering where they will go, for
there is no longer any link with any town.

The connection of moral courage and lonely individualism is even   4
tighter for that other, more modern American hero, the hard-boiled
detective. From Sam Spade to Serpico, the detective is a loner. He is
often unsuccessful in conventional terms, working out of a shabby office
where the phone never rings. Wily, tough, smart, he is nonetheless
unappreciated. But his marginality is also his strength. When a bit of

business finally comes their way, Philip Marlowe, Lew Archer, and Travis McGee are tenacious. They pursue justice and help the unprotected even when it threatens to unravel the fabric of society itself. Indeed, what is remarkable about the American detective story is less its hero than its image of crime. When the detective begins his quest, it appears to be an isolated incident. But as it develops, the case turns out to be linked to the powerful and privileged of the community. Society, particularly "high society," is corrupt to the core. It is this boring into the center of society to find it rotten that constitutes the fundamental drama of the American detective story. It is not a personal but a social mystery that the detective must unravel.[1]

To seek justice in a corrupt society, the American detective must be tough, and above all, he must be a loner. He lives outside the normal bourgeois pattern of career and family. As his investigations begin to lead him beyond the initial crime to the glamorous and powerful center of the society, its leaders make attempts to buy off the detective, to corrupt him with money, power, or sex. This counterpoint to the gradual unravelling of the crime is the battle the detective wages for his own integrity, in the end rejecting the money of the powerful and spurning (sometimes jailing or killing) the beautiful woman who has tried to seduce him. The hard-boiled detective, who may long for love and success, for a place in society, is finally driven to stand alone, resisting the blandishments of society, to pursue a lonely crusade for justice. Sometimes, as in the film *Chinatown*, corruption is so powerful and so total that the honest detective no longer has a place to stand and the message is one of unrelieved cynicism.

Both the cowboy and the hard-boiled detective tell us something important about American individualism. The cowboy, like the detective, can be valuable to society only because he is a completely autonomous individual who stands outside it. To serve society, one must be able to stand alone, not needing others, not depending on their judgment, and not submitting to their wishes. Yet this individualism is not selfishness. Indeed, it is a kind of heroic selflessness. One accepts the necessity of remaining alone in order to serve the values of the group. And this obligation to aloneness is an important key to the American moral imag-

[1]On individualism in nineteenth-century American literature see D. H. Lawrence, *Studies in Classic American Literature* (1923; Garden City, N.Y.: Doubleday, Anchor Books, 1951). On the image of the cowboy see Will Wright, *Sixguns and Society: A Structural Study of the Western* (Berkeley and Los Angeles: University of California Press, 1975). On cowboys and detectives see John G. Cawelti, *Adventure, Mystery, and Romance: Formula Stories as Art and Popular Culture* (Chicago: University of Chicago Press, 1976). [Author's note]

ination. Yet is is part of the profound ambiguity of the mythology of American individualism that its moral heroism is always just a step away from despair. For an Ahab, and occasionally for a cowboy or a detective, there is no return to society, no moral redemption. The hero's lonely quest for moral excellence ends in absolute nihilism.[2]

If we may turn from the mythical heroes of fiction to a mythic, but 7 historically real, hero, Abraham Lincoln, we may begin to see what is necessary if the nihilistic alternative is to be avoided. In many respects, Lincoln conforms perfectly to the archetype of the lonely, individualistic hero. He was a self-made man, never comfortable with the eastern upper classes. His dual moral commitment to the preservation of the Union and the belief that "all men are created equal" roused the hostility of abolitionists and southern sympathizers alike. In the war years, he was more and more isolated, misunderstood by Congress and cabinet, and unhappy at home. In the face of almost universal mistrust, he nonetheless completed his self-appointed task of bringing the nation through its most devastating war, preaching reconciliation as he did so, only to be brought down by an assassin's bullet. What saved Lincoln from nihilism was the larger whole for which he felt it was important to live and worthwhile to die. No one understood better the meaning of the Republic and of the freedom and equality that it only very imperfectly embodies. But it was not only civic republicanism that gave his life value. Reinhold Niebuhr[3] has said that Lincoln's biblical understanding of the Civil War was deeper than that of any contemporary theologian. The great symbols of death and rebirth that Lincoln invoked to give meaning to the sacrifice of those who died at Gettysburg, in a war he knew to be senseless and evil, came to redeem his own senseless death at the hand of an assassin. It is through his identification with a community and a tradition that Lincoln became the deeply and typically American individual that he was.[4]

[2]On the hero's avoidance of women and society see Leslie Fiedler, *Love and Death in the American Novel* (New York: Stein and Day, 1966), and Ann Swidler, "Love and Adulthood in American Culture," in *Themes of Work and Love in Adulthood*, ed. Neil J. Smelser and Erik H. Erikson (Cambridge, Mass.: Harvard University Press, 1980), pp. 120–47. [Author's note]

[3]*Reinhold Niebuhr:* American theologian (1892–1971), best known for a series of books on Christianity, politics, and history.

[4]The best book on Lincoln's meaning for American public life is Harry V. Jaffa, *Crisis of the House Divided: An Interpretation of the Lincoln-Douglas Debates* (Garden City, N.Y.: Doubleday, 1959). Reinhold Niebuhr's remarks appear in his essay "The Religion of Abraham Lincoln," in *Lincoln and the Gettysburg Address*, ed. Allan Nevins (Urbana, Ill.: University of Illinois Press, 1964), p. 72. [Author's note]

The Social Sources of Ambivalence

Individualism is deeply rooted in America's social history. Here the bondservant became free, the tenant became a small landowner, and what Benjamin Franklin called the self-respecting "middling" condition of men became the norm. Yet the incipient "independent citizen" of colonial times found himself in a cohesive community, the "peaceable kingdoms" that were colonial towns, where ties to family and church and respect for the "natural leaders" of the community were still strong.[5] Individualism was so embedded in the civic and religious structures of colonial life that it had not yet found a name, even though John Locke's ideas about individual autonomy were well known. It took the geographical and economic expansion of the new nation, especially in the years after 1800, to produce the restless quest for material betterment that led Tocqueville[6] to use the word "individualism" to describe what he saw.[7] . . .   8

Tocqueville was quick to point out one of the central ambiguities in the new individualism — that it was strangely compatible with conformism. He described the American insistence that one always rely on one's own judgment, rather than on received authority, in forming one's opinions and that one stand by one's own opinions. We have . . . heard many examples of this attitude . . . — in the assertion, for example, that compromise with others is desirable, but not if you sacrifice your own "values." But, as Tocqueville observed, when one can no longer rely on tradition or authority, one inevitably looks to others for confirmation of one's judgments. Refusal to accept established opinion and anxious conformity to the opinions of one's peers turn out to be two sides of the same coin.[8]   9

There has been a long-standing anxiety that the American individualist, who flees from home and family leaving the values of community and   10

---

[5]See, particularly, Michael Zuckerman, *Peaceable Kingdoms: New England Towns in the Eighteenth Century* (New York: Random House, 1970). The phrase "peaceable kingdom" is, of course, eschatological in its reference. It is what the New Englanders aspired to be, not what they claimed they were. [Author's note]

[6]*Tocqueville:* Alexis de Tocqueville (1805–1859), French politician and writer. (See p. 341.)

[7]On the introduction of the term individualism by Tocqueville and the American response see Yehoshua Arieli, *Individualism and Nationalism in American Ideology* (Cambridge, Mass.: Harvard University Press, 1964), pp. 183–210, 246–76. On the emergence of the term in the European context see Koenraad W. Swart, "Individualism in the Mid-Nineteenth Century," *Journal of the History of Ideas* 23 (1962): 77–90. [Author's note]

[8]Alexis de Tocqueville, *Democracy in America*, trans. George Lawrence, ed. J. P. Mayer (New York: Doubleday, Anchor Books, 1969), vol. 2, part 1, chapters 1 and 2. [Author's note]

tradition behind, is secretly a conformist. Mark Twain depicted the stultifying conformity of the mid-nineteenth-century town of his youth in recounting the adventures of boys who tried to break free of it and never quite succeeded. As late as the 1920s, Sinclair Lewis identified a classic American type in his portrait of *Babbitt*, the small town businessman too afraid of censure from neighbors and family to develop his political convictions or pursue his own happiness in love. The advice Babbitt gives his son not to make the mistake he has made is typical: "Don't be scared of the family. No, nor all of Zenith. Nor of yourself, the way I've been."

In the past hundred years, individualism and its ambiguities have   11
been closely linked to middle-class status. The "middle class" that began to emerge in the later part of the nineteenth century differed from the old "middling condition." In the true sense of the term, the middle class is defined not merely by the desire for material betterment but by a conscious, calculating effort to move up the ladder of success. David Schneider and Raymond Smith usefully define the middle class as a "broad but not undifferentiated category which includes those who have certain attitudes, aspirations, and expectations toward status mobility, and who shape their actions accordingly." Status mobility has increasingly depended on advanced education and competence in managerial and professional occupations that require specialized knowledge. For middle-class Americans, a calculating attitude toward educational and occupational choice has been essential and has often spilled over into determining criteria for the choice of spouse, friends, and voluntary associations. From the point of view of lower-class Americans, these preoccupations do not necessarily seem natural. As one of Schneider and Smith's informants put it, "To be a square dude is hard work, man."[9]

For those oriented primarily to upward mobility, to "success," major   12
features of American society appear to be "the normal outcome of the operation of individual achievement." In this conception, individuals, unfettered by family or other group affiliation, are given the chance to make the best of themselves, and, though equality of opportunity is essential, inequality of result is natural. But the ambiguities of individualism for the middle-class person arise precisely from lack of certainty about what the "best" we are supposed to make of ourselves is. Schneider and Smith note that "there are no fixed standards of behavior which serve to mark status. The only clearly defined cultural standards against which status can be measured are the gross standards of income, consumption,

[9]David M. Schneider and Raymond T. Smith, *Class Differences and Sex Roles in American Kinship and Family Structure* (Englewood Cliffs, N.J.: Prentice-Hall, 1973), pp. 19, 20. [Author's note]

and conformity to rational procedures for attaining ends." Middle-class individuals are thus motivated to enter a highly autonomous and demanding quest for achievement and then left with no standard against which achievement is to be measured except the income and consumption levels of their neighbors, exhibiting anew the clash between autonomy and conformity that seems to be the fate of American individualism.[10]

But perhaps Schneider and Smith's third cultural standard, "rational 13 procedures for attaining ends," offers a way of asserting individual autonomy without the anxious glance at the neighbor. In the case of middle-class professionals whose occupation involves the application of technical rationality to the solution of new problems, the correct solution of a problem or, even more, an innovative solution to a problem, provides evidence of "success" that has intrinsic validity. And where such competence operates in the service of the public good — as, for example, in medical practice at its best — it expresses an individualism that has social value without being conformist.[11]

But to the extent that technical competence is enclosed in the life 14 pattern that we have designated "career," concern for rational problem solving (not to speak of social contribution) becomes subordinated to standards of success measured only by income and consumption. When this happens, as it often does to doctors, lawyers, and other professionals, it raises doubts about the intrinsic value of the work itself. These doubts become all the more insistent when, as is often the case, the professional must operate in the context of a large public or private bureaucracy where much ingenuity must be spent, not on solving external problems, but on manipulating the bureaucratic rules and roles, both in order to get anything done and in order to move ahead in one's career. Anxieties about whether an "organization man" can be a genuine individual long predate William H. Whyte's famous book *The Organization Man*.[12] The cowboy and the detective began to appear as popular heroes when business corporations emerged as the focal institutions of American life. The fantasy of a lonely, but morally impeccable, hero corresponds to doubts about the integrity of the self in the context of modern bureaucratic organization.

The irony of present-day middle-class American individualism derives 15 from the fact that while a high degree of personal initiative, competence, and rationality are still demanded from individuals, the autonomy of the

[10]Ibid., p. 24. [Author's note]
[11]Ibid., p. 46. [Author's note]
[12]William H. Whyte, *The Organization Man* (New York: Simon and Schuster, 1956). [Author's note]

successful individual and even the meaning of "success" are increasingly in doubt. . . . One response to this situation is to make occupational achievement, for so long the dominating focus of middle-class individualism, no longer an end in itself, but merely an instrument for the attainment of a private lifestyle lived, perhaps, in a lifestyle enclave. Yet this solution . . . is subject to doubt. The same inner contradictions that undermined occupational success as a life goal also threaten to deprive private life of meaning when there is no longer any purpose to involvement with others except individual satisfaction.

The ambiguity and ambivalence of American individualism derive from 16
both cultural and social contradictions. We insist, perhaps more than ever before, on finding our true selves independent of any cultural or social influence, being responsible to that self alone, and making its fulfillment the very meaning of our lives. Yet we spend much of our time navigating through immense bureaucratic structures — multiversities, corporations, government agencies — manipulating and being manipulated by others. In describing this situation, Alasdair MacIntyre has spoken of "bureaucratic individualism," the form of life exemplified by the manager and the therapist.[13] In bureaucratic individualism, the ambiguities and contradictions of individualism are frighteningly revealed, as freedom to make private decisions is bought at the cost of turning over most public decisions to bureaucratic managers and experts. A bureaucratic individualism in which the consent of the governed, the first demand of modern enlightened individualism, has been abandoned in all but form, illustrates the tendency of individualism to destroy its own conditions.

But in our interviews, though we saw tendencies toward bureaucratic 17
individualism, we cannot say that it has yet become dominant. Rather we found all the classic polarities of American individualism still operating: the deep desire for autonomy and self-reliance combined with an equally deep conviction that life has no meaning unless shared with others in the context of community; a commitment to the equal right to dignity of every individual combined with an effort to justify inequality of reward, which, when extreme, may deprive people of dignity; an insistence that life requires practical effectiveness and "realism" combined with the feeling that compromise is ethically fatal. The inner tensions of American individualism add up to a classic case of ambivalence. We strongly assert the value of our self-reliance and autonomy. We deeply feel the emptiness of a life without sustaining social commitments. Yet we are hesitant to articulate our sense that we need one another as much as we need to

[13]Alasdair MacIntyre, *After Virtue* (South Bend, Ind.: University of Notre Dame Press, 1981), p. 33. [Author's note]

stand alone, for fear that if we did we would lose our independence altogether. The tensions of our lives would be even greater if we did not, in fact, engage in practices that constantly limit the effects of an isolating individualism, even though we cannot articulate those practices nearly as well as we can the quest for autonomy.

Engaging the Text

1. Define "modern individualism." What problems do the authors see with unbridled, absolute individualism? Why are one's peers, PARADOXICALLY, so important in individualistic American society, according to the authors?

2. What constraints (people, institutions, beliefs, etc.) keep you from doing anything you want as an individual? (Note that not all these constraints need be negative.) Which, if any, are under your control to some extent?

3. According to this reading selection, what roles do women play in the American MYTHOLOGY of individualism?

4. Bellah and his coauthors argue that the IMAGE of the isolated but virtuous hero "corresponds to doubts about the integrity of the self in the context of modern bureaucratic organization." Working in small groups, discuss why bureaucracy threatens one's sense of individuality and how the heroes described by the authors represent a response to this threat. Think of additional examples of heroes who have "bucked the system" and compare notes with other groups.

Exploring Connections

1. Reread the Declaration of Independence. Does it contain any passages that could be interpreted as endorsing the notion of individualism? What conception of the individual emerges from this document?

2. Look back at Turner's definition of the frontier earlier in this chapter. How would an extreme individualist, in the authors' sense of the term, fit into this environment?

3. How well does the description of the "cowboy" in this piece fit Henry Blanton in Jane Kramer's "Cowboy" (p. 25)? In particular, to what extent does Blanton reflect the tension between individualism and the need for community expressed in this selection?

Extending the Critical Context

1. Watch a film or read a story about either a cowboy or a detective. How well do the authors' generalizations hold up? Point to specifics in your story that support, complicate, or contradict the mythic types defined here.

2. Bellah and his coauthors suggest that when the desire for autonomy is unchecked

by a deep commitment to community it can lead to a destructive "nihilism." Do you agree with this analysis? In your view, which poses the greater danger for society — the extreme individual or the extreme CONFORMIST?

Charlie Sabatier

JOHN LANGSTON GWALTNEY

Charlie Sabatier, speaker of the following monologue, offers another view of individualism American style. A paraplegic veteran of the Vietnam War, Sabatier returned to the United States to become an activist for the disabled. This interview with Charlie Sabatier originally appeared in John Langston Gwaltney's The Dissenters. *No stranger himself to the problems encountered by the physically challenged, Gwaltney is a blind anthropologist who has made a career of studying the attitudes of marginalized groups; his first major book,* Drylongso, *is a collection of first-person accounts of what it means to be a black American. Gwaltney is a professor of anthropology at Syracuse University.*

Combat duty in Southeast Asia left Charlie Sabatier with a need for 1 *a wheelchair, but it is difficult for me to think of him as confined. The truth is, his mind is infinitely freer now than it was for most of his pre-Vietnam life. In that pre-Vietnam, South Texas existence, Charlie and I would probably not have had very much to do with one another. But in July of 1982 we met and talked in his suburban Boston home and he turned out to be civil, hospitable, direct, and a formidable raconteur. The talking and listening were facilitated by the array of thick sandwiches and cold beer he provided. Late in the afternoon of our day of talking and listening Charlie's wife, Peggy, phoned. He maneuvered his wheelchair out of the house they are remodeling, down the drive, and into his car and drove off to pick her up.*

The May 1982 issue of the American Coalition of Citizens with Disabilities 2 *newsletter had carried a story about Charlie's successful battle with Delta Airlines over one of their policies regarding disabled persons. The story read, in part:*

On March 17, 1982, in East Boston, Charles Sabatier fought with 3
Delta Airlines over evacuation. Sabatier was arrested when he refused
to comply with a Delta Airlines safety policy which stipulates that a
disabled person must sit on a blanket while in transit so that he/she
can be evacuated in case of emergency. . . . When Sabatier refused to
sit on the blanket (which was folded), the flight was delayed, and Sabatier
was eventually arrested for disorderly conduct.

The court in which he was charged was located in an inaccessible 4
courthouse. Sabatier refused to be carried up the courthouse steps and
was therefore arraigned on the steps. The location of the trial was then
moved to an accessible courthouse. Charges against Sabatier were dismissed
in court when the parties reached a pretrial settlement. Delta agreed to
change its policy so that use of a blanket to evacuate persons will be
optional and paid Sabatier $2,500.00 for legal fee expenses, $1.00 of
which would be for punitive damages at Sabatier's request. Sabatier
agreed not to sue Delta over the incident.

This blanket thing had happened to me at least a dozen times before, 5
and in the last three years I've flown at least three dozen times. I mean,
I've been *everywhere*. I've been to Seattle and Los Angeles and San
Francisco and New Orleans and Chicago and any place you can name
that's on the map, practically, any major city, I've been there in the
last three years. I've been subjected to that probably ninety percent of
the times I flew Delta or Eastern. I would protest. I would get on just
like this time. I would get on out of the wheelchair and into this aisle
chair that Delta, by the way, likes to call the "invalid" chair — I've
even written them letters about that. You know, about how language
means things. Like you don't call black people niggers and you don't
call women broads and chick and honey and you don't call disabled
people cripples and invalids. You know, I told 'em what an invalid meant.
That that's somebody in a bed, totally helpless. I said, "I'm not totally
helpless and stop calling me names." And I'd write them nice bureaucratic-
type letters. Yeah, they write back all the time, bureaucratic-type things.
They got a standard-type letter, I'm telling ya. They hire somebody,
you know, whose only qualification is — can you write a bureaucratic
meaningless letter? You know, at least a one-pager. That guy's probably
paid twenty-five thousand dollars a year to answer people like me. And
I never got anywhere by it, but that didn't stop me from writing them.
I had to write to get it out of my system, I think. One of the things I
contended was that the whole damn policy was arbitrary and capricious
because it happened to me a dozen times before and I always talked
my way off the blanket! I'd get in there and argue with 'em and talk

about my rights and all this self-worth, dignity, humiliation, and stigma and they'd go "Jesus Christ! Get him out of here. Forget about it." You know, "Just go sit down." They'd go, "Hey, we gotta take off, man!" So they'd say "Listen, forget it." And so that's what would happen. They would just forget about their dumb policy. And so I expected the same thing to happen this time. I mean, they're gonna subject me to this and I'll argue and get away with it. And this time I ran into a captain. The stewardess actually said forget it, and I went down — that's how I got into the seat. 'Cause this all happened at the door of the plane by the captain's cabin when I transferred from my chair to the aisle chair that gets me down the narrow aisle. And we argued and someone behind said, "Forget it." And so we went down. I got in the chair, got in the seat, had my seat belt on, they moved the chair out of the aisle and she comes down and says, "I'm sorry, the captain insists that you sit on the blanket." I said, "Look, you tell the captain what I told you. That I'm not about to sit on this blanket." And we went through this whole thing and I argued with every Delta person in probably the whole terminal over the course of about forty-five minutes and naturally, you know, this plane's going to Miami and everybody's saying, "Let's get going!" Yeah, I mean, it's not like it's wintertime and you're going to Minneapolis. They wanted to get going. Everybody's kinda wondering. I think the people on the plane, who saw me coming on, see, in this chair, they figured, this guy is sick or something and they were pretty nice. Well, finally the stewardess got irritated about this delay and she walks down the aisle and she used to like stoop down to talk to me but this time she comes down and just stands there and says, "Look, if you don't sit on the blanket, we're gonna have to de-board the plane and cancel the flight." Out loud, see? So everybody said, "Wait a minute, this guy's not sick. This delay's just 'cause he won't sit on a blanket." So some guy yells out, like about five rows behind me, "You mean to tell me that this delay is because this guy won't sit on a blanket?" And she says "Yes!" And he says, "Look, man, if I sit on a blanket, will you sit on a blanket?" And I said, "No. But if everybody sits on a blanket, I'll sit on a blanket." And he says, "Well, why do you have to sit on a blanket?" And she says, "It's for his safety." He says, "It's for your own good, do it." I said, "Look, seat belts are for people's safety. *Everybody* gets one. If blankets are for my safety, I want everybody to get one, Okay? If it's so good for my safety, it's so good for everybody else's. But if I'm the only one that has to do it, it's like puttin' a bag over an ugly man's head, you know? I mean, that's a stigma. So the guy says, "Okay, then we'll all sit on blankets." Everybody says, "Yeah!" So half these people started chanting, "We want blankets! We want blankets! We want blankets!" I kinda enjoyed it, 'cause I was getting some support finally. I was getting a kick out of it, but at the same time I was a little bit nervous. It was funny except for the fact that the State Police officer was comin' down the aisle at the same time they were chanting on the plane. So he says, "Either you sit on this blanket or I'm gonna have to arrest you." I said, "What charge? Where's the blanket charge?" He says, "Disorderly conduct." And that got me mad. Disorderly conduct? *These* are the people chanting "We want blankets," it's their conduct. I said, "If anybody's being disorderly, it's them. And it's this airline that's treating me like dirt who should be arrested." I said, "Besides, you don't work for the airline. You work for the State of Massachusetts, just like me. You shouldn't be arresting people that are violating some policy they have. This is not a Federal Aviation Administration regulation. And even if it was, it should be the feds making the arrest here, not you. You're out of your jurisdiction." Well, he didn't get ahold of all that and goes, "Oh well, I don't care. Look, these people are gonna have to get off, you're interrupting and costing them a lot of money. I'm going to arrest you. I'll worry about that later." I says, "You bet you will, 'cause I'm gonna sue you for false arrest. I got two attorneys sitting right here, right next to me, and I've got their cards and they've already said that I haven't done anything wrong and they're gonna be witnesses. You'd better write down your own witnesses 'cause you're gonna need 'em." I found out later that I was right. That I wasn't guilty of disorderly conduct.

But an ironic thing was that the guy who arrested me had a twelve-year-old son with multiple sclerosis who was in an electric wheelchair! When I was in his office taking care of the paperwork we were talking about his son and I said, "I'll tell you something. I feel better about taking a stand and doing this than I *ever* felt about my role in the war in Vietnam. I know that what I'm doing right here is right. I know right from wrong and I know that this policy humiliates people and irregardless of its intention to evacuate people in the event of a survivable crash, and that was even suspect if that was the real intention, it's categoric discrimination," I said. "Because when they see me as a nonambulatory person they categorically discriminated against me because they have me stereotyped as being helpless. I have no problem about how they get me out of the plane, *if* they get me out. I've got a problem about how they treat me *before* the crash. They could put the blanket above the seat in the compartment, they could put it under the seat. Do they think I'm gonna sit there and twiddle my thumbs in the seat waitin' for the stewardess to come back and get me on the blanket? I weigh two hundred pounds! Give me a break! I'm gonna be out of that seat just like I got in it, 'cause I know that when people start headin' for the exits, they're not comin' back for their purse, right? I mean, they're gonna be in the aisle, right down back, and there's gonna be this big cluster of people around the doors jumpin' out and I'll be right behind 'em. There are like eighty-, ninety-year-old people who get on that plane with the help of a walker and their grandson and they help 'em sit down and they kiss 'em good-bye. I'm telling you, if there was a survivable crash, those people, because of arthritis and age, couldn't get out. They'd be more helpless in a situation than I would, but they're ambulatory, you see, so they don't have to sit on a blanket. I mean, I had 'em cold, it was just unbelievable. I could have brought paraplegics in there who can lift five hundred pounds. I mean, I can prove that paraplegics are not helpless people.

If I had been in that pilot's place, of course I wouldn't have done 7 what he did. 'Course not, because I think I have more common sense than he had. I mean, I think I'd realize that if there was really a survivable crash, you're just gonna grab somebody and try to drag 'em out, no one's going to think about which one. I'll tell you something that I've always suspected. In their minds, they didn't just see me as a helpless person, they saw me as an incontinent person. They had probably had experiences of people who were paralyzed and incontinent and they're trying to protect the upholstery of their seats. That's not unusual, that paternalism. You know, I lobby all the time. I'll talk to people a half hour in their office — senators, congressmen — and on the way out I'll get patted on the back like I'm a little kid. I mean, even very high officials. They're so far out of tune with what's goin' on in the disabled movement and the women's movement, the black movement, I mean, they're just so engrossed, I guess, in doing their job, that they lose contact.

I've got a blind friend who we see every once in a while. One day 8 I'm walking down the street with this guy — and he's got dark glasses and a white cane — and a guy pulls over and says to me, "Hey! Could you tell me how to get to the Prudential Building?" Well, I had been here only a year and a half and I know the major roads, but I don't know the names of the streets so my friend starts talkin' and tells the guy how to get there and the guy pulls off and like five feet later pulls over and asks somebody else, 'cause he says to himself, "Blind guys don't know where anything is." But my friend can get around that town as well as anybody else. If anybody's gonna memorize how to get around, he is. But yeah, that's not untypical of the nondisabled population.

One of the things that happens when you stigmatize people is, you 9 see, if I can call people "niggers" in my mind, I don't think of these people as human beings. There's not equality, you know. They're not my peers. If I call a Vietnamese a gook, it's easier to kill him than Mr.

Hung Yung or whatever his name would be, right? So we do it. Americans do it, everyone, man. We call people krauts, limeys, gooks, niggers, and handicapped. People are refusing to recognize people as people, as having human traits. It's easier to just stereotype a large group of people than it is to deal with the problems and the need.

We always deal with problems in this country either technologically 10 or monetarily, and that's how this country has decided to deal with disabled people. Hey, I get my butt shot up in Vietnam, I come back here, they're not interested in what I'm gonna do, you know. They're not interested in my head problems about Vietnam or getting over all that trauma. It's later for that. We'll dump some money on you, just like, stay home. But if I say, "Look, later with your money. Stop subsidizing my life, just allow me equal opportunity to make my way in this life to the best that I can and all I want you to do is provide me accessible transportation so that I can get to and from my job, or make that post office that's two blocks away from here accessible so I can mail a letter and maintain my dignity while I'm doing it, rather than have somebody go up and do it for me," they refuse to do that. They'll dump money on you though, so you can stay home.

I don't even know if I could really give an answer as to why I didn't 11 sit on the blanket. I know good people, good friends of mine, who have sat on that blanket, and I consider them to be real advocates. They did it because, I guess, it was like the easiest course to take. Most people's lives, I think, probably are like water. Water runs to the easiest course and most people would prefer to go around a confrontation than actually confront somebody. Oh for sure I would have preferred that. I mean, nobody enjoys confrontation, really. I think you'd have to be sick to really enjoy confrontation. There's a lot that's gone on in my life that goes way back. There's building blocks, I guess, and you see things and it takes time. You are what you are today because of what you were yesterday and the day before. We are an accumulation.

I think by the time I got out of the army, I said to myself, "I'm gonna 12 start making the decisions in my life." Because I was always saying, "I should have listened to myself." Well, I started really making decisions for myself for the first time when I was layin' in a bloody mess in Vietnam. It was the first time, okay? Up until then I'd always been doing these crazy things on the advice of other people. I grew up in a time where we saw too many John Wayne movies, okay? I was a World War II baby, I was born in July of forty-five and I grew up with all this Audie Murphy, John Wayne type of thing. The good guy goes to war, gets a bullet in the shoulder, meets and marries the pretty nurse, and they live happily ever after. That was war to me — and besides, we always won. We were always the good guys and we were always moral and ethical and all that. That was the propaganda that I was fed all my life, through movies, television. When I was young, "Combat" was the big show. Vic Morrow, who just died, was the buck sergeant. I grew up in South Texas, my dad was a marine in World War II. I fell for it. I don't think that the movie industry really thought that they were propagandizing, but that's what it is. 'Cause you were subjected to only one side. I mean, the Nazis were always bad, every Nazi was bad, every bad guy had a foreign accent. The Japanese were the people who were always torturing people. My God, we'd never do a thing like that! Oh no! But I believed it. I mean, I was twenty years old and I believed it. I had *never learned* to question.

Actually I started questioning before I got shot but that changed my 13 life completely. When I got shot I took a different road, I guess, from the one I might have taken. I probably would have come back from 'Nam and gone back to school and been workin' in a bank with a couple kids, probably divorced, I'm sure, that type of thing. But it's strange, you know. Being shot has made my life probably a lot more exciting. I would have probably lived a normal, average mundane kind of life. But it's like I entered a whole new field. I started learning real fast that disabled people were not considered the general population and I started wondering why.

I learned what things meant and the language and semantics got 14 important to me. I was six foot two, a hundred seventy-five pounds, I'd never been disabled or in a hospital in my life. I had never seen anybody die before, then all of a sudden in a short period of time I'm killing people, people are trying to kill me, then I do get shot and almost killed. I get back and *then* I'm subjected to the worst bunch of crap I've ever seen in my life. I started being treated like dirt. It was ironic. Up until the time I got shot I was like Number One citizen. My country was spendin' *billions* of dollars for me. Thousands of dollars just to train me how to kill, thousands more dollars to send me halfway around the world to save us from "Communism." And they let it thrive ninety miles away! When I got in the army, that's when I started thinkin', wait a minute. Like I'm on this airplane and all of a sudden I realized, this is a one-way ticket! I'd been enslaved to keep this country "free." I'd been drafted for two years and if you don't think it's slavery, you just try to walk away from it! And so I said, okay, number one, I'm a slave, then I say, where am I? I'm goin' halfway around the world 'cause we had to pick a fight with some little Southeast Asian country to save the world from

Communism! I had never even met a Vietnamese. I didn't even know what one *looked* like. I couldn't tell one from a Japanese and I'm going to go over there and kill these people? I thought, "This is ridiculous."

I was like twenty-one when I got there and the average age of everybody   15 in 'Nam was nineteen. Which meant that the average age of the infantry, the guy on the line, was about seventeen and a half. And I just couldn't believe it. I just couldn't believe what was goin' on there. And we were goin' around in circles, you know, killin' people, and they were killin' us and it was like no war that we ever had. You never took ground, you never went north — you know, *that's* where the enemy is, Goddamn!

I think that we are a nation of dissenters. Our nation was created by   16 dissenters. Anybody that's ever made a major change in this world has been someone who was a dissenter. It's been done by somebody, you know, who you would call an unreasonable person. It was George Bernard Shaw who said the reasonable man looks at the world as it is and tries to adapt himself to suit the world. And the unreasonable man sees the world as it is and tries to change the world to suit himself. Therefore, said Shaw, all progress depends on the unreasonable man. I think that's absolutely true! And it's those dissenters that I think really are like a drumbeat ahead, you know, from the rest of the band. They are the people that are leading. Hey! If there were no dissenters, if there were no "unreasonable" people there'd just simply be the status quo. We'd still be goin' around as cave men. But somebody had to have a better idea. And it seems like every time somebody's got a better idea, the status quo is there to start callin' him names.

Like what I did. People would say, "Man, that was an unnatural thing   17 to do." And it *is* unnatural, because thousands of people have sat on the damn blanket before me. I guess they didn't consider it unnatural. But I'm telling ya, people are going to *have* to start becoming more unnatural, if that's what you want to call it, more unreasonable; less tolerant with those greedy people.

I don't know what makes people principled dissenters. I'll tell ya,   18 you're searching for somethin' and it's kinda like searching for something smaller than the atom. You *know* something's there, but it's those building blocks or the makeup or whatever that substance is that makes people good people or bad people. You know something's there, you're tryin' to search for it but I just don't think that we're there yet. I don't think we know what it is. I don't know. Everybody's different in their intellect, their ability. I'm no genius. I'm not really great with the books. I have to study real hard. I'm not super smart or anything, but I just think I was born with the right genes or something that just gave me good *common sense*. Good common sense to know right from wrong, good from bad and make good decisions in my life. And every once in a while we blow it.

I remember the first time I ever recognized discrimination in my life. 19 I was on a bus and this great big, huge black lady gets on the bus and sits down and faces me and the bus driver stopped the bus and said, "I'm sorry, lady, you're gonna have to move to the back of the bus." And she says somethin' like, "Look I have a right to sit here. I don't have to sit back there. My feet are hurtin' me. I've been working all day. I don't want to walk back down there." Just like Rosa Parks.[1] And he says, "Look, that's the law! Either you sit in the back of the bus or this bus don't go anywhere." So she was at that tired, worn-out stage and says okay, I'm ready for a rest. So *she* was a principled dissenter as far as I'm concerned. First one I ever heard of. And she says, "Then you do what you have to do. I'm gonna sit here, I'm tired." So he got off the bus, went to the corner, and got this cop who was directin' traffic, and this cop come on and like put a handcuff on her and took her off the bus. Boy! I thought, what's goin' on here? I never realized, see, up until that time that black people had to sit in the back of the bus. I just thought, they wanted to sit there, that they liked it there. I guess I was about nine. I thought, well, I guess I'm always sittin' near white people 'cause I want to, but I never thought about goin' back there. I just never thought of it. And then, all of a sudden, boom! I started thinkin' about it. All the way when I was goin' home I was thinkin', what'd she do? I didn't see her do anything. I thought maybe she had pickpocketed or robbed a purse. I didn't know. Why did they take her off the bus? I didn't know anything about it. And so I went home and I said to my mother, "What happened? This lady was arrested. I don't understand. Why couldn't she sit there?" And my mother said, "That's just the way things are. They've always been like that and that's the way they're always gonna be. Don't worry about it. Go outside and play." So I went outside and I remember sittin' on the porch for a long time and thinkin' about it, and *knowin'* that, now, I'm not getting the right answer here. Somethin's goin' on here, you know, like, even if it's always been that way and it's always goin' to be that way, well, why? Why is it that way? That's what I asked. I didn't get any answer to my question and back then that's probably the first time I started questioning like an adult would do. You know, I never thought of that again from that time on until after I got shot and I was in the VA hospital. The nurses were

[1] *Rosa Parks:* The black woman whose refusal to sit at the back of the bus initiated a bus boycott in Montgomery, Alabama, in 1955.

leavin' at four-thirty to go out and stand on the bus stop and take the bus and somebody said, "Why don't we go and take a bus and go down and have a drink with the nurses?" And everybody laughed. Ha. Ha. And there it went — boy! When that guy said that, I went back, back, seeing that person on the bus. And all of a sudden I went, "I don't believe this!" That's the first time that I had ever been discriminated against in my life!

I had been fortunate to live until that time as a white person in this 20 racist society, and I'd never experienced any kind of discrimination, none. All of a sudden I realized — you know my life was so screwed up, it was like a big jigsaw puzzle and I had found one piece to start putting my life back together and I wanted to talk about it. Like, hey! There's a big puzzle out here and I know that if we can fit all the pieces together I'll understand everything that's happening to me. And that was the first significant piece of the puzzle I found out.

Listen, I'll tell you a story. This happened to me in New York. I came 21 back from Los Angeles on TWA and I got to the terminal at Kennedy International and I was getting a transfer to Delta, okay? It had nothin' to do with the blanket, but another problem. Delta's terminal is in a separate terminal. It's about a half a mile around. And there's no curb cuts or anything. So I get there, it's midnight, and I get my bags on my lap and I'm goin' out and I figure I'll catch a cab around. So I ask a guy about cabs and he says, "Well, you're gonna have a hard time. Those cabbies have been sittin' in the line two hours and they want a big fare to go downtown." I says, "Well, I'll get one." So I went out and I told this lady who was the dispatcher. "I want a cab." She says, "Where ya goin'?" I said, "Delta Airlines." She says, "Nope! Nobody'll take ya!" So I say, "Look, then if I can't get over there, I want to go downtown, stay in a hotel overnight." She says, "Okay." Cab comes up, I get in, the guy puts my chair in the trunk and he says, "Where ya goin'?" "Delta Airlines." "Nope. I'm waiting here for a fare to go downtown." And I says, "Well, I ain't goin' downtown, I want to go to Delta Airlines." The dispatcher says, "You said you were goin' downtown." I said, "I changed my mind." He says, "Get out of the cab, I'm not goin' to take you over there. I've been sittin' here two hours." "No, I'm not going to get out." So *he* gets out and he takes my chair out of the trunk. I locked his doors. And he says, "Look, I'll call the police." And I said, "Call 'em. You call 'em and then I'll sue *you*." I says, "If you call 'em you're gonna be involved the whole damn night, you won't get another fare the whole night. Either you want to do that or take me to Delta. I don't know specifically what the law is here but I guarantee you you can't refuse to take me where I want to go. That's discrimination. Besides,

if you don't take me to Delta, I'm not gonna letcha back in the cab!"
And he says, "Look, man, don't make me break into my own cab!" I
says, "I'm gonna tell ya, take me to Delta or I'm gonna crawl over this
seat and drive this goddamned cab myself over there!" We went to Delta
Airlines. That has happened to me, like, three times! I've locked the
door. I'm just not gonna do that you know. And I know damn well
ninety-nine percent of disabled people would *never* do anything like
that because the movement is in its infancy stage. But we're getting
there.

It *bugs* me that people in this country are always talkin' about civil   22
rights, you know. When I think of rights, I think of something more —
a civil right is something that is written in law and that's all bullshit
anyway. We don't need any laws, we don't need any constitution, we
don't need the Declaration of Independence. All we need to do is treat
people with respect.

I grew up about twenty miles from this town called Alvin, Texas, and   23
there used to be a sign out there — I was in junior high school the last
time I saw it. I think since then they've had to take the thing down. It
was a sign out in front of the town that said, "Nigger, don't let the sun
set on your head." Not until I was twenty years old did I get out of
South Texas. I'm not a racist. I might have been. I remember one time
I pushed the button on the water fountain marked "white" and no water
would come out of it, so I pushed the button marked "colored" and
water came out, but I would not drink it. At that time we would think
nothing about tellin' a racist joke — and laughing. Maybe that's a way
of finding out who's a real racist. Something's happened to me. I don't
think I've lost my sense of humor, I'm pretty funny, I laugh — we've
been laughing here — but I just don't appreciate those kinds of jokes.
The important thing was, I think, not just one incident, but I kept seeing
incidents like that.

When I went into the army I was in Germany and I had never   24
associated a whole lot with black people before, and suddenly I'm sleeping
next to black people and showering with black people, drinkin' with
black people and *fightin'* with black people. And I remember we were
sittin' down on a cot and it was Christmastime and this one guy who
was black got this big long bar of candy with these nuts all around it
and he took this big bite out of it and handed it to me for me to get a
bite of. Man! It was like somebody had handed me a piece of *shit* to
take a bite of. Boy! Did that candy look good! But I hesitated you know,
and he says, "Oh, forgit it!" And I said, "Hey, no, give it here." I still
think of it and that was 1967 and Jesus! It makes you realize that, you
know, they got me. They got a piece of me. There we were, havin' a

good time, drinkin' beer and everything's great until I did somethin' like that, and I realized, well here I am, I'm a prejudiced ass. We grow though, we grow, hopefully.

What made me not like what was happening, those jokes, the water 25 fountain, what made me dislike that or understand that it's not right, I don't know. I think that's what you're really looking for. Why would somebody young and immature know in his soul and his heart and his mind that this is not right? Actually I did think about it a lot then. When I would see things like that happening, I would dwell on them. And I could look in the eyes of people when they were being done a number on and I could see it. I could see the hate, frustration, anger and I could see that what was happening here, this policy that would create that kind of reaction by somebody, is a policy that should be eliminated. We should have no policies that create that kind of tension in somebody, that kind of anxiety, that sense of disaster. I think I probably always felt that way. Not just for the racist-type things I saw, but as I grew up if I saw some kid being punished by his father or something, you know, when the punishment far surpassed what was just, if I saw somebody getting beat up on the playground, I was just the kind of person that would kind of go help the person.

I remember one time. It got me in really bad trouble. I was in eighth 26 grade and I was a big kid. I was six feet tall and we had this one guy who was the only disabled person I'd ever met in my life. He had CP[2] and he couldn't talk very good and we were friends. Well, it had been rainin' on the playground and some kid threw him in this hole. Just for fun! Boy, I'll tell ya, when they threw this guy into the mud, it just made me sick and I ran over there to help him and these people were gonna throw *me* in the mud! And then we were both so muddy — it was raining like cats and dogs. And then when we were almost out of the hole, these kids kicked mud in our faces. So I told the kid, "I want to see you after school. I'll get you." And before I realized what I was sayin', I was talkin' to like one of the toughest guys in the school! And later I was sittin' in my class and my knees were almost shakin'. I'm thinkin', "I'm gonna get killed. What do I do now? If I back down now I'll be *dirt* for four years, all through high school." So I said, "Jeez, I gotta go get beat up." So I went over and met him at the drugstore. And I thought, "If I let this guy hit me, I'm gonna die, so I'm gonna get the first punch in anyway." So I walked out of this drugstore door, it was like eight steps down to the sidewalk and the glass door was framed in wood and it was closing behind this guy and he walked out

---

[2]*CP:* cerebral palsy, a condition caused by damage to the brain before or during birth, characterized by muscular uncoordination and speech disturbances.

and took that first step and I caught him in midair. I turned around and *smacked* this guy right in the face. I connected so good in his face that I could just feel the guy's nose crack. Blood went all over and he flew back and went right through the glass door. Just flew! And then all of a sudden I changed from being wimpo, like "I'm gonna get killed," to "Come on, man! Let's get going!" Yeah, I was *bad* you know. Next thing I knew, I was worried 'cause the guy wasn't wakin' up. And I'm goin', "Wheow! What power!" Next thing I know, they call the police and I ran. No one squealed on me. I got away with the whole thing. I mean, the guy was so bad, if it had ever been a fair fight, I would have been dead. But the guy had some kind of respect for that kind of power and I just didn't. I had no respect for myself, see, 'cause I had sucker punched the guy, right? I hadn't really used any kind of power and after that he's thinkin' I'm this bad dude, don't mess with Sabatier, man. I had this great big reputation for nothin'. I said, "Thank God, nobody else'd pick a fight with me!" So I never really had much respect, I think, for strength as far as authority over other people. Maybe those kinds of things that happen throughout your life kinda teach that just because somebody has authority over you, has the power to do a number on you, doesn't make them the kind of person you have to respect. I don't think, when you fight, there's anything fair about it. When you fight, it's kinda like war — you win. The *only* thing that counts is to win. You defend yourself by destroying another person, that's all there is to it. I don't care what anybody says.

I enjoyed the fighting and I enjoyed being able to defend myself. 27 That's a nice thing — to know that you can defend yourself. That you don't take much guff. That's good and every kid needs that, at least men in our society need that. It was just demanded when we were kids. If you grow up wimpy, brother! People are going to start stepping on you so you have to be able to take care of yourself. No one ever really got hurt. That's the thing women miss most, I think, the fact that there's nothin' like winnin' a fight. If you get in a fight and you win, boy! The feeling of success and victory and power — there's somethin' about it that is a *good* feeling. And that's why when we get to be adults we get into violence. We like the violence.

It's kinda strange what happened to me. Just killing somebody, you 28 know, is something that you never get over, and when I left Vietnam I think I was more committed to learning as much as I could and trying to understand and be empathetic about people and I gained more respect for human life than I ever had before. I was put in a situation that had little respect for human life — either on our side or theirs. We had free fire zones and in the free-fire zone, anybody walking, you kill. You know, no respect. You don't ask any questions, in the free-fire zone you just kill 'em. And I think killin' somebody close up is more of an experience than doing a number on somebody in a bush that you don't see. You just fire at the bush or something and you walk by and you don't know what happened.

I had some really close experiences where I have actually killed somebody 29 *very* close. And I killed a woman who was unarmed and *that* was somethin' I will *never* shake. We had set up this perimeter and we were there eleven days and every day we'd run out, search and destroy, and come back. Well, it just so happened that there were about thirty Vietcong who were digging these tunnels, and we had caught them out in the open and didn't know it and when we set up our perimeter it was right on top of them. They hadn't dug the other entrance and so they were all closed in. They were like, after eleven days, tryin' to sneak out of the perimeter. They didn't have any food, they'd run out of water and they were on their way out. And it was about four o'clock in the morning. I'd just got off guard duty and I was going to sleep and I heard this guy on this tank next to my armored personnel carrier. He started yelling, "Infantry, there's somebody in the perimeter. There's gooks in the pe-rimeter!" And I said, "Okay, we'll go check it out." So I jumped up, I took a couple of guys from my squad and I went to the other side of this tank and he says, "There's somebody in the bomb crater. I killed two on the side of the bomb crater." We saw their bodies, they weren't moving and we could hear someone in the bomb crater. I had this tunnel light, this big flashlight that we used when we'd go through tunnels, and I shined it in the bomb crater and this guy's got these two big old bullet holes right on each side of his neck and he's breathing, erh, arh, erh, arh, like that, and blood's burbling right out of the holes in his neck and he's *buck* naked and he's got a grenade in each hand and he's layin' on his back and the tanker yells, "Go get a medic." And I says, "There's no medic going to go down there. The guy's dyin', man," I says. "Besides, he's got grenades in his hands. What fool's goin' to go down there?" So the guy calls the medic and the medic wouldn't go down there and the guy ended up, like five minutes later he died. But I wouldn't have gone down there either. And so I said, "Look, let's fan out around this bomb crater." I'm right next to the bomb crater and there's a guy like two feet to my left and two feet to his left there's another and we're gonna walk around this bomb crater and then I realize, hey! I'm the guy that has the light! So I thought, I can use my power here, you know, I'm a sergeant. I could say, "Hey, psst, take this light." But they'd say, "Take *this*." So I didn't say that. I said to myself, "Wow! What am I gonna do?" So I held this light wa-a-ay out to my left and I could feel this guy's hand pushing it back over toward me, so I went way over to my right, where nobody was and I take one step and it was so dark I couldn't see anything and I took one step and this gal jumped up in front of me on her knees and screamed out something, two or three words, and I just *instinctively* pulled the trigger on my M-16 and I just used up a whole ammo pack, twenty rounds, just destroyed her. Blood flew on me and she like flew forward and then backward and she hit me as I jumped down. I thought any second, after that, everybody's gonna open up and this guy's gonna start shootin' back or his friends will or something, but no one did. I jumped down and when I jumped down I jumped on her and I rolled off and I reached over. I was ready to fight this person, right? And of course she was dead and I grabbed her and when I grabbed her I thought, "Boy this is a little person," you know, "this is like grabbing my little niece or something." So, it was real quiet. We just lay there for a second or two and then I took the light and I said, "Let's take a look." And I put the light on her and she had her hair all up on top of her head and I cut this string that she had tied it with and boy! She had beautiful hair. It went all the way down, like past her knees.

Beautiful long black hair. And I searched her and she had this wallet, the only thing in it was a picture of her and a guy that was probably her husband and two little kids and a razor blade, an old rusty razor blade. I don't know why she had that, but that's all that was in her wallet. So I took the picture. We went around and ended up killing three or four more people and capturing about eight others and the next morning, the sun came up and the CO[3] called me over and said, "What's the statistics here?" And I told him how many dead and how many captured and he says, "Was there a woman there?" And I said, "Yeah, there was a woman." And he said, "Was she armed?" And I says, "No, we didn't find any weapons." But hell, I didn't have time to say, "Hey, do you have a weapon?" There were bullet holes in her ankles, in her arms, in her face, it was terrible. So he says, "Well, who killed her?" And I says, "I did." And this fool, he's got one of these guys that we captured and he happened to be her husband. He's in his tent and he's having this conversation with this guy with the interpreter and the interpreter tells the guy that I'm the one that killed his wife. So right away, man, the guy comes *runnin'* at me, you know, his hands are tied behind his back, and I just threw him down on the ground. And the guy just went berserk, you know, crazy. I mean, he was like a chicken with its head cut off. He wasn't comin' at anybody, he just went runnin' into everything, throwing dirt up into the air and kicking and hollerin'

30

[3]*CO:* commanding officer.

and screamin' and like he'd lost his mind, which he did. So there I was, you know, and that night everybody's callin' me the woman killer. Like it's a big joke. You know, the woman killer, it's a joke. That was the heaviest thing that's ever happened to me. And so I think, Jesus, I don't know whatever happened to that guy. Whether he ever got his mind together. I don't know what happened to her kids. I don't know if they're dead or alive. Unbelievable! The next day we ended up gettin' in a big firefight and burning down by accident, by all the fire and ammo and everything, all these hooches and stuff and the captain told me that that was the village that this lady lived in. So in a day I had killed an unarmed lady, seen her husband go crazy, and then burned down her village — and I'm the *good* guy! I'm the good guy? And I'm thinkin', I've gotta get out of here." God, she wasn't even armed. She was diggin' a tunnel, you know, carrying water back and forth for these people and what are they doin'? They're trying to get these foreigners out of their country, you know. That was us.

You know, I called them gooks. I used this term and everything. I 31 played that game but I never, never really thought that I was going to be in a position — that's how stupid and naïve I was — I never thought that *I* would really have to shoot somebody and that I would get shot. It was just stupid, just so stupid. I am convinced, I've talked to all those guys, you know, *none* of those people ever thought that they were actually gonna pull a trigger on somebody or that they would ever get killed. You know, what happens is that the country confused the war with the warriors. We lost the war, therefore the warriors are losers. We can make jokes about them. They're psychos, they're nuts, they're baby killers, they're losers! We are discriminated against as much as if we had been the ones over there being killed.

I thought a *lot* about that when I didn't have nothin' to do except 32 think. I was always in the field and sneakin' all the time and walkin' down trails and thinking, what am I doing? If I get killed today, will I go to hell or heaven? Am I guilty or innocent? Am I a war criminal? Am I violating people's human rights? Would I appreciate them in my country doing this? I'd walk in people's hooches and I mean, we'd go through a village at four-thirty in the morning. We don't knock on the door, we walk through and they're sleeping with their wives and babies and they're scared, you know, and you see these people, their faces. I felt like I was the Gestapo in World War II, walking in somebody's house without knocking on the door. 'Course that bothers me. I don't like doin' that. I'm not that kind of a person. But what am I gonna do? Refuse to go on a search-and-destroy mission? Jesus, so all I was hopin' to do was stay alive and get home and never find myself in that position again.

And so I *really* started thinking about all this right and wrong, good 33
and bad and human rights, and what I would die for, what I wouldn't
die for. And I came to the conclusion that there's just human rights.
Human rights, not civil rights. And human rights are not conditional.
Any commitment to a *conditional* human right is no commitment at all.
And that's exactly what we got, we disabled people. Here's a President
who says he's committed to social justice and all this business and at
the same time it's being conditioned on your ability to get on the bus,
or on your ability to see something. Things that really shouldn't matter.
And so a commitment for conditional human rights to me is no commitment
at all. Exactly none. And I'll do everything in my power to make sure
that people understand that if you're gonna be committed toward something
you can't talk commitment and in your actions do something else. You
can't say you're in favor of affirmative action and then go out and
discriminate.

I mean all the people of the different populations should recognize 34
things like that. Not many people look inward. They look outward to
see where the problem is. They don't look in and say, "Yeah, I've wasted
twenty people off the face of the earth and for what? You know, I'm
guilty, okay, from there I'll make sure this never happens again and I'll
try to stop it whenever I see it." You know, whenever I see that current
of hate or that current of discrimination, or see that president or that
mayor or the governor or somebody making bad decisions, whenever I
see it, I got to stand up and stop it. At least I owe those people, or
their souls that! I have to. I figure, if *I* don't, who will? I owe it.

Engaging the Text

1. Sabatier places great value on learning to question one's assumptions; how
and why does he learn to question his?
2. Debate Sabatier's assertion that "We don't need any laws, we don't need any
constitutions, we don't need the Declaration of Independence. All we need to
do is treat people with respect."
3. Do you agree with Sabatier and Shaw that "all progress depends on the
unreasonable man"? Why or why not?

Exploring Connections

1. Stage a "conversation" in class between Charlie Sabatier and Henry Blanton
of "Cowboy" (p. 25). What could they learn from each other? How might this
conversation change them? The conversation itself may take the form of a brief
play with a specific SETTING and may involve other, incidental CHARACTERS.

2. Write an essay comparing and contrasting Charlie Sabatier to Henry Blanton. In your search for points of comparison, be sure to consider their temperaments, their values, and their personal histories. Is there a critical difference between them? Is either of them heroic?

3. To what extent does the discussion of bureaucracy and individualism by Bellah and his coauthors in the preceding essay explain Sabatier's experience with the airline and his reaction to the incident?

4. How might Carol Gilligan (Chapter Four, "Women") explain Sabatier's remarks about fighting and violence?

Extending the Critical Context

1. Reread the newspaper account of the Delta incident that Gwaltney quotes in his introduction. Compare this version of the story to Sabatier's. What information does the news story highlight, and what does it omit? Is one version more "true" than the other? Why or why not?

2. Write a journal entry describing a time in your life when you began to question your own assumptions: What led you to re-evaluate your beliefs? Did you change as a result?

The Gospel of Wealth[1]

ANDREW CARNEGIE

Andrew Carnegie (1835–1919) immigrated to the United States from Scotland with his family at the age of thirteen. He rose rapidly through a series of jobs in a cotton mill and in his mid-twenties became a superintendent for the Pennsylvania Railroad. He invested in iron and steel manufacturing, and when he retired in 1901, his Carnegie Steel Company was producing one quarter of all steel in the United States. A strong believer in sharing his immense wealth, Carnegie donated hundreds of millions of dollars to libraries, scholarships, and public buildings like Carnegie Hall. This essay argues for the usefulness, even the necessity, of such charity or philanthropy; its most interesting features,

[1]Published originally in the *North American Review*, CXLVIII (June 1889), 653–664, and CXLIX (December 1889), 682–698. [Editor's note]

however, are the assumptions it contains about individualism, wealth, and the public good.

The problem of our age is the proper administration of wealth, that the ties of brotherhood may still bind together the rich and poor in harmonious relationship. The conditions of human life have not only been changed, but revolutionized, within the past few hundred years. In former days there was little difference between the dwelling, dress, food, and environment of the chief and those of his retainers. The Indians are today where civilized man then was. When visiting the Sioux, I was led to the wigwam of the chief. It was like the others in external appearance, and even within the difference was trifling between it and those of the poorest of his braves. The contrast between the palace of the millionaire and the cottage of the laborer with us today measures the change which has come with civilization. This change, however, is not to be deplored, but welcomed as highly beneficial. It is well, nay, essential, for the progress of the race that the houses of some should be homes for all that is highest and best in literature and the arts, and for all the refinements of civilization, rather than that none should be so. Much better this great irregularity than universal squalor. Without wealth there can be no Mæcenas.[2] The "good old times" were not good old times. Neither master nor servant was as well situated then as today. A relapse to old conditions would be disastrous to both — not the least so to him who serves — and would sweep away civilization with it. But whether the change be for good or ill, it is upon us, beyond our power to alter, and, therefore, to be accepted and made the best of it. It is a waste of time to criticize the inevitable. 1

It is easy to see how the change has come. One illustration will serve for almost every phase of the cause. In the manufacture of products we have the whole story. It applies to all combinations of human industry, as stimulated and enlarged by the inventions of this scientific age. Formerly, articles were manufactured at the domestic hearth, or in small shops which formed part of the household. The master and his apprentices worked side by side, the latter living with the master, and therefore subject to the same conditions. When these apprentices rose to be masters, there was little or no change in their mode of life, and they, in turn, educated succeeding apprentices in the same routine. There 2

[2]*Mæcenas:* Roman statesman and patron of the arts (70?–8 B.C.); friend to the poets Horace and Virgil.

was, substantially, social equality, and even political equality, for those engaged in industrial pursuits had then little or no voice in the State.

The inevitable result of such a mode of manufacture was crude articles 3 at high prices. Today the world obtains commodities of excellent quality at prices which even the preceding generation would have deemed incredible. In the commercial world similar causes have produced similar results, and the race is benefited thereby. The poor enjoy what the rich could not before afford. What were the luxuries have become the necessaries of life. The laborer has now more comforts than the farmer had a few generations ago. The farmer has more luxuries than the landlord had, and is more richly clad and better housed. The landlord has books and pictures rarer and appointments more artistic than the king could then obtain.

The price we pay for this salutary change is, no doubt, great. We 4 assemble thousands of operatives in the factory, and in the mine, of whom the employer can know little or nothing, and to whom he is little better than a myth. All intercourse between them is at an end. Rigid castes are formed, and, as usual, mutual ignorance breeds mutual distrust. Each caste is without sympathy with the other, and ready to credit anything disparaging in regard to it. Under the law of competition, the employer of thousands is forced into the strictest economies, among which the rates paid to labor figure prominently, and often there is friction between the employer and the employed, between capital and labor, between rich and poor. Human society loses homogeneity.

The price which society pays for the law of competition, like the price 5 it pays for cheap comforts and luxuries, is also great; but the advantages of this law are also greater still than its cost — for it is to this law that we owe our wonderful material development, which brings improved conditions in its train. But, whether the law be benign or not, we must say of it, as we say of the change in the conditions of men to which we have referred: It is here; we cannot evade it; no substitutes for it have been found; and while the law may be sometimes hard for the individual, it is best for the race, because it insures the survival of the fittest in every department. We accept and welcome, therefore, as conditions to which we must accommodate ourselves, great inequality of environment; the concentration of business, industrial and commercial, in the hands of a few; and the law of competition between these, as being not only beneficial, but essential to the future progress of the race. Having accepted these, it follows that there must be great scope for the exercise of special ability in the merchant and in the manufacturer who has to conduct affairs upon a great scale. That this talent for organization and management is rare among men is proved by the fact that it invariably secures enormous rewards for its possessor, no matter where or under what laws or conditions. The experienced in affairs always rate the MAN whose services can be obtained as a partner as not only the first consideration, but such as render the question of his capital[3] scarcely worth considering: for able men soon create capital; in the hands of those without the special talent required, capital soon takes wings. Such men become interested in firms or corporations using millions; and, estimating only simple interest to be made upon the capital invested, it is inevitable that their income must exceed their expenditure and that they must, therefore, accumulate wealth. Nor is there any middle ground which such men can occupy, because the great manufacturing or commercial concern which does not earn at least interest upon its capital soon becomes bankrupt. It must either go forward or fall behind; to stand still is impossible. It is a condition essential to its successful operation that it should be thus far profitable, and even that, in addition to interest on capital, it should make profit. It is a law, as certain as any of the others named, that men possessed of this peculiar talent for affairs, under the free play of economic forces must, of necessity, soon be in receipt of more revenue than can be judiciously expended upon themselves; and this law is as beneficial for the race as the others.

Objections to the foundations upon which society is based are not in order, because the condition of the race is better with these than it has been with any other which has been tried. Of the effect of any new substitutes proposed we cannot be sure. The Socialist or Anarchist who seeks to overturn present conditions is to be regarded as attacking the foundation upon which civilization itself rests, for civilization took its start from the day when the capable, industrious workman said to his incompetent and lazy fellow, "If thou dost not sow, thou shalt not reap,"[4] and thus ended primitive Communism by separating the drones from the bees. One who studies this subject will soon be brought face to face with the conclusion that upon the sacredness of property civilization itself depends — the right of the laborer to his hundred dollars in the savings-bank, and equally the legal right of the millionaire to his millions. Every man must be allowed "to sit under his own vine and fig-tree, with none to make afraid,"[5] if human society is to advance, or even to remain so far advanced as it is. To those who propose to substitute

6

---

[3]*capital:* wealth, especially money available for investment.

[4]*"If thou . . . reap":* Loose reference to a common Biblical image. Compare to Galatians 6:7 — ". . . whatsoever a man soweth, that shall he also reap."

[5]*"to sit . . . make afraid":* a biblical reference to the safety and prosperity of King Solomon's reign at its height. (See 1 Kings 4:25.)

Communism for this intense Individualism, the answer therefore is: The race has tried that. All progress from that barbarous day to the present time has resulted from its displacement. Not evil, but good, has come to the race from the accumulation of wealth by those who have had the ability and energy to produce it. But even if we admit for a moment that it might be better for the race to discard its present foundation, Individualism, — that it is a nobler ideal that man should labor, not for himself alone, but in and for a brotherhood of his fellows, and share with them all in common . . . even admit all this, and a sufficient answer is, This is not evolution, but revolution. It necessitates the changing of human nature itself — a work of eons, even if it were good to change it, which we cannot know.

It is not practicable in our day or in our age. Even if desirable the- 7 oretically, it belongs to another and long-succeeding sociological stratum. Our duty is with what is practicable now — with the next step possible in our day and generation. It is criminal to waste our energies in endeavoring to uproot, when all we can profitably accomplish is to bend the universal tree of humanity a little in the direction most favorable to the production of good fruit under existing circumstances. We might as well urge the destruction of the highest existing type of man because he failed to reach our ideal as to favor the destruction of Individualism, Private Property, the Law of Accumulation of Wealth, and the Law of Competition; for these are the highest result of human experience, the soil in which society, so far, has produced the best fruit. Unequally or unjustly, perhaps, as these laws sometimes operate, and imperfect as they appear to the Idealist, they are, nevertheless, like the highest type of man, the best and most valuable of all that humanity has yet accomplished.

We start, then, with a condition of affairs under which the best interests 8 of the race are promoted, but which inevitably gives wealth to the few. Thus far, accepting conditions as they exist, the situation can be surveyed and pronounced good. The question then arises, — and if the foregoing be correct, it is the only question with which we have to deal, — What is the proper mode of administering wealth after the laws upon which civilization is founded have thrown it into the hands of the few? And it is of this great question that I believe I offer the true solution. It will be understood that fortunes are here spoken of, not moderate sums saved by many years of effort, the returns from which are required for the comfortable maintenance and education of families. This is not wealth, but only competence, which it should be the aim of all to acquire, and which it is for the best interests of society should be acquired.

This, then, is held to be the duty of the man of wealth: To set an 9 example of modest, unostentatious living, shunning display or extravagance;

to provide moderately for the legitimate wants of those dependent upon him; and, after doing so, to consider all surplus revenues which come to him simply as trust funds, which he is called upon to administer, and strictly bound as a matter of duty to administer in the manner which, in his judgment, is best calculated to produce the most beneficial results for the community — the man of wealth thus becoming the mere trustee and agent for his poorer brethren, bringing to their service his superior wisdom, experience, and ability to administer, doing for them better than they would or could do for themselves.

. . . Those who would administer wisely must, indeed, be wise; for one of the serious obstacles to the improvement of our race is indiscriminate charity. It were better for mankind that the millions of the rich were thrown into the sea than so spent as to encourage the slothful, the drunken, the unworthy. Of every thousand dollars spent in so-called charity today, it is probable that nine hundred and fifty dollars is unwisely spent — so spent, indeed, as to produce the very evils which it hopes to mitigate or cure. A well-known writer of philosophic books admitted the other day that he had given a quarter of a dollar to a man who approached him as he was coming to visit the house of his friend. He knew nothing of the habits of this beggar, knew not the use that would be made of this money, although he had every reason to suspect that it would be spent improperly. This man professed to be a disciple of Herbert Spencer;[6] yet the quarter-dollar given that night will probably work more injury than all the money will do good which its thoughtless donor will ever be able to give in true charity. He only gratified his own feelings, saved himself from annoyance — and this was probably one of the most selfish and very worst actions of his life, for in all respects he is most worthy.

In bestowing charity, the main consideration should be to help those who will help themselves; to provide part of the means by which those who desire to improve may do so; to give those who desire to rise the aids by which they may rise; to assist, but rarely or never to do all. Neither the individual nor the race is improved by almsgiving. Those worthy of assistance, except in rare cases, seldom require assistance. . . .

The best means of benefiting the community is to place within its reach the ladders upon which the aspiring can rise — free libraries, parks, and means of recreation, by which men are helped in body and mind; works of art, certain to give pleasure and improve the public taste;

[6]*Herbert Spencer:* English philosopher and social theorist (1820–1903).

and public institutions of various kinds, which will improve the general condition of the people; in this manner returning their surplus wealth to the mass of their fellows in the forms best calculated to do them lasting good.

Thus is the problem of rich and poor to be solved. The laws of accumulation will be left free, the laws of distribution free. Individualism will continue, but the millionaire will be but a trustee for the poor, intrusted for a season with a great part of the increased wealth of the community, but administering it for the community far better than it could or would have done for itself. The best minds will thus have reached a stage in the development of the race in which it is clearly seen that there is no mode of disposing of surplus wealth creditable to thoughtful and earnest men into whose hands it flows, save by using it year by year for the general good. This day already dawns. Men may die without incurring the pity of their fellows, still sharers in great business enterprises from which their capital cannot be or has not been withdrawn, and which is left chiefly at death for public uses; yet the day is not far distant when the man who dies leaving behind him millions of available wealth, which was free to him to administer during life, will pass away "unwept, unhonored, and unsung," [7] no matter to what uses he leaves the dross which he cannot take with him. Of such as these the public verdict will then be: "The man who dies thus rich dies disgraced." 13

Such, in my opinion is the true gospel concerning wealth, obedience to which is destined some day to solve the problem of the rich and the poor, and to bring "Peace on earth, among men good will." 14

[7] "unwept, unhonored, and unsung": Carnegie is quoting Sir Walter Scott, The Lay of the Last Minstrel (1805).

Engaging the Text

1. How does Carnegie define progress? Do you accept his definition?

2. According to Carnegie, what are the costs and benefits of industrialization?

3. What IMAGE of poor and working-class people does this selection convey? How, by contrast, does it portray the rich? What are Carnegie's attitudes toward each?

4. How would you explain the religious TONE of this "gospel" of wealth?

5. Throughout the selection, Carnegie relies on words and ideas that are generally associated with objective science. Find several instances of this practice. What

effect does it have on the reader? How valid are Carnegie's "scientific" generalizations about wealth, poverty, and society?

Exploring Connections

1. How does Carnegie's notion of the individual compare with the ideal of the rugged frontiersman presented by Frederick Jackson Turner earlier in this chapter?
2. Look ahead to Christopher Lasch's "The Original Meaning of the Work Ethic" in Chapter Seven, "Making a Living." Where would Lasch place Carnegie in the evolution of the American idea of success?

Extending the Critical Context

1. Using your library's resources, write brief profiles of two or three contemporary Americans whom Carnegie might number among the wealthy elite. Do their actions confirm his idea that great wealth necessarily entails great social responsibility?
2. Research Social Darwinism. Begin by checking several encyclopedias and your library's card catalog. How does Carnegie use this theory to support his arguments?
3. What is the "highest and best in literature and the arts" today (see page 71)? Who defines it? Who has access to it?

Stephen Cruz

STUDS TERKEL

Studs Terkel (b. 1912) is probably the best known practitioner of oral history in the United States. He has compiled several books by interviewing dozens of widely varying people — ordinary people, for the most part — about important subjects like work, World War II, and the Depression. The edited versions of these interviews are often surprisingly powerful crystallizations of American social history, and Terkel's subjects give voice to the frustrations and hopes of whole generations of Americans. The speaker here, Stephen Cruz, is a man who at first glance seems to be living the American dream of success and upward mobility; he is never content, however, and he comes to question his own values and his place in the predominantly Anglo society where he is "successful."

He is thirty-nine.   1

"The family came in stages from Mexico. Your grandparents usually   2
came first, did a little work, found little roots, put together a few bucks,
and brought the family in, one at a time. Those were the days when
controls at the border didn't exist as they do now."

You just tried very hard to be whatever it is the system wanted of   3
you. I was a good student and, as small as I was, a pretty good athlete.
I was well liked, I thought. We were fairly affluent, but we lived down
where all the trashy whites were. It was the only housing we could get.
As kids, we never understood why. We did everything right. We didn't
have those Mexican accents, we were never on welfare. Dad wouldn't
be on welfare to save his soul. He woulda died first. He worked during
the depression. He carries that pride with him, even today.

Of the five children, I'm the only one who really got into the business   4
world. We learned quickly that you have to look for opportunities and
add things up very quickly. I was in liberal arts, but as soon as Sputnik
went up, well, golly, hell, we knew where the bucks were. I went right
over to the registrar's office and signed up for engineering. I got my
degree in '62. If you had a master's in business as well, they were just
paying all kinds of bucks. So that's what I did. Sure enough, the market
was super. I had fourteen job offers. I could have had a hundred if I
wanted to look around.

I never once associated these offers with my being a minority. I was   5
aware of the Civil Rights Act of 1964, but I was still self-confident enough
to feel they wanted me because of my abilities. Looking back, the reason
I got more offers than the other guys was because of the government
edict. And I thought it was because I was so goddamned brilliant. (Laughs.)
In 1962, I didn't get as many offers as those who were less qualified.
You have a tendency to blame the job market. You just don't want to
face the issue of discrimination.

I went to work with Procter & Gamble. After about two years, they   6
told me I was one of the best supervisors they ever had and they were
gonna promote me. Okay, I went into personnel. Again, I thought it
was because I was such a brilliant guy. Now I started getting wise to
the ways of the American Dream. My office was glass-enclosed, while
all the other offices were enclosed so you couldn't see into them. I was
the visible man.

They made sure I interviewed most of the people that came in. I just   7
didn't really think there was anything wrong until we got a new plant
manager, a southerner. I received instructions from him on how I should
interview blacks. Just check and see if they smell, okay? That was the

beginning of my training program. I started asking: Why weren't we hiring more minorities? I realized I was the only one in a management position.

I guess as a Mexican I was more acceptable because I wasn't really 8 black. I was a good compromise. I was visibly good. I hired a black secretary, which was *verboten*. When I came back from my vacation, she was gone. My boss fired her while I was away. I asked why and never got a good reason.

Until then, I never questioned the American Dream. I was convinced 9 if you worked hard, you could make it. I never considered myself different. That was the trouble. We had been discriminated against a lot, but I never associated it with society. I considered it an individual matter. Bad people, my mother used to say. In '68 I began to question.

I was doing fine. My very first year out of college, I was making twelve 10 thousand dollars. I left Procter & Gamble because I really saw no opportunity. They were content to leave me visible, but my thoughts were not really solicited. I may have overreacted a bit, with the plant manager's attitude, but I felt there's no way a Mexican could get ahead here.

I went to work for Blue Cross. It's 1969. The Great Society[1] is in full 11 swing. Those who never thought of being minorities before are being turned on. Consciousness raising is going on. Black programs are popping up in universities. Cultural identity and all that. But what about the one issue in this country: economics? There were very few management jobs for minorities, especially blacks.

The stereotypes popped up again. If you're Oriental, you're real good 12 in mathematics. If you're Mexican, you're a happy guy to have around, pleasant but emotional. Mexicans are either sleeping or laughing all the time. Life is just one big happy kind of event. *Mañana*. Good to have as part of the management team, as long as you weren't allowed to make decisions.

I was thinking there were two possibilities why minorities were not 13 making it in business. One was deep, ingrained racism. But there was still the possibility that they were simply a bunch of bad managers who just couldn't cut it. You see, until now I believed everything I was taught about the dream: the American businessman is omnipotent and fair. If we could show these turkeys there's money to be made in hiring minorities, these businessmen — good managers, good decision makers — would respond. I naïvely thought American businessmen gave a damn about

---

[1]*the Great Society:* President Lyndon B. Johnson's term for the American society he hoped to establish through social reforms, including an antipoverty program.

society, that given a choice they would do the right thing. I had that faith.

I was hungry for learning about decision-making criteria. I was still 14 too far away from top management to see exactly how they were working. I needed to learn more. Hey, just learn more and you'll make it. That part of the dream hadn't left me yet. I was still clinging to the notion of work your ass off, learn more than anybody else, and you'll get in that sphere.

During my fifth year at Blue Cross, I discovered another flaw in the 15 American Dream. Minorities are as bad to other minorities as whites are to minorities. The strongest weapon the white manager had is the old divide and conquer routine. My mistake was thinking we were all at the same level of consciousness.

I had attempted to bring together some blacks with the other minorities. 16 There weren't too many of them anyway. The Orientals never really got involved. The blacks misunderstood what I was presenting, perhaps I said it badly. They were on the cultural kick: a manager should be crucified for saying "Negro" instead of "black." I said as long as the Negro or the black gets the job, it doesn't mean a damn what he's called. We got into a huge hassle. Management, of course, merely smiled. The whole struggle fell flat on its face. It crumpled from divisiveness. So I learned another lesson. People have their own agenda. It doesn't matter what group you're with, there is a tendency to put the other guy down regardless.

The American Dream began to look so damn complicated, I began to 17 think: Hell, if I wanted, I could just back away and reap the harvest myself. By this time, I'm up to twenty-five thousand dollars a year. It's beginning to look good, and a lot of people are beginning to look good. And they're saying: "Hey, the American Dream, you got it. Why don't you lay off?" I wasn't falling in line.

My bosses were telling me I had all the "ingredients" for top man- 18 agement. All that was required was to "get to know our business." This term comes up all the time. If I could just warn all minorities and women whenever you hear "get to know our business," they're really saying "fall in line." Stay within that fence, and glory can be yours. I left Blue Cross disillusioned. They offered me a director's job at thirty thousand dollars before I quit.

All I had to do was behave myself. I had the "ingredients" of being 19 a good Chicano, the equivalent of the good nigger. I was smart. I could articulate well. People didn't know by my speech patterns that I was of Mexican heritage. Some tell me I don't look Mexican, that I have a certain amount of Italian, Lebanese, or who knows. (Laughs.)

One could easily say: "Hey, what's your bitch? The American Dream 20 has treated you beautifully. So just knock it off and quit this crap you're spreading around." It was a real problem. Every time I turned around, America seemed to be treating me very well.

Hell, I even thought of dropping out, the hell with it. Maybe get a 21 job in a factory. But what happened? Offers kept coming in. I just said to myself: God, isn't this silly? You might as well take the bucks and continue looking for the answer. So I did that. But each time I took the money, the conflict in me got more intense, not less.

Wow, I'm up to thirty-five thousand a year. This is a savings and loan 22 business. I have faith in the executive director. He was the kind of guy I was looking for in top management: understanding, humane, also looking for the formula. Until he was up for consideration as executive v.p. of the entire organization. All of a sudden everything changed. It wasn't until I saw this guy flip-flop that I realized how powerful vested interests are. Suddenly he's saying: "Don't rock the boat. Keep a low profile. Get in line." Another disappointment.

Subsequently, I went to work for a consulting firm. I said to myself: 23 Okay, I've got to get close to the executive mind. I need to know how they work. Wow, a consulting firm.

Consulting firms are saving a lot of American businessmen. They're 24 doing it in ways that defy the whole notion of capitalism. They're not allowing these businesses to fail. Lockheed was successful in getting U.S. funding guarantees because of the efforts of consulting firms working on their behalf, helping them look better. In this kind of work, you don't find minorities. You've got to be a proven success in business before you get there.

The American Dream, I see now, is governed not by education, op- 25 portunity, and hard work, but by power and fear. The higher up in the organization you go, the more you have to lose. The dream is *not losing*. This is the notion pervading America today: Don't lose.

When I left the consulting business, I was making fifty thousand dollars 26 a year. My last performance appraisal was: You can go a long way in this business, you can be a partner, but you gotta know our business. It came up again. At this point, I was incapable of being disillusioned any more. How easy it is to be swallowed up by the same set of values that governs the top guy. I was becoming that way. I was becoming concerned about losing that fifty grand or so a year. So I asked other minorities who had it made. I'd go up and ask 'em: "Look, do you owe anything to others?" The answer was: "We owe nothing to anybody." They drew from the civil rights movement but felt no debt. They've quickly forgotten how it happened. It's like I was when I first got out of college. Hey, it's really me, I'm great. I'm as angry with these guys as I am with the top guys.

Right now, it's confused. I've had fifteen years in the business world as "a success." Many Anglos would be envious of my progress. Fifty thousand dollars a year puts you in the one or two top percent of all Americans. Plus my wife making another thirty thousand. We had lots of money. When I gave it up, my cohorts looked at me not just as strange, but as something of a traitor. "You're screwing it up for all of us. You're part of our union, we're the elite, we should govern. What the hell are you doing?" So now I'm looked at suspiciously by my peer group as well. 27

I'm teaching at the University of Wisconsin at Platteville. It's nice. My colleagues tell me what's on their minds. I got a farm next-door to Platteville. With farm prices being what they are (laughs), it's a losing proposition. But with university work and what money we've saved, we're gonna be all right. 28

The American Dream is getting more elusive. The dream is being governed by a few people's notion of what the dream is. Sometimes I feel it's a small group of financiers that gets together once a year and decides all the world's issues. 29

It's getting so big. The small-business venture is not there any more. Business has become too big to influence. It can't be changed internally. A counterpower is needed. 30

Engaging the Text

1. Write a paragraph describing what you would like to achieve in order to consider yourself "a success" in life. How do your values compare to Cruz's? Is he a success?

2. Describe the stages Stephen Cruz goes through in his life vis-à-vis believing in the American Dream. Give each stage a name and describe its key features. Is there a pattern to the stages, or does Cruz just keep changing his mind about things randomly? Which stage most closely reflects your own attitudes right now?

3. As Cruz moves up the economic ladder, he experiences growing conflict that keeps him from being content and proud of his accomplishments. To what do you attribute his discontent? Is his "solution" the one you would recommend?

4. Cruz says that the real force in America is the dream of "not losing." What does he mean by this?

5. What, according to Stephen Cruz, is wrong with the American Dream? Write an essay in which you first define and then either defend or refute his position.

Exploring Connections

1. The authors of "The Paradox of Individualism," which appears earlier in this chapter, claim that we as a people are divided between our need to define ourselves as individuals and our need for a sense of community. Analyze Stephen Cruz's statement for traces of this AMBIVALENCE.

2. Compare and contrast Stephen Cruz's attitudes with those of Charlie Sabatier in Gwaltney's interview earlier in this chapter. How would you characterize the differences in their approaches to the challenges they encounter? Which seems more typically "American"?

3. Write a detailed analysis of Stephen Cruz's problem from the POINT OF VIEW of Andrew Carnegie. Or, write a CRITIQUE of Carnegie's philosophy from Cruz's point of view.

Extending the Critical Context

1. According to Cruz, in 1969 few management positions were open to members of minority groups. Working in pairs or small groups, go to the library and look up current statistics on minorities in business (e.g., the number of large, successful minority-owned companies; the number of minority chief executives among major corporations; the distribution of minorities among top management, middle management, supervisory, and clerical positions). Compare notes with classmates and discuss.

2

Justice for All

The Problem of Equality

When the Founding Fathers promised liberty and justice for all, they consciously excluded most of the residents of the new country: "all" in this case referred only to propertied white men. This chapter features a chorus of voices on the subject of social equality and race relations in the United States. The essays in the first section of this chapter, Theories of Prejudice, set up an interplay between concrete examples and explanatory theories. The selections by Gordon W. Allport, Peter Loewenberg, and James Boggs propose three quite different models for the dynamics of racial prejudice. Each of these readings is followed by a personal account of prejudice (biographical or literary); our intention is that you will probe the validity of the theories according to their ability to explain the narrated events. You'll hear the voices of a Jewish writer and a feminist, an exceptional black student who is allowed to address his white audience only after participating in a blindfolded brawl, and an ex-Klansman turned labor leader.

The second part of the chapter, Confronting Racism, focuses on reactions to prejudice, hints at the historical dimensions of the problem in the United States, and suggests some of the ways individuals and communities have resisted racial oppression. Luis M. Valdez's *Los Vendidos*, a one-act play, uses savage humor to fight several pernicious stereotypes of Mexicans. Next, Native American poet Wendy Rose protests against the economic exploitation of her people. The reading by Ida B. Wells and

John Tateishi's interview with Mary Tsukamoto are highly personal accounts of specific instances of racial discrimination (a lynching in Memphis and the World War II relocation of Japanese-Americans). Janice Mirikitani's "We, the Dangerous" concludes the chapter by establishing a broad perspective on the modern history of America and Asia; this compact poem links the relocation centers Tsukamoto describes to both Hiroshima and Vietnam.

Before Reading . . .

Do some contemplative journal writing about the ethnic group or groups of your own family. What stereotypes exist now or existed in the past that helped or hindered members of each group? How strong is your allegiance to or identification with any ethnic group? In what ways is this connection to a group displayed, and of what value is it to you? What problems, if any, does it create?

THEORIES OF PREJUDICE

Formation of In-Groups
GORDON W. ALLPORT

Gordon W. Allport (1897–1967) published The Nature of Prejudice, *from which the passage below is excerpted, in 1954. It served then as a cornerstone for the scientific study of racial prejudice and still provides a theoretical foundation for many psychologists and sociologists. In this section, Allport analyzes how people join and are excluded from various groups, relating these processes to the notion of stereotyping. When his work appeared, the idea that a person's behavior might be determined by individual characteristics learned throughout life rather than by innate drives was highly controversial. Allport was educated at Harvard and at Cambridge, England; throughout a career spanning some fifty years he taught psychology at Harvard and authored more than a dozen books and two hundred articles.*

The proverb *familiarity breeds contempt* contains considerably less 1
than a half-truth. While we sometimes do become bored with our daily
routine of living and with some of our customary companions, yet the
very values that sustain our lives depend for their force upon their
familiarity. What is more, what is familiar tends to *become a value*. We
come to like the style of cooking, the customs, the people, we have
grown up with.

Psychologically, the crux of the matter is that the familiar provides 2
the indispensable basis of our existence. Since existence is good, its
accompanying groundwork seems good and desirable. A child's parents,
neighborhood, region, nation are given to him — so too his religion,
race, and social traditions. To him all these affiliations are taken for
granted. Since he is part of them, and they are part of him, they are
good.

As early as the age of five, a child is capable of understanding that 3
he is a member of various groups. He is capable, for example, of a sense
of ethnic identification. Until he is nine or ten he will not be able to
understand just what his membership signifies — how, for example,
Jews differ from gentiles, or Quakers from Methodists, but he does not
wait for this understanding before he develops fierce in-group loyalties.

Some psychologists say that the child is "rewarded" by virtue of his 4
memberships, and that this reward creates the loyalty. That is to say,
his family feeds and cares for him, he obtains pleasure from the gifts
and attentions received from neighbors and compatriots. Hence he learns
to love them. His loyalties are acquired on the basis of such rewards.
We may doubt that this explanation is sufficient. A colored child is seldom
or never rewarded for being a Negro — usually just the opposite, and
yet he normally grows up with a loyalty to his racial group. Thoughts
of Indiana arouse a glow in the breast of a native Hoosier[1] — not
necessarily because he passed a happy childhood there, but simply because
he *came* from there. It is still, in part, the ground of his existence.

Rewards may, of course, help the process. A child who has plenty of 5
fun at a family reunion may be more attached thereafter to his own clan
because of the experience. But normally he would be attached to his
clan anyway, simply because it is an inescapable part of his life.

[1]*Hoosier:* common name for residents of the state of Indiana.

Happiness (i.e., "reward") is not then the only reason for our loyalties. 6
Few of our group memberships seem to be sustained by the pleasures
they provide — an exception perhaps being our recreational memberships.
And it takes a major unhappiness, a prolonged and bitter experience,
to drive us away from loyalties once formed. And sometimes no amount
of punishment can make us repudiate our loyalty.

This principle of the *ground* in human learning is important. We do 7
not need to postulate a "gregarious instinct" to explain why people like
to be with people: They have simply found people lock-stitched into the
very fabric of their existence. Since they affirm their own existence as
good, they will affirm social living as good. Nor do we need to postulate
a "consciousness of kind" to explain why people adhere to their own
families, clans, ethnic groups. The self could not be itself without them.

Scarcely anyone ever wants to be anybody else. However handicapped 8
or unhappy he feels himself, he would not change places with other
more fortunate mortals. He grumbles over his misfortunes and wants
his lot improved; but it is *his* lot and *his* personality that he wants
bettered. This attachment to one's own being is basic to human life. I
may say that I envy *you*. But I do not want to *be* you; I only want to
have for myself some of your attributes or possessions. And along with
this beloved self go all of the person's basic memberships. Since he
cannot alter his family stock, its traditions, his nationality, or his native
language, he does well to accept them. Their accent dwells in the heart
as well as on the tongue.

Oddly enough, it is not necessary for the individual to have direct 9
acquaintance with all his in-groups. To be sure, he usually knows the
members of his immediate family. (An orphan, however, may be pas-
sionately attached to parents he has never seen.) Some groups, such as
clubs, schools, neighborhoods, are known through personal contacts. But
others depend largely on symbols or hearsay. No one can have direct
acquaintance with his race as a whole, nor with all his lodge brothers
or co-religionists. The young child may sit enthralled while he hears of
the exploits of the great-grandfather whose role as a sea-captain, a frontiersman, or nobleman sets a tradition with which the child identifies
himself. The words he hears provide him just as authentic a ground for
his life as do his daily experiences. By symbols one learns family traditions,
patriotism, and racial pride. Thus in-groups that are only verbally defined
may be nonetheless firmly knit.

What Is an In-group?

In a static society it would be fairly easy to predict just what loyalties 10
the individual will form — to what region, to what phratry, or to what

social class. In such a static society kinship, status, even place of residence, may be rigidly prescribed.

> In ancient China at one time residential arrangements actually coincided with social distance. Where one lived indicated all of one's memberships. The inner circle of a region was the Tribute Holding where government officials only were permitted to reside. A second circle contained the nobility. Beyond this an outer but defended area, known as the Peaceful Tenures, contained literary workers and other citizens of repute. Farther out lay the Prohibited territory divided between foreigners and transported convicts. Finally came the Unstrained territory, where only barbarians and ostracized felons were allowed to dwell.[2]

In a more mobile, technological society such as ours no such rigidity exists.

There is one law — universal in all human societies — that assists us 11 in making an important prediction. *In every society on earth the child is regarded as a member of his parents' groups.* He belongs to the same race, stock, family tradition, religion, caste, and occupational status. To be sure, in our society, he may when he grows older escape certain of these memberships, but not all. The child is ordinarily expected to acquire his parents' loyalties and prejudices; and if the parent because of his group-membership is an object of prejudice, the child too is automatically victimized.

Although this rule holds in our society, it is less infallible than in more 12 "familistic" regions of the world. While the American child normally acquires a strong sense of family membership and a certain loyalty to his parents' country of origin, race, and religion, he has considerable latitude respecting his attachments. Each individual pattern will be somewhat different. An American child is free to accept some of his parents' memberships and to reject others.

It is difficult to define an in-group precisely. Perhaps the best that 13 can be done is to say that members of an in-group all use the term *we* with the same essential significance. Members of a family do so, likewise schoolmates, members of a lodge, labor union, club, city, state, nation. In a vaguer way members of international bodies may do the same. Some we-organizations are transitory (e.g., an evening party), some are permanent (e.g., a family or clan).

---

[2]W. G. Old. *The Shu King, or the Chinese Historical Classic.* New York: J. Lane, 1904, 50–51. See also J. Legge (Transl.), Texts of Confucianism, in *The Sacred Books of the East.* Oxford: Clarendon Press, 1879, Vol. III, 75–76. [Author's note]

Sam, a middle-aged man of only average sociability, listed his own   14
in-group memberships as follows:

his paternal relatives
his maternal relatives
family of orientation (in which he grew up)
family of procreation (his wife and children)
his boyhood circle (now a dim memory)
his grammar school (in memory only)
his high school (in memory only)
his college as a whole (sometimes revisited)
his college class (reinforced by reunions)
his present church membership (shifted when he was 20)
his profession (strongly organized and firmly knit)
his firm (but especially the department in which he works)
a "bunch" (group of four couples who take a good deal of recreation
    together)
surviving members of a World War I company of infantry (growing
    dim)
state where he was born (a fairly trivial membership)
town where he now lives (a lively civic spirit)
New England (a regional loyalty)
United States (an average amount of patriotism)
United Nations (in principle firmly believed in but psychologically loose
    because he is not clear concerning the "we" in this case)
Scotch-Irish stock (a vague feeling of kinship with others who have this
    lineage)
Republican party (he registers Republican in the primaries but has little
    additional sense of belonging)

Sam's list is probably not complete — but from it we can reconstruct
fairly well the membership ground on which he lives.

In his list Sam referred to a boyhood circle. He recalls that at one   15
time this in-group was of desperate importance to him. When he moved
to a new neighborhood at the age of 10 he had no one of his own age
to pal with, and he much desired companionship. The other boys were
curious and suspicious. Would they admit him? Was Sam's style compatible
with the gang's style? There was the usual ordeal by fistfight, set in
motion at some slight pretext. This ritual — as is customary in boys'
gangs — is designed to provide a swift and acceptable test of the stranger's
manners and morale. Will he keep within the limits set by the gang,
and show just enough boldness, toughness, and self-control to suit the
other boys? Sam was fortunate in this ordeal, and was forthwith admitted
to the coveted in-group. Probably he was lucky that he had no additional

handicaps in terms of his racial, religious, or status memberships. Otherwise the probation would have been longer and the tests more exacting; and perhaps the gang would have excluded him forever.

Thus some in-group memberships have to be fought for. But many are conferred automatically by birth and by family tradition. In terms of modern social science the former memberships reflect *achieved* status; the latter, *ascribed* status. 16

Sex as an In-group

Sam did not mention his membership (ascribed status) in the male sex. Probably at one time it was consciously important to him — and may still be so. 17

The in-group of sex makes an interesting case study. A child of two normally makes no distinction in his companionships: a little girl or a little boy is all the same to him. Even in the first grade the awareness of sex-groups is relatively slight. Asked whom they would choose to play with, first-grade children on the average choose opposite-sexed children at least a quarter of the time. By the time the fourth grade is reached these cross-sexed choices virtually disappear: Only two percent of the children want to play with someone of the opposite sex. When the eighth grade is reached friendships between boys and girls begin to re-emerge, but even then only eight percent extend their choices across the sex boundary.[3] 18

For some people — misogynists[4] among them — the sex-grouping remains important throughout their lives. Women are viewed as a wholly different species from men, usually an inferior species. Such primary and secondary sex differences as exist are greatly exaggerated and are inflated into imaginary distinctions that justify discrimination. With half of mankind (his own sex) the male may feel an in-group solidarity, with the other half, an irreconcilable conflict. 19

> Lord Chesterfield,[5] who in his letters often admonished his son to guide his life by reason rather than by prejudice, nevertheless has this to say about women:
>
> "Women, then, are only children of a larger growth; they have an entertaining tattle, and sometimes wit; but for solid reasoning, good

[3]J. L. Moreno. *Who shall survive?* Washington: Nervous & Mental Disease Pub. Co., 1934, 24. These data are somewhat old. At the present time there are grounds for believing that the sex boundary is not so important among children as formerly. [Author's note]
[4]*misogynist:* a person who hates women.
[5]*Lord Chesterfield:* English statesman and author (1694–1773), remembered for his *Letters to His Son*.

sense, I never knew in my life one that had it, or who reasoned or acted consequentially for four and twenty hours together. . . .

"A man of sense only trifles with them, plays with them, humors and flatters them, as he does a sprightly, forward child; but he neither consults them about, nor trusts them with serious matters; though he often makes them believe that he does both; which is the thing in the world that they are most proud of. . . ."[6]

"Women are much more like each other than men; they have in truth but two passions, vanity and love: These are their universal characteristics."[7]

Schopenhauer's[8] views were much like Chesterfield's. Women, he   20
wrote, are big children all their life long. A fundamental fault of the female character is that it has no sense of justice. This is mainly due to the fact, Schopenhauer insisted, that women are defective in the powers of reasoning and deliberation.[9]

Such antifeminism reflects the two basic ingredients of prejudice —   21
denigration and gross overgeneralization. Neither of these famous men of intellect allows for individual differences among women, nor asks whether their alleged attributes are in fact more common in the female than in the male sex.

What is instructive about this antifeminism is the fact that it implies   22
security and contentment with one's own sex-membership. To Chesterfield and to Schopenhauer the cleavage between male and female was a cleavage between accepted in-group and rejected out-group. But for many people this "war of the sexes" seems totally unreal. They do not find in it a ground for prejudice.

The Shifting Nature of In-groups

Although each individual has his own conception of in-groups important   23
to himself, he is not unaffected by the temper of the times. During the past century, national and racial memberships have risen in importance, while family and religious memberships have declined (though they are still exceedingly prominent). The fierce loyalties and rivalries between Scottish clans is almost a thing of the past — but the conception of a

[6]C. Strachey (Ed.). *The Letters of the Earl of Chesterfield to His Son*. New York: G. P. Putnam's Sons, 1925, Vol. I, 261. [Author's note]

[7]*Ibid.*, Vol. II, 5. [Author's note]

[8]*Schopenhauer:* Arthur Schopenhauer, German philosopher (1788–1860) whose pessimistic view of human existence stressed the dominance of will over intelligence.

[9]E. B. Bax (Ed.). *Selected Essays of Schopenhauer*. London: G. Bell & Sons, 1914, 340. [Author's note]

"master race"[10] has grown to threatening proportions. The fact that women in Western countries have assumed roles once reserved for men makes the antifeminism of Chesterfield and Schopenhauer seem old-fashioned indeed.

A change in the conception of the national in-group is seen in the   24 shifting American attitude toward immigration. The native American nowadays seldom takes an idealistic view of immigration. He does not feel it a duty and privilege to offer a home to oppressed people — to include them in his in-group. The legend on the Statue of Liberty, engraved eighty years ago, already seems out of date:

> Give me your tired, your poor,
> Your huddled masses yearning to breathe free,
> The wretched refuse of your teeming shore.
> Send these, the homeless, the tempest-tossed to me.
> I lift my lamp beside the golden door.

The lamp was virtually extinguished by the anti-immigration laws   25 passed in the period 1918–1924. The lingering sentiment was not strong enough to relax the bars appreciably following the Second World War when there were more homeless and tempest-tost than ever before crying for admission. From the standpoint of both economics and humanitarianism there were strong arguments for relaxing the restrictions; but people had grown fearful. Many conservatives feared the importation of radical ideas; many Protestants felt their own precarious majority might be further reduced; some Catholics dreaded the arrival of Communists; anti-Semites wanted no more Jews; some labor-union members feared that jobs would not be created to absorb the newcomers and that their own security would suffer.

During the 124 years for which data are available, approximately   26 40,000,000 immigrants came to America, as many as 1,000,000 in a single year. Of the total immigration 85 percent came from Europe. Until a generation ago, few objections were heard. But today nearly all applicants are refused admission, and few champions of "displaced persons" are heard. Times have changed, and whenever they change for the worse, as they have, in-group boundaries tend to tighten. The stranger is suspect and excluded.

Not only do the strength and definition of in-groups change over the   27 years in a given culture, but a single individual, too, may have occasion at one time to affirm one group-loyalty and at a different time another.

---

[10] *master race:* term used in Nazi Germany to distinguish those of Aryan ancestry from other supposedly inferior ethnic groups.

The following amusing passage from H. G. Wells's[11] *A Modern Utopia* illustrates this elasticity. The passage depicts a snob — a person whose group loyalties are narrow. But even a snob, it appears, must have a certain flexibility, for he finds it convenient to identify himself sometimes with one in-group and sometimes with another.

The passage illustrates an important point: In-group memberships are [28] not permanently fixed. For certain purposes an individual may affirm one category of membership, for other purposes a slightly larger category. It depends on his need for self-enhancement.

Wells is describing the loyalties of a certain botanist: [29]

> He has a strong feeling for systematic botanists as against plant phys-
> iologists, whom he regards as lewd and evil scoundrels in this relation;
> but he has a strong feeling for all botanists and indeed all biologists,
> as against physicists, and those who profess the exact sciences, all of
> whom he regards as dull, mechanical, ugly-minded scoundrels in this
> relation; but he has a strong feeling for all who profess what he calls
> Science, as against psychologists, sociologists, philosophers, and literary
> men, whom he regards as wild, foolish, immoral scoundrels in this
> relation; but he has a strong feeling for all educated men as against the
> working man, whom he regards as a cheating, lying, loafing, drunken,
> thievish, dirty scoundrel in this relation; but as soon as the working
> man is comprehended together with these others, as *Englishmen* . . .
> he holds them superior to all sorts of Europeans, whom he regards. . . .[12]

Thus the sense of belonging is a highly personal matter. Even two [30] members of the same actual in-group may view its composition in widely divergent ways. Take, for instance, the definition that two Americans might give to their own national in-group. [See Fig. 1.]

The narrowed perception of Individual A is the product of an arbitrary [31] categorization, one that he finds convenient (functionally significant) to hold. The larger range of perception on the part of Individual B creates a wholly different conception of the national in-group. It is misleading to say that both belong to the same in-group. Psychologically, they do not.

Each individual tends to see in his in-group the precise pattern of [32] security that he himself requires. An instructive example comes from a recent resolution of the convention of the Democratic Party in South Carolina. To the gentlemen assembled the Party was an important in-

[11]*H. G. Wells:* English novelist, historian, and sociologist (1866–1946), best known as author of *The Time Machine* and *War of the Worlds.*

[12]Reprinted by permission of Chapman & Hall, Ltd., from *A Modern Utopia.* London, 1905, 322 [Author's note] and A. P. Watt Ltd. on behalf of the Literary Executors of the Estate of H. G. Wells.

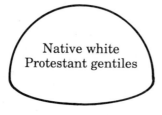

Native white Protestant gentiles	Native white Protestant gentiles, Negroes, Catholics, Jews, Immigrants, etc.
As seen by Individual A	As seen by Individual B

FIG. 1.   The national in-group as perceived by two Americans.

group. But the definition of Party (as stated in its national platform) was unacceptable. Hence in order to re-fence the in-group so that each member could feel secure, the category "Democrat" was redefined to "include those who believe in local self-government as against the idea of a strong centralized, paternalistic government; and exclude those whose ideas or leadership are inspired by foreign influences, Communism, Nazism, Fascism, statism, totalitarianism, or the Fair Employment Practices Commission."

Thus in-groups are often recreated to fit the needs of individuals, and when the needs are strongly aggressive — as in this case — the redefinition of the in-group may be primarily in terms of the hated out-groups. 33

In-groups and Reference Groups

We have broadly defined an in-group as any cluster of people who can use the term "we" with the same significance. But the reader has noted that individuals may hold all manner of views concerning their membership in in-groups. A first-generation American may regard his Italian background and culture as more important than do his children, who are second-generation Italian-Americans. Adolescents may view their neighborhood gang as a far more important in-group than their school. In some instances an individual may actively repudiate an in-group, even though he cannot escape membership in it. 34

In order to clarify this situation, modern social science has introduced the concept of reference group. Sherif and Sherif have defined reference groups as "those groups to which the individual relates himself as a part, 35 or to which he aspires to relate himself psychologically."[13] Thus a reference group is an in-group that is warmly accepted, or a group in which the individual wishes to be included.

Now usually an in-group is also a reference group, but not always. A 36 Negro may wish to relate himself to the white majority in his community. He would like to partake of the privileges of this majority, and be considered one of its members. He may feel so intensely about the matter that he repudiates his own in-group. He develops a condition that Kurt Lewin has called "self-hate" (i.e., hatred for his own in-group). Yet the customs of the community force him to live with, work with, and be classified with the Negro group. In such a case his in-group membership is not the same as his reference group.

Or take the case of a clergyman of Armenian descent ministering in 37 a small New England town. His name is foreign. Townsmen classify him as an Armenian. Yet he himself seldom thinks of his ancestry, though he does not actively reject his background. His reference groups (his main interests) are his church, his family, and the community in which he lives. Unfortunately for him, his fellow townsmen persist in regarding him as an Armenian; they regard this ethnic in-group as far more important than he himself does.

The Negro and the Armenian cleric occupy *marginal* roles in the 38 community. They have difficulty relating themselves to their reference groups because the pressures of the community force them always to tie to in-groups of small psychological importance to them.

To a considerable degree all minority groups suffer from the same 39 state of marginality, with its haunting consequences of insecurity, conflict, and irritation. Every minority group finds itself in a larger society where many customs, many values, many practices are prescribed. The minority group member is thus to some degree forced to make the dominant majority his reference group in respect to language, manners, morals, and law. He may be entirely loyal to his minority in-group, but he is at the same time always under the necessity of relating himself to the standards and expectations of the majority. The situation is particularly clear in the case of the Negro. Negro culture is almost entirely the same as white American culture. The Negro must relate himself to it. Yet whenever he tries to achieve this relatedness he is likely to suffer rebuff. Hence there is in his case an almost inevitable conflict between his biologically defined in-group and his culturally defined reference group.

[13]M. and Carolyn W. Sherif. *Groups in Harmony and Tension*. New York: Harper, 1953, 161. [Author's note]

If we follow this line of thinking we see why all minority groups, to some degree, occupy a marginal position in society with its unhappy consequents of apprehension and resentment.

The concepts of in-group and reference group help us to distinguish   40
two levels of belongingness. The former indicates the sheer fact of membership; the latter tells us whether the individual prizes that membership or whether he seeks to relate himself with another group. In many cases, as we have said, there is a virtual identity between in-groups and reference groups; but it is not always so. Some individuals, through necessity or by choice, continually compare themselves with groups which for them are not in-groups.

Social Distance

The distinction between in-group and reference group is well brought   41
out in studies of social distance. This familiar technique, invented by E. S. Bogardus, asks respondents to indicate to which steps on the following scale they would admit members of various ethnic and national groups:

1. to close kinship by marriage
2. to my club as personal chums
3. to my street as neighbors
4. to employment in my occupation
5. to citizenship in my country
6. as visitors only to my country
7. would exclude from my country

Now the most striking finding from this procedure is that a similar   42
pattern of preference is found across the country, varying little with income, region, education, occupation, or even with ethnic group. Most people, whoever they are, find the English and Canadians acceptable as citizens, as neighbors, as social equals, and as kinsmen. These ethnic stocks have the least social distance. At the other extreme come Hindus, Turks, Negroes. The ordering — with a few minor shifts — stays substantially constant.[14]

While members of the unfavored groups tend to put their own groups   43
high in the list, yet in all other respects they choose the prevailing order

[14]The order found by Bogardus in 1928 (E. S. Bogardus, *Immigration and Race Attitudes*, Boston: D. C. Heath, 1928) was found essentially unchanged by Hartley in 1946, and again by Spoerl in 1951. (Cf. E. L. Hartley, *Problems in Prejudice*, New York: Kings Crown Press, 1946; and Dorothy T. Spoerl, Some aspects of prejudice as affected by religion and education, *Journal of Social Psychology*, 1951, 33, 69–76). [Author's note]

of acceptability. In one study of Jewish children, for example, it was found that the standard pattern of social distance existed excepting only that most Jewish children place Jews high in acceptability.[15] In similar investigations it turns out that on the average the Negro places the Jew at about the same distance as does the white gentile; and the Jew ordinarily places the Negro low on his list.

From such results we are forced to conclude that the member of an 44 ethnic minority tends to fashion his attitudes as does the dominant majority. In other words, the dominant majority is for him a *reference group*. It exerts a strong pull upon him, forcing attitudinal conformity. The conformity, however, rarely extends to the point of repudiating his own in-group. A Negro, or Jew, or Mexican will ordinarily assert the acceptability of his own in-group, but in other respects he will decide as does his larger reference group. Thus, both in-group and reference group are important in the formation of attitudes.

The Group-Norm Theory of Prejudice

We are now in a position to understand and appreciate a major theory 45 of prejudice. It holds that all groups (whether in-groups or reference groups) develop a way of living with characteristic codes and beliefs, standards and "enemies" to suit their own adaptive needs. The theory holds also that both gross and subtle pressures keep every individual member in line. The in-group's preferences must be his preference, its enemies his enemies. The Sherifs, who advance this theory, write:

> Ordinarily the factors leading individuals to form attitudes of prejudice are not piecemeal. Rather, their formation is functionally related to becoming a group member — to adopting the group and its values (norms) as the main anchorage in regulating experience and behavior.[16]

A strong argument in favor of this view is the relative ineffectiveness 46 of attempts to change attitudes through influencing individuals. Suppose the child attends a lesson in intercultural education in the classroom. The chances are this lesson will be smothered by the more embracing norms of his family, gang, or neighborhood. To change the child's attitudes it would be necessary to alter the cultural equilibrium of these, to him, more important groups. It would be necessary for the family, the gang, or the neighborhood to sanction tolerance before he as an individual could practice it.

[15] Rose Zeligs. Racial attitudes of Jewish children. *Jewish Education*, 1937, 9, 148–152. [Author's note]
[16] M. and Carolyn W. Sherif. *Op. cit.*, 218. [Author's note]

This line of thought has led to the dictum, "It is easier to change   47
group attitudes than individual attitudes." Recent research lends some
support to the view. In certain studies whole communities, whole housing
projects, whole factories, or whole school systems have been made the
target of change. By involving the leaders, the policies, the rank and
file, new norms are created, and when this is accomplished, it is found
that individual attitudes tend to conform to the new group norm.[17]

While we cannot doubt the results, there is something unnecessarily   48
"collectivistic" about the theory. Prejudice is by no means exclusively
a mass phenomenon. Let the reader ask himself whether his own social
attitudes do in fact conform closely to those of his family, social class,
occupational group, or church associates. Perhaps the answer is yes; but
more likely the reader may reply that the prevailing prejudices of his
various reference groups are so contradictory that he cannot, and does
not, "share" them all. He may also decide that his pattern of prejudice
is unique, conforming to none of his membership groups.

Realizing this individual play of attitudes, the proponents of the theory   49
speak of a "range of tolerable behavior," admitting thereby that only
approximate conformity is demanded within any system of group norms.
People may deviate in their attitudes to some extent, but not too much.

As soon as we allow, however, for a "range of tolerable behavior" we   50
are moving toward a more individualistic point of view. We do not need
to deny the existence of group norms and group pressure in order to
insist that each person is uniquely organized. Some of us are avid conformists to what we believe the group requirement to be. Others of us
are passive conformists. Still others are nonconformists. Such conformism
as we show is the product of individual learning, individual needs, and
individual style of life.

In dealing with problems of attitude formation it is always difficult to   51
strike a proper balance between the collective approach and the individual
approach. This volume maintains that prejudice is ultimately a problem
of personality formation and development; no two cases of prejudice are
precisely the same. No individual would mirror his group's attitude
unless he had a personal need, or personal habit, that leads him to do
so. But it likewise maintains that one of the frequent sources, perhaps

[17] Among the studies of this type we may refer especially to: A. Morrow and J. French,
Changing a stereotype in industry, *Journal of Social Issues*, 1945, 1, 33–37; R. Lippitt,
Training in Community Relations, New York: Harper, 1949; Margot H. Wormser and
Claire Selltiz, *How to Conduct a Community Self-survey of Civil Rights*, New York:
Association Press, 1951; K. Lewin, Group decision and social change in T. M. Newcomb
and E. L. Hartley (Eds.), *Readings in Social Psychology*, New York: Holt, 1947. [Author's
note]

the most frequent source, of prejudice lies in the needs and habits that reflect the influence of in-group memberships upon the development of the individual personality. It is possible to hold the individualistic type of theory without denying that the major influences upon the individual may be collective.

Can There Be an In-group Without an Out-group?

Every line, fence, or boundary marks off an inside from an outside. 52 Therefore, in strict logic, an in-group always implies the existence of some corresponding out-group. But this logical statement by itself is of little significance. What we need to know is whether one's loyalty to the in-group automatically implies disloyalty, or hostility, or other forms of negativism, toward out-groups.

The French biologist, Felix le Dantec, insisted that every social unit 53 from the family to the nation could exist only by virtue of having some "common enemy." The family unit fights many threatening forces that menace each person who belongs to the unit. The exclusive club, the American Legion, the nation itself, exists to defeat the common enemies of its members. In favor of Le Dantec's view is the well-known Machiavellian trick of creating a common enemy in order to cement an in-group. Hitler created the Jewish menace not so much to demolish the Jews as to cement the Nazi hold over Germany. At the turn of the century the Workingmen's Party in California whipped up an anti-Oriental sentiment to consolidate its own ranks which, without a common enemy, were indifferent and wavering. School spirit is never so strong as when the time for an athletic contest with the traditional "enemy" approaches. Instances are so numerous that one is tempted to accept the doctrine. Studying the effect of strangers entering a group of nursery school children, Susan Isaacs reports, "The existence of an outsider is in the beginning an essential condition of any warmth or togetherness within the group."[18]

So deeply was William James[19] impressed by the fact that social co- 54 hesiveness seems to require a common enemy that he wrote a famous essay on the subject. In *The Moral Equivalent for War* he recognized the adventuresomeness, the aggression, and the competitiveness that marked human relationships, especially among young people of military

[18]Susan Isaacs, *Social Development in Young Children*. New York: Harcourt, Brace, 1933, 250. [Author's note]

[19]*William James:* American psychologist and philosopher (1842–1910), and leading exponent of pragmatism, the philosophical approach that measures the validity of a theory in terms of its practical result.

age. In order that they themselves might live at peace he recommended that they find an enemy that would not violate man's growing sense of loyalty to humanity. His advice was: Fight nature, fight disease, fight poverty.

Now there is no denying that the presence of a threatening common enemy will cement the in-group sense of any organized aggregate of people. A family (if it is not already badly disrupted) will grow cohesive in the face of adversity, and a nation is never so unified as in time of war. But the psychological emphasis must be placed primarily on the desire for security, not on hostility itself. 55

One's own family is an in-group; and by definition all other families on the street are out-groups; but seldom do they clash. A hundred ethnic groups compose America, and while serious conflict occasionally occurs, the majority rub along in peace. One knows that one's lodge has distinctive characteristics that mark it off from all others, but one does not necessarily despise the others. 56

The situation, it seems, can best be stated as follows: although we could not perceive our own in-groups excepting as they contrast to out-groups, still the in-groups are psychologically primary. We live in them, by them, and, sometimes, for them. Hostility toward out-groups helps strengthen our sense of belonging, but it is not required. 57

Because of their basic importance to our own survival and self-esteem we tend to develop a partisanship and ethnocentricism in respect to our in-groups. Seven-year-old children in one town were asked, "Which are better, the children in this town or in Smithfield (a neighboring town)?" Almost all replied, "The children in this town." When asked why, the children usually replied, "I don't know the kids in Smithfield." This incident puts the initial in-group and out-group situation in perspective. The familiar is *preferred*. What is alien is regarded as somehow inferior, less "good," but there is not necessarily hostility against it. 58

Thus while a certain amount of predilection is inevitable in all in-group memberships, the reciprocal attitude toward out-groups may range widely. At one extreme they may be viewed as a common enemy to be defeated in order to protect the in-group and strengthen its inner loyalties. At the other extreme the out-group may be appreciated, tolerated, even liked for its diversity. 59

Engaging the Text

1. Summarize the social and psychological reasons Allport gives for maintaining group loyalty. Is his analysis convincing? Can you think of any different explanations? Are there any social or psychological rewards for *changing* group loyalties?

2. How do in-groups and reference groups enforce values and prejudices? Think of examples from your own experience, from the experience of family members and friends, from things you've read or seen.

3. Explain what Allport means by "marginal." Do you agree with him that all minorities occupy marginal roles? Is there any sense in which women, although not a minority, also constitute a marginal group?

Exploring Connections

1. In "The Paradox of Individualism" in the previous chapter, the authors suggest that Americans have an intense need to feel part of a community. Given what Allport says in this essay, do you think it is possible to be part of a community without also creating an out-group? In other words, does community necessarily involve prejudice?

Extending the Critical Context

1. List the in-groups you belong to and identify whether each is ascribed or achieved. Rank the groups in order of their importance to you. Have these rankings ever been different from what they are now? If so, how and why? Write an essay explaining the way you ranked your in-groups and discussing how their importance has changed at different times in your life.

Split at the Root:
An Essay on Jewish Identity
ADRIENNE RICH

Academic concepts like "in-groups," "out-groups," and "marginalization" are easy to handle when abstracted from personal experience. But they can have a devastating impact when they are translated into real effects on individual lives. In the following selection, Adrienne Rich assesses the personal costs of growing up in a world divided by prejudice.

Adrienne Rich (b. 1929) is one of America's premier poets and an ardent feminist. Her poetry often addresses themes of social injustice, women's consciousness, and the need for an authentic human community. In 1974, she won the National Book Award for poetry for Diving into the Wreck. *This selection is taken from* Blood, Bread and Poetry: Selected

Prose, 1979–1985. *She is professor of English and feminist studies at Stanford University.*

For about fifteen minutes I have been sitting chin in hand in front of 1
the typewriter, staring out at the snow. Trying to be honest with myself,
trying to figure out why writing this seems to be so dangerous an act,
filled with fear and shame, and why it seems so necessary. It comes to
me that in order to write this I have to be willing to do two things: I
have to claim my father, for I have my Jewishness from him and not
from my gentile mother; and I have to break his silence, his taboos; in
order to claim him I have in a sense to expose him.

And there is, of course, the third thing: I have to face the sources 2
and the flickering presence of my own ambivalence as a Jew; the daily,
mundane anti-Semitisms of my entire life.

These are stories I have never tried to tell before. Why now? Why, 3
I asked myself sometime last year, does this question of Jewish identity
float so impalpably, so ungraspably around me, a cloud I can't quite see
the outlines of, which feels to me to be without definition?

And yet I've been on the track of this longer than I think. 4

In a long poem written in 1960, when I was thirty-one years old, I 5
described myself as "Split at the root, neither Gentile nor Jew,/Yankee
nor Rebel."[1] I was still trying to have it both ways: to be neither/nor,
trying to live (with my Jewish husband and three children more Jewish
in ancestry than I) in the predominantly gentile Yankee academic world
of Cambridge, Massachusetts.

But this begins, for me, in Baltimore, where I was born in my father's 6
workplace, a hospital in the Black ghetto, whose lobby contained an
immense white marble statue of Christ.

My father was then a young teacher and researcher in the department 7
of pathology at the Johns Hopkins Medical School, one of the very few
Jews to attend or teach at that institution. He was from Birmingham,
Alabama; his father, Samuel, was Ashkenazic,[2] an immigrant from Austria-
Hungary and his mother, Hattie Rice, a Sephardic[3] Jew from Vicksburg,

---

[1] Adrienne Rich, "Readings of History," in *Snapshots of a Daughter-in-Law* (New York: W. W. Norton, 1967), pp. 36–40. [Author's note]

[2] *Ashkenazic:* pertaining to descendants of the Jews who settled in middle and northern Europe after the Babylonian captivity (597–538 B.C.).

[3] *Sephardic:* pertaining to descendants of the Jews who settled in Spain and Portugal.

Mississippi. My grandfather had had a shoe store in Birmingham, which did well enough to allow him to retire comfortably and to leave my grandmother income on his death. The only souvenirs of my grandfather, Samuel Rich, were his ivory flute, which lay on our living-room mantel and was not to be played with; his thin gold pocket watch, which my father wore; and his Hebrew prayer book, which I discovered among my father's books in the course of reading my way through his library. In this prayer book there was a newspaper clipping about my grandparents' wedding, which took place in a synagogue.

My father, Arnold, was sent in adolescence to a military school in the   8
North Carolina mountains, a place for training white southern Christian gentlemen. I suspect that there were few, if any, other Jewish boys at Colonel Bingham's, or at "Mr. Jefferson's university" in Charlottesville, where he studied as an undergraduate. With whatever conscious fore-thought, Samuel and Hattie sent their son into the dominant southern WASP culture to become an "exception," to enter the professional class. Never, in describing these experiences, did he speak of having suffered — from loneliness, cultural alienation, or outsiderhood. Never did I hear him use the word *anti-Semitism*.

It was only in college, when I read a poem by Karl Shapiro beginning   9
"To hate the Negro and avoid the Jew / is the curriculum," that it flashed on me that there was an untold side to my father's story of his student years. He looked recognizably Jewish, was short and slender in build with dark wiry hair and deep-set eyes, high forehead and curved nose.

My mother is a gentile. In Jewish law I cannot count myself a Jew.   10
If it is true that "we think back through our mothers if we are women" (Virginia Woolf[4]) — and I myself have affirmed this — then even according to lesbian theory, I cannot (or need not?) count myself a Jew.

The white southern Protestant woman, the gentile, has always been   11
there for me to peel back into. That's a whole piece of history in itself, for my gentile grandmother and my mother were also frustrated artists and intellectuals, a lost writer and a lost composer between them. Readers and annotators of books, note takers, my mother a good pianist still, in her eighties. But there was also the obsession with ancestry, with "back-ground," the southern talk of family, not as people you would necessarily know and depend on, but as heritage, the guarantee of "good breeding." There was the inveterate romantic heterosexual fantasy, the mother telling the daughter how to attract men (my mother often used the word

[4]*Virginia Woolf*: English feminist, critic, and innovator in modern British fiction (1882–1941), best known for her novels *Mrs. Dalloway* and *To the Lighthouse*.

"fascinate"); the assumption that relations between the sexes could only be romantic, that it was in the woman's interest to cultivate "mystery," conceal her actual feelings. Survival tactics of a kind, I think today, knowing what I know about the white woman's sexual role in the southern racist scenario. Heterosexuality as protection, but also drawing white women deeper into collusion with white men.

It would be easy to push away and deny the gentile in me — that 12 white southern woman, that social christian. At different times in my life I have wanted to push away one or the other burden of inheritance, to say merely *I am a woman; I am a lesbian*. If I call myself a Jewish lesbian, do I thereby try to shed some of my southern gentile white woman's culpability? If I call myself only through my mother, is it because I pass more easily through a world where being a lesbian often seems like outsiderhood enough?

According to Nazi logic, my two Jewish grandparents would have made 13 me a *Mischling, first-degree* — nonexempt from the Final Solution.[5]

The social world in which I grew up was christian virtually without 14 needing to say so — christian imagery, music, language, symbols, assumptions everywhere. It was also a genteel, white, middle-class world in which "common" was a term of deep opprobrium. "Common" white people might speak of "niggers"; *we* were taught never to use that word — *we* said "Negroes" (even as we accepted segregation, the eating taboo, the assumption that Black people were simply of a separate species). Our language was more polite, distinguishing us from the "red-necks" or the lynch-mob mentality. But so charged with negative meaning was even the word "Negro" that as children we were taught never to use it in front of Black people. We were taught that any mention of skin color in the presence of colored people was treacherous, forbidden ground. In a parallel way, the word "Jew" was not used by polite gentiles. I sometimes heard my best friend's father, a Presbyterian minister, allude to "the Hebrew people" or "people of the Jewish faith." The world of acceptable folk was white, gentile (christian, really), and had "ideals" (which colored people, white "common" people, were not supposed to have). "Ideals" and "manners" included not hurting someone's feelings by calling her or him a Negro or a Jew — naming the hated identity. This is the mental framework of the 1930s and 1940s in which I was raised.

[5] *Final Solution:* euphemistic name for the Nazi plan to execute all members of the Jewish race in "death camps" like Auschwitz and Dachau.

(Writing this, I feel dimly like the betrayer: of my father, who did 15
not speak the word; of my mother, who must have trained me in the
messages; of my caste and class; of my whiteness itself.)

Two memories: I am in a play reading at school of *The Merchant of* 16
Venice. Whatever Jewish law says, I am quite sure I was *seen* as Jewish
(with a reassuringly gentile mother) in that double vision that bigotry
allows. I am the only Jewish girl in the class, and I am playing Portia.
As always, I read my part aloud for my father the night before, and he
tells me to convey, with my voice, more scorn and contempt with the
word "Jew": "Therefore, Jew . . ." I have to say the word out, and say
it loudly. I was encouraged to pretend to be a non-Jewish child acting
a non-Jewish character who has to speak the word "Jew" emphatically.
Such a child would not have had trouble with the part. But *I* must have
had trouble with the part, if only because the word itself was really
taboo. I can see that there was a kind of terrible, bitter bravado about
my father's way of handling this. And who would not dissociate from
Shylock in order to identify with Portia? As a Jewish child who was also
a female, I loved Portia — and, like every other Shakespearean heroine,
she proved a treacherous role model.

A year or so later I am in another play, *The School for Scandal*, in 17
which a notorious spendthrift is described as having "many excellent
friends . . . among the Jews." In neither case was anything explained,
either to me or to the class at large, about this scorn for Jews and the
disgust surrounding Jews and money. Money, when Jews wanted it, had
it, or lent it to others, seemed to take on a peculiar nastiness; Jews and
money had some peculiar and unspeakable relation.

At this same school — in which we had Episcopalian hymns and 18
prayers, and read aloud through the Bible morning after morning — I
gained the impression that Jews were in the Bible and mentioned in
English literature, that they had been persecuted centuries ago by the
wicked Inquisition, but that they seemed not to exist in everyday life.
These were the 1940s, and we were told a great deal about the Battle
of Britain, the noble French Resistance fighters, the brave, starving
Dutch — but I did not learn of the resistance of the Warsaw ghetto
until I left home.

I was sent to the Episcopal church, baptized and confirmed, and 19
attended it for about five years, though without belief. That religion
seemed to have little to do with belief or commitment; it was liturgy
that mattered, not spiritual passion. Neither of my parents ever entered
that church, and my father would not enter *any* church for any reason
— wedding or funeral. Nor did I enter a synagogue until I left Baltimore.
When I came home from church, for a while, my father insisted on

reading aloud to me from Thomas Paine's *The Age of Reason* — a diatribe against institutional religion. Thus, he explained, I would have a balanced view of these things, a choice. He — they — did not give me the choice to be a Jew. My mother explained to me when I was filling out forms for college that if any question was asked about "religion," I should put down "Episcopalian" rather than "none" — to seem to have no religion was, she implied, dangerous.

But it was white social christianity, rather than any particular christian sect, that the world was founded on. The very word *Christian* was used as a synonym for virtuous, just, peace-loving, generous, etc., etc.[6] The norm was christian: "religion: none" was indeed not acceptable. Anti-Semitism was so intrinsic as not to have a name. I don't recall exactly being taught that the Jews killed Jesus — "Christ killer" seems too strong a term for the bland Episcopal vocabulary — but certainly we got the impression that the Jews had been caught out in a terrible mistake, failing to recognize the true Messiah, and were thereby less advanced in moral and spiritual sensibility. The Jews had actually allowed *moneylenders in the Temple* (again, the unexplained obsession with Jews and money). They were of the past, archaic, primitive, as older (and darker) cultures are supposed to be primitive; christianity was lightness, fairness, peace on earth, and combined the feminine appeal of "The meek shall inherit the earth" with the masculine stride of "Onward, Christian Soldiers."

Sometime in 1946, while still in high school, I read in the newspaper that a theater in Baltimore was showing films of the Allied liberation of the Nazi concentration camps. Alone, I went downtown after school one afternoon and watched the stark, blurry, but unmistakable newsreels. When I try to go back and touch the pulse of that girl of sixteen, growing up in many ways so precocious and so ignorant, I am overwhelmed by a memory of despair, a sense of inevitability more enveloping than any I had ever known. Anne Frank's diary and many other personal narratives of the Holocaust were still unknown or unwritten. But it came to me that every one of those piles of corpses, mountains of shoes and clothing had contained, simply, individuals, who had believed, as I now believed of myself, that they were intended to live out a life of some kind of meaning, that the world possessed some kind of sense and order; yet *this* had happened to them. And I, who believed my life was intended to be so interesting and meaningful, was connected to those dead by

20

21

---

[6]In a similar way the phrase "That's white of you" implied that you were behaving with the superior decency and morality expected of white but not of Black people. [Author's note]

something — not just mortality but a taboo name, a hated identity. Or
was I — did I really have to be? Writing this now, I feel belated rage
that I was so impoverished by the family and social worlds I lived in,
that I had to try to figure out by myself what this did indeed mean for
me. That I had never been taught about resistance, only about passing.
That I had no language for anti-Semitism itself.

When I went home and told my parents where I had been, they were 22
not pleased. I felt accused of being morbidly curious, not healthy, sniffing
around death for the thrill of it. And since, at sixteen, I was often not
sure of the sources of my feelings or of my motives for doing what I
did, I probably accused myself as well. One thing was clear: there was
nobody in my world with whom I could discuss those films. Probably
at the same time, I was reading accounts of the camps in magazines and
newspapers; what I remember were the films and having questions that
I could not even phrase, such as *Are those men and women "them" or
"us"?*

To be able to ask even the child's astonished question *Why do they* 23
hate us so? means knowing how to say "we." The guilt of not knowing,
the guilt of perhaps having betrayed my parents or even those victims,
those survivors, through mere curiosity — these also froze in me for
years the impulse to find out more about the Holocaust.

1947: I left Baltimore to go to college in Cambridge, Massachusetts, 24
left (I thought) the backward, enervating South for the intellectual, vital
North. New England also had for me some vibration of higher moral
rectitude, of moral passion even, with its seventeenth-century Puritan
self-scrutiny, its nineteenth-century literary "flowering," its abolitionist
righteousness, Colonel Shaw and his Black Civil War regiment depicted
in granite on Boston Common. At the same time, I found myself, at
Radcliffe, among Jewish women. I used to sit for hours over coffee with
what I thought of as the "real" Jewish students, who told me about
middle-class Jewish culture in America. I described my background —
for the first time to strangers — and they took me on, some with
amusement at my illiteracy, some arguing that I could never marry into
a strict Jewish family, some convinced I didn't "look Jewish," others that
I did. I learned the names of holidays and foods, which surnames are
Jewish and which are "changed names"; about girls who had had their
noses "fixed," their hair straightened. For these young Jewish women,
students in the late 1940s, it was acceptable, perhaps even necessary,
to strive to look as gentile as possible; but they stuck proudly to being
Jewish, expected to marry a Jew, have children, keep the holidays, carry
on the culture.

I felt I was testing a forbidden current, that there was danger in these 25 revelations. I bought a reproduction of a Chagall[7] portrait of a rabbi in striped prayer shawl and hung it on the wall of my room. I was admittedly young and trying to educate myself, but I was also doing something that *is* dangerous: I was flirting with identity.

One day that year I was in a small shop where I had bought a dress 26 with a too-long skirt. The shop employed a seamstress who did alterations, and she came in to pin up the skirt on me. I am sure that she was a recent immigrant, a survivor. I remember a short, dark woman wearing heavy glasses, with an accent so foreign I could not understand her words. Something about her presence was very powerful and disturbing to me. After marking and pinning up the skirt, she sat back on her knees, looked up at me, and asked in a hurried whisper: "You Jewish?" Eighteen years of training in assimilation sprang into the reflex by which I shook my head, rejecting her, and muttered, "No."

What was I actually saying "no" to? She was poor, older, struggling 27 with a foreign tongue, anxious; she had escaped the death that had been intended for her, but I had no imagination of her possible courage and foresight, her resistance — I did not see in her a heroine who had perhaps saved many lives, including her own. I saw the frightened immigrant, the seamstress hemming the skirts of college girls, the wandering Jew. But I was an American college girl having her skirt hemmed. And I was frightened myself, I think, because she had recognized me ("It takes one to know one," my friend Edie at Radcliffe had said) even if I refused to recognize myself or her, even if her recognition was sharpened by loneliness or the need to feel safe with me.

But why should she have felt safe with me? I myself was living with 28 a false sense of safety.

There are betrayals in my life that I have known at the very moment 29 were betrayals: this was one of them. There are other betrayals committed so repeatedly, so mundanely, that they leave no memory trace behind, only a growing residue of misery, of dull, accreted self-hatred. Often these take the form not of words but of silence. Silence before the joke at which everyone is laughing: the anti-woman joke, the racist joke, the anti-Semitic joke. Silence and then amnesia. Blocking it out when the oppressor's language starts coming from the lips of one we admire, whose courage and eloquence have touched us: *She didn't really mean that; he didn't really say that.* But the accretions build up out of sight, like scale inside a kettle.

[7]*Chagall:* Marc Chagall, Russian painter (1887–1985), famous for surreal, dreamlike works inspired by his Jewish heritage.

1948: I come home from my freshman year at college, flaming with   30
new insights, new information. I am the daughter who has gone out into
the world, to the pinnacle of intellectual prestige, Harvard, fulfilling my
father's hopes for me, but also exposed to dangerous influences. I have
already been reproved for attending a rally for Henry Wallace[8] and the
Progressive party. I challenge my father: "Why haven't you told me that
I am Jewish? Why do you never talk about being a Jew?" He answers
measuredly, "You know that I have never denied that I am a Jew. But
it's not important to me. I am a scientist, a deist. I have no use for
organized religion. I choose to live in a world of many kinds of people.
There are Jews I admire and others whom I despise. I am a person,
not simply a Jew." The words are as I remember them, not perhaps
exactly as spoken. But that was the message. And it contained enough
truth — as all denial drugs itself on partial truth — so that it remained
for the time being unanswerable, leaving me high and dry, split at the
root, gasping for clarity, for air.

At that time Arnold Rich was living in suspension, waiting to be   31
appointed to the professorship of pathology at Johns Hopkins. The appointment was delayed for years, no Jew ever having held a professional
chair in that medical school. And he wanted it badly. It must have been
a very bitter time for him, since he had believed so greatly in the
redeeming power of excellence, of being the most brilliant, inspired man
for the job. With enough excellence, you could presumably make it stop
mattering that you were Jewish; you could become the *only* Jew in the
gentile world, a Jew so "civilized," so far from "common," so attractively
combining southern gentility with European cultural values that no one
would ever confuse you with the raw, "pushy" Jews of New York, the
"loud, hysterical" refugees from eastern Europe, the "overdressed" Jews
of the urban South.

We — my sister, mother, and I — were constantly urged to speak   32
quietly in public, to dress without ostentation, to repress all vividness
or spontaneity, to assimilate with a world which might see us as too
flamboyant. I suppose that my mother, pure gentile though she was,
could be seen as acting "common" or "Jewish" if she laughed too loudly
or spoke aggressively. My father's mother, who lived with us half the
year, was a model of circumspect behavior, dressed in dark blue or
lavender, retiring in company, ladylike to an extreme, wearing no jewelry
except a good gold chain, a narrow brooch, or a string of pearls. A few
times, within the family, I saw her anger flare, felt the passion she was

[8]*Henry Wallace:* (1888–1965), American journalist, politician, and agriculturalist who
was the Progressive Party's candidate for the presidency in 1948.

repressing. But when Arnold took us out to a restaurant or on a trip, the Rich women were always tuned down to some WASP level my father believed, surely, would protect us all — maybe also make us unrecognizable to the "real Jews" who wanted to seize us, drag us back to the *shtetl*, the ghetto, in its many manifestations.

For, yes, that *was* a message — that some Jews would be after you,   33 once they "knew," to rejoin them, to re-enter a world that was messy, noisy, unpredictable, maybe poor — "even though," as my mother once wrote me, criticizing my largely Jewish choice of friends in college, "some of them will be the most brilliant, fascinating people you'll ever meet." I wonder if that isn't one message of assimilation — of America — that the unlucky or the unachieving want to pull you backward, that to identify with them is to court downward mobility, lose the precious chance of passing, of token existence. There was always within this sense of Jewish identity a strong class discrimination. Jews might be "fascinating" as individuals but came with huge unruly families who "poured chicken soup over everyone's head" (in the phrase of a white southern male poet). Anti-Semitism could thus be justified by the bad behavior of certain Jews; and if you did not effectively deny family and community, there would always be a remote cousin claiming kinship with you who was the "wrong kind" of Jew.

I have always believed his attitude toward other Jews depended on   34 *who they were. . . . It was my impression that Jews of this background looked down on Eastern European Jews, including Polish Jews and Russian Jews, who generally were not as well educated.* This from a letter written to me recently by a gentile who had worked in my father's department, whom I had asked about anti-Semitism there and in particular regarding my father. This informant also wrote me that it was hard to perceive anti-Semitism in Baltimore because the racism made so much more intense an impression: *I would almost have to think that blacks went to a different heaven than the whites, because the bodies were kept in a separate morgue, and some white persons did not even want blood transfusions from black donors.* My father's mind was predictably racist and misogynist;[9] yet as a medical student he noted in his journal that southern male chivalry stopped at the point of any white man in a streetcar giving his seat to an old, weary Black woman standing in the aisle. Was this a Jewish insight — an outsider's insight, even though the outsider was striving to be on the inside?

Because what isn't named is often more permeating than what is, I   35 believe that my father's Jewishness profoundly shaped my own identity

[9]*misogynist:* a person who hates women.

and our family existence. They were shaped both by external anti-Semitism and my father's self-hatred, and by his Jewish pride. What Arnold did, I think, was call his Jewish pride something else: achievement, aspiration, genius, idealism. Whatever was unacceptable got left back under the rubric of Jewishness or the "wrong kind" of Jews — uneducated, aggressive, loud. The message I got was that we were really superior: nobody else's father had collected so many books, had traveled so far, knew so many languages. Baltimore was a musical city, but for the most part, in the families of my school friends, culture was for women. My father was an amateur musician, read poetry, adored encyclopedic knowledge. He prowled and pounced over my school papers, insisting I use "grown-up" sources; he criticized my poems for faulty technique and gave me books on rhyme and meter and form. His investment in my intellect and talent was egotistical, tyrannical, opinionated, and terribly wearing. He taught me, nevertheless, to believe in hard work, to mistrust easy inspiration, to write and rewrite; to feel that I *was* a person of the book, even though a woman; to take ideas seriously. He made me feel, at a very young age, the power of language and that I could share in it.

The Riches were proud, but we also had to be very careful. Our behavior had to be more impeccable than other people's. Strangers were not to be trusted, nor even friends; family issues must never go beyond the family; the world was full of potential slanderers, betrayers, *people who could not understand*. Even within the family, I realize that I never in my whole life knew what my father was really feeling. Yet he spoke — monologued — with driving intensity. You could grow up in such a house mesmerized by the local electricity, the crucial meanings assumed by the merest things. This used to seem to me a sign that we were all living on some high emotional plane. It was a difficult force field for a favored daughter to disengage from. 36

Easy to call that intensity Jewish; and I have no doubt that passion 37 is one of the qualities required for survival over generations of persecution. But what happens when passion is rent from its original base, when the white gentile world is softly saying "Be more like us and you can be almost one of us"? What happens when survival seems to mean closing off one emotional artery after another? His forebears in Europe had been forbidden to travel or expelled from one country after another, had special taxes levied on them if they left the city walls, had been forced to wear special clothes and badges, restricted to the poorest neighborhoods. He had wanted to be a "free spirit," to travel widely, among "all kinds of people." Yet in his prime of life he lived in an increasingly withdrawn world, in his house up on a hill in a neighborhood where Jews were not supposed to be able to buy property, depending almost exclusively on interactions with his wife and daughters to provide emotional connectedness. In his home, he created a private defense system so elaborate that even as he was dying, my mother felt unable to talk freely with his colleagues or others who might have helped her. Of course, she acquiesced in this.

The loneliness of the "only," the token, often doesn't feel like loneliness 38 but like a kind of dead echo chamber. Certain things that ought to don't resonate. Somewhere Beverly Smith writes of women of color "inspiring the behavior" in each other. When there's nobody to "inspire the behavior," act out of the culture, there is an atrophy, a dwindling, which is partly invisible.

Sometimes I feel I have seen too long from too many disconnected 39 angles: white, Jewish, anti-Semite, racist, anti-racist, once-married, lesbian, middle-class, feminist, exmatriate southerner, *split at the root* — that I will never bring them whole. I would have liked, in this essay, to bring together the meanings of anti-Semitism and racism as I have experienced them and as I believe they intersect in the world beyond my life. But I'm not able to do this yet. I feel the tension as I think, make notes: *If you really look at the one reality, the other will waver and disperse*. Trying in one week to read Angela Davis and Lucy Davidowicz;[10] trying to hold throughout to a feminist, a lesbian, perspective — what does this mean? Nothing has trained me for this. And sometimes I feel inadequate to make any statement as a Jew; I feel the history of denial within me like an injury, a scar. For assimilation has affected *my* perceptions; those early lapses in meaning, those blanks, are with me still. My ignorance can be dangerous to me and to others.

Yet we can't wait for the undamaged to make our connections for us; 40 we can't wait to speak until we are perfectly clear and righteous. There is no purity and, in our lifetimes, no end to this process.

This essay, then, has no conclusions: it is another beginning for me. 41 Not just a way of saying, in 1982 Right Wing America, *I, too, will wear the yellow star*. It's a moving into accountability, enlarging the range of accountability. I know that in the rest of my life, the next half century or so, every aspect of my identity will have to be engaged. The middle-class white girl taught to trade obedience for privilege. The Jewish lesbian raised to be a heterosexual gentile. The woman who first heard oppression named and analyzed in the Black Civil Rights struggle. The woman with

[10]Angela Y. Davis, *Women, Race and Class* (New York: Random House, 1981); Lucy S. Davidowicz, *The War against the Jews 1933–1945* (1975) (New York: Bantam, 1979). [Author's note]

three sons, the feminist who hates male violence. The woman limping with a cane, the woman who has stopped bleeding are also accountable. The poet who knows that beautiful language can lie, that the oppressor's language sometimes sounds beautiful. The woman trying, as part of her resistance, to clean up her act.

Engaging the Text

1. In this personal reminiscence, Rich dissects her identity, analyzing her consciousness into separate, often antagonistic selves that compete for recognition. Work through her essay to identify these various selves and discuss how and why they conflict with one another.

2. Analyze the motives that underlie Arnold Rich's racism and his denial of his own Jewish HERITAGE.

3. Why are other ETHNIC minority groups important to Rich?

4. When Rich mentions buying a Chagall portrait of a rabbi (para. 25), she writes, "but I was also doing something that *is* dangerous: I was flirting with identity." What does she mean? Why is exploring her own identity a "dangerous" act?

Exploring Connections

1. Review Gordon Allport's definitions of in-groups and out-groups in the previous essay. List all the in-groups that Rich's family identifies with. What features or behaviors describe each group? What out-groups is each defined against? What, according to Rich, are the personal costs of in-group and out-group relations, and of mobility between groups?

Extending the Critical Context

1. Try your hand at writing your own self-analysis: How many separate selves do you contain? What demands do they make of you? How do they conflict? What does it mean for you to be "accountable" to them?

The Psychology of Racism

PETER LOEWENBERG

This excerpt provides a second but substantially different psychological approach to the workings of racial prejudice. Loewenberg (b. 1933) defines two concepts — "projection" and "displacement" — which may help explain some of the behavior you will read about in personal narratives or historical overviews that follow. Loewenberg's special interest is the psychological approach to history, and in that sense he occupies an intermediate position between Gordon W. Allport's purely psychological approach and James Boggs's sociohistorical argument, which follows. A professor at the University of California, Los Angeles, Loewenberg is a widely published analyst of racial issues in American history.

When we turn to how prejudice actually works in the mind, we find 1 that all men, white and black, harbor desires that are inadmissible to consciousness because these wishes are not socially sanctioned and therefore arouse guilt. These desires — voluptuous, murderous, and incestuous — are kept hidden in the unconscious. One means of defense against unconscious wishes is projection. Projection is perceiving in others that which one wishes to deny in oneself. It is the process of saying: "the evil impulses are out there, not here in me." What is outside can be repudiated and destroyed. One of the classic themes in modern literature and drama concerns persons whose guilt about their own erotic feelings is assuaged by condemning them in others. The minister in Somerset Maugham's *Rain* is a poignant example of this. He castigates the prostitute for her promiscuity when the true, unrecognized seat of sexual craving is in himself. In Robert Anderson's *Tea and Sympathy*, and Arthur Miller's *View from the Bridge*, the heroes perceive homoerotic feelings in others in order to defend against admitting such feelings in themselves.

When forbidden desires emerge in a white man, he can facilitate their 2 repression by projecting them onto blacks or members of other racial minorities. In the unconscious of the bigot the black represents his own repressed instincts which he fears and hates and which are forbidden by his conscience as it struggles to conform to the values professed by society. This is why the black man becomes the personification of sexuality, lewdness, laziness, dirtiness, and unbridled hostility. He is the symbol of voluptuousness and the immediate gratification of pleasure. In the deepest recesses of the minds of white Americans, Negroes are associated with lowly and debased objects or with sexuality and violence. In our society children are taught at an early age that their excrement is disgusting, smelly, and dirty, and that sexual and hostile feelings are bad and dangerous. These feelings are easily associated with low status or tabooed groups such as Negroes. Blacks are pictured in the unconscious imagery of the white majority as dark and odorous, aggressive, libidinal, and threatening.

Internal ambivalence — the experiencing of contradictory feelings at   3
the same time — frequently is resolved by projection. All elements of the population in the United States are in conflict over the emotionally loaded issue of race. The official ideal of equality teaches that each man has inalienable rights to be protected by the democratic political system. Yet in reality, American society condones the ghetto and other discriminatory situational and institutional practices. White people who practice discrimination must repress in themselves their own equalitarian impulses and project them onto white liberal "nigger lovers" who are then seen as the sole source of integrationist sentiment. On the other hand, white advocates of civil rights must repress in themselves racist stereotypes and view such ideas as emanating exclusively from bigoted segregationists. The difference between the white liberal and the white bigot is chiefly a difference in ideals. The liberal feels shame and guilt for his prejudiced ideas and therefore tries to make his conduct conform to the demands of his democratic ideals and his conscience; the bigot does not.

The process of projection becomes dangerous to the bigot when he   4
perceives that he is hated as the exploiter and oppressor and that he must fear the revenge of the blacks. It has become apparent in recent years that centuries of denigration and humiliation have been unsuccessful in keeping the Negro "in his place." Blacks, sometimes with the initial aid of whites, have persisted in rising on all fronts: educationally, socially, legally, and politically. These efforts have often been interpreted in the white mind as preludes to hostile vengefulness by blacks. This, again, is largely a projection. Bigoted whites cannot imagine blacks who are not vengeful because they identify projectively with the targets of their prejudice and they know how revengeful they themselves would be in similar circumstances. White ambivalence vitiates the capacity of the majority to understand black militancy. Many whites overreact to black militancy and violence by conjuring up fantasies of revenge: that the oppressed will now conquer and rule their oppressors. This is pure fantasy since no black group or leader has advocated ruling over the whites. Most whites interpret black threats as final intentions of annihilation rather than tests of reality by those who have until now been powerless. Such overanxious whites reason, on a primitive archaic level, that an

injury can be undone or must be punished by a similar deed inflicted on themselves. Whites accordingly are preoccupied with protecting themselves from black violence, which blacks in turn misapprehend as a preparation for accelerated white oppression and even genocide.

The mechanism of projection frequently coincides with and is complemented by displacement. This is when the anxiety, frustration, or cause of misery, whether social or instinctual, is attributed to a person or object which is less threatening and more accessible than the real source. The classic example is the man who is mistreated or misunderstood by his boss at work, and then comes home to yell at his wife and beat his children. It is safe to express his anger against them. His hostility is displaced from its true source, which is too remote or powerful to be attacked, to a closer defenseless object. Small children often express their rage against their parents by abusing their pets. It is far too dangerous to risk the loss of mother's love, so the anger is displaced onto a kitten or puppy which is easily available and without means of retaliation.

Displacement is seen dramatically in a famous study correlating lynchings of Negroes in the South to the price of cotton during the years from 1882 to 1930. Whenever the income from cotton declined and economic hardship ensued, the number of lynchings rose, suggesting that material frustration caused anger that could not effectively or immediately be directed at an abstract social and economic system, and that this hostility was instead discharged by being displaced onto blacks.

Another important dimension of the psychology of racism concerns interracial sex relations. People with the most guilt about their own sexual desires also have the greatest prejudice involving sexual fears. A study of prison inmates showed that men with high sexual anxiety are more hostile toward racial minorities and tend to commit more sexual offenses than men who are sexually more secure.

A southern author, Wilbur J. Cash has brilliantly portrayed the sexual patterns of southern men who have historically exploited black women. In *The Mind of the South*, Cash stresses the mental mechanism of guilt which has impelled these men to make white women into desexualized objects of worship. This is the peculiar southern variant of a common tendency in the mind of the Western world to divide women into mutually exclusive categories. The first, which corresponds to what Denis De Rougemont has called courtly romantic love, views woman as a spiritualized pure image to be worshiped from a distance. The other regards her as a debased, voluptuous, and sensual creature to be used for sexual pleasure. These images coexist in the mind and are split, or ascribed to different women. In a society with a highly differentiated class or racial structure, the erotic and sensual qualities tend to be ascribed to the women of a minority race or a lower social class, while the women of the dominant or upper-class group are depicted as pure, virginal, desexualized, domestic — and therefore more incestually taboo. This is why in the South white womanhood was glorified in courtly chivalric terms while sexual gratification was obtained from the black women of the slave quarters and shanty towns.

Though Cash does not explore the linkage between the guilt induced   9
by this emotional splitting and white attitudes toward black men, the connection is apparent. If he desires and sexually uses black women, the white man fantasizes and fears that black men will claim the same right and desire. Thus the white man who uses black women sexually perceives the black man as a menace to him and his women. By projection, the black man is seen as the one who lusts after white womanhood. This projection — "it is he, not I, who is lascivious" — is both guilt-evading and self-assuring because the evil doer who violates social morality is the other man, not oneself. Thus the "badness" is externalized.

However, Negroes are not only equated with dirt and uncontrolled   10
violence in the mind of white America. The emotions of race are much more conflicted and ambivalent than that. In the same white minds Negroes are also the symbols of warmth, fecundity, and wild voluptuousness. Two such apparently contradictory feelings may coexist with equanimity because elements of mystery and forbiddenness heighten attraction in a society which places, as does our own, many inhibitions on the enjoyment of the body and the senses. What is attractive must therefore also be degraded and forbidden.

A number of outstanding works of American literature vividly present   11
the theme of the erotic attraction of the white imagination to the tabooed people of dark skin. To cite from three classics: James Fenimore Cooper's Natty Bumppo and Chingachgook, Herman Melville's Ishmael and Queequeg, and Mark Twain's Huck and Jim give to each other the love, trust, tenderness, and comradeship which they could not find in the world of women. In each case two men, one dark hued, the other light skinned, shared what the critic Leslie A. Fiedler has called the "archetypal relationship" which "haunts the American psyche."[1] It is highly suggestive that the favorite epithet of bigots for the white liberal is "Niggerlover." The very word itself suggests that those who use it are enmeshed in their own projected feelings of attraction.

Gordon W. Allport illustrates this phenomenon by citing the response   12

[1] Leslie A. Fiedler, *Love and Death in the American Novel* (Cleveland and New York, 1960), p. 187. [Author's note]

of an urban housewife when questioned as to whether she would object to Negroes moving on to her street:

> I wouldn't want to live with Negroes. They smell too much. They're of a different race. That's what creates racial hatreds. When I sleep with a Negro in the same bed, I'll live with them. But you know we can't.[2]

We are startled to see how a woman's unconscious sexual fantasies 13 have intruded themselves into an unrelated problem, namely residence on the same street. After all, the fact of living on the same block is not the criterion by which most people select their sexual partners. We note that her mind first goes to the supposed distinctive unpleasant odor of Negroes, an assumption for which there is no scientific evidence. The woman's mental associations then move from images of body products that are intimate and disgusting to the theme of forbidden sexuality. We may see here how unconscious aggressive, sexual, and other repressed feelings emerge into consciousness in association with Negroes and are defended against by projection and displacement onto Negroes. This is one reason that repression of Negroes is maintained with such vehemence and that reaction to efforts at social or residential racial mixing is so irrational and intense. The deepest emotions concerning body products and repressed desires threaten to burst out of control. Inner panic must be avoided by new defenses against unconscious wishes; hence outer social segregation must be re-enforced.

The social effect of sexual projection and the inequality of the admin- 14 istration of justice in the United States are dramatically displayed in the pattern of criminal convictions for interracial sex offenders. The conviction of black males for sex offenses with white women has been dispropor- tionately heavy, although the majority of interracial sex offenses are committed by white men. In thirteen southern states where blacks made up 24 percent of the population 15 whites and 187 Negroes were executed for rape between 1938 and 1948.

We are often led to ask: why are some people more susceptible than 15 others to racial hatred? In recent years social scientists have conducted extensive research on the personalities of prejudiced people in search of an answer to this question. Their work demonstrates a correlation between personality, ideas, and racial prejudice. Feelings of personal

---

[2] Gordon W. Allport, *The Nature of Prejudice* (Cambridge, Mass., 1954), p. 373. [Author's note]

insecurity, deprivation, anxiety, and hostility are all linked to prejudice. N. W. Ackerman and Marie Jahoda have described anti-Semitism as a culturally provided projective test, "the Jewish inkblot," onto which people project all the negative feelings of which they disapprove.

A famous study, by T. W. Adorno and his associates, *The Authoritarian Personality*, found that the primary feature of the racially prejudiced personality is authoritarianism — a preoccupation with issues of power such as who is strong and who is weak. The study used questionnaires, in-depth interviews, and projective tests. The central finding is that prejudiced attitudes express inner needs. The authoritarian individual is a weak and dependent person who lacks the capacity for genuine experience of himself or others. Behind his façade of strength lurks a shaky sense of order and safety. His world is one of rigidly stereotyped categories of power, success, and punitive moralism. He seeks to align himself with the conventional, and with what is regarded by others as good and strong. But these are not his own values. He has underlying feelings of weakness and self-contempt which he suppresses and projects onto ethnic minorities and other outgroups. The authoritarian thinks in rigid categories of dominance and submission, those who command and those who obey, masters and slaves. For him weakness is contemptuous. It is associated with guilt. His identification with those in power is a reaction to deep feelings of inadequacy and weakness. He acts the role of the "tough guy," trying to appear hypermasculine, while in reality he has strong feminine dependent tendencies that he denies. His conceptions of masculinity and femininity are exaggerated and rigid. Therefore he fears and rejects all that appears as soft, feminine, or weak. 16

Authoritarian personalities tend to describe their fathers as distant, stern, and bad tempered. The relationship between father and child is cold and remote. The son tends to see his father as an oppressor, but his unconscious hostility is concealed from himself and others by an attitude of submission and admiration. This submission to the father, a relation of love for the powerful man, determines the later projection of the dominance-submission dimension on all relationships. It also creates a compelling fear of weakness which is defended against by a façade of toughness. There follows a projection of all sinful, aggressive, and sexual impulses on outgroups and condemnation of these groups because of this projection. The authors of *The Authoritarian Personality* concluded: 17

> Thus a basically hierarchical, authoritarian, exploitative parent-child relationship is apt to carry over into a power-oriented . . . political philosophy and social outlook which has no room for anything but a

desperate clinging to what appears to be strong and a disdainful rejection of whatever is relegated to the bottom.[3]

Thus, a close relationship exists between sexual anxiety and intense prejudice. Men who hate racial minorities show "masculine" protest against sexual passivity, semi-impotence, or homosexual trends. They defend against these passive and feminine feelings by exaggerated toughness, pseudomasculinity, hostility, and racial prejudice.

Something vital is missing, however, from the extensive scholarship 18 on prejudice carried out after World War II. The thrust of this scholarship was to suggest that prejudiced people were emotionally sick and that emotionally healthy people were ethnically tolerant. A direct relationship was posited between neurosis and prejudice. What this formulation disregards is the covering over and apparently strengthening qualities that may be conferred by racial prejudice. The greater the underlying anxiety of a person, the more prejudiced he is, because the pressure of his anxiety weakens his personal controls. Thus weakened, he seeks relief through prejudice, which serves to reduce anxiety because prejudice facilitates the discharge of hostility. If hostility is discharged, regardless of whether it is toward the "realistic" object of hate or not, anxiety is reduced. Prejudice suggests to the person that he is better than others, hence he does not need to feel so anxious. Thus prejudice can help a person protect his individuality and maintain the emotional balance of a distorted personality.

One of the striking changes in the views of several prominent social 19 scientists, such as Bettelheim[4] and Janowitz,[5] in recent years is the discovery that prejudice may indeed be an integrating psychological force. The prejudiced person needs his hate to maintain his feeling of selfhood. The chief psychiatrist for the Netherlands army in World War II described the ego-strengthening effect of the release of hatred on some of his patients:

> Hatred gives man new social status among all those who share his feelings, and a feeling of magic power. The hater lives in a constant inner ecstasy. Even a pathological idiot assumes a pseudo-personality when he preaches hate and destruction. Several egoless patients of mine became (in their own estimation) new personalities when the

[3]T. W. Adorno, Else Frenkel-Brunswick, Daniel J. Levinson, R. Nevitt Sanford, and collaborators, *The Authoritarian Personality* (New York, 1950), p. 971. [Author's note]
[4]*Bettelheim:* Bruno Bettelheim, American psychologist and educationalist (b. 1903), famous for his work on children and the nature of prejudice.
[5]*Janowitz:* Morris Janowitz, American sociologist (b. 1919), best known as coauthor of *The Dynamics of Prejudice* (1950) with Bruno Bettelheim.

Nazis, who occupied their homeland, gave them the opportunity to feel real hatred. The reality hatred cured them of their obsessive defenses against their inner hostility.[6]

Thus we can see how prejudice may permit the bigot to function 20 better in society. A discharge of tension through racial hostility (projection and displacement onto minorities) permits the re-establishment of control over the rest of his instinctual forces. Prejudice may meet the need for emotional strength and personal control. For those who fail to achieve an effective personal identity, prejudice may become a permanent part of their identity. This reaction is involved whenever a person is threatened by self-doubt, feelings of confusion about who he is, a fear that he may be a "nobody." When a person has strong doubts about his ethnic, sexual, vocational, social, national, or personal identity, he may unconsciously adopt prejudice against others to compensate for a lack of certainty about who or what he is.

[6]Joost A. M. Meerloo, *That Difficult Peace* (Great Neck, N.Y., 1961), p. 69. [Author's note]

Engaging the Text

1. Summarize Loewenberg's discussion of "projection." What is it and what are its psychological motives? Write a paragraph defining "displacement" and describing its connection to projection.

2. Write a one-paragraph definition of the "authoritarian personality" as Loewenberg describes it. What examples of authoritarian personalities can you find in advertising, TV, politics, or other areas?

3. Carefully reread paragraph 18. When Loewenberg refers to the "apparently strengthening qualities" of racism, is he defending racist attitudes? Can something that benefits an individual nevertheless be bad or harmful? Find specific language in the paragraph that reveals Loewenberg's argument.

Exploring Connections

1. Compare and contrast Loewenberg's analysis of the psychology of racism with that of Gordon Allport earlier in this chapter.

Extending the Critical Context

1. Peter Loewenberg mentions that Western cultures often divide women into two categories: "a spiritualized pure image to be worshipped from a distance,"

and "a debased, voluptuous, and sensual creature to be used for sexual pleasure."
Do you find this division in the images of women you see in advertising, TV,
and movies? Write an essay identifying several women from history, literature,
or the media who fit these categories and several others who do not. In each
case, discuss specific details of dress, language, and behavior that reveal why
the woman does or does not fit the STEREOTYPES.

From *Invisible Man*

RALPH ELLISON

In 1965, a Book Week *poll of some two hundred writers and critics
named* Invisible Man *the most distinguished novel since World War II.
Some of the novel's strengths are apparent in this selection from the
Prologue and the opening chapter: unusual situations, an intriguing
narrator, intricate symbolism, and a crisp, forceful style. Here we witness,
from the victim's point of view, a racist culture in operation. Bear in
mind that the attitudes of the anonymous narrator change markedly as
the novel progresses, so you cannot simply equate his views here with
Ellison's own. Ellison (b. 1914) was born in Oklahoma and was educated
at Tuskegee Institute in Alabama before establishing himself as a writer
and critic in New York City. Since the publication of* Invisible Man
*Ellison has taught at several universities, including Columbia, Yale, and
New York University, and has published a book of essays,* Going to the
Territory *(1986).*

Prologue

I am an invisible man. No, I am not a spook like those who haunted 1
Edgar Allan Poe;[1] nor am I one of your Hollywood-movie ectoplasms.
I am a man of substance, of flesh and bone, fiber and liquids — and I
might even be said to possess a mind. I am invisible, understand, simply
because people refuse to see me. Like the bodiless heads you see sometimes
in circus sideshows, it is as though I have been surrounded by mirrors

[1]*Edgar Allan Poe:* American poet, critic, essayist, and short story writer (1809–1849);
famed for tales of suspense and horror.

of hard, distorting glass. When they approach me they see only my surroundings, themselves, or figments of their imagination — indeed, everything and anything except me.

Nor is my invisibility exactly a matter of a bio-chemical accident to my epidermis. That invisibility to which I refer occurs because of a peculiar disposition of the eyes of those with whom I come in contact. A matter of the construction of their *inner* eyes, those eyes with which they look through their physical eyes upon reality. I am not complaining, nor am I protesting either. It is sometimes advantageous to be unseen, although it is most often rather wearing on the nerves. Then too, you're constantly being bumped against by those of poor vision. Or again, you often doubt if you really exist. You wonder whether you aren't simply a phantom in other people's minds. Say, a figure in a nightmare which the sleeper tries with all his strength to destroy. It's when you feel like this that, out of resentment, you begin to bump people back. And, let me confess, you feel that way most of the time. You ache with the need to convince yourself that you do exist in the real world, that you're a part of all the sound and anguish, and you strike out with your fists, you curse and you swear to make them recognize you. And, alas, it's seldom successful. 2

One night I accidentally bumped into a man, and perhaps because of the near darkness he saw me and called me an insulting name. I sprang at him, seized his coat lapels and demanded that he apologize. He was a tall blond man, and as my face came close to his he looked insolently out of his blue eyes and cursed me, his breath hot in my face as he struggled. I pulled his chin down sharp upon the crown of my head, butting him as I had seen the West Indians do, and I felt his flesh tear and the blood gush out, and I yelled, "Apologize! Apologize!" But he continued to curse and struggle, and I butted him again and again until he went down heavily, on his knees, profusely bleeding. I kicked him repeatedly, in a frenzy because he still uttered insults though his lips were frothy with blood. Oh yes, I kicked him! And in my outrage I got out my knife and prepared to slit his throat, right there beneath the lamplight in the deserted street, holding him in the collar with one hand, and opening the knife with my teeth — when it occurred to me that the man had not *seen* me, actually; that he, as far as he knew, was in the midst of a walking nightmare! And I stopped the blade, slicing the air as I pushed him away, letting him fall back to the street. I stared at him hard as the lights of a car stabbed through the darkness. He lay there, moaning on the asphalt; a man almost killed by a phantom. It unnerved me. I was both disgusted and ashamed. I was like a drunken man myself, wavering about on weakened legs. Then I was amused: 3

Something in this man's thick head had sprung out and beaten him within an inch of his life. I began to laugh at this crazy discovery. Would he have awakened at the point of death? Would Death himself have freed him for wakeful living? But I didn't linger. I ran away into the dark, laughing so hard I feared I might rupture myself. The next day I saw his picture in the *Daily News*, beneath a caption stating that he had been "mugged." Poor fool, poor blind fool, I thought with sincere compassion, mugged by an invisible man!

Chapter 1

It goes a long way back, some twenty years. All my life I had been 4 looking for something, and everywhere I turned someone tried to tell me what it was. I accepted their answers too, though they were often in contradiction and even self-contradictory. I was naïve. I was looking for myself and asking everyone except myself questions which I, and only I, could answer. It took me a long time and much painful boomeranging of my expectations to achieve a realization everyone else appears to have been born with: That I am nobody but myself. But first I had to discover that I am an invisible man!

And yet I am no freak of nature, nor of history. I was in the cards, 5 other things having been equal (or unequal) eighty-five years ago. I am not ashamed of my grandparents for having been slaves. I am only ashamed of myself for having at one time been ashamed. About eighty-five years ago they were told that they were free, united with others of our country in everything pertaining to the common good, and, in everything social, separate like the fingers of the hand. And they believed it. They exulted in it. They stayed in their place, worked hard, and brought up my father to do the same. But my grandfather is the one. He was an odd old guy, my grandfather, and I am told I take after him. It was he who caused the trouble. On his deathbed he called my father to him and said, "Son, after I'm gone I want you to keep up the good fight. I never told you, but our life is a war and I have been a traitor all my born days, a spy in the enemy's country ever since I give up my gun back in the Reconstruction. Live with your head in the lion's mouth. I want you to overcome 'em with yeses, undermine 'em with grins, agree 'em to death and destruction, let 'em swoller you till they vomit or bust wide open." They thought the old man had gone out of his mind. He had been the meekest of men. The younger children were rushed from the room, the shades drawn and the flame of the lamp turned so low that it sputtered on the wick like the old man's breathing. "Learn it to the younguns," he whispered fiercely; then he died.

But my folks were more alarmed over his last words than over his 6 dying: It was as though he had not died at all, his words caused so much anxiety. I was warned emphatically to forget what he had said and, indeed, this is the first time it has been mentioned outside the family circle. It had a tremendous effect upon me, however. I could never be sure of what he meant. Grandfather had been a quiet old man who never made any trouble, yet on his deathbed he had called himself a traitor and a spy, and he had spoken of his meekness as a dangerous activity. It became a constant puzzle which lay unanswered in the back of my mind. And whenever things went well for me I remembered my grandfather and felt guilty and uncomfortable. It was as though I was carrying out his advice in spite of myself. And to make it worse, everyone loved me for it. I was praised by the most lily-white men of the town. I was considered an example of desirable conduct — just as my grandfather had been. And what puzzled me was that the old man had defined it as *treachery*. When I was praised for my conduct I felt a guilt that in some way I was doing something that was really against the wishes of the white folks, that if they had understood they would have desired me to act just the opposite, that I should have been sulky and mean, and that that really would have been what they wanted, even though they were fooled and thought they wanted me to act as I did. It made me afraid that some day they would look upon me as a traitor and I would be lost. Still I was more afraid to act any other way because they didn't like that at all. The old man's words were like a curse. On my graduation day I delivered an oration in which I showed that humility was the secret, indeed, the very essence of progress. (Not that I believed this — how could I, remembering my grandfather? — I only believed that it worked.) It was a great success. Everyone praised me and I was invited to give the speech at a gathering of the town's leading white citizens. It was a triumph for our whole community.

It was in the main ballroom of the leading hotel. When I got there 7 I discovered that it was on the occasion of a smoker,[2] and I was told that since I was to be there anyway I might as well take part in the battle royal to be fought by some of my schoolmates as part of the entertainment. The battle royal came first.

All of the town's big shots were there in their tuxedoes, wolfing down 8 the buffet foods, drinking beer and whiskey and smoking black cigars. It was a large room with a high ceiling. Chairs were arranged in neat rows around three sides of a portable boxing ring. The fourth side was clear, revealing a gleaming space of polished floor. I had some misgivings over the battle royal, by the way. Not from a distaste for fighting, but

---

[2] *smoker:* an informal social gathering for men.

because I didn't care too much for the other fellows who were to take part. They were tough guys who seemed to have no grandfather's curse worrying their minds. No one could mistake their toughness. And besides, I suspected that fighting a battle royal might detract from the dignity of my speech. In those pre-invisible days I visualized myself as a potential Booker T. Washington.[3] But the other fellows didn't care too much for me either, and there were nine of them. I felt superior to them in my way, and I didn't like the manner in which we were all crowded together into the servants' elevator. Nor did they like my being there. In fact, as the warmly lighted floors flashed past the elevator we had words over the fact that I, by taking part in the fight, had knocked one of their friends out of a night's work.

We were led out of the elevator through a rococo hall into an anteroom 9 and told to get into our fighting togs. Each of us was issued a pair of boxing gloves and ushered out into the big mirrored hall, which we entered looking cautiously about us and whispering, lest we might accidentally be heard above the noise of the room. It was foggy with cigar smoke. And already the whiskey was taking effect. I was shocked to see some of the most important men of the town quite tipsy. They were all there — bankers, lawyers, judges, doctors, fire chiefs, teachers, merchants. Even one of the more fashionable pastors. Something we could not see was going on up front. A clarinet was vibrating sensuously and the men were standing up and moving eagerly forward. We were a small tight group, clustered together, our bare upper bodies touching and shining with anticipatory sweat; while up front the big shots were becoming increasingly excited over something we still could not see. Suddenly I heard the school superintendent, who had told me to come, yell, "Bring up the shines, gentlemen! Bring up the little shines!"

We were rushed up to the front of the ballroom, where it smelled 10 even more strongly of tobacco and whiskey. Then we were pushed into place. I almost wet my pants. A sea of faces, some hostile, some amused, ringed around us, and in the center, facing us, stood a magnificent blonde — stark naked. There was dead silence. I felt a blast of cold air chill me. I tried to back away, but they were behind me and around me. Some of the boys stood with lowered heads, trembling. I felt a wave of irrational guilt and fear. My teeth chattered, my skin turned to goose flesh, my knees knocked. Yet I was strongly attracted and looked in spite of myself. Had the price of looking been blindness, I would have looked. The hair was yellow like that of a circus kewpie doll, the face

[3]*Booker T. Washington:* U.S. educator and black leader (1856–1915), who advocated training black people for skilled labor jobs before seeking integration and equality.

heavily powdered and rouged, as though to form an abstract mask, the eyes hollow and smeared a cool blue, the color of a baboon's butt. I felt a desire to spit upon her as my eyes brushed slowly over her body. Her breasts were firm and round as the domes of East Indian temples, and I stood so close as to see the fine skin texture and beads of pearly perspiration glistening like dew around the pink and erected buds of her nipples. I wanted at one and the same time to run from the room, to sink through the floor, or go to her and cover her from my eyes and the eyes of the others with my body; to feel the soft thighs, to caress her and destroy her, to love her and murder her, to hide from her, and yet to stroke where below the small American flag tattooed upon her belly her thighs formed a capital V. I had a notion that of all in the room she saw only me with her impersonal eyes.

And then she began to dance, a slow sensuous movement; the smoke 11 of a hundred cigars clinging to her like the thinnest of veils. She seemed like a fair bird-girl girdled in veils calling to me from the angry surface of some gray and threatening sea. I was transported. Then I became aware of the clarinet playing and the big shots yelling at us. Some threatened us if we looked and others if we did not. On my right I saw one boy faint. And now a man grabbed a silver pitcher from a table and stepped close as he dashed ice water upon him and stood him up and forced two of us to support him as his head hung and moans issued from his thick bluish lips. Another boy began to plead to go home. He was the largest of the group, wearing dark red fighting trunks much too small to conceal the erection which projected from him as though in answer to the insinuating low-registered moaning of the clarinet. He tried to hide himself with his boxing gloves.

And all the while the blonde continued dancing, smiling faintly at the 12 big shots who watched her with fascination, and faintly smiling at our fear. I noticed a certain merchant who followed her hungrily, his lips loose and drooling. He was a large man who wore diamond studs in a shirtfront which swelled with the ample paunch underneath, and each time the blonde swayed her undulating hips he ran his hand through the thin hair of his bald head and, with his arms upheld, his posture clumsy like that of an intoxicated panda, wound his belly in a slow and obscene grind. This creature was completely hypnotized. The music had quickened. As the dancer flung herself about with a detached expression on her face, the men began reaching out to touch her. I could see their beefy fingers sink into the soft flesh. Some of the others tried to stop them and she began to move around the floor in graceful circles, as they gave chase, slipping and sliding over the polished floor. It was mad. Chairs went crashing, drinks were spilt, as they ran laughing and howling after her. They caught her just as she reached a door, raised her from the floor, and tossed her as college boys are tossed at a hazing, and above her red, fixed-smiling lips I saw the terror and disgust in her eyes, almost like my own terror and that which I saw in some of the other boys. As I watched, they tossed her twice and her soft breasts seemed to flatten against the air and her legs flung wildly as she spun. Some of the more sober ones helped her to escape. And I started off the floor, heading for the anteroom with the rest of the boys.

Some were still crying and in hysteria. But as we tried to leave we   13 were stopped and ordered to get into the ring. There was nothing to do but what we were told. All ten of us climbed under the ropes and allowed ourselves to be blindfolded with broad bands of white cloth. One of the men seemed to feel a bit sympathetic and tried to cheer us up as we stood with our backs against the ropes. Some of us tried to grin. "See that boy over there?" one of the men said. "I want you to run across at the bell and give it to him right in the belly. If you don't get him, I'm going to get you. I don't like his looks." Each of us was told the same. The blindfolds were put on. Yet even then I had been going over my speech. In my mind each word was as bright as flame. I felt the cloth pressed into place, and frowned so that it would be loosened when I relaxed.

But now I felt a sudden fit of blind terror. I was unused to darkness.   14 It was as though I had suddenly found myself in a dark room filled with poisonous cottonmouths. I could hear the bleary voices yelling insistently for the battle royal to begin.

"Get going in there!"   15

"Let me at that big nigger!"   16

I strained to pick up the school superintendent's voice, as though to   17 squeeze some security out of that slightly more familiar sound.

"Let me at those black sonsabitches!" someone yelled.   18

"No, Jackson, no!" another voice yelled. "Here, somebody, help me   19 hold Jack."

"I want to get at that ginger-colored nigger. Tear him limb from limb,"   20 the first voice yelled.

I stood against the ropes trembling. For in those days I was what they   21 called ginger-colored, and he sounded as though he might crunch me between his teeth like a crisp ginger cookie.

Quite a struggle was going on. Chairs were being kicked about and   22 I could hear voices grunting as with a terrific effort. I wanted to see, to see more desperately than ever before. But the blindfold was tight as a thick skin-puckering scab and when I raised my gloved hands to push the layers of white aside a voice yelled, "Oh, no you don't, black bastard! Leave that alone!"

"Ring the bell before Jackson kills him a coon!" someone boomed in 23
the sudden silence. And I heard the bell clang and the sound of the
feet scuffling forward.

A glove smacked against my head. I pivoted, striking out stiffly as 24
someone went past, and felt the jar ripple along the length of my arm
to my shoulder. Then it seemed as though all nine of the boys had
turned upon me at once. Blows pounded me from all sides while I struck
out as best I could. So many blows landed upon me that I wondered if
I were not the only blindfolded fighter in the ring, or if the man called
Jackson hadn't succeeded in getting me after all.

Blindfolded, I could no longer control my motions. I had no dignity. 25
I stumbled about like a baby or a drunken man. The smoke had become
thicker and with each new blow it seemed to sear and further restrict
my lungs. My saliva became like hot bitter glue. A glove connected with
my head, filling my mouth with warm blood. It was everywhere. I could
not tell if the moisture I felt upon my body was sweat or blood. A blow
landed hard against the nape of my neck. I felt myself going over, my
head hitting the floor. Streaks of blue light filled the black world behind
the blindfold. I lay prone, pretending that I was knocked out, but felt
myself seized by hands and yanked to my feet. "Get going, black boy!
Mix it up!" My arms were like lead, my head smarting from blows. I
managed to feel my way to the ropes and held on, trying to catch my
breath. A glove landed in my mid-section and I went over again, feeling
as though the smoke had become a knife jabbed into my guts. Pushed
this way and that by the legs milling around me, I finally pulled erect
and discovered that I could see the black, sweat-washed forms weaving
in the smoky-blue atmosphere like drunken dancers weaving to the rapid
drum-like thuds of blows.

Everyone fought hysterically. It was complete anarchy. Everybody 26
fought everybody else. No group fought together for long. Two, three,
four, fought one, then turned to fight each other, were themselves
attacked. Blows landed below the belt and in the kidney, with the gloves
open as well as closed, and with my eye partly opened now there was
not so much terror. I moved carefully, avoiding blows, although not too
many to attract attention, fighting from group to group. The boys groped
about like blind, cautious crabs crouching to protect their mid-sections,
their heads pulled in short against their shoulders, their arms stretched
nervously before them, with their fists testing the smoke-filled air like
the knobbed feelers of hypersensitive snails. In one corner I glimpsed
a boy violently punching the air and heard him scream in pain as he
smashed his hand against a ring post. For a second I saw him bent over
holding his hand, then going down as a blow caught his unprotected
head. I played one group against the other, slipping in and throwing a

punch then stepping out of range while pushing the others into the melee to take the blows blindly aimed at me. The smoke was agonizing and there were no rounds, no bells at three minute intervals to relieve our exhaustion. The room spun around me, a swirl of lights, smoke, sweating bodies surrounded by tense white faces. I bled from both nose and mouth, the blood spattering upon my chest.

The men kept yelling, "Slug him, black boy! Knock his guts out!" 27

"Uppercut him! Kill him! Kill that big boy!" 28

Taking a fake fall, I saw a boy going down heavily beside me as though 29
we were felled by a single blow, saw a sneaker-clad foot shoot into his groin as the two who had knocked him down stumbled upon him. I rolled out of range, feeling a twinge of nausea.

The harder we fought the more threatening the men became. And 30
yet, I had begun to worry about my speech again. How would it go? Would they recognize my ability? What would they give me?

I was fighting automatically when suddenly I noticed that one after 31
another of the boys was leaving the ring. I was surprised, filled with panic, as though I had been left alone with an unknown danger. Then I understood. The boys had arranged it among themselves. It was the custom for the two men left in the ring to slug it out for the winner's prize. I discovered this too late. When the bell sounded two men in tuxedoes leaped into the ring and removed the blindfold I found myself facing Tatlock, the biggest of the gang. I felt sick at my stomach. Hardly had the bell stopped ringing in my ears than it clanged again and I saw him moving swiftly toward me. Thinking of nothing else to do I hit him smash on the nose. He kept coming, bringing the rank sharp violence of stale sweat. His face was a black blank of a face, only his eyes alive — with hate of me and aglow with a feverish terror from what had happened to us all. I became anxious. I wanted to deliver my speech and he came at me as though he meant to beat it out of me. I smashed him again and again, taking his blows as they came. Then on a sudden impulse I struck him lightly and as we clinched, I whispered, "Fake like I knocked you out, you can have the prize."

"I'll break your behind," he whispered hoarsely. 32

"For *them?*" 33

"For *me,* sonofabitch!" 34

They were yelling for us to break it up and Tatlock spun me half 35
around with a blow, and as a joggled camera sweeps in a reeling scene, I saw the howling red faces crouching tense beneath the cloud of blue-gray smoke. For a moment the world wavered, unraveled, flowed, then my head cleared and Tatlock bounced before me. That fluttering shadow before my eyes was his jabbing left hand. Then falling forward, my head against his damp shoulder, I whispered,

"I'll make it five dollars more." 36

"Go to hell!" 37

But his muscles relaxed a trifle beneath my pressure and I breathed, 38
"Seven?"

"Give it to your ma," he said, ripping me beneath the heart. 39

And while I still held him I butted him and moved away. I felt myself 40
bombarded with punches. I fought back with hopeless desperation. I
wanted to deliver my speech more than anything else in the world,
because I felt that only these men could judge truly my ability, and now
this stupid clown was ruining my chances. I began fighting carefully
now, moving in to punch him and out again with my greater speed. A
lucky blow to his chin and I had him going too — until I heard a loud
voice yell, "I got my money on the big boy."

Hearing this, I almost dropped my guard. I was confused: Should I 41
try to win against the voice out there? Would not this go against my
speech, and was not this a moment for humility, for nonresistance? A
blow to my head as I danced about sent my right eye popping like a
jack-in-the-box and settled my dilemma. The room went red as I fell.
It was a dream fall, my body languid and fastidious as to where to land,
until the floor became impatient and smashed up to meet me. A moment
later I came to. An hypnotic voice said FIVE emphatically. And I lay
there, hazily watching a dark red spot of my own blood shaping itself
into a butterfly, glistening and soaking into the soiled gray world of the
canvas.

When the voice drawled TEN I was lifted up and dragged to a chair. 42
I sat dazed. My eye pained and swelled with each throb of my pounding
heart and I wondered if now I would be allowed to speak. I was wringing
wet, my mouth still bleeding. We were grouped along the wall now.
The other boys ignored me as they congratulated Tatlock and speculated
as to how much they would be paid. One boy whimpered over his
smashed hand. Looking up front, I saw attendants in white jackets rolling
the portable ring away and placing a small square rug in the vacant
space surrounded by chairs. Perhaps, I thought, I will stand on the rug
to deliver my speech.

Then the M.C. called to us, "Come on up here boys and get your 43
money."

We ran forward to where the men laughed and talked in their chairs, 44
waiting. Everyone seemed friendly now.

"There it is on the rug," the man said. I saw the rug covered with 45
coins of all dimensions and a few crumpled bills. But what excited me,
scattered here and there, were the gold pieces.

"Boys, it's all yours," the man said. "You get all you grab." 46

"That's right, Sambo," a blond man said, winking at me confidentially. 47

I trembled with excitement, forgetting my pain. I would get the gold 48
and the bills, I thought. I would use both hands. I would throw my
body against the boys nearest me to block them from the gold.

"Get down around the rug now," the man commanded, "and don't 49
anyone touch it until I give the signal."

"This ought to be good," I heard. 50

As told, we got around the square rug on our knees. Slowly the man 51
raised his freckled hand as we followed it upward with our eyes.

I heard, "These niggers look like they're about to pray!" 52

Then, "Ready," the man said. "Go!" 53

I lunged for a yellow coin lying on the blue design of the carpet, 54
touching it and sending a surprised shriek to join those rising around
me. I tried frantically to remove my hand but could not let go. A hot,
violent force tore through my body, shaking me like a wet rat. The rug
was electrified. The hair bristled up on my head as I shook myself free.
My muscles jumped, my nerves jangled, writhed. But I saw that this
was not stopping the other boys. Laughing in fear and embarrassment,
some were holding back and scooping up the coins knocked off by the
painful contortions of the others. The men roared above us as we struggled.

"Pick it up, goddamnit, pick it up!" someone called like a bass-voiced 55
parrot. "Go on, get it!"

I crawled rapidly around the floor, picking up the coins, trying to 56
avoid the coppers and to get greenbacks and the gold. Ignoring the shock
by laughing, as I brushed the coins off quickly, I discovered that I could
contain the electricity — a contradiction, but it works. Then the men
began to push us onto the rug. Laughing embarrassedly, we struggled
out of their hands and kept after the coins. We were all wet and slippery
and hard to hold. Suddenly I saw a boy lifted into the air, glistening
with sweat like a circus seal, and dropped, his wet back landing flush
upon the charged rug, heard him yell and saw him literally dance upon
his back, his elbows beating a frenzied tattoo upon the floor, his muscles
twitching like the flesh of a horse stung by many flies. When he finally
rolled off, his face was gray and no one stopped him when he ran from
the floor amid booming laughter.

"Get the money," the M.C. called. "That's good hard American cash!" 57

And we snatched and grabbed, snatched and grabbed. I was careful 58
not to come too close to the rug now, and when I felt the hot whiskey
breath descend upon me like a cloud of foul air I reached out and grabbed
the leg of a chair. It was occupied and I held on desperately.

"Leggo, nigger! Leggo!" 59

The huge face wavered down to mine as he tried to push me free. 60
But my body was slippery and he was too drunk. It was Mr. Colcord,

who owned a chain of movie houses and "entertainment palaces." Each time he grabbed me I slipped out of his hands. It became a real struggle. I feared the rug more than I did the drunk, so I held on, surprising myself for a moment by trying to topple *him* upon the rug. It was such an enormous idea that I found myself actually carrying it out. I tried not to be obvious, yet when I grabbed his leg, trying to tumble him out of the chair, he raised up roaring with laughter, and, looking at me with soberness dead in the eye, kicked me viciously in the chest. The chair leg flew out of my hand and I felt myself going and rolled. It was as though I had rolled through a bed of hot coals. It seemed a whole century would pass before I would roll free, a century in which I was seared through the deepest levels of my body to the fearful breath within me and the breath seared and heated to the point of explosion. It'll all be over in a flash, I thought as I rolled clear. It'll all be over in a flash.

But not yet, the men on the other side were waiting, red faces swollen   61
as though from apoplexy as they bent forward in their chairs. Seeing their fingers coming toward me I rolled away as a fumbled football rolls off the receiver's fingertips, back into the coals. That time I luckily sent the rug sliding out of place and heard the coins ringing against the floor and the boys scuffling to pick them up and the M.C. calling, "All right, boys, that's all. Go get dressed and get your money."

I was limp as a dish rag. My back felt as though it had been beaten   62
with wires.

When we had dressed the M.C. came in and gave us each five dollars,   63
except Tatlock, who got ten for being last in the ring. Then he told us to leave. I was not to get a chance to deliver my speech, I thought. I was going out into the dim alley in despair when I was stopped and told to go back. I returned to the ballroom, where the men were pushing back their chairs and gathering in groups to talk.

The M.C. knocked on a table for quiet. "Gentlemen," he said, "we   64
almost forgot an important part of the program. A most serious part, gentlemen. This boy was brought here to deliver a speech which he made at his graduation yesterday . . ."

"Bravo!"   65

"I'm told that he is the smartest boy we've got out there in Greenwood.   66
I'm told that he knows more big words than a pocket-sized dictionary."

Much applause and laughter.   67

"So now, gentlemen, I want you to give him your attention."   68

There was still laughter as I faced them, my mouth dry, my eye   69
throbbing. I began slowly, but evidently my throat was tense, because they began shouting, "Louder! Louder!"

"We of the younger generation extol the wisdom of that great leader   70 and educator," I shouted, "who first spoke these flaming words of wisdom: 'A ship lost at sea for many days suddenly sighted a friendly vessel. From the mast of the unfortunate vessel was seen a signal: "Water, water; we die of thirst!" The answer from the friendly vessel came back: "Cast down your bucket where you are." The captain of the distressed vessel, at last heeding the injunction, cast down his bucket, and it came up full of fresh sparkling water from the mouth of the Amazon River.' And like him I say, and in his words, 'To those of my race who depend upon bettering their condition in a foreign land, or who underestimate the importance of cultivating friendly relations with the Southern white man, who is his next-door neighbor, I would say: "Cast down your bucket where you are" — cast it down in making friends in every manly way of the people of all races by whom we are surrounded . . .'"

I spoke automatically and with such fervor that I did not realize that   71
the men were still talking and laughing until my dry mouth, filling up with blood from the cut, almost strangled me. I coughed, wanting to stop and go to one of the tall brass, sand-filled spittoons to relieve myself, but a few of the men, especially the superintendent, were listening and I was afraid. So I gulped it down, blood, saliva and all, and continued. (What powers of endurance I had during those days! What enthusiasm! What a belief in the rightness of things!) I spoke even louder in spite of the pain. But still they talked and still they laughed, as though deaf with cotton in dirty ears. So I spoke with greater emotional emphasis. I closed my ears and swallowed blood until I was nauseated. The speech seemed a hundred times as long as before, but I could not leave out a single word. All had to be said, each memorized nuance considered, rendered. Nor was that all. Whenever I uttered a word of three or more syllables a group of voices would yell for me to repeat it. I used the phrase "social responsibility" and they yelled:

"What's that word you say, boy?"   72
"Social responsibility," I said.   73
"What?"   74
"Social . . ."   75
"Louder."   76
". . . responsibility."   77
"More!"   78
"Respon — "   79
"Repeat!"   80
" — sibility."   81
The room filled with the uproar of laughter until, no doubt, distracted   82
by having to gulp down my blood, I made a mistake and yelled a phrase

I had often seen denounced in newspaper editorials, heard debated in private.

"Social . . ." 83

"What?" they yelled. 84

". . . equality — " 85

The laughter hung smokelike in the sudden stillness. I opened my 86 eyes, puzzled. Sounds of displeasure filled the room. The M.C. rushed forward. They shouted hostile phrases at me. But I did not understand.

A small dry mustached man in the front row blared out, "Say that 87 slowly, son!"

"What, sir?" 88

"What you just said!" 89

"Social responsibility, sir," I said. 90

"You weren't being smart, were you, boy?" he said, not unkindly. 91

"No, sir!" 92

"You sure that about 'equality' was a mistake?" 93

"Oh, yes, sir," I said. "I was swallowing blood." 94

"Well, you had better speak more slowly so we can understand. We 95 mean to do right by you, but you've got to know your place at all times. All right, now, go on with your speech."

I was afraid. I wanted to leave but I wanted also to speak and I was 96 afraid they'd snatch me down.

"Thank you, sir," I said, beginning where I had left off, and having 97 them ignore me as before.

Yet when I finished there was a thunderous applause. I was surprised 98 to see the superintendent come forth with a package wrapped in white tissue paper, and, gesturing for quiet, address the men.

"Gentlemen you see that I did not overpraise this boy. He makes a 99 good speech and some day he'll lead his people in the proper paths. And I don't have to tell you that that is important in these days and times. This is a good, smart boy, and so to encourage him in the right direction, in the name of the Board of Education I wish to present him a prize in the form of this . . ."

He paused, removing the tissue paper and revealing a gleaming calfskin 100 brief case.

". . . in the form of this first-class article from Shad Whitmore's shop." 101

"Boy," he said, addressing me, "take this prize and keep it well. 102 Consider it a badge of office. Prize it. Keep developing as you are and some day it will be filled with important papers that will help shape the destiny of your people."

I was so moved that I could hardly express my thanks. A rope of 103 bloody saliva forming a shape like an undiscovered continent drooled upon the leather and I wiped it quickly away. I felt an importance that I had never dreamed.

"Open it and see what's inside," I was told. 104

My fingers a-tremble, I complied, smelling the fresh leather and finding 105 an official-looking document inside. It was a scholarship to the state college for Negroes. My eyes filled with tears and I ran awkwardly off the floor.

I was overjoyed; I did not even mind when I discovered that the gold 106 pieces I had scrambled for were brass pocket tokens advertising a certain make of automobile.

When I reached home everyone was excited. Next day the neighbors 107 came to congratulate me. I even felt safe from grandfather, whose deathbed curse usually spoiled my triumphs. I stood beneath his photograph with my brief case in hand and smiled triumphantly into his stolid black peasant's face. It was a face that fascinated me. The eyes seemed to follow everywhere I went.

That night I dreamed I was at a circus with him and that he refused 108 to laugh at the clowns no matter what they did. Then later he told me to open my brief case and read what was inside and I did, finding an official envelope stamped with the state seal; and inside the envelope I found another and another, endlessly, and I thought I would fall of weariness. "Them's years," he said. "Now open that one." And I did and in it I found an engraved document containing a short message in letters of gold. "Read it," my grandfather said. "Out loud!"

"To Whom It May Concern," I intoned. "Keep This Nigger-Boy 109 Running."

I awoke with the old man's laughter ringing in my ears. 110

(It was a dream I was to remember and dream again for many years 111 after. But at that time I had no insight into its meaning. First I had to attend college.)

Engaging the Text

1. In what way is the NARRATOR of the Prologue invisible? Why does he react so violently to the man he accidentally runs into? Review Allport's discussion of in-groups and out-groups: How might it help to explain the white man's and/or the narrator's behavior?

2. The boxing scene in this passage offers a SYMBOLIC image of how racism affects minorities. What is particularly symbolic in this scene? Pay attention to details like the narrator's speech, the blindfolds, and so on. What does Ellison

seem to be saying about the impact of racism on individual members of minority groups?

3. What does the narrator's grandfather represent to him? Why does the old man refer to his grandson's success as "treachery"? Discuss the significance of the narrator's dream of his grandfather at the end of the chapter.

4. Define "irony." What irony do you find in the narrator's speech to the white businessmen? What other ironies do you see in this passage?

Exploring Connections

1. Use Gordon Allport's discussion of in-groups, out-groups, and reference groups in the opening selection of this chapter to analyze the feelings and behavior of the CHARACTERS in this selection.

2. Read or review Peter Loewenberg's definition of "projection" in the preceding essay: What CHARACTERISTICS do the white men project onto the black teenagers in the "battle royal" scene?

3. Recalling Loewenberg's notion that racism grows out of repressed sexual desires, discuss the symbolic implications of the stripper and her dance. (Note small details, such as the dancer's tattoo, as well as the general symbolism of the scene.)

Uprooting Racism and Racists in the United States[1]

JAMES BOGGS

This essay, like Allport's and Loewenberg's, offers a theoretical explanation of racism, but there the similarity ends. Boggs (b. 1919) has little use for psychology, asserting instead that racism is the product of systematic historical and cultural forces, not individual psychological "flaws." Before emerging as a powerful leftist voice in the 1960s, Boggs worked as a field hand, ice cutter, and auto worker, and these experiences clearly helped shape his radical, even revolutionary views. He now lives in Detroit, where he works with the National Organization for American

---

[1]This paper was written with Grace Lee Boggs. [Author's note]

Revolution. His most recent book is Revolution and Evolution in the Twentieth Century *(1980).*

The first thing we have to understand is that racism is not a "mental quirk" or a "psychological flaw" on an individual's part.[2] Racism is the systematized oppression by one race of another. In other words, the various forms of oppression within every sphere of social relations — economic exploitation, military subjugation, political subordination, cultural devaluation, psychological violation, sexual degradation, verbal abuse, etc. — together make up a whole of interacting and developing processes which operate so normally and naturally and are so much a part of the existing institutions of the society that the individuals involved are barely conscious of their operation. As Fanon[3] says, "The racist in a culture with racism is therefore normal." 1

This kind of systematic oppression of one race by another was unknown to mankind in the thousands of years of recorded history before the emergence of capitalism four hundred years ago — although racial prejudice was not unknown. For example, some Chinese in the third century B.C. considered yellow-haired, green-eyed people in a distant province barbarians. In Ancient Egypt the ruling group, which at different times was red or yellow or black or white, usually regarded the others as inferior. 2

Slave oppression had also existed in earlier times, but this was usually on the basis of military conquest and the conquerors — the ancient Greeks and Romans — did not develop a theory of racial superiority to rationalize their right to exploit their slaves. 3

Just as mankind, prior to the rise of capitalism, had not previously experienced an economic system which naturally and normally pursues the expansion of material productive forces at the expense of human forces, so it had never known a society which naturally and normally pursues the systematic exploitation and dehumanization of one race of people by another. An organic link between capitalism and racism is therefore certainly suggested. 4

The parallel between the rise of capitalism and the rise of racism has 5

[2]See Frantz Fanon, "Racism and Culture," in *Toward the African Revolution* (New York and London: Monthly Review Press, 1967). [Author's note]

[3]*Fanon:* Frantz Fanon, West-Indian psychiatrist (1925–1961), who wrote several important works on racism and colonial liberation based on his experiences during the French-Algerian War.

been traced by a number of scholars. The Portuguese, who were the first Europeans to come into contact with Africans at the end of the fifteenth and beginning of the sixteenth centuries, treated them as natural friends and allies. They found African customs strange and exotic but also found much to admire in their social and political organization, craftsmanship, architecture, and so on. At this point the chief technological advantages enjoyed by the Europeans were their navigation skills and firepower (both, by the way, originally learned from the Chinese). In the next four centuries these two advantages would be used to plunder four continents of their wealth in minerals and people and thereby to increase the technological superiority of Europeans by leaps and bounds.

Africa was turned into a hunting ground for slaves to work the land 6 of the West Indies and the Southern colonies that had been stolen from the Indians. As the slave trade expanded, its enormous profits concentrated capital in Europe and America for the expansion of commerce, industry, and invention, while in Africa the social fabric was torn apart. In the Americas the blood and sweat of African slaves produced the sugar, tobacco, and later cotton to feed the refineries, distilleries, and textile mills, first of Western Europe and then of the Northern United States.

The more instrumental the slave trade in destroying African culture, 7 the more those involved directly and indirectly in the slave traffic tried to convince themselves and others that there had never been any African culture in the first place. The more brutal the methods needed to enforce slavery against rebellious blacks, the more the brutalizers insisted that the submissiveness of slavery was the natural state of black people. The more valuable the labor of blacks to Southern agriculture, precisely because of the relatively advanced stage of agriculture in their African homeland, the more white Americans began to insist that they had done the African savage a favor by bringing him to a land where he could be civilized by agricultural labor. Thus, step by step, in order to justify their mutually reinforcing economic exploitation and forceful subjugation of blacks, living, breathing white Americans created a scientifically cloaked theory of white superiority and black inferiority.

In order to understand the ease with which racism entrenched itself 8 in Europe and North America, it is important to emphasize that not only the big merchants, manufacturers, and shipowners benefited from the slave trade and slavery. All kinds of little people on both sides of the Atlantic drew blood money directly from the slave traffic. Thus, "though a large part of the Liverpool slave traffic was monopolized by about ten large firms, many of the small vessels in the trade were fitted out by attorneys, drapers, grocers, barbers, and tailors. The shares in the ventures were subdivided, one having one-eighth, another one-fifteenth, a third one-thirty-second part of a share and so on. . . . 'almost every order of people is interested in a Guinea cargo.'"[4]

The middle classes benefited indirectly from the general economic 9 prosperity created by the slave trade. "Every port to which the slave ships returned saw the rise of manufactures in the eighteenth century — refineries, cottons, dyeworks, sweetmaking — in increasing numbers which testified to the advance of business and industry."[5] In the expanding economy the shopkeeper found a growing number of customers for his goods, the farmer for his produce, the doctor and lawyer for their skills.

To white workers at the very bottom of white society, African slavery 10 also brought substantial benefits. First, the expanding industry made possible by the profits of slave trafficking created jobs at an expanding rate. Second, in the Americas particularly, white indentured servants were able to escape from the dehumanization of plantation servitude only because of the seemingly inexhaustible supply of constantly imported African slaves to take their place.

Contrary to racist mythology, blacks did not thrive any better in the 11 rice swamps and on the sugar and cotton plantations than whites. Nor had blacks been treated significantly worse than white indentured servants in the early days of colonial settlement when convicts and poor whites, kidnapped off the wharfs of Liverpool and London, had been crowded onto dirty transatlantic ships en route to Southern plantations to work as white indentured servants. These whites had been bracketed with blacks and treated as "white trash." But they had one advantage denied the blacks: They were of the same color as their masters. Therefore, when their contracts expired or they were able to escape, they could not be easily detected, and, *because there were blacks to take their place*, the slave masters did not put out the great effort which would have been needed to capture them. Thus the ex-indentured servant climbed into the free society as farmer or worker on the backs of black slaves.

It is only when we understand this immediate economic and social 12 stake which not only the slave owners and the capitalist entrepreneurs but the entire white population — including doctors, lawyers, bakers, and candlestickmakers (but not, of course, the Indian chiefs whose lands were taken for the plantations and farms) — had in the enslavement of

[4]Eric Williams, *Capitalism and Slavery* (New York: G. P. Putnam, 1966). [Author's note]

[5]Ernest Mandel, *Marxist Economic Theory* (New York: Monthly Review Press, 1969), p. 444. [Author's note]

blacks that we can understand the realities of racism in this country. Racism was real because there were real people with a stake in racism — racists — and these real people were ready to resort to force to protect their stake. As Eugene Genovese has pointed out, blacks were often safer on the slave plantation than off it because of the hostile, armed non-slaveholding whites.[6]

Radical historians have tended to underplay these realities, pointing 13
out how, in the final analysis, slavery impoverished the soil, drove the free farmers farther West, kept down the wages of white workers, etc. This is because these historians, usually white, have begun their analysis with the plight of white workers in the process of capitalist production and then have tried to fit the grievances and revolt of blacks into this theoretical framework. Hence, . . . they have failed to prepare us for the surfacing of white racist workers. Also, addressing themselves chiefly to white workers and trying to convince these workers of the need to destroy capitalism, they have insisted that black and white workers are "really" (i.e., according to their theory) allies, kept apart only by a vertical color line which the evil slave owners and capitalists have conspired to draw down the middle between them.

The historical fact is that without African slavery the class struggle 14
between capitalists and workers could not even have been joined in the first place. For the capitalist, it served the functions of primitive accumulation. That is, it provided both the initial capital *and* the labor force freed from the means of production which is a prerequisite for the process of capitalist accumulation inside the factory.

For the individual white indentured servant or laborer, African slavery 15
meant the opportunity to rise above the status of slave and become farmer or free laborer. Thus, early in the history of this country a pattern was created which persists to this day: physical and social mobility for white workers into and within increasingly modernized industries, possible only because there is a reserve army of black labor to scavenge the dirty, unskilled jobs in the fields and sweatshops.

Instead of the vertical color line dreamed up by white radicals, there 16
has actually existed a horizontal platform resting on the backs of blacks and holding them down, while on top white workers have been free to move up the social and economic ladder of advancing capitalism. This horizontal platform, a ceiling for blacks and a floor for whites, has created

---

[6]Eugene Genovese, *The Legacy of Slavery and the Roots of Black Nationalism*, a speech delivered at the 1966 Socialist Scholars Conference and reprinted by the New England Free Press. [Author's note]

and maintained a black labor force serving the economic needs of advancing capitalism.

Engaging the Text

1. Summarize Boggs's theory about the connection between economics and racism. What is his most important supporting evidence?

2. If money and class are the key issues for Boggs, what role *does* racial prejudice play?

3. Create extended glossary entries for the terms listed below (they are common in Marxist theory). First try to define them from context and from whatever knowledge of the terms you already have. Then split up the work of finding more complete definitions and examples, and meet again to share and compile your work. Possible sources include dictionaries, encyclopedias, and political science texts.

The terms: *capitalists, workers, class struggle, means of production.*

Exploring Connections

1. Compare and contrast Boggs's explanation of the sources and dynamics of racism to those offered by Gordon Allport and Peter Loewenberg earlier in this chapter. Are the views irreconcilable? Which argument (or what combination of arguments) do you find most persuasive and why?

2. Use Boggs to explain the events narrated by Ida B. Wells or Mary Tsukamoto later in this chapter. How well can Boggs's theory account for these events? Where does it fall short?

Extending the Critical Context

1. Contact the affirmative action office on your campus and find out the ETHNIC breakdown for the following categories of employee: (a) professors/instructors; (b) managers/administrators; (c) clerical and support staff; and (d) janitorial/maintenance personnel. Report on your findings to the class: Do they support Boggs's theory?

C. P. Ellis

STUDS TERKEL

The following interview brings us uncomfortably close to concrete, everyday racial prejudice: C. P. Ellis is a former Ku Klux Klan member who claims to have overcome his racist (and sexist) attitudes; he speaks here as a union leader who feels an alliance to other workers, including blacks and women. The story of his "transformation" is not only fascinating reading in its own right but also provides a real, complex example on which various theories like Boggs's and Loewenberg's (pp. 137, 114) can be tested. For a brief introduction to Studs Terkel (b. 1912) and his method of compiling oral histories, see the headnote to the Terkel selection in Chapter One, "American Dreams" (p. 77).

We're in his office in Durham, North Carolina. He is the business 1 *manager of the International Union of Operating Engineers. On the wall is a plaque: "Certificate of Service, in recognition to C. P. Ellis, for your faithful service to the city in having served as a member of the Durham Human Relations Council. February 1977."*

At one time, he had been president (exalted cyclops) of the Durham 2 *chapter of the Ku Klux Klan. . . .*

He is fifty-three years old. 3

My father worked in a textile mill in Durham. He died at forty-eight 4 years old. It was probably from cotton dust. Back then, we never heard of brown lung. I was about seventeen years old and had a mother and sister depending on somebody to make a livin'. It was just barely enough insurance to cover his burial. I had to quit school and go to work. I was about eighth grade when I quit.

My father worked hard but never had enough money to buy decent 5 clothes. When I went to school, I never seemed to have adequate clothes to wear. I always left school late afternoon with a sense of inferiority. The other kids had nice clothes, and I just had what Daddy could buy. I still got some of those inferiority feelin's now that I have to overcome once in a while.

I loved my father. He would go with me to ball games. We'd go fishin' 6 together. I was really ashamed of the way he'd dress. He would take this money and give it to me instead of putting it on himself. I always had the feeling about somebody looking at him and makin' fun of him and makin' fun of me. I think it had to do somethin' with my life.

My father and I were very close, but we didn't talk about too many 7
intimate things. He did have a drinking problem. During the week, he would work every day, but weekends he was ready to get plastered. I can understand when a guy looks at his paycheck and looks at his bills, and he's worked hard all the week, and his bills are larger than his paycheck. He'd done the best he could the entire week, and there seemed to be no hope. It's an illness thing. Finally you just say: "The heck with it. I'll just get drunk and forget it."

My father was out of work during the depression, and I remember 8
going with him to the finance company uptown, and he was turned down. That's something that's always stuck.

My father never seemed to be happy. It was a constant struggle with 9
him just like it was for me. It's very seldom I'd see him laugh. He was just tryin' to figure out what he could do from one day to the next.

After several years pumping gas at a service station, I got married. 10
We had to have children. Four. One child was born blind and retarded, which was a real additional expense to us. He's never spoken a word. He doesn't know me when I go to see him. But I see him, I hug his neck. I talk to him, tell him I love him. I don't know whether he knows me or not, but I know he's well taken care of. All my life, I had work, never a day without work, worked all the overtime I could get and still could not survive financially. I began to say there's somethin' wrong with this country. I worked my butt off and just never seemed to break even.

I had some real great ideas about this great nation. (Laughs.) They 11
say to abide by the law, go to church, do right and live for the Lord, and everything'll work out. But it didn't work out. It just kept gettin' worse and worse.

I was workin' a bread route. The highest I made one week was seventy- 12
five dollars. The rent on our house was about twelve dollars a week. I will never forget: outside of this house was a 265-gallon oil drum, and I never did get enough money to fill up that oil drum. What I would do every night, I would run up to the store and buy five gallons of oil and climb up the ladder and pour it in that 265-gallon drum. I could hear that five gallons when it hits the bottom of that oil drum, splatters, and it sounds like it's nothin' in there. But it would keep the house warm for the night. Next day you'd have to do the same thing.

I left the bread route with fifty dollars in my pocket. I went to the 13
bank and I borrowed four thousand dollars to buy the service station.

I worked seven days a week, open and close, and finally had a heart attack. Just about two months before the last payments of that loan. My wife had done the best she could to keep it runnin'. Tryin' to come out of that hole, I just couldn't do it.

I really began to get bitter. I didn't know who to blame. I tried to find somebody. I began to blame it on black people. I had to hate somebody. Hatin' America is hard to do because you can't see it to hate it. You gotta have somethin' to look at to hate. (Laughs.) The natural person for me to hate would be black people, because my father before me was a member of the Klan. As far as he was concerned, it was the savior of the white people. It was the only organization in the world that would take care of the white people. So I began to admire the Klan. 14

I got active in the Klan while I was at the service station. Every Monday night, a group of men would come by and buy a Coca-Cola, go back to the car, take a few drinks, and come back and stand around talkin'. I couldn't help but wonder: Why are these dudes comin' out every Monday? They said they were with the Klan and have meetings close-by. Would I be interested? Boy, that was an opportunity I really looked forward to! To be part of somethin'. I joined the Klan, went from member to chaplain, from chaplain to vice-president, from vice-president to president. The title is exalted cyclops. 15

The first night I went with the fellas, they knocked on the door and gave the signal. They sent some robed Klansmen to talk to me and give me some instructions. I was led into a large meeting room, and this was the time of my life! It was thrilling. Here's a guy who's worked all his life and struggled all his life to be something, and here's the moment to be something. I will never forget it. Four robed Klansmen led me into the hall. The lights were dim, and the only thing you could see was an illuminated cross. I knelt before the cross. I had to make certain vows and promises. We promised to uphold the purity of the white race, fight communism, and protect white womanhood. 16

After I had taken my oath, there was loud applause goin' throughout the buildin', musta been at least four hundred people. For this one little ol' person. It was a thrilling moment for C. P. Ellis. 17

It disturbs me when people who do not really know what it's all about are so very critical of individual Klansmen. The majority of 'em are low-income whites, people who really don't have a part in something. They have been shut out as well as the blacks. Some are not very well educated either. Just like myself. We had a lot of support from doctors and lawyers and police officers. 18

Maybe they've had bitter experiences in this life and they had to hate somebody. So the natural person to hate would be the black person. 19

He's beginnin' to come up, he's beginnin' to learn to read and start votin' and run for political office. Here are white people who are supposed to be superior to them, and we're shut out.

I can understand why people join extreme right-wing or left-wing groups. They're in the same boat I was. Shut out. Deep down inside, we want to be part of this great society. Nobody listens, so we join these groups. 20

At one time, I was state organizer of the National Rights party. I organized a youth group for the Klan. I felt we were getting old and our generation's gonna die. So I contacted certain kids in schools. They were havin' racial problems. On the first night, we had a hundred high school students. When they came in the door, we had "Dixie" playin'. These kids were just thrilled to death. I begin to hold weekly meetin's with 'em, teachin' the principles of the Klan. At that time, I believed Martin Luther King had Communist connections. I began to teach that Andy Young was affiliated with the Communist party. 21

I had a call one night from one of our kids. He was about twelve. He said: "I just been robbed downtown by two niggers." I'd had a couple of drinks and that really teed me off. I go downtown and couldn't find the kid. I got worried. I saw two young black people. I had the .32 revolver with me. I said: "Nigger, you seen a little young white boy up here? I just got a call from him and was told that some niggers robbed him of fifteen cents." I pulled my pistol out and put it right at his head. I said: "I've always wanted to kill a nigger and I think I'll make you the first one." I nearly scared the kid to death, and he struck off. 22

This was the time when the civil rights movement was really beginnin' to peak. The blacks were beginnin' to demonstrate and picket downtown stores. I never will forget some black lady I hated with a purple passion. Ann Atwater. Every time I'd go downtown, she'd be leadin' a boycott. How I hated — pardon the expression, I don't use it much now — how I just hated that black nigger. (Laughs.) Big, fat, heavy woman. She'd pull about eight demonstrations, and first thing you know they had two, three blacks at the checkout counter. Her and I have had some pretty close confrontations. 23

I felt very big, yeah. (Laughs.) We're more or less a secret organization. We didn't want anybody to know who we were, and I began to do some thinkin'. What am I hidin' for? I've never been convicted of anything in my life. I don't have any court record. What am I, C. P. Ellis, as a citizen and a member of the United Klansmen of America? Why can't I go the city council meeting and say: "This is the way we feel about the matter? We don't want you to purchase mobile units to set in our schoolyards. We don't want niggers in our schools." 24

We began to come out in the open. We would go to the meetings, 25
and the blacks would be there and we'd be there. It was a confrontation
every time. I didn't hold back anything. We began to make some inroads
with the city councilmen and county commissioners. They began to call
us friend. Call us at night on the telephone: "C. P., glad you came to
that meeting last night." They didn't want integration either, but they
did it secretively, in order to get elected. They couldn't stand up openly
and say it, but they were glad somebody was sayin' it. We visited some
of the city leaders in their home and talk to 'em privately. It wasn't long
before councilmen would call me up: "The blacks are comin' up tonight
and makin' outrageous demands. How about some of you people showin'
up and have a little balance?" I'd get on the telephone: "The niggers is
comin' to the council meeting tonight. Persons in the city's called me
and asked us to be there."

We'd load up our cars and we'd fill up half the council chambers, and 26
the blacks the other half. During these times, I carried weapons to the
meetings, outside my belt. We'd go there armed. We would wind up
just hollerin' and fussin' at each other. What happened? As a result of
our fightin' one another, the city council still had their way. They didn't
want to give up control to the blacks nor the Klan. They were usin' us.

I began to realize this later down the road. One day I was walkin' 27
downtown and a certain city council member saw me comin'. I expected
him to shake my hand because he was talkin' to me at night on the
telephone. I had been in his home and visited with him. He crossed
the street. Oh shit, I began to think, somethin's wrong here. Most of
'em are merchants or maybe an attorney, an insurance agent, people
like that. As long as they kept low-income whites and low-income blacks
fightin', they're gonna maintain control.

I began to get that feeling after I was ignored in public. I thought: 28
Bullshit, you're not gonna use me any more. That's when I began to do
some real serious thinkin'.

The same thing is happening in this country today. People are being 29
used by those in control, those who have all the wealth. I'm not espousing
communism. We got the greatest system of government in the world.
But those who have it simply don't want those who don't have it to have
any part of it. Black and white. When it comes to money, the green,
the other colors make no difference. (Laughs.)

I spent a lot of sleepless nights. I still didn't like blacks. I didn't want 30
to associate with 'em. Blacks, Jews, or Catholics. My father said: "Don't
have anything to do with 'em." I didn't until I met a black person and
talked with him, eyeball to eyeball, and met a Jewish person and talked
to him, eyeball to eyeball. I found out they're people just like me. They

cried, they cussed, they prayed, they had desires. Just like myself. Thank God, I got to the point where I can look past labels. But at that time, my mind was closed.

I remember one Monday night Klan meeting. I said something was wrong. Our city fathers were using us. And I didn't like to be used. The reactions of the others was not too pleasant: "Let's just keep fightin' them niggers."

I'd go home at night and I'd have to wrestle with myself. I'd look at a black person walkin' down the street, and the guy'd have ragged shoes or his clothes would be worn. That began to do somethin' to me inside. I went through this for about six months. I felt I just had to get out of the Klan. But I wouldn't get out.

Then something happened. The state AFL-CIO received a grant from the Department of HEW, a $78,000 grant: how to solve racial problems in the school system. I got a telephone call from the president of the state AFL-CIO. "We'd like to get some people together from all walks of life." I said: "All walks of life? Who you talkin' about?" He said: "Blacks, whites, liberals, conservatives, Klansmen, NAACP people."

I said: "No way am I comin' with all those niggers. I'm not gonna be associated with those type of people." A White Citizens Council guy said: "Let's go up there and see what's goin' on. It's tax money bein' spent." I walk in the door, and there was a large number of blacks and white liberals. I knew most of 'em by face 'cause I seen 'em demonstratin' around town. Ann Atwater was there. (Laughs.) I just forced myself to go in and sit down.

The meeting was moderated by a great big black guy who was bushy-headed. (Laughs.) That turned me off. He acted very nice. He said: "I want you all to feel free to say anything you want to say." Some of the blacks stand up and say it's white racism. I took all I could take. I asked for the floor and I cut loose. I said: "No, sir, it's black racism. If we didn't have niggers in the schools, we wouldn't have the problems we got today."

I will never forget. Howard Clements, a black guy, stood up. He said: "I'm certainly glad C. P. Ellis come because he's the most honest man here tonight." I said: "What's that nigger tryin' to do?" (Laughs.) At the end of that meeting, some blacks tried to come up shake my hand, but I wouldn't do it. I walked off.

Second night, same group was there. I felt a little more easy because I got some things off my chest. The third night, after they elected all the committees, they want to elect a chairman. Howard Clements stood up and said: "I suggest we elect two co-chairpersons." Joe Beckton, executive director of the Human Relations Commission, just as black as he can be, he nominated me. There was a reaction from some blacks. Nooo. And, of all things, they nominated Ann Atwater, that big old fat black gal that I had just hated with a purple passion, as co-chairman. I thought to myself: Hey, ain't no way I can work with that gal. Finally, I agreed to accept it, 'cause at this point, I was tired of fightin', either for survival or against black people or against Jews or against Catholics.

A Klansman and a militant black woman, co-chairmen of the school 38 committee. It was impossible. How could I work with her? But after about two or three days, it was in our hands. We had to make it a success. This give me another sense of belongin', a sense of pride. This helped this inferiority feelin' I had. A man who has stood up publicly and said he despised black people, all of a sudden he was willin' to work with 'em. Here's a chance for a low-income white man to be somethin'. In spite of all my hatred for blacks and Jews and liberals, I accepted the job. Her and I began to reluctantly work together. (Laughs.) She had as many problems workin' with me as I had workin' with her.

One night, I called her: "Ann, you and I should have a lot of differences 39 and we got 'em now. But there's somethin' laid out here before us, and if it's gonna be a success, you and I are gonna have to make it one. Can we lay aside some of these feelin's?" She said: "I'm willing if you are." I said: "Let's do it."

My old friends would call me at night: "C. P., what the hell is wrong 40 with you? You're sellin' out the white race." This begin to make me have guilt feelin's. Am I doin' right? Am I doin' wrong? Here I am all of a sudden makin' an about-face and tryin' to deal with my feelin's, my heart. My mind was beginnin' to open up. I was beginnin' to see what was right and what was wrong. I don't want the kids to fight forever.

We were gonna go ten nights. By this time, I had went to work at 41 Duke University, in maintenance. Makin' very little money. Terry Sanford give me this ten days off with pay. He was president of Duke at the time. He knew I was a Klansman and realized the importance of blacks and whites getting along.

I said: "If we're gonna make this thing a success, I've got to get to 42 my kind of people." The low-income whites. We walked the streets of Durham, and we knocked on doors and invited people. Ann was goin' into the black community. They just wasn't respondin' to us when we made these house calls. Some of 'em were cussin' us out. "You're sellin' us out, Ellis, get out of my door. I don't want to talk to you." Ann was gettin' the same response from blacks: "What are you doin' messin' with that Klansman?"

One day, Ann and I went back to the school and we sat down. We 43 began to talk and just reflect. Ann said: "My daughter came home cryin' every day. She said her teacher was makin' fun of me in front of the other kids." I said: "Boy, the same thing happened to my kid. White liberal teacher was makin' fun of Tim Ellis's father, the Klansman. In front of other peoples. He came home cryin'." At this point — (he pauses, swallows hard, stifles a sob) — I begin to see, here we are, two people from the far ends of the fence, havin' identical problems, except hers bein' black and me bein' white. From that moment on, I tell ya, that gal and I worked together good. I begin to love the girl, really. (He weeps.)

The amazing thing about it, her and I, up to that point, had cussed 44
each other, bawled each other, we hated each other. Up to that point, we didn't know each other. We didn't know we had things in common.

We worked at it, with the people who came to these meetings. They 45
talked about racism, sex education, about teachers not bein' qualified. After seven, eight nights of real intense discussion, these people, who'd never talked to each other before, all of a sudden came up with resolutions. It was really somethin', you had to be there to get the tone and feelin' of it.

At that point, I didn't like integration, but the law says you do this 46
and I've got to do what the law says, okay? We said: "Let's take these resolutions to the school board." The most disheartening thing I've ever faced was the school system refused to implement any one of these resolutions. These were recommendations from the people who pay taxes and pay their salaries. (Laughs.)

I thought they were good answers. Some of 'em I didn't agree with, 47
but I been in this thing from the beginning, and whatever comes of it, I'm gonna support it. Okay, since the school board refused, I decided I'd just run for the school board.

I spent eighty-five dollars on the campaign. The guy runnin' against 48
me spent several thousand. I really had nobody on my side. The Klan turned against me. The low-income whites turned against me. The liberals didn't particularly like me. The blacks were suspicious of me. The blacks wanted to support me, but they couldn't muster up enough to support a Klansman on the school board. (Laughs.) But I made up my mind that what I was doin' was right, and I was gonna do it regardless what anybody said.

It bothered me when people would call and worry my wife. She's 49
always supported me in anything I wanted to do. She was changing, and my boys were too. I got some of my youth corps kids involved. They still followed me.

I was invited to the Democratic women's social hour as a candidate. 50
Didn't have but one suit to my name. Had it six, seven, eight years. I

had it cleaned, put on the best shirt I had and a tie. Here were all this high-class wealthy candidates shakin' hands. I walked up to the mayor and stuck out my hand. He give me that handshake with that rag type of hand. He said: "C. P., I'm glad to see you." But I could tell by his handshake he was lyin' to me. This was botherin' me. I know I'm a low-income person. I know I'm not wealthy. I know they were sayin': "What's this little ol' dude runnin' for school board?" Yet they had to smile and make like they're glad to see me. I begin to spot some black people in that room. I automatically went to 'em and that was a firm handshake. They said: "I'm glad to see you, C. P." I knew they meant it — you can tell about a handshake.

Every place I appeared, I said I will listen to the voice of the people. 51 I will not make a major decision until I first contacted all the organizations in the city. I got 4,640 votes. The guy beat me by two thousand. Not bad for eighty-five bucks and no constituency.

The whole world was openin' up, and I was learnin' new truths that 52 I had never learned before. I was beginnin' to look at a black person, shake hands with him, and see him as a human bein'. I hadn't got rid of all this stuff. I've still got a little bit of it. But somethin' was happenin' to me.

It was almost like bein' born again. It was a new life. I didn't have 53 these sleepless nights I used to have when I was active in the Klan and slippin' around at night. I could sleep at night and feel good about it. I'd rather live now than at any other time in history. It's a challenge.

Back at Duke, doin' maintenance, I'd pick up my tools, fix the commode, 54 unstop the drains. But this got in my blood. Things weren't right in this country, and what we done in Durham needs to be told. I was so miserable at Duke, I could hardly stand it. I'd go to work every morning just hatin' to go.

My whole life had changed. I got an eighth-grade education, and I 55 wanted to complete high school. Went to high school in the afternoons on a program called PEP — Past Employment Progress. I was about the only white in class, and the oldest. I begin to read about biology. I'd take my books home at night, 'cause I was determined to get through. Sure enough, I graduated. I got the diploma at home.

I come to work one mornin' and some guy says: "We need a union." 56 At this time I wasn't pro-union. My daddy was anti-labor, too. We're not gettin' paid much, we're havin' to work seven days in a row. We're all starvin' to death. The next day, I meet the international representative of the Operating Engineers. He give me authorization cards. "Get these cards out and we'll have an election." There was eighty-eight for the union and seventeen no's. I was elected chief steward for the union.

Shortly after, a union man come down from Charlotte and says we 57
need a full-time rep. We've got only two hundred people at the two
plants here. It's just barely enough money comin' in to pay your salary.
You'll have to get out and organize more people. I didn't know nothin'
about organizin' unions, but I knew how to organize people, stir people
up. (Laughs.) That's how I got to be business agent for the union.

When I began to organize, I began to see far deeper. I began to see 58
people again bein' used. Blacks against whites. I say this without any
hesitancy: Management is vicious. There's two things they want to keep:
all the money and all the say-so. They don't want these poor workin'
folks to have none of that. I begin to see management fightin' me with
everything they had. Hire anti-union law firms, badmouth unions. The
people were makin' a dollar ninety-five an hour, barely able to get
through weekends. I worked as a business rep for five years and was
seein' all this.

Last year, I ran for business manager of the union. He's elected by 59
the workers. The guy that ran against me was black, and our membership
is seventy-five percent black. I thought: Claiborne, there's no way you
can beat that black guy. People know your background. Even though
you've made tremendous strides, those black people are not gonna vote
for you. You know how much I beat him? Four to one. (Laughs.)

The company used my past against me. They put out letters with a 60
picture of a robe and a cap: Would you vote for a Klansman? They
wouldn't deal with the issues. I immediately called for a mass meeting.
I met with the ladies at an electric component plant. I said: "Okay, this
is Claiborne Ellis. This is where I come from. I want you to know right
now, you black ladies here, I was at one time a member of the Klan.
I want you to know, because they'll tell you about it."

I invited some of my old black friends. I said: "Brother Joe, Brother 61
Howard, be honest now and tell these people how you feel about me."
They done it. (Laughs.) Howard Clements kidded me a little bit. He
said: "I don't know what I'm doin' here, supportin' an ex-Klansman."
(Laughs.) He said: "I know what C. P. Ellis come from. I knew him
when he was. I knew him as he grew, and growed with him. I'm tellin'
you now: Follow, follow this Klansman." (He pauses, swallows hard.)
"Any questions?" "No," the black ladies said. "Let's get on with the
meeting, we need Ellis." (He laughs and weeps.) Boy, black people
sayin' that about me. I won one thirty-four to forty-one. Four to one.

It makes you feel good to go into a plant and butt heads with professional 62
union busters. You see black people and white people join hands to
defeat the racist issues they use against people. They're tryin' the same
things with the Klan. It's still happenin' today. Can you imagine a guy

who's got an adult high school diploma runnin' into professional college graduates who are union busters? I gotta compete with 'em. I work seven days a week, nights and on Saturday and Sunday. The salary's not that great, and if I didn't care, I'd quit. But I care and I can't quit. I got a taste of it. (Laughs.)

I tell people there's a tremendous possibility in this country to stop   63
wars, the battles, the struggles, the fights between people. People say: "That's an impossible dream. You sound like Martin Luther King." An ex-Klansman who sounds like Martin Luther King. (Laughs.) I don't think it's an impossible dream. It's happened in my life. It's happened in other people's lives in America.

I don't know what's ahead of me. I have no desire to be a big union   64
official. I want to be right out here in the field with the workers. I want to walk through their factory and shake hands with that man whose hands are dirty. I'm gonna do all that one little ol' man can do. I'm fifty-two years old, and I ain't got many years left, but I want to make the best of 'em.

When the news came over the radio that Martin Luther King was   65
assassinated, I got on the telephone and begin to call other Klansmen. We just had a real party at the service station. Really rejoicin' 'cause that son of a bitch was dead. Our troubles are over with. They say the older you get, the harder it is for you to change. That's not necessarily true. Since I changed, I've set down and listened to tapes of Martin Luther King. I listen to it and tears come to my eyes 'cause I know what he's sayin' now. I know what's happenin'.

POSTSCRIPT: *The phone rings. A conversation.*   66

"This was a black guy who's director of Operation Breakthrough in   67
Durham. I had called his office. I'm interested in employin' some young black person who's interested in learnin' the labor movement. I want somebody who's never had an opportunity, just like myself. Just so he can read and write, that's all."

Engaging the Text

1. How does Ellis battle the racism he finds in himself? What gives him the strength to change? What specific changes does he undergo, and does he entirely overcome racist attitudes?

2. Would Ellis say that economic class is more important than race in determining job placement and occupational mobility? Find specific passages that reveal Ellis's beliefs about the connections between economic class, race, and success in American society.

3. How well does Ellis seem to understand himself, his feelings, his motives? Give evidence for your assertions.

4. What is Terkel's role in the C. P. Ellis selection? Is he helping to rationalize or justify the actions of the Ku Klux Klan?

Exploring Connections

1. To what extent does Ellis's experience illustrate Gordon Allport's concept of in-groups and out-groups? Of group mobility? Find specific examples that support your assertions. (Allport's essay opens this chapter.)

2. Does Ellis's experience seem to offer a way of overcoming misunderstanding and hatred between races? Thinking about the explanations Allport, Loewenberg, and Boggs offer for the persistence of racism, do you think Ellis's "solution" would be workable on a large scale? Why or why not?

3. Review Loewenberg's description of "displacement." Discuss C. P. Ellis's decision to join the Ku Klux Klan as an example of displacement.

4. Reread Peter Loewenberg's definition of the "authoritarian personality" earlier in the chapter. Which details of C. P. Ellis's life seem to fit that definition, and which do not?

CONFRONTING RACISM

Los Vendidos[1]

LUIS M. VALDEZ

In this one-act play, Valdez ridicules stereotypical thinking by following up on an oddball symbolic premise: the sale of Mexican robots to then-governor Ronald Reagan's administration in California. Valdez (b. 1940) has been a major force in the establishment of Chicano theater in the

[1] *Los Vendidos:* sellouts.

United States. *His best-known plays are* Zoot Suit *and* I Don't Have to Show You No Stinking Badges. *Recently he wrote and directed the hit movie* La Bamba.

Characters

HONEST SANCHO	JOHNNY
SECRETARY	REVOLUCIONARIO
FARM WORKER	MEXICAN-AMERICAN

Scene: Honest Sancho's Used Mexican Lot and Mexican Curio Shop. Three models are on display in Honest Sancho's shop: to the right, there is a Revolucionario, complete with sombrero, carrilleras,[2] and carabina 30–30. At center, on the floor, there is the Farm Worker, under a broad straw sombrero. At stage left is the Pachuco, filero[3] in hand.

(Honest Sancho is moving among his models, dusting them off and preparing for another day of business.)

SANCHO: Bueno, bueno, mis monos, vamos a ver a quien vendemos 1
ahora, ¿no? *(To audience.)* ¡Quihubo![4] I'm Honest Sancho and this is
my shop. Antes fui contratista pero ahora logré tener mi negocito.[5]
All I need now is a customer. *(A bell rings offstage.)* Ay, a customer!

SECRETARY *(Entering)*: Good morning, I'm Miss Jiménez from — 2

SANCHO: ¡Ah, una chicana! Welcome, welcome Señorita Jiménez. 3

SECRETARY *(Anglo pronunciation)*: JIM-enez. 4

SANCHO: ¿Qué? 5

SECRETARY: My name is Miss JIM-enez. Don't you speak English? What's 6
wrong with you?

SANCHO: Oh, nothing, Señorita JIM-enez. I'm here to help you. 7

SECRETARY: That's better. As I was starting to say, I'm a secretary from 8
Governor Reagan's office, and we're looking for a Mexican type for
the administration.

SANCHO: Well, you come to the right place, lady. This is Honest Sancho's 9

---

[2]*carrilleras:* literally chin straps, but may refer to cartridge belts.

[3]*Pachuco:* Chicano slang for a 1940s zoot suiter; *filero:* blade.

[4]*Bueno, bueno, . . . Quihubo:* "Good, good, my cute ones, let's see who we can sell now, O.K.?"

[5]*Antes fui . . . negocito:* "I used to be a contractor, but now I've succeeded in having my little business."

Used Mexican lot, and we got all types here. Any particular type you want?

SECRETARY: Yes, we were looking for somebody suave — 10

SANCHO: Suave. 11

SECRETARY: Debonair. 12

SANCHO: De buen aire. 13

SECRETARY: Dark. 14

SANCHO: Prieto. 15

SECRETARY: But of course not too dark. 16

SANCHO: No muy prieto. 17

SECRETARY: Perhaps, beige. 18

SANCHO: Beige, just the tone. Así como cafecito con leche,[6] ¿no? 19

SECRETARY: One more thing. He must be hard-working. 20

SANCHO: That could only be one model. Stop right over here to the center of the shop, lady. (*They cross to the Farm Worker.*) This is our standard farm worker model. As you can see, in the words of our beloved Senator George Murphy, he is "built close to the ground." Also take special notice of his four-ply Goodyear huaraches, made from the rain tire. This wide-brimmed sombrero is an extra added feature — keeps off the sun, rain, and dust. 21

SECRETARY: Yes, it does look durable. 22

SANCHO: And our farmworker model is friendly. Muy amable.[7] Watch. (*Snaps his fingers.*) 23

FARM WORKER (*Lifts up head*): Buenos días, señorita. (*His head drops.*) 24

SECRETARY: My, he's friendly. 25

SANCHO: Didn't I tell you? Loves his patrones! But his most attractive feature is that he's hard working. Let me show you. (*Snaps fingers. Farm Worker stands.*) 26

FARM WORKER: ¡El jale![8] (*He begins to work.*) 27

SANCHO: As you can see, he is cutting grapes. 28

SECRETARY: Oh, I wouldn't know. 29

SANCHO: He also picks cotton. (*Snap. Farm Worker begins to pick cotton.*) 30

SECRETARY: Versatile isn't he? 31

SANCHO: He also picks melons. (*Snap. Farm Worker picks melons.*) That's his slow speed for late in the season. Here's his fast speed. (*Snap. Farm Worker picks faster.*) 32

SECRETARY: ¡Chihuahua! . . . I mean, goodness, he sure is a hard worker. 33

[6]*Así como . . . leche:* like coffee with milk.
[7]*Muy amable:* very friendly.
[8]*El jale:* the job.

SANCHO *(Pulls the Farm Worker to his feet)*: And that isn't the half of 34
it. Do you see these little holes on his arms that appear to be pores?
During those hot sluggish days in the field, when the vines or the
branches get so entangled, it's almost impossible to move; these holes
emit a certain grease that allow our model to slip and slide right
through the crop with no trouble at all.

SECRETARY: Wonderful. But is he economical? 35

SANCHO: Economical? Señorita, you are looking at the Volkswagen of 36
Mexicans. Pennies a day is all it takes. One plate of beans and tortillas
will keep him going all day. That, and chile. Plenty of chile. Chile
jalapenos, chile verde, chile colorado. But, of course, if you do give
him chile *(Snap. Farm Worker turns left face. Snap. Farm Worker
bends over.)* then you have to change his oil filter once a week.

SECRETARY: What about storage? 37

SANCHO: No problem. You know these new farm labor camps our Hon- 38
orable Governor Reagan has built out by Parlier or Raisin City? They
were designed with our model in mind. Five, six, seven, even ten in
one of those shacks will give you no trouble at all. You can also put
him in old barns, old cars, river banks. You can even leave him out
in the field overnight with no worry!

SECRETARY: Remarkable. 39

SANCHO: And here's an added feature: Every year at the end of the 40
season, this model goes back to Mexico and doesn't return, automatically,
until next Spring.

SECRETARY: How about that. But tell me: does he speak English? 41

SANCHO: Another outstanding feature is that last year this model was 42
programmed to go out on STRIKE! *(Snap.)*

FARM WORKER: ¡HUELGA! ¡HUELGA! Hermanos, sálganse de esos 43
files.[9] *(Snap. He stops.)*

SECRETARY: No! Oh no, we can't strike in the State Capitol. 44

SANCHO: Well, he also scabs. *(Snap.)* 45

FARM WORKER: Me vendo barato, ¿y qué?[10] *(Snap.)* 46

SECRETARY: That's much better, but you didn't answer my question. 47
Does he speak English?

SANCHO: Bueno . . . no, pero[11] he has other — 48

SECRETARY: No. 49

SANCHO: Other features. 50

SECRETARY: NO! He just won't do! 51

SANCHO: Okay, okay pues. We have other models. 52

[9]*HUELGA! HUELGA! . . . esos files:* "Strike! Strike! Brothers, leave those rows."
[10]*Me vendo . . . qué:* "I come cheap, so what?"
[11]*Bueno . . . no, pero:* "Well, no, but . . ."

SECRETARY: I hope so. What we need is something a little more 53
sophisticated.

SANCHO: Sophisti — ¿qué? 54

SECRETARY: An urban model. 55

SANCHO: Ah, from the city! Step right back. Over here in this corner 56
of the shop is exactly what you're looking for. Introducing our new
1969 JOHNNY PACHUCO model! This is our fast-back model.
Streamlined. Built for speed, low-riding, city life. Take a look at some
of these features. Mag shoes, dual exhausts, green chartreuse paint-
job, dark-tint windshield, a little poof on top. Let me just turn him
on. (*Snap. Johnny walks to stage center with a pachuco bounce.*)

SECRETARY: What was that? 57

SANCHO: That, señorita, was the Chicano shuffle. 58

SECRETARY: Okay, what does he do? 59

SANCHO: Anything and everything necessary for city life. For instance, 60
survival: He knife fights. (*Snap. Johnny pulls out switch blade and
swings at Secretary.*)

(*Secretary screams.*)

SANCHO: He dances. (*Snap.*) 61

JOHNNY (*Singing*): "Angel Baby, my Angel Baby . . ." (*Snap.*) 62

SANCHO: And here's a feature no city model can be without. He gets 63
arrested, but not without resisting, of course. (*Snap.*)

JOHNNY: ¡En la madre, la placa![12] I didn't do it! I didn't do it! (*Johnny* 64
*turns and stands up against an imaginary wall, legs spread out, arms
behind his back.*)

SECRETARY: Oh no, we can't have arrests! We must maintain law and 65
order.

SANCHO: But he's bilingual! 66

SECRETARY: Bilingual? 67

SANCHO: Simón que yes.[13] He speaks English! Johnny, give us some 68
English. (*Snap.*)

JOHNNY (*Comes downstage*): Fuck-you! 69

SECRETARY (*Gasps*): Oh! I've never been so insulted in my whole life! 70

SANCHO: Well, he learned it in your school. 71

SECRETARY: I don't care where he learned it. 72

SANCHO: But he's economical! 73

SECRETARY: Economical? 74

[12]*En la . . . placa:* "Wow, the police!"
[13]*Simón . . . yes:* yeah, sure.

SANCHO: Nickels and dimes. You can keep Johnny running on hamburgers,   75
Taco Bell tacos, Lucky Lager beer, Thunderbird wine, yesca —

SECRETARY: Yesca?   76

SANCHO: Mota.   77

SECRETARY: Mota?   78

SANCHO: Leños[14] . . . Marijuana. *(Snap; Johnny inhales on an imaginary*   79
joint.)

SECRETARY: That's against the law!   80

JOHNNY *(Big smile, holding his breath)*: Yeah.   81

SANCHO: He also sniffs glue. *(Snap. Johnny inhales glue, big smile.)*   82

JOHNNY: Tha's too much man, ése.   83

SECRETARY: No, Mr. Sancho, I don't think this —   84

SANCHO: Wait a minute, he has other qualities I know you'll love. For   85
example, an inferiority complex. *(Snap.)*

JOHNNY *(To Sancho)*: You think you're better than me, huh ése? *(Swings*   86
switch blade.)

SANCHO: He can also be beaten and he bruises, cut him and he bleeds;   87
kick him and he — *(He beats, bruises and kicks Pachuco.)* would you
like to try it?

SECRETARY: Oh, I couldn't.   88

SANCHO: Be my guest. He's a great scapegoat.   89

SECRETARY: No, really.   90

SANCHO: Please.   91

SECRETARY: Well, all right. Just once. *(She kicks Pachuco.)* Oh, he's   92
so soft.

SANCHO: Wasn't that good? Try again.   93

SECRETARY *(Kicks Pachuco)*: Oh, he's so wonderful! *(She kicks him*   94
again.)

SANCHO: Okay, that's enough, lady. You ruin the merchandise. Yes, our   95
Johnny Pachuco model can give you many hours of pleasure. Why,
the L.A.P.D. just bought twenty of these to train their rookie cops
on. And talk about maintenance. Señorita, you are looking at an entirely
self-supporting machine. You're never going to find our Johnny Pachuco
model on the relief rolls. No, sir, this model knows how to liberate.

SECRETARY: Liberate?   96

SANCHO: He steals. *(Snap. Johnny rushes the Secretary and steals her*   97
purse.)

JOHNNY: ¡Dame esa bolsa, vieja![15] *(He grabs the purse and runs. Snap*   98
by Sancho. He stops.)

---

[14]*Leños:* "joints" of marijuana.
[15]*Dame esa . . . , viega:* "Gimme that bag, old lady!"

(Secretary runs after Johnny and grabs purse away from him, kicking him as she goes.)

SECRETARY: No, no, no! We can't have any *more* thieves in the State 99
    Administration. Put him back.

SANCHO: Okay, we still got other models. Come on, Johnny, we'll sell 100
    you to some old lady. *(Sancho takes Johnny back to his place.)*

SECRETARY: Mr. Sancho, I don't think you quite understand what we 101
    need. What we need is something that will attract the women voters.
    Something more traditional, more romantic.

SANCHO: Ah, a lover. *(He smiles meaningfully.)* Step right over here, 102
    señorita. Introducing our standard Revolucionario and/or Early California
    Bandit type. As you can see he is well-built, sturdy, durable. This is
    the International Harvester of Mexicans.

SECRETARY: What does he do? 103

SANCHO: You name it, he does it. He rides horses, stays in the mountains, 104
    crosses deserts, plains, rivers, leads revolutions, follows revolutions,
    kills, can be killed, serves as a martyr, hero, movie star — did I say
    movie star? Did you ever see *Viva Zapata? Viva Villa? Villa Rides?*
    Pancho Villa Returns? *Pancho Villa Goes Back? Pancho Villa Meets*
    Abbott and Costello —

SECRETARY: I've never seen any of those. 105

SANCHO: Well, he was in all of them. Listen to this. *(Snap.)* 106

REVOLUCIONARIO *(Scream)*: ¡VIVA VILLAAAAA! 107

SECRETARY: That's awfully loud. 108

SANCHO: He has a volume control. *(He adjusts volume. Snap.)* 109

REVOLUCIONARIO *(Mousey voice)*: ¡Viva Villa! 110

SECRETARY: That's better. 111

SANCHO: And even if you didn't see him in the movies, perhaps you 112
    saw him on TV. He makes commercials. *(Snap.)*

REVOLUCIONARIO: Is there a Frito Bandito in your house? 113

SECRETARY: Oh yes, I've seen that one! 114

SANCHO: Another feature about this one is that he is economical. He 115
    runs on raw horsemeat and tequila!

SECRETARY: Isn't that rather savage? 116

SANCHO: Al contrario,[16] it makes him a lover. *(Snap.)* 117

REVOLUCIONARIO *(To Secretary)*: ¡Ay, mamasota, cochota, ven pa'ca! 118
    (He grabs Secretary and folds her back — Latin-Lover style.)

SANCHO *(Snap. Revolucionario goes back upright.)*: Now wasn't that 119
    nice?

---

[16] *Al contrario:* on the contrary.

SECRETARY: Well, it was rather nice. 120

SANCHO: And finally, there is one outstanding feature about this model 121
I KNOW the ladies are going to love: He's a GENUINE antique! He
was made in Mexico in 1910!

SECRETARY: Made in Mexico? 122

SANCHO: That's right. Once in Tijuana, twice in Guadalajara, three times 123
in Cuernavaca.

SECRETARY: Mr. Sancho, I thought he was an American product. 124

SANCHO: No, but — 125

SECRETARY: No, I'm sorry. We can't buy anything but American-made 126
products. He just won't do.

SANCHO: But he's an antique! 127

SECRETARY: I don't care. You still don't understand what we need. It's 128
true we need Mexican models such as these, but it's more important
that he be *American*.

SANCHO: American? 129

SECRETARY: That's right, and judging from what you've shown me, I 130
don't think you have what we want. Well, my lunch hour's almost
over; I better —

SANCHO: Wait a minute! Mexican but American? 131

SECRETARY: That's correct. 132

SANCHO: Mexican but . . . *(A sudden flash.)* AMERICAN! Yeah, I think 133
we've got exactly what you want. He just came in today! Give me a
minute. *(He exits. Talks from backstage.)* Here he is in the shop. Let
me just get some papers off. There. Introducing our new 1970 Mexican-
American! Ta-ra-ra-ra-ra-ra-RA-RAAA!

*(Sancho brings out the Mexican-American model, a clean-shaven middle-
class type in a business suit, with glasses.)*

SECRETARY *(Impressed)*: Where have you been hiding this one? 134

SANCHO: He just came in this morning. Ain't he a beauty? Feast your 135
eyes on him! Sturdy US STEEL frame, streamlined, modern. As a
matter of fact, he is built exactly like our Anglo models except that
he comes in a variety of darker shades: naugahyde, leather, or leatherette.

SECRETARY: Naugahyde. 136

SANCHO: Well, we'll just write that down. Yes, señorita, this model 137
represents the apex of American engineering! He is bilingual, college
educated, ambitious! Say the word "acculturate" and he accelerates.
He is intelligent, well-mannered, clean — did I say clean? *(Snap.
Mexican-American raises his arm.)* Smell.

SECRETARY *(Smells)*: Old Sobaco, my favorite. 138

SANCHO *(Snap. Mexican-American turns toward Sancho.)*: Eric! *(To* 139

Secretary.) We call him Eric García. *(To Eric.)* I want you to meet Miss JIM-enez, Eric.

MEXICAN-AMERICAN: Miss JIM-enez, I am delighted to make your ac- 140
quaintance. *(He kisses her hand.)*

SECRETARY: Oh, my, how charming! 141

SANCHO: Did you feel the suction? He has seven especially engineered 142
suction cups right behind his lips. He's a charmer all right!

SECRETARY: How about boards? Does he function on boards? 143

SANCHO: You name them, he is on them. Parole boards, draft boards, 144
school boards, taco quality control boards, surf boards, two-by-fours.

SECRETARY: Does he function in politics? 145

SANCHO: Señorita, you are looking at a political MACHINE. Have you 146
ever heard of the OEO, EOC, COD, WAR ON POVERTY? That's
our model! Not only that, he makes political speeches.

SECRETARY: May I hear one? 147

SANCHO: With pleasure. *(Snap.)* Eric, give us a speech. 148

MEXICAN-AMERICAN: Mr. Congressman, Mr. Chairman, members of 149
the board, honored guests, ladies and gentlemen. *(Sancho and Secretary
applaud.)* Please, please. I come before you as a Mexican-American
to tell you about the problems of the Mexican. The problems of the
Mexican stem from one thing and one thing alone: He's stupid. He's
uneducated. He needs to stay in school. He needs to be ambitious,
forward-looking, harder-working. He needs to think American, American,
American, AMERICAN, AMERICAN, AMERICAN. GOD BLESS
AMERICA! GOD BLESS AMERICA! GOD BLESS AMERICA!! *(He
goes out of control.)*

*(Sancho snaps frantically and the Mexican-American finally slumps for-
ward, bending at the waist.)*

SECRETARY: Oh my, he's patriotic too! 150

SANCHO: Sí, señorita, he loves his country. Let me just make a little 151
adjustment here. *(Stands Mexican-American up.)*

SECRETARY: What about upkeep? Is he economical? 152

SANCHO: Well, no, I won't lie to you. The Mexican-American costs a 153
little bit more, but you get what you pay for. He's worth every extra
cent. You can keep him running on dry Martinis, Langendorf bread.

SECRETARY: Apple pie? 154

SANCHO: Only Mom's. Of course, he's also programmed to eat Mexican 155
food on ceremonial functions, but I must warn you: an overdose of
beans will plug up his exhaust.

SECRETARY: Fine! There's just one more question: HOW MUCH DO 156
YOU WANT FOR HIM?

SANCHO: Well, I tell you what I'm gonna do. Today and today only, 157 because you've been so sweet, I'm gonna let you steal this model from me! I'm gonna let you drive him off the lot for the simple price of — let's see taxes and license included — $15,000.

SECRETARY: Fifteen thousand DOLLARS? For a MEXICAN!   158

SANCHO: Mexican? What are you talking, lady? This is a Mexican-   159
AMERICAN! We had to melt down two pachucos, a farm worker and three gabachos to make this model! You want quality, but you gotta pay for it! This is no cheap run-about. He's got class!

SECRETARY: Okay, I'll take him.   160

SANCHO: You will?   161

SECRETARY: Here's your money.   162

SANCHO: You mind if I count it?   163

SECRETARY: Go right ahead.   164

SANCHO: Well, you'll get your pink slip in the mail. Oh, do you want   165
me to wrap him up for you? We have a box in the back.

SECRETARY: No, thank you. The Governor is having a luncheon this   166
afternoon, and we need a brown face in the crowd. How do I drive him?

SANCHO: Just snap your fingers. He'll do anything you want.   167

(Secretary snaps. Mexican-American steps forward.)

MEXICAN-AMERICAN: RAZA QUERIDA, ¡VAMOS LEVANTANDO AR-   168
MAS PARA LIBERARNOS DE ESTOS DESGRACIADOS GABA-
CHOS QUE NOS EXPLOTAN! VAMOS.[17]

SECRETARY: What did he say?   169

SANCHO: Something about lifting arms, killing white people, etc.   170

SECRETARY: But he's not supposed to say that!   171

SANCHO: Look, lady, don't blame me for bugs from the factory. He's   172
your Mexican-American; you bought him, now drive him off the lot!

SECRETARY: But he's broken!   173

SANCHO: Try snapping another finger.   174

(Secretary snaps. Mexican-American comes to life again.)

MEXICAN-AMERICAN: ¡ESTA GRAN HUMANIDAD HA DICHO BASTA!   175
Y SE HA PUESTO EN MARCHA! ¡BASTA! ¡BASTA! ¡VIVA LA RAZA!
¡VIVA LA CAUSA! ¡VIVA LA HUELGA! ¡VIVAN LOS BROWN BE-
RETS! ¡VIVAN LOS ESTUDIANTES! ¡CHICANO POWER![18]

---

[17]*RAZA QUERIDA, . . . VAMOS:* "Beloved Raza, let's pick up arms to liberate ourselves from those damned whites that exploit us! Let's go."

[18]*ESTA GRAN . . . CHICANO POWER:* "This great mass of humanity has said enough! And it begins to march! Enough! Enough! Long live La Raza! Long live the Cause! Long live the strike! Long live the Brown Berets! Long live the students! Chicano Power!

(The Mexican-American turns toward the Secretary, who gasps and backs up. He keeps turning toward the Pachuco, Farm Worker, and Revolucionario, snapping his fingers and turning each of them on, one by one.)

PACHUCO *(Snap. To Secretary)*: I'm going to get you, baby! ¡Viva La Raza!   176

FARM WORKER *(Snap. To Secretary)*: ¡Viva la huelga! ¡Viva la Huelga! ¡VIVA LA HUELGA!   177

REVOLUCIONARIO *(Snap. To Secretary)*: ¡Viva la revolución! ¡VIVA LA REVOLUCION!   178

(The three models join together and advance toward the Secretary who backs up and runs out of the shop screaming. Sancho is at the other end of the shop holding his money in his hand. All freeze. After a few seconds of silence, the Pachuco moves and stretches, shaking his arms and loosening up. The Farm Worker and Revolucionario do the same. Sancho stays where he is, frozen to his spot.)

JOHNNY: Man, that was a long one, ése. *(Others agree with him.)*   179

FARM WORKER: How did we do?   180

JOHNNY: Perty good, look all that lana, man! *(He goes over to Sancho and removes the money from his hand. Sancho stays where he is.)*   181

REVOLUCIONARIO: En la madre, look at all the money.   182

JOHNNY: We keep this up, we're going to be rich.   183

FARM WORKER: They think we're machines.   184

REVOLUCIONARIO: Burros.   185

JOHNNY: Puppets.   186

MEXICAN-AMERICAN: The only thing I don't like is — how come I always got to play the godamn Mexican-American?   187

JOHNNY: That's what you get for finishing high school.   188

FARM WORKER: How about our wages, ése?   189

JOHNNY: Here it comes right now. $3,000 for you, $3,000 for you, $3,000 for you, and $3,000 for me. The rest we put back into the business.   190

MEXICAN-AMERICAN: Too much, man. Heh, where you vatos going tonight?   191

FARM WORKER: I'm going over to Concha's. There's a party.   192

JOHNNY: Wait a minute, vatos. What about our salesman? I think he needs an oil job.   193

REVOLUCIONARIO: Leave him to me.   194

(The Pachuco, Farm Worker, and Mexican-American exit, talking loudly about their plans for the night. The Revolucionario goes over to Sancho, removes his derby hat and cigar, lifts him up and throws him over his shoulder. Sancho hangs loose, lifeless.)

REVOLUCIONARIO *(To audience)*: He's the best model we got! ¡Ajua! 195
(Exit.)

(End.)

Engaging the Text

1. Who is Honest Sancho? Who would buy his products? What is Valdez saying about American society through this CHARACTER?

2. What is the point of the discussion about Ms. Jiménez's name? What does she want, and what does she represent in the play?

3. Whom does Valdez attack in the play, and how? How can you be sure of Valdez's position?

4. Write a short essay explaining the significance of the play's conclusion.

5. Why is the play primarily in English? How different would its effect be if it were entirely in English or Spanish? Who is the ideal audience for the play?

Exploring Connections

1. Explain the RATIONALE behind the scam perpetrated by the four Chicanos in *Los Vendidos* and the grandfather's advice to the NARRATOR in Ralph Ellison's *Invisible Man*.

Extending the Critical Context

1. Working in groups, classify the common STEREOTYPES for another group (for example, college students — by major or by living group; residents of your city; members of a different ETHNIC group). In what ways do these stereotypes oversimplify or distort reality? To extend the assignment, write an essay comparing and contrasting the stereotyped image of the group to its reality as you know it.

2. Describe the characters and plot of the play if you were to rewrite it for an Asian or black audience.

Three Thousand Dollar Death Song

WENDY ROSE

*Many Native American authors have noted and decried the tendency
to treat their heritage as something dead and gone, something to be
studied like the fossil record of extinct animals. Rose's poem is a proud
song of protest against this dehumanization. Wendy Rose (b. 1948) is a
half-Hopi poet and visual artist as well as a lecturer at the University
of California, Berkeley in Native American studies. Besides illustrating
numerous books and journals, she has published several books of poetry
and contributed to many anthologies, sometimes under the pseudonym
Chiron Khanshendel.*

> Nineteen American Indian Skeletons from Nevada . . . valued at
> $3000 . . .
>
> — MUSEUM INVOICE, 1975

Is it in cold hard cash? the kind
that dusts the insides of men's pockets
lying silver-polished surface along the cloth.
Or in bills? papering the wallets of they
who thread the night with dark words. Or   5
checks? paper promises weighing the same
as words spoken once on the other side
of the grown grass and dammed rivers
of history. However it goes, it goes
Through my body it goes   10
assessing each nerve, running its edges
along my arteries, planning ahead
for whose hands will rip me
into pieces of dusty red paper,
whose hands will smooth or smatter me   15
into traces of rubble. Invoiced now,
it's official how our bones are valued
that stretch out pointing to sunrise
or are flexed into one last foetal bend,
that are removed and tossed about,   20
catalogued, numbered with black ink
on newly-white foreheads.

As we were formed to the white soldier's voice,
so we explode under white students' hands.
Death is a long trail of days   25
in our fleshless prison.

From this distant point we watch our bones
auctioned with our careful beadwork,
our quilled medicine bundles, even the bridles
of our shot-down horses. You: who have   30
priced us, you who have removed us: at what cost?
What price the pits where our bones share
a single bit of memory, how one century
turns our dead into specimens, our history
into dust, our survivors into clowns.   35
Our memory might be catching, you know;
picture the mortars, the arrowheads, the labrets[1]
shaking off their labels like bears
suddenly awake to find the seasons have ended
while they slept. Watch them touch each other,   40
measure reality, march out the museum door!
Watch as they lift their faces
and smell about for us; watch our bones rise
to meet them and mount the horses once again!
The cost, then, will be paid   45
for our sweetgrass-smelling having-been
in clam shell beads and steatite,[2]
dentalia[3] and woodpecker scalp, turquoise
and copper, blood and oil, coal
and uranium, children, a universe   50
of stolen things.

[1] *labrets:* ornaments of wood or bone worn in holes pierced through the lip.
[2] *steatite:* a soft, easily carved stone; soapstone.
[3] *dentalia:* a type of mollusk shell resembling a tooth.

Engaging the Text

1. What do the Indian skeletons mentioned in the EPIGRAPH represent?

2. How do time, place, and POINT OF VIEW shift in the poem? How do these
shifts contribute to the poem's meaning?

3. What is the "distant point" Rose mentions in the second STANZA?

4. What item seems unusual or out of place in the catalogue of "stolen things" that ends the poem? Why does Rose include it in the list? In what way were all these things stolen from the Indians?

Exploring Connections

1. Playing the roles of Rose and Frederick Jackson Turner (Chapter One, "American Dreams"), debate the benefits and the costs of frontier settlement.

Extending the Critical Context

1. Play the role of museum director. Write a letter to the Reno *Times* explaining and defending the purchase of the skeletons. Make up any circumstances you think plausible. As an extra, separate step, you may wish to evaluate the effectiveness of your defense.

Lynching at the Curve
IDA B. WELLS

This selection from The Autobiography of Ida B. Wells *documents a lynching in Memphis in 1892 and the responses of the black community there — a streetcar boycott and mass migration westward. As the passages make clear, Wells (1869–1931) was a journalist and a prominent opponent of lynching. In fact, she fled Memphis, where she was editor and co-owner of the weekly* Free Speech, *after exposing the lynching described below. She continued her crusade by writing from New York and Chicago and remained an important spokesperson for black Americans. The excerpt provides a glimpse of the historical roots of the modern civil rights movement and highlights a neglected aspect of frontier settlement.*

While I was thus carrying on the work of my newspaper, happy in   1
the thought that our influence was helpful and that I was doing the work
I loved and had proved that I could make a living out of it, there came
the lynching in Memphis which changed the whole course of my life.
I was on one of my trips away from home. I was busily engaged in

Natchez when word came of the lynching of three men in Memphis. It came just as I had demonstrated that I could make a living by my newspaper and need never tie myself down to school teaching.

Thomas Moss, Calvin McDowell, and Henry Stewart owned and op- 2
erated a grocery store in a thickly populated suburb. Moss was a letter carrier and could only be at the store at night. Everybody in town knew and loved Tommie. An exemplary young man, he was married and the father of one little girl, Maurine, whose godmother I was. He and his wife Betty were the best friends I had in town. And he believed, with me, that we should defend the cause of right and fight wrong wherever we saw it.

He delivered mail at the office of the *Free Speech*, and whatever 3
Tommie knew in the way of news we got first. He owned his little home, and having saved his money he went into the grocery business with the same ambition that a young white man would have had. He was the president of the company. His partners ran the business in the daytime.

They had located their grocery in the district known as the "Curve" 4
because the streetcar line curved sharply at that point. There was already a grocery owned and operated by a white man who hitherto had had a monopoly on the trade of this thickly populated colored suburb. Thomas's grocery changed all that, and he and his associates were made to feel that they were not welcome by the white grocer. The district being mostly colored and many of the residents belonging either to Thomas's church or to his lodge, he was not worried by the white grocer's hostility.

One day some colored and white boys quarreled over a game of 5
marbles and the colored boys got the better of the fight which followed. The father of the white boys whipped the victorious colored boy, whose father and friends pitched in to avenge the grown white man's flogging of a colored boy. The colored men won the fight, whereupon the white father and grocery keeper swore out a warrant for the arrest of the colored victors. Of course the colored grocery keepers had been drawn into the dispute. But the case was dismissed with nominal fines. Then the challenge was issued that the vanquished whites were coming on Saturday night to clean out the People's Grocery Company.

Knowing this, the owners of the company consulted a lawyer and were 6
told that as they were outside the city limits and beyond police protection, they would be justified in protecting themselves if attacked. Accordingly the grocery company armed several men and stationed them in the rear of the store on that fatal Saturday night, not to attack but to repel a threatened attack. And Saturday night was the time when men of both races congregated in their respective groceries.

About ten o'clock that night, when Thomas was posting his books for 7
the week and Calvin McDowell and his clerk were waiting on customers

preparatory to closing, shots rang out in the back room of the store. The men stationed there had seen several white men stealing through the rear door and fired on them without a moment's pause. Three of these men were wounded, and others fled and gave the alarm.

Sunday morning's paper came out with lurid headlines telling how 8 officers of the law had been wounded while in the discharge of their duties, hunting up criminals whom they had been told were harbored in the People's Grocery Company, this being "a low dive in which drinking and gambling were carried on: a resort of thieves and thugs." So ran the description in the leading white journals of Memphis of this successful effort of decent black men to carry on a legitimate business. The same newspaper told of the arrest and jailing of the proprietor of the store and many of the colored people. They predicted that it would go hard with the ringleaders if these "officers" should die. The tale of how the peaceful homes of that suburb were raided on that quiet Sunday morning by police pretending to be looking for others who were implicated in what the papers had called a conspiracy, has been often told. Over a hundred colored men were dragged from their homes and put in jail on suspicion.

All day long on that fateful Sunday white men were permitted in the 9 jail to look over the imprisoned black men. Frenzied descriptions and hearsays were detailed in the papers, which fed the fires of sensationalism. Groups of white men gathered on the street corners and meeting places to discuss the awful crime of Negroes shooting white men.

There had been no lynchings in Memphis since the Civil War, but 10 the colored people felt that anything might happen during the excitement.[1] Many of them were in business there. Several times they had elected a member of their race to represent them in the legislature in Nashville. And a Negro, Lymus Wallace, had been elected several times as a member of the city council and we had had representation on the school board several times. Mr. Fred Savage was then our representative on the board of education.

The manhood which these Negroes represented went to the county 11 jail and kept watch Sunday night.[2] This they did also on Monday night,

[1]There had been a riot, however, in 1866, in which forty-four Negroes and two whites were killed. Gerald M. Capers, Jr., *The Biography of a River Town: Memphis; Its Heroic Age* (Chapel Hill: University of North Carolina Press, 1939), pp. 177, 178. [Author's note]
[2]"The Tennessee Rifles guarded the jail for three nights." Interview with Thomas Jackson of Chicago, Illinois, who was a young man then and remembered vividly the events of the lynching and subsequent events on 14 August 1892. "The court . . . ordered the sheriff to take charge of the arms of the Tennessee Rifles, a Negro guard, whose armory is near Hernando and Union Streets." See also the *Memphis Commercial*, 10 March 1892. [Author's note]

guarding the jail to see that nothing happened to the colored men during this time of race prejudice, while it was thought that the wounded white men would die. On Tuesday following, the newspapers which had fanned the flame of race prejudice announced that the wounded men were out of danger and would recover. The colored men who had guarded the jail for two nights felt that the crisis was past and that they need not guard the jail the third night.

While they slept a body of picked men was admitted to the jail, which was a modern Bastille.[3] This mob took out of their cells Thomas Moss, Calvin McDowell, and Henry Stewart, the three officials of the People's Grocery Company. They were loaded on a switch engine of the railroad which ran back of the jail, carried a mile north of the city limits, and horribly shot to death. One of the morning papers held back its edition in order to supply its readers with the details of that lynching.

From its columns was gleaned the above information, together with details which told that "It is said that Tom Moss begged for his life for the sake of his wife and child and his unborn baby"; that when asked if he had anything to say, told them to "tell my people to go West — there is no justice for them here"; that Calvin McDowell got hold of one of the guns of the lynchers and because they could not loosen his grip a shot was fired into his closed fist. When the three bodies were found, the fingers of McDowell's right hand had been shot to pieces and his eyes were gouged out. This proved that the one who wrote that news report was either an eyewitness or got the facts from someone who was.[4]

The shock to the colored people who knew and loved both Moss and McDowell was beyond description. Groups of them went to the grocery and elsewhere and vented their feelings in talking among themselves, but they offered no violence. Word was brought to the city hall that Negroes were massing at the "Curve" where the grocery had been located. Immediately an order was issued by the judge of the criminal court sitting on the bench, who told the sheriff to "take a hundred men, go out to the Curve at once, and shoot down on sight any Negro who appears to be making trouble."

The loafers around the courts quickly spread the news, and gangs of them rushed into the hardware stores, armed themselves, boarded the cars and rushed out to the Curve. They obeyed the judge's orders literally and shot into any group of Negroes they saw with as little compunction

---

[3]*Bastille:* a castle-like fortress built in Paris in 1369 and used as a prison until destroyed in 1789 during the French Revolution; its destruction is commemorated on Bastille Day, July 14.

[4]Interview with Thomas Jackson of Chicago, Illinois, p. 1. [Author's note]

as if they had been on a hunting trip. The only reason hundreds of Negroes were not killed on that day by the mobs was because of the forebearance of the colored men. They realized their helplessness and submitted to outrages and insults for the sake of those depending upon them.

This mob took possession of the People's Grocery Company, helping themselves to food and drink, and destroyed what they could not eat or steal. The creditors had the place closed and a few days later what remained of the stock was sold at auction. Thus, with the aid of the city and county authorities and the daily papers, that white grocer had indeed put an end to his rival Negro grocer as well as to his business. 16

As said before, I was in Natchez, Mississippi, when the worst of this horrible event was taking place. Thomas Moss had already been buried before I reached home. Although stunned by the events of that hectic week, the *Free Speech* felt that it must carry on. Its leader for that week said: 17

> The city of Memphis has demonstrated that neither character nor standing avails the Negro if he dares to protect himself against the white man or become his rival. There is nothing we can do about the lynching now, as we are out-numbered and without arms. The white mob could help itself to ammunition without pay, but the order was rigidly enforced against the selling of guns to Negroes. There is therefore only one thing left that we can do; save our money and leave a town which will neither protect our lives and property, nor give us a fair trial in the courts, but takes us out and murders us in cold blood when accused by white persons.

This advice of the *Free Speech*, coupled with the last words of Thomas Moss, was taken up and reechoed among our people throughout Memphis. Hundreds disposed of their property and left. Rev. R. N. Countee and Rev. W. A. Brinkley, both leading pastors, took their whole congregations with them as they, too, went West. Memphis had never seen such an upheaval among colored people. Business was practically at a standstill, for the Negro was famous then, as now, for spending his money for fine clothes, furniture, jewelry, and pianos and other musical instruments, to say nothing of good things to eat. Music houses had more musical instruments, sold on the installment plan, thrown back on their hands than they could find storage for. Housewives found a hitherto unknown scarcity of help and resorted to the expedient of paying their servants only half the wages due them at the end of the week. 18

Six weeks after the lynching the superintendent and treasurer of the City Railway Company came into the office of the *Free Speech* and asked 19 us to use our influence with the colored people to get them to ride on the streetcars again. When I asked why they came to us the reply was that colored people had been their best patrons, but that there had been a marked falling off of their patronage. There were no jim crow[5] streetcars in Memphis then. I asked what they thought was the cause. They said they didn't know. They had heard Negroes were afraid of electricity, for Memphis already had streetcars run by electricity in 1892. They wanted us to assure our people that there was no danger and to tell them that any discourtesy toward them would be punished severely.

But I said that I couldn't believe it, because "electricity has been the [20] motive power here for over six months and you are just now noticing the slump. How long since you have observed the change?" "About six weeks," said one of them. "You see it's a matter of dollars and cents with us. If we don't look after the loss and remedy the cause the company will get somebody else who will."

"So your own job then depends on Negro patronage?" I asked. And [21] although their faces flushed over the question they made no direct reply. "You see it is like this," said the superintendent. "When the company installed electricity at a cost of thousands of dollars last fall, Negro labor got a large share of it in wages in relaying tracks, grading the streets, etc. And so we think it is only fair that they should give us their patronage in return."

Said I, "They were doing so until six weeks ago, yet you say you don't [22] know the cause of the falling off. Why, it was just six weeks ago that the lynching took place." "But the streetcar company had nothing to do with the lynching," said one of the men. "It is owned by northern capitalists." "And run by southern lynchers," I retorted. "We have learned that every white man of any standing in town knew of the plan and consented to the lynching of our boys. Did you know Tom Moss, the letter carrier?" "Yes," he replied.

"A finer, cleaner man than he never walked the streets of Memphis," [23] I said. "He was well liked, a favorite with everybody; yet he was murdered with no more consideration than if he had been a dog, because he as a man defended his property from attack. The colored people feel that every white man in Memphis who consented to his death is as guilty as those who fired the guns which took his life, and they want to get away from this town.

"We told them the week after the lynching to save their nickels and [24]

[5] *jim crow:* refers to laws that sanctioned racial discrimination in the South by mandating "separate but equal" institutions and accommodations for blacks and whites.

dimes so that they could do so. We had no way of knowing that they were doing so before this, as I have walked more than I ever did in my life before. No one has been arrested or punished about that terrible affair nor will they be because all are equally guilty."

"Why don't the colored people find the guilty ones?" asked one of 25 them. "As if they could. There is strong belief among us that the criminal court judge himself was one of the lynchers. Suppose we had the evidence; could we get it before that judge? Or a grand jury of white men who had permitted it to be? Or force the reporter of the *Appeal* to tell what he saw and knows about that night? You know very well that we are powerless to do any of these things."

"Well we hope you will do what you can for us and if you know of 26 any discourtesy on the part of our employees let us know and we will be glad to remedy it."

When they left the office I wrote this interview for the next issue of 27 the *Free Speech* and in the article told the people to keep up the good work. Not only that, I went to the two largest churches in the city the next Sunday, before the paper came out, and told them all about it. I urged them to keep on staying off the cars.

Every time word came of people leaving Memphis, we who were left 28 behind rejoiced. Oklahoma was about to be opened up, and scores sold or gave away property, shook Memphis dust off their feet, and went out West as Tom Moss had said for us to do.

Engaging the Text

1. Outline the key events of this reading passage. Then discuss the extent to which different people in the excerpt are motivated by the following:

peer pressure	self-preservation/self-promotion
moral/ethical grounds	sense of duty
economic motives	ignorance/mistaken assumptions

Overall, what seems most important to the black men, to the white men, and to Wells?

2. Identify the various Memphis "institutions" mentioned by Wells: the courts, the church, the press, and so on. Then analyze them: How do they function, whom do they serve, which are most powerful, and which are most culpable in the murders?

3. What different kinds of progress had the black community made before the lynching? Were these accomplishments entirely lost after the lynching? Do not limit yourself to considering economic gains.

Exploring Connections

1. Review the essay by James Boggs earlier in this chapter. How would he explain the lynching?
2. What specific details of Thomas Moss's life could be interpreted as attempts to achieve some version of the American Dream, as described in Chapter One? Does Moss's life end tragically for any reason other than his color?
3. To what extent do the black pioneers who left Memphis for Oklahoma in the aftermath of the lynching fit Frederick Jackson Turner's THESIS (excerpted in Chapter One, "American Dreams") about the function of the American West?

Extending the Critical Context

1. Write an imaginary dialogue between one of the black pioneers in Oklahoma and a Native American displaced by the opening of the territory to settlers.

Mary Tsukamoto

JOHN TATEISHI

Following the bombing of Pearl Harbor, many military and government officials feared that the presence of Japanese-Americans threatened the security of the war effort on the West Coast. On February 19, 1942, President Franklin D. Roosevelt signed Executive Order 9066, authorizing the secretary of war to exclude "any or all" persons from designated "military areas." As a result, over a hundred twenty thousand Japanese-Americans, most of them U.S. citizens, were forced to leave their homes and businesses on the west coast and travel to inland prison camps. This selection describes how these events wrenched apart the Japanese-American community in one rural California town.

Mary Tsukamoto (b. 1915) has coauthored We the People: A History of Internment in America *(1987). Her narrative appears in an oral history of the detention camps. The editor, John Tateishi, was himself relocated as a child and has been active in the national movement seeking redress for the victims of the internment.*

I was born in San Francisco. My parents came from Okinawa and had 1
the Capitol Laundry on Geary Street, where I lived when I was very
little. Then my father moved to Turlock. When I was ten, he moved
his family to Florin to raise strawberries, and became one of the bigger
strawberry farmers there. From ten on I grew up in Florin, where I
had the shock of attending the Florin Elementary School, because a few
years before we arrived, the school was segregated. Until then we hadn't
really encountered that kind of prejudice. Everyone whispered, and you
felt kind of ashamed and afraid, and it made you kind of tighten up your
body.

When Al and I were married, we became members of the Florin 2
JACL[1] which was organized in 1935. In 1939 we decided we wanted to
do something for the community. So we wondered if we couldn't ask
the school trustees and the county superintendent if the school might
be integrated. Surprisingly, the superintendent didn't object, and the
trustees and the principal were agreeable. So the segregated school lasted
about fifteen years, from 1923 to 1939.

We went to Elk Grove High School, which was not segregated, but 3
it was an experience to come out of a school where there were only
Japanese children and then go on to Elk Grove High School. It was a
traumatic experience for many of us who were very sensitive during
those teenage years. I remember how we meekly walked around and
we huddled together, and very reluctantly responded to invitations to
various activities. But as we developed, amazingly, the boys who were
athletic got involved, and they were more popular. But the kids who
weren't very athletic often got beat up. The Manchurian crisis[2] was in
the news then and caused many of the kids to get into fights. Some of
the teachers were trying to help us develop better feeling among the
students, but it wasn't very easy because the community went along
with a strong Native Sons and Daughters of the Golden West organization.
Everyone was affected by their propaganda.

I remember we had an annual oratorical contest sponsored by the 4
Native Sons and Daughters, and I ended up one of the nine qualifying
competitors. Then the principal and the teacher called me in and told
me that I couldn't be in it because of my ancestry. I was relieved I
didn't have to do another oration, but the teacher didn't let me forget.
She was upset and so discouraged that the Native Sons wouldn't change

[1]*JACL:* the Japanese American Citizens League — a human and civil rights organization
representing over 30,000 Americans of Japanese ancestry.

[2]*Manchurian crisis:* the Japanese invasion and occupation of Manchuria, a territory in
northeast China.

their position. She was really angry because it was a whole class assignment, given to every one of the children who took public speaking. That they would discriminate made her very angry, but she couldn't do anything about it. She was the one that was responsible in getting me to college because of that experience — to the College of the Pacific. I graduated from high school in 1933. That teacher was poor herself, but before my dad knew anything about it, she had arranged to get me a $150 scholarship. She even had to go and ask Dad if he would let me go and not help at home because every child was needed for the strawberries at that time. Every child and everybody in the family worked together to eke out a living. My dad was so deeply touched, of course, he let me go.

But there were other things he had learned about this country too. 5 He was chased out of Turlock, where there was a great deal of anti-Japanese sentiment. He had always had a difficult time because he didn't know the language. There was a time when the Japanese farmers lost a lot of money because they couldn't even write contracts, and they lost a lot of money by verbal agreements. And all of this was part of what he remembered, but also he remembered this wonderful teacher who got me to college. That's how I ended up being a schoolteacher, and for that I feel very grateful.

Florin was an unusual community because more than 60 percent were 6 Japanese people who were farming. There were also a lot of Japanese townspeople working in the basket factory or cover factory. They would work in the fields as laborers during the harvest season but lived in the town of Florin the rest of the time. Altogether there were 2,500 Japanese people making a living here, depending on each other. We raised strawberries, and then in the fall we harvested grapes.

Way back in 1892, when Grandpa Tsukamoto, Al's father, came to 7 Florin for the first time, he already found Mr. Nakayama growing straw-berries. He had figured out a way of making the patches just so wide so he could also nurture the new young grapevines. They realized that it took four or five years for the grapes to start producing. But in the meantime they were able to harvest strawberries to make a living, and so, by combining the two crops, they managed to survive.

Anyway, because grape growing was a very profitable way of making 8 a living, the white owners were very happy to have the Japanese farmers come into this area. This is how Florin grew, and by 1942 we had a very large Japanese colony. It was sort of a mistake beyond our control. There were too many Japanese compared to the Caucasian people. I found out that sociologists said it was a mistake to overpopulate with a foreign group that should be in the minority if we were to work together happily. But that wasn't so here. We had no control over it, because we were encouraged to come, and we were welcomed by the landowners. But some people around us didn't quite like what was happening. They were afraid and spoke out. The Native Sons and Daughters and the American Legion and the California Federation of Labor and the Hearst papers and the McClatchy papers all claimed that the Japanese were going to own all of California, that we were going to take over the land. So, many people decided that they wanted to try to get us out. Publicity would periodically appear in the papers, and the campaign seemed to hit us every election year. Prejudice was deliberately manufactured, and people had to work hard to create and stir it up. We were innocent victims, but we have to understand this background if we are to understand what happened when the war broke out.

I remember some of the boys. We just knew when we were walking 9 home from school that they would throw stones at us and call us Japs, but we just couldn't do anything back. The thing is, when the legislature was working on the alien land law in Sacramento, a small group of white landowners who were very kind and friends to Japanese were alarmed at what was going to happen. They tried to go to protest, but they weren't given an opportunity to speak in favor of the Japanese. It just wasn't the popular thing to do. They were very disappointed that they weren't given a chance to be heard and tried to get it into the papers. But, of course, with McClatchy and Hearst, they just didn't have a chance.

I do remember Pearl Harbor day. I was about twenty-seven, and we 10 were in church. It was a December Sunday, so we were getting ready for our Christmas program. We were rehearsing and having Sunday School class, and I always played the piano for the adult Issei[3] service. Of course, because there were so many Japanese, all of it was in Japanese; the minister was a Japanese, and he preached in Japanese. But after the service started, my husband ran in. He had been home that day and heard on the radio. We just couldn't believe it, but he told us that Japan attacked Pearl Harbor. I remember how stunned we were. And suddenly the whole world turned dark. We started to speak in whispers, and because of our experience in Florin, we immediately sensed something terrible was going to happen. We just prayed that it wouldn't, but we sensed the things would be very difficult. The minister and all of the leaders discussed matters, and we knew that we needed to be prepared for the worst.

Then, of course, within a day or two, we heard that the FBI had taken 11

[3]*Issei:* a first-generation Japanese immigrant, as distinguished from a second-generation Japanese-American, or a Nisei.

Mr. Tanigawa and Mr. Tsuji. I suppose the FBI had them on their list, and it wasn't long before many of them were taken. We had no idea what they were going through. We should have been more aware. One Issei, Mr. Iwasa, committed suicide. So all of these reports and the anguish and the sorrow made the whole world very dark. Then rumors had it that we were supposed to turn in our cameras and our guns, and they were called in. Every day there was something else about other people being taken by the FBI. Then gradually we just couldn't believe the newspapers and what people were saying. And then there was talk about sending us away, and we just couldn't believe that they would do such a thing. It would be a situation where the whole community would be uprooted. But soon enough we were reading reports of other communities being evacuated from San Pedro and from Puget Sound. After a while we became aware that maybe things weren't going to just stop but would continue to get worse and worse.

We read about President Roosevelt's Executive Order 9066. I remember   12
the JACL people had a convention in San Francisco in March. We realized that we needed to be able to rise to the occasion to help in whatever way we could in our community. We came home trying to figure out just how we could do that. We had many meetings at night and the FBI was always lurking around. We were told we couldn't stay out after eight o'clock in the evening.

Meanwhile, Hakujin [white] neighbors were watching us and reporting   13
to the FBI that we were having secret meetings. We were not supposed to meet after eight o'clock, but often we couldn't cut off our JACL meeting at eight o'clock, and so we would have tea or coffee and keep talking. We would be reported, and the police would come. There were so many people making life miserable for us. Then we heard that we had been restricted to traveling five miles from our homes; it was nine miles to Sacramento, and at that time everything was in Sacramento, like doctors, banks, and grocery stores. So it just was a terrible, fearful experience. Every time we went anywhere more than five miles away, we were supposed to go to the WCCA office in Sacramento, nine miles away, to get a permit. It was ridiculous.

A lot of little things just nagged at us and harassed us, and we were   14
frightened, but even in that atmosphere I remember we frantically wanted to do what was American. We were Americans and loyal citizens, and we wanted to do what Americans should be doing. So we were wrapping Red Cross bandages and trying to do what we could to help our country. By May 1942, more than a hundred of our boys were already drafted. We worried about them, and they were worried about what was going to happen to their families. We knew what we wanted to do. We started

to buy war bonds, and we took first aid classes with the rest of the Hakujin people in the community. We went out at night to go to these classes, but we worried about being out after eight o'clock. It was a frightening time. Every little rule and regulation was imposed only on the Japanese people. There were Italian and German people in the community, but it was just us that had travel restrictions and a curfew.

And we were still trying to think about how we could serve the 15 community. I finally opened a JACL office near the end of March, and I was running in and out of the Wartime Civilian Control Administration (WCCA) office. They finally decided to send some people out to work with me to advise me and the welfare office and the Federal Reserve Bank and the Farm Security Agency. They were to help the people who were asking questions and trying to get ready for this terrible ordeal that was ahead of them. Not knowing for sure, many of them kept hoping and wishing that we would not have to go, that somehow things would change and we wouldn't have to leave.

We tried to get everybody instructions, and the WCCA would tell 16 me one thing one day, and I would then tell everybody this is what we're going to need to do, and then the next week the whole regulation was changed, and we just ended up being liars right and left. It was such a state of confusion and anger, everyone being so upset at what was happening. I remember I was crying inside and I just felt like I was put through a hamburger machine. I was human and worried and scared for myself too, but worried about everybody else and trying to help people.

I remember Ida Onga. Her husband was taken by the FBI, and she 17 came in here so big; she was going to have a baby in a month or so. She cried because she was supposed to go and see the doctor, and she didn't know that she had to have a traveler's permit. She had come from Folsom and had traveled more than five miles. I needed to get her into town so she could get to the doctor, and so I took her to the WCCA office for a travel permit. There we found out that Mrs. Tsuji's husband was taken away by the FBI. But nobody thought about the family left behind needing food and money. We finally arranged for the WCCA welfare office to provide food, and she cried because Japanese people are proud and they weren't willing to accept handouts. They never had been on welfare before, and she felt terrible because here she ended up receiving food. But we told her this was different, because her husband was taken and because it's what you have to do. She had three children. These things were happening.

I remember Mrs. Kuima, whose son was thirty-two years old and 18 retarded. She took care of him. They had five other boys, but she took care of this boy at home. The welfare office said No, she couldn't take him, that the families have to institutionalize a child like that. It was a very tragic thing for me to have to tell her, and I remember going out to the field — she was hoeing strawberries — and I told her what they told us, that you can't take your son with you. And so she cried, and I cried with her. A few days before they were evacuated they came to take him away to an institution. It was very hard for me to face that family. I felt as though I was the messenger that carried such tragic news for them. It was only about a month after we got to Fresno Assembly Center that they sent us a wire saying he died. All these years she loved him and took care of him, he only knew Japanese and ate Japanese food. I was thinking of the family; they got over it quietly; they endured it. I just felt guilty, you know, just for having been involved.

I had anxieties for Grandpa and Grandma. They were old and had 19 farmed all their lives, and after more than fifty years here, the thought of uprooting these people and taking them away from their farm and the things they loved was terrible. Grandpa growing tea and vegetables, and Grandma growing her flowers. It was a cruel thing to do to them in their twilight years. But we had to get them ready to leave, anxious for their health and their safety. And my daughter, who was five, had to be ready to go to school. Al had had a hemorrhage that winter, so we all had our personal grief as well.

The Farm Security Administration (FSA) told us that we should work 20 until the very last moment. Yet we had to worry about selling our car and our refrigerator and about what we should do with our chickens and our pets. And we worried about trying to buy the right kind of things to get ready for a place we knew nothing about. We thought about camping. They said "camp," so we thought about going up in the mountains somewhere. I even bought boots thinking we would be up in the mountains where there might be snakes. Just ridiculous all the funny things we thought about!

In those days women didn't wear slacks much, but we all bought 21 them, and we were running around trying to get ourselves ready. I was busy almost to the last day at the JACL office, sending the weekly bulletins and handling the personal problems of everybody. And I wrote to the President of the United States and the principal of the high school and the newspaper editors thanking them for whatever they did for us. I don't know if I was crazy to do this, but I felt that history was happening, and I felt that it was important to say good-bye in a proper way, speaking for the people who were leaving and trying to tell our friends that we were loyal Americans and that we were sorry that this was happening. We needed to say something, and that's what I did.

We left early in the morning on May 29. Two days earlier we sold 22
our car for eight hundred dollars, which was just about giving it away.
We also had to sell our refrigerator. But some wonderful friends came
to ask if they could take care of some things we couldn't store. Mr.
Lernard, a principal of a high school, took my piano, and his daughter
took our dining table set, which was a wedding gift. They did that for
us. Other things we had to sell, and still other things we had to crate.
The Japanese community hall was declared the "federal reserve bank,"
a warehouse, and some of our things were stored there as well as in the
Buddhist Church gymnasium. So people were bringing their stuff, crating
it, stacking it up, and storing it. Some were working until the very last
minute.

A few days earlier signs had been nailed to the telephone poles saying 23
that we were to report to various spots. They told us to register as
families. We had to report to the Elk Grove Masonic Building where
we were given our family number, No. 2076. In the family I was *B* and
my husband was *A*, and we were registered. We found out we were
going to the Fresno Assembly Center.

It happened so suddenly to our community. You know, we grew up 24
together, we went through the hardships of the Depression, and then
finally things were picking up. People who had mortgages on their land
were beginning to be able to make payments back to the bank. They
were going to own the land that they had worked so hard to have. Then
we had to evacuate. So there were still some people who owed some
money on their property, and they lost the property because, of course,
they couldn't make mortgage payments.

These were our people, and we loved them. We wept with them at 25
their funerals and laughed with them and rejoiced at their weddings.
And suddenly we found out that the community was going to be split
up. The railroad track was one dividing line, and Florin Road the other
dividing line. We were going to Fresno; the ones on the other side went
to Manzanar; and the ones on the west side went to Tule. The ones on
the west and north went to Pinedale and Poston. We never dreamed
we would be separated — relatives and close friends, a community. The
village people, we were just like brothers and sisters. We endured so
much together and never dreamed we would be separated. Suddenly
we found out we wouldn't be going to the same place. That was a
traumatic disappointment and a great sadness for us. We were just tied
up in knots, trying to cope with all of this happening at once and so
fast. I can't understand why they had to do this. I don't know why they
had to split us up.

We'll never forget the shock and grief and the sorrow on top of 26
everything else that was happening to us. You know, every day we were
supposed to pick berries, and that was important, because in those days
we were barely making a living. We had to borrow ahead from companies
and stores, and we had to borrow to buy groceries until we had our
crop, and then we paid them. This is how we managed with the produce-
shipping companies too. They loaned us money ahead, advanced it. So
every day the berries being harvested and turned in was important to
us so that we could get out from under a debt. We all tried very hard
to pay our debts. If New Year's time came and we welcomed the new
year with debts, it was a shame. That was an inherent part of the culture.

At the JACL office, we handled all kinds of problems. Let's say a big 27
family came in. You can't split that family up. So we'd ask some smaller
family that had signed up earlier for a different camp if they would be
willing to go to Manzanar instead. Everybody got angry about things
like that. We urged them to go somewhere else, and some of them
didn't want to, because they were going to be separated from their
friends and relatives. That was a tragic thing, and some of us were
blamed for people being shipped to Manzanar. A lot of terrible things
were said, and we were at each other's throats. The Japanese people
were blaming me and the JACL for sending people every which way
and keeping our personal friends together.

I don't know, we had been a very happy family. When we left, we 28
swept our house and left it clean, because that's the way Japanese feel
like leaving a place. I can just imagine everyone's emotions of grief and
anger when they had to leave, when the military police (MPs) came and
told them, "Get ready right now. You've got two hours to get ready to
catch this train."

Early in the morning, Margaret and George File came after us in 29
their car because we no longer had one to move our things. We had
taken our luggage the day before on the pickup. We were very fortunate.
Al had a very dear friend, Bob Fletcher, who was going to stay at our
place and run our farm, our neighbor's farm, and Al's cousin's farm. So
these three adjoining farms would be taken care of, at least the grape
vineyards would be. Bob would stay at our place, and we left our dog
with him. Nobody could take pets, and this was a sad thing for my
daughter. There were tears everywhere; Grandma couldn't leave her
flowers, and Grandpa looked at his grape vineyard. We urged him to
get into the car and leave. I remember that sad morning when we realized
suddenly that we wouldn't be free. It was such a clear, beautiful day,
and I remember as we were driving, our tears. We saw the snow-clad

Sierra Nevada mountains that we had loved to see so often, and I thought about God and about the prayer that we often prayed.

I remember one scene very clearly: On the train, we were told not to look out the window, but people were peeking out. After a long time on the train somebody said, "Oh, there's some Japanese standing over there." So we all took a peek, and we saw this dust, and rows and rows of barracks, and all these tan, brown Japanese people with their hair all bleached. They were all standing in a huddle looking at us, looking at this train going by. Then somebody on the train said, "Gee, that must be Japanese people in a camp." We didn't realize who they were before, but I saw how terrible it looked: the dust, no trees — just barracks and a bunch of people standing against the fence, looking out. Some children were hanging onto the fence like animals, and that was my first sight of the assembly center. I was so sad and discouraged looking at that, knowing that, before long, we would be inside too. 30

As we arrived, there were all these people, peeking out from behind the fence, wondering what group would be coming next, and, of course, looking for their friends too. Suddenly you realized that human beings were being put behind fences just like on the farm where we had horses and pigs in corrals. 31

It was hot, and everybody was perspiring. We were tired from the train trip, and here they were just staring at us. It is humiliating to be stared at like that. These were *Nihonjin* ("Japanese") people staring at us, Nihonjin people. We came in dragging suitcases and luggage and all our clothing. We felt so self-conscious to be stared at, but of course I looked right back to see if I recognized anybody. My father and mother and my cousins had gone a day or two ahead of us. I was looking for them, and they came looking for us. There were joyous greetings and gladness of reunion. 32

Then we began to realize what it meant to stand in line — long hours standing for eating in the mess hall, standing in line in front of the latrine, standing in line for our bath. That was a shock, but I guess the Army's latrine is the same everywhere. For us women and children, this was something which we just couldn't . . . it was just a shock. I remember we got sick . . . we couldn't go . . . we didn't want to go. It was smelly, and it was dirty. In the shower, the water was poured over you, and there were no partitions, and it was so cramped that we almost touched each other. It was very humiliating. It sure helped when the kids had a variety show. Many were quite talented, and one night they made us all laugh, and we cried with laughter because it was so funny. There were five or six boys standing in a row, dramatizing the time when we go to the latrine. 33

I guess we needed to laugh it off like that, and soon we learned to   34
cope, and we managed to enjoy whatever we could and got busy. I
taught English to Isseis, which was a delightful experience. I also taught
public speaking. This was thrilling to me, because I found out that the
Isseis really wanted to learn something that they never had the opportunity
to learn before. Some dear old ladies and old men who could hardly
hear, hardly see, hardly hold a pencil, realized that this was a chance
to learn English. One mother said, "I want to be able to write my son
a letter. I'm always asking other people to write for me. When he's in
the service and worried, I want him to know I'm all right. I want him
to understand from my own letters that I care for him and that I am
okay."

We used unfinished buildings for temporary classrooms, and we hastily   35
tried to keep everybody busy. Soon surprising things began to happen.
The Issei ladies were making crepe-paper flowers. They were taking
classes from old Mrs. Nagao, who was a farmer's wife, brown and tanned
and wrinkled. All I knew was that she was a strawberry grower's wife,
and I knew that she could pick strawberries. Here she was a teacher of
this crepe paper flower making class.

Other hidden talents began to emerge. Everett Sasaki was in charge   36
of the victory garden. He was one of the JACL people in Florin. Quiet
little old Everett was directing that project and planting all kinds of
vegetables. Soon they were producing more than we could use at Fresno.
There were a lot of other things going on. Baseball games. Obachan
("grandmother") loved baseball, and they got busy going to baseball
games, watching baseball games. My mother and father and uncle and
aunt got busy playing Chinese checkers and things like that.

We would be just so angered because we had to wash the sheets, and   37
we had to borrow old-fashioned washboards to do it. But within a few
weeks somebody had already planted a garden. Soon somebody would
give us a little cucumber or one tomato. Before we left in October, the
whole camp was transformed. Who but Nihonjins would leave a place
like that in beauty? It was an inspiring sight. I felt proud that the
Nihonjins who had coped through the heat of the summer had faith
enough to plant a garden. We left it beautiful. Of course, it was probably
torn down quickly because it was a Fresno fairground.

That's the way we drove out of the camp. I remember seeing the   38
morning-glory vines covering the tar-paper barracks. And the sight of
just so many beautiful flowers and vegetables, so lush and green. And
we drove away knowing that even a place like that could become a part
of us, our home, because our loved ones were there.

I remember another thing. We had our Fourth of July program.   39

Because we couldn't think of anything to do, we decided to recite the Gettysburg Address as a verse choir. We had an artist draw a big picture of Abraham Lincoln with an American flag behind him. Some people had tears in their eyes; some people shook their heads and said it was so ridiculous to have that kind of thing recited in a camp. It didn't make sense, but it was our hearts' cry. We wanted so much to believe that this was a government by the people and for the people and that there was freedom and justice. So we did things like that to entertain each other, to inspire each other, to hang on to things that made sense and were right.

We were finally moved from Fresno in October 1942 to the Jerome 40 relocation camp in Arkansas. After we were there awhile, all of a sudden cold weather arrived, and they didn't have enough wood to heat the rooms. We were on the edge of the Mississippi River, the swamplands of Arkansas. We had to go into the woods to chop wood. All the men stopped everything; school, everything, was closed and the young people were told to go out and work. They brought the wood in, and the women helped to saw it. Then, of course, we can stoop so low as human beings; we get so greedy and selfish. People started to hoard wood. There wouldn't be enough for some people. I felt sorry for the block manager who had to go in and check every apartment. When we're unhappy and miserable, our sense of values and our behavior change. We can become hateful people.

In Fresno, I remember, we heard language from over the partitions, 41 language I didn't want my daughter to grow up hearing. There was talking back to parents, young people shouting, fathers shouting and angry. All of that made me hate people, and I was ashamed of being a part of a group of people who would be so hateful to each other. But after a while, we all got on each other's nerves. It was a terrible, terrible time of adjustment when we were in Fresno.

I remember Dr. Allen Hunter, who spoke to us. Some of us asked 42 him to teach us how to pray. I said we feel like hating everybody; we just can't stand so many people all around us. Wherever we go we're with everybody, and there is no privacy. He said, tomorrow morning when you get up, you just know that every single person in that camp, 5,600 people, every one of them has a halo over his head. Each one is trying to grow tall enough to fit under that halo. He said that each one of us is trying his very best to be a good person, and I never forgot that.

After all I had gone through and when I had an opportunity to speak, 43 when people asked me to tell them the story, why didn't I have the courage to tell the truth? I realized that I needed to be angry not just for myself personally, but for what happened to our people. And also for our country because I really believe it wasn't just Japanese Americans that were betrayed, but America itself. I'm saying that for the kids — for the *Yonsei* ("fourth generation") kids and for their children and their friends and all the generations that are coming. For their sakes, we need to be angry enough to do something about it so that it will never happen again. It's not anger because I'm bitter or disappointed that it happened to me. I'm disappointed for America that it had to happen, and I want the record to be straight.

I remember my daughter was five, and she cried for a whole week   44
— she cried and cried and cried. She was so upset, because she wanted to go home; she wanted to get away from camp. Adults felt the same way, but we weren't children and so could not dare to cry. I remember I always felt like I was dangling and crying deep inside, and I was hurt.

I know many Niseis who say, That was all so long ago. Let's forget   45
it and leave well enough alone. But I just say, we were the ones that went through it — the tears and the shame and the shock. We need to leave our legacy to our children. And also our legacy to America, from our tears, what we learned.

Engaging the Text

1. What does Tsukamoto mean when she says that the relocation was a betrayal of America itself?

2. Tsukamoto says that the internees' LEGACY is what they learned; what lessons do you draw from the experiences she describes?

3. Using evidence from the text to support your decisions, arrange the values of the Japanese-American community into a HIERARCHY. How do these compare to traditional American values?

Exploring Connections

1. Examine Tsukamoto's conflicting feelings toward America and toward her own people. Analyze these conflicts in light of Allport's discussion of in-groups and reference groups (p. 85).

Extending the Critical Context

1. Tsukamoto describes writing to President Roosevelt thanking him. Why do you think she did this? Write your own letter to the president expressing your feelings about his decision.

2. Check a newspaper or periodicals index and find articles about efforts to win reparation for Japanese-American citizens interned during World War II. Summarize the issues, arguments, and outcome of the debate.

We, the Dangerous
Janice Mirikitani

Janice Mirikitani (b. 1942) presents a sobering catalog of injustice, oppression, and violence that the United States has inflicted on Asian and Asian-American people. Yet this poem also celebrates the persistence, pride, and courage that have enabled them to endure. Mirikitani is a poet, choreographer, teacher, and community activist. Her latest book is a collection of poetry and prose, Shedding Silence (1987).

I swore
it would not devour me
I swore
it would not humble me
I swore   5
it would not break me.

    And they commanded we dwell in the desert
    Our children be spawn of barbed wire and barracks

We, closer to the earth,
squat, short thighed,   10
knowing the dust better.

    And they would have us make the garden
    Rake the grass to soothe their feet

We, akin to the jungle,
plotting with the snake,   15
tails shedding in civilized America.

    And they would have us skin their fish
    deft hands like blades/sliding back flesh/bloodless

We, who awake in the river
Ocean's child   20
Whale eater.

    And they would have us strange scented women,
    Round shouldered/strong and yellow/like the moon
    to pull the thread to the cloth
    to loosen their backs massaged in myth   25

We, who fill the secret bed,
the sweat shops
the laundries.

    And they would dress us in napalm,
    Skin shred to clothe the earth,   30
    Bodies filling pock marked fields.
    Dead fish bloating our harbors.

We, the dangerous,
Dwelling in the ocean.
Akin to the jungle.   35
Close to the earth.

    Hiroshima
    Vietnam
    Tule Lake[1]

And yet we were not devoured.   40
And yet we were not humbled
And yet we are not broken.

[1]*Tule Lake:* the largest of the camps where Japanese immigrants and their children were
imprisoned in the United States during World War II.

Engaging the Text

1. Who are "they," and what values and CHARACTERISTICS does Mirikitani
associate with them?

2. List the IMAGES associated with Asian people in the poem. What values and
characteristics do these images suggest, and why are they "dangerous"?

3. Discuss the significance of the shift from "I" to "we" between STANZAS 1
and 2.

4. What does the poem suggest about the social and economic status of Asians
in the United States?

Exploring Connections

1. Compare and contrast the attitudes of Mary Tsukamoto (in the preceding essay) and Mirikitani toward relocation.

2. Compare the roles of the SPEAKERS in Wendy Rose's "Three Thousand Dollar Death Song" (p. 166) and "We, the Dangerous."

3

One Nation or Many?

Immigration and Assimilation

Our identity as a nation has been shaped and reshaped by successive waves of immigration. We pay homage to the diversity of a culture whose population comes from every continent, yet many "established" Americans blame new immigrants for straining the economy or threatening traditional customs and values. Do the ethnic differences that distinguish us also divide us?

The first section of this chapter, The Immigrant Experience, weighs the historical and personal impact of immigration. Alistair Cooke offers a broad survey of European immigration to the United States in the nineteenth and early twentieth centuries. The short story that follows, by Anzia Yezierska, records the struggles of one Russian Jewish immigrant as she searches for the America of her dreams. Two poems round out this section: Joseph Bruchac's tribute to his ancestors embodies the conflict between nation-building immigrants and the tribal nations they displaced, while Dadi Piñero, in "Puerto Rico's Reply," looks at the Americanization of the land the immigrants left behind.

Ethnic Identity and Majority Culture examines assimilation, the difficult process of balancing the demands of conflicting cultural values. Milton Gordon summarizes three models of assimilation, each promoting a different relationship between the dominant society and immigrant or minority groups. In "Letter to My Mother," Vietnamese immigrant Tran Thi Nga sums up the daily gains and losses of life in a new culture. Hank López speaks as a thoroughly assimilated but still self-divided American, and Maxine Hong Kingston recalls the psychological cost of Americanization — an experience that left her silent for a year as she fought American-style schooling and the English language. "Para Teresa," Inés Hernández's powerful bilingual poem, counterpoints Gordon's essay by offering two models of response to the forces of assimilation. Finally, Kwame Toure argues that American blacks, as involuntary immigrants, must reject integration for economic and political self-determination.

Before Reading . . .

Write your own family's history: begin by interviewing family members who can provide you with information on family origins. You should not only explain how and why your ancestors became residents of the United States but also describe the challenges they faced and how they met them.

The Immigrant Experience

The Huddled Masses

Alistair Cooke

From 1840 to 1920, the United States experienced an unprecedented explosion in the number of immigrants who came seeking freedom and fortune in what they saw as the land of opportunity. This chapter from Alistair Cooke's America *offers a narrative history of those tumultuous years. Originally presented in 1970 as part of the acclaimed television series of the same name, this panoramic view of the immigrant experience helps us grasp the magnitude of this first great wave of U.S. immigration and gives us insight into the motives that brought immigrants to our shores.*

An immigrant himself, Alistair Cooke (b. 1908) left his native England for the United States in 1937. As a broadcaster, commentator, and journalist, he has made a career of interpreting American institutions and American culture to the world.

"We call England the Mother country," Robert Benchley,[1] once re- 1 marked, "because most of us come from Poland or Italy." It's not quite as drastic as that, but today the chances of an American being of wholly English stock are, outside the South, no more than one in four. Only the English visitor is still surprised by this palpable fact. When a German makes his first trip across the Atlantic, he can go into almost any large city between southern Pennsylvania and the Great Lakes, and on across the prairie into the small towns of Kansas, and he will find himself among people whose physique is familiar, who share many of his values and his tastes in food and drink. The Scandinavian will be very much at home with the landscape and the farming of Minnesota, and he will not be surprised to hear that the state is represented in Congress by men named Langen and Olson and Nelsen. A Polish Catholic would easily pass as a native among the sandy potato fields, the lumbering wooden churches, and the Doroskis and Stepnoskis of eastern Long Island.

For three quarters of the population that hears itself so often hailed 2 as "the American people" are the descendants of immigrants from Asia and Africa and, most of all, from the continent of Europe. They brought over with them their religions and folkways and their national foods, not least their national prejudices, which for a long time in the new country turned the cities of the Northeast and the Midwest into adjoining compounds of chauvinists, distrustful not only of immigrants from other nations everywhere but too often of their neighbors three or four blocks away.

But even the most clannish of them sooner or later had to mix with 3 the peoples already there and learn among other things a new kind of politics, in which the dominant power went to men who knew how to balance the needs of one national group against another. The American delicatessen became an international store for the staples that the old immigrant could not do without. Few American children, certainly in the cities, need to be told that goulash comes from Hungary, liverwurst from Germany, borscht from Russia, and lasagne from Italy. And even

---

[1] *Robert Benchley:* American humorist (1889–1945).

Gentiles who never tasted the combination probably know that lox — smoked salmon — and the doughnut-shaped rolls called bagels are as inseparable, in Jewish households of any nationality, as an Englishman's — and an Anglo-Saxon American's — bacon and eggs.

Why did they come? Why do they still come? For a mesh of reasons 4 and impulses that condition any crucial decision in life. But the most powerful was one common to most of the immigrants from the 1840s on — hard times in the homeland. They chose America because, by the early nineteenth century, Europeans, especially if they were poor, had heard that the Americans had had a revolution that successfully overthrew the old orders of society. Madame de Staël[2] could tell a Boston scholar, in 1817, "You are the advance guard of the human race." And Goethe,[3] ten years later, wrote for anybody to read: "Amerika, du hast es besser als unser Kontinent" (which may be loosely translated as: "America, you have things better over there.") He was thinking of the freedom from the binding force of "useless traditions." But people who had never heard of Madame de Staël and Goethe picked up the new belief that there was a green land far away preserved "from robbers, knights and ghosts afrighting." Whenever life could hardly be worse at home, they came to believe that life was better in America.

In Ireland in the middle 1840s human life had touched bottom. Ironically, 5 two causes of the Irish plight came *from* America. The rising competition of American agriculture made thousands of very small farmers (300,000 of Ireland's 685,000 farms had less than three acres) shift from tillage to grazing, on barren ground. And the potato blight, which was to putrefy vast harvests in a few weeks, had crossed the Atlantic from America in 1845. Within five years the potato famine had claimed almost a million Irish lives, over twenty thousand of them dropping in the fields from starvation.

The young Queen Victoria was informed that the state of Ireland was 6 "alarming" and that the country was so full of "inflammable matter" that it could explode in rebellion. So she paid a royal visit, serenely admired the beauty of the scenery, and was relieved that the people "received us with the greatest enthusiasm." Nevertheless, at Kingston and at Cork she noted: "You see more ragged and wretched people here than I ever saw anywhere else." One of those ragged people could well have been

[2]*Madame de Staël:* Swiss-French writer (1766–1817), remembered for her literary criticism, novels, and flamboyant life.
[3]*Goethe:* Johann Wolfgang von Goethe, German poet, philosopher, scientist, and dramatist (1749–1832), famous as the author of *Faust*.

a bankrupt farmer from Wexford County who had gone to Cork. Most such, with any energy left over after the famine, retreated to the towns and either joined sedition societies or headed for America. This one chose America, and, like very many of the Irish who came after, his destination was chosen for him by the simple fact that Boston was the end of the Cunard line. His name was Patrick Kennedy, great-grandfather of the thirty-fifth President of the United States. He was one of the 1,700,000 Irish — a little less than one quarter of the whole population when the famine began — who left for America in the 1840s and 1850s.

Hunger, then, was the spur in Ireland. There were other, equally   7
fearful incentives. In the single year of 1848 political storms swept across Europe — in Austria, an abdication, arrests, and executions; in Italy, a revolution and a declaration of war by the Pope against Austria; in Sicily, an uprising against the King of Naples; in Germany, a liberal revolution that failed. Both then and throughout the rest of the century and on into our own, in any troubled country, whether or not its mischief could be laid to known culprits, there was always the ancient scapegoat of the Jew. In eastern and central Europe the ghettos had long been routine targets for the recruiting sergeant and the secret police, and their inhabitants were acquainted from childhood with what one of them called "the stoniest sound in the world: the midnight knock on the door." It would be hard to calculate but easy to guess at the millions of American Jews whose forefathers were harried and haunted by these persecutors. It is something hardly thought of by most of us who came here by free choice, or were born here without ever having to make a choice.

In some cities of Europe, Jews were permitted to practice their religion   8
in compounds. But in many more places, where the Jews had been systematically vilified for fifteen hundred years, authorities considered their rituals to be as sinister as black magic, and the more daring or devout worshiped in stealth. In America, they had heard, they could worship openly in their own fashion, Orthodox, Reform, Conservative — or, as radical Reconstructionists, they could look to the United States as a permitted rallying ground on which to muster the faithful for the return to Palestine. I dwell on the Jews because, in the great tidal wave of the late nineteenth- and early twentieth-century immigration, they were the most numerous of those who saw America as the Land of Canaan;[4] because their story offers the most dramatic and arduous exercise in the struggle to assimilate; and because, as much or more than other

[4] *Land of Canaan:* the land promised to the Israelites in the Old Testament.

peoples, they created the American polyglot metropolis against which, in 1924, the Congress protested with restrictive legislation that tried, too late, to restore the United States to its northern European origins.

So late as 1880, there were only a quarter of a million Jews in the 9 United States. By 1924 there were four and a half million, the product of a westward movement that started in the early nineteenth century with their exodus from the ghettos of eastern Europe into the new factories of western Europe. They had moved in that direction earlier throughout the Thirty Years War[5] and then after the later Cossack[6] massacres and peasant revolts. But the factory system provided them with a legal right to flee from their inferior citizenship in Germany and from pogroms[7] in Russia, Poland, and Romania. In the last quarter of the nineteenth century, both city and rural Jews were the willing quarry of emigration agents from America carrying glowing broadsides from house to house about the high wages, good clothes, abundant food, and civil liberties available in the New World. The sweet talk of these promoters might be sensibly discounted, but not the bags of mail containing "America letters" from relatives who had made the voyage and whose more practical accounts of an attainable decent life were read aloud in cottages, markets, and factories.

The word spread beyond the factories and the ghettos to the farmers 10 of southern and central Europe. And whereas before 1890 the immigrant stream had flowed out of Scandinavia, Germany, Ireland, England, and Canada, in the next thirty years the mass of immigrants came from Italy, Austria-Hungary, Russia, and again and always Ireland.

The Germans formed a strong and special current in the mainstream 11 of immigration. There were already a quarter of a million of them in the United States at the time of the Declaration of Independence, and in the thirty years between 1860 and 1890 they contributed more refugees than any other nation, among them more varied social types, more professionals, and more scholars than the others. They also settled far and wide. The German Jews, beginning as small merchants, prospered more conspicuously and founded many of the great banking families of New York. Wherever the Germans went, they tended to establish them-selves, both by superiority of talent and a marked gift of clannishness, at the head of the social hierarchy of Jewry. The Sephardic Jews[8] and

[5]*Thirty Years War:* a series of European political and religious wars (1618–1648).
[6]*Cossack:* Nineteenth-century Russian cavalryman.
[7]*pogroms:* organized persecution or attacks on minority groups, especially Jewish settlements.
[8]*Sephardic Jews:* descendants of the Jews who settled in Spain and Portugal.

the German Jews were at the top, and at the bottom were the Lithuanians and the Hungarians, elements in a social system that discouraged intermarriage between its upper and lower strata the defiance of which has probably caused as much snobbish anguish as the love matches of Jews and Gentiles in other immigrant families.

All told, in the first two decades of this century, an unbelievable 12 fourteen and a half million immigrants arrived. They were mostly the persecuted and the poor, "the wretched refuse of your teeming shore" apostrophized by Emma Lazarus,[9] a wealthy and scholarly young lady whose poetic dramas and translations of Heine[10] are forgotten in the thunder of five lines inscribed on the Statue of Liberty. These unlettered millions were, for the most part, to become the "huddled masses" who, in the tenements of the American cities, would have quite a time of it "yearning to breathe free." They had never heard of Thomas Jefferson or George Washington. But they were the easy victims of the absurd myth that the streets of America were paved with gold — not much, perhaps, but enough to offer striking proof, in sepia photographs sent back to Poland or Hungary, of well-fed families who looked you in the eye, of a father or a cousin wearing a suit and shiny shoes, just like a doctor or a merchant in the old country.

Long before they arrived at the ports of embarkation — Constantinople, 13 Piraeus, Antwerp, Bremen — emigrant trains had started deep inside Russia. Most of them were linked box cars, sometimes with benches, the men in one car, the women and children in another. Every few hundred miles the train would be shunted on to a siding in order to pick up other new armies, of Austrians, Hungarians, Lithuanians, and finally a troop of Germans, before they came to, say, Hamburg. There they were corralled and checked to see if they had the three essential passports to America: an exit paper, twenty-five spare dollars to prevent their becoming a public charge, and the price of the passage. By the 1890s lively rate wars between steamship lines had halved the steerage fare from about twenty dollars to ten. In an enclosure outside Hamburg they would be bathed, de-loused, and fed, and their baggage and clothes fumigated. Then they were ferried out to the big ship and stowed aboard, as many as nine hundred in steerage.

In the floating commune of the emigrant ship, the status symbols were 14 few but well defined. A suitcase, however battered, was most likely the

[9]*Emma Lazarus:* American poet and essayist (1849–1887), whose sonnet, *The New Colossus,* is a tribute to the Statue of Liberty.
[10]*Heine:* Heinrich Heine, German romantic poet and essayist (1797–1856).

mark of a city man. To a poor peasant, a wicker basket was elegance enough. Most people tied everything up in a blanket or a sheet. They had brought with them what they thought to be indispensable to a decent life afloat. First, the necessity of a pillow, goose-feather, if they were lucky — a point of pride, a relic, and a symbol that some families kept throughout their lives. Village girls took along their only certain dowry, a special extra petticoat and, for formal occasions, a corset. Many of the young women were engaged to men from the home town on the other side of the Atlantic. It was well understood that the ambitious male, engaged or already married, went on ahead to stake out the fortune, which was more often the bare living that could sustain a family. Many of these engagements were broken once for all on the way over by the rude proximity of the males in steerage.

Like all travelers, both simple and sophisticated, they were deeply 15 suspicious of the other nation's food. It was a common thing to take along a cooking pot, a few raw vegetables, and a hunk of sausage or some other final reminder of the favorite snack. The religious invariably took with them the tokens of their faith, a cross or a prayer book or phylacteries;[11] and a member of a closely-knit family would cherish an heirloom yielded up in the moment of parting. It could be nothing more pretentious than a brass candlestick or a lock of hair.

For two weeks or eight days, depending on the size of the ship, they 16 sewed, played cards, sang to harmonicas or tin whistles, counted their savings, continually checked their exit papers, complained about the atrocious food and the ubiquity of the rats. The ones who could read, probably less than half the flock, recited the cheering promise of the emigrant agents' broadsides and pamphlets. The young women nursed the elders and the chronically seasick and resisted, or succumbed to, the advances of spry bachelors. There was no possibility of privacy in the swarm of steerage.

But as America came nearer, some of them suffered from nervous 17 recall of the stratagems that had got them this far. Bright youngsters who had carefully failed their high school examinations in order to prove their unfitness for military service. Oldsters who began to mask a fever with massive doses of medicine. Embezzlers, petty criminals, and betrothed men skipping breach-of-promise suits who had obviously had the wit to fake an exit pass or steal the passage money. A lot of people had a lot to hide.

Far down in the lower bay of New York City, they crowded to the 18

[11] *phylacteries:* small leather cases containing slips inscribed with scriptural passages, worn by Jewish men during morning prayers.

rail to eye their first Americans in the persons of the immigration inspectors, two men and a woman in uniform clambering up a ladder from a cutter that had nosed alongside. The captain was required to note on the ship's manifest the more flagrant cases of contagious disease, for only seventy years ago they were still on the lookout for yellow fever and leprosy. The unlucky victims of such ailments were taken off in a quarantine boat to a special island to be deported as soon as possible.

The harbor was sometimes choked with ships at anchor. In the early 1900s there could be as many as fifteen thousand immigrants arriving in one day, and the ships had to drop anchor and wait. But eventually the engines would rumble again, and there, like a battleship on the horizon, stood what the song calls "Manhattan, an isle of joy." Closer, it grew into a cluster of pinnacles known as skyscrapers. And then the midtown skyscrapers topped the ones first seen. It was unlike any other city, and to the European it was always audacious and magical, and threatening.

Soon the newcomers would be on the docks sorting their bundles and baggage in a babble of languages, and when that was done they were tagged with numbers. Until 1892 they were cleared for entry at Castle Garden, once a fort, then a theater and a public amusement place down at the Battery. However, the volume of immigrants grew so great, and so many of them managed to disappear into Manhattan before being "processed," that a larger and more isolated sorting point had to be found. So, from 1892 on, once the immigrants had been tagged with numbers they were shipped aboard a ferry or a barge to what was to be known in several languages as "the isle of tears," the clearing station, Ellis Island.

It had been used by the early Dutch as a picnic ground. Much later its three acres were increased by landfill into twenty-seven, and it became a government arsenal. Today, it looks like a rather imposing college recently gutted by fire. It is totally derelict, a frowzy monument to the American habit of junking and forgetting whatever wears out. But wandering through its great central hall and tattered corridors, seeing the offices with their rusting files, the broken lavatories, and upturned dining tables, one can imagine the bedlam of its heyday, when the milling swarm of strangers was served and interrogated by hundreds of inspectors, wardens, interpreters, doctors, nurses, waiters, cooks, and agents of immigrant aid societies; and all the while a guerrilla army of con men, land swindlers, and hackmen passed out fresh broadsides boosting the heavenly prospects of the inland towns and unheard-of settlements on the prairie.

The newcomers crowded into the main building and the first thing they heard over the general bedlam were the clarion voices of inspectors bellowing out numbers in Italian, German, Polish, Hungarian, Russian, and Yiddish. According to assigned numbers they were herded into groups of thirty and led through long tiled corridors up a wide staircase into the biggest hall most of them had ever seen. Its dimensions, its pillars, its great soaring windows still suggest the grand ballroom of some abdicated monarch. Once they were assembled there in their thousands, the clearance procedure began. I recently pressed an aged immigrant to describe it. "Procedure?" he squealed incredulously. "Din, confusion, bewilderment, madness!"

They moved in single file through a stockyard maze of passageways 23 and under the eye of a doctor in a blue uniform who had in his hand a piece of chalk. He was a tough instant diagnostician. He would look at the hands, the hair, the faces and rap out a few questions. He might spot a panting old man with purple lips, and he would chalk on his back a capital "H" for suspected heart disease. Any facial blotches, a hint of gross eczema brought forth a chalked "F," for facial rash. Children in arms were made to stand down to see if they rated an "L" for the limp of rickets or some other deficiency disease. There was one chalk mark that every family dreaded, for it guaranteed certain deportation. It was a circle with a cross in the middle, and it indicated "feeble-minded."

Next they moved on to two doctors dipping into bowls of disinfectant 24 and snapping back the eyelids of suspects, usually with a buttonhook. They were looking for a disease very common then in southern and eastern Europe, trachoma.[12] If you had it, an "E" was chalked on your back, and your first days in the New World were surely your last.

About eight in ten survived this scrutiny and passed to the final ordeal, 25 the examination before an immigration inspector standing with an interpreter. Not noticeably gracious types, for they worked ten hours a day, seven days a week, they droned out an unchanging catechism: Who paid your passage? How many dependents? Ever been in prison? Can you read and write? (There was for a long time no legal obligation to be able to do either.) Is there a job waiting for you? (This was a famous catch, since a law called the Contract Labor Law forbade immigrants from signing up abroad for any work at all.) Finally, your name was checked against the ship's manifest. Many people were lucky to emerge into the new life with their old name. An Irish inspector glancing down at what to him was the gobbledygook of "Ouspenska" wrote on the landing card "Spensky." A Norwegian with an unpronounceable name

[12]*trachoma:* a contagious form of conjunctivitis characterized by inflammation of the inner eyelid.

was asked for the name of the town he had left. It was Dröbak. The inspector promptly wrote down what he thought he'd heard. Another Norwegian standing nearby philosophically realized that his own name was just as unmanageable and decided that what was good enough for his friend was good enough for him. To this day the progeny of both families rejoice in the name of Robeck.

But a new identity was better than none, and it gave you a landing   26 card. With it you were now ready to pay a visit to a currency booth to change your lire or drachmas, or whatever, into dollars. This exchange could entail prolonged haggling and not a few fist fights with the cashiers, who for many years were short-change artists. But at last you were handed over to the travel agent or the railroad men, if you were going far afield, or you sought the help of an aid society or a beckoning politician, if New York was to be the end of the line. Most immigrants could speak hardly a word of English except the one they had memorized as the town of their destination. A man would unfold a scrap of paper and point to a blockprinted word: "Pringvilliams." Maybe he eventually arrived in Springfield, Massachusetts, and maybe he didn't. But at this point the immigrants' only concern was to get off Ellis Island. All of them looked in relief for the door that was marked "Push to New York." And they pushed.

Now, after another ferry ride, they set foot on the earth of the land   27 that was paved with gold. I once asked a successful but unfailingly cynical immigrant if the reality hadn't meant a shattering disillusion. "But there *was* gold," he said, "to us. There were markets groaning with food and clothes. There were streetcars all over town. You could watch the automobiles. There was no military on horseback and no whips. The neighbors were out in the open, trading and shouting, enjoying free fights. And to a boy like me it was a ball, a friendship club. The streets were an open road." Admittedly, here was a man who had always been able to cope.

There were probably many more who soon came to feel that, at best,   28 they had traded a fearful time in the homeland for a baffling or brutal time in the slums of the cities. Such people went for help to the immigrant aid societies, which proliferated for the needy and the puzzled of the separate nations. The Jews of any nation gravitated to a newspaper office, that of the *Jewish Daily Forward*. It still survives, as the last Yiddish daily left in the United States. Starting in 1897 it attained a high circulation of two hundred and fifty thousand. Today, only seventy-five thousand New Yorkers need or choose to read the daily news in Yiddish. But the desperate immigrants didn't buy it for the news alone. Some went to its office clutching painfully written letters for publication in a daily feature that for nearly eighty years has served as a first-aid station to the immigrant. It is called the "Bintel Brief," and from the beginning the column advertised the various plights of the stranded and helped parted relatives to come together again. It was a blessing to many a wife yearning to find her husband. And, of course, it was a curse to many a husband yearning not to find his wife. But in the main it listened to and advised immigrant Jews who were exploited or bewildered by the polyglot society they had moved into.

> DEAR EDITOR: I was born in a small town in Russia, and until I was sixteen I studied in *Talmud Torahs*[13] and *yeshivas*,[14] but when I came to America I changed quickly. I . . . became a freethinker. . . . When I go past a synagogue during these days and hear a cantor chanting the melodies of the prayers, I become very gloomy and my depression is so great that I cannot endure it . . . what is your opinion of this?

> DEAR EDITOR: For a long time I worked in a shop with a Gentile girl, and we began to go out together and fell in love. We agreed that I would remain a Jew and she a Christian. But after we had been married for a year, I realized that it would not work. . . . Advise me what to do now. I could never convert and there's no hope for me to keep her from going to church.

> DEAR EDITOR: In the name of all the workers of our shop, I write these words to you . . . we make raincoats. With us is a thirteen-year-old boy who works hard for the two and half dollars a week he earns. Just lately it happened that the boy came to work ten minutes late. This was a "crime" the bosses couldn't overlook and for the lost ten minutes they docked him two cents.

> DEAR EDITOR: I am a girl from Galicia and in the shop where I work I sit near a Russian Jew . . . once, in a short debate, he stated that all Galicians were no good. . . . According to him the *Galitzianer* are inhuman savages . . . Dear Editor, does he really have a right to say this? I hope you will print my letter and give your opinion.

The files of the "Bintel Brief" ache with troubles: of parents grieved 29 that the American-born son refuses to keep *kosher*;[15] of students who quit chemistry or law books because they were told no Jew could graduate; of a son in a torment of conscience because he feels he must go back

---

[13] *Talmud Torah:* the collection of writings that constitutes Jewish civil and religious law.
[14] *yeshivas:* Orthodox Jewish schools for Talmudic study, or any Orthodox Jewish schools for religious and secular education.
[15] *kosher:* conforming to Jewish dietary laws.

and defend his mother and sisters from a new pogrom; of the ignorance and brutality of sweatshop bosses; of the hopelessness of escaping from the bigotry of the neighborhood and the slights of the Gentile shopkeepers. Very many of these Jews found out what the Irish in New York had found out before them — that however much they felt imprisoned with their own kind, they were unwanted on the outside. After the first wave of Jews from southern and eastern Europe, the newspaper advertisements were dotted with new variations on the old warning, "No Irish need apply."

In the early years of this century, you could have gone down to New 30 York's Lower East Side, and to similar parts of Pittsburgh and Chicago, and looked on the roaring maelstroms of any street scene as proof positive that the immigrants of many nations were already bubbling together in the melting pot. Yet, if you went closer and listened, you would know that they were all bustling within the confines of Little Italy or Little Russia. Mike Royko[16] has pointed out that until as late as the 1950s Chicago

> was a place where people stayed put for a while, creating tightly knit nighborhoods as small-townish as any village in the wheat fields. The neighborhood towns were part of larger ethnic states. To the north of the Loop was Germany. To the northwest Poland. To the west were Italy and Israel. To the southwest were Bohemia and Lithuania. And to the south was Ireland.

Officially, you changed from a foreigner into an American citizen after 31 filing naturalization papers, painfully boning up on a few elementary facts of American government, taking an indulgent verbal examination in these mysteries, and finally appearing before a judge to take the oath. But becoming an American was more complicated and for most more painful. It entailed at first the enormous obstacle of the language, and there are countless thousands of aged immigrants today who have managed with American life with the barest pidgin English.

On young families raising first-generation Americans, the pressure to 32 learn the language was intense as the children grew and went through the public school, which, in immigrant neighborhoods, had the dual purpose of teaching the rudiments of mathematics and geography and also of Americanizing the small stranger within the gates. Then the children went home and saw their parents reading an Italian or Russian

[16] *Mike Royko:* writer (b. 1932), for the *Chicago Tribune* and a nationally syndicated columnist.

or Yiddish paper and they began to notice thick accents. They felt uncomfortable and then they felt ashamed. This slow but sure discovery that the parents were odd, and to the extent of their oddity figures of fun, is a great and tragic theme in American life and literature. And the parents' shameful awareness of it sent them off in droves to night school, to make the final capitulation to the new land by learning the language of their sons and daughters.

I mentioned earlier that all you needed to get to America was an exit pass, twenty-five dollars, and reasonable health, but that what you were forbidden to have was a contract for a job in the new country. Toward the end of the Civil War, labor was so scarce that Congress made labor contracts signed abroad valid and protected by the courts. The subsequent rush into Europe of factory and railroad agents to sign up intending immigrants threatened a flood of cheap labor bound to industrial serfdom, and within four years the act was repealed. 33

In 1885 Congress decided to discourage unskilled immigrants by enacting a Contract Labor Law that prohibited the signing of foreigners to contract jobs, unless those jobs were professional or otherwise skilled. But the flood of the unskilled was not stopped, and the effect of the act was exactly the reverse of its intention. It meant that the really welcome immigrant was jobless, and in the high tide of immigration southern and central Europe was a bottomless pool of cheap labor. In the Midwest, they poured into the steel and coke factories and the railroad shops; in New York, into the garment factories. Among them were not only city people but peasants and poor farmers who had found themselves transplanted to a city block and were terrified of venturing further into the unknown Siberia of the countryside. Many thousands of them arrived just after the invention of such labor-saving devices as the sewing machine, which had been touted as a boon to the housewife, but was a curse to the seamstress. The labor that she had done for forty cents an hour was now being done by machines, and she had no choice but to stay on and work them for eight cents an hour. 34

The industrialists, the steel men, the iron and tin and railroad barons, came very easily to make the same large assumption about the inexhaustibility of cheap labor. But . . . the immigrant did not stay cowed forever. Henry Frick,[17] [Andrew] Carnegie's[18] bosom partner in his steel enterprises, was a fanatical opponent of labor unions, but he was quick 35

[17] *Henry Frick:* Henry Clay Frick, American coal and steel magnate (1849–1919).
[18] *Carnegie:* Andrew Carnegie, American industrialist and philanthropist (1835–1919); founder of the U.S. Steel Corporation.

to see that the latest wave of immigrants could be employed as strike-breakers. One year he employed Hungarians to break a strike. But within a year or two he had to hire Italians to break a strike of Hungarians, who by then were beginning to learn a specialty. In an irritable moment Frick got off a profound remark. "The immigrant," he complained, "however illiterate or ignorant he may be, always learns too soon." Not soon enough, however, to deny these industrial tycoons their imperial hold on the raw materials of industry and, in the person of John Pierpont Morgan,[19] on the national economy itself.

. . . For forty years after the Civil War the true national power lay with the oil monopoly, the steel trust, the railroad combines. They had all voted enthusiastically to elect [Theodore] Roosevelt Vice President. But when he got to the White House after McKinley's assassination, he looked at the ways, beginning with the standby stratagems of the holding companies, in which the Barons preserved their immunity from the law. He determined, if not to break them, to bring them under the control of Congress.   36

He had started, as Police Commissioner of New York, going after all the petty grafters who made life hell for the immigrants, and had achieved the feat of making Ellis Island decent and its inspectors able and courteous. As Governor of New York he went after the sweatshop owners and the tenement landlords. As President he charged up and down the social scale, flagellating everybody from food packagers to bankers, challenging them in the name of the federal government. The men who ran the trusts he called, in his squeaky but blazing fashion, "malefactors of great wealth." The trust he saw as an octopus whose longest tentacles bound the immigrants "as dwellers in a polyglot boarding house." His bravest mission was to try and see, through social legislation and new resources of education, that the immigrants should no longer be looked on as nationally identifiable pools of cheap labor. The country must stop talking about German-Americans and Italian-Americans and Polish-Americans: "We have room for but one language here, and that is the English language, for we intend to see that the crucible turns our people out as Americans." There must be no more "hyphenated Americans."   37

Roosevelt's aim was a double one: to liberate the immigrant from his daily grind in a polyglot compound, and to set him free from the hampering liabilities of his native tongue. The first aim did not begin to be achieved until 1911, when there was an appalling fire in New York's Triangle Shirtwaist Factory. It took a hundred and forty lives, roused the needle   38

[19]*John Pierpont ("J. P.") Morgan:* American financier and banker (1837–1913).

workers to go on strike and wakened the public conscience. And at the end of it, the airless sweatshop, with its two exits leading to one rickety staircase, was abolished by New York State law. So was the peddling out of piecework to the immigrant's home. It took this trauma to start the Jewish garment workers organizing in unions for decent hours and tolerable wages, and it marked the fiery beginning of their emergence into New York politics. Within a year William Howard Taft[20] would confide to reporters that "Jews make the best Republicans." (Forty years later, Adlai Stevenson,[21] with equal conviction, confided that "Jews make the best Democrats.")

The liberation of the immigrant from his mother tongue was something   39
that only time and two generations of American schoolchildren would achieve. By, say, the Second World War, it had been done. But in the past ten years or so there has appeared a new strain of ethnic pride, almost an insistence on reverting to hyphenated Americanism. The blacks who, arguing that "black is beautiful," refused to be assimilated in the white man's world may have led the way, but a similar pride in national origin is now being flaunted by immigrants old and new. As early as the first decade of the century, there were protests and small riots outside burlesque and vaudeville theaters against the caricaturing of German and Italian and Jewish traits. In the 1930s the motion picture industry devised a code to eliminate the representation of Greeks as conniving merchants, Italians as gangsters, Negroes as shiftless clowns. This new pride springs, I think, partly from a desperate desire of the underdog in the faceless cities to claim an identity, partly from the pragmatic aim of new immigrants — the Puerto Ricans after the Second World War, the Cubans after Castro's coup, the Hungarians after the Soviet invasion — to arrest at once their automatic consignment to the bottom of the labor market. They do not necessarily succeed, but at least they organize and agitate for the rights of equal pay and first-class citizenship.

Today the tenements are seventy years older than when the Poles   40
and Italians and Lithuanians and Russians climbed into them, and they were old then. They are the crumbling homes of the newer refugees, and most of all of the native blacks who began sixty years ago to be refugees from the South and from the countryside everywhere. Today, in the cities, the masses are as huddled as ever, and they no longer come expecting El Dorado.[22] More often than not they exchange a rural

[20] *William Howard Taft:* twenty-seventh president of the United States (1909–1913).
[21] *Adlai Stevenson:* American politician (1900–1965); Democratic candidate for the presidency in 1952 and 1956.
[22] *El Dorado:* an imaginary Latin American country rich in gold and precious gems that was the object of early Spanish explorers.

slum for a city hovel. They know it — and they hate it. And the threat of "the fire next time"[23] is an ever-present one wherever the comfortable whites and the impoverished blacks grow farther apart.

But in the wake of the immigrant flood that we have been talking   41
about, paupers became shopkeepers, and the sons and daughters of peasants bound for centuries to slivers of poor soil turned into clerks and nurses and accountants and schoolteachers and druggists and cab drivers and lawyers and doctors. Looking back on those sheepish legions, we should not pretend that they were ever rollicking characters in a musical comedy. But we should not forget, either, the millions who struggled for a decent and tidy life, and made it, and still do.

[23] *"the fire next time"*: According to James Baldwin, who used the phrase as a book title, a "prophecy, re-created from the Bible in a song by a slave: 'God gave Noah the rainbow sign,/No more water, the fire next time!' "

Engaging the Text

1. According to Cooke, what motivated immigrants to come to the United States? How did they interpret or extend the American Dream?

2. How does Cooke portray early immigrants? What qualities or CHARACTERISTICS does he attribute to them as a group?

3. What forces kept people of the same ETHNIC background together in the United States? What forces pushed them to mix with other people?

Exploring Connections

1. In "Uprooting Racism and Racists in the United States" (p. 137), James Boggs takes the position that the root cause of racism is economic EXPLOITATION. Try to apply Boggs's economic analysis to the events described by Cooke: Is it possible to explain the mass migration of immigrants into the United States in terms of economic exploitation?

2. Working in groups, compare the STYLE and method of Cooke's historical NARRATIVE to that of Milton Gordon later in this chapter. How do their purposes differ? What audience does each seem to address? What characteristics of Cooke's language, organization, and selection of detail suggest that this passage was primarily intended to be heard rather than read?

3. Cooke speaks of "liberating" the immigrant from the "hampering liability of his native tongue." Does Yezierska's NARRATOR share this view of her first language as an impediment? Do Hank López, Maxine Hong Kingston, and Tran Thi Nga? Why or why not? (These readings all appear in this chapter.)

Extending the Critical Context

1. Assume that you have been hired by the federal government to "Americanize" new immigrants. What specifically would it mean to "Americanize" a person, and how would you go about it?

2. Cooke highlights the experiences of only a few of the many groups that immigrated to the United States before World War II. Using library resources like the *Harvard Encyclopedia of American Ethnic Groups*, write a narrative documenting the experience of a group that Cooke either neglects or only mentions in passing.

America and I

ANZIA YEZIERSKA

In this heavily autobiographical short story, Anzia Yezierska (1885?–1970) recounts the struggles of a Russian immigrant to find the "real" America. Arriving in New York with her family, the fifteen-year-old Yezierska, like her protagonist, worked at a series of menial jobs while studying English at night. Her novels and short stories, detailing the lives of Jewish immigrants on New York's Lower East Side, attained popular and critical success in the 1920s.

As one of the dumb, voiceless ones I speak. One of the millions of 1
immigrants beating, beating out their hearts at your gates for a breath of understanding.

Ach! America! From the other end of the earth where I came, America 2
was a land of living hope, woven of dreams, aflame with longing and desire.

Choked for ages in the airless oppression of Russia, the Promised Land 3
rose up — wings for my stifled spirit — sunlight burning through my darkness — freedom singing to me in my prison — deathless songs turning prison-bars into strings of a beautiful violin.

I arrived in America. My young, strong body, my heart and soul 4
pregnant with the unlived lives of generations clamoring for expression.

What my mother and father and their mother and father never had 5
a chance to give out in Russia, I would give out in America. The hidden

sap of centuries would find release; colors that never saw light — songs that died unvoiced — romance that never had a chance to blossom in the black life of the Old World.

In the golden land of flowing opportunity I was to find my work that 6 was denied me in the sterile village of my forefathers. Here I was to be free from the dead drudgery for bread that held me down in Russia. For the first time in America, I'd cease to be a slave of the belly. I'd be a creator, a giver, a human being! My work would be the living joy of fullest self-expression.

But from my high visions, my golden hopes, I had to put my feet 7 down on earth. I had to have food and shelter. I had to have the money to pay for it.

I was in America, among the Americans, but not of them. No speech, 8 no common language, no way to win a smile of understanding from them, only my young, strong body and my untried faith. Only my eager, empty hands, and my full heart shining from my eyes!

God from the world! Here I was with so much richness in me but 9 my mind was not wanted without the language. And my body, unskilled, untrained, was not even wanted in the factory. Only one of two chances was left open to me: the kitchen, or minding babies.

My first job was as a servant in an Americanized family. Once, long 10 ago, they came from the same village from where I came. But they were so well-dressed, so well-fed, so successful in America, that they were ashamed to remember their mother tongue.

"What were to be my wages?" I ventured timidly, as I looked up to 11 the well-fed, well-dressed "American" man and woman.

They looked at me with a sudden coldness. What have I said to draw 12 away from me their warmth? Was it so low from me to talk of wages? I shrank back into myself like a low-down bargainer. Maybe they're so high up in well-being they can't any more understand my low thoughts for money.

From his rich height the man preached down to me that I must not 13 be so grabbing for wages. Only just landed from the ship and already thinking about money when I should be thankful to associate with "Americans."

The woman, out of her smooth, smiling fatness assured me that this 14 was my chance for a summer vacation in the country with her two lovely children. My great chance to learn to be a civilized being, to become an American by living with them.

So, made to feel that I was in the hands of American friends, invited 15 to share with them their home, their plenty, their happiness, I pushed out from my head the worry for wages. Here was my first chance to begin my life in the sunshine, after my long darkness. My laugh was all over my face as I said to them: "I'll trust myself to you. What I'm worth you'll give me." And I entered their house like a child by the hand.

The best of me I gave them. Their house cares were my house cares. 16 I got up early. I worked till late. All that my soul hungered to give I put into the passion with which I scrubbed floors, scoured pots, and washed clothes. I was so grateful to mingle with the American people, to hear the music of the American language, that I never knew tiredness.

There was such a freshness in my brains and such a willingness in my 17 heart that I could go on and on — not only with the work of the house, but work with my head — learning new words from the children, the grocer, the butcher, the iceman. I was not even afraid to ask for words from the policeman on the street. And every new word made me see new American things with American eyes. I felt like a Columbus, finding new worlds through every new word.

But words alone were only for the inside of me. The outside of me 18 still branded me for a steerage immigrant. I had to have clothes to forget myself that I'm a stranger yet. And so I had to have money to buy these clothes.

The month was up. I was so happy! Now I'd have money. *My own,* 19 *earned* money. Money to buy a new shirt on my back — shoes on my feet. Maybe yet an American dress and hat!

Ach! How high rose my dreams! How plainly I saw all that I would 20 do with my visionary wages shining like a light over my head!

In my imagination I already walked in my new American clothes. How 21 beautiful I looked as I saw myself like a picture before my eyes! I saw how I would throw away my immigrant rags tied up in my immigrant shawl. With money to buy — free money in my hands — I'd show them that I could look like an American in a day.

Like a prisoner in his last night in prison, counting the seconds that 22 will free him from his chains, I trembled breathlessly for the minute I'd get the wages in my hand.

Before dawn I rose. 23

I shined up the house like a jewel-box. 24

I prepared breakfast and waited with my heart in my mouth for my 25 lady and gentleman to rise. At last I heard them stirring. My eyes were jumping out of my head to them when I saw them coming in and seating themselves by the table.

Like a hungry cat rubbing up to its boss for meat, so I edged and 26 simpered around them as I passed them the food. Without my will, like a beggar, my hand reached out to them.

The breakfast was over. And no word yet from my wages.   27

"*Gottuniu!*" I thought to myself. Maybe they're so busy with their   28
own things they forgot it's the day for my wages. Could they who have
everything know what I was to do with my first American dollars? How
could they, soaking in plenty, how could they feel the longing and the
fierce hunger in me, pressing up through each visionary dollar? How
could they know the gnawing ache of my avid fingers for the feel of my
own, earned dollars? *My* dollars that I could spend like a free person.
My dollars that would make me feel with everybody alike!

Breakfast was long past.   29

Lunch came. Lunch past.   30

Oi-i weh! Not a word yet about my money.   31

It was near dinner. And not a word yet about my wages.   32

I began to set the table. But my head — it swam away from me. I   33
broke a glass. The silver dropped from my nervous fingers. I couldn't
stand it any longer. I dropped everything and rushed over to my American
lady and gentleman.

"*Oi weh!* The money — my money — my wages!" I cried breathlessly.   34

Four cold eyes turned on me.   35

"Wages? Money?" The four eyes turned into hard stone as they looked   36
me up and down. "Haven't you a comfortable bed to sleep, and three
good meals a day? You're only a month here. Just came to America.
And you already think about money. Wait till you're worth any money.
What use are you without knowing English? You should be glad we
keep you here. It's like a vacation for you. Other girls pay money yet
to be in the country."

It went black for my eyes. I was so choked no words came to my lips.   37
Even the tears went dry in my throat.

I left. Not a dollar for all my work.   38

For a long, long time my heart ached and ached like a sore wound.   39
If murderers would have robbed me and killed me it wouldn't have hurt
me so much. I couldn't think through my pain. The minute I'd see
before me how they looked at me, the words they said to me — then
everything began to bleed in me. And I was helpless.

For a long, long time the thought of ever working in an "American"   40
family made me tremble with fear, like the fear of wild wolves. No —
never again would I trust myself to an "American" family, no matter
how fine their language and how sweet their smile.

It was blotted out in me all trust in friendship from "Americans." But   41
the life in me still burned to live. The hope in me still craved to hope.
In darkness, in dirt, in hunger and want, but only to live on!

There had been no end to my day — working for the "American" family.   42

Now rejecting false friendships from higher-ups in America, I turned 43
back to the Ghetto. I worked on a hard bench with my own kind on
either side of me. I knew before I began what my wages were to be. I
knew what my hours were to be. And I knew the feeling of the end of
the day.

From the outside my second job seemed worse than the first. It was 44
in a sweat-shop of a Delancey Street basement, kept up by an old,
wrinkled woman that looked like a black witch of greed. My work was
sewing on buttons. While the morning was still dark I walked into a
dark basement. And darkness met me when I turned out of the basement.

Day after day, week after week, all the contact I got with America 45
was handling dead buttons. The money I earned was hardly enough to
pay for bread and rent. I didn't have a room to myself. I didn't even
have a bed. I slept on a mattress on the floor in a rat-hole of a room
occupied by a dozen other immigrants. I was always hungry — oh, so
hungry! The scant meals I could afford only sharpened my appetite for
real food. But I felt myself better off than working in the "American"
family, where I had three good meals a day and a bed to myself. With
all the hunger and darkness of the sweat-shop, I had at least the evening
to myself. And all night was mine. When all were asleep, I used to
creep up on the roof of the tenement and talk out my heart in silence
to the stars in the sky.

"Who am I? What am I? What do I want with my life? Where is 46
America? Is there an America? What is this wilderness in which I'm
lost?"

I'd hurl my questions and then think and think. And I could not tear 47
it out of me, the feeling that America must be somewhere, somehow
— only I couldn't find it — *my America,* where I would work for love
and not for a living. I was like a thing following blindly after something
far off in the dark!

"*Oi weh!*" I'd stretch out my hand up in the air. "My head is so lost 48
in America! What's the use of all my working if I'm not in it? Dead
buttons is not me."

Then the busy season started in the shop. The mounds of buttons 49
grew and grew. The long day stretched out longer. I had to begin with
the buttons earlier and stay with them till later in the night. The old
witch turned into a huge greedy maw for wanting more and more buttons.

For a glass of tea, for a slice of herring over black bread, she would 50
buy us up to stay another and another hour, till there seemed no end
to her demands.

One day, the light of self-assertion broke into my cellar darkness. 51

"I don't want the tea. I don't want your herring," I said with terrible 52
boldness. "I only want to go home. I only want the evening to myself!"

"You fresh mouth, you!" cried the old witch. "You learned already 53 too much in America. I want no clock-watchers in my shop. Out you go!"

I was driven out to cold and hunger. I could no longer pay for my 54 mattress on the floor. I no longer could buy the bite in the mouth. I walked the streets. I knew what it is to be alone in a strange city, among strangers.

But I laughed through my tears. So I learned too much already in 55 America because I wanted the whole evening to myself? Well America has yet to teach me still more: how to get not only the whole evening to myself, but a whole day a week like the American workers.

That sweat-shop was a bitter memory but a good school. It fitted me 56 for a regular factory. I could walk in boldly and say I could work at something, even if it was only sewing on buttons.

Gradually, I became a trained worker. I worked in a light, airy factory, 57 only eight hours a day. My boss was no longer a sweater and a blood-squeezer. The first freshness of the morning was mine. And the whole evening was mine. All day Sunday was mine.

Now I had better food to eat. I slept on a better bed. Now, I even 58 looked dressed up like the American-born. But inside of me I knew that I was not yet an American. I choked with longing when I met an American-born, and I could say nothing.

Something cried dumb in me. I couldn't help it. I didn't know what 59 it was I wanted. I only knew I wanted. I wanted. Like the hunger in the heart that never gets food.

An English class for foreigners started in our factory. The teacher had 60 such a good, friendly face, her eyes looked so understanding, as if she could see right into my heart. So I went to her one day for an advice:

"I don't know what is with me the matter," I began. "I have no rest 61 in me. I never yet done what I want."

"What is it you want to do, child?" she asked me. 62

"I want to do something with my head, my feelings. All day long, 63 only with my hands I work."

"First you must learn English." She patted me as if I was not yet 64 grown up. "Put your mind on that, and then we'll see."

So for a time I learned the language. I could almost begin to think 65 with English words in my head. But in my heart the emptiness still hurt. I burned to give, to give something, to do something, to be something. The dead work with my hands was killing me. My work left only hard stones on my heart.

Again I went to our factory teacher and cried to her: "I know already 66 to read and write the English language, but I can't put it into words what I want. What is it in me so different that can't come out?"

She smiled at me down from her calmness as if I were a little bit out 67
of my head. "What *do you want* to do?"

"I feel. I see. I hear. And I want to think it out. But I'm like dumb 68
in me. I only feel I'm different — different from everybody."

She looked at me close and said nothing for a minute. "You ought to 69
join one of the social clubs of the Women's Association," she advised.

"What's the Women's Association?" I implored greedily. 70

"A group of American women who are trying to help the working-girl 71
find herself. They have a special department for immigrant girls like
you."

I joined the Women's Association. On my first evening there they 72
announced a lecture: "The Happy Worker and His Work," by the Welfare
director of the United Mills Corporation.

"Is there such a thing as a happy worker at his work?" I wondered. 73
Happiness is only by working at what you love. And what poor girl can
ever find it to work at what she loves? My old dreams about my America
rushed through my mind. Once I thought that in America everybody
works for love. Nobody has to worry for a living. Maybe this welfare
man came to show me the *real* America that till now I sought in vain.

With a lot of polite words the head lady of the Women's Association 74
introduced a higher-up that looked like the king of kings of business.
Never before in my life did I ever see a man with such a sureness in
his step, such power in his face, such friendly positiveness in his eye
as when he smiled upon us.

"Efficiency is the new religion of business," he began. "In big business 75
houses, even in up-to-date factories, they no longer take the first comer
and give him any job that happens to stand empty. Efficiency begins at
the employment office. Experts are hired for the one purpose, to find
out how best to fit the worker to his work. It's economy for the boss to
make the worker happy." And then he talked a lot more on efficiency
in educated language that was over my head.

I didn't know exactly what it meant — efficiency — but if it was to 76
make the worker happy at his work, then that's what I had been looking
for since I came to America. I only felt from watching him that he was
happy by his job. And as I looked on this clean, well-dressed, successful,
one, who wasn't ashamed to say he rose from an office-boy, it made me
feel that I, too, could lift myself up for a person.

He finished his lecture, telling us about the Vocational-Guidance Center 77
that the Women's Association started.

The very next evening I was at the Vocational-Guidance Center. There 78
I found a young, college-looking woman. Smartness and health shining
from her eyes! She, too, looked as if she knew her way in America. I

could tell at the first glance: here is a person that is happy by what she does.

"I feel you'll understand me," I said right away. 79

She leaned over with pleasure in her face: "I hope I can." 80

"I want to work by what's in me. Only, I don't know what's in me. 81 I only feel I'm different."

She gave me a quick, puzzled look from the corner of her eyes. "What 82 are you doing now?"

"I'm the quickest shirtwaist hand on the floor. But my heart wastes 83 away by such work. I think and think, and my thoughts can't come out."

"Why don't you think out your thoughts in shirtwaists? You could 84 learn to be a designer. Earn more money."

"I don't want to look on waists. If my hands are sick from waists, how 85 could my head learn to put beauty into them?"

"But you must earn your living at what you know, and rise slowly 86 from job to job."

I looked at her office sign: "Vocational Guidance." "What's your vocational 87 guidance?" I asked. "How to rise from job to job — how to earn more money?"

The smile went out from her eyes. But she tried to be kind yet. "What 88 *do* you want?" she asked, with a sigh of last patience.

"I want America to want me." 89

She fell back in her chair, thunderstruck with my boldness. But yet, 90 in a low voice of educated self-control, she tried to reason with me:

"You have to *show* that you have something special for America before 91 America has need of you."

"But I never had a chance to find out what's in me, because I always 92 had to work for a living. Only, I feel it's efficiency for America to find out what's in me so different, so I could give it out by my work."

Her eyes half closed as they bored through me. Her mouth opened 93 to speak, but no words came from her lips. So I flamed up with all that was choking in me like a house on fire:

"America gives free bread and rent to criminals in prison. They got 94 grand houses with sunshine, fresh air, doctors and teachers, even for the crazy ones. Why don't they have free boarding-schools for immigrants — strong people — willing people? Here you see us burning up with something different, and America turns her head away from us."

Her brows lifted and dropped down. She shrugged her shoulders away 95 from me with the look of pity we give to cripples and hopeless lunatics.

"America is no Utopia. First you must become efficient in earning a 96 living before you can indulge in your poetic dreams."

I went away from the vocational-guidance office with all the air out 97 of my lungs. All the light out of my eyes. My feet dragged after me like dead wood.

Till now there had always lingered a rosy veil of hope over my emptiness, a hope that a miracle would happen. I would open my eyes some day and suddenly find the America of my dreams. As a young girl hungry for love sees always before her eyes the picture of lover's arms around her, so I saw always in my heart the vision of Utopian America. 98

But now I felt that the America of my dreams never was and never could be. Reality had hit me on the head as with a club. I felt that the America that I sought was nothing but a shadow — an echo — a chimera of lunatics and crazy immigrants. 99

Stripped of all illusion, I looked about me. The long desert of wasting days of drudgery stared me in the face. The drudgery that I had lived through, and the endless drudgery still ahead of me rose over me like a withering wilderness of sand. In vain were all my cryings, in vain were all frantic efforts of my spirit to find the living waters of understanding for my perishing lips. Sand, sand was everywhere. With every seeking, every reaching out I only lost myself deeper and deeper in a vast sea of sand. 100

I knew now the American language. And I knew now, if I talked to the Americans from morning till night, they could not understand what the Russian soul of me wanted. They could not understand *me* anymore than if I talked to them in Chinese. Between my soul and the American soul were worlds of difference that no words could bridge over. What was that difference? What made the Americans so far apart from me? 101

I began to read the American history. I found from the first pages that America started with a band of Courageous Pilgrims. They had left their native country as I had left mine. They had crossed an unknown ocean and landed in an unknown country, as I. 102

But the great difference between the first Pilgrims and me was that they expected to make America, build America, create their own world of liberty. I wanted to find it ready made. 103

I read on. I delved deeper down into the American history. I saw how the Pilgrim Fathers came to a rocky desert country, surrounded by Indian savages on all sides. But undaunted, they pressed on — through danger — through famine, pestilence, and want — they pressed on. They did not ask the Indians for sympathy, for understanding. They made no demands on anybody, but on their own indomitable spirit of persistence. 104

And I — I was forever begging a crumb of sympathy, a gleam of understanding from strangers who could not sympathize, who could not understand. 105

I, when I encountered a few savage Indian scalpers, like the old witch 106
of the sweat-shop, like my "Americanized" countryman, who cheated
me of my wages — I, when I found myself on the lonely, untrodden
path through which all seekers of the new world must pass, I lost heart
and said: "There is no America!"

Then came a light — a great revelation! I saw America — a big idea 107
— a deathless hope — a world still in the making. I saw that it was the
glory of America that it was not yet finished. And I, the last comer, had
her share to give, small or great, to the making of America, like those
Pilgrims who came in the *Mayflower*.

Fired up by this revealing light, I began to build a bridge of under- 108
standing between the American-born and myself. Since their life was
shut out from such as me, I began to open up my life and the lives of
my people to them. And life draws life. In only writing about the Ghetto
I found America.

Great chances have come to me. But in my heart is always a deep 109
sadness. I feel like a man who is sitting down to a secret table of plenty,
while his near ones and dear ones are perishing before his eyes. My
very joy in doing the work I love hurts me like secret guilt, because all
about me I see so many with my longings, my burning eagerness, to
do and to be, wasting their days in drudgery they hate, merely to buy
bread and pay rent. And America is losing all that richness of the soul.

The Americans of to-morrow, the America that is every day nearer 110
coming to be, will be too wise, too open-hearted, too friendly-handed,
to let the least last-comer at their gates knock in vain with his gifts
unwanted.

Engaging the Text

1. What does America represent to Yezierska's NARRATOR? What is her dream?

2. What things does Yezierska value that she finds it hard to have in America,
at least at first? Why are these things hard to get?

3. Which of Yezierska's complaints or dissatisfactions would be solved with
greater material wealth? Which would not? What's the connection for Yezierska
between material goods and satisfaction?

4. The immigrant experience may be seen as a kind of education — a schooling
in the ways of a new culture, a new set of values, a new way of doing things,
a new set of social relations. Using this PERSPECTIVE, what are the stages of
Yezierska's "American education"? What lessons does she learn? What does
becoming an American mean to her?

5. In this story, the narrator's language often departs from conventional English

usage; working in pairs or small groups, rewrite a paragraph or two in standard English. Read both versions aloud and discuss the differences you detect in sound and effect.

Exploring Connections

1. What does Yezierska mean when she says that she wants to work for "love, not for a living"? Looking ahead to Chapter Seven, "Making a Living," compare her attitudes toward the relationship between labor and life with those of Mike Lefevre, Willie, and Jane Ellen Wilson.

2. To what extent does Andrew Carnegie's formula for success (Chapter One, "American Dreams") apply to the narrator's experience? Support your argument with specific examples from both texts.

Extending the Critical Context

1. At one point the narrator suggests that the United States would ultimately benefit by providing free boarding schools for immigrants. Discuss the benefits and drawbacks of such a proposal.

2. Working in groups, discuss how the United States might tap the rich potential of new immigrants that, according to the story, is being wasted in drudgery.

Ellis Island

JOSEPH BRUCHAC

"Ellis Island" reminds us of another side of American immigration — the dispossession of Native Americans as expanding settlement pushed them from their ancestral lands. Of mixed immigrant and American Indian ancestry, Joseph Bruchac III (b. 1942) notes that "much of my writing and my life relates to the problem of being an American." Bruchac has published widely as a poet, novelist, editor, and translator of West African and Iroquois literature.

Beyond the red brick of Ellis Island
where the two Slovak children

who became my grandparents
waited the long days of quarantine,
after leaving the sickness,   5
the old Empires of Europe,
a Circle Line ship slips easily
on its way to the island
of the tall woman, green
as dreams of forests and meadows   10
waiting for those who'd worked
a thousand years
yet never owned their own.

Like millions of others,
I too come to this island,   15
nine decades the answerer
of dreams.

Yet only one part of my blood loves that memory.
Another voice speaks
of native lands   20
within this nation.
Lands invaded
when the earth became owned.
Lands of those who followed
the changing Moon,   25
knowledge of the seasons
in their veins.

Engaging the Text

1. What is Bruchac's attitude toward the immigrants and their dream?

2. How is the SPEAKER in the poem "the answerer/of dreams"?

3. Who is the "tall woman" referred to in line 9? What does it mean to describe her as "green/as dreams of forests and meadows"?

4. Who are "those who followed/the changing Moon"?

Extending the Critical Context

1. Write a poem about, or addressed to, your own grandparents and ancestors, placing their history within the larger history of the United States. For background, refer to Cooke (p. 192) and consult a historical encyclopedia to find out more about the national events that occurred during their lifetimes.

Puerto Rico's Reply

Dadi Piñero

Puerto Rico is both a part of and apart from the rest of the United States, as can be seen in the recurring debate over the advantages and disadvantages of statehood. This poem offers insight into the human side of the often uneasy relationship between Puerto Rico and the rest of the country. It is taken from Nuyorican Poetry, *edited by Miguel Algarín and Miguel Gomez Piñero, two New York City writer–playwrights who were born in Puerto Rico.*

Roll around in a VW around
the beautiful beaches of Puerto Rico
smiling Burger Kings and McDonald's
heading to Gurabo my hometown
we stopped for a while and kept   5
moving around we're going
up a hill Miguel is puzzled
his mind seems to wander out to
the streets he is
checking the beat he's   10
thundering inside glitter in his eyes
stop the car don't go no more
I want to see if there is
any Puerto Rican out here
in beautiful Puerto Rico   15
we get ready to watch Miguel
get hit in the eye we grab the pipe
Miguel stepped out he stopped a
man then quietlike and scared
he said to the man "are there any Puerto   20
Ricans in Puerto Rico?" we got ready
for static the man replied
Miguel came back surprised
we asked him what he
replied Miguel said   25
"I don't know I don't know
I don't think so."

Engaging the Text

1. Miguel asks an odd question in this poem, "Are there any Puerto Ricans in Puerto Rico?" What would the answer "Yes" mean? What would "No" mean? Why do you think the stranger says, "I don't know"?
2. What is the SPEAKER's attitude toward "Burger Kings and McDonald's"? How can you tell? Why would fast-food restaurants seem to be an important issue?
3. What is the dominant feeling at the end of the poem?
4. Why is there so little punctuation in the poem?

Extending the Critical Context

1. Survey recent immigrants about their attitudes toward their native country. Have they returned there (either to visit or to live for an extended period)? Do they hope or plan to return? Why or why not? Report your findings to the rest of the class. If two or more people or groups tackle this assignment, one could design and use actual survey forms while another carried out less formal interviews. What differences are there in the type of information elicited in these two different ways? Which method of investigation seems more valuable in this case?

ETHNIC IDENTITY AND MAJORITY CULTURE

Assimilation in America

MILTON GORDON

Since its publication in 1964, Milton Gordon's Assimilation in American Life *has become a basic text for sociologists and students of American culture. In this excerpt, Gordon defines the three dominant models of how immigrants are assimilated into U.S. culture and provides a framework for analyzing the personal accounts that follow. Gordon (b. 1918) is a professor emeritus of sociology at the University of Massachusetts, Amherst. He has recently published* The Scope of Sociology *(1988).*

Three ideologies or conceptual models have competed for attention 1
on the American scene as explanations of the way in which a nation, in the beginning largely white, Anglo-Saxon, and Protestant, has absorbed over 41 million immigrants and their descendants from variegated sources and welded them into the contemporary American people. These ideologies are Anglo-conformity, the melting pot, and cultural pluralism. They have served at various times, and often simultaneously, as explanations of what has happened — descriptive models — and of what should happen — goal models. Not infrequently they have been used in such a fashion that it is difficult to tell which of these two usages the writer has had in mind. In fact, one of the more remarkable omissions in the history of American intellectual thought is the relative lack of close analytical attention given to the theory of immigrant adjustment in the United States by its social scientists.

Anglo-Conformity

"Anglo-conformity"[1] is a broad term used to cover a variety of viewpoints 2
about assimilation and immigration; they all assume the desirability of maintaining English institutions (as modified by the American Revolution), the English language, and English-oriented cultural patterns as dominant and standard in American life. However, bound up with this assumption are related attitudes. These may range from discredited notions about race and "Nordic" and "Aryan" racial superiority, together with the nativist political programs and exclusionist immigration policies which such notions entail, through an intermediate position of favoring immigration from northern and western Europe on amorphous, unreflective grounds ("They are more like us"), to a lack of opposition to any source of immigration, as long as these immigrants and their descendants duly adopt the standard Anglo-Saxon cultural patterns. There is by no means any necessary equation between Anglo-conformity and racist attitudes.

It is quite likely that "Anglo-conformity" in its more moderate aspects, 3
however explicit its formulation, has been the most prevalent ideology of assimilation goals in America throughout the nation's history. As far back as colonial times, Benjamin Franklin recorded concern about the

---

[1]The phrase is the Coles's. See Stewart G. Cole and Mildred Wiese Cole, *Minorities and the American Promise* (New York, Harper & Brothers, 1954), ch. 6. [Author's note]

clannishness of the Germans in Pennsylvania, their slowness in learning English, and the establishment of their own native-language press.[2] Others of the founding fathers had similar reservations about large-scale immigration from Europe. In the context of their times they were unable to foresee the role such immigration was to play in creating the later greatness of the nation. They were not at all men of unthinking prejudices. The disestablishment of religion[3] and the separation of church and state (so that no religious group — whether New England Congregationalists, Virginian Anglicans, or even all Protestants combined — could call upon the federal government for special favors or support, and so that man's religious conscience should be free) were cardinal points of the new national policy they fostered. "The Government of the United States," George Washington had written to the Jewish congregation of Newport during his first term as president, "gives to bigotry no sanction, to persecution no assistance."

Political differences with ancestral England had just been written in blood; but there is no reason to suppose that these men looked upon their fledgling country as an impartial melting pot for the merging of the various cultures of Europe, or as a new "nation of nations," or as anything but a society in which, with important political modifications, Anglo-Saxon speech and institutional forms would be standard. Indeed, their newly won victory for democracy and republicanism made them especially anxious that these still precarious fruits of revolution should not be threatened by a large influx of European peoples whose life experiences had accustomed them to the bonds of despotic monarchy. Thus, although they explicitly conceived of the new United States of America as a haven for those unfortunates of Europe who were persecuted and oppressed, they had characteristic reservations about the effects of too free a policy. "My opinion, with respect to immigration," Washington wrote to John Adams in 1794, "is that except of useful mechanics and some particular descriptions of men or professions, there is no need of encouragement, while the policy or advantage of its taking place in a body (I mean the settling of them in a body) may be much questioned; for, by so doing, they retain the language, habits and principles (good

4

---

[2]Maurice R. Davie, *World Immigration* (New York, Macmillan, 1936), p. 36, and (cited therein) "Letter of Benjamin Franklin to Peter Collinson, 9th May, 1753, on the condition and character of the Germans in Pennsylvania," in *The Works of Benjamin Franklin, with notes and a life of the author*, by Jared Sparks (Boston, 1828), vol. 7, pp. 71–73. [Author's note]

[3]*disestablishment of religion:* the act of a state when it breaks off official affiliation with religious groups.

or bad) which they bring with them."[4] Thomas Jefferson, whose views on race and attitudes towards slavery were notably liberal and advanced for his time, had similar doubts concerning the effects of mass immigration on American institutions, while conceding that immigrants, "if they come of themselves . . . are entitled to all the rights of citizenship."[5]

Anglo-conformity received its fullest expression in the so-called Americanization movement which gripped the nation during World War I. While "Americanization" in its various stages had more than one emphasis, it was essentially a consciously articulated movement to strip the immigrant of his native culture and attachments and make him over into an American along Anglo-Saxon lines — all this to be accomplished with great rapidity. To use an image of a later day, it was an attempt at "pressure-cooking assimilation." It had prewar antecedents, but it was during the height of the world conflict that federal agencies, state governments, municipalities, and a host of private organizations joined in the effort to persuade the immigrant to learn English, take out naturalization papers, buy war bonds, forget his former origins and culture, and give himself over to patriotic hysteria.

The Melting Pot

While Anglo-conformity in various guises has probably been the most prevalent ideology of assimilation in the American historical experience, a competing viewpoint with more generous and idealistic overtones has had its adherents and exponents from the eighteenth century onward. Conditions in the virgin continent, it was clear, were modifying the institutions which the English colonists brought with them from the mother country. Arrivals from non-English homelands such as Germany, Sweden, and France were similarly exposed to this fresh environment. Was it not possible, then, to think of the evolving American society not as a slightly modified England but rather as a totally new blend, culturally and biologically, in which the stocks and folkways of Europe, figuratively speaking, were indiscriminately mixed in the political pot of the emerging nation and fused by the fires of American influence and interaction into a distinctly new type?

Such, at any rate, was the conception of the new society which motivated that eighteenth-century French-born writer and agriculturalist, J. Hector

---

[4]*The Writings of George Washington*, collected and edited by W. C. Ford (New York, G. P. Putnam's Sons, 1889), vol. 12, p. 489. [Author's note]
[5]Thomas Jefferson, "Notes on Virginia, Query 8"; in *The Writings of Thomas Jefferson*, ed. A. E. Bergh (Washington, The Thomas Jefferson Memorial Association, 1907), vol. 2, p. 121. [Author's note]

St. John Crèvecoeur, who, after many years of American residence, published his reflections and observations in *Letters from an American Farmer*.[6] Who, he asks, is the American?

> He is either an European, or the descendant of an European, hence that strange mixture of blood, which you will find in no other country. I could point out to you a family whose grandfather was an Englishman, whose wife was Dutch, whose son married a French woman, and whose present four sons have now four wives of different nations. *He* is an American, who leaving behind him all his ancient prejudices and manners, receives new ones from the new mode of life he has embraced, the new government he obeys, and the new rank he holds. He becomes an American by being received in the broad lap of our great *Alma Mater*. Here individuals of all nations are melted into a new race of men, whose labours and posterity will one day cause great changes in the world.

Some observers have interpreted the open-door policy on immigration of the first three-quarters of the nineteenth century as reflecting an underlying faith in the effectiveness of the American melting pot, in the belief "that all could be absorbed and that all could contribute to an emerging national character."[7] No doubt many who observed with dismay the nativist agitation of the times felt as did Ralph Waldo Emerson[8] that such conformity-demanding and immigrant-hating forces represented a perversion of the best American ideals. In 1845, Emerson wrote in his Journal:[9]

> I hate the narrowness of the Native American Party.[10] It is the dog in the manger. It is precisely opposite to all the dictates of love and magnanimity; and therefore, of course, opposite to true wisdom. . . . Man is the most composite of all creatures. . . . Well, as in the old burning of the Temple at Corinth, by the melting and intermixture of silver and gold and other metals a new compound more precious than any, called Corinthian brass, was formed; so in this continent — asylum of all nations — the energy of Irish, Germans, Swedes, Poles, and

[6]J. Hector St. John Crèvecoeur, *Letters from an American Farmer* (New York, Albert and Charles Boni, 1925; reprinted from the 1st edn., London, 1782), pp. 54–55. [Author's note]

[7]Oscar Handlin, ed., *Immigration as a Factor in American History* (Englewood, Prentice-Hall, 1959), p. 146. [Author's note]

[8]*Ralph Waldo Emerson:* American essayist, philosopher, and poet (1803–1882).

[9]Quoted by Stuart P. Sherman in his Introduction to *Essays and Poems of Emerson* (New York, Harcourt Brace, 1921), p. xxxiv. [Author's note]

[10]*Native American Party:* a minor U.S. political party (1844–1850) founded to oppose Catholic immigration.

Cossacks, and all the European tribes — of the Africans, and of the Polynesians — will construct a new race, a new religion, a new state, a new literature, which will be as vigorous as the new Europe which came out of the smelting-pot of the Dark Ages, or that which earlier emerged from the Pelasgic and Etruscan barbarism.[11] *La Nature aime les croisements.*[12]

Eventually, the melting-pot hypothesis found its way into historical scholarship and interpretation. While many American historians of the late nineteenth century, some fresh from graduate study at German universities, tended to adopt the view that American institutions derived in essence from Anglo-Saxon (and ultimately Teutonic) sources, others were not so sure.[13] One of these was Frederick Jackson Turner, a young historian from Wisconsin, not long emerged from his graduate training at Johns Hopkins. Turner presented a paper to the American Historical Association, meeting in Chicago in 1893. Called "The Significance of the Frontier in American History," this paper proved to be one of the most influential essays in the history of American scholarship, and its point of view, supported by Turner's subsequent writings and his teaching, pervaded the field of American historical interpretation for at least a generation. Turner's thesis was that the dominant influence in the shaping of American institutions and American democracy was not this nation's European heritage in any of its forms, nor the forces emanating from the eastern seaboard cities, but rather the experiences created by a moving and variegated western frontier. Among the many effects attributed to the frontier environment and the challenges it presented was that it acted as a solvent for the national heritages and the separatist tendencies of the many nationality groups which had joined the trek westward, including the Germans and Scotch-Irish of the eighteenth century and the Scandinavians and Germans of the nineteenth. "The frontier," asserted Turner, "promoted the formation of a composite nationality for the American people. . . . In the crucible of the frontier the immigrants were Americanized, liberated, and fused into a mixed race, English in neither nationality nor characteristics. The process has gone on from the early days to our own." And later, in an essay on the role of the Mississippi Valley, he refers to "the tide of foreign immigration which has risen so

9

---

[11]*Pelasgic and Etruscan barbarism:* refers to the crude, barbaric state of the ancient inhabitants of the lands that were to become the sites of classical Greek and Roman civilization.

[12]*"La Nature aime les croisements":* [roughly translated] nature loves hybrids.

[13]See Edward N. Saveth, *American Historians and European Immigrants, 1875–1925,* New York, Columbia University Press, 1948. [Author's note]

steadily that it has made a composite American people whose amalgamation is destined to produce a new national stock."[14]

Cultural Pluralism

Probably all the non-English immigrants who came to American shores in any significant numbers from colonial times onward — settling either in the forbidding wilderness, the lonely prairie, or in some accessible urban slum — created ethnic enclaves and looked forward to the preservation of at least some of their native cultural patterns. Such a development, natural as breathing, was supported by the later accretion of friends, relatives, and countrymen seeking out oases of familiarity in a strange land, by the desire of the settlers to rebuild (necessarily in miniature) a society in which they could communicate in the familiar tongue and maintain familiar institutions, and, finally, by the necessity to band together for mutual aid and mutual protection against the uncertainties of a strange and frequently hostile environment. This was as true of the "old" immigrants as of the "new." In fact, some of the liberal intellectuals who fled to America from an inhospitable political climate in Germany in the 1830's, 1840's, and 1850's looked forward to the creation of an all-German state within the union, or, even more hopefully, to the eventual formation of a separate German nation, as soon as the expected dissolution of the union under the impact of the slavery controversy should have taken place.[15] Oscar Handlin,[16] writing of the sons of Erin[17] in mid-nineteenth-century Boston, recent refugees from famine and economic degradation in their homeland, points out: "Unable to participate in the normal associational affairs of the community, the Irish felt obliged to erect a society within a society, to act together in their own way. In every contact therefore the group, acting apart from other sections of the community, became intensely aware of its peculiar and exclusive identity."[18] Thus cultural pluralism was a fact in American

[14] Frederick Jackson Turner, *The Frontier in American History* (New York, Henry Holt, 1920), pp. 22–23, 190 [Author's note]

[15] Nathan Glazer, "Ethnic Groups in America: From National Culture to Ideology," in Morroe Berger, Theodore Abel, and Charles H. Page, eds., *Freedom and Control in Modern Society* (New York, D. Van Nostrand, 1954), p. 161; Marcus Lee Hansen, *The Immigrant in American History* (Cambridge, Harvard University Press, 1940), pp. 129–140; John A. Hawgood, *The Tragedy of German-America* (New York, Putnam's, 1940), *passim*. [Author's note]

[16] *Oscar Handlin:* American historian (b. 1915); winner of the Pulitzer Prize for his work on U.S. immigration.

[17] *sons of Erin:* Irish immigrants.

[18] Oscar Handlin, *Boston's Immigrants* (Cambridge, Harvard University Press, 1959, rev. edn.), p. 176. [Author's note]

society before it became a theory — a theory with explicit relevance for the nation as a whole, and articulated and discussed in the English-speaking circles of American intellectual life.

Early in 1915 there appeared in the pages of *The Nation* two articles under the title "Democracy *versus* the Melting-Pot." Their author was Horace Kallen, a Harvard-educated philosopher with a concern for the application of philosophy to societal affairs, and, as an American Jew, himself derivative of an ethnic background which was subject to the contemporary pressures for dissolution implicit in the "Americanization," or Anglo-conformity, and the melting-pot theories. In these articles Kallen vigorously rejected the usefulness of these theories as models of what was actually transpiring in American life or as ideals for the future. Rather he was impressed by the way in which the various ethnic groups in America were coincident with particular areas and regions, and with the tendency for each group to preserve its own language, religion, communal institutions, and ancestral culture. All the while, he pointed out, the immigrant has been learning to speak English as the language of general communication, and has participated in the over-all economic and political life of the nation. These developments in which "the United States are in the process of becoming a federal state not merely as a union of geographical and administrative unities, but also as a cooperation of cultural diversities, as a federation or commonwealth of national cultures,"[19] the author argued, far from constituting a violation of historic American political principles, as the "Americanizers" claimed, actually represented the inevitable consequences of democratic ideals, since individuals are implicated in groups, and since democracy for the individual must by extension also mean democracy for his group.

The processes just described, however, as Kallen develops his argument, are far from having been thoroughly realized. They are menaced by "Americanization" programs, assumptions of Anglo-Saxon superiority, and misguided attempts to promote "racial" amalgamation. Thus America stands at a kind of cultural crossroads. It can attempt to impose by force an artificial, Anglo-Saxon oriented uniformity on its peoples, or it can consciously allow and encourage its ethnic groups to develop democratically, each emphasizing its particular cultural heritage. If the latter course is followed, as Kallen puts it at the close of his essay, then,[20]

11

12

---

[19] Horace M. Kallen, "Democracy *versus* the Melting-Pot," *The Nation*, 18 and 25 February 1915; reprinted in his *Culture and Democracy in the United States*, New York, Boni and Liveright, 1924; the quotation is on p. 116. [Author's note]
[20] Kallen, *Culture and Democracy . . .* , p. 124. [Author's note]

The outlines of a possible great and truly democratic commonwealth become discernible. Its form would be that of the federal republic; its substance a democracy of nationalities, cooperating voluntarily and autonomously through common institutions in the enterprise of self-realization through the perfection of men according to their kind. The common language of the commonwealth, the language of its great tradition, would be English, but each nationality would have for its emotional and involuntary life its own peculiar dialect or speech, its own individual and inevitable esthetic and intellectual forms. The political and economic life of the commonwealth is a single unit and serves as the foundation and background for the realization of the distinctive individuality of each *nation* that composes it and of the pooling of these in a harmony above them all. Thus "American civilization" may come to mean the perfection of the cooperative harmonies of "European civilization" — the waste, the squalor and the distress of Europe being eliminated — a multiplicity in a unity, an orchestration of mankind.

Engaging the Text

1. Explain and illustrate the difference between the melting pot and cultural PLURALISM.

2. Gordon distinguishes between "descriptive models" and "goal models." Write a paragraph explaining the distinction. If possible, include your own examples.

3. Gordon roughly defines three varieties of "Anglo-conformity" in paragraph 2. Imagine that it is 1925 and that you support one of these three types of ASSIMILATION. Write a paragraph defining and defending a desirable immigration policy from that POINT OF VIEW. Then switch viewpoints and write a second paragraph, then a third.

4. To follow up on the previous assignment, work with classmates to formulate a response to or a rebuttal of these policies from the point of view of someone who favors cultural pluralism.

Exploring Connections

1. Which IDEOLOGY of assimilation seems to dominate in Alistair Cooke's "The Huddled Masses"? Which ideology would seem to be most consistent with Anzia Yezierska's view of the immigrant? With Crèvecoeur's essay in Chapter One, "American Dreams"?

2. Would Kwame Toure (p. 250) agree with Gordon that "there is by no means any necessary equation between Anglo-conformity and racist attitudes"? Explain.

3. Drawing on all the personal NARRATIVES and poems in this chapter, evaluate the strengths and limitations of Gordon's classification scheme. Propose an alternate model for describing the varieties and degrees of assimilation you see in these readings.

Extending the Critical Context

1. What qualities, CHARACTERISTICS, values, and behaviors would an immigrant have to adopt to conform with ANGLO culture in the United States today?

2. What METAPHORS besides "melting pot" have you heard used to describe assimilation in American society (e.g., "mosaic," "salad")? In what ways does each metaphor make sense or tell us something about the United States, and in what ways (if any) is each metaphor limited, misleading, or inaccurate?

3. Look up the word "ideology" in the glossary and an encyclopedia. Using this information and examples drawn from your own experience, write an essay explaining what an ideology is and how it works.

Letter to My Mother

TRAN THI NGA

Tran Thi Nga was born in China in 1927 and educated in Hanoi, Vietnam, and South Wales, Great Britain. She has worked as a social worker in Vietnam and as a journalist in both Asia and the United States. She currently lives in Connecticut. The following piece, which might be considered a prose poem, speaks eloquently of an immigrant's ties not only to her mother, but to her mother country.

Dear Mother,

I do not know if you are receiving my letters, but I will keep writing   1
to you as you are always in my mind.

We have been here three years now. I have moved from Greenwich   2
and have a wooden shingled house in Cos Cob. We have a garden in
the back where we plant vegetables, flowers in the front the way we
used to when we were together. I have a pink dogwood tree that blooms
in spring. It looks like the Hoa dai tree, but has no leaves, only flowers.

We worked for months to clear away the poison ivy, a plant that turns   3
your skin red and makes you itch.

We are near a beach, a school and a shopping center. Green lawns   4
go down to the streets and there are many cars and garages. I am even
learning to drive.

When we got our new house, people from the church came and took us to "Friendly's" for ice cream. Americans celebrate with ice cream. They have so many kinds — red like watermelon, green for pistachio, orange sherbet like Buddha's robes, mint chocolate chip. You buy it fast and take it away to eat. 5

Our house is small, but a place to be together and discuss our daily life. At every meal we stare at the dishes you used to fix for us and think about you. We are sorry for you and for ourselves. 6

If we work hard here, we have everything, but we fear you are hungry and cold and lonesome. Last week we made up a package of clothes. We all tried to figure out how thin you must be now. I do not know if you will ever receive that package wrapped with all our thoughts. 7

I remember the last days when you encouraged us to leave the country and refused to go yourself. You said you were too old, did not want to leave your home and would be a burden to us. We realize now that you sacrificed yourself for our well-being. 8

You have a new grandson born in the United States. Thanh looked beautiful at her wedding in a red velvet dress and white veil, a yellow turban in her dark hair. She carried the chrysanthemums you love. 9

You always loved the fall in Hanoi. You liked the cold. We don't. We have just had the worst winter in a century, snow piled everywhere. I must wear a heavy coat, boots, fur gloves, and a hat. I look like a ball running to the train station. I feel that if I fell down, I could never get up. 10

Your grandson is three, in nursery school. He speaks English so well that we are sad. We made a rule. We must speak Vietnamese at home so that the children will not forget their mother tongue. 11

We have made an altar to Father. We try to keep up our traditions so that we can look forward to the day we can return to our country, although we do not know when that will be. 12

Here we are materially well off, but spiritually deprived. We miss our country. Most of all we miss you. Should Buddha exist, we should keep praying to be reunited. 13

Dear Mother, keep up your mind. Pray to Buddha silently. We will have a future and I hope it will be soon. 14

We want to swim in our own pond. 15
Clear or stinky, still it is ours.

Your daughter,

Nga

Engaging the Text

1. Make two columns, one for each culture referred to in Tran's letter, and list specific details in each column. Based on this data, what are the SPEAKER'S attitudes toward America in the poem? Toward Vietnam?

2. Why is the family sad that the grandson speaks English so well?

3. In what sense are Tran and her family "spiritually deprived"?

Exploring Connections

1. Compare and contrast Tran's attitudes toward America and her native land with those expressed by Anzia Yezierska's NARRATOR earlier in this chapter.

2. Which of Milton Gordon's three models of ASSIMILATION (see "Assimilation in America" earlier in this chapter) comes closest to describing the attitudes of the speaker in this letter? In what ways do these models fail to account for or capture the reactions of this individual immigrant to America?

3. Taking the role of an "experienced" immigrant like Hank López from the next selection, "Back to Bachimba," write a letter to Tran, advising her how best to cope with the unfamiliar ways of her adopted country. Read these letters aloud in class and discuss.

Back to Bachimba
ENRIQUE "HANK" LÓPEZ

Enrique "Hank" López (1921–1985) distinguished himself in the Chicano community as the first Hispanic graduate of Harvard Law School and as a dedicated educator, author, and activist. Having apparently achieved the immigrant's dream of success, López felt the pressures and the personal ambivalence that often accompany assimilation. In "Back to Bachimba," he describes the complex feelings of people who see themselves as "hyphenated Americans."

I am a *pocho* from Bachimba, a rather small Mexican village in the   1
state of Chihuahua, where my father fought with the army of Pancho
Villa.[1] He was, in fact, the only private in Villa's army.

[1]*Pancho Villa:* Mexican revolutionary and folk hero (1878–1923) who led guerrilla raids into U.S. territory in 1915.

Pocho is ordinarily a derogatory term in Mexico (to define it succinctly,   2
a *pocho* is a Mexican slob who has pretensions of being a gringo sonofabitch),
but I use it in a very special sense. To me that word has come to mean
"uprooted Mexican," and that's what I have been all my life. Though
my entire upbringing and education took place in the United States, I
have never felt completely American, and when I am in Mexico, I
sometimes feel like a displaced gringo with a curiously Mexican name
— Enrique Preciliano López y Martinez de Sepulveda de Sapien de
Quien-sabe-quien. One might conclude that I'm either a schizo-cultural
Mexican or a cultured schizoid American.

In any event, the schizo-ing began a long time ago, when my father   3
and many of Pancho Villa's troops fled across the border to escape the
oncoming *federales*[2] who eventually defeated Villa. My mother and I,
traveling across the hot desert plains in a buckboard wagon, joined my
father in El Paso, Texas, a few days after his hurried departure. With
more and more Villistas swarming into El Paso every day, it was quickly
apparent that jobs would be exceedingly scarce and insecure; so my
parents packed our few belongings and we took the first available bus
to Denver. My father had hoped to move to Chicago because the name
sounded so Mexican, but my mother's meager savings were hardly enough
to buy tickets for Colorado.

There we moved into a ghetto of Spanish-speaking residents who chose   4
to call themselves Spanish Americans and resented the sudden migration
of their brethren from Mexico, whom they sneeringly called *surumatos*
(slang for "southerners"). These so-called Spanish Americans claimed
direct descent from the original *conquistadores*[3] of Spain. They also
insisted that they had *never* been Mexicans, since their region of New
Spain (later annexed to the United States) was never a part of Mexico.
But what they claimed most vociferously — and erroneously — was an
absence of Indian ancestry. It made no difference that any objective
observer could see by merely looking at them the results of considerable
fraternization between the conquering Spaniards and the Comanche and
Navaho women who crossed their paths. Still, these *manitos*, as they
were snidely labeled by the *surumatos*, stubbornly refused to be identified
with Mexico, and would actually fight anyone who called them Mexican.
So intense was this intergroup rivalry that the bitterest "race riots" I
have ever witnessed — and engaged in — were between the look-alike,
talk-alike *surumatos* and *manitos* who lived near Denver's Curtis Park.

[2]*federales:* U.S. troops.
[3]*conquistadores:* leaders of the sixteenth-century Spanish conquest of America.

In retrospect the harsh conflicts between us were all the more silly and self-defeating when one recalls that we were all lumped together as "spiks" and "greasers" by the Anglo-Saxon community.

Predictably enough, we *surumatos* began huddling together in a sub- 5 neighborhood within the larger ghetto, and it was there that I became painfully aware that my father had been the only private in Pancho Villa's army. Most of my friends were the sons of captains, colonels, majors, and even generals, though a few fathers were admittedly mere sergeants and corporals. My father alone had been a lowly private in that famous Division del Norte. Naturally, I developed a most painful complex, which led me to all sorts of compensatory fibs. During one brief spell I fancied my father as a member of the dreaded *los dorados*, the "golden ones," who were Villa's favorite henchmen. (Later I was to learn that my father's cousin, Martin López, was a genuine and quite notorious *dorado*.) But all my inventions were quickly un-invented by my very own father, who seemed to take a perverse delight in being Pancho's only private.

No doubt my chagrin was accentuated by the fact that Pancho Villa's 6 exploits were a constant topic of conversation in our household. My entire childhood seems to be shadowed by his presence. At our dinner table, almost every night, we would listen to endlessly repeated accounts of this battle, that stratagem, or some great act of Robin Hood kindness by *el centauro del norte*.[4] I remember how angry my parents were when they saw Wallace Beery[5] in *Viva Villa!* "Garbage by stupid gringos," they called it. They were particularly offended by the sweaty, unshaven sloppiness of Beery's portrayal. "Pancho Villa was clean and orderly, no matter how much he chased after women. This man's a dirty swine."

As if to deepen our sense of *Villismo*, my parents also taught us 7 "Adelita" and "*Se llevaron el cañon para Bachimba*" ("They took the cannons to Bachimba"), the two most famous songs of the Mexican revolution. Some twenty years later (during my stint at Harvard Law School), while strolling along the Charles River, I would find myself softly singing "*Se llevaron el cañon para Bachimba, para Bachimba, para Bachimba*" over and over again. That's all I could remember of that poignant rebel song. Though I had been born there, I had always regarded "Bachimba" as a fictitious, made-up, Lewis Carroll[6] kind of word. So that eight years ago, when I first returned to Mexico, I was

---

[4]*el centauro del norte:* [Spanish] the centaur of the North — referring to Pancho Villa.
[5]*Wallace Beery:* American film actor (1885–1949).
[6]*Lewis Carroll:* pen name of English writer and mathematician Charles Dodgson (1832–1898), best known for *Alice's Adventures in Wonderland*.

literally stunned when I came to a crossroad south of Chihuahua and saw an old road marker: "Bachimba 18 km." Then it really exists — I shouted inwardly — Bachimba is a real town! Swinging onto the narrow, poorly paved road, I gunned the motor and sped toward the town I'd been singing about since infancy. It turned out to be a quiet, dusty village with a bleak worn-down plaza that was surrounded by nondescript buildings of uncertain vintage.

Aside from the songs about Bachimba and Adelita and all the folk tales 8 about Villa's guerrilla fighters, my early years were strongly influenced by our neighborhood celebrations of Mexico's two most important patriotic events: Mexican Independence Day on September 16 and the anniversary of the battle of Puebla on May 5. On those two dates Mexicans all over the world are likely to become extremely chauvinistic.[7] In Denver we would stage annual parades that included three or four floats skimpily decorated with crepe paper streamers, a small band, several adults in threadbare battle dress, and hundreds of kids marching in wild disorder. It was during one of these parades — I was ten years old then — that I was seized with acute appendicitis and had to be rushed to a hospital. The doctor subsequently told my mother that I had made a long, impassioned speech about the early revolutionist Miguel Hidalgo while the anesthetic was taking hold, and she explained with pardonable pride that it was the speech I was to make at Turner Hall that evening. Mine was one of the twenty-three *discursos* scheduled on the postparade program, a copy of which my mother still retains. My only regret was missing the annual *discurso* of Don Miguel Gómez, my godfather, a deep-throated orator who would always climax his speech by falling to his knees and dramatically kissing the floor, almost weeping as he loudly proclaimed: "*Ay, Mexico! Beso tu tierra, tu mero corazon*" ("Ah, Mexico! I kiss your sacred soil, the very heart of you"). He gave the same oration for seventeen years, word for word and gesture for gesture, and it never failed to bring tears to his eyes. But not once did he return to Chihuahua, even for a brief visit.

My personal Mexican-ness eventually produced serious problems for 9 me. Upon entering grade school I learned English rapidly, and rather well, always ranking either first or second in my class; yet the hard core of me remained stubbornly Mexican. This chauvinism may have been a reaction to the constant racial prejudice we encountered on all sides. The neighborhood cops were always running us off the streets and calling

---

[7]*chauvinistic:* characterized by excessive attachment to any group or nationality.

us "dirty greasers," and most of our teachers frankly regarded us as totally inferior. I still remember the galling disdain of my sixth-grade teacher, whose constant mimicking of our heavily accented speech drove me to a desperate study of *Webster's Dictionary* in the hope of acquiring a vocabulary larger than hers. Sadly enough, I succeeded only too well, and for the next few years I spoke the most ridiculous high-flown rhetoric in the Denver public schools. One of my favorite words was "indubitably," and it must have driven everyone mad. I finally got rid of my accent by constantly reciting "Peter Piper picked a peck of pickled peppers" with little round pebbles in my mouth. Somewhere I had read about Demosthenes.[8]

During this phase of my childhood the cultural tug of war known as   10 "Americanization" almost pulled me apart. There were moments when I would identify completely with the gringo world (what could have been more American than my earnest high-voiced portrayal of George Washington, however ridiculous the cotton wig my mother had fashioned for me?); then quite suddenly I would feel so acutely Mexican that I would stammer over the simplest English phrase. I was so ready to take offense at the slightest slur against Mexicans that I would imagine prejudice where none existed. But on other occasions, in full confidence of my belonging, I would venture forth into social areas that I should have realized were clearly forbidden to little chicanos from Curtis Park. The inevitable rebuffs would leave me floundering in self-pity; it was small comfort to know that other minority groups suffered even worse rebuffs than we did.

The only non-Mexican boy on our street was a Negro named Leroy   11 Logan, who was probably my closest childhood friend. Leroy was the best athlete, the best whistler, the best liar, the best horseshoe player, the best marble shooter, the best mumblety-pegger, and the best shoplifter in our neighborhood. He was also my "partner," and I thus entitled myself to a fifty-fifty share of all his large triumphs and petty thefts. Because he considered "Mexican" a derogatory word bordering on obscenity, Leroy would pronounce it "Mesican" so as to soften its harshness. But once in a while, when he'd get angry with me, he would call me a "lousy Mesican greasy spik" with the most extraordinarily effective hissing one can imagine. And I'm embarrassed to admit that I would retaliate by calling him "alligator bait." As a matter of fact, just after I had returned from the hospital, he came to visit me, and I thoughtlessly

[8]*Demosthenes:* celebrated Greek orator and politician (385–322 B.C.).

greeted him with a flippant, "Hi, alligator ba —" I never finished the phrase because Leroy whacked me on the stomach with a Ping-Pong paddle and rushed out of my house with great, sobbing anger.

Weeks later, when we had re-established a rather cool rapport, I tried 12 to make up for my stupid insult by helping him steal cabbages from the vegetable trucks that rumbled through our neighborhood on their way to the produce markets. They would come down Larimer Street in the early dawn, and Leroy and I would sneak up behind them at the 27th Street stop sign, where they were forced to pause for cross traffic. Then Leroy, with a hooked pole he had invented, would stab the top cabbages and roll them off the truck. I would be waiting below to catch them with an open gunny sack. Our system was fabulously successful for a while, and we found a ready market for the stolen goods; but one morning, as I started to unfurl my sack, a fairly large cabbage conked me on the head. Screaming with pain, I lunged at Leroy and tried to bite him. He, laughing all the while — it was obviously a funny scene — glided out of my reach, and finally ran into a nearby alley. We never engaged in commercial affairs thereafter.

Still and all, I remember him with great affection and a touch of 13 sadness. I say sadness because eventually Leroy was to suffer the misery of being an outsider in an already outside ghetto. As he grew older, it was apparent that he longed to be a Mexican, that he felt terribly dark and alone. "Sometimes," he would tell me, "I feel like my damn skin's too tight, like I'm gonna bust out of it." One cold February night I found him in the coal shed behind Pacheco's store, desperately scraping his forearm with sandpaper, the hurt tears streaming down his face. "I got to get this off, man. I can't stand all this blackness." We stood there quietly staring at the floor for a long, anguished moment, both of us miserable beyond word or gesture. Finally he drew a deep breath, blew his nose loudly, and mumbled half audibly, "Man, you sure lucky to be a Mesican."

Not long after this incident Leroy moved out of Denver to live with 14 relatives in Georgia. When I saw him off at the bus station, he grabbed my shoulder and whispered huskily, "You gonna miss me, man. You watch what I tellya." "Indubitably," I said. "Aw, man, cut that stuff. You the most fancy-pants Mesican I know." Those were his last words to me, and they caused a considerable dent in my ego. Not enough, however, to diminish my penchant for fancy language. The dictionary continued to be my comic book well into high school.

Speaking of language, I am reminded of a most peculiar circumstance: 15 almost every Mexican American lawyer that I've ever met speaks English with a noticeable Spanish accent, this despite the fact that they have all been born, reared, and educated exclusively in America. Of the forty-eight lawyers I have in mind, only three of us are free of any accent. Needless to say, our "cultural drag" has been weighty and persistent. And one must presume that our ethnic hyphens shall be with us for many years to come.

My own Mexican-ness, after years of decline at Harvard University, suddenly burst forth again when I returned to Chihuahua and stumbled on the town of Bachimba. I had long conversations with an uncle I'd never met before, my father's younger brother, Ramón. It was Tío Ramón who chilled my spine with eyewitness stories about Pancho Villa's legendary *dorados*, one of whom was Martin López. "He was your second cousin. The bravest young buck in Villa's army. And he became a *dorado* when he was scarcely seventeen years old because he dared to defy Pancho Villa himself. As your papa may have told you, Villa had a bad habit of burying treasure up in the mountains and also burying the man he took with him to dig the hole for it. Well, one day he chose Martin López to go with him. Deep in the mountains they went, near Parral. And when they got to a suitably lonely place, Pancho Villa told him to dig a hole with pick and shovel. Then, when Martin had dug down to his waist, Villa leveled a gun at the boy. "Say your prayers, *muchacho*. You shall stay here with the gold — forever." But Martin had come prepared. In his large right boot he had a gun, and when he rose from his bent position, he was pointing that gun at Villa. They stood there, both ready to fire, for several seconds, and finally Don Pancho started to laugh in that wonderful way of his. *"Bravo, bravo, muchacho!* You've got more guts than a man. Get out of that hole, boy. I need you for my *dorados*."

Tío Ramón's eyes were wet with pride. "But what is more important, he died with great valor. Two years later, after he had terrorized the *federales* and Pershing's[9] gringo soldiers, he was finally wounded and captured here in Bachimba. It was a bad wound in his leg, finally turning to gangrene. Then one Sunday morning they hauled Martin López and three other prisoners to the plaza. One by one they executed the three lesser prisoners against that wall. I was up on the church tower watching it all. Finally it was your uncle's turn. They dragged him off the buckboard wagon and handed him his crutches. Slowly, painfully, he hobbled to the wall and stood there. Very straight he stood. 'Do you have any last words?' asked the captain of the firing squad. With great pride Martin tossed his crutches aside and stood very tall on his one good leg. 'Give

[9]*Pershing:* John Joseph Pershing, American general (1860–1948), led troops against Pancho Villa in 1916.

me, you yellow bastards, give me a gun — and I'll show you who is the man among . . .' Eight bullets crashed into his chest and face, and I never heard that final word. That was your second cousin. You would have been proud to know him."

As I listened to Tio Ramón's soft nostalgic voice that evening, there 18 in the sputtering light of the kerosene lamp on his back patio, I felt as intensely Mexican as I shall ever feel.

But not for long. Within six weeks I was destined to feel *less* Mexican 19 than I had ever felt. The scene of my trauma was the Centro Mexicano de Escritores, where the finest young writers of Mexico met regularly to discuss works in progress and to engage in erudite literary and philosophical discussions. Week after week I sat among them, dumbstruck by my inadequacy in Spanish and my total ignorance of their whole frame of reference. How could I have possibly imagined that I was Mexican? Those conversations were a dense tangle of local and private allusions, and the few threads I could grasp only magnified my ignorance. The novelist Juan Rulfo was then reading the initial drafts of his *Pedro Páramo*, later to be acclaimed the best avant-garde[10] fiction in Mexican literature. Now that I have soaked myself in the *ambiance* of Mexico, Rulfo's novel intrigues me beyond measure; but when he first read it at the Centro, he might just as well have been reading "Jabberwocky"[11] in Swahili for all I understood of it. And because all of the other Mexican writers knew and greatly appreciated *Páramo*, I could only assume that I was really "too gringo" to comprehend it. For this reason, I, a person with no great talent for reticence, never opened my mouth at the Centro. In fact, I was so shell-shocked by those sessions that I even found it difficult to converse with my housekeeper about such simple matters as dirty laundry or the loose doorknob in the bathroom.

Can any of us really go home again? I, for one, am convinced that I 20 have no true home, that I must reconcile myself to a schizo-cultural limbo, with a mere hyphen to provide some slight cohesion between my split selves. This inevitable splitting is a plague and a pleasure. Some mornings as I glide down the Paseo de la Reforma, perhaps the most beautiful boulevard in the world, I am suddenly angered by the *machismo*, or aggressive maleness, of Mexican drivers who crowd and bully their screeching machines through dense traffic. What terrible insecurity, what awful dread of emasculation, produces such assertive bully-boy conduct behind a steering wheel? Whatever the reasons, there is a part of me

---

[10] *avant-garde:* pertaining to unorthodox and experimental art or artists.

[11] *Jabberwocky:* a nonsense poem from Lewis Carroll's *Through the Looking Glass*.

that can never accept this much-celebrated *machismo*. Nor can I accept the exaggerated nationalism one so frequently encounters in the press, on movie screens, over the radio, in daily conversations — that shrill barrage of slogans proclaiming that "there is only one Mexico."

Recently, when I expressed these views to an old friend, he smiled quite knowingly: "Let's face it, Hank, you're not really a Mexican — despite that long, comical name of yours. You're an American through and through." But that, of course, is a minority view and almost totally devoid of realism. One could just as well say that Martin Luther King was not a Negro, that he was merely an American. But the plain truth is that neither I nor the Martin Luther Kings of our land can escape the fact that we are Mexican and Negro with roots planted so deeply in the United States that we have grown those strong little hyphens that make us Mexican-American and Negro-American. This assertion may not please some idealists who would prefer to blind themselves to our obvious ethnic and racial differences, who are unwittingly patronizing when they insist that we are all alike and indistinguishable. But the politicians, undoubtedly the most pragmatic creatures in America, are completely aware that ethnic groups *do* exist and that they seem to huddle together, bitch together, and sometimes vote together.

When all is said and done, we hyphenated Americans are here to stay, bubbling happily or unhappily in the great non-melting pot. Much has been gained and will be gained from the multiethnic aspects of the United States, and there is no useful purpose in attempting to wish it away or to homogenize it out of existence. In spite of the race riots in Watts[12] and ethnic unrest elsewhere, there would appear to be a kind of modus vivendi[13] developing on almost every level of American life.

And if there are those of us who may never feel completely at home, we can always make that brief visit to Bachimba.

[12] *race riots in Watts:* refers to the 1965 civil insurrection in Watts, a predominantly black community in Los Angeles, California.
[13] *modus vivendi:*[Latin] manner of living; way of life.

Engaging the Text

1. What does Bachimba represent to López? Why was he "stunned" to discover that it was a real town? Did its significance change for him after he had seen it in person?

2. Why is Pancho Villa such an important figure for the López family and the Mexican-American community as a whole? What does López mean when he describes his father as "the only private in Villa's army"?

3. Based on the information López provides, diagram the social HIERARCHY of ETHNIC groups in Denver: *surumatos, manitos,* blacks, ANGLOS, and Indians. Who is at the top of the ladder? At the bottom? Does there seem to be a consistent explanation for each group's position in this hierarchy?

4. At the end of "Back to Bachimba," López offers some conclusions about ASSIMILATION, politics, hyphenated Americans, and related topics. How clearly do his conclusions follow from his experiences? Explain.

Exploring Connections

1. Read or review "Formation of In-Groups" by Gordon Allport in Chapter Two, "Justice for All." How would Allport explain the bitter conflict between the *surumatos* and the *manitos*?

2. Compare López's account of what it means to grow up between two cultures with that of Adrienne Rich (p. 101). Write an essay in which you explore and try to account for the differences between their experiences.

3. López's feeling of "Mexican-ness" seems to arise in part from the stories, songs, and *discursos* he learned from his family. Compare and contrast the role of stories in creating personal identity in this essay and in Paula Gunn Allen's "Where I Come From Is Like This" in Chapter Four, "Women."

Extending the Critical Context

1. In "Back to Bachimba," López seems to imply that we need personal dreams, personal MYTHS about our family and our origins, perhaps both to give us a sense of our own special identity as we enter the "melting pot" and to reaffirm our sense of community and continuity with the past. What myths about origins fulfill this function in your family?

From *The Woman Warrior*

MAXINE HONG KINGSTON

To the Chinese immigrant, white Americans are "ghosts" — threatening and, at times, comical specters who speak an incomprehensible tongue. For many immigrants, becoming American means living among "ghosts," finding a new voice, adopting new values, defining a new self. This selection, from Maxine Hong Kingston's enormously popular autobiography,

The Woman Warrior, describes the conflicts experienced by a young Chinese girl as she struggles to adapt to new ways in her American school.

Maxine Hong Kingston (b. 1940) taught in several high schools and private business schools before The Woman Warrior *brought her national recognition in 1975. Since then, she has published* China Men *(1980). She currently teaches at the University of Hawaii.*

Long ago in China, knot-makers tied string into buttons and frogs, and rope into bell pulls. There was one knot so complicated that it blinded the knot-maker. Finally an emperor outlawed this cruel knot, and the nobles could not order it anymore. If I had lived in China, I would have been an outlaw knot-maker. 1

Maybe that's why my mother cut my tongue. She pushed my tongue up and sliced the frenum. Or maybe she snipped it with a pair of nail scissors. I don't remember her doing it, only her telling me about it, but all during childhood I felt sorry for the baby whose mother waited with scissors or knife in hand for it to cry — and then, when its mouth was wide open like a baby bird's, cut. The Chinese say "a ready tongue is an evil." 2

I used to curl up my tongue in front of the mirror and tauten my frenum into a white line, itself as thin as a razor blade. I saw no scars in my mouth. I thought perhaps I had had two frena, and she had cut one. I made other children open their mouths so I could compare theirs to mine. I saw perfect pink membranes stretching into precise edges that looked easy enough to cut. Sometimes I felt very proud that my mother committed such a powerful act upon me. At other times I was terrified — the first thing my mother did when she saw me was to cut my tongue. 3

"Why did you do that to me, Mother?" 4

"I told you." 5

"Tell me again." 6

"I cut it so that you would not be tongue-tied. Your tongue would be able to move in any language. You'll be able to speak languages that are completely different from one another. You'll be able to pronounce anything. Your frenum looked too tight to do those things, so I cut it." 7

"But isn't 'a ready tongue an evil'?" 8

"Things are different in this ghost country." 9

"Did it hurt me? Did I cry and bleed?" 10

"I don't remember. Probably." 11

She didn't cut the other children's. When I asked cousins and other 12
Chinese children whether their mothers had cut their tongues loose,
they said, "What?"

"Why didn't you cut my brothers' and sisters' tongues?" 13
"They didn't need it." 14
"Why not? Were theirs longer than mine?" 15
"Why don't you quit blabbering and get to work?" 16

If my mother was not lying she should have cut more, scraped away 17
the rest of the frenum skin, because I have a terrible time talking. Or
she should not have cut at all, tampering with my speech. When I went
to kindergarten and had to speak English for the first time, I became
silent. A dumbness — a shame — still cracks my voice in two, even
when I want to say "hello" casually, or ask an easy question in front of
the check-out counter, or ask directions of a bus driver. I stand frozen,
or I hold up the line with the complete, grammatical sentence that
comes squeaking out at impossible length. "What did you say?" says the
cab driver, or "Speak up," so I have to perform again, only weaker the
second time. A telephone call makes my throat bleed and takes up that
day's courage. It spoils my day with self-disgust when I hear my broken
voice come skittering out into the open. It makes people wince to hear
it. I'm getting better, though. Recently I asked the postman for special-
issue stamps; I've waited since childhood for postmen to give me some
of their own accord. I am making progress, a little every day.

My silence was thickest — total — during the three years that I 18
covered my school paintings with black paint. I painted layers of black
over houses and flowers and suns, and when I drew on the blackboard,
I put a layer of chalk on top. I was making a stage curtain, and it was
the moment before the curtain parted or rose. The teachers called my
parents to school, and I saw they had been saving my pictures, curling
and cracking, all alike and black. The teachers pointed to the pictures
and looked serious, talked seriously too, but my parents did not understand
English. ("The parents and teachers of criminals were executed," said
my father.) My parents took the pictures home. I spread them out (so
black and full of possibilities) and pretended the curtains were swinging
open, flying up, one after another, sunlight underneath, mighty operas.

During the first silent year I spoke to no one at school, did not ask 19
before going to the lavatory, and flunked kindergarten. My sister also
said nothing for three years, silent in the playground and silent at lunch.
There were other quiet Chinese girls not of our family, but most of them
got over it sooner than we did. I enjoyed the silence. At first it did not
occur to me I was supposed to talk or to pass kindergarten. I talked at
home and to one or two of the Chinese kids in class. I made motions

and even made some jokes. I drank out of a toy saucer when the water spilled out of the cup, and everybody laughed, pointing at me, so I did it some more. I didn't know that Americans don't drink out of saucers.

I liked the Negro students (Black Ghosts) best because they laughed 20 the loudest and talked to me as if I were a daring talker too. One of the Negro girls had her mother coil braids over her ears Shanghai-style like mine; we were Shanghai twins except that she was covered with black like my paintings. Two Negro kids enrolled in Chinese school, and the teachers gave them Chinese names. Some Negro kids walked me to school and home, protecting me from the Japanese kids, who hit me and chased me and stuck gum in my ears. The Japanese kids were noisy and tough. They appeared one day in kindergarten, released from concentration camp,[1] which was a tic-tac-toe mark, like barbed wire, on the map.

It was when I found out I had to talk that school became a misery, 21 that the silence became a misery. I did not speak and felt bad each time that I did not speak. I read aloud in first grade, though, and heard the barest whisper with little squeaks come out of my throat. "Louder," said the teacher, who scared the voice away again. The other Chinese girls did not talk either, so I knew the silence had to do with being a Chinese girl.

Reading out loud was easier than speaking because we did not have 22 to make up what to say, but I stopped often, and the teacher would think I'd gone quiet again. I could not understand "I." The Chinese "I" has seven strokes, intricacies. How could the American "I," assuredly wearing a hat like the Chinese, have only three strokes, the middle so straight? Was it out of politeness that this writer left off strokes the way a Chinese has to write her own name small and crooked? No, it was not politeness; "I" is a capital and "you" is a lower-case. I stared at that middle line and waited so long for its black center to resolve into tight strokes and dots that I forgot to pronounce it. The other troublesome word was "here," no strong consonant to hang on to, and so flat, when "here" is two mountainous ideographs.[2] The teacher, who had already told me every day how to read "I" and "here," put me in the low corner under the stairs again, where the noisy boys usually sat.

When my second grade class did a play, the whole class went to the 23 auditorium except the Chinese girls. The teacher, lovely and Hawaiian,

---

[1]*concentration camp:* refers to one of the U.S. camps where Japanese-Americans were imprisoned during World War II.

[2]*ideographs:* composite characters in Chinese writing made by combining two or more other characters.

should have understood about us, but instead left us behind in the classroom. Our voices were too soft or nonexistent, and our parents never signed the permission slips anyway. They never signed anything unnecessary. We opened the door a crack and peeked out, but closed it again quickly. One of us (not me) won every spelling bee, though.

I remember telling the Hawaiian teacher, "We Chinese can't sing 24 'land where our fathers died.' " She argued with me about politics, while I meant because of curses. But how can I have that memory when I couldn't talk? My mother says that we, like the ghosts, have no memories.

After American school, we picked up our cigar boxes, in which we 25 had arranged books, brushes, and an inkbox neatly, and went to Chinese school, from 5:00 to 7:30 P.M. There we chanted together, voices rising and falling, loud and soft, some boys shouting, everybody reading together, reciting together and not alone with one voice. When we had a memorization test, the teacher let each of us come to his desk and say the lesson to him privately, while the rest of the class practiced copying or tracing. Most of the teachers were men. The boys who were so well behaved in the American school played tricks on them and talked back to them. The girls were not mute. They screamed and yelled during recess, when there were no rules; they had fistfights. Nobody was afraid of children hurting themselves or of children hurting school property. The glass doors to the red and green balconies with the gold joy symbols were left wide open so that we could run out and climb the fire escapes. We played capture-the-flag in the auditorium, where Sun Yat-sen and Chiang Kai-shek's pictures hung at the back of the stage, the Chinese flag on their left and the American flag on their right. We climbed the teak ceremonial chairs and made flying leaps off the stage. One flag headquarters was behind the glass door and the other on stage right. Our feet drummed on the hollow stage. During recess the teachers locked themselves up in their office with the shelves of books, copybooks, inks from China. They drank tea and warmed their hands at a stove. There was no play supervision. At recess we had the school to ourselves, and also we could roam as far as we could go — downtown, Chinatown stores, home — as long as we returned before the bell rang.

At exactly 7:30 the teacher again picked up the brass bell that sat on 26 his desk and swung it over our heads, while we charged down the stairs, our cheering magnified in the stairwell. Nobody had to line up.

Not all of the children who were silent at American school found voice 27 at Chinese school. One new teacher said each of us had to get up and recite in front of the class, who was to listen. My sister and I had memorized the lesson perfectly. We said it to each other at home, one chanting, one listening. The teacher called on my sister to recite first.

It was the first time a teacher had called on the second-born to go first. My sister was scared. She glanced at me and looked away; I looked down at my desk. I hoped that she could do it because if she could, then I would have to. She opened her mouth and a voice came out that wasn't a whisper, but it wasn't a proper voice either. I hoped that she would not cry, fear breaking up her voice like twigs underfoot. She sounded as if she were trying to sing through weeping and strangling. She did not pause or stop to end the embarrassment. She kept going until she said the last word, and then she sat down. When it was my turn, the same voice came out, a crippled animal running on broken legs. You could hear splinters in my voice, bones rubbing jagged against one another. I was loud, though. I was glad I didn't whisper. There was one little girl who whispered.

Engaging the Text

1. After reading the whole selection, explain the significance of the first paragraph and Kingston's assertion that she "would have been an outlaw knot-maker."

2. Did Kingston's mother literally cut her tongue? If so, why, and what was the result? If not, why does Kingston create this elaborate and graphic story?

3. Why is Kingston silent? What's the connection between her silence and her being Chinese? Between her silence and her being female?

4. Working in groups, identify the ways Chinese and American cultures conflict with each other as described in this selection.

Exploring Connections

1. Compare and contrast Kingston's "voicelessness" with the "invisibility" of the NARRATOR of the selection from Ellison's *Invisible Man* in Chapter Two, "Justice for All."

2. In "The Achievement of Desire" (Chapter Six, "Grading American Education"), Richard Rodriguez also reports a period of silence and discomfort in school. How does his situation compare with Kingston's? Are the differences you see merely a matter of degree, or were the two students silent for different reasons?

Extending the Critical Context

1. How would the teachers, counselors, and administrators of Kingston's school most likely have interpreted her behavior? In what different ways might school authorities respond to such behavior? What could have been done to help Kingston adapt to the ways of this new system?

Para Teresa[1]

INÉS HERNÁNDEZ

Hernández's poem represents an attempt to resolve an old conflict between the speaker and her schoolmate, two Chicanas who chose radically different strategies for dealing with the majority culture. Inés Hernández (b. 1947) has taught at the University of Texas at Austin. She has published a volume of poetry, Con Razon, Corazón.

A tí-Teresa Compean
Te dedico las palabras estás
que explotan de mi corazón[2]

That day during lunch hour
at Alamo which-had-to-be-its-name   5
Elementary
my dear raza
That day in the bathroom
Door guarded
Myself cornered   10
I was accused by you, Teresa
Tú y las demás de tus amigas
Pachucas todas
Eran Uds. cinco.[3]

Me gritaban que porque me creía tan grande[4]   15
What was I trying to do, you growled
Show you up?
Make the teachers like me, pet me,
Tell me what a credit to my people I was?
I was playing right into their hands, you challenged   20
And you would have none of it.
I was to stop.

[1] For Teresa. [Author's note]
[2] To you, Teresa Compean, I dedicate these words that explode from my heart. [Author's note]
[3] You and the rest of your friends, all Pachucas, there were five of you. [Author's note]
[4] You were screaming at me, asking me why I thought I was so hot. [Author's note]

I was to be like you
I was to play your game of deadly defiance
Arrogance, refusal to submit.   25
The game in which the winner takes nothing
Asks for nothing
Never lets his weaknesses show.

But I didn't understand.
My fear salted with confusion   30
Charged me to explain to you
I did nothing *for the teachers*.
I studied for my parents and for my grandparents
Who cut out honor roll lists
Whenever their nietos'[5] names appeared   35
For my shy mother who mastered her terror
to demand her place in mother's clubs
For my carpenter-father who helped me patiently with my math.
For my abuelos que me regalaron lápices en la Navidad[6]
And for myself.   40

Porque reconocí en aquel entonces
una verdad tremenda
que me hizo a mi un rebelde
Aunque tú no te habías dadocuenta[7]
We were not inferior   45
You and I, y las demás de tus amigas
Y los demás de nuestra gente[8]
I knew it the way I know I was alive
We were good, honorable, brave
Genuine, loyal, strong   50

And smart.
Mine was a deadly game of defiance, also.
My contest was to prove
beyond any doubt
that we were not only equal but superior to them.   55
That was why I studied.
If I could do it, we all could.

[5]Grandchildren's. [Author's note]
[6]Grandparents who gave me gifts of pencils at Christmas. [Author's note]
[7]Because I recognized a great truth then that made me a rebel, even though you didn't
realize it. [Author's note]
[8]And the rest of your friends/And the rest of our people. [Author's note]

You let me go then,
Your friends unblocked the way
I who-did-not-know-how-to-fight   60
was not made to engage with you-who-grew-up-fighting
Tu y yo, Teresa[9]
We went in different directions
Pero fuimos juntas.[10]

In sixth grade we did not understand   65
Uds. with the teased, dyed-black-but-reddening hair,
Full petticoats, red lipsticks
and sweaters with the sleeves
pushed up
Y yo conformándome con lo que deseaba mi mamá[11]   70
Certainly never allowed to dye, to tease, to paint myself
I did not accept your way of anger,
Your judgements
You did not accept mine.

But now in 1975, when I am twenty-eight   75
Teresa Compean
I remember you.
Y sabes —
Te comprendo,
Es más, te respeto.   80
Y, si me permites,
Te nombro — "hermana."[12]

[9]You and I. [Author's note]
[10]But we were together. [Author's note]
[11]And I conforming to my mother's wishes. [Author's note]
[12]And do you know what, I understand you. Even more, I respect you. And, if you
permit me, I name you my sister. [Author's note]

Engaging the Text

1. The SPEAKER says that she didn't understand Teresa at the time of the incident
she describes. Why didn't she understand? How have her views of Teresa and
of herself changed since then? What seems to have brought about this change?

2. What attitudes toward ASSIMILATION do Teresa and the speaker represent?
In what way are both girls playing a "deadly game of defiance"?

3. Speculate about why Hernández chose to write the poem in both Spanish

and English: What does it say about the speaker's life? About her change of attitude toward Teresa?

Exploring Connections

1. Do you see any similarities between the speaker's confrontation with Teresa and the rivalry between the *surumatos* and the *manitos* described by López in "Back to Bachimba" earlier in this chapter? Between López's feelings about his Mexican HERITAGE and Hernández's feelings about hers?

2. Compare and contrast the experience of the speaker in "Para Teresa" with Maxine Hong Kingston's in the passage from *The Woman Warrior,* which appears earlier in this chapter. Consider each girl's relationship to her family, her attitude toward ANGLO society, and her strategy for coping with or fitting into that society.

Extending the Critical Context

1. Was there a person or group you disliked, feared, or fought with in elementary school? Has your understanding of your adversary or of your own motives changed since then? If so, what brought about this change?

What We Want

KWAME TOURE (STOKELY CARMICHAEL)

Separatism — the determination of a particular group of people to resist assimilating to the majority culture — has a long history in the United States. Nearly every wave of immigrants to this country has at least initially tried to maintain the integrity of its native culture. Some, like the Amish, have succeeded. Early in this century, Jamaican-born Marcus Garvey urged American blacks to reject the dream of integration and to return to Africa. Garvey's philosophy of Pan-Africanism re-emerged in the 1960s in the cry for "black power." The following excerpt from Kwame Toure's "What We Want" offers an articulate rationale for the notion of an independent black community.

Kwame Toure (Stokely Carmichael, b. 1941), was an organizer of the Student Nonviolent Coordinating Committee (SNCC) during its involvement in the freedom marches of 1965–1967. He later became prime minister of the Black Panther Party, a radical black "self-defense" organization. He has lived in Guinea, West Africa since 1969.

Ultimately, the economic foundations of this country must be shaken 1 if black people are to control their lives. The colonies of the United States — and this includes the black ghettoes within its borders, north and south — must be liberated. For a century, this nation has been like an octopus of exploitation, its tentacles stretching from Mississippi and Harlem to South America, the Middle East, southern Africa, and Vietnam; the form of exploitation varies from area to area but the essential result has been the same — a powerful few have been maintained and enriched at the expense of the poor and voiceless colored masses. This pattern must be broken. As its grip loosens here and there around the world, the hopes of black Americans become more realistic. For racism to die, a totally different America must be born.

This is what the white society does not wish to face; this is why that 2 society prefers to talk about integration. But integration speaks not at all to the problem of poverty, only to the problem of blackness. Integration today means the man who "makes it," leaving his black brothers behind in the ghetto as fast as his new sports car will take him. It has no relevance to the Harlem wino or to the cottonpicker making three dollars a day. As a lady I know in Alabama once said, "the food that Ralph Bunche[1] eats doesn't fill my stomach."

Integration, moreover, speaks to the problem of blackness in a despicable 3 way. As a goal, it has been based on complete acceptance of the fact that *in order to have* a decent house or education, blacks must move into a white neighborhood or send their children to a white school. This reinforces, among both black and white, the idea that "white" is automatically better and "black" is by definition inferior. This is why integration is a subterfuge for the maintenance of white supremacy. It allows the nation to focus on a handful of Southern children who get into white schools, at great price, and to ignore the 94 percent who are left behind in unimproved all-black schools. Such situations will not change until black people have power — to control their own school boards, in this case. Then Negroes become equal in a way that means something, and integration ceases to be a one-way street. Then integration doesn't mean draining skills and energies from the ghetto into white neighborhoods;

[1]*Ralph Bunche:* black American educator (1904–1971); United Nations statesman and recipient of the Nobel Peace Prize in 1950.

then it can mean white people moving from Beverly Hills into Watts, white people joining the Lowndes County Freedom Organization.[2] Then integration becomes relevant.

White America will not face the problem of color, the reality of it. 4 The well-intended say: "We're all human, everybody is really decent, we must forget color." But color cannot be "forgotten" until its weight is recognized and dealt with. White America will not acknowledge that the ways in which the country sees itself are contradicted by being black — and always have been. Whereas most of the people who settled this country came here for freedom or for economic opportunity, blacks were brought here to be slaves. When the Lowndes County Freedom Organization chose the black panther as its symbol, it was christened by the press "the Black Panther Party" — but the Alabama Democratic Party, whose symbol is a rooster, has never been called the White Cock Party. No one ever talked about "white power" because power in this country *is* white. All this adds up to more than merely identifying a group phenomenon by some catchy name or adjective. The furor over that black panther reveals the problems that white America has with color and sex; the furor over "black power" reveals how deep racism runs and the great fear which is attached to it.

Whites will not see that I, for example, as a person oppressed because 5 of my blackness, have common cause with other blacks who are oppressed because of blackness. This is not to say that there are no white people who see things as I do, but that it is black people I must speak to first. It must be the oppressed to whom SNCC addresses itself primarily, not to friends from the oppressing group.

From birth, black people are told a set of lies about themselves. We 6 are told that we are lazy — yet I drive through the Delta area of Mississippi and watch black people picking cotton in the hot sun for fourteen hours. We are told, "If you work hard, you'll succeed" — but if that were true, black people would own this country. We are oppressed because we are black — not because we are ignorant, not because we are lazy, not because we're stupid (and got good rhythm), but because we're black.

I remember that when I was a boy, I used to go to see Tarzan movies 7 on Saturday. White Tarzan used to beat up the black natives. I would sit there yelling, "Kill the beasts, kill the savages, kill 'em!" I was saying:

[2]*Lowndes County Freedom Organization:* a civil rights group in Lowndes County, Alabama (near Montgomery); a stronghold of white resistance to the civil rights movement, Lowndes County was the setting for both legal and physical battles.

Kill *me*. It was as if a Jewish boy watched Nazis taking Jews off to concentration camps and cheered them on. Today, I want the chief to beat hell out of Tarzan and send him back to Europe. But it takes time to become free of the lies and their shaming effect on black minds. It takes time to reject the most important lie: that black people inherently can't do the same things white people can do, unless white people help them.

The need for psychological equality is the reason why SNCC today 8 believes that blacks must organize in the black community. Only black people can convey the revolutionary idea that black people are able to do things themselves. Only they can help create in the community an aroused and continuing black consciousness that will provide the basis for political strength. In the past, white allies have furthered white supremacy without the whites involved realizing it — or wanting it, I think. Black people must do things for themselves; they must get poverty money they will control and spend themselves, they must conduct tutorial programs themselves so that black children can identify with black people. This is one reason Africa has such importance: The reality of black men ruling their own nations gives blacks elsewhere a sense of possibility, of power, which they do not now have.

This does not mean we don't welcome help, or friends. But we want 9 the right to decide whether anyone is, in fact, our friend. In the past, black Americans have been almost the only people whom everybody and his momma could jump up and call their friends. We have been tokens, symbols, objects — as I was in high school to many young whites, who liked having "a Negro friend." We want to decide who is our friend, and we will not accept someone who comes to us and says: "If you do X, Y, and Z, then I'll help you." We will not be told whom we should choose as allies. We will not be isolated from any group or nation except by our own choice. We cannot have the oppressors telling the oppressed how to rid themselves of the oppressor.

I have said that most liberal whites react to "black power" with the 10 question, What about me?, rather than saying: Tell me what you want me to do and I'll see if I can do it. There are answers to the right question. One of the most disturbing things about almost all white supporters of the movement has been that they are afraid to go into their own communities — which is where the racism exists — and work to get rid of it. They want to run from Berkeley[3] to tell us what to do in Mississippi; let them look instead at Berkeley. They admonish blacks to

[3]*Berkeley:* University of California, Berkeley — site of many student protests during the 1960s and '70s.

be nonviolent; let them preach nonviolence in the white community. They come to teach me Negro history; let them go to the suburbs and open up freedom schools for whites. Let them work to stop America's racist foreign policy; let them press this government to cease supporting the economy of South Africa.

There is a vital job to be done among poor whites. We hope to see, 11 eventually, a coalition between poor blacks and poor whites. That is the only coalition which seems acceptable to us, and we see such a coalition as the major internal instrument of change in American society. SNCC has tried several times to organize poor whites; we are trying again now, with an initial training program in Tennessee. It is purely academic today to talk about bringing poor blacks and whites together, but the job of creating a poor-white power bloc must be attempted. The main responsibility for it falls upon whites. Black and white can work together in the white community where possible; it is not possible, however, to go into a poor Southern town and talk about integration. Poor whites everywhere are becoming more hostile — not less — partly because they see the nation's attention focussed on black poverty and nobody coming to them. Too many young middle-class Americans, like some sort of Pepsi generation, have wanted to come alive through the black community; they've wanted to be where the action is — and the action has been in the black community.

Black people do not want to "take over" this country. They don't want 12 to "get Whitey"; they just want to get him off their backs, as the saying goes. It was for example the exploitation by Jewish landlords and merchants which first created black resentment toward Jews — not Judaism. The white man is irrelevant to blacks, except as an oppressive force. Blacks want to be in his place, yes, but not in order to terrorize and lynch and starve him. They want to be in his place because that is where a decent life can be had.

But our vision is not merely of a society in which all black men have 13 enough to buy the good things of life. When we urge that black money go into black pockets, we mean the communal pocket. We want to see money go back into the community and used to benefit it. We want to see the cooperative concept applied in business and banking. We want to see black ghetto residents demand that an exploiting landlord or store keeper sell them, at minimal cost, a building or a shop that they will own and improve cooperatively; they can back their demand with a rent strike, or a boycott, and a community so unified behind them that no one else will move into the building or buy at the store. The society we seek to build among black people, then, is not a capitalist one. It is a society in which the spirit of community and humanistic love prevail. The word love is suspect; black expectations of what it might produce have been betrayed too often. But those were expectations of a response from the white community, which failed us. The love we seek to encourage is within the black community, the only American community where men call each other "brother" when they meet. We can build a community of love only where we have the ability and power to do so; among blacks.

As for white America, perhaps it can stop crying out against "black supremacy," "black nationalism," "racism in reverse," and begin facing reality. The reality is that this nation, from top to bottom, is racist; that racism is not primarily a problem of "human relations" but of an exploitation maintained — either actively or through silence — by the society as a whole. Camus[4] and Sartre[5] have asked, can a man condemn himself? Can whites, particularly liberal whites, condemn themselves? Can they stop blaming us, and blame their own system? Are they capable of the shame which might become a revolutionary emotion? 14

We have found that they usually cannot condemn themselves, and so we have done it. But the rebuilding of this society, if at all possible, is basically the responsibility of whites — not blacks. We won't fight to save the present society, in Vietnam or anywhere else. We are just going to work, in the way *we* see fit, and on goals *we* define, not for civil rights but for all our human rights. 15

[4]*Camus:* Albert Camus, French-Algerian novelist, essayist, and dramatist (1913–1960); recipient of the Nobel Prize for Literature in 1957.
[5]*Sartre:* Jean Paul Sartre, renowned French philosopher, writer, and social critic (1905–1980); the leading exponent of existentialism, a philosophical approach that emphasizes the absurdity of life and the importance of the individual's will.

Engaging the Text

1. What's wrong with INTEGRATION, according to Toure? What arguments does he advance for independent black action?

2. Explain what Toure means by "psychological equality." How does psychological equality differ from political and economic equality?

3. Why does Toure believe that economic revolution must accompany political equality?

4. In what sense can shame be understood as a "revolutionary emotion"?

5. What audience is Toure addressing in this essay? How does he take his audience into account?

Exploring Connections

1. Compare Toure's position on economic revolution with James Boggs's analysis of the causes of racism in Chapter Two, "Justice for All."

2. Look ahead to Howard and Hammond's article "Rumors of Inferiority" in Chapter Six, "Grading American Education." How does their analysis of the challenges faced by American blacks compare to Toure's? Are they also arguing for a kind of SEPARATISM?

Extending the Critical Context

1. Working in groups, research the Student Nonviolent Coordinating Committee (SNCC), Marcus Garvey's "Back to Africa Movement," or the Black Panther Party in an encyclopedia or other reference book and summarize its history and accomplishments.

2. Research the position of other famous black leaders on the topic of assimilation and integration. Where, for example, did the Reverend Martin Luther King, Jr., Sojourner Truth, or W. E. B. Du Bois stand on this issue?

4

Women

The Emerging Majority

In his 1832 treatise on American democracy, James Fenimore Cooper noted that "females are, almost generally, excluded from the possession of political rights." The feminist movement has remedied many of those early inequities, winning women the right to vote in 1920 and the right to equal educational and employment opportunities in the 1970s. But attitudes are more difficult to change than laws, and there is more to feminism than battling for legal equality. This chapter suggests some dramatic ways in which feminist perspectives can influence our understanding of our culture and ourselves.

The first group of essays, Gender Roles: Tradition and Change, looks at gender roles — the conventional patterns of feeling and behavior we learn to associate with each sex. The opening selection by Janet Saltzman Chafetz provides a summary of stereotypical gender role advantages and disadvantages; the oral history that follows, "Nora Quealey," provides a case in point — a portrait of a woman deeply ambivalent about her roles as mother, wife, and blue-collar worker. Paula Gunn Allen eloquently argues that tribal heritage offers more strong, positive female roles than does the Western European tradition. Reinterpreting traditional roles, Carol Gilligan, Lorenza Calvillo Craig, and Marilyn French propose that typically devalued "feminine" qualities such as cooperation and nurturance are better indicators of psychological health and moral development than more highly regarded "masculine" traits like competition and power.

The next section, Racism, Sexism, and Heterosexism, addresses the experiences of women whose voices are not always heard in the feminist movement. Bell Hooks indicts middle-class white feminists for historically neglecting black women and for maintaining a privileged social status through racism. In an autobiographical excerpt, Maya Angelou describes the shifting relationship between a black servant and her white employer. Rose Weitz analyzes heterosexism — prejudice against homosexuals — as a reaction against perceived threats to male power. "The Two," Gloria Naylor's story about a lesbian couple, offers a sympathetic psychological study and invites you to test Weitz's thesis.

Before Reading . . .

Divide into small groups by gender and discuss the advantages and disadvantages you associate with each sex. First compare notes with the other groups of the same sex, and then with the class as a whole.

GENDER ROLES:
TRADITION AND CHANGE

Some Individual Costs
of Gender Role Conformity

JANET SALTZMAN CHAFETZ

In 1971, Chafetz surveyed male and female college students to evaluate how they perceived the advantages and disadvantages of their own and each other's gender roles. Here she reports her results: The magnitude of the male/female differences may surprise you. Chafetz (b. 1942), who teaches sociology at the University of Houston, has written or contributed to several books on the sociology of gender roles. Her most recent work is Feminist Sociology: An Overview of Contemporary Theories *(1988).*

It is probably true that very few individuals conform totally to their 1
sex-relevant stereotypes. Roles of all kinds . . . are sociocultural givens,
but this is not to say that people play them in the same way. Indeed,
individuals, like stage actors and actresses, interpret their roles and
create innovations for their "parts." The fact remains that there is a
"part" to be played, and it does strongly influence the actual "performance."

It is also important to recall that the precise definitions of gender role 2
stereotypes vary within the broader culture by social class, region, race
and ethnicity, and other subcultural categories. Thus, for instance, more
than most other Americans, the various Spanish-speaking groups in this
country (Mexican-American, Puerto Rican, Cuban) stress domesticity,
passivity, and other stereotypical feminine traits, and dominance, aggressiveness, physical prowess, and other stereotypical masculine traits.
Indeed, the masculine gender role for this group is generally described
by reference to the highly stereotyped notion of *machismo*. In fact, a
strong emphasis on masculine aggressiveness and dominance may be
characteristic of most groups in the lower ranges of the socioeconomic
ladder (McKinley, 1964, pp. 89, 93, 112; Yorburg, 1974). Conversely,
due to historical conditions beyond its control, black America has had
to rely heavily on the female as provider and, more often than in the
rest of society, as head of the household. Thus, the feminine stereotype
discussed above has traditionally been less a part of the cultural heritage
of blacks than that of whites (Staples, 1970; Yorburg, 1974). It is also
clear that, at least at the verbal level, both gender role stereotypes have
historically been taken more seriously in Dixie than elsewhere (see Scott,
1970, especially chap. 1). Although today this difference is probably
declining, along with most other regional differences, personal experience
leads me to conclude that it nonetheless remains. The pioneer past of
the Far West, where survival relied upon strong, productive, independent
females as well as males, may have dampened the emphasis on some
aspects of the traditional feminine stereotype in that area of the country.

Much research remains to be done by way of documenting differences 3
in gender role stereotypes between various groups, but there is little
doubt that such differences exist. It is important to note, however, that,
with the exception of explicitly countercultural groups, such as the "hippies"
of the 1960s, even among subcultures with relatively strong traditions

of their own the cultural definitions of the dominant society exert substantial pressure toward conformity. Minorities — namely, all those who are not part of the socioculturally dominant white, northern European, Protestant, middle and upper classes — exist within a society that defines them to a greater or lesser extent as inferior. To some degree such definitions are internalized by many members of the various minority groups and accepted as valid, a phenomenon known in the literature on minority groups as racial or ethnic "self-hatred" (Adelson, 1958, pp. 486, 489; Allport, 1958, pp. 147–48; Frazier, 1957, pp. 217, 226; Simpson & Yinger, 1965, pp. 227–29).

To the extent that individual minority members engage in such group 4 self-hatred, they are led to attempt, within the limits of opportunity and the resources allowed by the dominant group, to "live up to" the norms and roles of the dominant society. Given limited economic opportunities, the result is often a parody of the values and behaviors of the dominant society, as exemplified by the strong emphasis on aggression, sexual exploitation, and physical prowess by lower class males of most ethnic groups. Similarly, large numbers of blacks, many highly educated and involved in radical politics, have accepted the negative (and false) description of their family structure as "matriarchal"[1] which has been propounded by Daniel Moynihan (1965) and other whites. Moreover, many black males and females are now engaged in efforts to change this structure to conform to the major cultural pattern of male as dominant partner and breadwinner, and female as subservient homemaker. However, less biased research (Hill, 1972; Rhodes, 1971; Stack, 1974; Myers, 1975; Dietrich, 1975) suggests that the traditional black family structure is and has been very functional in enabling the black to survive in this society. This structure is not the pathological, weak, disorganized entity usually conveyed by the term "matriarchy."

Individuals of all levels of society who reject traditional gender role 5 stereotypes are labeled "nonconformist" and subjected to the wrath of most members of the society. The harsh treatment of longhaired males in the 1960s by police, possible employers, and ordinary citizens speaks eloquently of the "cost" of nonconformity, as does the "wallflower" status of competitive, intellectually gifted, or career-oriented females. But costs are also paid by those who generally conform to gender role stereotypes (or any other kind, for that matter), and these are usually more "hidden."

---

[1] *matriarchal:* family structure in which the mother holds the power and authority.

Perceived Costs and Benefits

In 1971, students in a sex role class were asked to form single-sex 6
groups to discuss the advantages of the other gender role and the disadvantages of their own. This exercise was a replication of the study
done by Barbara Polk and Robert Stein (1972) at a northern university,
using 250 students of highly diverse backgrounds, and the results parallel
theirs almost exactly. Results of the class study are reported in Tables
1 and 2.

When the advantages and disadvantages of the gender roles are com- 7
pared, the most striking finding relates to the relative length of the
various lists. There seem to be many more disadvantages adhering to
the feminine role as perceived by females than to the masculine role as
perceived by males (or else the females were simply and stereotypically
more loquacious!). Conversely, more advantages are seen as accruing to
the masculine role by females than to the feminine role by males. More
relevant to the question of costs, however, is the finding that the perceived
advantages of one sex are the disadvantages of the other. If it is a
masculine disadvantage not to be able to show emotions, it is a feminine

Table 1   Disadvantages of Same Gender Role and Advantages of Other One
as Perceived by Males

MALE DISADVANTAGES	FEMALE ADVANTAGES
Can't show emotions (P)	Freedom to express emotions (R)
Must be provider (O)	Fewer financial obligations; parents support longer (S)
Pressure to succeed, be competitive (O)	Less pressure to succeed (P)
Alimony and child support (O)	Alimony and insurance benefits (S)
Liable to draft (O)	Free from draft (S)
Must take initiative, make decisions (O)	Protected (S)
Limit on acceptable careers (P)	
Expected to be mechanical, fix things (O)	
	More leisure (S)
	Placed on pedestal; object of courtesy (S)

Note: Letters enclosed in parentheses refer to a fourfold categorization of roles (Polk &
Stein, 1972): P = proscription; O = obligation; R = right; S = structural benefit.

Table 2 Disadvantages of Same Gender Role and Advantages of Other One as Perceived by Females

FEMALE DISADVANTAGES	MALE ADVANTAGES
Job opportunities limited; discrimination; poor pay (P)	Job opportunities greater (S)
Legal and financial discrimination (P)	Financial and legal opportunity (S)
Educational opportunities limited; judged mentally inferior; opinion devalued; intellectual life stifled (P)	Better educational and training opportunities; opinions valued (S)
Single status stigmatized; stigma for divorce and unwed pregnancy (P)	Bachelorhood glamorized (R)
Socially and sexually restricted; double standard (P)	More freedom sexually and socially (R)
Must bear and rear children; no abortions (in many places); responsible for birth control (O)	No babies (S)
Must maintain good outward appearance; dress, make-up (O)	Less fashion demand and emphasis on appearance (R)
Domestic work (O)	No domestic work (R)
Must be patient; give in; subordinate self; be unaggressive; wait to be asked out on dates (P)	Can be aggressive, dating and otherwise (O)
Inhibited motor control; not allowed to be athletic (P)	More escapism allowed (R)

Note: Letters enclosed in parentheses refer to a fourfold categorization of roles (Polk & Stein, 1972): P = proscription; O = obligation; R = right; S = structural benefit.

advantage to be able to do so. Likewise, if it is a feminine disadvantage to face limited job opportunities, the converse is a masculine advantage. Summarizing similar findings, Polk and Stein (1972) conclude: "The extent to which this relationship exists strongly suggests that there is general agreement on the desirable characteristics for any individual, regardless of sex" (p. 16).

Polk and Stein's fourfold categorization of role components as rights, obligations, proscriptions, and structural benefits is useful in examining the nature of specific perceived costs and benefits of the two roles. According to Polk and Stein, "Rights allow the individual the freedom to commit an act or refrain from an act without receiving sanctions for either choice" (p. 19). Obligations and proscriptions are different in that individuals are negatively sanctioned, in the first case for not doing something, in the second for doing it. Structural benefits refer to "advantages derived from the social structure or from actions of others" on the basis of sex alone (p. 21). Each advantage and disadvantage listed in Tables 1 and 2 is followed by a letter in parentheses which represents my judgment as to whether that characteristic is a right (R), a proscription (P), an obligation (O), or a structural benefit (S). Masculine disadvantages consist overwhelmingly of obligations with a few proscriptions, while the disadvantages of the feminine role arise primarily from proscriptions, with a few obligations. Thus females complain about what they can't do, males about what they must do. Females complain that they cannot be athletic, aggressive, sexually free, or successful in the worlds of work and education; in short, they complain of their passivity. Males complain that they must be aggressive and must succeed; in short, of their activity. The (sanctioned) requirement that males be active and females passive in a variety of ways is clearly unpleasant to both.

The nature of the types of advantages seen as accruing to each of the   9
two roles by the other sex supports the stereotyped dichotomy between activity and passivity still further. Females are seen as overwhelmingly enjoying structural benefits, namely, advantages that accrue to them without reference to what they do. Males believe females have only one right. Females believe males also enjoy structural benefits but have considerably more rights, namely, choices of action or inaction. These findings generally agree with those of Polk and Stein, who found that altogether the masculine role had 14 obligations compared to 8 for the feminine role; 6 rights compared to 0; 4 proscriptions compared to 15; and 6 structural benefits compared to 4 (pp. 20–21, Table 2).

Economic Costs and Benefits

How helpful or costly would the masculine or feminine gender role   10
stereotype traits . . . be for a competitor in the highest echelons of our economy and society? One measure of such success is occupation. Robert Hodge, Paul Siegel, and Peter Rossi (1966) studied the relative prestige of a large number of occupations in the United States and found that the four most prestigious were: U.S. Supreme Court Justice, physician, scientist, and state governor. Table 3 [p. 264] summarizes the data on which stereotypical traits are clearly helpful in attaining and performing well in these occupational roles and which are harmful. While the designation as "helpful" or "harmful" for some few traits is debatable, the overall picture probably is not. Stereotypical feminine traits patently do not equip those who might try to live up to them to compete in the world of social and economic privilege, power, and prestige; the exact opposite is the case for masculine characteristics. Where 15 feminine

Table 3 Gender Role Traits Helpful and Harmful in Acquiring and
Performing Well in Prestigious Occupational Roles

STEREOTYPED TRAITS	HARMFUL	HELPFUL
Masculine	Sloppy	Breadwinner, provider
	Dogmatic	Stoic, unemotional
		Logical, rational, objective, scientific
		Practical
		Mechanical (for scientist and physician)
		Public awareness
		Leader
		Disciplinarian
		Independent
		Demanding
		Aggressive
		Ambitious
		Proud, confident
		Moral, trustworthy
		Decisive
		Competitive
		Adventurous

traits are classified as "harmful," only 2 masculine ones are so designated. Conversely, where 17 masculine traits are classified as "helpful," the analogous number of feminine traits is 7. The cost of femininity for those who would enter the world outside the home could scarcely be more clear: The more a female conforms, the less is she capable of functioning in roles that are other than domestic.

Indeed, gender roles are so deeply ingrained that even among successful 11 business executives, women, unlike men, often attribute their success to luck rather than their own hard work and competence. Moreover, women tend to understate the extent of their achievements (Hennig & Jardim, 1977). On the other hand, reared in a culture that emphasizes the myth that hard work and personal worth will result in job success, many males, especially in the middle class, suffer feelings of personal inadequacy and failure if they are not highly successful in a material sense. In short, the feminine role stereotype gears women for economic failure, and if that is not the case, women explain their success in terms external to themselves. The masculine role stereotype gears men for economic success, and if that is not forthcoming men perceive themselves as personally responsible for their "failure."

Table 3 — Continued Gender Role Traits Helpful and Harmful in Acquiring and Performing Well in Prestigious Occupational Roles

STEREOTYPED TRAITS	HARMFUL	HELPFUL
Feminine	Worry about appearance and age	Compassionate
	Sensual	Intuitive
	Domestic	Humanistic
	Seductive, flirtatious	Perceptive
	Emotional, sentimental	Idealistic
	Nervous, insecure, fearful	Patient
	Scatterbrained, frivolous	Gentle
	Impractical	
	Petty, coy, gossipy	
	Dependent, overprotected	
	Follower, submissive	
	Self-conscious; easily intimidated	
	Not aggressive, passive	
	Tardy	
	Noncompetitive	

Works Cited

Adelson, Joseph. "A Study of Minority Group Authoritarianism." In Marshall Sklare (ed.), *The Jews: Social Patterns of an American Group*, pp. 475–92. Glencoe, Ill.: Free Press, 1958.

Allport, Gordon. *The Nature of Prejudice*. Garden City, N.Y.: Doubleday Anchor Books, 1958; first published 1954.

Dietrich, Kathryn. "The Re-examination of the Myth of Black Matriarchy." *Journal of Marriage and the Family* 37 (May 1975): 367–74.

Frazier, E. Franklin. *Black Bourgeoisie*. Glencoe, Ill.: Free Press, 1957.

Hennig, Margaret, and Jardim, Anne. *The Managerial Woman*. New York: Anchor-Doubleday, 1977.

Hill, Robert B. *The Strengths of Black Families*. New York: Emerson Hall Publishers, 1972.

Hodge, Robert; Siegel, Paul; and Rossi, Peter. "Occupational Prestige in the United States: 1925–1963." In Reinhard Bendix and S. M. Lipset (eds.), *Class, Status and Power*, pp. 322–34. 2nd ed. Glencoe, Ill.: Free Press, 1966.

McKinley, Donald G. *Social Class and Family Life*. Glencoe, Ill.: Free Press, 1964.

Moynihan, Daniel P. *The Negro Family: The Case for National Action*. Washington, D.C.: U.S. Department of Labor, 1965.

Myers, Lena Wright. "Black Women and Self-Esteem." In Marcia Millman and

Rosabeth Kanter (eds.), *Another Voice*, pp. 240–50. Garden City, N.Y.: Anchor Books, 1975.

Polk, Barbara Bovee, and Stein, Robert B. "Is the Grass Greener on the Other Side?" In Constantina Safilios-Rothschild (ed.), *Toward a Sociology of Women*, pp. 14–23. Lexington, Mass.: Xerox College Publishing Co., 1972.

Rhodes, Barbara. "The Changing Role of the Black Woman." In Robert Staples (ed.), *The Black Family*, pp. 145–49. Belmont, Calif.: Wadsworth Publishing Co., 1971.

Scott, Anne Firor. *The Southern Lady*. Chicago: University of Chicago Press, 1970.

Simpson, George E., and Yinger, J. Milton. *Racial and Cultural Minorities*. 3rd ed. New York: Harper & Row, 1965.

Stack, Carol. *All Our Kin: Strategies for Survival in a Black Community*. New York: Harper & Row, 1974.

Staples, Robert. "The Myth of the Black Matriarchy." *Black Scholar* 1 (January-February, 1970): 8–16.

Yorburg, Betty. *Sexual Identity: Sex Roles and Social Change*. New York: John Wiley & Sons, 1974.

Engaging the Text

1. What, according to Chafetz, is "machismo"?

2. In paragraph 2, Chafetz defines several different female gender role STE-REOTYPES. Try to describe other female stereotypes specific to particular regions, SOCIOECONOMIC levels, or ETHNIC groups. What similarities and differences do you see in these stereotypes?

3. Chafetz mentions the "cost" of NONCONFORMITY to gender role stereotypes. Working in groups, list some of the specific costs that nonconformists might pay. Have you ever been penalized for failing to live up to your expected masculine or feminine role?

Exploring Connections

1. Reread the description of the American hero in "The Paradox of Individualism" (Robert Bellah et al., Chapter One, "American Dreams"). How many "heroic" traits are compatible with the traditional feminine role as defined by Chafetz? Redefine heroism to include more positive "feminine" traits: What women and men from history, fiction, film, or public life exemplify this new heroism?

2. How would Gordon Allport (Chapter Two, "Justice for All") interpret the results of Chafetz's research? Is it possible to consider men as a "reference group" for women?

Extending the Critical Context

1. Watch your favorite TV show, noting the number of times it depicts gender role stereotypes and the number of times it calls them into question. Use this evidence to analyze the degree to which the program reinforces traditional gender roles.

2. Design a study similar to Chafetz's that probes attitudes about ETHNICITY rather than gender. Write a detailed description of how your study would work — i.e., your methods — and then HYPOTHESIZE as to expected results. Time and circumstances permitting, carry out the study and write up the actual results.

Nora Quealey

JEAN REITH SCHROEDEL

This interview reveals the thoughts of a woman who has encountered sexism (as well as the simple exploitation of workers, male and female) in a traditionally male occupation — assembly-line work on trucks. Quealey is proud, strong, insightful . . . and thinks she would prefer being a housewife. Schroedel (b. 1951) began collecting oral histories of blue-collar working women when she was an undergraduate at the University of Washington and published these interviews in Alone in a Crowd *(1985). She herself has worked as a machinist and a union organizer, and, fittingly, she supported her work on the book by driving a bus.*

I was a housewife until five years ago. The best part was being home 1 when my three kids came in from school. Their papers and their junk that they made from kindergarten on up — they were my total, whole life. And then one day I realized when they were grown up and gone, graduated and married, I was going to be left with nothing. I think there's a lot of women that way, housewives, that never knew there were other things and people outside of the neighborhood. I mean the block got together once a week for coffee and maybe went bowling, but that was it. My whole life was being there when the kids came home from school.

I never disliked anything. It was just like everything else in a marriage, 2 there never was enough money to do things that you wanted — never to take a week's vacation away from the kids. If we did anything, it was just to take the car on Saturday or Sunday for a little, short drive. But there was never enough money. The extra money was the reason I decided to go out and get a job. The kids were getting older, needed more, wanted more, and there was just not enough.

See, I don't have a high school diploma, so when I went to Boeing 3 and put an application in, they told me not to come back until I had a diploma or a G.E.D.[1] On the truck line they didn't mind that I hadn't finished school. I put an application in and got hired on the spot.

My dad works over at Bangor[2] in the ammunition depot, so I asked 4 him what it would be like working with all men. The only thing he told me was if I was gonna work with a lot of men, that I would have to *listen* to swear words and some of the obscene things, but still *act* like a lady, or I'd never fit in. You can still be treated like a lady and act like a lady and work like a man. So I just tried to fit in. It's worked, too. The guys come up and they'll tell me jokes and tease me and a lot of them told me that I'm just like one of the guys. Yet they like to have me around because I wear make-up and I do curl my hair, and I try to wear not really frilly blouses, see-through stuff, but nice blouses.

We had one episode where a gal wore a tank top and when she bent 5 over the guys could see her boobs or whatever you call it, all the way down. Myself and a couple other women went and tried to complain about it. We wanted personnel to ask her to please wear a bra, or at least no tank tops. We were getting a lot of comebacks from the guys like, "When are you gonna dress like so-and-so," or "When are *you* gonna go without a bra," and "We wanna see what *you've* got." And I don't feel any need to show off; you know, I know what I've got. There were only a few women there, so that one gal made a very bad impression. But personnel said there was nothing they could do about it.

But in general the guys were really good. I started out in cab building 6 hanging radio brackets and putting heaters in. It was all hand work, and at first I really struggled with the power screwdrivers and big reamers, but the guy training me was super neato. I would think, "Oh, dear, can I ever do this, can I really prove myself or come up to their expectations?" But the guys never gave me the feeling that I was taking the job from a man or food from his family's mouth. If I needed help, I didn't even have to ask, if they saw me struggling, they'd come right over to help.

I've worked in a lot of different places since I went to work there. I 7 was in cab build for I don't know how long, maybe six months, eight

[1]*G.E.D.:* a high school equivalency certificate.
[2]*Bangor:* site of a Trident nuclear submarine base in the state of Washington.

months. Then they took me over to sleeper boxes, where I stayed for about two-and-one-half years. I put in upholstery, lined the head liners and the floor mats. After that I went on the line and did air conditioning. When the truck came to me, it had hoses already on it, and I'd have to hook up a little air-condition-pump-type thing and a suction that draws all the dust and dirt from the lines. Then you close that off, put freon in, and tie down the line. Then I'd tie together a bunch of color-coded electrical wires with tie straps and electrical tape to hook the firewall to the engine. Sometimes I also worked on the sleeper boxes by crawling underneath and tightening down big bolts and washers. Next they sent me over to the radiator shop. I was the first woman ever to do radiators. That I liked. A driver would bring in the radiators and you'd put it on a hoist, pick it up and put it on a sling, and work on one side putting your fittings on and wiring and putting in plugs. Then they bounced me back to sleeper boxes for a while and finally ended up putting me in the motor department, where I am now. The motors are brought in on a dolly. The guy behind me hangs the transmission and I hang the pipe with the shift levers and a few other little things and that's about it. Except that we have to work terribly fast.

I was moved into the motor department after the big layoff. At that time we were doing ten motors a day. Now we're up to fourteen without any additional help. When we were down, the supervisor came to me and said we had to help fill in and give extra help to the other guys, which is fine. But the minute production went up, I still had to do my own job plus putting on parts for three different guys. These last two weeks have been really tough. I've been way behind. They've got two guys that are supposed to fill in when you get behind, but I'm stubborn enough that I won't go over and ask for help. The supervisor should be able to see that I'm working super-duper hard while some other guys are taking forty-five minutes in the can and having a sandwich and two cups of coffee. Sometimes I push myself so hard that I'm actually in a trance. And I have to stop every once in a while and ask, "What did I do?" I don't even remember putting parts on, I just go from one to the other, just block everything out — just go, go, go, go. And that is bad, for myself, my own sanity, my own health. I don't take breaks. I don't go to the bathroom. There's so much pressure on me, physical and mental stress. It's hard to handle because then I go home and do a lot of crying and that's bad for my kids because I do a lot of snapping and growling at them. When I'm down, depressed, aching, and sore, to come home and do that to the kids is not fair at all. The last couple of days the attitude I've had is, I don't care whether I get the job done or not. If they can't see I'm going under, then I don't care. And I'll take five or ten minutes to just go to the bathroom, sit on the floor, and take a couple of deep breaths, just anything to get away.

The company doesn't care about us at all. Let me give you an example. 9 When we were having all this hot weather, I asked them please if we couldn't get some fans in here. Extension cords even, because some guys had their own fans. I wasn't just asking for myself, but those guys over working by the oven. They've got a thermometer there and it gets to a hundred and fifteen degrees by that oven! They've got their mouths open, can hardly breathe, and they're barely moving. So I said to the supervisor, "Why can't we have a fan to at least circulate the air?" "Oh, yeah, we'll look at it," was as far as it went. We're human. We have no right to be treated like animals. I mean you go out to a dairy farm and you've got air conditioning and music for those cows. I'm a person, and I don't like feeling weak and sick to my stomach and not feel like eating. Then to have the supervisor expect me to put out production as if I was mechanical — a thing, just a robot. I'm human.

You know, I don't even know what my job title is. I'm not sure if it's 10 trainee or not. But I do know I'll never make journeyman. I'll never make anything. I tried for inspection — took all the classes they offered at the plant, went to South Seattle Community College on my own time, studied blueprinting, and worked in all the different areas like they said I had to. I broke ground for the other girls, but they won't let me move up. And it all comes down to one thing, because I associated with a black man. I've had people in personnel tell me to stop riding to work with the man, even if it meant taking the bus to and from work. I said no one will make my decisions as to who I ride with and who my friends are. Because you walk into a building with a person, have lunch with him, let him buy you a cup of coffee, people condemn you. They're crazy, because when I have a friend, I don't turn my back on them just because of what people think. What I do outside the plant after quitting time is my own business. If they don't like it, that's their problem. But in that plant I've conducted myself as a lady and have nothing to be ashamed of. I plant my feet firmly and I stand by it.

Early on, I hurt my neck, back, and shoulder while working on sleeper 11 boxes. When I went into the motor department I damaged them more by working with power tools above my head and reaching all day long. I was out for two weeks and then had a ten-week restriction. Personnel said I had to go back to my old job, and if I couldn't handle it I would have to go home. They wouldn't put me anywhere else, which is ridiculous, with all the small parts areas that people can sit down and work in while they are restricted. My doctor said if I went back to doing what I was doing when I got hurt, I had a fifty-fifty chance of completely paralyzing myself from the waist down. But like a fool I went back. Some of the guys helped me with the bending and stooping over. Then the supervisor borrowed a ladder with three steps and on rollers from the paint department. He wanted me to stand on the top step while working on motors which are on dollies on a moving chain. I'd be using two press-wrenches to tighten fittings down while my right knee was on the transmission and the left leg standing up straight. All this from the top step of a ladder on rollers. One slip and it would be all over. I backed off and said it wouldn't work. By this time I'd gotten the shop steward there, but he didn't do anything. In fact, the next day he left on three weeks' vacation without doing anything to help me. I called the union hall and was told they'd send a business rep down the next day. I never saw or heard from the man.

Anyhow, I'm still doing the same job as when I got hurt. I can feel   12
the tension in my back and shoulder coming up. I can feel the spasms start and muscles tightening up. Things just keep gettin' worse and they don't care. People could be rotated and moved rather than being cramped in the same position, like in the sleeper boxes, where you never stand up straight and stretch your neck out. It's eight, ten, twelve hours a day all hunched over. In the next two years I've got to quit. I don't know what I'll do. If I end up paralyzed from the neck down, the company doesn't give a damn, the union doesn't give a damn, who's gonna take care of me? Who's gonna take care of my girls? I'm gonna be put in some moldy, old, stinkin' nursing home. I'm thirty-seven years old. I could live another thirty, forty years. And who's gonna really care about me?

I mean my husband left me. He was very jealous of my working with   13
a lot of men and used to follow me to work. When I joined the bowling team, I tried to get him to come and meet the guys I worked with. He came but felt left out because there was always an inside joke or something that he couldn't understand. He resented that and the fact that I made more money than he did. And my not being home bothered him. But he never said, "I want you to quit," or "We'll make it on what I get." If he had said that I probably would have quit. Instead we just muddled on. With me working, the whole family had to pitch in and help. When I come home at night my daughter has dinner waiting, and I do a couple loads of wash and everybody folds their own clothes. My husband pitched in for a while. Then he just stopped coming home. He found another lady that didn't work, had four kids, and was on welfare.

It really hurt and I get very confused still. I don't have the confidence   14
and self-assurance I used to have. I think, "Why did I do that," or "Maybe I shouldn't have done it," and I have to force myself to say,

"Hey, I felt and said what I wanted to and there's no turning back." It came out of me and I can't be apologizing for everything that I do. And, oh, I don't know, I guess I'm in a spell right now where I'm tired of being dirty. I want my fingernails long and clean. I want to not go up to the bathroom and find a big smudge of grease across my forehead. I want to sit down and be pampered and pretty all day. Maybe that wouldn't satisfy me, but I just can't imagine myself at fifty or sixty or seventy years old trying to climb on these trucks. I've been there for five years. I'm thirty-seven and I want to be out of there before I'm forty. And maybe I will. I've met this nice guy and he's talking of getting married. At the most, I would have to work for one more year and then I could stay at home, go back to being a housewife.

Engaging the Text

1. What are Nora Quealey's attitudes toward domesticity? Toward work? Toward being a housewife?

2. Quealey's life is in some ways tragic. What are the greatest blows she has suffered? Do you think she could have avoided any of them? How — and at what price?

3. What motivates Quealey to persevere in her career in the face of the difficulties she encounters? List as many possible motivations as you can, and review the text to find evidence of them.

4. Is Quealey a feminist?

Exploring Connections

1. How many of the gender role advantages and disadvantages listed by Chafetz in the previous selection apply to Nora Quealey? To what extent, if any, does her experience illustrate Chafetz's assertion that "the feminine role stereotype gears women for economic failure"?

2. Read the selections by Carol Gilligan and Marilyn French later in this chapter. How would they interpret Nora Quealey's story?

Extending the Critical Context

1. Play Ann Landers. Imagine that Quealey has written you a long letter — namely, the text you've just read. Write a confidential letter back to her giving advice, encouragement, or an analysis of her situation or feelings, as you see fit. Then provide a RATIONALE for your answer.

2. Write a letter of response to Nora Quealey, playing the role of a male

coworker, the female coworker who wore the low-cut tank top, a male foreman, a union representative, or the husband who left her. Share your letter with classmates who chose different roles.

Where I Come from Is Like This

PAULA GUNN ALLEN

Where Paula Gunn Allen comes from is a life as a Laguna Pueblo/Sioux woman. In this essay she discusses some of the ways in which traditional images of women in her Native American culture differ from images of women in mainstream American culture. A professor of Native American and Ethnic Studies at the University of California, Berkeley, Allen (b. 1939) is also widely recognized for her books of poetry and for the novel The Woman Who Owned the Shadows *(1983).*

I

Modern American Indian women, like their non-Indian sisters, are 1 deeply engaged in the struggle to redefine themselves. In their struggle they must reconcile traditional tribal definitions of women with industrial and postindustrial non-Indian definitions. Yet while these definitions seem to be more or less mutually exclusive, Indian women must somehow harmonize and integrate both in their own lives.

An American Indian woman is primarily defined by her tribal identity. 2 In her eyes, her destiny is necessarily that of her people, and her sense of herself as a woman is first and foremost prescribed by her tribe. The definitions of woman's roles are as diverse as tribal cultures in the Americas. In some she is devalued, in others she wields considerable power. In some she is a familial/clan adjunct, in some she is as close to autonomous as her economic circumstances and psychological traits permit. But in no tribal definitions is she perceived in the same way as are women in western industrial and postindustrial cultures.

In the west, few images of women form part of the cultural mythos, 3 and these are largely sexually charged. Among Christians, the madonna is the female prototype, and she is portrayed as essentially passive: her contribution is simply that of birthing. Little else is attributed to her and she certainly possesses few of the characteristics that are attributed to mythic figures among Indian tribes. This image is countered (rather than balanced) by the witch-goddess/whore characteristics designed to reinforce cultural beliefs about women, as well as western adversarial and dualistic perceptions of reality.

The tribes see women variously, but they do not question the power of femininity. Sometimes they see women as fearful, sometimes peaceful, sometimes omnipotent and omniscient, but they never portray women as mindless, helpless, simple, or oppressed. And while the women in a given tribe, clan, or band may be all these things, the individual woman is provided with a variety of images of women from the interconnected supernatural, natural, and social worlds she lives in.

As a half-breed American Indian woman, I cast about in my mind for negative images of Indian women, and I find none that are directed to Indian women alone. The negative images I do have are of Indians in general and in fact are more often of males than of females. All these images come to me from non-Indian sources, and they are always balanced by a positive image. My ideas of womanhood, passed on largely by my mother and grandmothers, Laguna Pueblo women, are about practicality, strength, reasonableness, intelligence, wit, and competence. I also remember vividly the women who came to my father's store, the women who held me and sang to me, the women at Feast Day, at Grab Days,[1] the women in the kitchen of my Cubero home, the women I grew up with; none of them appeared weak or helpless, none of them presented herself tentatively. I remember a certain reserve on those lovely brown faces; I remember the direct gaze of eyes framed by bright-colored shawls draped over their heads and cascading down their backs. I remember the clean cotton dresses and carefully pressed hand-embroidered aprons they always wore; I remember laughter and good food, especially the sweet bread and the oven bread they gave us. Nowhere in my mind is there a foolish woman, a dumb woman, a vain woman, or a plastic woman, though the Indian women I have known have shown a wide range of personal style and demeanor.

My memory includes the Navajo woman who was badly beaten by her Sioux husband; but I also remember that my grandmother abandoned her Sioux husband long ago. I recall the stories about the Laguna woman beaten regularly by her husband in the presence of her children so that the children would not believe in the strength and power of femininity. And I remember the women who drank, who got into fights with other

[1]*Grab Days:* Laguna ritual in which women throw food and small items (like pieces of cloth) to those attending.

women and with the men, and who often won those battles. I have memories of tired women, partying women, stubborn women, sullen women, amicable women, selfish women, shy women, and aggressive women. Most of all I remember the women who laugh and scold and sit uncomplaining in the long sun on feast days and who cook wonderful food on wood stoves, in beehive mud ovens, and over open fires outdoors.

Among the images of women that come to me from various tribes as 7 well as my own are White Buffalo Woman, who came to the Lakota long ago and brought them the religion of the Sacred Pipe which they still practice; Tinotzin the goddess who came to Juan Diego to remind him that she still walked the hills of her people and sent him with her message, her demand and her proof to the Catholic bishop in the city nearby. And from Laguna I take the images of Yellow Woman, Coyote Woman, Grandmother Spider (Spider Old Woman), who brought the light, who gave us weaving and medicine, who gave us life. Among the Keres she is known as Thought Woman who created us all and who keeps us in creation even now. I remember Iyatiku, Earth Woman, Corn Woman, who guides and counsels the people to peace and who welcomes us home when we cast off this coil of flesh as huskers cast off the leaves that wrap the corn. I remember Iyatiku's sister, Sun Woman, who held metals and cattle, pigs and sheep, highways and engines and so many things in her bundle, who went away to the east saying that one day she would return.

II

Since the coming of the Anglo-Europeans beginning in the fifteenth 8 century, the fragile web of identity that long held tribal people secure has gradually been weakened and torn. But the oral tradition has prevented the complete destruction of the web, the ultimate disruption of tribal ways. The oral tradition is vital; it heals itself and the tribal web by adapting to the flow of the present while never relinquishing its connection to the past. Its adaptability has always been required, as many generations have experienced. Certainly the modern American Indian woman bears slight resemblance to her forebears — at least on superficial examination — but she is still a tribal woman in her deepest being. Her tribal sense of relationship to all that is continues to flourish. And though she is at times beset by her knowledge of the enormous gap between the life she lives and the life she was raised to live, and while she adapts her mind and being to the circumstances of her present life, she does so in tribal ways, mending the tears in the web of being from which she takes her existence as she goes.

My mother told me stories all the time, though I often did not recognize 9 them as that. My mother told me stories about cooking and childbearing; she told me stories about menstruation and pregnancy; she told me stories about gods and heroes, about fairies and elves, about goddesses and spirits; she told me stories about the land and the sky, about cats and dogs, about snakes and spiders; she told me stories about climbing trees and exploring the mesas; she told me stories about going to dances and getting married; she told me stories about dressing and undressing, about sleeping and waking; she told me stories about herself, about her mother, about her grandmother. She told me stories about grieving and laughing, about thinking and doing; she told me stories about school and about people; about darning and mending; she told me stories about turquoise and about gold; she told me European stories and Laguna stories; she told me Catholic stories and Presbyterian stories; she told me city stories and country stories; she told me political stories and religious stories. She told me stories about living and stories about dying. And in all of those stories she told me who I was, who I was supposed to be, whom I came from, and who would follow me. In this way she taught me the meaning of the words she said, that all life is a circle and everything has a place within it. That's what she said and what she showed me in the things she did and the way she lives.

Of course, through my formal, white, Christian education, I discovered 10 that other people had stories of their own — about women, about Indians, about fact, about reality — and I was amazed by a number of startling suppositions that others made about tribal customs and beliefs. According to the un-Indian, non-Indian view, for instance, Indians barred menstruating women from ceremonies and indeed segregated them from the rest of the people, consigning them to some space specially designed for them. This showed that Indians considered menstruating women unclean and not fit to enjoy the company of decent (nonmenstruating) people, that is, men. I was surprised and confused to hear this because my mother had taught me that white people had strange attitudes toward menstruation: they thought something was bad about it, that it meant you were sick, cursed, sinful, and weak and that you had to be very careful during that time. She taught me that menstruation was a normal occurrence, that I could go swimming or hiking or whatever else I wanted to do during my period. She actively scorned women who took to their beds, who were incapacitated by cramps, who "got the blues."

As I struggled to reconcile these very contradictory interpretations of 11 American Indians' traditional beliefs concerning menstruation, I realized that the menstrual taboos were about power, not about sin or filth. My conclusion was later borne out by some tribes' own explanations, which, as you may well imagine, came as quite a relief to me.

The truth of the matter as many Indians see it is that women who 12
are at the peak of their fecundity are believed to possess power that
throws male power totally out of kilter. They emit such force that, in
their presence, any male-owned or -dominated ritual or sacred object
cannot do its usual task. For instance, the Lakota say that a menstruating
woman anywhere near a yuwipi man, who is a special sort of psychic,
spirit-empowered healer, for a day or so before he is to do his ceremony
will effectively disempower him. Conversely, among many if not most
tribes, important ceremonies cannot be held without the presence of
women. Sometimes the ritual woman who empowers the ceremony must
be unmarried and virginal so that the power she channels is unalloyed,
unweakened by sexual arousal and penetration by a male. Other ceremonies
require tumescent women, others the presence of mature women who
have borne children, and still others depend for empowerment on post-
menopausal women. Women may be segregated from the company of
the whole band or village on certain occasions, but on certain occasions
men are also segregated. In short, each ritual depends on a certain
balance of power, and the positions of women within the phases of
womanhood are used by tribal people to empower certain rites. This
does not derive from a male-dominant view; it is not a ritual observance
imposed on women by men. It derives from a tribal view of reality that
distinguishes tribal people from feudal and industrial people.

Among the tribes, the occult power of women, inextricably bound to 13
our hormonal life, is thought to be very great; many hold that we possess
innately the blood-given power to kill — with a glance, with a step, or
with a judicious mixing of menstrual blood into somebody's soup. Medicine
women among the Pomo of California cannot practice until they are
sufficiently mature; when they are immature, their power is diffuse and
is likely to interfere with their practice until time and experience have
it under control. So women of the tribes are not especially inclined to
see themselves as poor helpless victims of male domination. Even in
those tribes where something akin to male domination was present,
women are perceived as powerful, socially, physically, and metaphysically.
In times past, as in times present, women carried enormous burdens
with aplomb. We were far indeed from the "weaker sex," the designation
that white aristocratic sisters unhappily earned for us all.

I remember my mother moving furniture all over the house when she 14
wanted it changed. She didn't wait for my father to come home and
help — she just went ahead and moved the piano, a huge upright from
the old days, the couch, the refrigerator. Nobody had told her she was
too weak to do such things. In imitation of her, I would delight in loading
trucks at my father's store with cases of pop or fifty-pound sacks of flour.

Even when I was quite small I could do it, and it gave me a belief in my own physical strength that advancing middle age can't quite erase. My mother used to tell me about the Acoma Pueblo women she had seen as a child carrying huge ollas (water pots) on their heads as they wound their way up the tortuous stairwell carved into the face of the "Sky City" mesa, a feat I tried to imitate with books and tin buckets. ("Sky City" is the term used by the Chamber of Commerce for the mother village of Acoma, which is situated atop a high sandstone table mountain.) I was never very successful, but even the attempt reminded me that I was supposed to be strong and balanced to be a proper girl.

Of course, my mother's Laguna people are Keres Indian, reputed to be the last extreme mother-right people on earth. So it is no wonder that I got notably nonwhite notions about the natural strength and prowess of women. Indeed, it is only when I am trying to get non-Indian approval, recognition, or acknowledgment that my "weak sister" emotional and intellectual ploys get the better of my tribal woman's good sense. At such times I forget that I just moved the piano or just wrote a competent paper or just completed a financial transaction satisfactorily or have supported myself and my children for most of my adult life. 15

Nor is my contradictory behavior atypical. Most Indian women I know are in the same bicultural bind: we vacillate between being dependent and strong, self-reliant and powerless, strongly motivated and hopelessly insecure. We resolve the dilemma in various ways: some of us party all the time; some of us drink to excess; some of us travel and move around a lot; some of us land good jobs and then quit them; some of us engage in violent exchanges; some of us blow our brains out. We act in these destructive ways because we suffer from the societal conflicts caused by having to identify with two hopelessly opposed cultural definitions of women. Through this destructive dissonance we are unhappy prey to the self-disparagement common to, indeed demanded of, Indians living in the United States today. Our situation is caused by the exigencies of a history of invasion, conquest, and colonization whose searing marks are probably ineradicable. A popular bumper sticker on many Indian cars proclaims: "If You're Indian You're In," to which I always find myself adding under my breath, "Trouble." 16

III

No Indian can grow to any age without being informed that her people were "savages" who interfered with the march of progress pursued by respectable, loving, civilized white people. We are the villains of the scenario when we are mentioned at all. We are absent from much of white history except when we are calmly, rationally, succinctly, and 17 systematically dehumanized. On the few occasions we are noticed in any way other than as howling, bloodthirsty beings, we are acclaimed for our noble quaintness. In this definition, we are exotic curios. Our ancient arts and customs are used to draw tourist money to state coffers, into the pocketbooks and bank accounts of scholars, and into support of the American-in-Disneyland promoters' dream.

As a Roman Catholic child I was treated to bloody tales of how the savage Indians martyred the hapless priests and missionaries who went among them in an attempt to lead them to the one true path. By the time I was through high school I had the idea that Indians were people who had benefited mightily from the advanced knowledge and superior morality of the Anglo-Europeans. At least I had, perforce, that idea to lay beside the other one that derived from my daily experience of Indian life, an idea less dehumanizing and more accurate because it came from my mother and the other Indian people who raised me. That idea was that Indians are a people who don't tell lies, who care for their children and their old people. You never see an Indian orphan, they said. You always know when you're old that someone will take care of you — one of your children will. Then they'd list the old folks who were being taken care of by this child or that. No child is ever considered illegitimate among the Indians, they said. If a girl gets pregnant, the baby is still part of the family, and the mother is too. That's what they said, and they showed me real people who lived according to those principles. 18

Of course the ravages of colonization have taken their toll; there are orphans in Indian country now, and abandoned, brutalized old folks; there are even illegitimate children, though the very concept still strikes me as absurd. There are battered children and neglected children, and there are battered wives and women who have been raped by Indian men. Proximity to the "civilizing" effects of white Christians has not improved the moral quality of life in Indian country, though each group, Indian and white, explains the situation differently. Nor is there much yet in the oral tradition that can enable us to adapt to these inhuman changes. But a force is growing in that direction, and it is helping Indian women reclaim their lives. Their power, their sense of direction and of self will soon be visible. It is the force of the women who speak and work and write, and it is formidable. 19

Through all the centuries of war and death and cultural and psychic destruction have endured the women who raise the children and tend the fires, who pass along the tales and the traditions, who weep and bury the dead, who are the dead, and who never forget. There are always the women, who make pots and weave baskets, who fashion clothes and cheer their children on at powwow, who make fry bread 20 and piki bread, and corn soup and chili stew, who dance and sing and remember and hold within their hearts the dream of their ancient peoples — that one day the woman who thinks will speak to us again, and everywhere there will be peace. Meanwhile we tell the stories and write the books and trade tales of anger and woe and stories of fun and scandal and laugh over all manner of things that happen every day. We watch and we wait.

My great-grandmother told my mother: Never forget you are Indian. 21 And my mother told me the same thing. This, then, is how I have gone about remembering, so that my children will remember too.

Engaging the Text

1. Outline the ways Allen's views of women are different from traditional Anglo-American views.

2. How has reading this selection changed your perception of Native American cultures, and especially of women's roles in such cultures?

3. As the title suggests, much of the passage is *personal* recollection. Try to "translate" some of this information into more straightforward statements of THEME or message (e.g., you might write, "Women's roles in Native American cultures are maintained through example, through oral tradition, and through ceremonial tribal practices.") What is gained, what lost in such "translations"?

Exploring Connections

1. Compare the "bicultural bind" Allen describes to the cultural conflict experienced by Hank López or Maxine Hong Kingston in Chapter Three, "One Nation or Many?"

2. How do you think Allen might respond to Marilyn French's call (p. 290) for the prominence of a women's morality? Is her notion of tribal connectedness compatible with French's view of women's superior morality? Would Allen accept French's generalizations about women?

3. Compare the significance of stories in creating identity for Allen with their importance for López in "Back to Bachimba" (p. 232).

Extending the Critical Context

1. Do you feel that women are torn between media images or other dominant cultural images and what they really are? What are some of the most powerful of these images? What are the dominant STEREOTYPES of American men? To what extent are men pulled in conflicting directions?

2. Are you struggling to reconcile different definitions of what you should be? Write an essay or journal entry exploring this issue. (For example, are family, friends, and school pushing you in different directions?)

Images of Relationships
CAROL GILLIGAN

Carol Gilligan (b. 1936) reports here on an elegant study of female/male psychology. She presented college students with simple pictures (some suggesting personal intimacy, others suggesting professional achievement) and asked them to write stories for each image. Male and female students responded in markedly different ways; for example, women protected trapeze artists with a net while men sent one or both acrobats to their death. Gilligan is an associate professor of education at Harvard University; this selection is from her book In a Different Voice: Psychological Theory and Women's Development *(1982).*

. . . A study of the images of violence that appear in stories written   1
by college students to pictures on the TAT[1] . . . report[s] statistically significant sex differences in the places where violence is seen and in the substance of violent fantasies as well. The themes of separation and connection are central to the study, conducted by Susan Pollak and myself and based on analysis of stories, written prior to the study, by students as a class exercise in a psychology course on motivation (Pollak and Gilligan, 1982). The study began with Pollak's observation of seemingly bizarre imagery of violence in men's stories about a picture of what appeared to be a tranquil scene, a couple sitting on a bench by a river next to a low bridge. In response to this picture, more than 21 percent of the eighty-eight men in the class had written stories containing

[1]*TAT:* Thematic Apperception Test; according to Gilligan, "The TAT presents for interpretation an ambiguous cue — a picture about which a story is to be written or a segment of a story that is to be completed. Such stories . . . are considered by psychologists to reveal . . . the concepts and interpretations [people] bring to their experience and thus presumably the kind of sense they make of their lives" (*In a Different Voice*, 14).

incidents of violence — homicide, suicide, stabbing, kidnapping, or rape. In contrast, none of the fifty women in the class had projected violence into this scene.

This observation of violence in men's stories about intimacy appeared 2 to us as a possible corollary to Horner's (1968) report of imagery of violence in women's stories about competitive success. Horner, exemplifying her category of "bizarre or violent imagery" in depicting women's anticipation of negative consequences following success, cites a story that portrays a jubilant Anne, at the top of her medical school class, physically beaten and maimed for life by her jealous classmates. The corollary observation of violent imagery in men's fantasies of intimate relationships is illustrated by a story written by one of the men in the class to the picture of the riverbench scene:

> Nick saw his life pass before his eyes. He could feel the cold penetrating ever deeper into his body. How long had it been since he had fallen through the ice — thirty seconds, a minute? It wouldn't take long for him to succumb to the chilling grip of the mid-February Charles River. What a fool he had been to accept the challenge of his roommate Sam to cross the frozen river. He knew all along that Sam hated him. Hated him for being rich and especially hated him for being engaged to Mary, Sam's childhood sweetheart. But Nick never realized until now that Mary also hated him and really loved Sam. Yet there they were, the two of them, calmly sitting on a bench in the riverbend, watching Nick drown. They'd probably soon be married, and they'd probably finance it with the life insurance policy for which Mary was the beneficiary.

Calling attention to the eye of the observer in noting where danger 3 is seen, Pollak and I wondered whether men and women perceive danger in different situations and construe danger in different ways. Following the initial observation of violence in men's stories about intimacy, we set out to discover whether there were sex differences in the distribution of violent fantasies across situations of achievement and affiliation and whether violence was differentially associated by males and females with intimacy and competitive success. The findings of the resulting images of violence study corroborate previous reports of sex differences in aggression (Terman and Tyler, 1953; Whiting and Pope, 1973; Maccoby and Jacklin, 1974) by revealing a far greater incidence of violence in stories written by men. Of the eighty-eight men in the motivation class, 51 percent wrote at least one story containing images of violence, in comparison to 20 percent of the fifty women in the class, and no woman wrote more than one story in which violence appeared. But the study also revealed sex differences in the distribution and substance of violent fantasies, indicating a difference between the way in which men and women tend to imagine relationships.

Four of the six pictures that comprised the test were chosen for the 4 purposes of this analysis since they provided clear illustrations of achievement and affiliation situations. Two of the pictures show a man and a woman in close personal affiliation — the couple on the bench in the river scene, and two trapeze artists grasping each other's wrists, the man hanging by his knees from the trapeze and the woman in mid-air. Two pictures show people at work in impersonal achievement situations — a man sitting alone at his desk in a high-rise office building, and two women, dressed in white coats, working in a laboratory, the woman in the background watching while the woman in the foreground handles the test tubes. The study centered on a comparison between the stories written about these two sets of pictures.

The men in the class, considered as a group, projected more violence 5 into situations of personal affiliation than they did into impersonal situations of achievement. Twenty-five percent of the men wrote violent stories only to the pictures of affiliation, 19 percent to pictures of both affiliation and achievement, and 7 percent only to pictures of achievement. In contrast, the women saw more violence in impersonal situations of achievement than in situations of affiliation; 16 percent of the women wrote violent stories to the achievement pictures and 6 percent to the pictures of affiliation.

As the story about Nick, written by a man, illustrates the association 6 of danger with intimacy, so the story about Miss Hegstead, written by a woman, exemplifies the projection of violence into situations of achievement and the association of danger with competitive success:

> Another boring day in the lab and that mean bitchy Miss Hegstead always breathing down the students' backs. Miss Hegstead has been at Needham Country High School for 40 years and every chemistry class is the same. She is watching Jane Smith, the model student in the class. She always goes over to Jane and comments to the other students that Jane is always doing the experiment right and Jane is the only student who really works hard, etc. Little does Miss Hegstead know that Jane is making some arsenic to put in her afternoon coffee.

If aggression is conceived as a response to the perception of danger, 7 the findings of the images of violence study suggest that men and women may perceive danger in different social situations and construe danger in different ways — men seeing danger more often in close personal affiliation than in achievement and construing danger to arise from intimacy, women perceiving danger in impersonal achievement situations and construing danger to result from competitive success. The danger men describe in their stories of intimacy is a danger of entrapment or betrayal, being caught in a smothering relationship or humiliated by rejection and deceit. In contrast, the danger women portray in their tales of achievement is a danger of isolation, a fear that in standing out or being set apart by success, they will be left alone. In the story of Miss Hegstead, the only apparent cause of the violence is Jane's being singled out as the best student and thus set apart from her classmates. She retaliates by making arsenic to put in the teacher's afternoon coffee, yet all Miss Hegstead did was to praise Jane for her good work.

As people are brought closer together in the pictures, the images of violence in the men's stories increase, while as people are set further apart, the violence in the women's stories increases. The women in the class projected violence most frequently into the picture of the man at his desk (the only picture portraying a person alone), while the men in the class most often saw violence in the scene of the acrobats on the trapeze (the only picture in which people touched). Thus, it appears that men and women may experience attachment and separation in different ways and that each sex perceives a danger which the other does not see — men in connection, women in separation.

But since the women's perception of danger departs from the usual mode of expectation, the acrobats seeming to be in far greater danger than the man at his desk, their perception calls into question the usual mode of interpretation. Sex differences in aggression are usually interpreted by taking the male response as the norm, so that the absence of aggression in women is identified as the problem to be explained. However, the disparate location of violence in the stories written by women and men raises the question as to why women see the acrobats as safe.

The answer comes from the analysis of the stories about the trapeze. Although the picture of acrobats shows them performing high in the air without a net, 22 percent of the women in the study added nets in the stories they wrote. In contrast, only 6 percent of the men imagined the presence of a net, while 40 percent either explicitly mentioned the absence of a net or implied its absence by describing one or both acrobats as plummeting to their deaths. Thus, the women saw the scene on the trapeze as safe because, by providing nets, they had made it safe, protecting the lives of the acrobats in the event of a fall. Yet failing to imagine the presence of nets in the scene on the trapeze, men, interpreting women's responses, readily attribute the absence of violence in women's stories to a denial of danger or to a repression of aggression (May, 1981) rather than to the activities of care through which the women make the acrobats safe. As women imagine the activities through which relationships are woven and connection sustained, the world of intimacy — which appears so mysterious and dangerous to men — comes instead to appear increasingly coherent and safe.

If aggression is tied, as women perceive, to the fracture of human 11
connection, then the activities of care, as their fantasies suggest, are the activities that make the social world safe, by avoiding isolation and preventing aggression rather than by seeking rules to limit its extent. In this light, aggression appears no longer as an unruly impulse that must be contained but rather as a signal of a fracture of connection, the sign of a failure of relationship. From this perspective, the prevalence of violence in men's fantasies, denoting a world where danger is everywhere seen, signifies a problem in making connection, causing relationships to erupt and turning separation into a dangerous isolation. Reversing the usual mode of interpretation, in which the absence of aggression in women is tied to a problem with separation, makes it possible to see the prevalence of violence in men's stories, its odd location in the context of intimate relationships, and its association with betrayal and deceit as indicative of a problem with connection that leads relationships to become dangerous and safety to appear in separation. Then rule-bound competitive achievement situations, which for women threaten the web of connection, for men provide a mode of connection that establishes clear boundaries and limits aggression, and thus appears comparatively safe.

A story written by one of the women about the acrobats on the trapeze 12
illustrates these themes, calling into question the usual opposition of achievement and affiliation by portraying the continuation of the relationship as the predicate for success:

> These are two Flying Gypsies, and they are auditioning for the big job with the Ringling Brothers Circus. They are the last team to try out for the job, and they are doing very well. They have grace and style, but they use a safety net which some teams do not use. The owners say that they'll hire them if they forfeit the net, but the Gypsies decide that they would rather live longer and turn down the job than take risks like that. They know the act will be ruined if either got hurt and see no sense in taking the risk.

For the Gypsies in the story, it is not the big job with the circus that is of paramount importance but rather the well-being of the two people involved. Anticipating negative consequences from a success attained at the risk of their lives, they forfeit the job rather than the net, protecting their lives but also their act, which "would be ruined if either got hurt."

While women thus try to change the rules in order to preserve re- 13
lationships, men, in abiding by these rules, depict relationships as easily

replaced. Projecting most violence into this scene, they write stories about infidelity and betrayal that end with the male acrobat dropping the woman, presumably replacing the relationship and going on with the act:

> The woman trapeze artist is married to the best friend of the male who has just discovered (before the show) that she has been unfaithful to his friend (her husband). He confronted her with this knowledge and told her to tell her husband but she refused. Not having the courage to confront him himself, the trapeze artist creates an accident while 100 feet above ground, letting the woman slip out of his grasp in mid-flight. She is killed in the incident but he feels no guilt, believing that he has rectified the situation.

The prevalence of violence in male fantasy . . . is consonant with the view of aggression as endemic in human relationships. But these male fantasies and images also reveal a world where connection is fragmented and communication fails, where betrayal threatens because there seems to be no way of knowing the truth. Asked if he ever thinks about whether or not things are real, eleven-year-old Jake says that he wonders a lot about whether people are telling the truth, about "what people say, like one of my friends says, 'Oh yeah, he said that,' and sometimes I think, 'Is he actually saying the truth?' " Considering truth to lie in math and certainty to reside in logic, he can see "no guidelines" for establishing truth in English class or in personal relationships. 14

Thus, although aggression has been construed as instinctual and separation has been thought necessary for its constraint, the violence in male fantasy seems rather to arise from a problem in communication and an absence of knowledge about human relationships. But as . . . women in their fantasies create nets of safety where men depict annihilation, the voices of women comment on the problem of aggression that both sexes face, locating the problem in the isolation of self and in the hierarchical construction of human relationships. 15

. . . The images of hierarchy and web, drawn from the texts of men's and women's fantasies and thoughts, convey different ways of structuring relationships and are associated with different views of morality and self. But these images create a problem in understanding because each distorts the other's representation. As the top of the hierarchy becomes the edge of the web and as the center of a network of connection becomes the middle of a hierarchical progression, each image marks as dangerous the place which the other defines as safe. Thus the images of hierarchy and web inform different modes of assertion and response: the wish to be alone at the top and the consequent fear that others will get too close; the wish to be at the center of connection and the consequent fear of 16 being too far out on the edge. These disparate fears of being stranded and being caught give rise to different portrayals of achievement and affiliation, leading to different modes of action and different ways of assessing the consequences of choice.

The reinterpretation of women's experience in terms of their own 17 imagery of relationships thus clarifies that experience and also provides a nonhierarchical vision of human connection. Since relationships, when cast in the image of hierarchy, appear inherently unstable and morally problematic, their transposition into the image of web changes an order of inequality into a structure of interconnection. But the power of the images of hierarchy and web, their evocation of feelings and their recurrence in thought, signifies the embeddedness of both of these images in the cycle of human life. The experiences of inequality and interconnection, inherent in the relation of parent and child, then give rise to the ethics of justice and care, the ideals of human relationship — the vision that self and other will be treated as of equal worth, that despite differences in power, things will be fair; the vision that everyone will be responded to and included, that no one will be left alone or hurt. These disparate visions in their tension reflect the paradoxical truths of human experience — that we know ourselves as separate only insofar as we live in connection with others, and that we experience relationship only insofar as we differentiate other from self.

Works Cited

Horner, Matina S. "Sex Differences in Achievement Motivation and Performance in Competitive and Noncompetitive Situations." Ph.D. Diss., University of Michigan, 1968. University Microfilms #6912135.

Maccoby, Eleanor, and Jacklin, Carol. *The Psychology of Sex Differences*. Stanford: Stanford University Press, 1974.

Pollak, Susan, and Gilligan, Carol. "Images of Violence in Thematic Apperception Test Stories." *Journal of Personality and Social Psychology* 42, no. 1 (1982): 159–167.

Terman, L., and Tyler, L. "Psychological Sex Differences." In L. Carmichael, ed., *Manual of Child Psychology*. 2nd ed. New York: John Wiley and Sons, 1954.

Whiting, Beatrice, and Pope, Carolyn. "A Cross-cultural Analysis of Sex Difference in the Behavior of Children Age Three to Eleven." *Journal of Social Psychology* 91 (1973): 171–188.

Engaging the Text

1. Break into single-gender groups. Discuss and CRITIQUE Gilligan's study, its findings, and her interpretations. Then combine the groups and compare notes. Do you find Gilligan's interpretations of her results convincing? Is she attacking men?

2. Does a man's aggressive attitude toward intimacy, as revealed by a test like the one described here, constitute either sexism or a psychological problem? Debate.

Exploring Connections

1. Compare the ways Gilligan and Paula Gunn Allen (in the previous essay) use the IMAGE of the web to illustrate their arguments about female and tribal values.

2. Apply the psychological concept of "projection" discussed by Loewenberg (Chapter Two, "Justice for All") to explain the way that men interpret women's behavior — for example, to explain why men might label women's lack of aggression "timidity."

Extending the Critical Context

1. Suppose for the moment that it is true, as Gilligan asserts, that many men fear intimacy and that many women fear success. Speculate as to *why* this is the case. What kinds of evidence would you need to validate your speculations?

Men

LORENZA CALVILLO CRAIG

This poem indicts men's failure to understand the spirit of women and predicts dire consequences as a result of that failure. Lorenza Calvillo Craig (b. 1943) is an educator, lawyer, and poet.

suffering/afflicted
with a seemingly
congenital blindness:
  bodyofawoman
while they apparently   5
are able to see
the body and spirit
of men,
a few men,
they are totally unable   10

to see beyond
the body of a woman.
they cannot see and
erroneously decree
that a woman hath   15
no spirit
no soul.
this eye disease
moreover
frequently spreads   20
to include
   other men
   children
   trees
   butterflies   25
   black men
   chicanos
   indians
   communists
   students   30
   own children
   all insects
   animals
   academicians

soon   35
the man is alone
unable to see
any spirit but his own
he dies
in the midst of life.   40

Engaging the Text

1. What does Craig mean when she says that men cannot "see" the spirit of women?

2. Study the long indented list in the second half of the poem. What elements in the list are most interesting or surprising? How does Craig's argument develop here?

3. Is Craig attacking all men, many men, or just a few men? On what do you base your answer? Is Craig fair? Does a writer from a minority or oppressed group have the same responsibilities to fairness as anyone else?

Exploring Connections

1. To what extent does Carol Gilligan's research, reported in the previous selection, support the poem's assumption that men isolate themselves from others?

Extending the Critical Context

1. Craig's poem uses strong assertions and IMAGES — for example, the METAPHOR of blindness. Rewrite the poem as a short prose passage, striving for a reasonable, noninflammatory tone. What is lost in the "translation"? Is anything gained?

The Ideal of Equality

MARILYN FRENCH

Having herself experienced the traditional roles of marriage and motherhood, Marilyn French (b. 1929) has also become a leading voice in contemporary feminism. She electrified readers in 1977 with her radical condemnation of women's domestic roles in her novel, The Women's Room. *This excerpt comes from French's analysis of the future of the feminist movement,* Beyond Power: On Women, Men, and Models *(1985). Women today, according to French, need to fight for more than legal equality with men: What women should be aiming at is nothing short of a revolution of consciousness — a new morality and a new set of values. French's latest book is* Her Mothers' Daughter *(1987).*

Some of the earliest feminists — the brilliant Mary Wollstonecraft,[1]   1
for example, or some of the suffragists[2] — did not suggest that they wanted equality with men.

But equality has been a major demand of second-wave feminists, who   2

[1]*Mary Wollstonecraft:* English intellectual and writer (1759–1797); published *A Vindication of the Rights of Woman* in 1792.
[2]*suffragists:* feminists who campaigned for the extension of voting rights to women. In the United States, the crusade for woman suffrage extended from the mid-nineteenth century until 1920, when the Nineteenth Amendment was ratified.

realized that the right to vote, the right to go to school, and even the right to hold a job above the menial level did not give women a voice — as individuals, as a caste, or as a moral constituency. They thus began a movement for equality based on the black civil rights movement. Using the principles of the foundations of the state — enunciated in the Declaration of Independence, the Constitution and the Bill of Rights that is its heart — blacks and women began what seemed a campaign for assimilation. Unlike other social protest movements — the labor movement, the campaign against anti-Semitism — the civil rights movements of blacks and women have been only moderately successful. Because blacks and women are symbolic of elements patriarchy[3] was designed to transcend, they cannot be assimilated into society as it stands. For members of these groups to be absorbed into society, they would have to transform themselves into white males. They would have to enunciate the values and standards of the white male world, adopt its modes of behavior, dress, and life style, and prove their devotion to the principle of stratified power, to hierarchy. Women and blacks who have been able to do this are treated as almost equal by the white male world. It is the best status they will ever achieve, since they cannot change their sex or their skin color.

Equality continues to be the goal of many women's and black groups, however. Because of the unbridgeable gap between white and black, male and female, every gain made in the name of the latter groups is rescinded the next day and must be earned again and again. The resistance to receiving women and blacks as equals of white males is so profound, so undying, and so implanted in the culture, that the example of one woman or black doing a good job is not enough to ease the lot of the next; and assimilative acts performed under political (or moral, or social) pressure are often undone as soon as the pressure is removed. It is impossible to rely on the endurance of improvements in hiring practices, promotion, or pay, in assimilated dwelling, education, or work (for blacks), in ownership of rights over one's own body and reproduction, assimilated work, or political representation (for women). Only warily can blacks or women attempt to use past accomplishments as foundation stones to build on, because so often, in a month, or a year, or three, these advances are annulled, the struggle must be refought against an opponent whose resources are so much greater, whose life is so much more comfortable, that it can afford to sit back and litigate: for years. 3

There are those who, seeing this immovability, this intransigence, and 4

[3] *patriarchy:* a form of society in which economic and political power are monopolized by males and those who subscribe to traditionally male values.

perceiving the rigidity of the society, advocate violent overthrow of the present system and the creation of a new one from the ground up. The problem with this idea (quite apart from the fact that it is unlikely to succeed) is that the new society would be created only from the ground up, with the old roots still in place. Those who hold such a position, however, scorn the fight for equality, finding equality in an unworthy society an unworthy goal.

Nevertheless, given the intransigence of our institutions, their rigidity 5 toward symbolic entities that are actual people, the struggle for equality continues to be necessary, both for its potential to improve life for some people, and because it provides a course of action and thus a cause for pride (if also frustration and despair) to those engaged in it and those who benefit from it.

At the same time it is essential to keep in mind the kind of equality 6 we desire. Assimilation in an unworthy society *is* an unworthy goal. The white male world offers an unhappy and unworthy standard. The equality we must fight for is political and economic sufficiency: a position strong and broad enough to give us a voice in the large decisions affecting our culture, a position rich and admirable enough to allow alteration of that culture through example and influence.

There has been, and remains, a tendency within feminism to hold the 7 white male world up for emulation, to compare white male and general female modes and find the latter lacking. I doubt if there is a feminist alive who has not sat up late for nights in conflict over what to do in a given situation. For example, a woman may suspect that a male colleague has done something unprofessional which has harmed her, perhaps run her down to an important customer. Her first thought may be: What would a man do? She may decide that a man would first obtain clear evidence of the colleague's act and then complain to their superior. But she feels reluctant to do that; what she wants to do is confront the colleague and ask him why he tried to harm her. She knows, however, that he will be evasive. She also knows that for her, a woman, to use a man's mode of handling the situation may turn the superior officer against her. She also has deep emotional reservations about using this method. She wants revenge — it would satisfy her; but she does not want to be the kind of person who acts in vengeance, partly because she has been socialized not to be aggressive. The method she wants to use is typical of a woman and is almost guaranteed to fail; and it may violate her feminist principles, which require her to assert herself. There is no adequate model for this woman within the white male world; nor is there any possibility that her action, whatever it may be, will be interpreted as it would be if a white male performed it.

Equality is not possible in a world that worships power and tran- 8
scendence. Women's dilemmas in functioning in a misogynistic world
are insoluble; if women make decisions using equality as a standard,
they violate principles they have learned to cherish and frequently fail
anyway. At best, they become pseudo-men. What is necessary is the
development of a set of moral standards that women feel comfortable
with, that express their value structure, and that are generally disseminated.
Women must build a morality that can stand in the world despite its
difference from male morality. And the first step in the creation of such
a morality is broadening or even altering present standards of evaluation.

In the past two decades, considerable research comparing men and 9
women has been done in three major areas of experience: in the area
of motivation (success or success avoidance); in language; and in morality.
The initial research showed women to be in some way different and
therefore less adequate than men in these areas. Later research was
based on a broader perspective and opened up questions that men as
well as women need to confront; it challenged current (male) standards.

The earliest work on achievement motivation was done by David 10
McClelland and associates. Their book, based on studies done in 1953,
was nine hundred pages long and discussed achievement motivation as
if the authors' theory applied to everyone. Only one footnote informs
the careful reader that data on females do not fit into the theory.[4]

In the late 1960s, Matina Horner published the first studies of women's 11
attitudes toward success.[5] She and her coworkers presented college students
with the opening of a story and asked them to finish it. The opening
described a young woman aiming for a career in medicine, a traditional
success ladder. Most of the women who took the test gave the story an
ambiguous or unhappy conclusion, showing that they had unpleasant
associations with success. Horner interpreted this response as expressing
a fear that success would lead a woman to be socially rejected and to
lose her "femininity."

Horner's interpretation was based on a male standard: that is, men 12
show a desire for success; if women do not, they demonstrate an inadequacy.
Such an interpretation offers those who wish to use it a pseudoscientific
basis for the fact that women are so rarely successful, and for continued
male exclusion of them. Although Horner herself did not foster such

[4]The book is David McClelland, John Atkinson, R. A. Clark, and E. L. Lowell, *The
Achievement Motive* (New York, 1953). The comment is from Joanna Rohrbaugh, *Women:
Psychology's Puzzle* (New York, 1979), p. 219. [Author's note]

[5]Matina S. Horner, "Women's Need to Fail," *Psychology Today*, Nov. 1969; "Toward
an Understanding of Achievement-Related Conflicts in Women," *Journal of Social Issues*
28, 9 (1972):157–175. [Author's note]

ideas, her work was widely cited in support of them. After it was published other researchers studied the subject; most attempted to challenge Horner's results rather than her interpretation. Success avoidance remained strong among white college women, but — during an era of doubt and hostility toward institutions — also appeared in an increasing number of white college men.[6] Other studies showed that black women had less avoidance of success, and that the higher a young woman's socioeconomic class, the greater her fear of succeeding.[7]

Little was made of tests showing that men who desired success believed   13
it would bring them not only money and status but love and intimacy as well, whereas the behavior required of a successful man impedes his capacity for love and intimacy. Not until 1976 was there a suggestion that the women in Horner's experiment were less afraid of success than of the negative consequences for those who deviate from traditional sex-role expectations, and that Horner's subjects displayed not a deep-seated psychological condition but a realistic appraisal of the ways of the world.[8] In addition, John Condry and Sharon Dyer suggested that to describe success in terms of doing well in school or having career goals is to limit that term unduly. Other recent researchers have found that women do express the desire to achieve in areas designated as feminine, especially those of affiliation and affective ties.[9] No one seems to have given such tests to older women.

But Martha Mednick, Sandra Tangri, and Lois Hoffman[10] conclude   14
that to judge female motivation by male standards is ultimately destructive. Both men and women must give up important parts of themselves to succeed in prestigious careers like medicine. They hypothesize that the reluctance of young women to do this testifies to their possession of more integrated personalities, a conception of what a life should be that is wider and richer than "success." That young women from the higher socioeconomic class — that class whose members have achieved worldly success — are most likely to wish to avoid that kind of success is an

[6]L. W. Hoffman, "Fear of Success in Males and Females: 1965 and 1972," *Journal of Consulting and Clinical Psychology* (1974). [Author's note]

[7]Several studies are published and discussed in *Women and Achievement*, ed. Martha Mednick, Sandra Tangri, and Lois Hoffman (New York, 1975). [Author's note]

[8]John Condry and Sharon Dyer, "Fear of Success: Attribution of Cause to the Victim," *Journal of Social Issues* 32, 3 (Summer 1976):63–83. See also Lenore J. Weitzman, "Sex-Role Socialization," in Freeman, *Women*. [Author's note]

[9]Harriet Holter, "Sex Roles and Social Change," Mednick et al., *Women and Achievement*. [Author's note]

[10]Martha Mednick, Sandra Tangri, and Lois Hoffman, eds., *Women and Achievement* (New York: Hemisphere Publishing, 1975).

implicit criticism of their families, probably especially their fathers. Young women may be saying they do not want lives like those lived by their parents.

Horner's work was important because she bothered to test women at 15 all and to take her results seriously. Her use of a male standard in judging women was inevitable at the time. But researchers have lately been opening their minds to new positions: that female standards are not identical to men's; that the difference may not indicate inferiority; and, although this suggestion usually remains implicit, that men might be better off with female standards.

Considering the great stress many men live with, their shorter life 16 spans, greater loneliness, and relative incapacity for intimacy, community, and love, it is possible that women's values are superior to men's. Perhaps we should not be asking why women do not on the whole want to be president of General Motors, and ask why men do. It is conceivable that success in our world is not a desirable goal for anyone, that any enterprise requiring the sacrifice of expressiveness, interrelatedness, compassion, and (often) humane standards is not worth what it costs. Men are socialized to believe that worldly success will automatically bring them love, in- terrelatedness, and acceptance, as well as money and status: women know better, for themselves at least. A more useful guide to attitudes and motivation might be a question about what people believe constitutes a successful life, rather than a question about motivation to success in current worldly terms.

Early work on women and language began with the same bias. This 17 complex area of study involves at least three subareas: gender in language; comparative study of how men and women are described by language; and comparative study of how women and men use language.[11] The third category has been the subject of considerable research in the past decade, and at first both male and female researchers tended to hold up male use of language as a standard that demonstrated the "weakness" shown in female deviations from it.[12]

An early (1972) article on the dialect of Norwich, England, discusses 18

[11]For an overview, see Marilyn French, "Women in Language," *Soundings* 59, 3 (Fall 1976):329–344. [Author's note]

[12]The way people speak is called "language behavior" in the jargon. For research on this subject, see *Language and Sex*, ed. Barrie Thorne and Nancy Henley (Rowley, Mass., 1975); Mary Ritchie Key, *Male/Female Language* (Metuchen, N.J., 1975); Elizabeth Aries, "Interaction Patterns and Themes of Males, Females, and Mixed Groups," *Small Group Behavior* 7, 1 (1976):1–18; Casey Miller and Kate Swift, *Words and Women* (London, 1977); Karen Adams and Norma C. Ware, "Sexism and the English Language: The Linguistic Implications of Being a Woman," in Freeman, *Women*. [Author's note]

the more grammatical language of the local women, the cruder, rougher language of the men.[13] The data stand: but the interpretation put upon them belongs to the researcher, Peter Trudgill, who implicitly accepts the male dialect as basic and realistic, the language of real men, and considers the women's more correct and refined language pretentious, an attempt by status-conscious people to raise their status. Since male language is equally status-conscious (although a different kind of status is involved), this interpretation is biased.

In 1973 Robin Lakoff published what was probably the most influential 19 early article (later expanded into a book) on female language behavior.[14] The article concentrated on three instances of difference in female (as opposed to male) speech, and its stance is condescending to women: Lakoff believes their speech illegitimates them, deprives them of male authority and force. Her strong male standard was probably responsible for the wide dissemination of her conclusions in popular organs — again, her work seemed to justify women's inferior status; it was also responsible for a host of follow-up studies by female researchers.

The first characteristic that Lakoff discusses is women's use of tag 20 questions. Women, she writes, are far more likely than men to attach a question to a statement, as in, "This war in Vietnam is terrible, isn't it?" A man might say, "This war in Vietnam is an atrocity!" Lakoff thinks tag questions display unsureness about the self, a fear of assertiveness and a need for reassurance from others, whereas male utterances display authority and confidence.

Second, women, but not men, use a questioning tone in answering 21 questions. Thus if one asks a woman, "What time will dinner be ready?" she may reply, "Oh . . . around six o'clock?" To Lakoff this shows the speaker's lack of confidence, a lack so profound as to require confirmation and support even in a situation she ostensibly controls.

Finally, women avoid strong statements; here Lakoff's examples compare 22 commands to questions. A man is more likely to order, "Close the door!" or "Do close the door." A woman is more likely to request, "Will you close the door?" or "Please close the door?" or even, in the negative phrasing that invites rebellion, "Won't you close the door?" Again Lakoff concludes that such locutions reinforce women's lack of authority.

Later researchers have questioned some of Lakoff's results. One study 23 demonstrates male use of tag questions either as veiled threat ("You

[13]Peter Trudgill, "Sex, Covert Prestige and Linguistic Change in the Urban British English of Norwich," *Language in Society* 1, 2 (1973):179–195. [Author's note]

[14]Robin Lakoff, "Language and Woman's Place," *Language in Society* 2, 1 (1973):45–79; *Language and Woman's Place* (New York, 1975). [Author's note]

agree with me, don't you?") or to make a real question sound like an assertion, so that the man appears to be in control of a situation ("That is the case, isn't it?")[15] But a larger issue than the accuracy of Lakoff's data is the implicit bias of her interpretation. The question we should be asking is not why women are different from men, or how women's behavior or attitudes perpetuate inferiority; but, as Susanne Langer[16] asked about each art form, *What does it create?* Let us assume that Lakoff's report on women's language is correct: I, at least, see no reason to doubt it. We are facing two different ways of using language: What does each create?

Men's statements, unmodified by questions, tend to be pronouncements: these silence discussion, shut people out, intimidate them, and thus impoverish conversation. Men's statements could easily be interpreted as a sign of fear rather than confidence: they brook no contradiction, risk no argument, admit no equality. The use of tag questions could be seen as a sign of grace, generosity, and sociability, since they invite discussion, include others, and provide opening instead of closure. Similar comments apply to Lakoff's other points. No one, not even the most insecure woman, would respond, "Oh . . . about six o'clock?" if the question were "What time does the plane leave?" Responding to a question with a question in the way Lakoff describes is a shorthand way of making a statement. The woman is saying, "Well, I thought we'd eat around six, but if that's inconvenient, if you need to go out early, or if you're not hungry, we could make it a little earlier or later." Responding with a question to a question is a tacit way of suggesting that an item is negotiable, that the speaker is not rigidly committed to one plan, that she is open to the needs and desires of others. This device too opens up a situation, shows a will toward harmony and mutual satisfaction in a matter that *is* adjustable. The flexibility implicit in such an answer is another sign of grace.

And anyone, anyone at all, would prefer to be asked to close a door, or open a window, walk the dog, whatever, than to be ordered to do so. Orders are *always* humiliating; humiliation may be lessened or removed when orders are the ritual form of communication, as in military services, or when orders are shorthand requests made of intimates. But a request shows respect for others and sensitivity to them, both of which require

24

25

---

[15] Betty Lou Dubois and Isabel Crouch, "The Question of Tag Questions in Women's Speech: They Don't Really Use More of Them, Do They?" *Language in Society* 4, 4 (1975):289–294. [Author's note]

[16] *Susanne Langer:* American philosopher (1895–1985) who did pioneering work in aesthetics — the philosophy of art.

some degree of personal strength and self-assurance. Command shows neither and requires of the commander nothing internal whatever, only external status, the right to command.

It is, of course, possible that women's language shows timidity and 26 lack of confidence; many women feel these things (so do many men), and express them not just in the words they use and their tonality, but in voicing, facial aspect, and general demeanor. But it is also true that in general women's language aims for harmony with others rather than an expression of control over them, and that the former seems preferable to the latter as a societal standard. . . .

There are many other areas of life in which males are seen as providing 27 the standard and women the deviation, but perhaps none is more dismaying than the area of morality. Despite the daily evidence of eye and ear, it remains a byword of patriarchy that women as a sex are by nature deficient in moral sense and character. This belief has been "proven" anew by each new wave of patriarchal thought. . . .

The most recent of such theories is that of Lawrence Kohlberg, who 28 devised several tests of sex-role behavior, among them a test of moral development. Upon giving the test to men and women, he found that few if any women developed very far. Kohlberg's scale has three ascending levels, each with two stages, a lower and a higher.

Level I, the lowest, is concerned with morality as act. In Stage 1, the 29 lower stage of this level, a person behaves as he does because he fears punishment or desires approval from others. (I use *he* throughout this discussion because Kohlberg's published results refer only to males.) Stage 2, the upper stage of this level, includes behavior based on what will satisfy the self. To consider the self in isolation seems to Kohlberg a higher state of morality than to consider the self in relation to others.

As a boy matures, he reaches Level II and becomes concerned with 30 morality as role. At Stage 3 he has a "good-boy orientation," and tries to gain approval by helping others. He learns to conform to stereotypical images of his sex and age, and begins to judge others less by deeds than by intentions. It is at this stage that Kohlberg locates most women: they want to win affection and acceptance from others, and do not progress beyond this posture. The next Stage, 4, is similar, but more public: at this level people defer to patterns of authority and convention: they do their duty to win respect, rather than affection. Both these stages focus on how one is viewed from the outside.

Level III, the highest and most rarely attained, is described thus: 31 "Moral right resides in conformity by the self to shared or shareable standards, rights, and duties." That is, it involves a morality based on principle. Its lower stage is legalistic: people who reach it act according to contract or agreement; they accept the "rules of the game," whatever they may be or however arbitrary. Relationships with other people are based on mutual distance, on "avoidance of violation of the rights of others." Stage 6, the highest of all, the level of saints, is reached when people act according to universal principle. The rather opaque description of this stage is, "Orientation not only to actually ordained social rules but to principles of choice involving appeal to logical universality and consistency." One's own conscience functions as one's guide and points toward "mutual respect and trust."[17] It is hard to know where that *trust* came from, since there is nothing in the earlier stages suggesting that other people may be trustworthy, or are anything but hindrances to self-development.

Indeed, it is hard to know how Kohlberg's saints become apprised of 32 "universality," since all his stages focus on the person separated from others. Whether a boy acts in a particular way because he fears punishment or desires approval from others, or because he wants approval and so learns to help others, he is utterly divided from those others, who are merely instruments manipulated to satisfy his desires. At the highest level of moral development, according to Kohlberg, a man detaches himself from others totally, in order to act according to contract (Stage 5), or principles of choice (Stage 6), which involve universality. Kohlberg's scale is actually a scale of power: in the early stages the person must defer to others to gain a sense of rightness and identity; in the late stages the person transcends other people entirely, and guides his behavior by legal or moral codes. At the very highest level, achieved by only a few humans, according to Kohlberg, the moral relation between the person and the world is characterized by distance, formality, and judgment. Kohlberg's vision of the self in the world is antisocial, rooted in traditional male values — independence, isolation, and disconnectedness.

What is conspicuously lacking in many male versions of human relations 33 is any connection apart from power exchanges. Nancy Hartsock describes exchange theorists in sociology who depict human relations as power trade-offs, assuming that people are fundamentally isolated from each other and that encounters between people emerge from opposing interests. She comments that such a view of society is unrealistic: people are born helpless and survive only because of the dedication to them of their

[17] All preceding references to Kohlberg's work are from Lawrence Kohlberg, "Stage and Sequence: The Cognitive-Developmental Approach to Socialization," in *Handbook of Socialization Theory and Research*, ed. David A. Goslin (Chicago, 1969). [Author's note]

mothers or mother figures, a relation that cannot be described as a power exchange.[18] But male accounts of life omit the feminine: females and "feminine" qualities. . . .

Women and men — in general — have different moralities because 34 they have different goals. Male morals are designed to permit male transcendence. Life — that mass of breathing flesh, sweating pores, darting sensation, uncontrollable being — is rooted in nature, in the fetid swamp, the foul murk into which manufactured nature — cities — seems always about to sink. Above these, stark, pure, beyond the pull of heart or genitals, soar a rigid set of principles, rules, taboos. To prove his full manhood (which is sainthood) a man must cleave to these and abandon the other, which is the realm of woman. Since actual transcendence is not possible, transcendence is postulated in a beyond which is death. That even in death one cannot transcend, but is transformed into the very materials of the murk and swamp, the minerals that feed plants and animals, thus becoming nourishment for the very element one despises, is ignored, for this material part is despised, and the spirit, it is presumed, will rise into the ethereal.

Female morals are designed to permit survival. Life *is* the highest 35 good (*pace* Hannah Arendt):[19] not necessarily one's personal life, but life itself, of plants and animals and humans, the community, the tribe, the family, the children. Violence has been committed in an effort to save the child, the relative, the friend; but such violence is minuscule compared to that committed in the effort to prove the rightness or truth of some transcendent doctrine, or to gain power over others.

Female morals foster survival: which means they foster those elements, 36 both material and immaterial, that are necessary to life. Women grow much of the world's food, and everywhere women prepare food for those they live with. They do this because they are expected to, because they expect to, because they want to: so that the act is seen as nonvolitional and unnecessary to reward. It is rewarded by the well-being of those fed. This is true. What kind of morality teaches us to see this as contemptible?

But women everywhere provide food for the soul as well as the body, 37 offering compassion and support, touching, praising, loving. Germaine Tillion has written of her experience in the Ravensbrück concentration

[18]Nancy Hartsock, *Money, Sex, and Power: Toward a Feminist Historical Materialism* (New York, 1983), pp. 41–42. [Author's note]
[19]*Hannah Arendt:* German-born American political philosopher (1906–1975) best known for her writings on the Holocaust.

camp, an environment sufficient to kill every shred of the dignity necessary to sustain life. Tillion writes of the bonds that formed among the women, sometimes between a mother and daughter, sometimes women from the same town who had been seized at the same time, sometimes between sisters. "This tenuous web of friendship was . . . almost submerged by the stark brutality of selfishness and the struggle for survival, but somehow everyone in the camp was invisibly woven into it."[20] This caring connectedness allowed many women to survive, emotionally and physically, through sharing of resources. Another survivor of the camps recalls a moment when women, in a railroad car stopped en route to Bergen-Belsen, saw men in a car across the tracks. Although the women and men were both "skeletons, in identical stripes . . . the men's bodies reflected so much more pessimism than did ours. . . . We reached for our little morsels of bread and threw them to the men."[21] A group of female survivors report that relationships with other women were critical to survival: "Bonding with other women was of supreme importance," asserts a woman who was interned in Theresienstadt, Auschwitz, and Ravensbrück. There were no rules: although the survival of children was linked to their mothers, for some children it was the physical connection with the mother that meant salvation and for others it was separation. Some mothers kept their children, others gave them away: both sets of mothers acted as they did in the hope that the children could survive.[22]

In a world in which transcendence means power, in which there is 38 contention among nations that wish to demonstrate their possession of the greatest, the superior, the supreme power, and in which the only way to do this is to use that power to destroy, we might consider the benefits of a morality of survival and well-being, rather than one of transcendence and superiority. A similar position can be taken toward other dimensions in which men and women are compared and males are seen as the standard.

Equality is an abstract notion that can never be substantiated. It is a 39 principle intended to guide attitude, so that different people can receive, not identical human treatment, but identical consideration by rule and law. Equality is a principle necessary only in societies dominated by rule and law rather than by affection and bonding.

---

[20] Germaine Tillion, *Ravensbrück: An Eyewitness Account of a Women's Concentration Camp* (New York, 1975), p. xxii. [Author's note]
[21] Nadine Brozan, "Holocaust Women: A Study in Survival," *New York Times*, March 23, 1983. Quotation from Jolly Zeleny. [Author's note]
[22] Brozan, "Holocaust Women," *New York Times*, March 23, 1983. Quotation from Susan Cernyak-Spatz. [Author's note]

Equality is not similarity or identity. To be equal to men does not   40
mean to be like them. It is essential that women confront the pervasive
attitude that what men do and how they do it represents a *human*
standard with the question: What do these actions create? And what is
created by women's behavior in this situation? Doing so, women — and
men — might discover their own unarticulated moralities, and perhaps
even the nature of their real desires, for power, for love.

Engaging the Text

1. Summarize French's discussion of research on motivation, language, and
morality.

2. French writes that "assimilation in an unworthy society *is* an unworthy goal.
The white male world offers an unhappy and unworthy standard." Why does
she reject equality as a goal for women?

3. French wants women to attain a power that would allow "alteration of [our]
culture." What does she mean by this phrase?

4. French presents in paragraph 7 a detailed example of a woman trapped
between choosing effective actions that she thinks a man might use and, on the
other hand, morally superior but less pragmatic behavior. If you have faced a
similar situation, explain it in a paragraph or two. Then describe how you acted
and what resulted.

5. Do you agree with French that men have a "relative incapacity for intimacy,
community, and love"? Write an essay responding to this claim.

Exploring Connections

1. How does French account for the fear of success noted in the readings by
Carol Gilligan and Janet Chafetz earlier in this chapter?

2. Compare the way French and Bell Hooks (see the next reading) discuss the
connection between feminism and the civil rights movement.

3. The dream of the frontier is a peculiarly masculine idea. How would French
and Gilligan interpret the specifically masculine tone of the dream of the frontier?
From their PERSPECTIVE, what has this American ideal contributed to our culture?

Extending the Critical Context

1. French and Gilligan both point to examples of feminists and psychologists
assuming that what is true of males is the correct norm or standard for *humans*.
Can you cite other examples where this "logic of dominance" seems to be
operating? (You can look at politics, the media, your family, history, literature,

etc.) Can you cite counterexamples where women have a separate norm or where they set the standard for men?

2. If women agree with French, what should they do? What about men?

Racism, Sexism, and Heterosexism

Racism and Feminism

Bell Hooks

In this provocative essay, Hooks reinterprets the feminist movement from the perspective of black women. Grounding her argument in historical analysis, she questions the extent to which contemporary feminists represent the needs of all women — especially working-class, poor, and minority women. The essay thus seriously complicates the picture of the women's movement presented by earlier readings. Bell Hooks is the pen name of Gloria Watkins (b. 1952), who teaches at Oberlin College and contributes regularly to Zeta Magazine.

I am a black woman. I attended all-black public schools. I grew up 1
in the south where all around me was the fact of racial discrimination, hatred, and forced segregation. Yet my education as to the politics of race in American society was not that different from that of white female students I met in integrated high schools, in college, or in various women's groups. The majority of us understood racism as a social evil perpetuated by prejudiced white people that could be overcome through bonding between blacks and liberal whites, through militant protest, changing of laws or racial integration. Higher educational institutions did nothing to increase our limited understanding of racism as a political ideology. Instead professors systematically denied us truth, teaching us

to accept racial polarity in the form of white supremacy and sexual polarity in the form of male dominance.

American women have been socialized, even brainwashed, to accept 2 a version of American history that was created to uphold and maintain racial imperialism in the form of white supremacy and sexual imperialism in the form of patriarchy. One measure of the success of such indoctrination is that we perpetuate both consciously and unconsciously the very evils that oppress us. I am certain that the black female sixth grade teacher who taught us history, who taught us to identify with the American government, who loved those students who could best recite the pledge of allegiance to the American flag was not aware of the contradiction; that we should love this government that segregated us, that failed to send schools with all black students supplies that went to schools with only white pupils. Unknowingly she implanted in our psyches a seed of the racial imperialism that would keep us forever in bondage. For how does one overthrow, change, or even challenge a system that you have been taught to admire, to love, to believe in? Her innocence does not change the reality that she was teaching black children to embrace the very system that oppressed us, that she encouraged us to support it, to stand in awe of it, to die for it.

That American women, irrespective of their education, economic status, 3 or racial identification, have undergone years of sexist and racist socialization that has taught us to blindly trust our knowledge of history and its effect on present reality, even though that knowledge has been formed and shaped by an oppressive system, is nowhere more evident than in the recent feminist movement. The group of college-educated white middle and upper class women who came together to organize a women's movement brought a new energy to the concept of women's rights in America. They were not merely advocating social equality with men. They demanded a transformation of society, a revolution, a change in the American social structure. Yet as they attempted to take feminism beyond the realm of radical rhetoric and into the realm of American life, they revealed that they had not changed, had not undone the sexist and racist brainwashing that had taught them to regard women unlike themselves as Others. Consequently, the Sisterhood they talked about has not become a reality, and the women's movement they envisioned would have a transformative effect on American culture has not emerged. Instead, the hierarchical pattern of race and sex relationships already established in American society merely took a different form under "feminism": the form of women being classed as an oppressed group under affirmative action programs further perpetuating the myth that the social status of all women in America is the same; the form of women's studies programs being established with all-white faculty teaching literature almost exclusively by white women about white women and frequently from racist perspectives; the form of white women writing books that purport to be about the experience of American women when in fact they concentrate solely on the experience of white women; and finally the form of endless argument and debate as to whether or not racism was a feminist issue.

Every women's movement in America from its earliest origin to the present day has been built on a racist foundation — a fact which in no way invalidates feminism as a political ideology. The racial apartheid social structure that characterized 19th and early 20th century American life was mirrored in the women's rights movement. The first white women's rights advocates were never seeking social equality for all women; they were seeking social equality for white women. Because many 19th century white women's rights advocates were also active in the abolitionist movement,[1] it is often assumed they were anti-racist. Historiographers and especially recent feminist writing have created a version of American history in which white women's rights advocates are presented as champions of oppressed black people. This fierce romanticism has informed most studies of the abolitionist movement. In contemporary times there is a general tendency to equate abolitionism with a repudiation of racism. In actuality, most white abolitionists, male and female, though vehement in their anti-slavery protest, were totally opposed to granting social equality to black people. Joel Kovel, in his study *White Racism: A Psychohistory*, emphasizes that the "actual aim of the reform movement, so nobly and bravely begun, was not the liberation of the black, but the fortification of the white, conscience and all."

It is a commonly accepted belief that white female reformist empathy with the oppressed black slave, coupled with her recognition that she was powerless to end slavery, led to the development of a feminist consciousness and feminist revolt. Contemporary historiographers and in particular white female scholars accept the theory that the white women's rights advocates' feelings of solidarity with black slaves were an indication that they were anti-racist and were supportive of social equality of blacks. It is this glorification of the role white women played that leads Adrienne Rich to assert:

> . . . It is important for white feminists to remember that — despite lack of constitutional citizenship, educational deprivation, economic bondage to men, laws and customs forbidding women to speak in public

[1] *abolitionist movement:* campaign led by free blacks and liberal whites in the North to abolish slavery in the United States. The movement was active from the early 1800s until 1865, when the Thirteenth Amendment was ratified.

or to disobey fathers, husbands, and brothers — our white foresisters have, in Lillian Smith's words, repeatedly been "disloyal to civilization" and have "smelled death in the word 'segregation'," often defying patriarchy for the first time, not on their own behalf but for the sake of black men, women, and children. We have a strong anti-racist female tradition despite all efforts by the white patriarchy to polarize its creature-objects, creating dichotomies of privilege and caste, skin color, and age and condition of servitude.

There is little historical evidence to document Rich's assertion that 6 white women as a collective group or white women's rights advocates are part of an anti-racist tradition. When white women reformers in the 1830s chose to work to free the slave, they were motivated by religious sentiment. They attacked slavery, not racism. The basis of their attack was moral reform. That they were not demanding social equality for black people is an indication that they remained committed to white racist supremacy despite their anti-slavery work. While they strongly advocated an end to slavery, they never advocated a change in the racial hierarchy that allowed their caste status to be higher than that of black women or men. In fact, they wanted that hierarchy to be maintained. Consequently, the white women's rights movement which had a lukewarm beginning in earlier reform activities emerged in full force in the wake of efforts to gain rights for black people precisely because white women wanted to see no change in the social status of blacks until they were assured that their demands for more rights were met.

White women's rights advocate and abolitionist Abby Kelly's comment, 7 "We have good cause to be grateful to the slave for the benefit we have received to ourselves, in working for him. In striving to strike his irons off, we found most surely, that we were manacled ourselves," is often quoted by scholars as evidence that white women became conscious of their own limited rights as they worked to end slavery. Despite popular 19th century rhetoric, the notion that white women had to learn from their efforts to free the slave of their own limited rights is simply erroneous. No 19th century white woman could grow to maturity without an awareness of institutionalized sexism. White women did learn via their efforts to free the slave that white men were willing to advocate rights for blacks while denouncing rights for women. As a result of negative reaction to their reform activity and public effort to curtail and prevent their anti-slavery work, they were forced to acknowledge that without outspoken demands for equal rights with white men they might ultimately be lumped in the same social category with blacks — or even worse, black men might gain a higher social status than theirs.

It did not enhance the cause of oppressed black slaves for white women 8 to make synonymous their plight and the plight of the slave. Despite Abby Kelly's dramatic statement, there was very little if any similarity between the day-to-day life experiences of white women and the day-to-day experiences of the black slave. Theoretically, the white woman's legal status under patriarchy may have been that of "property," but she was in no way subjected to the de-humanization and brutal oppression that was the lot of the slave. When white reformers made synonymous the impact of sexism on their lives, they were not revealing an awareness of or sensitivity to the slave's lot; they were simply appropriating the horror of the slave experience to enhance their own cause.

The fact that the majority of white women reformers did not feel 9 political solidarity with black people was made evident in the conflict over the vote. When it appeared that white men might grant black men the right to vote while leaving white women disenfranchised, white suffragists did not respond as a group by demanding that all women and men deserved the right to vote. They simply expressed anger and outrage that white men were more committed to maintaining sexual hierarchies than racial hierarchies in the political arena. Ardent white women's rights advocates like Elizabeth Cady Stanton who had never before argued for women's rights on a racially imperialistic platform expressed outrage that inferior "niggers" should be granted the vote while "superior" white women remained disenfranchised. Stanton argued:

> If Saxon men have legislated thus for their own mothers, wives and daughters, what can we hope for at the hands of Chinese, Indians, and Africans? . . . I protest against the enfranchisement of another man of any race or clime until the daughters of Jefferson, Hancock, and Adams are crowned with their rights.

White suffragists felt that white men were insulting white womanhood by refusing to grant them privileges that were to be granted black men. They admonished white men not for their sexism but for their willingness to allow sexism to overshadow racial alliances. Stanton, along with other white women's rights supporters, did not want to see blacks enslaved, but neither did she wish to see the status of black people improved while the status of white women remained the same.

Animosity between black and white women's liberationists was not 10 due solely to disagreement over racism within the women's movement; it was the end result of years of jealously, envy, competition, and anger between the two groups. Conflict between black and white women did not begin with the 20th century women's movement. It began during slavery. The social status of white women in America has to a large extent been determined by white people's relationship to black people. It was the enslavement of African people in colonized America that marked the beginning of a change in the social status of white women. Prior to slavery, patriarchal law decreed white women were lowly inferior beings, the subordinate group in society. The subjugation of black people allowed them to vacate their despised position and assume the role of a superior.

Consequently, it can be easily argued that even though white men   11
institutionalized slavery, white women were its most immediate bene-
ficiaries. Slavery in no way altered the hierarchical social status of the white male but it created a new status for the white female. The only way that her new status could be maintained was through the constant assertion of her superiority over the black woman and man. All too often colonial white women, particularly those who were slave mistresses, chose to differentiate their status from the slave's by treating the slave in a brutal and cruel manner. It was in her relationship to the black female slave that the white woman could best assert her power. Individual black slave women were quick to learn that sex-role differentiation did not mean that the white mistress was not to be regarded as an authority figure. Because they had been socialized via patriarchy to respect male authority and resent female authority, black women were reluctant to acknowledge the "power" of the white mistress. When the enslaved black woman expressed contempt and disregard for white female authority, the white mistress often resorted to brutal punishment to assert her authority. But even brutal punishment could not change the fact that black women were not inclined to regard the white female with the awe and respect they showed to the white male.

By flaunting their sexual lust for the bodies of black women and their   12
preference for them as sexual partners, white men successfully pitted white women and enslaved black women against one another. In most instances, the white mistress did not envy the black female slave her role as sexual object; she feared only that her newly acquired social status might be threatened by white male sexual interaction with black women. His sexual involvement with black women (even if that involvement was rape) in effect reminded the white female of her subordinate position in relationship to him. For he could exercise his power as racial imperialist and sexual imperialist to rape or seduce black women, while white women were not free to rape or seduce black men without fear of punishment. Though the white female might condemn the actions of a white male who chose to interact sexually with black female slaves, she was unable to dictate to him proper behavior. Nor could she retaliate by engaging in sexual relationships with enslaved or free black men.

Not surprisingly, she directed her anger and rage at the enslaved black women. In those cases where emotional ties developed between white men and black female slaves, white mistresses would go to great lengths to punish the female. Severe beatings were the method most white women used to punish black female slaves. Often in a jealous rage a mistress might use disfigurement to punish a lusted-after black female slave. The mistress might cut off her breast, blind an eye, or cut off another body part. Such treatment naturally caused hostility between white women and enslaved black women. To the enslaved black woman, the white mistress living in relative comfort was the representative symbol of white womanhood. She was both envied and despised — envied for her material comfort, despised because she felt little concern or compassion for the slave woman's lot. Since the white woman's privileged social status could only exist if a group of women were present to assume the lowly position she had abdicated, it follows that black and white women would be at odds with one another. If the white woman struggled to change the lot of the black slave woman, her own social position on the race-sex hierarchy would be altered.

Manumission[2] did not bring an end to conflicts between black and white women; it heightened them. To maintain the apartheid structure slavery had institutionalized, white colonizers, male and female, created a variety of myths and stereotypes to differentiate the status of black women from that of white women. White racists and even some black people who had absorbed the colonizer's mentality depicted the white woman as a symbol of perfect womanhood and encouraged black women to strive to attain such perfection by using the white female as her model. The jealousy and envy of white women that had erupted in the black woman's consciousness during slavery was deliberately encouraged by the dominant white culture. Advertisements, newspaper articles, books, etc., were constant reminders to black women of the difference between their social status and that of white women, and they bitterly resented it. Nowhere was this dichotomy as clearly demonstrated as in the materially privileged white household where the black female domestic worked as an employee of the white family. In these relationships, black women workers were exploited to enhance the social standing of white families. In the white community, employing domestic help was a sign of material privilege and the person who directly benefited from a servant's work was the white woman, since without the servant she would have performed domestic chores. Not surprisingly, the black female domestic

[2]*Manumission:* the abolition of slavery.

tended to see the white female as her "boss," her oppressor, not the white male whose earnings usually paid her wage.

Throughout American history white men have deliberately promoted 14 hostility and divisiveness between white and black women. The white patriarchal power structure pits the two groups against each other, preventing the growth of solidarity between women and ensuring that woman's status as a subordinate group under patriarchy remains intact. To this end, white men have supported changes in the white woman's social standing only if there exists another female group to assume that role. Consequently, the white patriarch undergoes no radical change in his sexist assumption that woman is inherently inferior. He neither relinquishes his dominant position nor alters the patriarchal structure of society. He is, however, able to convince many white women that fundamental changes in "woman's status" have occurred because he has successfully socialized her, via racism, to assume that no connection exists between her and black women.

Because women's liberation has been equated with gaining privileges 15 within the white male power structure, white men — and not women, either white or black — have dictated the terms by which women are allowed entrance into the system. One of the terms male patriarchs have set is that one group of women is granted privileges that they obtain by actively supporting the oppression and exploitation of other groups of women. White and black women have been socialized to accept and honor these terms, hence the fierce competition between the two groups; a competition that has always been centered in the arena of sexual politics, with white and black women competing against one another for male favor. This competition is part of an overall battle between various groups of women to be the chosen female group.

The contemporary move toward feminist revolution was continually 16 undermined by competition between various factions. In regards to race, the women's movement has become simply another arena in which white and black women compete to be the chosen female group. This power struggle has not been resolved by the formation of opposing interest groups. Such groups are symptomatic of the problem and are no solution. Black and white women have for so long allowed their idea of liberation to be formed by the existing status quo that they have not yet devised a strategy by which we can come together. They have had only a slave's idea of freedom. And to the slave, the master's way of life represents the ideal free lifestyle.

Women's liberationists, white and black, will always be at odds with 17 one another as long as our idea of liberation is based on having the power white men have. For that power denies unity, denies common connections, and is inherently divisive. It is woman's acceptance of divisiveness as a natural order that has caused black and white women to cling religiously to the belief that bonding across racial boundaries is impossible, to passively accept the notion that the distances that separate women are immutable.

Engaging the Text

1. Rewrite some of Hooks's main ideas into a five-minute speech to be delivered to a women's group in your community.

2. In what different ways does Hooks attempt to persuade the reader of the truth of her argument? What kind(s) of evidence or reasoning would be necessary to contradict her?

3. Hooks claims that the women's movement can truly succeed only if it overcomes racism and represents all women. Do you think that this essay could bring closer a coalition of white and minority women?

4. Hooks wields an impressive vocabulary and employs many abstract concepts in this essay (e.g., "manumission," "patriarchy," "racial imperialism"). Find other examples of this verbal and conceptual complexity. What is the intended effect of setting the DISCOURSE at this level of sophistication? Is that its effect on you as a reader?

Exploring Connections

1. Read or review the analyses of racism offered by Gordon Allport, Peter Loewenberg, and James Boggs (Chapter Two, "Justice for All"). Which of these would Hooks be most likely to accept? Why is this type of understanding of racism important to her THESIS?

2. How would Nora Quealey (p. 267) probably react to Hooks's statements about white women and their role in the oppression of blacks? Does Quealey's story challenge any of Hooks's assumptions?

Extending the Critical Context

1. Suppose that a handful of influential white feminists accepted Hooks's thesis. What should they do?

2. Marilyn French (p. 290) and Hooks both assert that the success of a few women does not guarantee progress for women in general. What is the value to the women's movement of spectacularly successful women (e.g., famous writers, politicians, astronauts)? Does the success of such women pose any problems for the women's movement?

From *I Know Why the Caged Bird Sings*

Maya Angelou

By the time she had reached her early twenties, Maya Angelou (b. 1928) had been a maid, a cocktail waitress, a Creole cook, an unwed mother, and a sometime prostitute and drug addict. Today, she is an internationally celebrated author, poet, playwright, actor, singer, and civil rights activist. The following chapter from I Know Why the Caged Bird Sings, *the first of her five autobiographical works, tells of her early experience as a domestic servant and her rebellion against her employer. It speaks eloquently about the courage a young girl needs to rise above the limitations of gender, class, and race.*

Recently a white woman from Texas, who would quickly describe   1
herself as a liberal, asked me about my hometown. When I told her
that in Stamps my grandmother had owned the only Negro general
merchandise store since the turn of the century, she exclaimed, "Why,
you were a debutante." Ridiculous and even ludicrous. But Negro girls
in small Southern towns, whether poverty-stricken or just munching
along on a few of life's necessities, were given as extensive and irrelevant
preparations for adulthood as rich white girls shown in magazines. Admittedly the training was not the same. While white girls learned to
waltz and sit gracefully with a tea cup balanced on their knees, we were
lagging behind, learning the mid-Victorian values with very little money
to indulge them. (Come and see Edna Lomax spending the money she
made picking cotton on five balls of ecru tatting thread. Her fingers are
bound to snag the work and she'll have to repeat the stitches time and
time again. But she knows that when she buys the thread.)

We were required to embroider and I had trunkfuls of colorful dishtowels,   2
pillowcases, runners and handkerchiefs to my credit. I mastered the art
of crocheting and tatting, and there was a lifetime's supply of dainty
doilies that would never be used in sacheted dresser drawers. It went
without saying that all girls could iron and wash, but the finer touches
around the home, like setting a table with real silver, baking roasts and
cooking vegetables without meat, had to be learned elsewhere. Usually
at the source of those habits. During my tenth year, a white woman's
kitchen became my finishing school.

Mrs. Viola Cullinan was a plump woman who lived in a three-bedroom 3 house somewhere behind the post office. She was singularly unattractive until she smiled, and then the lines around her eyes and mouth which made her look perpetually dirty disappeared, and her face looked like the mask of an impish elf. She usually rested her smile until late afternoon when her women friends dropped in and Miss Glory, the cook, served them cold drinks on the closed-in porch.

The exactness of her house was inhuman. This glass went here and 4 only here. That cup had its place and it was an act of impudent rebellion to place it anywhere else. At twelve o'clock the table was set. At 12:15 Mrs. Cullinan sat down to dinner (whether her husband had arrived or not). At 12:16 Miss Glory brought out the food.

It took me a week to learn the difference between a salad plate, a 5 bread plate and a dessert plate.

Mrs. Cullinan kept up the tradition of her wealthy parents. She was 6 from Virginia. Miss Glory, who was a descendant of slaves that had worked for the Cullinans, told me her history. She had married beneath her (according to Miss Glory). Her husband's family hadn't had their money very long and what they had "didn't 'mount to much."

As ugly as she was, I thought privately, she was lucky to get a husband 7 above or beneath her station. But Miss Glory wouldn't let me say a thing against her mistress. She was very patient with me, however, over the housework. She explained the dishware, silverware and servants' bells.

The large round bowl in which soup was served wasn't a soup bowl, 8 it was a tureen. There were goblets, sherbet glasses, ice-cream glasses, wine glasses, green glass coffee cups with matching saucers, and water glasses. I had a glass to drink from, and it sat with Miss Glory's on a separate shelf from the others. Soup spoons, gravy boat, butter knives, salad forks and carving platter were additions to my vocabulary and in fact almost represented a new language. I was fascinated with the novelty, with the fluttering Mrs. Cullinan and her Alice-in-Wonderland house.

Her husband remains, in my memory, undefined. I lumped him with 9 all the other white men that I had ever seen and tried not to see.

On our way home one evening, Miss Glory told me that Mrs. Cullinan 10 couldn't have children. She said that she was too delicate-boned. It was hard to imagine bones at all under those layers of fat. Miss Glory went on to say that the doctor had taken out all her lady organs. I reasoned that a pig's organs included the lungs, heart and liver, so if Mrs. Cullinan was walking around without those essentials, it explained why she drank alcohol out of unmarked bottles. She was keeping herself embalmed.

When I spoke to Bailey[1] about it, he agreed that I was right, but he also informed me that Mr. Cullinan had two daughters by a colored lady and that I knew them very well. He added that the girls were the spitting image of their father. I was unable to remember what he looked like, although I had just left him a few hours before, but I thought of the Coleman girls. They were very light-skinned and certainly didn't look very much like their mother (no one ever mentioned Mr. Coleman). 11

My pity for Mrs. Cullinan preceded me the next morning like the Cheshire cat's smile. Those girls, who could have been her daughters, were beautiful. They didn't have to straighten their hair. Even when they were caught in the rain, their braids still hung down straight like tamed snakes. Their mouths were pouty little cupid's bows. Mrs. Cullinan didn't know what she missed. Or maybe she did. Poor Mrs. Cullinan. 12

For weeks after, I arrived early, left late and tried very hard to make up for her barrenness. If she had had her own children, she wouldn't have had to ask me to run a thousand errands from her back door to the back door of her friends. Poor old Mrs. Cullinan. 13

Then one evening Miss Glory told me to serve the ladies on the porch. After I set the tray down and turned toward the kitchen, one of the women asked, "What's your name, girl?" It was the speckled-faced one. Mrs. Cullinan said, "She doesn't talk much. Her name's Margaret."

"Is she dumb?" 15

"No. As I understand it, she can talk when she wants to but she's usually quiet as a little mouse. Aren't you, Margaret?" 16

I smiled at her. Poor thing. No organs and couldn't even pronounce my name correctly. 17

"She's a sweet little thing, though." 18

"Well, that may be, but the name's too long. I'd never bother myself. I'd call her Mary if I was you." 19

I fumed into the kitchen. That horrible woman would never have the chance to call me Mary because if I was starving I'd never work for her. I decided I wouldn't pee on her if her heart was on fire. Giggles drifted in off the porch and into Miss Glory's pots. I wondered what they could be laughing about. 20

Whitefolks were so strange. Could they be talking about me? Everybody knew that they stuck together better than the Negroes did. It was possible that Mrs. Cullinan had friends in St. Louis who heard about a 21

---

[1]*Bailey:* Angelou's brother.

girl from Stamps being in court and wrote to tell her. Maybe she knew about Mr. Freeman.[2]

My lunch was in my mouth a second time and I went outside and   22
relieved myself on the bed of four-o'clocks. Miss Glory thought I might
be coming down with something and told me to go on home, that Momma
would give me some herb tea, and she'd explain to her mistress.

I realized how foolish I was being before I reached the pond. Of   23
course Mrs. Cullinan didn't know. Otherwise she wouldn't have given
me the two nice dresses that Momma cut down, and she certainly
wouldn't have called me a "sweet little thing." My stomach felt fine,
and I didn't mention anything to Momma.

That evening I decided to write a poem on being white, fat, old and   24
without children. It was going to be a tragic ballad. I would have to
watch her carefully to capture the essence of her loneliness and pain.

The very next day, she called me by the wrong name. Miss Glory   25
and I were washing up the lunch dishes when Mrs. Cullinan came to
the doorway. "Mary?"

Miss Glory asked, "Who?"   26

Mrs. Cullinan, sagging a little, knew and I knew. "I want Mary to go   27
down to Mrs. Randall's and take her some soup. She's not been feeling
well for a few days."

Miss Glory's face was a wonder to see. "You mean Margaret, ma'am.   28
Her name's Margaret."

"That's too long. She's Mary from now on. Heat that soup from last   29
night and put it in the china tureen and, Mary, I want you to carry it
carefully."

Every person I knew had a hellish horror of being "called out of his   30
name." It was a dangerous practice to call a Negro anything that could
be loosely construed as insulting because of the centuries of their having
been called niggers, jigs, dinges, blackbirds, crows, boots and spooks.

Miss Glory had a fleeting second of feeling sorry for me. Then as she   31
handed me the hot tureen she said, "Don't mind, don't pay that no
mind. Sticks and stones may break your bones, but words . . . You
know, I been working for her for twenty years."

She held the back door open for me. "Twenty years. I wasn't much   32
older than you. My name used to be Hallelujah. That's what Ma named
me, but my mistress give me 'Glory,' and it stuck. I likes it better too."

---

[2]Mr. Freeman, a friend of her mother's, raped Angelou when she was a child living in
St. Louis. Freeman was convicted of the crime, and shortly after the trial, was found
beaten to death. Angelou, traumatized by these events, felt responsible for his death.

I was in the little path that ran behind the houses when Miss Glory 33
shouted, "It's shorter too."

For a few seconds it was a tossup over whether I would laugh (imagine 34
being named Hallelujah) or cry (imagine letting some white woman
rename you for her convenience). My anger saved me from either outburst.
I had to quit the job, but the problem was going to be how to do it.
Momma wouldn't allow me to quit for just any reason.

"She's a peach. That woman is a real peach." Mrs. Randall's maid was 35
talking as she took the soup from me, and I wondered what her name
used to be and what she answered to now.

For a week I looked into Mrs. Cullinan's face as she called me Mary. 36
She ignored my coming late and leaving early. Miss Glory was a little
annoyed because I had begun to leave egg yolk on the dishes and wasn't
putting much heart in polishing the silver. I hoped that she would
complain to our boss, but she didn't.

Then Bailey solved my dilemma. He had me describe the contents 37
of the cupboard and the particular plates she liked best. Her favorite
piece was a casserole shaped like a fish and the green glass coffee cups.
I kept his instructions in mind, so on the next day when Miss Glory
was hanging out clothes and I had again been told to serve the old
biddies on the porch, I dropped the empty serving tray. When I heard
Mrs. Cullinan scream, "Mary!" I picked up the casserole and two of the
green glass cups in readiness. As she rounded the kitchen door I let
them fall on the tiled floor.

I could never absolutely describe to Bailey what happened next, because 38
each time I got to the part where she fell on the floor and screwed up
her ugly face to cry, we burst out laughing. She actually wobbled around
on the floor and picked up shards of the cups and cried, "Oh, Momma.
Oh, dear Gawd. It's Momma's china from Virginia. Oh, Momma, I
sorry."

Miss Glory came running in from the yard and the women from the 39
porch crowded around. Miss Glory was almost as broken up as her
mistress. "You mean to say she broke our Virginia dishes? What we
gone do?"

Mrs. Cullinan cried louder, "That clumsy nigger. Clumsy little black 40
nigger."

Old speckled-face leaned down and asked, "Who did it, Viola? Was 41
it Mary? Who did it?"

Everything was happening so fast I can't remember whether her action 42
preceded her words, but I know that Mrs. Cullinan said, "Her name's
Margaret, goddamn it, her name's Margaret!" And she threw a wedge
of the broken plate at me. It could have been the hysteria which put

her aim off, but the flying crockery caught Miss Glory right over her ear and she started screaming.

I left the front door wide open so all the neighbors could hear.   43

Mrs. Cullinan was right about one thing. My name wasn't Mary.   44

Engaging the Text

1. Why is the issue of "being called out of name" apparently more important than the vast differences in wealth, power, and SOCIAL STATUS that exist between the NARRATOR and Mrs. Cullinan?

2. Why didn't Angelou say anything in protest when Mrs. Cullinan began calling her Mary?

3. Most readers applaud the author's retaliation against Mrs. Cullinan. What limits would you set for the author's right to take revenge, and on what are these limits based?

Exploring Connections

1. How would Gordon Allport (p. 85) explain Miss Glory's willingness to identify with Mrs. Cullinan?

2. Compare and contrast Angelou's resistance in this story to the resistance of the black community in Ida B. Wells's "Lynching at the Curve" (p. 168).

3. How would Bell Hooks (p. 303) analyze the relationship between the young Angelou and Mrs. Cullinan?

What Price Independence?
Social Reactions to Lesbians, Spinsters, Widows, and Nuns
ROSE WEITZ

This short essay addresses the history of women who have been excluded by their societies. In these pages, Weitz marshals a considerable body of historical fact to demonstrate that the social order stigmatizes lesbians and other independent women because they threaten the foundation of male dominance upon which it is built. Besides documenting misogyny and "gynophobia" in the West, she also considers the Hindu practice of suttee — the ritual burning of wives on their husbands' funeral pyres. Rose Weitz (b. 1952) teaches in the sociology department at Arizona State University and has written Labor Pains: Modern Midwives and Home Birth *(1988).*

For seven days in 1981, nineteen-year-old Stephanie Riethmiller was 1 held captive by two men and a woman in a secluded Alabama cabin. During that time, according to Riethmiller, her captors constantly harangued her on the sinfulness of homosexuality, and one captor raped her nightly. Riethmiller's parents, who feared that their daughter was involved in a lesbian relationship with her roommate, had paid $8,000 for this "deprogramming"; her mother remained in the next room throughout her captivity. When the kidnappers were brought to trial, the jury, in the opinion of the judge, "permit[ted] their moral evaluations to enter into their legal conclusions" and failed to bring in a guilty verdict (Raskin 1982, 19).

As the Riethmiller case shows, the individual who identifies herself 2 as a lesbian — or who is so labeled by others — may face severe social, economic, and legal sanctions. Along with communists, the diseased, and the insane, persons who openly acknowledge their homosexuality may be denied admission to the United States. In most U.S. jurisdictions, discrimination against homosexuals in housing, employment, child custody, and other areas of life is legal, while homosexual behavior is illegal. Gay persons are not covered under any of the national civil rights acts, and most court decisions have held that they are not covered under the equal protection clause of the United States Constitution. (For an excellent review of the legal status of homosexuality, see Rivera 1979.)

These legal restrictions reflect generally held social attitudes. Surveys 3 conducted during the 1970s using large national probability samples found that between 70 percent and 75 percent of the Americans interviewed believed that sexual relations between two members of the same sex were always wrong (Glenn and Weaver 1979).

Cross-cultural and Historical Views of Lesbianism

To most Americans, stigmatization and punishment of lesbianism seem 4 perfectly natural. Yet such has not always been the case. In fact, a study of attitudes toward homosexuality in seventy-six cultures around the world found that in 64 percent of those cultures "homosexual activities of one sort or another are considered normal and socially acceptable for certain members of the community" (Ford and Beach 1951, 130).

In the western world, male homosexuality, which had been an accepted 5 part of Greek and Roman culture, was increasingly rejected by society as the power of the Christian church grew (Barrett 1979). Yet lesbianism generally remained unrecognized legally and socially until the beginning of the modern age. Instead, beginning with the Renaissance, intimate "romantic friendships" between women were a common part of life, at least among the middle and upper classes (Faderman 1981).[1]

> Women who were romantic friends were everything to each other. They lived to be together. They thought of each other constantly. They made each other deliriously happy or horribly miserable by the increase or abatement of their proffered love. They were jealous of other female friends (and certainly of male friends) who impinged on their beloved's time or threatened to carry away a portion of her affections. They vowed that if it were at all possible they would someday live together, or at least die together, and they declared that both eventualities would be their greatest happiness. They embraced and kissed and walked hand in hand, and some even held each other all night in sleep. But unless they were transvestites or considered "unwomanly" in some male's conception, there was little chance that their relationships would be considered lesbian [Faderman 1981, 84].

We cannot know whether most romantic friends expressed their love 6 for women genitally, and we do know that most were married to men (at least in part for economic survival). A reading of letters and journals from this period leaves no doubt, however, of the erotic and emotional intensity of these relationships between women and little doubt that in another era the relationships would have been expressed sexually (Smith-Rosenberg 1975; Faderman 1981). Yet belief in the purity of these relationships lingered even into the twentieth century. For example, when the British Parliament attempted in 1885 to add mention of lesbianism to its criminal code, Queen Victoria refused to sign the bill, on the ground that such behavior did not exist (Ettorre 1980).

Given that lesbianism has not always elicited negative social reactions, 7 the current intolerance of it cannot derive from some universal biological or ethical law. What, then, causes these negative social reactions? I suggest in this article that at least part of the answer lies in the threat

[1]We have little first-hand data about the intimate lives of lower-class women. Few poorer women could write, and, even if they could and did record their lives, their letters and journals were rarely preserved. [Author's note]

that lesbianism presents to the power of males in society. Furthermore, I suggest that whenever men fear women's sexual or economic independence, all unmarried women face an increased risk of stigmatization and punishment. The experience of such diverse groups as lesbians, medieval nuns, and Hindu widows shows the interrelated social fates of all women not under the direct control of men.

Lesbians and the Threat to Male Power

Western culture teaches that women are the weaker sex, that they   8
cannot flourish — or perhaps even survive — without the protection of men. Women are taught that they cannot live happy and fulfilled lives without a Prince Charming, who is superior to them in all ways. In the struggle to find and keep their men, women learn to view each other as untrustworthy competitors. They subordinate the development of their own psychological, physical, and professional strengths to the task of finding male protectors who will make up for their shortcomings. In this way, western culture keeps women from developing bonds with each other, while it maintains their dependence on men.

Lesbians[2] throw a large wrench into the works of this cultural system.   9
In a society that denigrates women, lesbians value women enough to spend their lives with women rather than with men. Lesbians therefore do not and cannot rely on the protection of men. Knowing that they will not have that protection, lesbians are forced to develop their own resources. The very survival of lesbians therefore suggests the potential strength of all women and their ability to transcend their traditional roles. At the same time, since lesbians do not have even the illusion of male protection that marriage provides, and since they are likely to see their fate as tied to other women rather than to individual men, lesbians may be more likely than heterosexual women to believe in the necessity of fighting for women's rights; the heavy involvement of lesbians in the feminist movement seems to support this thesis (Abbott and Love 1972).

Lesbians also threaten the dominant cultural system by presenting,   10
or at least appearing to present, an alternative to the typical inequality of heterosexual relationships. Partners attempting to equalize power in a heterosexual relationship must first neutralize deeply ingrained traditional sex roles. Since lesbian relationships generally contain no built-in as-

[2]I am using the terms *lesbian* and *heterosexual* as nouns simply to ease the flow of the writing. This article focuses on stigmatization, not on some intrinsic quality of individuals. Hence, in this article, *lesbian* and *heterosexual* refer to persons who adopt a particular life-style or who are labeled as doing so by significant others. These terms reflect shared social fates, not some essential, inflexible aspect of the individual. [Author's note]

sumption of the superiority of one partner,[3] developing an egalitarian relationship may be easier. Lesbian relationships suggest both that a love between equals is possible and that an alternative way of obtaining such a love may exist. Regardless of the actual likelihood of achieving equality in a lesbian relationship, the threat to the system remains, as long as lesbian relationships are believed to be more egalitarian. This threat increases significantly when, as in the past few years, lesbians express pride in and satisfaction with their life-style.

If lesbianism incurs social wrath because of the threat it presents to   11
existing sexist social arrangements, then we should find that lesbianism is most negatively viewed by persons who hold sexist beliefs. Evidence from various studies (summarized in Weinberger and Millham 1979) supports this hypothesis. Homophobia (i.e., fear and hatred of homosexuals) appears strongly correlated with support for traditional sex roles. Survey data suggest that support for traditional sex roles explains homophobia better than do negative or conservative attitudes toward sex in general (MacDonald et al. 1973; MacDonald and Games 1974).

Historical data on when and under what circumstances lesbianism   12
became stigmatized also support the contention of a link between that stigma and the threat lesbianism poses to male power. As described above, romantic friendships between women were common in both Europe and America from the Renaissance through the late nineteenth century. The women involved were generally accepted or at least tolerated by society even in the few cases where their relationships were openly sexual. That acceptance ceased, however, if either of the women attempted to usurp male privilege in some way — by wearing men's clothing, using a dildo, or passing as a man. Only in these circumstances were pre-modern-era lesbians likely to suffer social sanctions. In looking at both historical records and fiction from the thirteenth through the nineteenth centuries, Faderman (1981) found that women were, at most, lightly punished for lesbianism unless they wore male clothing.[4] She therefore concludes that "at the base it was not the sexual aspects of lesbianism as much as the attempted usurpation of male prerogative by women who behaved like men that many societies appeared to find most disturbing" (Faderman 1981, 17).

[3]While there is no way to ascertain exactly what proportion of lesbian couples adopted butch-femme relationships in the past, recent studies suggest that such relationships have all but disappeared, especially among younger and more feminist lesbians (Wolf 1979; Tanner 1978). [Author's note]

[4]The crime for which Joan of Arc was eventually condemned was not witchcraft but the heretical act of wearing male clothing. [Author's note]

As long as the women involved did not attempt to obtain male privileges, 13
romantic friends ran little risk of censure before the late nineteenth
century. The factors behind the shift in attitude that occurred at that
time again suggest the importance of the threat that lesbianism seemed
to pose to male power.

Before the twentieth century, only a small number of independently 14
wealthy women (such as the Ladies of Llangollen [Mavor 1973]) were
able to establish their own households and live out their lives with their
female companions (Faderman 1981). By the second half of the nineteenth
century, however, the combined effects of the Civil War in this country
and of male migration away from rural areas in both the United States
and Europe had created a surplus of unmarried women in many communities. At the same time, the growth of the feminist movement had
led to increased educational opportunities for women. These factors,
coupled with the growth of industrialization, opened the possibility of
employment and an independent existence to significant numbers of
women.

Once female independence became a real economic possibility, it 15
became a serious concern to those intent on maintaining the sexual status
quo. Relationships between women, which previously had seemed harm-
less, now took on a new and threatening appearance. Only at this point
do new theories emerge that reject the Victorian image of the passionless
woman (Cott 1978), acknowledge females as sexual beings, and define
lesbianism as pathological.

Stereotypes of lesbianism, first developed in the early twentieth century, 16
reduce the threat to existing social arrangements by defusing the power
of lesbianism as a viable alternative life-style. According to these stereotypes, all lesbians are either butches or femmes, and their relationships
merely mimic heterosexual relationships. Lesbianism, therefore, seems
to offer no advantages over heterosexuality.

Cultural stereotypes defuse lesbian sexuality by alternately denying 17
and exaggerating it. These stereotypes hold that women become lesbians
because of either their inability to find a man or their hatred of men.
Such stereotypes deny that lesbianism may be a positive choice, while
suggesting that lesbianism can be cured by the right man. The supposed
futility of lesbian sexuality was summed up by best-selling author Dr.
David Reuben in the phrase, "one vagina plus another vagina still equals
zero" (1969, 217). (Reuben further invalidated lesbianism by locating his
entire discussion of the subject within his chapter on prostitution; male
homosexuality was "honored" with its own chapter.) In other cultural
arenas, lesbians and lesbianism are defined in purely sexual terms, stripped
of all romantic, social, or political content. In this incarnation, lesbianism

can be subverted into a vehicle for male sexual pleasure; in the world of pornographic films, men frequently construct lesbian scenes to play out their own sexual fantasies.

In sum, strong evidence suggests that the negative social reactions to 18 lesbianism reflect male fears of female independence, and the social sanctions and cultural stereotypes serve to lessen the threat that these independent women pose to male power.

If this hypothesis is true, then it should also hold for other groups of 19 women not under direct male control. Next, I briefly discuss how, historically, negative social reactions to such women seem most likely to develop whenever men fear women's sexual or economic independence.

Spinsters, Widows, and Women Religious

The inquisition against witches that occurred from the fifteenth through 20 the seventeenth centuries represents the most extreme response in the western world to the threat posed by independent women. The vast majority of the persons executed for witchcraft were women; estimates of the number killed range from under one hundred thousand to several million (Daly 1978). Accusations of witchcraft typically involved charges that the women healed sickness, engaged in prohibited sexual practices, or controlled reproduction (Ehrenreich and English 1973). Such activities threatened the power of the church by giving individuals (especially women) greater control over their own lives, reducing their dependence on the church for divine intervention while inhibiting the natural increase of the Catholic population.

The witchcraft trials occurred in a society undergoing the first throes 21 of industrialization and urbanization (Nelson 1979). The weakening of the rural extended family forced many women to look for employment outside the home. These unattached women proved especially vulnerable to accusations of witchcraft (Nelson 1979; Daly 1978). As Mary Daly points out, "The targets of attack in the witchcraze were not women defined by assimilation into the patriarchal family. Rather, the witchcraze focused predominantly upon women who had rejected marriage (Spinsters) [sic] and some who had survived it (widows)" (1978, 184).

Contemporary theological beliefs regarding female sexuality magnified 22 the perceived economic and social threat posed by unmarried women. The medieval church viewed all aspects of female sexuality with distrust; unless a woman was virginal or proven chaste, she was believed to be ruled by her sexual desires (Ehrenreich and English 1973). Catholic doctrine blamed Eve's licentiousness for the fall from grace in the Garden of Eden. According to the most popular medieval "manual" for witch-hunters, the *Malleus Maleficarum*, most witches were women because "all witchcraft comes from carnal lust, which is in women insatiable" (Kramer and Sprenger 1971, 120). Given this theology, any woman not under the direct sexual control of a man would appear suspect, if not outright dangerous.

For most women living before the nineteenth century who wished to 23 or were forced to remain unmarried, entering the religious life was the only socially acceptable option.[5] During the Middle Ages, a woman could either become a nun or join one of the "secular convents" known as *Beguines* (Nelson 1979; Boulding 1976). Beguines arose to serve the population of surplus unmarried women that had developed in the early European cities. Residents of Beguines took a vow of chastity and obedience while living there, but they could marry thereafter. They spent their days in work and prayer.

Beguines threatened the monopolies of both the guilds and the church. 24 The guilds feared the economic competition of these organized skilled women workers, while the church feared their social and religious independence (Nelson 1979); the Beguines' uncloistered life seemed likely to lead women into sin, while the lack of perpetual vows freed them from direct church supervision. For these reasons, the church in the fourteenth century ordered the Beguine houses dissolved, although some have continued nonetheless to the present day. Residents were urged either to marry or to become nuns (Boulding 1976).

The history of convents similarly illustrates the church's distrust of 25 independent women (Eckenstein 1963). In the early medieval period, many nuns lived with their families. Some nuns showed their religious vocation through the wearing of a veil, while others wore no distinctive dress. Convents served as centers of learning for women, providing educational opportunities not available elsewhere. During this period, many "double monasteries" flourished, in which male and female residents lived and shared decision-making authority.

Given medieval ideas regarding the spiritual weakness and inherent 26 carnality of women, the independence of early medieval nuns could not be allowed to last long. The developing laws of feudalism increasingly restricted the right of women to own land, so that, by the Renaissance, women faced increasing difficulties in attempting to found or to endow convents, while friars began to take over the management of existing convents (Eckenstein 1963). The church gradually closed all double monasteries, pressuring nuns to enter cloisters and to wear religious habits.

[5]However, it should be realized that convent life was not always a chosen refuge. Just as a father could marry his daughter to whatever man he chose, so too could he "marry" his daughter to the church. [Author's note]

Education for nuns increasingly seemed unnecessary or even dangerous. For this reason, by the sixteenth century church authorities had significantly decreased the educational opportunities available in most convents, although some convents did manage to preserve their intellectual traditions. Once Latin ceased to be taught, nuns were effectively excluded from all major church decisions.

As Protestant ideas began to infiltrate Europe, the status of unmarried 27 women declined. One of the few areas in which Catholics and early Protestants agreed was the danger presented by independent women. Responding to flagrant sexual offenses in medieval monasteries, Protestants concluded that few men — let alone women, given their basically carnal nature — could maintain a celibate life. They therefore viewed "the religious profession [as] a thing of evil and temptation in which it was not possible to keep holy" (Charitas Perckheimer, quoted in Eckenstein 1963, 467). To Protestants, "marriage was the most acceptable state before God and . . . a woman has no claim to consideration except in her capacity as wife and mother" (Eckenstein 1963, 433). These beliefs, coupled with the political aims of Protestant rulers, culminated in the forced dissolution of convents and monasteries in many parts of Europe. In Protestant Europe, women were left without a socially acceptable alternative to marriage, while, in Catholic Europe, nuns had been stripped of their autonomy.

The belief in female carnality continued until the nineteenth century. 28 At that point, while lower-class women were still considered sexually wanton by their social betters, prescriptive literature began to paint an image of upper-class women as passionless (Cott 1978). In this situation, unmarried lower-class women continued to suffer severe social sanctions as real or suspected prostitutes. Unmarried upper-class women continued to be stigmatized as unnatural, since they were not fulfilling their allotted role as wives and mothers. These upper-class women did not seem particularly threatening, however, since they were assumed, at least in public discourse, to be asexual beings. As a result, social sanctions against them diminished sharply, not to emerge again until women's new-found economic independence significantly changed the social context of romantic friendships among women.

In this historical overview I have so far discussed only events in the 29 western world. In the West, widows probably evoke less of a sense of threat than do other unmarried women, since widows do not generally seem to have chosen their fate. It is instructive to compare the fate of Hindu widows, who are believed to have caused their husbands' deaths by sins they committed in this or a previous life (Daly 1978; Stein 1978).

Since a Hindu woman's status is determined by her relationship to a 30 man, and since Hindu custom forbids remarriage, widows literally have no place in that society. A widow is a superfluous economic burden on her family. She is also viewed as a potential source of dishonor, since Hindus believe that "women are by nature sexually unreliable and incapable of leading chaste lives without a husband to control them" (Stein 1978, 255). For the benefit of her family and for her own happiness in future lives, a widow was in the past expected to commit suttee — to throw herself alive onto her husband's burning funeral pyre.[6] The horror of suttee was multiplied by the practice of polygamy and by the practice of marrying young girls to grown men, which resulted in the widowing of many young girls before they even reached puberty (Stein 1978; Daly 1978). Suttee, child marriage, and polygamy are illegal under the current government, but they do still occur.

As her only alternative to suttee, a widow was allowed to adopt a life 31 of such poverty and austerity that she rarely survived for long. Her life was made even more miserable by the fact that only faithful wives were permitted to commit suttee. The refusal to commit suttee might therefore be regarded as an admission of infidelity. If a woman declined to immolate herself, her relatives might force her to do so, to protect both her honor and the honor of her family.

Stigmatization of Male Homosexuals

Reflecting the basic concerns of this book, this article has discussed 32 male homosexuality only in passing. Nevertheless, it cannot be ignored that the sanctions against male homosexuality appear even stronger than those against lesbianism. Why might this be so? First, I would argue that anything women do is considered relatively trivial — be it housework, mothering, or lesbianism. Second, whereas lesbians threaten the status quo by refusing to accept their inferior position as women, gay males may threaten it even more by appearing to reject their privileged status as men. Prevailing cultural mythology holds that lesbians want to be males. In a paradoxical way, therefore, lesbians may be perceived as upholding "male" values. Male homosexuality, on the other hand, is regarded as a rejection of masculine values; gay males are regarded as feminized "sissies" and "queens." Thus male homosexuality, with its implied rejection of male privilege, may seem even more incomprehensible and threatening than lesbianism. Finally, research indicates that people in general are more fearful and intolerant of homosexuals of their own

[6]Suttee was most common among the upper castes (where a widow meant an extra mouth, but not an extra pair of hands), but it occurred throughout Hindu society (Stein 1978). [Author's note]

sex than of homosexuals belonging to the opposite sex (Weinberger and Millham 1979). The greater stigmatization of male than female homosexuality may therefore simply reflect the greater ability of males to enforce their prejudices.

Conclusions

The stigmatization of independent women — whether spinster, widow, 33 nun, or lesbian — is neither automatic nor natural. Rather, it seems to derive from a particular social constellation in which men fear women's sexual and economic independence. Sociological theory explains how stigmatizing individuals as deviant may serve certain purposes for the dominant community, regardless of the accuracy of the accusations leveled (Erikson 1962). First, particularly when social norms are changing rapidly, labeling and punishing certain behaviors as deviant emphasizes the new or continued unacceptability of those behaviors. The stigmatization of "romantic friendships" in the early twentieth century, for example, forced all members of society to recognize that social norms had changed and that such relationships would no longer be tolerated. Second, stigmatizing certain groups as deviant may increase solidarity within the dominant group, as the dominant group unites against its common enemy. Third, stigmatizing as deviant the individuals who challenge traditional ideas may reduce the threat of social change, if those individuals either lose credibility or are removed from the community altogether.

These principles apply to the stigmatization of independent women, 34 from the labeling of nontraditional women as witches in medieval society to the condemnation of lesbians in contemporary society. Medieval inquisitors used the label *witch* to reinforce the normative boundaries of their community, to unite that community against the perceived source of its problems, and to eliminate completely women who seemed to threaten the social order. Currently, the word *lesbian* is used not only to describe women who love other women but also to censure women who overstep the bounds of the traditional female role and to teach all women that such behavior will not be tolerated. Feminists, women athletes, professional women, and others risk being labeled lesbian for their actions and beliefs. Awareness of the potential social consequences of that label exerts significant pressure on all women to remain in their traditional roles.

Antifeminist forces have used the lesbian label to denigrate all feminists, 35 incite community wrath against them, and dismiss their political claims. In 1969 and 1970, some feminists responded to this social pressure by purging lesbians from their midst and proclaiming their moral purity (Abbott and Love 1972). This tactic proved extremely self-destructive, as movement organizations collapsed in bitterness and dissension. In addition, eliminating lesbian members had little effect, since lesbian-baiting by antifeminists was equally damaging to the movement whether or not it was accurate.

By late 1970, many feminists had realized that trying to remove lesbians 36 from their organizations was both self-destructive and ineffective. In response to this knowledge, various feminist organizations went on record acknowledging sexual preference as a feminist and a civil rights issue and supporting the rights of lesbians (Abbott and Love 1972). In a press conference held in December 1970, various women's liberation activists stated:

> Women's Liberation and Homosexual Liberation are both struggling toward a common goal: a society free from defining and categorizing people by virtue of gender and/or sexual preference. "Lesbian" is a label used as a psychic weapon to keep women locked into their male-defined "feminine role." The essence of that role is that a woman is defined in terms of her relationship to men. A woman is called a Lesbian when she functions autonomously. Women's autonomy is what Women's Liberation is all about [quoted in Abbott and Love 1972, 124].

A leaflet distributed the same month by the New York branch of the National Organization for Women acknowledged that, when charges of lesbianism are made, "it is not one woman's sexual preference that is under attack — it is the freedom of all women to openly state values that fundamentally challenge the basic structure of patriarchy" (quoted in Abbott and Love 1972, 122).

It seems, then, that the fates of feminists and lesbians are inextricably 37 intertwined. Unless and until women's independence is accepted, lesbians will be stigmatized, and unless and until the stigma attached to lesbianism diminishes, the lesbian label will be used as a weapon against those who work for women's independence.

Works Cited

Abbott, Sidney, and Barbara Love. *Sappho Was a Right-on Woman: A Liberated View of Lesbianism*. New York: Stein and Day Publishers, 1972.

Barrett, Ellen M. "Legal Homophobia and the Christian Church." *Hastings Law Journal* 30(4): 1019–27, 1979.

Boulding, Elise. *The Underside of History*. Boulder, Colo.: Westview Press, 1976.

Cott, Nancy. "Passionlessness: An Interpretation of Victorian Sexual Ideology, 1790–1850." *Signs: Journal of Women in Culture and Society* 4(2): 219–36, 1978.

Daly, Mary. *Gyn/ecology: The Metaethics of Radical Feminism*. Boston: Beacon Press, 1978.

Eckenstein, Lina. *Women under Monasticism*. New York: Russell and Russell, 1963.

Ehrenreich, Barbara, and Deirdre English. *Witches, Midwives and Nurses: A History of Women Healers*. Old Westbury, N.Y.: Feminist Press, 1973.

Erikson, Kai T. "Notes on the Sociology of Deviance." *Social Problems* 9(spring): 307–14, 1962.

Ettorre, E. M. *Lesbians, Women and Society*. London: Routledge and Kegan Paul, 1980.

Faderman, Lillian. *Surpassing the Love of Men: Romantic Friendship and Love between Women from the Renaissance to the Present*. New York: William Morrow and Co., 1981.

Ford, Clellan S., and Frank A. Beach. *Patterns of Sexual Behavior*. New York: Harper and Row, 1951.

Glenn, Norval D., and Charles N. Weaver. "Attitudes towards Premarital, Extramarital and Homosexual Relationships in the United States in the 1970s." *Journal of Sex Research* 15(2): 108–17, 1979.

Kramer, H., and J. Sprenger. *Malleus Maleficarum*. Translated by Montague Summers. New York: Dover Publications, 1971.

MacDonald, A. P., and R. G. Games. "Some Characteristics of Those Who Hold Positive and Negative Attitudes towards Homosexuals." *Journal of Homosexuality* 1(1): 9–28, 1974.

MacDonald, A. P., J. Huggins, S. Young, and R. A. Swanson. "Attitudes towards Homosexuality: Preservation of Sex Morality or the Double Standard." *Journal of Consulting and Clinical Psychology* 40(1): 161, 1973.

Mavor, Elizabeth. *The Ladies of Llangollen: A Study of Romantic Friendship*. New York: Penguin Books, 1973.

Nelson, Mary. "Why Witches Were Women." In Jo Freeman (ed.), *Women: A Feminist Perspective*, 2d ed. Palo Alto, Calif.: Mayfield Publishing Co., 1979.

Raskin, Richard. "The 'Deprogramming' of Stephanie Riethmiller," *Ms.*, Sept. 1982, 19.

Reuben, David. *Everything You Always Wanted to Know about Sex But Were Afraid to Ask*. New York: David McKay Co., 1969.

Rivera, Rhonda R. "Our Straight-laced Judges: The Legal Position of Homosexual Persons in the United States." *Hastings Law Journal* 30(4): 799–956, 1979.

Smith-Rosenberg, Carroll. "The Female World of Love and Ritual: Relations between Women in Nineteenth Century America." *Signs: Journal of Women in Culture and Society* 1(1): 1–29, 1975.

Stein, Dorothy K. "Women to Burn: Suttee as a Normative Institution." *Signs: Journal of Women in Culture and Society* 4(2): 253–68, 1978.

Tanner, Donna M. *The Lesbian Couple*. Lexington, Mass.: D.C. Heath and Co., 1978.

Weinberger, Linda E., and Jim Millham. "Attitudinal Homophobia and Support of Traditional Sex Roles." *Journal of Homosexuality* 4(3): 237–45, 1979.

Wolf, Deborah Goleman. *The Lesbian Community*. Berkeley: University of California Press, 1979.

Engaging the Text

1. How does Weitz explain her assertion that lesbianism was not STIGMATIZED until very recently in history?

2. Outline the structure of Weitz's argument. What kind of evidence does she rely on in making her case? Overall, do you find her convincing?

3. In your own words, explain how the Prince Charming syndrome works. Illustrate your explanation with examples drawn from your own experience and from contemporary culture.

Exploring Connections

1. To what extent does Weitz's analysis of prejudice against independent women draw on the different theories of prejudice offered by Gordon Allport (p. 85), Peter Loewenberg (p. 114), and James Boggs (p. 137)?

Extending the Critical Context

1. Working in groups, make a list of independent women (real and fictional) from history, public life, movies, and TV. Do you see any evidence that such women are still stigmatized in American society?

2. Go to the library and research the Salem witchcraft trials. How do the depictions you find of these events compare with Weitz's? Do you find any support for her point of view?

3. Debate Weitz's assertion that typical male-female relationships are hierarchical, patriarchal, and undemocratic.

The Two

GLORIA NAYLOR

This story from Gloria Naylor's The Women of Brewster Place *paints a fictional portrait of a black lesbian couple as their neighbors begin to discover their secret. As they emerge in the story, Lorraine and Theresa prompt us to reconsider stereotypes of homosexuals. Gloria Naylor (b. 1950) holds a master's degree in Afro-American Studies from Yale University.* The Women of Brewster Place *brought her national recognition and critical acclaim when it won the American Book Award for First*

Fiction in 1983. She has recently published two other novels, Linden Hills *(1985) and* Mama Day *(1988).*

At first they seemed like such nice girls. No one could remember 1
exactly when they had moved into Brewster. It was earlier in the year
before Ben[1] was killed — of course, it had to be before Ben's death.
But no one remembered if it was in the winter or spring of that year
that the two had come. People often came and went on Brewster Place
like a restless night's dream, moving in and out in the dark to avoid
eviction notices or neighborhood bulletins about the dilapidated condition
of their furnishings. So it wasn't until the two were clocked leaving in
the mornings and returning in the evenings at regular intervals that it
was quietly absorbed that they now claimed Brewster as home. And
Brewster waited, cautiously prepared to claim them, because you never
knew about young women, and obviously single at that. But when no
wild music or drunken friends careened out of the corner building on
weekends, and especially, when no slightly eager husbands were encouraged to linger around that first-floor apartment and run errands for
them, a suspended sigh of relief floated around the two when they
dumped their garbage, did their shopping, and headed for the morning
bus.

The women of Brewster had readily accepted the lighter, skinny one. 2
There wasn't much threat in her timid mincing walk and the slightly
protruding teeth she seemed so eager to show everyone in her bell-like
good mornings and evenings. Breaths were held a little longer in the
direction of the short dark one — too pretty, and too much behind. And
she insisted on wearing those thin Qiana dresses that the summer breeze
molded against the maddening rhythm of the twenty pounds of rounded
flesh that she swung steadily down the street. Through slitted eyes, the
women watched their men watching her pass, knowing the bastards were
praying for a wind. But since she seemed oblivious to whether these
supplications went answered, their sighs settled around her shoulders
too. Nice girls.

And so no one even cared to remember exactly when they had moved 3
into Brewster Place, until the rumor started. It had first spread through
the block like a sour odor that's only faintly perceptible and easily
ignored until it starts growing in strength from the dozen mouths it had
been lying in, among clammy gums and scum-coated teeth. And then

---

[1]*Ben:* the resident caretaker for the apartments in Brewster Place.

it was everywhere — lining the mouths and whitening the lips of everyone as they wrinkled up their noses at its pervading smell, unable to pinpoint the source or time of its initial arrival. Sophie could — she had been there.

It wasn't that the rumor had actually begun with Sophie. A rumor 4 needs no true parent. It only needs a willing carrier, and it found one in Sophie. She had been there — on one of those August evenings when the sun's absence is a mockery because the heat leaves the air so heavy it presses the naked skin down on your body, to the point that a sheet becomes unbearable and sleep impossible. So most of Brewster was outside that night when the two had come in together, probably from one of those air-conditioned movies downtown, and had greeted the ones who were loitering around their building. And they had started up the steps when the skinny one tripped over a child's ball and the darker one had grabbed her by the arm and around the waist to break her fall. "Careful, don't wanna lose you now." And the two of them had laughed into each other's eyes and went into the building.

The smell had begun there. It outlined the image of the stumbling 5 woman and the one who had broken her fall. Sophie and a few other women sniffed at the spot and then, perplexed, silently looked at each other. Where had they seen that before? They had often laughed and touched each other — held each other in joy or its dark twin — but where had they seen *that* before? It came to them as the scent drifted down the steps and entered their nostrils on the way to their inner mouths. They had seen that — done that — with their men. That shared moment of invisible communion reserved for two and hidden from the rest of the world behind laughter or tears or a touch. In the days before babies, miscarriages, and other broken dreams, after stolen caresses in barn stalls and cotton houses, after intimate walks from church and secret kisses with boys who were now long forgotten or permanently fixed in their lives — that was where. They could almost feel the odor moving about in their mouths, and they slowly knitted themselves together and let it out into the air like a yellow mist that began to cling to the bricks on Brewster.

So it got around that the two in 312 were *that* way. And they had 6 seemed like such nice girls. Their regular exits and entrances to the block were viewed with a jaundiced eye. The quiet that rested around their door on the weekends hinted of all sorts of secret rituals, and their friendly indifference to the men on the street was an insult to the women as a brazen flaunting of unnatural ways.

Since Sophie's apartment windows faced theirs from across the air 7 shaft, she became the official watchman for the block, and her opinions were deferred to whenever the two came up in conversation. Sophie took her position seriously and was constantly alert for any telltale signs that might creep out around their drawn shades, across from which she kept a religious vigil. An entire week of drawn shades was evidence enough to send her flying around with reports that as soon as it got dark they pulled their shades down and put on the lights. Heads nodded in knowing unison — a definite sign. If doubt was voiced with a "But I pull my shades down at night too," a whispered "Yeah, but you're not *that* way" was argument enough to win them over.

Sophie watched the lighter one dumping their garbage, and she went 8 outside and opened the lid. Her eyes darted over the crushed tin cans, vegetable peelings, and empty chocolate chip cookie boxes. What do they do with all them chocolate chip cookies? It was surely a sign, but it would take some time to figure that one out. She saw Ben go into their apartment, and she waited and blocked his path as he came out, carrying his toolbox.

"What ya see?" She grabbed his arm and whispered wetly in his face. 9

Ben stared at her squinted eyes and drooping lips and shook his head 10 slowly. "Uh, uh, uh, it was terrible."

"Yeah?" She moved in a little closer. 11

"Worst busted faucet I seen in my whole life." He shook her hand 12 off his arm and left her standing in the middle of the block.

"You old sop bucket," she muttered, as she went back up on her 13 stoop. A broken faucet, huh? Why did they need to use so much water?

Sophie had plenty to report that day. Ben had said it was terrible in 14 there. No, she didn't know exactly what he had seen, but you can imagine — and they did. Confronted with the difference that had been thrust into their predictable world, they reached into their imaginations and, using an ancient pattern, weaved themselves a reason for its existence. Out of necessity they stitched all of their secret fears and lingering childhood nightmares into this existence, because even though it was deceptive enough to try and look as they looked, talk as they talked, and do as they did, it had to have some hidden stain to invalidate it — it was impossible for them both to be right. So they leaned back, supported by the sheer weight of their numbers and comforted by the woven barrier that kept them protected from the yellow mist that enshrouded the two as they came and went on Brewster Place.

Lorraine was the first to notice the change in the people on Brewster 15 Place. She was a shy but naturally friendly woman who got up early, and had read the morning paper and done fifty sit-ups before it was time to leave for work. She came out of her apartment eager to start her day by greeting any of her neighbors who were outside. But she noticed that some of the people who had spoken to her before made a point of having something else to do with their eyes when she passed, although she could almost feel them staring at her back as she moved on. The ones who still spoke only did so after an uncomfortable pause, in which they seemed to be peering through her before they begrudged her a good morning or evening. She wondered if it was all in her mind and she thought about mentioning it to Theresa, but she didn't want to be accused of being too sensitive again. And how would Tee even notice anything like that anyway? She had a lousy attitude and hardly ever spoke to people. She stayed in that bed until the last moment and rushed out of the house fogged-up and grumpy, and she was used to being stared at — by men at least — because of her body.

Lorraine thought about these things as she came up the block from work, carrying a large paper bag. The group of women on her stoop parted silently and let her pass.   16

"Good evening," she said, as she climbed the steps.   17

Sophie was standing on the top step and tried to peek into the bag. "You been shopping, huh? What ya buy?" It was almost an accusation.   18

"Groceries." Lorraine shielded the top of the bag from view and squeezed past her with a confused frown. She saw Sophie throw a knowing glance to the others at the bottom of the stoop. What was wrong with this old woman? Was she crazy or something?   19

Lorraine went into her apartment. Theresa was sitting by the window, reading a copy of *Mademoiselle*. She glanced up from her magazine. "Did you get my chocolate chip cookies?"   20

"Why good evening to you, too, Tee. And how was my day? Just wonderful." She sat the bag down on the couch. "The little Baxter boy brought in a puppy for show-and-tell, and the damn thing pissed all over the floor and then proceeded to chew the heel off my shoe, but, yes, I managed to hobble to the store and bring you your chocolate chip cookies."   21

Oh, Jesus, Theresa thought, she's got a bug up her ass tonight.   22

"Well, you should speak to Mrs. Baxter. She ought to train her kid better than that." She didn't wait for Lorraine to stop laughing before she tried to stretch her good mood. "Here, I'll put those things away. Want me to make dinner so you can rest? I only worked half a day, and the most tragic thing that went down was a broken fingernail and that got caught in my typewriter."   23

Lorraine followed Theresa into the kitchen. "No, I'm not really tired, and fair's fair, you cooked last night. I didn't mean to tick off like that;   24 it's just that . . . well, Tee, have you noticed that people aren't as nice as they used to be?"

Theresa stiffened. Oh, God, here she goes again. "What people, Lorraine? Nice in what way?" 25

"Well, the people in this building and on the street. No one hardly speaks anymore. I mean, I'll come in and say good evening — and just silence. It wasn't like that when we first moved in. I don't know, it just makes you wonder; that's all. What are they thinking?" 26

"I personally don't give a shit what they're thinking. And their good evenings don't put any bread on my table." 27

"Yeah, but you didn't see the way that woman looked at me out there. They must feel something or know something. They probably —" 28

"They, they, they!" Theresa exploded. "You know, I'm not starting up with this again, Lorraine. Who in the hell are they? And where in the hell are we? Living in some dump of a building in this God-forsaken part of town around a bunch of ignorant niggers with the cotton still under their fingernails because of you and your theys. They knew something in Linden Hills, so I gave up an apartment for you that I'd been in for the last four years. And then they knew in Park Heights, and you made me so miserable there we had to leave. Now these mysterious theys are on Brewster Place. Well, look out that window, kid. There's a big wall down that block, and this is the end of the line for me. I'm not moving anymore, so if that's what you're working yourself up to — save it!" 29

When Theresa became angry she was like a lump of smoldering coal, and her fierce bursts of temper always unsettled Lorraine. 30

"You see, that's why I didn't want to mention it." Lorraine began to pull at her fingers nervously. "You're always flying up and jumping to conclusions — no one said anything about moving. And I didn't know your life has been so miserable since you met me. I'm sorry about that," she finished tearfully. 31

Theresa looked at Lorraine, standing in the kitchen door like a wilted leaf, and she wanted to throw something at her. Why didn't she ever fight back? The very softness that had first attracted her to Lorraine was now a frequent cause for irritation. Smoked honey. That's what Lorraine had reminded her of, sitting in her office clutching that application. Dry autumn days in Georgia woods, thick bloated smoke under a beehive, and the first glimpse of amber honey just faintly darkened about the edges by the burning twigs. She had flowed just that heavily into Theresa's mind and had stuck there with a persistent sweetness. 32

But Theresa hadn't known then that this softness filled Lorraine up to the very middle and that she would bend at the slightest pressure, 33 would be constantly seeking to surround herself with the comfort of everyone's goodwill, and would shrivel up at the least touch of disapproval. It was becoming a drain to be continually called upon for this nurturing and support that she just didn't understand. She had supplied it at first out of love for Lorraine, hoping that she would harden eventually, even as honey does when exposed to the cold. Theresa was growing tired of being clung to — of being the one who was leaned on. She didn't want a child — she wanted someone who could stand toe to toe with her and be willing to slug it out at times. If they practiced that way with each other, then they could turn back to back and beat the hell out of the world for trying to invade their territory. But she had found no such sparring partner in Lorraine, and the strain of fighting alone was beginning to show on her.

"Well, if it was that miserable, I would have been gone a long time 34 ago," she said, watching her words refresh Lorraine like a gentle shower.

"I guess you think I'm some sort of a sick paranoid, but I can't afford 35 to have people calling my job or writing letters to my principal. You know I've already lost a position like that in Detroit. And teaching is my whole life, Tee."

"I know," she sighed, not really knowing at all. There was no danger 36 of that ever happening on Brewster Place. Lorraine taught too far from this neighborhood for anyone here to recognize her in that school. No, it wasn't her job she feared losing this time, but their approval. She wanted to stand out there and chat and trade makeup secrets and cake recipes. She wanted to be secretary of their block association and be asked to mind their kids while they ran to the store. And none of that was going to happen if they couldn't even bring themselves to accept her good evenings.

Theresa silently finished unpacking the groceries. "Why did you buy 37 cottage cheese? Who eats that stuff?"

"Well, I thought we should go on a diet." 38

"If we go on a diet, then you'll disappear. You've got nothing to lose 39 but your hair."

"Oh, I don't know. I thought that we might want to try and reduce 40 our hips or something." Lorraine shrugged playfully.

"No, thank you. We are very happy with our hips the way they are," 41 Theresa said, as she shoved the cottage cheese to the back of the refrigerator. "And even when I lose weight, it never comes off there. My chest and arms just get smaller, and I start looking like a bottle of salad dressing."

The two women laughed, and Theresa sat down to watch Lorraine fix 42 dinner. "You know, this behind has always been my downfall. When I was coming up in Georgia with my grandmother, the boys used to promise me penny candy if I would let them pat my behind. And I used to love those jawbreakers — you know, the kind that lasted all day and kept changing colors in your mouth. So I was glad to oblige them, because in one afternoon I could collect a whole week's worth of jawbreakers."

"Really. That's funny to you? Having some boy feeling all over you." 43

Theresa sucked her teeth. "We were only kids, Lorraine. You know, 44 you remind me of my grandmother. That was one straight-laced old lady. She had a fit when my brother told her what I was doing. She called me into the smokehouse and told me in this real scary whisper that I could get pregnant from letting little boys pat my butt and that I'd end up like my cousin Willa. But Willa and I had been thick as fleas, and she had already given me a step-by-step summary of how she'd gotten into her predicament. But I sneaked around to her house that night just to double-check her story, since that old lady had seemed so earnest. 'Willa, are you sure?' I whispered through her bedroom window. 'I'm tellin' ya, Tee,' she said. 'Just keep both feet on the ground and you home free.' Much later I learned that advice wasn't too biologically sound, but it worked in Georgia because those country boys didn't have much imagination."

Theresa's laughter bounced off of Lorraine's silent, rigid back and died 45 in her throat. She angrily tore open a pack of the chocolate chip cookies. "Yeah," she said, staring at Lorraine's back and biting down hard into the cookie, "it wasn't until I came up north to college that I found out there's a whole lot of things that a dude with a little imagination can do to you even with both feet on the ground. You see, Willa forgot to tell me not to bend over or squat or —"

"Must you!" Lorraine turned around from the stove with her teeth 46 clenched tightly together.

"Must I what, Lorraine? Must I talk about things that are as much a 47 part of life as eating or breathing or growing old? Why are you always so uptight about sex or men?"

"I'm not uptight about anything. I just think it's disgusting when you 48 go on and on about —"

"There's nothing disgusting about it, Lorraine. You've never been 49 with a man, but I've been with quite a few — some better than others. There were a couple who I still hope to this day will die a slow, painful death, but then there were some who were good to me — in and out of bed."

"If they were so great, then why are you with me?" Lorraine's lips 50 were trembling.

"Because —" Theresa looked steadily into her eyes and then down at 51 the cookie she was twirling on the table. "Because," she continued slowly, "you can take a chocolate chip cookie and put holes in it and attach it to your ears and call it an earring, or hang it around your neck on a silver chain and pretend it's a necklace — but it's still a cookie. See — you can toss it in the air and call it a Frisbee or even a flying saucer, if the mood hits you, and it's still just a cookie. Send it spinning on a table — like this — until it's a wonderful blur of amber and brown light that you can imagine to be a topaz or rusted gold or old crystal, but the law of gravity has got to come into play, sometime, and it's got to come to rest — sometime. Then all the spinning and pretending and hoopla is over with. And you know what you got?"

"A chocolate chip cookie," Lorraine said.   52

"Uh-huh." Theresa put the cookie in her mouth and winked. "A   53 lesbian." She got up from the table. "Call me when dinner's ready, I'm going back to read." She stopped at the kitchen door. "Now, why are you putting gravy on that chicken, Lorraine? You know it's fattening."

Engaging the Text

1. What type of community does Naylor describe in her opening two paragraphs, and how, specifically, does she create this atmosphere? Why is this important to the THEME of the story?

2. Why does Naylor shift the story's POINT OF VIEW from that of the community to that of Lorraine and Theresa? How does this change of PERSPECTIVE affect the reader?

3. Why does Naylor make a point of details like drawn shades, chocolate chip cookies, and the broken faucet?

4. How important is sexuality in Lorraine and Theresa's relationship? What do they share besides lovemaking?

Exploring Connections

1. How would Rose Weitz (p. 317) explain the community's reaction to the presence of a lesbian couple in the neighborhood?

2. Does Lorraine and Theresa's relationship support Weitz's claim that lesbian couples are more "egalitarian" than heterosexual couples?

Extending the Critical Context

1. Find one or more psychology texts or articles authored before 1960 that cover homosexuality. How is it defined, described, and classified? How often is lesbianism specifically included in the discussion?

2. Investigate the official policy (if any) toward homosexual teachers at various schools in your locale. Are there restrictions, explicit or implicit, against homosexual teachers? Report to the class on your findings. Your sources might include interviews with teachers as well as school documents, laws, or court cases.

5

The Changing Family

What would an American political campaign be without wholesome photographs of the candidates' loving families and dozens of kissed babies? Politicians understand the symbolism of the family in America; they appreciate that the family is a sacred institution. Today's version of the perfect nuclear family — Dad, Mom, a couple of kids, maybe a dog, and a spacious suburban home — is a powerful ideal, a dream that millions of Americans work to fulfill. Yet this ideal scarcely reflects the realities of modern family life. Climbing divorce rates, the rise of the single-parent household, the impact of remarriages, the increase in two-paycheck families, and the stresses of urban life are transforming the family and challenging our myths about the value of family life.

The first section of this chapter, Reassessing Family Life, explores the strengths and limitations of traditional family arrangements. It begins with Alexis de Tocqueville's analysis of the influence of democracy on American family relationships. Arlene Skolnick follows by examining the costs of the myth of family perfection. Next, Adam Hochschild presents an intimate look at the quiet violence that can mar even the most "perfect" of families. The section closes with two selections that address the costs of growing up too fast in modern America: an excerpt from David Elkind's *The Hurried Child* and a short story by Lorrie Moore entitled "The Kid's Guide to Divorce."

Alternative Family Structures considers nontraditional patterns of family life. In the first selection, Joseph L. White suggests that black families cannot be understood in terms of conventional European family structures and values. Shirley Ann Grau's short story explores the love between a young black woman and her mother. Karen Lindsey argues that the traditional family is a primitive institution that can be replaced by voluntary associations of friends. Finally, Richard Goldstein reports on family arrangements in gay and lesbian communities.

Before Reading . . .

Spend ten minutes jotting down every word, phrase, or image you associate with the idea of "family." Write as freely as possible, without censoring your thoughts or worrying about grammatical correctness. Working in small groups, compare lists and try to categorize your responses. What assumptions about families do they reveal?

REASSESSING FAMILY LIFE

Influence of Democracy on the Family
ALEXIS DE TOCQUEVILLE

In 1831, Alexis de Tocqueville (1805–1859), a young French aristocrat, left Europe to study the American penal system. Democratic society left a deep impression on Tocqueville, and in 1835 he published his reflections on this new way of life in Democracy in America *— a work that has since become the point of departure for many studies of American culture. In the following passage from* Democracy in America, *Tocqueville comments on the "democratic" American family — an institution markedly different from the aristocratic families of his native Europe.*

It has been universally remarked, that, in our time, the several members   1
of a family stand upon an entirely new footing towards each other; that

the distance which formerly separated a father from his sons has been lessened; and that paternal authority, if not destroyed, is at least impaired.

Something analogous to this, but even more striking, may be observed 2 in the United States. In America, the family, in the Roman and aristocratic signification of the word, does not exist. All that remains of it are a few vestiges in the first years of childhood, when the father exercises, without opposition, that absolute domestic authority which the feebleness of his children renders necessary, and which their interest, as well as his own incontestable superiority, warrants. But as soon as the young American approaches manhood, the ties of filial obedience are relaxed day by day: Master of his thoughts, he is soon master of his conduct. In America, there is, strictly speaking, no adolescence: At the close of boyhood, the man appears, and begins to trace out his own path.

It would be an error to suppose that this is preceded by a domestic 3 struggle, in which the son has obtained by a sort of moral violence the liberty that his father refused him. The same habits, the same principles, which impel the one to assert his independence, predispose the other to consider the use of that independence as an incontestable right. The former does not exhibit any of those rancorous or irregular passions which disturb men long after they have shaken off an established authority; the latter feels none of that bitter and angry regret which is apt to survive a bygone power. The father foresees the limits of his authority long beforehand, and when the time arrives, he surrenders it without a struggle: The son looks forward to the exact period at which he will be his own master; and he enters upon his freedom without precipitation and without effort, as a possession which is his own, and which no one seeks to wrest from him.

It may, perhaps, be useful to show how these changes which take 4 place in family relations are closely connected with the social and political revolution which is approaching its consummation under our own eyes.

There are certain great social principles which a people either introduces 5 everywhere or tolerates nowhere. In countries which are aristocratically constituted with all the gradations of rank, the government never makes a direct appeal to the mass of the governed; as men are united together, it is enough to lead the foremost; the rest will follow. This is applicable to the family, as well as to all aristocracies which have a head. Amongst aristocratic nations, social institutions recognize, in truth, no one in the family but the father; children are received by society at his hands; society governs him, he governs them. Thus, the parent has not only a natural right, but he acquires a political right, to command them: He is the author and the support of his family; but he is also its constituted ruler.

In democracies, where the government picks out every individual 6
singly from the mass to make him subservient to the general laws of the
community, no such intermediate person is required: A father is there,
in the eye of the law, only a member of the community, older and richer
than his sons.

When most of the conditions of life are extremely unequal, and the 7
inequality of these conditions is permanent, the notion of a superior
grows upon the imaginations of men; if the law invested him with no
privileges, custom and public opinion would concede them. When, on
the contrary, men differ but little from each other, and do not always
remain in dissimilar conditions of life, the general notion of a superior
becomes weaker and less distinct: It is vain for legislation to strive to
place him who obeys very much beneath him who commands; the manners
of the time bring the two men nearer to one another, and draw them
daily towards the same level.

Although the legislation of an aristocratic people should grant no peculiar 8
privileges to the heads of families, I shall not be the less convinced that
their power is more respected and more extensive than in a democracy;
for I know that, whatsoever the laws may be, superiors always appear
higher, and inferiors lower, in aristocracies than amongst democratic
nations.

When men live more for the remembrance of what has been than for 9
the care of what is, and when they are more given to attend to what
their ancestors thought than to think themselves, the father is the natural
and necessary tie between the past and the present, — the link by which
the ends of these two chains are connected. In aristocracies, then, the
father is not only the civil head of the family, but the organ of its
traditions, the expounder of its customs, the arbiter[1] of its manners. He
is listened to with deference, he is addressed with respect, and the love
which is felt for him is always tempered with fear.

When the condition of society becomes democratic, and men adopt 10
as their general principle that it is good and lawful to judge of all things
for one's self, using former points of belief not as a rule of faith, but
simply as a means of information, the power which the opinions of a
father exercise over those of his sons diminishes, as well as his legal
power.

Perhaps the subdivision of estates[2] which democracy brings about 11
contributes more than anything else to change the relations existing

[1]*arbiter:* person with authority to judge or decide a dispute.
[2]*subdivision of estates:* In Europe, land and buildings were generally willed to the eldest
son alone. See paragraph 17.

between a father and his children. When the property of the father of a family is scanty, his son and himself constantly live in the same place, and share the same occupations: Habit and necessity bring them together, and force them to hold constant communication; the inevitable consequence is a sort of familiar intimacy, which renders authority less absolute, and which can ill be reconciled with the external forms of respect.

Now, in democratic countries, the class of those who are possessed 12 of small fortunes is precisely that which gives strength to the notions and a particular direction to the manners of the community. That class makes its opinions preponderate as universally as its will; and even those who are most inclined to resist its commands are carried away in the end by its example. I have known eager opponents of democracy, who allowed their children to address them with perfect colloquial equality.

Thus, at the same time that the power of aristocracy is declining, the 13 austere, the conventional, and the legal part of parental authority vanishes, and a species of equality prevails around the domestic hearth. I know not, upon the whole, whether society loses by the change, but I am inclined to believe that man individually is a gainer by it. I think that, in proportion as manners and laws become more democratic, the relation of father and son becomes more intimate and more affectionate; rules and authority are less talked of, confidence and tenderness are oftentimes increased, and it would seem that the natural bond is drawn closer in proportion as the social bond is loosened.

In a democratic family, the father exercises no other power than that 14 which is granted to the affection and the experience of age; his orders would perhaps be disobeyed, but his advice is for the most part authoritative. Though he be not hedged in with ceremonial respect, his sons at least accost him with confidence; they have no settled form of addressing him, but they speak to him constantly, and are ready to consult him every day: The master and the constituted ruler have vanished; the father remains.

Nothing more is needed in order to judge of the difference between 15 the two states of society in this respect, than to peruse the family correspondence of aristocratic ages. The style is always correct, ceremonious, stiff, and so cold that the natural warmth of the heart can hardly be felt in the language. In democratic countries, on the contrary, the language addressed by a son to his father is always marked by mingled freedom, familiarity, and affection, which at once show that new relations have sprung up in the bosom of the family.

A similar revolution takes place in the mutual relations of children. 16 In aristocratic families, as well as in aristocratic society, every place is marked out beforehand. Not only does the father occupy a separate rank, in which he enjoys extensive privileges, but even the children are not equal amongst themselves. The age and sex of each irrevocably determine his rank, and secure to him certain privileges: Most of these distinctions are abolished or diminished by democracy.

In aristocratic families, the eldest son, inheriting the greater part of the property, and almost all the rights of the family, becomes the chief, and, to a certain extent, the master, of his brothers. Greatness and power are for him; for them, mediocrity and dependence. But it would be wrong to suppose that, amongst aristocratic nations, the privileges of the eldest son are advantageous to himself alone, or that they excite nothing but envy and hatred around him. The eldest son commonly endeavors to procure wealth and power for his brothers, because the general splendor of the house is reflected back on him who represents it; the younger sons seek to back the elder brother in all his undertakings, because the greatness and power of the head of the family better enable him to provide for all its branches. The different members of an aristocratic family are therefore very closely bound together; their interests are connected, their minds agree, but their hearts are seldom in harmony. 17

Democracy also binds brothers to each other, but by very different means. Under democratic laws, all the children are perfectly equal, and consequently independent: Nothing brings them forcibly together, but nothing keeps them apart; and as they have the same origin, as they are trained under the same roof, as they are treated with the same care, and as no peculiar privilege distinguishes or divides them, the affectionate and frank intimacy of early years easily springs up between them. Scarcely anything can occur to break the tie thus formed at the outset of life, for brotherhood brings them daily together, without embarrassing them. It is not then by interest, but by common associations and by the free sympathy of opinion and of taste, that democracy unites brothers to each other. It divides their inheritance, but allows their hearts and minds to unite. 18

Such is the charm of these democratic manners, that even the partisans of aristocracy are attracted by it; and after having experienced it for some time, they are by no means tempted to revert to the respectful and frigid observances of aristocratic families. They would be glad to retain the domestic habits of democracy, if they might throw off its social conditions and its laws; but these elements are indissolubly united, and it is impossible to enjoy the former without enduring the latter. 19

The remarks I have made on filial love and fraternal affection are applicable to all the passions which emanate spontaneously from human nature itself. 20

If a certain mode of thought or feeling is the result of some peculiar condition of life, when that condition is altered nothing whatever remains of the thought or feeling. Thus, a law may bind two members of the 21 community very closely to one another; but that law being abolished, they stand asunder. Nothing was more strict than the tie which united the vassal to the lord under the feudal system: At the present day, the two men know not each other; the fear, the gratitude, and the affection which formerly connected them have vanished, and not a vestige of the tie remains.

Such, however, is not the case with those feelings which are natural 22 to mankind. Whenever a law attempts to tutor these feelings in any particular manner, it seldom fails to weaken them; by attempting to add to their intensity, it robs them of some of their elements, for they are never stronger than when left to themselves.

Democracy, which destroys or obscures almost all the old conventional 23 rules of society, and which prevents men from readily assenting to new ones, entirely effaces most of the feelings to which these conventional rules have given rise; but it only modifies some others, and frequently imparts to them a degree of energy and sweetness unknown before.

Perhaps it is not impossible to condense into a single proposition the 24 whole purport of this chapter, and of several others that preceded it. Democracy loosens social ties, but tightens natural ones; it brings kindred more closely together, whilst it throws citizens more apart.

Engaging the Text

1. What, according to Tocqueville, are the differences between the traditional European aristocratic family and the American family? What is the role of the father in each?

2. What connection does Tocqueville perceive between personal and public relationships (i.e., between intrafamily relations and the individual's relationship to the state and society at large)?

3. In the final paragraph, Tocqueville claims that democracy tightens natural ties. What does he mean by "natural," and why does a democracy foster such relationships?

Exploring Connections

1. Return to the selection from *Letters of an American Farmer* (Chapter One, "American Dreams") and compare Crèvecoeur's view of the American character to Tocqueville's.

Extending the Critical Context

1. Much has changed in the United States since Tocqueville made his observations on the American family. Working in groups, discuss what portions of his descriptions

of the family are no longer accurate, and why. What observations, if any, still hold true?

2. Tocqueville argues that in a democracy, the father may no longer function as "the organ of its traditions, the expounder of its customs, the arbiter of its manners." Yet family traditions, customs, and manners still exist in America. Who or what has taken over the role that Tocqueville once attributed to fathers?

3. Tocqueville says that in post-revolutionary America "there is, strictly speaking, no adolescence," since, contrary to the European pattern, American children moved relatively effortlessly into adult roles and responsibilities. Why do you suppose that today children in the United States go through a prolonged adolescence? Of what does that period mainly consist? Are contemporary American children less "free" or less accustomed to freedom than were their early American counterparts?

The Paradox of Perfection*

ARLENE SKOLNICK

The pressures of life in a highly industrialized urban society have taken their toll on the American family during the 150 years since Tocqueville first described it. Divorce is commonplace, mothers have joined fathers in the work force, remarriages have vastly complicated family relationships. Yet the ideal of the perfect family lives on in American mythology. In the following selection, Skolnick examines the myth and the effect it has on families that fail to live up to the expectations it creates. Arlene Skolnick (b. 1933) is a research psychologist at the Institute of Human Development at the University of California, Berkeley. She has edited or co-edited four books: Family in Transition, *4th ed. (1983),* The Intimate Environment *(1973),* Rethinking Childhood *(1976), and* The Psychology of Human Development *(1986).*

The American Family, as even readers of *Popular Mechanics* must   1
know by now, is in what Sean O'Casey[1] would have called "a terrible

*From the *Wilson Quarterly,* Summer 1980. Copyright 1980 by The Woodrow Wilson International Center for Scholars.
[1]*Sean O'Casey:* Irish playwright (1880–1964).

state of chassis." Yet, there are certain ironies about the much-publicized crisis that give one pause.

True, the statistics seem alarming. The U.S. divorce rate, though it 2 has reached something of a plateau in recent years, remains the highest in American history. The number of births out-of-wedlock among all races and ethnic groups continues to climb. The plight of many elderly Americans subsisting on low fixed incomes is well known.

What puzzles me is an ambiguity, not in the facts, but in what we 3 are asked to make of them. A series of opinion polls conducted in 1978 by Yankelovich, Skelley, and White, for example, found that 38 percent of those surveyed had recently witnessed one or more "destructive activities" (e.g., a divorce, a separation, a custody battle) within their own families or those of their parents or siblings. At the same time, 92 percent of the respondents said the family was highly important to them as a "personal value."

Can the family be at once a cherished "value" and a troubled institution? 4 I am inclined to think, in fact, that they go hand in hand. A recent "Talk of the Town" report in *The New Yorker* illustrates what I mean:

> A few months ago word was heard from Billy Gray, who used to play brother Bud in "Father Knows Best," the 1950s television show about the nice Anderson family who lived in the white frame house on a side street in some mythical Springfield — the house at which the father arrived each night swinging open the front door and singing out "Margaret, I'm home!" Gray said he felt "ashamed" that he had ever had anything to do with the show. It was all "totally false," he said, and had caused many Americans to feel inadequate, because they thought that was the way life was supposed to be and that their own lives failed to measure up.

As Susan Sontag[2] has noted in *On Photography*, mass-produced images 5 have "extraordinary powers to determine our demands upon reality." The family is especially vulnerable to confusion between truth and illusion. What, after all, is "normal"? All of us have a backstairs view of our own families, but we know The Family, in the aggregate, only vicariously.

Like politics or athletics, the family has become a media event. Television 6 offers nightly portrayals of lump-in-throat family "normalcy" (*The Waltons*, *Little House on the Prairie*) and even humorous "deviance" (*One Day at a Time*, *The Odd Couple*). Family advisers sally forth in syndicated newspaper columns to uphold standards, mend relationships, suggest counseling, and otherwise lead their readers back to the True Path. For

---

[2]*Susan Sontag:* contemporary American essayist and critic (b. 1933).

commercial purposes, advertisers spend millions of dollars to create stirring vignettes of glamorous-but-ordinary families, the kind of family most 11-year-olds wish they had.

All Americans do not, of course, live in such a family, but most share 7
an intuitive sense of what the "ideal" family should be — reflected in the precepts of religion, the conventions of etiquette, and the assumptions of law. And, characteristically, Americans tend to project the ideal back into the past, the time when virtues of all sorts are thought to have flourished.

We do not come off well by comparison with that golden age, nor 8
could we, for it is as elusive and mythical as Brigadoon.[3] If Billy Gray shames too easily, he has a valid point: While Americans view the family as the proper context for their own lives — 9 out of 10 people live in one — they have no realistic context in which to view the family. Family history, until recently, was as neglected in academe as it still is in the press. [The summer 1980] White House Conference on Families is "policy-oriented," which means present-minded. The familiar, depressing charts of "leading family indicators" — marriage, divorce, illegitimacy — in newspapers and newsmagazines rarely survey the trends before World War II. The discussion, in short, lacks ballast.

Let us go back to before the American Revolution. 9

Perhaps what distinguishes the modern family most from its colonial 10
counterpart is its newfound privacy. Throughout the 17th and 18th centuries, well over 90 percent of the American population lived in small rural communities. Unusual behavior rarely went unnoticed, and neighbors often intervened directly in a family's affairs, to help or to chastise.

The most dramatic example was the rural "charivari," prevalent in 11
both Europe and the United States until the early 19th century. The purpose of these noisy gatherings was to censure community members for familial transgressions — unusual sexual behavior, marriages between persons of grossly discrepant ages, or "household disorder," to name but a few. As historian Edward Shorter describes it in *The Making of the Modern Family*:

> Sometimes the demonstration would consist of masked individuals circling somebody's house at night, screaming, beating on pans, and blowing cow horns. . . . [O]n other occasions, the offender would be seized and marched through the streets, seated perhaps backwards on a donkey or forced to wear a placard describing his sins.

[3]*Brigadoon:* In the Broadway musical (and, later, film) by Alan Jay Lerner and Frederick Loewe, Brigadoon is a Scottish town that comes to life only once every hundred years. It thus remains almost unchanged, a utopian place "saved" from history.

The state itself had no qualms about intruding into a family's affairs by statute, if necessary. Consider 17th-century New England's "stubborn child" laws that, though never actually enforced, sanctioned the death penalty for chronic disobedience to one's parents.

If the boundaries between home and society seem blurred during the colonial era, it is because they were. People were neither very emotional nor very self-conscious about family life, and, as historian John Demos points out, family and community were "joined in a relation of profound reciprocity." In his *Of Domestical Duties*, William Gouge, a 17th-century Puritan preacher, called the family "a little community." The home, like the larger community, was as much an economic as a social unit; all members of the family worked, be it on the farm, or in a shop, or in the home.

There was not much to idealize. Love was not considered the basis for marriage but one possible result of it. According to historian Carl Degler, it was easier to obtain a divorce in colonial New England than anywhere else in the Western world, and the divorce rate climbed steadily throughout the 18th century, though it remained low by contemporary standards. Romantic images to the contrary, it was rare for more than two generations (parents and children) to share a household, for the simple reason that very few people lived beyond the age of 60. It is ironic that our nostalgia for the extended family — including grandparents and grandchildren — comes at a time when, thanks to improvements in health care, its existence is less threatened than ever before.

Infant mortality was high in colonial days, though not as high as we are accustomed to believe, since food was plentiful and epidemics, owing to generally low population density, were few. In the mid-1700s, the average age of marriage was about 24 for men, 21 for women — not much different from what it is now. Households, on average, were larger, but not startlingly so: A typical household in 1790 included about 5.6 members, versus about 3.5 today. Illegitimacy was widespread. Premarital pregnancies reached a high in 18th-century America (10 percent of all first births) that was not equalled until the 1950s.

Form Follows Function

In simple demographic terms, then, the differences between the American family in colonial times and today are not all that stark; the similarities are sometimes striking.

The chief contrast is psychological. While Western societies have always idealized the family to some degree, the *most vivid* literary portrayals of family life before the 19th century were negative or, at best, ambivalent.

In what might be called the "high tragic" tradition — including Sophocles,[4] Shakespeare, and the Bible, as well as fairy tales and novels — the family was portrayed as a high-voltage emotional setting, laden with dark passion, sibling rivalries, and violence. There was also the "low comic" tradition — the world of henpecked husbands and tyrannical mothers-in-law.

It is unlikely that our 18th-century ancestors ever left the Book of   18 Genesis or *Tom Jones* with the feeling that their own family lives were seriously flawed.

By the time of the Civil War, however, American attitudes toward   19 the family had changed profoundly. The early decades of the 19th century marked the beginnings of America's gradual transformation into an urban, industrial society. In 1820, less than 8 percent of the U.S. population lived in cities; by 1860, the urban concentration approached 20 percent, and by 1900 that proportion had doubled.

Structurally, the American family did not immediately undergo a com-   20 parable transformation. Despite the large families of many immigrants and farmers, the size of the *average* family declined — slowly but steadily — as it had been doing since the 17th century. Infant mortality remained about the same and may even have increased somewhat, owing to poor sanitation in crowded cities. Legal divorces were easier to obtain than they had been in colonial times. Indeed, the rise in the divorce rate was a matter of some concern during the 19th century, though death, not divorce, was the prime cause of one-parent families, as it was up to 1965.

Functionally, however, America's industrial revolution had a lasting   21 effect on the family. No longer was the household typically a group of interdependent workers. Now, men went to offices and factories and became breadwinners; wives stayed home to mind the hearth; children went off to the new public schools. The home was set apart from the dog-eat-dog arena of economic life; it came to be viewed as a utopian retreat or, in historian Christopher Lasch's[5] phrase, a "haven in a heartless world." Marriage was now valued primarily for its emotional attractions. Above all, the family became something to worry about.

The earliest and most saccharine "sentimental model" of the family   22 appeared in the new mass media that proliferated during the second quarter of the 19th century. Novels, tracts, newspaper articles, and ladies' magazines — there were variations for each class of society —

[4]*Sophocles:* Greek dramatist (495?–406? B.C.).
[5]*Christopher Lasch:* See p. 533.

elaborated a "Cult of True Womanhood" in which piety, submissiveness, and domesticity dominated the pantheon of desirable feminine qualities. This quotation from *The Ladies Book* (1830) is typical:

> See, she sits, she walks, she speaks, she looks — unutterable things! Inspiration springs up in her very paths — it follows her footsteps. A halo of glory encircles her, and illuminates her whole orbit. With her, man not only feels safe, but actually renovated.

In the late 1800s, science came into the picture. The "professionalization" of the housewife took two different forms. One involved motherhood and childrearing, according to the latest scientific understanding of children's special physical and emotional needs. (It is no accident that the publishing of children's books became a major industry during this period.) The other was the domestic science movement — "home economics," basically — which focused on woman as full-time homemaker, applying "scientific" and "industrial" rationality to shopping, making meals, and housework.   23

The new ideal of the family prompted a cultural split that has endured, one that Tocqueville[6] had glimpsed (and rather liked) in 1835. Society was divided more sharply into man's sphere and woman's sphere. Toughness, competition, and practicality were the masculine values that ruled the outside world. The softer values — affection, tranquility, piety — were worshipped in the home and the church. In contrast to the colonial view, the ideology of the "modern" family implied a critique of everything beyond the front door.   24

What is striking as one looks at the writings of the 19th-century "experts" — the physicians, clergymen, phrenologists,[7] and "scribbling ladies"[8] — is how little their essential message differs from that of the sociologists, psychiatrists, pediatricians, and women's magazine writers of the 20th century, particularly since World War II.   25

Instead of men's and women's spheres, of course, sociologists speak of "instrumental" and "expressive" roles. The notion of the family as a retreat from the harsh realities of the outside world crops up as "functional differentiation." And, like the 19th-century utopians who believed society could be regenerated through the perfection of family life, 20th-century   26

---

[6]*Tocqueville:* See p. 341.

[7]*phrenologists:* scientists who believed that certain mental characteristics could be indicated by the configuration of one's skull. Phrenology, which often supported racist arguments, has been discredited in this century.

[8]*scribbling ladies:* Nathaniel Hawthorne's derogatory term for female novelists who dealt with domestic themes and — not incidentally — often outsold Hawthorne's own works.

social scientists have looked at the failed family as the source of most American social problems.

None of these who promoted the sentimental model of the family — 27
neither the popular writers nor the academics — considered the paradox of perfectionism: the ironic possibility that it would lead to trouble. Yet it has. The image of the perfect, happy family makes ordinary families seem like failures. Small problems loom as big problems if the "normal" family is thought to be one where there are no real problems at all.

One sees this phenomenon at work on the generation of Americans 28
born and reared during the late 19th century, the first generation reared on the mother's milk of sentimental imagery. Between 1900 and 1920, the U.S. divorce rate doubled, from four to eight divorces annually per 1,000 married couples. The jump — comparable to the 100 percent increase in the divorce rate between 1960 and 1980 — is not attributable to changes in divorce laws, which were not greatly liberalized. Rather, it would appear that, as historian Thomas O'Neill believes, Americans were simply more willing to dissolve marriages that did not conform to their idea of domestic bliss — and perhaps try again.

A "Fun" Morality

If anything, family standards became even more demanding as the 29
20th century progressed. The new fields of psychology and sociology opened up whole new definitions of familial perfection. "Feelings" — fun, love, warmth, good orgasm — acquired heightened popular significance as the invisible glue of successful families.

Psychologist Martha Wolfenstein, in an analysis of several decades of 30
government-sponsored infant care manuals, has documented the emergence of a "fun morality." In former days, being a good parent meant carrying out certain tasks with punctilio;[9] if your child was clean and reasonably obedient, you had no cause to probe his psyche. Now, we are told, parents must commune with their own feelings and those of their children — an edict which has seeped into the ethos of education as well. The distinction is rather like that between religions of deed and religions of faith. It is one thing to make your child brush his teeth; it is quite another to transform the whole process into a joyous "learning experience."

The task of 20th-century parents has been further complicated by the 31
advice offered them. The experts disagree with each other and often contradict themselves. The kindly Dr. Benjamin Spock, for example, is

[9]*punctilio:* strictness or exactness.

full of contradictions. In a detailed analysis of *Baby and Child Care*, historian Michael Zuckerman observes that Spock tells mothers to relax ("trust yourself") yet warns them that they have an "ominous power" to destroy their children's innocence and make them discontented "for years" or even "forever."

As we enter the 1980s, both family images and family realities are in   32
a state of transition. After a century and a half, the web of attitudes and nostrums[10] comprising the "sentimental model" is beginning to unravel. Since the mid-1960s, there has been a youth rebellion of sorts, a new "sexual revolution," a revival of feminism, and the emergence of the two-worker family. The huge postwar Baby-Boom generation is pairing off, accounting in part for the upsurge in the divorce rate (half of all divorces occur within seven years of a first marriage). Media images of the family have become more "realistic," reflecting new patterns of family life that are emerging (and old patterns that are re-emerging).

Among social scientists, "realism" is becoming something of an ideal   33
in itself. For some of them, realism translates as pluralism: All forms of the family, by virtue of the fact that they happen to exist, are equally acceptable — from communes and cohabitation to one-parent households, homosexual marriages, and, come to think of it, the nuclear family. What was once labeled "deviant" is now merely "variant." In some college texts, "the family" has been replaced by "family systems." Yet, this new approach does not seem to have squelched perfectionist standards. Indeed, a palpable strain of perfectionism runs through the pop literature on "alternative" family lifestyles.

For the majority of scholars, realism means a more down-to-earth view   34
of the American household. Rather than seeing the family as a haven of peace and tranquility, they have begun to recognize that even "normal" families are less than ideal, that intimate relations of any sort inevitably involve antagonism as well as love. Conflict and change are inherent in social life. If the family is now in a state of flux, such is the nature of resilient institutions; if it is beset by problems, so is life. The family will survive.

[10]*nostrums:* quack medicines or, more generally, pet schemes to remedy social ills.

Engaging the Text

1. Summarize the three historical attitudes toward families that Skolnick describes. How does she account for the emergence of these different views?

2. What is PARADOXICAL about the desire to have a "perfect" family, according to Skolnick?

3. In Skolnick's view, what is "fun" morality and how has it affected family relationships?

4. Is Skolnick's conclusion about the future of the family consistent with the rest of the essay?

Exploring Connections

1. Would Tocqueville, author of the preceding essay, agree that the early American family was a "little commonwealth"? Do Skolnick and Tocqueville agree on the relationship of the early American family to society?

2. Skolnick suggests that in the past families and family relationships have often been depicted tragically. Look ahead to Karen Lindsey's "Friends as Family." How does her account of the patriarchal family help to explain this negative characterization?

Extending the Critical Context

1. What evidence do you see in families you know or in society at large of the "professionalization" of the housewife/mother?

2. Examine images of the family in contemporary media (television shows, films, song lyrics, etc.). How pervasive is the image of the perfect family? Are there differences in the ways the various media portray the family?

3. Skolnick describes how colonial communities intervened in family matters (para. 10). What sanctions, if any, are exercised today to punish "familial transgressions"?

From *Half the Way Home: A Memoir of Father and Son*

ADAM HOCHSCHILD

This selection is drawn from a widely praised portrait of a father-son relationship. It offers the son's retrospective view of a man who was publicly admired (he was a successful businessman and a generous supporter of civic causes) but privately cold and intimidating — at least in his son's eyes. After beginning his career as a reporter, Adam Hochschild (b. 1942) cofounded Mother Jones *magazine and currently serves as president of the nonprofit organization, Foundation for National Progress.*

All through my childhood, people would say, "Your father? Oh, of 1 course, what a wonderful man. I know him well." But our language is deficient. There should be two words, one for knowing a person as a friend or colleague, the other for knowing someone as a parent. I never felt that way about my mother. For her, one word would do. But Father was different. Others seemed only to see a man of wit, learning, and great integrity, someone who generously bestowed gifts and invitations on his wide circle of friends, a world traveler who spoke five languages, a businessman of unusual liberalism, and a self-taught expert on Adirondack history: In his spare time, he wrote a prize-winning book on the subject, and founded a fine museum. A somewhat uncomfortable man, true; shy, a bit distant, sometimes ill at ease, but still, how lucky you must be to have had him as a father! And besides, Adam, you had everything: Houses, chauffeurs, maids, money — the whole world was yours. How can you complain?

All this was true. But there was another side to Father, whose weight 2 only I seemed to feel. Where I most experienced it, even amid all the pleasures of Eagle Nest,[1] was in the recurring outbursts of his intense disapproval. These did not come daily, perhaps not even weekly. But they affected me so powerfully that they colored the time between them as well.

Like bouts of a disease, these episodes always followed a set pattern. 3 First was my crime itself. To begin with, Father disapproved of some of my hobbies, tentative as they were, thinking them frivolous. I used to listen to an old shortwave radio that had been *his*, even, which I found discarded in the attic and fixed up — until one day he solemnly said he thought I was spending too much time on this. Or sometimes my wrongdoing involved my being, in his eyes, too uncommunicative and not polite enough with a guest. Or it was the sin of not being grateful enough for something — not thanking someone with enough enthusiasm, say, for a present I really didn't want. But there was a treacherously narrow path between being not animated enough and being too much so. For, most often of all, my crime would be that of taking too much

[1]*Eagle Nest:* the name of the Hochschild family estate.

space, of talking too much: at the table, in a carload of family and guests en route to Eagle Nest, anywhere he and I were together with other people.

It was so easy to slip into this pattern, particularly if I had been 4 spending time with my mother: To her I was a precocious, entertaining child; she was endlessly delighted by my thoughts and questions and fantasies. When I was with her, there was no such thing as talking too much. I could chatter for hours and she loved it. But when Father and a group of his friends were there, I was surrounded by an invisible trip wire. I could never figure out in advance just where it lay, until suddenly I knew, with a sinking-stomach despair, that I had inadvertently stumbled against it. I would be talking and giggling, happily taking center stage, when I would see the moment at which Father found me guilty: a slight pursing of the lips, a raising of one eyebrow, a cryptic word or two which I knew would be expanded on later: "Adam! I think that's enough for now."

At this point some valve opened inside me, and I felt a pervasive 5 dread traveling through my whole body as if I had taken some powerful, swift-acting drug. Sometimes I tried desperately to win back his approval by being very affectionate, but it never worked.

The next stage, a few hours later, was confirmation of the verdict. 6 Often I overheard my parents talking, when they thought I was asleep, or when I hid behind a tree as they walked from the Club House to the Cottage. Always Father would bring up the subject:

"I thought Adam was talking too much at the table today." 7

"Yes, you're probably right, Harold," my mother would agree. She 8 never reprimanded me herself and never seemed angry with me. But she always agreed with him.

"I think I better speak to him about it," Father said. 9

"Yes, dear." 10

I went to sleep subdued. When I woke the next morning, it seemed 11 like a normal day until, a few moments after opening my eyes, I remembered. In the morning would come the announcement. He would say: "Adam, can I see you in my study at two o'clock, please?" Or perhaps he would be upstairs working, and my mother would be the messenger. "Father wants to see you at two o'clock. O.K., dear?"

The morning was long. I could not concentrate when I read. I was 12 cloaked in dread.

Two o'clock. I waited until maybe 2:03, but to wait any longer would 13 risk the additional crime of being late, something guaranteed at any time to make Father upset. I knocked on his door.

"Come in!" 14

"Hi . . . you wanted . . . to talk . . . to me?" 15

"Sit down, Adam. I'll be with you in a moment." 16

A shuffle of papers; a signature on a document; at last Father put the 17
work on his desk aside, and leaned back in his chair.

"I've been meaning to talk to you, Adam, about something that happened 18
yesterday. I thought it was quite rude when you were talking so much
at the table last night. Couldn't you see it was preventing people from
having their own conversation?"

It didn't last long. No spanking. No beating. No raised voice. Maybe 19
just two or three minutes of talk. Father's words were always carefully
chosen, balanced, never casual, as if each phrase had been inspected
and been found irrefutable before he permitted it to exit his lips.

I couldn't bring myself to look at him. I craved for an earthquake to 20
bring the session to an end. What made it so much worse was that
Father was always, it seemed, fully reasonable. He spoke in a voice
which carried in it the full weight of his authority, of his wide reputation
for morality, a voice whose very quietness contained the expectation of
unquestioning obedience.

After he had finished whatever he had to say — all of which I had 21
known was coming for perhaps a full twenty-four hours — Father would
pause for me to respond. He listened, it might be said, in a distinct
tone of voice: His right hand, leathery, mottled, crept up to his face to
support his chin with its thumb, while first and second fingers bracketed
his mouth, as if holding in his own speech while he heard me out. In
a way this was the most frightening moment of all, this careful, alert
listening from someone whose entire bearing and role in life was that
of a man who expected to be listened *to*. Of course I never really dared
argue; his evidence always seemed convincing.

At last, to put the seal on the encounter, Father would say, in words 22
which ostensibly dissipated, but in fact thickened, the cloud that hung
over me:

"All right? I think you now see what I mean. I won't speak about this 23
incident again."

Then he motioned for me to come around behind his desk so we could 24
exchange kisses on the cheek, that gesture between us in which there
was always an element of submission: Now it was a sign that I had
acknowledged my error and would reform. Our session was over.

The impact of one of these reprimands echoed in my head for days 25
afterward. Take one such incident; multiply it by a hundred. Add to the
picture the fact that I had no brothers or sisters, no allies, no witnesses
for the defense. Why did this process seem all the worse for his never
raising his voice, never striking me? I think because I therefore had no

chance to get angry *back;* I never doubted that he was merciful and that I was guilty.

My tendency automatically to assume my own guilt spread from those 26 sessions in Father's study over the rest of my life.

Once, when I was in seventh grade, my history teacher gave me a 27 book to read and report on to the class — a book about the battles of the Civil War. I still remember it: The cover was blue, with crossed swords and a soldier's cap. A few days after he gave it to me, I lost the book. I felt complete panic.

"What happened to that special report you were going to give us, 28 Hochschild?"

"I'm . . . working on it, sir." 29

Desperately, I searched everywhere: desk, locker, odd corners of the 30 classroom, my room at home. No book. Days went by. I avoided eye contact with the teacher and slipped out of class as soon as the bell rang so I would never find myself alone with him. At one level of awareness, I knew he was an absentminded man and might well have forgotten about the book. But I still lived in fear that he would remember.

I searched again and again. The school year ended. The summer was 31 an idyll of Europe and Eagle Nest, but every few days I would remember the lost book, wince, and feel my day darken.

Then, one day in the fall, I was studying in the school library. I looked 32 up for a moment, and there, on a shelf at my eye level, was the missing book, crossed swords and all. It had been a library book, and somebody must have seen it lying about and simply returned it. This was the one place I had never thought to look. A vast rush of relief swept through me; I could see the sky again.

Engaging the Text

1. Does Hochschild win your sympathy in this selection? Is he overdramatizing his situation? Do you attribute the unhealthiness of the relationship primarily to the father or the son?

2. What long-term consequences would you expect to result from the relationship described here?

3. Of what social standing is the Hochschild family? Do you think that this has anything to do with the father's behavior?

4. What does Hochschild's language — and particularly the language he uses to describe his father — tell us about their relationship? For example, what does Hochschild mean when he says that when his father listened to his explanations "he listened . . . in a distinct tone of voice"?

Exploring Connections

1. Compare Hochschild's relationship with his father to Adrienne Rich's relationship with Arnold Rich in Chapter Two, "Justice for All."

Extending the Critical Context

1. Play the role of Adam's mother. Write a letter to Dear Abby describing your husband's relationship with your son. Exchange letters with a classmate and write an answer.

From *The Hurried Child*

DAVID ELKIND

Throughout a long career, psychologist David Elkind has written or edited more than a dozen books, most of them dealing with child or adolescent psychology. In this piece from his popular book The Hurried Child, *Elkind points to what he sees as a major problem in family life today: a senseless and potentially destructive compulsion to rush children into maturity. This wide-ranging selection touches on, among other things, teenage suicide, media influence, and teenage sexuality. Elkind (b. 1931) is professor of child study at Tufts University and has recently published* Mis-Education: Preschoolers at Risk *(1987).*

The concept of childhood, so vital to the traditional American way of 1
life, is threatened with extinction in the society we have created. Today's child has become the unwilling, unintended victim of overwhelming stress — the stress borne of rapid, bewildering social change and constantly rising expectations. The contemporary parent dwells in a pressure-cooker of competing demands, transitions, role changes, personal and professional uncertainties, over which he or she exerts slight direction. We seek release from stress whenever we can, and usually the one sure ambit of our control is the home. Here, if nowhere else, we enjoy the fact (or illusion) of playing a determining role. If child-rearing necessarily entails

stress, then by hurrying children to grow up, or by treating them as adults, we hope to remove a portion of our burden of worry and anxiety and to enlist our children's aid in carrying life's load. We do not mean our children harm in acting thus — on the contrary, as a society we have come to imagine that it is good for young people to mature rapidly. Yet we do our children harm when we hurry them through childhood.

The principal architect of our modern notion of childhood was the 2 French philosopher Jean-Jacques Rousseau.[1] It was he who first criticized the educational methods for presenting materials from a uniquely adult perspective, reflecting adult values and interests. Classical *paideia*[2] — that is, the value of transmitting a cultural-social heritage — was a good thing, said Rousseau, but the learning process must take the child's perceptions and stage of development into account. In his classic work *Emile*, Rousseau wrote, "Childhood has its own way of seeing, thinking, and feeling, and nothing is more foolish than to try to substitute ours for theirs." More specifically, he observed that children matured in four stages, and just as each stage had its own characteristics, it should also have a corresponding set of appropriate educational objectives.[3]

This idea of childhood as a distinct phase preceding adult life became 3 inextricably interwoven with the modern concepts of universal education and the small, nuclear family (mother, father, children — not the extended family of earlier eras) in the late eighteenth and early nineteenth centuries, the heyday of the original Industrial Revolution. The transition is well explained by futurologist Alvin Toffler: "As work shifted out of the fields and the home, children had to be prepared for factory life. . . . If young people could be prefitted in the industrial system, it would vastly ease the problems of industrial discipline later on. The result was another central structure of all [modern] societies: mass education."[4]

In addition to free, universal, public education, the emergent society 4 tended to create smaller family units. Toffler writes, "To free workers for factory labor, key functions of the family were parcelled out to new specialized institutions. Education of the child was turned over to schools. Care of the aged was turned over to the poor houses or old-age homes or nursing homes. Above all, the new society required mobility. It needed workers who would follow jobs from place to place. . . . Torn

---

[1]*Jean-Jacques Rousseau:* French author and philosopher (1712–1778).
[2]*paideia:* Greek word for "education" in the broad sense of preparation to belong to a culture.
[3]J. J. Rousseau, *Emile.* New York: Dutton, 1957. [Author's note]
[4]A. Toffler, *The Third Wave.* New York: Bantam, 1980. [Author's note]

apart by migration to the cities, battered by economic storms, families stripped themselves of unwanted relatives, grew smaller, more mobile, more suited to the needs of the [work place]."[5]

Miniature Adults

Today's pressures on middle-class children to grow up fast begin in   5
early childhood. Chief among them is the pressure for early intellectual attainment, deriving from a changed perception of precocity. Several decades ago precocity was looked upon with great suspicion. The child prodigy, it was thought, turned out to be a neurotic adult; thus the phrase "early ripe, early rot!" Trying to accelerate children's acquisition of academic skills was seen as evidence of bad parenting.

A good example of this type of attitude is provided by the case of   6
William James Sidis, the son of a psychiatrist. Sidis was born at the turn of the century and became a celebrated child prodigy who entered Harvard College at the age of eleven. His papers on higher mathematics gave the impression that he would make major contributions in this area. Sidis soon attracted the attention of the media, who celebrated his feats as a child. But Sidis never went further and seemed to move aimlessly from one job to another. In 1930 James Thurber wrote a profile of Sidis in the *New Yorker* Magazine entitled "Where Are They Now?"; he described Sidis's lonely and pitiful existence in which his major preoccupation was collecting streetcar transfers from all over the world.

Such attitudes, however, changed markedly during the 1960s when   7
parents were bombarded with professional and semiprofessional dicta on the importance of learning in the early years. If you did not start teaching children when they were young, parents were told, a golden opportunity for learning would be lost. Today, tax-supported kindergartens are operating in almost every state, and children are admitted at increasingly earlier ages. (In many cities a child born before January 1 can enter kindergarten the preceding September, making his or her effective entrance age four.) Once enrolled in kindergarten, children are now often presented with formal instruction in reading and math once reserved for the later grades.

How did this radical turnabout in attitudes happen? There are probably   8
many reasons, but a major one was the attack on "progressive" education that occurred in the fifties and that found much education material dated. The Russian launching of the Sputnik in 1957 drove Americans into a frenzy of self-criticism about education and promoted the massive curriculum movement of the 1960s that brought academics from major universities into curriculum writing. Unfortunately, many academics knew

[5]Toffler, ibid. [Author's note]

their discipline but didn't know children and were unduly optimistic about how fast and how much children could learn. This optimism was epitomized in Jerome Bruner's famous phrase, "That any subject can be taught effectively in some intellectually honest form to any child at any stage of development."[6] What a shift from "early ripe, early rot"!

The trend toward early academic pressure was further supported by the civil rights movement, which highlighted the poor performance of disadvantaged children in our schools. Teachers were under attack by avant-garde educators such as John Holt,[7] Jonathan Kozol,[8] and Herbert Kohl,[9] and they were forced to defend their lack of success by shifting the blame. Their children did not do well because they came inadequately prepared. It was not what was going on in the classroom but what had not gone on at home that was the root of academic failure among the disadvantaged; hence Headstart, hence busing, which by integrating students would equalize background differences.

One consequence of all this concern for the early years was the demise of the "readiness" concept. The concept of readiness had been extolled by developmental psychologists such as Arnold Gesell who argued for the biological limitations on learning.[10] Gesell believed that children were not biologically ready for learning to read until they had attained a Mental Age (a test score in which children are credited with a certain number of months for each correct answer) of six and one-half years. But the emphasis on early intervention and early intellectual stimulation (even of infants) made the concept of readiness appear dated and old-fashioned. In professional educational circles readiness, once an honored educational concept, is now in disrepute.

The pressure for early academic achievement is but one of many contemporary pressures on children to grow up fast. Children's dress is another. Three or four decades ago, prepubescent boys wore short pants and knickers until they began to shave; getting a pair of long pants was a true rite of passage. Girls were not permitted to wear makeup or sheer stockings until they were in their teens. For both sexes, clothing set children apart. It signaled adults that these people were to be treated differently, perhaps indulgently; it made it easier for children to act as children. Today even preschool children wear miniature versions of adult

---

[6]J. Bruner, *The Process of Education*. Cambridge, Massachusetts: Harvard University Press, 1960. [Author's note]

[7]J. C. Holt, *How Children Fail*. New York: Pitman, 1964. [Author's note]

[8]J. Kozol, *Death at an Early Age*. Boston: Houghton Mifflin, 1967. [Author's note]

[9]H. R. Kohl, *36 Children*. New York: New American Library, 1967. [Author's note]

[10]Arnold L. Gesell, Louise B. Ames, and Frances L. Ilg, *Infant and Child in the Culture of Today*. New York: Harper & Row, 1943. [Author's note]

clothing. From overalls to LaCoste shirts to scaled-down designer fashions, a whole range of adult costumes is available to children. (Along with them is a wide choice of corresponding postures such as those of young teenagers modeling designer jeans.) Below is an illustration from a recent article by Susan Ferraro entitled "Hotsy Totsy."

> It was a party like any other: ice cream and cake, a donkey poster and twelve haphazard tails, and a door prize for everyone including Toby, the birthday girl's little brother who couldn't do anything but smear icing.

> "Ooh," sighed seven-year-old Melissa as she opened her first present. It was Calvin Klein jeans. "Aah," she gasped as the second box revealed a bright new top from Gloria Vanderbilt. There were Christian Dior undies from grandma — a satiny little chemise and matching bloomer bottoms — and mother herself had fallen for a marvelous party outfit from Yves St. Laurent. Melissa's best friend gave her an Izod sports shirt, complete with alligator emblem. Added to that a couple of books were, indeed, very nice and predictable — except for the fancy doll one guest's eccentric mother insisted on bringing.[11]

When children dress like adults they are more likely to behave as 12 adults do, to imitate adult actions. It is hard to walk like an adult male wearing corduroy knickers that make an awful noise. But boys in long pants can walk like men, and little girls in tight jeans can walk like women. It is more difficult today to recognize that children are children and not miniature adults, because children dress and move like adults.

Another evidence of the pressure to grow up fast is the change in the 13 programs of summer camps for children. Although there are still many summer camps that offer swimming, sailing, horseback riding, archery, and camp fires — activities we remember from our own childhood — an increasing number of summer camps offer specialized training in many different areas, including foreign languages, tennis, baseball, dance, music, and even computers.

Among such camps the most popular seem to be those that specialize 14 in competitive sports: softball, weight training, tennis, golf, football, basketball, hockey, soccer, lacrosse, gymnastics, wrestling, judo, figure skating, surfing. "Whatever the sport there's a camp (or ten or a hundred of them) dedicated to teaching the finer points. Often these camps are under the direction, actual or nominal, of a big name in a particular sport, and many have professional athletes on their staffs. The daily

[11]S. Ferraro, "Hotsy Totsy," *American Way Magazine*, April, 1981, p. 61. [Author's note]

routine is rigorous, with individual and/or group lessons, practice sessions and tournaments, complete with trophies. And, to cheer the athletes on with more pep and polish, cheerleaders and song girls can also attend."[12]

The change in the programs of summer camps reflects the new attitude 15 that the years of childhood are not to be frittered away by engaging in activities merely for fun. Rather, the years are to be used to perfect skills and abilities that are the same as those of adults. Children are early initiated into the rigors of adult competition. Competitive sports for children are becoming ever more widespread and include everything from Little League to Pee Wee hockey. The pressure to engage in organized, competitive sports at camp and at home is one of the most obvious pressures on contemporary children to grow up fast.

There are many other pressures as well. Many children today travel 16 across the country, and indeed across the world, alone. The so-called unaccompanied minor has become so commonplace that airlines have instituted special rules and regulations for them. The phenomenon is a direct result of the increase in middle-class divorces and the fact that one or the other parent moves to another part of the country or world. Consequently, the child travels to visit one parent or the other. Children also fly alone to see grandparents or to go to special camps or training facilities.

Other facets of society also press children to grow up fast. Lawyers, 17 for example, are encouraging children to sue their parents for a variety of grievances. In California, four-and-one-half-year-old Kimberely Ann Alpin, who was born out of wedlock, is suing her father for the right to visit with him. The father, who provides support payments, does not want to see Kimberely. Whatever the decision, or the merits of the case, it illustrates the tendency of child-advocates to accord adult legal rights to children. In West Hartford, Connecticut, David Burn, age 16, legally "divorced" his parents under a new state law in 1980. While such rights may have some benefits, they also put children in a difficult and often stressful position vis-à-vis their parents.

The media too, including music, books, films, and television, increasingly 18 portray young people as precocious and present them in more or less explicit sexual or manipulative situations. Such portrayals force children to think they should act grown up before they are ready. In the movie *Little Darlings* the two principals — teenage girls — are in competition as to who will lose her virginity first. Similarly, teen music extols songs

[12]C. Emerson, "Summer Camp, It's Not the Same Anymore," *Sky*, March 1981, 29–34. [Author's note]

such as "Take Your Time (Do It Right)" and "Do That to Me One More Time," which are high on the charts of teen favorites. Television also promotes teenage erotica with features detailing such themes as teenage prostitution. According to some teenagers, the only show on television where playing hard to get is not regarded as stupid is *Laverne and Shirley.*

The media promote not only teenage sexuality but also the wearing   19
of adult clothes and the use of adult behaviors, language, and interpersonal strategies. Sexual promotion occurs in the context of other suggestions and models for growing up fast. A Jordache jean commercial, which depicts a young girl piggyback on a young boy, highlights clothing and implicit sexuality as well as adult expressions, hairstyles, and so on. Likewise, in the film *Foxes*, four teenage girls not only blunder into sexual entanglements but also model provocative adult clothing, makeup, language, and postures. Thus the media reinforce the pressure on children to grow up fast in their language, thinking, and behavior.

But can young people be hurried into growing up fast emotionally as   20
well? Psychologists and psychiatrists recognize that emotions and feelings are the most complex and intricate part of development. Feelings and emotions have their own timing and rhythm and cannot be hurried. Young teenagers may look and behave like adults but they usually don't feel like adults. (Watch a group of teenagers in a children's playground as they swing on the swings and teeter on the teeter-totters.) Children can grow up fast in some ways but not in others. Growing up emotionally is complicated and difficult under any circumstances but may be especially so when children's behavior and appearance speak "adult" while their feelings cry "child."

The Child Inside

Some of the more negative consequences of hurrying usually become   21
evident in adolescence, when the pressures to grow up fast collide with institutional prohibitions. Children pushed to grow up fast suddenly find that many adult prerogatives — which they assumed would be their prerogative — such as smoking, drinking, driving, and so on, are denied them until they reach a certain age. Many adolescents feel betrayed by a society that tells them to grow up fast but also to remain a child. Not surprisingly, the stresses of growing up fast often result in troubled and troublesome behavior during adolescence.

In a recent article, Patricia O'Brien gave some examples of what she   22
called "the shrinking of childhood." Her examples reflect a rush to experiment that is certainly one consequence of growing up fast:

Martin L (not his real name) confronted his teenager who had stayed out very late the night before. The son replied, "Look, Dad, I've done it all — drugs, sex, and booze, there is nothing left I don't know about." This young man is twelve years old!

In Washington, D.C. area schools administrators estimate that many thousands of teenagers are alcoholics, with an estimated 30,000 such young people in Northern Virginia alone.[13]

The rush to experiment is perhaps most noticeable in teenage sexual 23 behavior. Although survey data are not always as reliable as one might wish, the available information suggests that there has been a dramatic increase in the number of sexually active teenage girls in the last decade. Melvin Zelnick and John F. Kanther, professors of public health at Johns Hopkins University in Baltimore, conclude that nearly 50 percent of the total population of teenage girls between the ages of fifteen and nineteen (about 10.3 million females) have had premarital sex. The percentage has nearly doubled since the investigators first undertook their study in 1971. "Things that supported remaining a virgin in the past — the fear of getting pregnant, being labelled the 'town pump,' or whatever have disappeared," observes Zelnick.[14]

Young people themselves are very much aware of this trend. "I'd say 24 half the girls in my graduating class are virgins," says an eighteen-year-old high school senior from New Iberia, Louisiana. "But you wouldn't believe those freshmen and sophomores. By the time they graduate there aren't going to be any virgins left."[15]

There are a number of disturbing consequences of this sexual liberation. 25 The number of teenage pregnancies is growing at a startling rate. About 10 percent of all teenage girls, one million in all, get pregnant each year and the number keeps increasing. About 600,000 teenagers give birth each year, and the sharpest increase in such births is for girls under fourteen! In addition, venereal disease is a growing problem among teenagers, who account for 25 percent of the one million or so cases of gonorrhea each year.

The causes of this enhanced sexual activity among young people today 26 are many and varied. The age of first menstruation, for example, has dropped from age seventeen about a century ago to age twelve and a half today. Fortunately this seems to be the lower limit made possible

[13]Patricia O'Brien, "Dope, Sex, Crime, What Happened to Childhood," *Chicago Tribune*, March 8, 1981. [Author's note]

[14]"The Games Teen Agers Play," *Newsweek*, September 1, 1980. [Author's note]

[15]Ibid. [Author's note]

by good health care and nutrition. However, this age of first menstruation has remained stable over the past decade, so it cannot account for the increased sexual activity of young women during this period. Other contributing factors include rapid changes in social values, women's liberation, the exploding divorce rate, the decline of parental and institutional authority, and the fatalistic sense, not often verbalized, that we are all going to die in a nuclear holocaust anyway, so "what the hell, have a good time."

Although the media are quick to pick up these sexual trends and exploit them for commercial purposes (for example, the cosmetics for girls four to nine years old currently being marketed by toy manufacturers), the immediate adult model is perhaps the most powerful and the most pervasive. Married couples are generally discreet about their sexuality in front of their offspring — in part because of a natural tendency to avoid exposing children to what they might not understand, but also because by the time the children are born, much of the romantic phase of the relationship for many couples is in the past. 27

But single parents who are dating provide a very different model for children. Quite aside from confrontations such as that in *Kramer vs. Kramer* wherein the son encounters the father's naked girlfriend, single parents are likely to be much more overtly sexual than married couples. With single parents, children may witness the romantic phase of courtship — the hand-holding, the eye-gazing, the constant touching and fondling. This overt sexuality, with all the positive affection it demonstrates, may encourage young people to look for something similar. 28

It is also true, as Professor Mavis Hetherington of the University of Virginia has found in her research, that daughters of divorced women tend to be more sexually oriented, more flirtatious with men than daughters of widowed mothers or daughters from two-parent homes.[16] Because there are more teenage daughters from single-parent homes today than ever before, this too could contribute to enhanced sexual activity of contemporary teenage girls. 29

While it is true that some young people in every past generation have engaged in sex at an early age, have become pregnant, contracted venereal disease, and so on, they were always a small proportion of the population. What is new today are the numbers, which indicate that pressures to grow up fast are social and general rather than familial and specific (reflecting parental biases and needs). The proportion of young people 30

[16] E. M. Hetherington, M. Cos, and R. Cox, "The Aftermath of Divorce." In J. H. Stevens, Jr. & M. Mathews (Eds.) *Mother-child, father-child relations*. Washington, D.C.: NAEYC, 1978. [Author's note]

who are abusing drugs, are sexually active, and are becoming pregnant is so great that we must look to the society as a whole for a full explanation, not to just the parents who mirror it.

Paralleling the increased sexuality of young people is an increase in children of what in adults are known as stress diseases. Pediatricians report a greater incidence of such ailments as headaches, stomachaches, allergic reactions, and so on in today's youngsters than in previous generations. Type A behavior (high-strung, competitive, demanding) has been identified in children and associated with heightened cholesterol levels. It has also been associated with parental pressure for achievement.   31

Another negative reflection of the pressure to grow up fast is teenage (and younger) crime. During 1980, for example, New York police arrested 12,762 children aged sixteen and under on felony charges. In Chicago the figure for the same period was 18,754 charges. Having worked for juvenile courts, I am sure that these figures are underestimated. Many children who have committed felonies are released without a formal complaint so that they will not have a police record. The children who are "booked" have usually had several previous encounters with the law.   32

The following examples, recent cases from the New York Police Department, illustrate the sort of activities for which children get arrested: 33

- On 27 February 1981, a boy who had to stand on tiptoes to speak to the bank teller made off with $118 that he had secured at gunpoint. He was nine years old, the youngest felon ever sought by the F.B.I.
- A ten-year-old Brooklyn girl was apprehended in December after she snatched a wallet from a woman's purse. Police said it was the girl's nineteenth arrest.
- One of four suspects captured in the murder of a policeman in Queens on 12 January 1981 was a fifteen-year-old youth.
- A thirteen-year-old Bronx boy was arrested in March 1981 on charges that he killed two elderly women during attempted purse snatchings.
- Another thirteen-year-old boy had a record of thirty-two arrests when seized last year on a charge of attempted murder. He later confessed to an incredible 200 plus felonies.[17]

Such crimes are not being committed just by poor disadvantaged youth who are acting out against a society prejudiced against them. Much teenage crime is committed by middle-class youngsters. However, it tends to be concealed because police and parents try to protect the children; but sometimes this is not possible. One case involved a thirteen-   34

[17]Michael Coakley, "Robert, a Robber at Age 9, and Just One of Thousands," *Chicago Tribune*, March 8, 1981. [Author's note]

year-old Long Island boy who was killed by three teenagers who stomped on him and strangled him by stuffing stones down his throat. He was attacked because he accidentally discovered that the other boys had stolen an old dirt bike worth only a couple of dollars. It was one of the most brutal and gruesome murders to be committed on Long Island.

. . . There are many . . . solutions to [the] pressure to achieve early. One such solution is to join a cult, such as the "Moonies."[18] What characterizes such cults is that they accept young people unconditionally, regardless of academic success or failure. The cults, in effect, provide an accepting family that does not demand achievement in return for love, although cults do demand obedience and adherence to a certain moral ethic. Even rebellious young people find it easy to adhere to these rules in the atmosphere of acceptance and lack of pressure and competition offered by the cult group. Cult membership is [a] form of negative identity in which young people adopt a group identity rather than an individual one. 35

A case in point is the Christ Commune (a pseudonym), a branch of the best-organized and most rapidly growing sect of what has been called the Jesus movement. The Commune is a summer camp where members come from their homes for a few months each year. The population (about one hundred) consists of young adults between the ages of fifteen and thirty (average age twenty-one) who are white and come from large (four to eight children), middle-class families. Most have completed high school and some have done college work. One gets the impression they are young people who have not distinguished themselves socially, academically, or athletically and who have held boring, low-paying jobs. 36

The group offers a strict moral code, a rigid behavioral program, and a sense of mission, of being chosen by and working for God through the mediation of Christ. The members work hard — they get up at 4:30 A.M. and go to sleep at 11:00 P.M. They seem happy with simple food (little meat, water to drink, peanut butter sandwiches for lunch) and strenuous work six days a week. Entertainment and recreation are limited to sitting in a common room, talking, singing spirituals, and engaging in spontaneous prayer. 37

Such communes, the Jesus movement, and other religious groups are attractive to young people whose personal styles are at variance with those of the larger society. Such groups offer recognition and status to young people who tend to be noncompetitive, anti-intellectual, and spiritual 38

---

[18]*Moonies:* disparaging term for the members of the Unification Church, a sect led by the Rev. Sun Myung Moon, prominent in the United States in the 1970s.

in orientation. Thus the groups provide a needed haven from the pressure to grow up fast, to achieve early, and to make a distinctive mark in life.

The last phenomenon in relation to hurrying to be discussed here is 39 teenage suicide. Currently, suicide is the third leading cause of death during the teen years — preceded only by death via accidents and homicide. An American Academy of Pediatrics report on teenage suicide indicates a large increase in the number of suicides by adolescents in the last decade — the number is now about 5000 per year. For young people between the ages of fifteen to nineteen, the number of suicides per year doubled during the period from 1968 to 1976. The data for young adolescents of ages ten to fourteen are even more distressing: The number of suicides was 116 in 1968 and rose to 158 by 1976.

For every suicide completed, some 50 to 200 are attempted but not 40 successful. Adolescents from all walks of life, all races, religions, and ethnic groups commit or attempt to commit suicide. Boys are generally more successful than girls because they use more lethal methods — boys tend to shoot or hang themselves whereas girls are more likely to overdose on pills or to cut their wrists. "For most adolescents," the pediatric report concludes, "suicide represents an attempt to resolve a difficult conflict, escape an intolerable living arrangement, or punish important individuals in their lives."

To illustrate how hurrying can contribute to teenage suicide, consider 41 the data from the most affluent suburbs of Chicago, a ten-mile stretch of communities along Chicago's northside lakefront that is one of the richest areas in the country. It is the locale chosen by director Robert Redford for the movie *Ordinary People*. The median income per family is about $60,000. Children in these areas attend excellent schools, travel about the world on vacations, are admitted to the best and most prestigious private colleges, and often drive their own cars (which can sometimes be a Mercedes). These are children of affluence who would seem to have it made.

And yet, this cluster of suburbs has the highest number of teenage 42 suicides per year in the state, and almost in the nation. There has been a 250 percent increase in suicides per year over the past decade. These figures are dismaying not only in and of themselves but because the community has made serious efforts at suicide prevention, including the training of teachers in suicide detection and the provision of a twenty-four-hour hot line. One hot line, provided by Chicago psychoanalyst Joseph Pribyl, receives some 150 calls per month. But the suicides continue.

A nineteen-year-old from Glencoe, Illinois, says, "We have an outrageous 43 number of suicides for a community our size." One of this teenager's friends cut her wrist and two others drove their cars into trees. "Growing up here you are handed everything on a platter, but something else is missing. The one thing parents don't give is love, understanding, and acceptance of you as a person." And Isadora Sherman, of Highland Park's Jewish Family and Community Service says, "People give their kids a lot materially, but expect a lot in return. No one sees his kids as average, and those who don't perform are made to feel like failures."[19]

Chicago psychiatrist Harold Visotsky succinctly states how pressure   44
to achieve at an early age, to grow up and be successful fast can contribute to teenage suicide: "People on the lower end of the social scale expect less than these people. Whatever anger the poor experience is acted out in antisocial ways — vandalism, homicide, riots — and the sense of shared misery in the lower income groups prevents people from feeling so isolated. With well-to-do kids, *the rattle goes in the mouth and the foot goes on the social ladder*. The competition ethic takes over, making a child feel even more alone. He's more likely to take it out on himself than society."[20]

Adolescents are very audience conscious. Failure is a public event,   45
and the adolescent senses the audience's disapproval. It is the sense that "everyone knows" that is so painful and that can lead to attempted and successful suicides in adolescents who are otherwise so disposed. Hurrying our children has, I believe, contributed to the extraordinary rise in suicide rates among young people over the past decade.

All Grown Up and No Place to Go

Sigmund Freud was once asked to describe the characteristics of maturity,   46
and he replied: *lieben und arbeiten* ("loving and working"). The mature adult is one who can love and allow himself or herself to be loved and who can work productively, meaningfully, and with satisfaction. Yet most adolescents, and certainly all children, are really not able to work or to love in the mature way that Freud had in mind. Children love their parents in a far different way from how they will love a real or potential mate. And many, probably most, young people will not find their life work until they are well into young adulthood.

When children are expected to dress, act, and think as adults, they   47
are really being asked to playact, because all of the trappings of adulthood do not in any way make them adults in the true sense of *lieben und arbeiten*. It is ironic that the very parents who won't allow their children

---

[19]"Suicide Belt," *Time Magazine*, September 1, 1980. [Author's note]
[20]Ibid. [Author's note]

to believe in Santa Claus or the Easter Bunny (because they are fantasy and therefore dishonest) allow their children to dress and behave as adults without any sense of the tremendous dishonesty involved in allowing children to present themselves in this grown-up way.

It is even more ironic that practices once considered the province of lower-class citizens now have the allure of middle-class chic. Divorce, single parenting, dual-career couples, and unmarried couples living together were common among the lower class decades ago. Such arrangements were prompted more often than not by economic need, and the children of low-income families were thus pressured to grow up fast out of necessity. They were pitied and looked down upon by upper- and middle-class parents, who helped provide shelters like the Home for Little Wanderers in Boston. 48

Today the middle class has made divorce its status symbol. And single parenting and living together without being married are increasingly commonplace. Yet middle-class children have not kept pace with the adjustments these adult changes require. In years past a child in a low-income family could appreciate the need to take on adult responsibilities early; families needed the income a child's farm or factory labor would bring, and chores and child-rearing tasks had to be allocated to even younger members of the family. But for the middle-income child today, it is hard to see the necessity of being relegated to a baby sitter or sent to a nursery school or a day care center when he or she has a perfectly nice playroom and yard at home. It isn't the fact of parents' being divorced that is so distressing to middle-class children, but rather that often it seems so unnecessary, so clearly a reflection of parent and not child need. . . . It is the feeling of being used, of being exploited by parents, of losing the identity and uniqueness of childhood without just cause that constitutes the major stress of hurrying and accounts for so much unhappiness among affluent young people today. 49

It is certainly true that the trend toward obscuring the divisions between children and adults is part of a broad egalitarian movement in this country that seeks to overcome the barriers separating the sexes, ethnic and racial groups, and the handicapped. We see these trends in unisex clothing and hairstyles, in the call for equal pay for equal work, in the demands for affirmative action, and in the appeals and legislation that provide the handicapped with equal opportunities for education and meaningful jobs. 50

From this perspective, the contemporary pressure for children to grow up fast is only one symptom of a much larger social phenomenon in this country — a movement toward true equality, toward the ideal expressed in our Declaration of Independence. While one can only applaud this 51 movement with respect to the sexes, ethnic and racial groups, and the handicapped, its unthinking extension to children is unfortunate.

Children need time to grow, to learn, and to develop. To treat them 52 differently from adults is not to discriminate against them but rather to recognize their special estate. Similarly, when we provide bilingual programs for Hispanic children, we are not discriminating against them but are responding to the special needs they have, which, if not attended to, would prevent them from attaining a successful education and true equality. In the same way, building ramps for handicapped students is a means to their attaining equal opportunity. Recognizing special needs is not discriminatory; on the contrary, it is the only way that true equality can be attained.

All children have, vis-à-vis adults, special needs — intellectual, social, 53 and emotional. Children do not learn, think, or feel in the same way as adults. To ignore these differences, to treat children as adults, is really not democratic or egalitarian. If we ignore the special needs of children, we are behaving just as if we denied Hispanic or Indian children bilingual programs, or denied the handicapped their ramps and guideposts. In truth, the recognition of a group's special needs and accommodation to those needs are the only true ways to insure equality and true equal opportunity.

Engaging the Text

1. Debate Elkind's central proposition that while children are being encouraged by their parents, the media, and other social forces to imitate adults, they remain children in terms of both understanding and emotional maturity.

2. In Elkind's view, how does formal education in the United States serve the needs of an industrial society? How has it contributed to the phenomenon of the hurried child?

3. What social pressures besides those mentioned by Elkind may promote the kind of precocious behavior he describes?

4. At the end of the selection, Elkind uses an ANALOGY comparing the special needs of children to the needs of other groups (nonnative speakers and disabled students). Discuss the logic and the effect of this analogy.

Exploring Connections

1. Is there any difference between Elkind's "hurried" children and the young Americans who Tocqueville claimed had "no adolescence" (p. 341)? How do you account for the authors' different views toward early maturation?

2. Where does Elkind stand on the democratization of the family that Tocqueville describes?

3. Is either Adrienne Rich (p. 101) or Adam Hochschild (p. 355) a typical "hurried" child?

Extending the Critical Context

1. Find one or two articles on one of the problems Elkind mentions (e.g., teen pregnancy, substance abuse, suicide, crime). Do these articles seem to share Elkind's idea that young people are pressured into becoming adults too soon? What other factors do they identify as causes of the problem you're studying? How do you suppose Elkind would respond to these articles?

The Kid's Guide to Divorce

LORRIE MOORE

This short story features a young narrator whom you might not want to baby-sit but whose voice you'll enjoy hearing. Lorrie Moore (Marie Lorena Moore, b. 1957), who teaches English at the University of Wisconsin, has published a novel, Anagrams *(1986), and a collection of short stories,* Self Help *(1985).*

Put extra salt on the popcorn because your mom'll say that she needs   1
it because the part where Inger Berman[1] almost dies and the camera
does tricks to elongate her torso sure gets her every time.

Think: Geeze, here she goes again with the Kleenexes.   2

She will say thanks honey when you come slowly, slowly around the   3
corner in your slippers and robe, into the living room with Grandma's
old used-to-be-salad-bowl piled high. I made it myself, remind her, and
accidentally drop a few pieces on the floor. Mittens will bat them around
with his paws.

---

[1]*Inger Berman:* actually international film star Ingrid Bergman. The reference is to Alfred Hitchcock's *Notorious* (1946) starring Bergman and Cary Grant.

Mmmmm, good to replenish those salts, she'll munch and smile soggily. 4

Tell her the school nurse said after a puberty movie once that salt is 5
bad for people's hearts.

Phooey, she'll say. It just makes it thump, that's all. Thump, thump, 6
thump — oh look! She will talk with her mouth full of popcorn. Cary
Grant is getting her out of there. Did you unplug the popper?

Pretend you don't hear her. Watch Inger Berman look elongated; 7
wonder what it means.

You'd better check, she'll say. 8

Groan. Make a little *tsk* noise with your tongue on the roof of your 9
mouth. Run as fast as you can because the next commercial's going to
be the end. Unplug the popper. Bring Mittens back in with you because
he is mewing by the refrigerator. He'll leave hair on your bathrobe.
Dump him in your mom's lap.

Hey baby, she'll coo at the cat, scratching his ears. Cuddle close to 10
your mom and she'll reach around and scratch one of your ears too,
kissing your cheek. Then she'll suddenly lean forward, reaching toward
the bowl on the coffee table, carefully so as not to disturb the cat. I
always think he's going to realize faster than he does, your mom will
say between munches, hand to hand to mouth. Men can be so dense
and frustrating. She will wink at you.

Eye the tube suspiciously. All the bad guys will let Cary Grant take 11
Inger Berman away in the black car. There will be a lot of old-fashioned
music. Stand and pull your bathrobe up on the sides. Hang your tongue
out and pretend to dance like a retarded person at a ball. Roll your
eyes. Waltz across the living room with exaggerated side-to-side motions,
banging into furniture. Your mother will pretend not to pay attention
to you. She will finally say in a flat voice: How wonderful, gee, you
really send me.

When the music is over, she will ask you what you want to watch 12
now. She'll hand you the *TV Guide*. Look at it. Say: The Late, Late
Chiller. She'll screw up one of her eyebrows at you, but say *please,
please* in a soft voice and put your hands together like a prayer. She
will smile back and sigh, okay.

Switch the channel and return to the sofa. Climb under the blue 13
afghan with your mother. Tell her you like this beginning cartoon part
best where the mummy comes out of the coffin and roars, *CHILLER!!*
Get up on one of the arms of the sofa and do an imitation, your hands
like claws, your elbows stiff, your head slumped to one side. Your mother
will tell you to sit back down. Snuggle back under the blanket with her.

When she says, Which do you like better, the mummy or the werewolf, 14
tell her the werewolf is scary because he goes out at night and does

things that no one suspects because in the day he works in a bank and has no hair.

What about the mummy? she'll ask, petting Mittens. 15

Shrug your shoulders. Fold in your lips. Say: The mummy's just the 16 mummy.

With the point of your tongue, loosen one of the chewed, pulpy kernels 17 in your molars. Try to swallow it, but get it caught in your throat and begin to gasp and make horrible retching noises. It will scare the cat away.

Good God, be careful, your mother will say, thwacking you on the 18 back. Here, drink this water.

Try groaning root beer, root beer, like a dying cowboy you saw on a 19 commercial once, but drink the water anyway. When you are no longer choking, your face is less red, and you can breathe again, ask for a Coke. Your mom will say: I don't think so; Dr. Atwood said your teeth were atrocious.

Tell her Dr. Atwood is for the birds. 20

What do you mean by that? she will exclaim. 21

Look straight ahead. Say: I dunno. 22

The mummy will be knocking down telephone poles, lifting them up, 23 and hurling them around like Lincoln Logs.

Wow, all wrapped up and no place to go, your mother will say. 24

Cuddle close to her and let out a long, low, admiring *Neato*. 25

The police will be in the cemetery looking for a monster. They won't 26 know whether it's the mummy or the werewolf, but someone will have been hanging out there leaving little smoking piles of bones and flesh that even the police dogs get upset and whine at.

Say something like gross-out, and close your eyes. 27

Are you sure you want to watch this? 28

Insist that you are not scared. 29

There's a rock concert on Channel 7, you know. 30

Think about it. Decide to try Channel 7, just for your mom's sake. 31 Somebody with greasy hair who looks like Uncle Jack will be saying something boring.

Your mother will agree that he does look like Uncle Jack. A little. 32

A band with black eyeshadow on will begin playing their guitars. Stand 33 and bounce up and down like you saw Julie Steinman do once.

God, why do they always play them down at their crotches? your 34 mom will ask.

Don't answer, simply imitate them, throwing your hair back and fiddling 35 bizarrely with the crotch of your pajama bottoms. Your mother will slap you and tell you you're being fresh.

Act hurt. Affect a slump. Pick up a magazine and pretend you're 36
reading it. The cat will rejoin you. Look at the pictures of the food.

Your mom will try to pep you up. She'll say: Look! Pat Benatar! Let's 37
dance.

Tell her you think Pat Benatar is stupid and cheap. Say nothing for 38
five whole minutes.

When the B-52's come on, tell her you think *they're* okay. 39

Smile sheepishly. Then the two of you will get up and dance like wild 40
maniacs around the coffee table until you are sweating, whooping to the
oo-ah-oo's, jumping like pogo sticks, acting like space robots. Do razz-
ma-tazz hands like your mom at either side of your head. During a
commercial, ask for an orange soda.

Water or milk, she will say, slightly out of breath, sitting back down. 41

Say shit, and when she asks what did you say, sigh: Nothing. 42

Next is Rod Stewart singing on a roof somewhere. Your mom will say: 43
He's sort of cute.

Tell her Julie Steinman saw him in a store once and said he looked 44
really old.

Hmmmm, your mother will say. 45

Study Rod Stewart carefully. Wonder if you could make your legs go 46
like that. Plan an imitation for Julie Steinman.

When the popcorn is all gone, yawn. Say: I'm going to bed now. 47

Your mother will look disappointed, but she'll say, okay, honey. She'll 48
turn the TV off. By the way, she'll ask hesitantly like she always does.
How did the last three days go?

Leave out the part about the lady and the part about the beer. Tell 49
her they went all right, that he's got a new silver dartboard and that
you went out to dinner and this guy named Hudson told a pretty funny
story about peeing in the hamper. Ask for a 7-Up.

Engaging the Text

1. In your opinion, what are the age and sex of the NARRATOR? What details
support your guesses?

2. Most of the time, this story focuses on the external behavior of the child and
mother. Working in groups, go through the story and list the possible motives
behind their words and actions.

3. How would you describe the relationship between mother and child in the
story? How well do the two understand each other? Is either CHARACTER in
trouble or heading for it?

4. What is Moore's attitude towards: the narrator? the mother?

5. Why is the story entitled "A Kid's Guide to Divorce"?

Exploring Connections

1. Analyze this story as an example of Elkind's "hurried child" syndrome, described in the preceding selection. To what extent does the narrator illustrate Elkind's concept?

Extending the Critical Context

1. In this story, the mother and child act out a number of rituals, such as the debate over what to watch on TV and the question about the child's father. Write a journal entry about a pattern of events or remarks that is lived out repeatedly in your family and thus becomes predictable. What are the causes and characteristics of the situation, and why does it recur?

ALTERNATIVE FAMILY STRUCTURES

Black Family Life

JOSEPH L. WHITE

In the following selection an eminent Afro-American researcher challenges some of the prevailing views of the black family. He argues that it is inaccurate to apply Western European standards and expectations to black families, to see them, essentially, as failed white families; the black family must, instead, be seen in the context of the cultural traditions and historical circumstances surrounding its development. White (b. 1932) is professor of psychology and psychiatry in the Department of Comparative Culture at the University of California, Irvine. This selection is from his book, The Psychology of Blacks: An Afro-American Perspective *(1984).*

The Deficit-deficiency Model

The view of the core structure of the Black family as an extended   1
family grouping is not shared by all observers. The traditional view of
the Black family, which has evolved from the works of Frazier (1939),
Elkins (1968), Moynihan (1965), and Rainwater (1970), is one of a disorganized, single-parent, subnuclear,[1] female-dominated social system.
This is essentially the deficit-deficiency model of Black family life. The
deficit-deficiency model begins with the historical assumption that there
was no carry-over from Africa to America of any sophisticated African-
based form of family life and communal living. Viable patterns of family
life either did not exist because Africans were incapable of creating them,
or they were destroyed beginning with slavery and the separation of
biological parents and children, forced breeding, the master's sexual
exploitation of Black women, and the accumulative effects of three hundred
years of economic and social discrimination. As a result of this background
of servitude, deprivation, second-class citizenship, and chronic unemployment, Black adults have not been able to develop marketable skills,
self-sufficiency, future orientation, and planning and decision-making
competencies, instrumental behaviors thought to be necessary for sustaining
a successful two-parent nuclear family while guiding the children through
the socialization process.

In a society that placed a premium on decisive male leadership in the   2
family, the Black male was portrayed as lacking the masculine sex role
behaviors characterized by logical thinking, willingness to take responsibility
for others, assertiveness, managerial skills, achievement orientation, and
occupational mastery. The Black male in essence had been psychologically
castrated and rendered ineffective by forces beyond his control. He is
absent within the family circle and unable to provide leadership and
command respect when he is present. After generations of being unable
to achieve the ideal male role in the family and in American society,
the Black male is likely to be inclined to compensate for his failure by
pursuing roles such as the pimp, player, hustler, and sweet daddy, which
are in conflict with the norms of the larger society. The appearance of
these roles in male behavior in the Black community, rather than being

[1]*subnuclear:* referring to families that appear to contain fewer members than the traditional
two-parent nuclear family.

interpreted as a form of social protest, reinforces the majority culture stereotypes of Black males as irresponsible, lazy, shiftless, and sociopathic.[2]

The Black woman does not fare much better in terms of how she is   3
portrayed in the deficit-deficiency model of Black family life. She is regarded as the head of the household, a matriarch[3] who initially received her power because the society was unwilling to permit the Black male to assume the legal, economic, and social positions necessary to become a dominant force within the family and community life. Having achieved this power by default, the Black female is unwilling to share it. Her unwillingness to share her power persists even when the Black male is present and willing to assume responsibility in the family circle, since she is not confident of the male's ability to follow through on his commitments. Confrontation over decision making and family direction is usually not necessary because the Black male is either not present in the household on any ongoing basis or is regarded as ineffective by the female when he is present.

The proponents of the pathology-oriented, matriarchal family model   4
did not consider the possibility that a single-parent Black mother could serve as an adequate role model for the children of both sexes. The notion that the mother could reflect a balance of the traditional male and female roles, with respect to mental toughness and emotional tenderness, was largely ignored because of the rigid classification of psychosexual roles in American society. In the Black community, however, the categorization of social role behaviors based on gender is not as inflexible. It is conceivable that a Black mother could project a combination of assertive and nurturant behaviors in the process of rearing children of both sexes as nonsexist adults.

With the reality of accelerating divorce rates, in recent years the single-   5
parent family headed by a woman has become a social reality in Euro-America. This reality has been accompanied by an attempt on the part of social scientists to legitimate family structures that represent alternatives to the nuclear family while reconceptualizing the social roles of males and females with less emphasis on exclusive behaviors. The concept of androgyny[4] has been introduced to cover the vast pool of human personality traits that can be developed by either sex (Rogers, 1978). A well-balanced person reflects a combination of both instrumental[5] and expressive[6] traits.

---

[2]*sociopathic:* characterized by anti-social behavior.
[3]*matriarch:* a female who rules or dominates a family group.
[4]*androgyny:* the condition of having both male and female characteristics.
[5]*instrumental:* of or relating to extrinsic purposes; active; aggressive.
[6]*expressive:* relating to feelings; emotional; affective.

The latter include feeling-oriented behaviors formerly considered feminine, such as tenderness, caring, and affection. Thus, it is conceptually possible for a white, single and androgynous female parent to rear psychologically healthy, emotionally integrated children. It is interesting how the sociology of the times makes available to white Americans psychological concepts designed to legitimatize changes in the family, in child-rearing patterns, and in relationships between the sexes. Yet, these same behaviors when first expressed by Afro-Americans were considered as pathological.

The Extended Family Model

The extended family, in contrast to the single-parent subnuclear family, 6 consists of a related and quasi-related group of adults, including aunts, uncles, parents, cousins, grandparents, boyfriends, and girlfriends linked together in a kinship or kinlike network. They form a cooperative interface[7] with each other in confronting the concerns of living and rearing the children. This model of family life, which seems able to capture not only the strength, vitality, resilience, and continuity of the Black family, but also the essence of Black values, folkways, and life styles, begins with a different set of assumptions about the development and evolution of Black family life in America.

The Black extended family is seen as an outgrowth of African patterns 7 of family and community life that survived in America. The Africans carried with them through the Mid-Atlantic passage and sale to the initial slave owners a well-developed pattern of kinship, exogamous mating,[8] and communal values, emphasizing collective survival, mutual aid, co-operation, mutual solidarity, interdependence, and responsibility for others (Nobles, 1974; Blassingame, 1972). These values became the basis for the Black extended family in America. They were retained because they were familiar and they allowed the slaves to have some power over destiny by enabling them to develop their own styles for family interaction. A consciousness of closeness to others, belongingness, and togetherness protected the slave from being psychologically destroyed by feelings of despair and alienation and the extended family provided a vehicle to pass the heritage on to the children (Fredrickson, 1976; Gutman, 1976). Slaves in essence created their own communal family space, regardless of whether the master was paternalistic[9] or conducted a Nazi-like concentration camp.

To understand the cultural continuity, it is necessary to depart from 8 the traditional hypothesis that slave masters and their descendants exercised

[7]*cooperative interface:* reciprocal or two-way relationship.
[8]*exogamous mating:* marriage outside of a specific group.
[9]*paternalistic:* relating to an apparently benevolent authority.

total psychological and social control over the development of Black family life and community institutions. The slaves were much more than empty psychological tablets on which the master imprinted an identity. These early Blacks were able to find ways of creating psychological space and implementing African cultural forms that whites were unaware of and did not understand. Once in the New World the African recreated a sense of tribal community within the plantation milieu[10] through a series of extended kin and kinlike family networks that carried on the cultural values of responsibility for others, mutual aid, and collective survival. First- and second-generation American slaves who were separated from biological kin by continued activity at the auction block and newly arriving slaves who were sold to different plantations were incorporated into the extended family structures of existing plantations. It was not essential for the survival of African conceptions of family life that biological or legal kinship ties be maintained. When a people share a philosophy of interdependence and collective survival, persons who are not biologically or legally related can become interwoven into newly created and existing kinlike networks. Cultural patterns once established seem to endure, especially if they work. The extended family survived because it provided Afro-Americans a support system within the context of a shared frame of reference. Along with other African customs and beliefs, an African family identity was passed along to the children as the link between generations through the oral tradition.

Once the philosophy of collective survival and interdependence was   9
set into place as the foundation for community living, the extended family evolved through a series of cycles of formation, breakup, and reformation as the slaves who were without the recourse to legal rights to protect kinship structures and conjugal unions were transferred from place to place. Much later, with the beginnings of the Industrial Revolution after the Civil War, the pattern of Black family life based on combinations of kinship and kinlike networks continued, despite the emergence of the nuclear family among Euro-Americans. The growth of the individual nuclear family in Euro-America seemed to correspond with the competitive and individualistic values of the market place. The cycles of formation, breakup, and reformation of the extended family continued as Blacks migrated farther north and west towards the cities at the turn of the century during the pre and post periods of the two world wars and into the modern age.

The Black extended family, with its grandparents, biological parents,   10
conjugal partners, aunts, uncles, cousins, older siblings, boyfriends, girl-

[10] *milieu:* environment; setting.

a story about moving his nephew, a high school student, from the boy's mother's residence in Louisiana to his household in Berkeley, California. There were no major psychosocial adjustment problems associated with the nephew's making the transition from the Louisiana branch of the Nobles extended family to the Berkeley, California, branch. The problem came about when Dr. Nobles attempted to explain to the Internal Revenue Service how he came by an adolescent dependent in the space of one year with no legal papers to back him up. If Professor Nobles, who holds a Ph.D. from Stanford University, had difficulty explaining the composition of his extended family with the addition of this adolescent nephew, try to imagine what low-income Black aunties or grandmothers go through when they are trying to get aid for dependent children residing in their household who are not their biological or legal offspring, or for that matter what Black college freshmen go through trying to explain the income of their multiple extended-family parents divided by the number of dependent cousins, siblings, nieces, nephews, and fictional kin to college financial aid officers.

The Black child growing up in the extended family is exposed to a   17
variety of role models covering a wide age span whose social behaviors are not completely regulated by conventional sex roles. This offers the children a greater opportunity to incorporate a balanced pattern of expressive and instrumental behaviors. Since parents may not be equally effective as role models at every stage of the child's development, the presence of a range of role models allows the children a series of options at any stage of their development in terms of adults they might seek out for guidance. . . .

Works Cited

Blassingame, John. *The Slave Community*. New York: Oxford University Press, 1972.

Elkins, Stanley. *Slavery: A Problem in American Institutions and Intellectual Life*. Chicago: University of Chicago Press, 1968.

Frazier, E. Franklin. *The Negro Family in the United States*. Chicago: University of Chicago Press, 1939.

Fredrickson, George. "The Gutman Report," *The New York Review*, September 30, 1976, pp. 18–22, 27.

Gutman, Herbert. *The Black Family in Slavery and Freedom, 1750–1925*. New York: Vintage Books, 1976.

McAdoo, Harriet. "Black Kinship," *Psychology Today*, May 1979, pp. 67–69, 79, 110.

Moynihan, Daniel Patrick. *The Negro Family: The Case for National Action*. Washington, D.C.: U.S. Government Printing Office, 1965.

Nobles, Wade. "Africanity: Its Role in Black Families," *The Black Scholar*, June 1974, pp. 10–17.

———. "Toward an Empirical and Theoretical Framework for Defining Black Families," *Journal of Marriage and Family*, November 1978, pp. 679–688.

Rainwater, Lee. *Behind Ghetto Walls: Black Family Life in a Federal Slum*. Chicago: Aldine, 1970.

Rogers, Dorothy. *Adolescence: A Psychological Perspective*, 2nd Edition. Monterey, Calif.: Brooks/Cole, 1978.

Stack, Carol. *All Our Kin: Strategies for Survival in a Black Community*. New York: Harper & Row, 1974.

Engaging the Text

1. In the beginning of this selection, White presents what he terms the "deficit-deficiency model" of black family life. Describe this model in your own words. What assumptions underlie it? What is White's final evaluation of its effectiveness?

2. What does White mean when he says that the extended black family is "equalitarian" in nature (para. 10)?

3. In what sense has the extended black family provided a means of surviving "oppressive economic and social conditions" (para. 11)?

4. How does White account for what he sees as earlier misinterpretations of the black American family? How persuasive do you find his arguments?

Exploring Connections

1. Contrast White's model of the extended black family with the "perfect" nuclear family described earlier in this chapter by Skolnick.

2. Examine the way that the mother in Shirley Ann Grau's story "The Beginning" (p. 388) balances or fails to balance sexual roles. Does she succeed in combining assertive ("instrumental") behaviors with nurturing ("expressive") ones? How might White evaluate her as a role model?

3. Compare and contrast White's notion of the extended black family with the tribal family described earlier by Paula Gunn Allen (p. 273).

Extending the Critical Context

1. Taking several generations into consideration, describe the structure of your family. Does it conform to the general features of either the traditional nuclear family or the extended family? Would you describe it as equalitarian, matriarchal, or patriarchal? Does it reflect a particular "ethos"?

2. Examine the ways that black family members are portrayed in popular movies and TV shows. Do these portrayals still depend on the "deficit-deficiency" model?

3. As a class, debate whether the traditional nuclear family is, in fact, becoming more like the Afro-American family.

4. *The Cosby Show* has been praised and criticized because of its portrayal of black family life (see, for example, the selections by Martha Bayles and Mark C. Miller in Chapter Eight, "Television and the Consumption of Images"). To what extent do the Huxtables conform to or diverge from the model of the extended black family presented in this selection?

The Beginning

SHIRLEY ANN GRAU

"The Beginning" depicts the intimate relationship between a young black woman and her mother. This short story is in some ways a mirror image of the Hochschild memoir earlier in the chapter. In that piece, we observed an outwardly successful family whose personal relationships were severely deficient; in Grau's story — also told from the point of view of an adult trying to recreate her childhood — we witness a non-traditional and socially marginalized family, which nevertheless maintains strong personal bonds. Grau (b. 1929) won the Pulitzer Prize in 1965 for The Keepers of the House, *a novel about three generations of a Southern family. "The Beginning" appears in her recent collection of short stories,* Nine Women *(1985).*

In the beginning there was just my mother and me.   1

"You are," my mother would say, "the queen of the world, the jewel   2 of the lotus, the pearl without price, my secret treasure."

She whispered words like that, singsonging them in her soft high voice   3 that had a little tiny crackle in it like a scratched record, to comfort me when I was a baby. Her light high whisper threaded through all my days, linking them tightly together, from the day of my birth, from that first moment when I slid from her body to lie in the softness of her bed, the same bed she slept in now. The one we took with us from place to place. And there were many different places. We were wanderers, my mother and I. I even had a wicker basket for my toys; I would pack and carry them myself.

It mattered little to me where we lived. I did not go outside. I did 4
not go for walks, nor play on park swings. On the one day my mother
was home, on Sunday, we worked together, all the while she sang her
murmured song to me. Secret treasure. Lotus flower. And in her murmuring way she told me all she knew about my father, a Hindu from
Calcutta, a salesman of Worthington pumps. Of all the many men my
mother had known, he was the only one she had loved. She told me
about his thin face and his large eyes black as oil, and his skin that was
only slightly lighter than her own.

"You have his eyes and his skin," she said as, after my bath, she 5
rubbed me with oil. (It was baby oil, its vanilla scent soon lost in her
heavier perfume.) "And you have his hair," she said, combing in more
oil.

And there is, to be sure, a certain look of India about me. Even now, 6
in the grown woman.

"You are a little queen," my mother would say, turning me around 7
and around. "You are exquisite, a princess of all the world. You must
have a lovely new dress."

And so I would. She made all my clothes, made and designed. Summer 8
dresses of handkerchief linen and soft smooth voile, winter dresses of
dark rich velvets, and monk's-cloth coats so heavily smocked across the
shoulders they were almost waterproof.

Of course we couldn't afford to buy fabrics like that, not in those days. 9
My mother worked as a stock girl for Lambert Brothers Department
Store. She had worked there for years, even before I was born. Ever
since she'd come out of the country. (That was the way she put it, as
if it were the bottom of a well or a deep hole.) And Lambert Brothers
provided our material, quite a lot of it over the years. It all began on
a city bus when my mother met a clerk from the Perfection Cloth Shoppe.
They began talking, casually at first and then with purpose. My mother
exchanged a bottle of perfume or a box of dusting powder or some
Lancôme lipsticks from Lambert Brothers for small lengths of expensive
material from the Perfection Cloth Shoppe.

My mother never told me how she smuggled the cosmetics out of the 10
store. I suppose she'd been there so long and so faithfully that they half-
trusted her. She did tell me how she and her friend robbed the Perfection
Cloth Shoppe — a simple plan that worked for years.

My mother's friend collected the fabrics over a period of weeks, hiding 11
them among the hundreds of stacked bolts. When she saw her chance,
she bundled the pieces tightly and dropped them in a box of trash,
making a small red check on the outside. My mother had only to pass
along the service drive at the back of the building, look for the mark,

remove the package. That evening we spread out the material on our kitchen table (the only table we had) and admired it together. Only once did something go wrong. Once the trash was collected an hour earlier than usual and my beautiful dress went to the city incinerator. My mother and I managed to laugh about that.

During those early years, during the long dull hours checking stock   12
in dusty rooms, my mother began planning a business of her own, as dressmaker. My stolen clothes were the beginning. I was her model, the body on which her work came to life, the living sketchbook. Too small to see above the knees of adults, but perfectly quiet and perfectly composed, I displayed her clothes. My mother did not need to teach me how to walk or to act. Remember your father is an Indian prince and you are his only daughter, she would say to me. And so we made our rounds, peddling our wares, much like my father and his Worthington pumps. If he had traveled farther, half a world, our merchandise was far more beautiful. My mother and I went to talent shows and beauty contests, to church services and choir rehearsals. Wherever ladies gathered and the admission was free, there we were. My mother sold her clothes, as it were, from off my back.

"We are selling very well in the Afro-American community," my mother   13
would say. "Soon I will open a small showroom. The walls will be painted white and the only thing on them will be pictures of you. On every wall, the entire way around."

And eventually she did just that. I remember it very clearly, the white   14
room, quite bare and businesslike and lined with pictures of me. They were color photographs, very expensive for a woman just starting in business, but they showed the details of the clothes beautifully. My face, I remember, was rather blurred, but the light always seemed to catch the smooth line of my long dark hair. When I modeled for the customers (seated in creaking folding chairs and reeking with conflicting perfumes), my hair was always swept forward over one shoulder. My mother ironed it carefully in the dressing room at the very last moment. I remember the glare of the naked light bulbs around the mirror and the smell of singeing as my mother pressed my hair on her ironing board.

I don't remember saying a single word at any time. I have since   15
noticed that people usually speak to a child, but no one spoke to me. Perhaps they did not think I was quite real.

Twice a month, in the evenings, my mother did her books. For years   16
these were my favorite times. I sat, in my nightgown (always ankle length, always with a drawn-lace yoke), in the corner of the sofa, its red velvet worn and prickling on the sides of my arms, and watched my mother with her checkbooks and her account books and her order books.

I watched her pencil picking away at the pages, flicking, stabbing, moving. She was a very good bookkeeper. In different circumstances I suppose she would have gone to college and earned a CPA to put behind her name. But she didn't. She just remained somebody who was very quick with numbers. And there was another strange thing about her, though I didn't notice it until many years later. She was so good with figures, she spoke so very well in soft tones as soothing as a cough lozenge — but she could hardly read at all. She wasn't illiterate, but she read street signs and phone books, business forms and contracts all the same way: carefully, taking a very long time, sounding out the words. As a child, I thought that muttering was the way everyone read. (The nuns at school soon corrected me.) Eventually I just fell asleep on the old sofa with that comforting whispering lullaby in my ears.

When my mother picked me up to carry me to bed, which was next to hers, she would always be smiling. "The figures dance so beautifully for me, my little love. The Afro-American community is contributing devotedly to the treasure of the mahal. The daughters saw her and blessed her, also the queens and the concubines." (Someone had once read the Bible to my mother; bits and pieces kept appearing in her talk.) 17

In the morning when I woke, she was gone. At first, when I was very small, when I first remember things, like wet diapers and throwing up in my bed, there was someone who stayed with me, an old old woman who sat in a rocker all day long and listened to the radio. Her name was Miss Beauty. I don't remember her ever feeding me, but I suppose she must have. She died one day, in her rocking chair. I thought she was asleep so I went on playing with my doll. My cat — we kept one to kill the mice that played all over the old house — jumped on Miss Beauty's lap, then jumped down again quickly, coming to sit next to me in the window. "You heard her snore," I whispered to the cat, very severely. "Don't wake her, she won't like that at all." At the usual time I heard my mother's key in the lock and the funny little nine-note tune she whistled every evening just inside the door. (It was from *Lucia di Lammermoor*,[1] I discovered years later in a college music appreciation class, and I rose in my seat with the impact of memory.) I put my finger to my lips and pointed silently to Miss Beauty. My mother hesitated, eyes flicking between us, nose wrinkling like an animal. Without moving, she bent forward toward Miss Beauty. Then quickly, so quickly, with a clatter of feet across the linoleum floor, she snatched me up and ran outside. 18

[1]*Lucia di Lammermoor:* tragic opera (1835) by Gaetano Donizetti.

After Miss Beauty's death, there was no one. I stayed by myself. We   19
moved to a nicer neighborhood, a street with trees and double cottages
behind small front gardens. (The landlord had paved over our garden
with pale green cement.) I never felt afraid. If I got lonely, I could sit
in the big front window and watch the neighborhood children play in
the street. I never joined them.

During these years I do not remember my mother having any friends.   20
I remember only one visitor. He was short and wore a plaid coat and
a wide-brimmed hat, and the ring on his left hand flashed colored lights.
He was waiting for my mother when she came home after work. They
talked briefly, standing at the curb next to his big white car, then the
two of them came into the house. He smiled at me, saying, "Well, well,
now, is that your little girl? Hello there, little girl." My mother went
straight to the red sofa, reached inside the top cushion. When she turned
around, there was a gun in her hand. She just stood there, her long
fingers wrapped around that small dull-blue gun, both hands holding it
firm and steady. The man stopped smiling and backed out the door. He
never said another word. Nor did my mother.

We moved again then, away from the house with the front yard of   21
green-tinted cement. This time we packed and moved quickly, far away
across town. My mother rented a truck and she hired two men to load
it for us. She hurried them too. Our beds, the red velvet sofa, the two
folding bridge chairs, the refrigerator and the gas stove, the enamel-
topped kitchen table, the armoire with the cracked mirrored doors —
they fitted neatly into the truck along with the boxes of clothes and
dishes and my mother's sewing machine, which was the only new thing
we owned.

"Hurry," my mother said, carrying some of the smaller things herself,   22
"we haven't got all day. I am paying you to be quick."

Grumbling and complaining, the men finished the loading and took   23
their money and stood on the sidewalk to watch us leave.

"Get in," my mother said to me. "Be quick."   24

We drove down highways lined with withered brown palm trees, past   25
endless intersections where traffic lights stabbed out their signals like
lighthouses. We waited, part of an impatient horn-blowing crowd, while
canal bridges opened to let gravel-filled barges glide past through oily
water.

And my mother said nothing at all. When I could wait no longer,   26
when the silence between us seemed more dangerous and frightening
than any nightmare, I asked, "Why are we running away?"

"To be safe," she said. 27

"Is it far?" 28

"It is far enough to be safe," she said. 29

When we finally reached the place where we would live, she hired 30
two more neighborhood men to take our things up the stairs. She had
moved without leaving a trace behind.

I guessed it had something to do with her visitor, but I did not worry. 31
In all the stories my mother had told me, there were always threats and
pursuits and enemies to be avoided. It was the way a princess lived.
And my mother was always there, to bring me to safety at last.

When we sat in our new home, in the clutter of boxes and furniture, 32
when we were safely inside, the door locked behind us, my mother
smiled at me, a great slow smile that showed square strong teeth in the
smooth darkness of her face. "My hidden princess," she said, "my lotus
flower . . ."

The accustomed endearments tumbled from her lips, the expected 33
exotic song of love and praise. I, young as I was, noted the change. For
the past few days, and on the drive across town, she had spoken rarely,
and then only in the crisp blunt language of everyday.

Now, by the smooth soft flow of her words, I knew that we were 34
indeed safe. We had passed through a series of lodgings — I think I
remember them all, even the one where I was born, the one with a
chinaberry tree outside the window — but we had finally gained our
castle, the one we had been searching for. There was even a turret, to
command the approaches and to defend against enemies.

The house stood on a corner. Its old clapboard walls rose directly from 35
the sidewalk through two stories of flaking gray paint to a roof decorated
with fancy wooden scallops; in the dark spaces under the eaves generations
of pigeons nested and fluttered. At the second-floor corner, jutting over
the sidewalk, was a small turret or tower, capped with a high pointed
roof like a clown's hat.

Inside the tower was a hinged seat of varnished wood entirely covered 36
by scratch drawings: flowers and initials and hearts, dancing stick figures
and even a face or two. Here we stored odd bits of things: old shoes,
an umbrella with a broken rib, a doll in a pink and blue gingham dress,
an Easter bunny of purple and yellow plush, a black patent purse.
Roaches lived there too; they ate the stuffing from the doll and the
feather from her hat, and they ate spots of fur from the Easter bunny
so that it looked burned. I thought they had also nibbled the edge of
the patent leather purse, but my mother said no, it was just use-worn.

Day after day, I sat on top that jumble of things, above the secret 37 workings of insects, and I watched through the windows, three panes of glass on the three sides of my tower, which my mother washed every month, so that I might see clearly.

Most of the floor below us was occupied by a drugstore, a small dark 38 place that smelled of disinfectant and sugar candy, of brown paper and cough medicine. On two of the other corners were small houses, one room wide, perched off the ground on low brick foundations and edged by foot-wide runners of grass. On the third corner, directly across from my window was Providence Manor, a home for the old. A tall iron fence enclosed an entire block of grass and trees and even occasional blooming flowers, a wilderness that stretched out of my sight. Just inside the fence was a gravel path where, on good days, the old people walked, some slowly on canes, some with arms flexing rapidly in a military march, some in chairs wheeled by nuns in black habits and white headdresses. They rotated past the spear points of the fence, every good day taking their quota of sun and exhaust-laden air. After dark, on rainy nights, the flashing sign in the drugstore window beat against those railings, broke and ran off down the shiny black street.

Downstairs too, directly below, in our small slice of the old house, 39 were the two rooms that were my mother's workshop and showroom. On our front door — up two wooden steps from the uneven brick sidewalk — was a small neat sign: MODISTE. My mother had lettered that herself; she had always been very clever with her hands. It was the first real shop she had.

I spent my days either at my window or in my mother's workrooms. 40 The rest of the house, the other two rooms, I don't remember at all. I was either a princess in my tower or a mannequin in my mother's clothes.

Not until years later did I realize that all the faces I saw were black. 41 (To me they had no color, no color at all.) The people walking on the street, the old on their therapeutic rounds, the Sisters of the Holy Family, the drivers impatiently threading their way through the heavy street traffic, my mother, and her customers — they all wore black skin.

As did the children in school. Eventually I had to go to school. My 42 mother did not send me when I was six, as the law said she must. For one extra year I dreamed and flaunted my beautiful dresses. I doubt that the authorities would have noticed had I not gone to school at all. I think it was my mother's new friend who finally persuaded her. For my mother at last had a friend, a good friend whose visits were regular and predictable. For him my mother bathed and did her hair and cooked specially and smiled when the doorbell rang.

My mother's friend was a tall, heavy man who came to church with 43 us every Sunday and afterwards held my hand as I walked along the top of the low wall that bordered the churchyard. He owned a small cab company — he drove one himself — whose insignia was a lightning bolt across a bright blue circle. His name was David Clark, and he took me to school and picked me up every day of my first year.

I went to parochial school. Navy skirts and white blouses and black 44 and white saddle oxfords, all of us. All of us, rows of little black raisins, waiting to be taught to read and to count and to love Lord Jesus. But I was the only one picked up by taxi every day at three o'clock. The children stared at me as I rode away, the Indian princess in her palanquin,[2] the treasure of the mahal above Leconte's Drugstore.

On the first day of school my mother went with me. I remember very little about that day — I was nauseated with excitement, gripped with fear — but I remember the dress she wore. She had made it herself of course, just as she had made my school uniform; it was brown linen, a long-sleeved blouse and an eight-gore[3] skirt. I saw the nuns' eyes flick over us in brief appraisal: We passed with honors. (I took it as my due. I wonder now how my mother felt.)

The school smelled of peanuts and garlic bologna. The floor of my 46 classroom was spotted with puddles of slimy liquid. Oddly enough, the other children's panic quieted me. In the reek of their nervousness, my own stomach settled, and when the harried janitor arrived with a bucket of sawdust to sprinkle on the vomit, I helped him by pushing aside the desks.

That first day was the longest I have ever known. And the hottest. It 47 was early September and the afternoon sun burned through the window shades to polish our faces with sweat — all except the teaching sister. Her face remained dry and dull as if coated with a film of dust.

I never grew used to the noise and rush of children leaving class. 48 When the bell sounded, I always waited while the room emptied. Then, in a pause disturbed only by the soft sounds of the teacher gathering her papers, I walked slowly through the door, last and alone. Always alone, except for once, years later when I was at boarding school at St. Mary's, mine the only dark face in a sea of Irish skin. (The other girls simply ignored me, saw through me as if I were invisible or transparent.) By the time I had gathered my books and reached the door, their departing backs were far down the hall. But at St. Mary's I was not alone. My companion was a moonfaced child of my own age who had rheumatoid arthritis, took massive doses of cortisone, and moved with

---

[2]*palanquin:* a covered passenger carriage carried by several men (found in India and other Asian countries).
[3]*gore:* a panel of cloth. An eight-gore skirt is quite elaborate.

the slow painful dignity of an ancient woman. She died in our second year of high school. I, along with every other girl in the school, wrote a letter of condolence to her parents. Mine was never acknowledged.

But that was in the future, in the time when I was no longer a child, 49 a good many years away.

For first grade, I had two skirts, made by my mother according to 50 the uniform dress code of the parochial school system, and two blouses. Every second day, when I came home, I was expected to wash my blouse carefully, using the kitchen sink and a small scrubbing board that my mother kept underneath, propped against the pipes. I then hung it on the back porch inside the screen, where no bird could soil it. Every so often my mother was dissatisfied with its whiteness and she would wash it again in bleach. The next time I wore that blouse I was certain to have a rash across my neck and shoulders where the fabric rubbed my skin.

Later on, when my growing required new blouses (the skirts had deep 51 hems to let down), my mother made them slightly different. She added small tucks down the front, two tiny rows on each side of the buttons. I noticed the nuns looking at me — they were very strict about uniforms in those days — and they must have written to my mother. My next blouses were perfectly plain. What the nuns couldn't know about were my slips. My mother made my slips too, and they had all the elaborate decorations that my blouses lacked. They were tucked, with drawn lace and wide bands of crochet at the shoulders, and a deep flounce of lace at the hem. Only one nun ever saw them and she wasn't really a nun. She was a novice: very young, shorter even than I was. She was cleaning the bathrooms and I, not noticing her, was fanning myself with my skirt against the heat. She stopped and fingered my slip. "What lovely work, what exquisite work." Then she looked shocked and ashamed — perhaps she had made a vow of silence — and she went hastily back to her pail and mop.

After the first year at school, I took the city bus home. The stop was 52 at our corner. All I had to do was cross the street and open the door. Once inside, I rushed to bathe, to brush my hair, to put on the dresses that my mother would sell. Wearing her clothes and her dreams, I would move carefully among her customers, gracefully, as only a princess can.

The lotus blossom. The treasure of the mahal. In the women's faces 53 I saw greed and covetousness. My mother's order books rustled busily. I myself drew spirit and sustenance from the flickering eyes and the fingers stretched out to touch. In the small crowded room, I had come into my castle and my kingdom.

And so I passed my childhood disguised to myself as a princess. I   54
thrived, grew strong and resilient. When the kingdom at last fell and
the castle was conquered, and I lost my crown and my birthright, when
I stood naked and revealed as a young black female of illegitimate birth,
it hardly mattered. By then the castle and the kingdom were within me
and I carried them away.

Engaging the Text

1. Describe the relationship between the NARRATOR and her mother. How do
you account for their social isolation?

2. Using specific evidence from the story, debate whether or not the mother
here is a "good mother."

3. Write a straightforward chronological account of the events in these CHARACTERS'
lives, being sure to fill in events that are hinted at but not narrated directly.
What effect does Grau's less direct storytelling have on your feelings toward the
characters?

4. What is the effect of the biblical ALLUSION in the story's first sentence?

Exploring Connections

1. Consider the role of the family as portrayed in Gloria Naylor's "The Two"
(Chapter Four, "Women"), as well as the role the immigrant family in the
experiences of writers like Hank López and Maxine Hong Kingston (Chapter
Three, "One Nation or Many?"). What effects does being outside MAINSTREAM
culture have on families?

Extending the Critical Context

1. The narrator of this story views her family differently than an outsider might.
Describe your own family, first as you think an outside observer would and then
as you see it yourself.

Friends as Family

KAREN LINDSEY

In this introduction to her book, Friends as Family *(1981),* Lindsey *proposes a tantalizing and controversial thesis — that families need not be defined by biological relationships, but may be "chosen." In clearing the ground to make this argument, she also offers some startling information about the history of the family. Lindsey (b. 1944) is a teacher, editor, and freelance writer whose work often reflects her radical feminist viewpoint.*

The traditional family isn't working. This should not come as a startling   1
revelation to anyone who picks up this book: It may be the single fact
on which every American, from the Moral Majority member. through
the radical feminist, agrees. Statistics abound: 50 percent of couples
married since 1970 and 33 percent of those married since 1950 are
divorced. One out of every six children under eighteen lives with only
one parent. The number of children living in families headed by women
more than doubled between 1954 and 1975.[1] The family no longer has
room for aged parents. Increasing numbers of the elderly live alone or
in nursing homes: Only 11 percent live with their children or with other
relatives.[2]

Even when the family stays together, it often does so under grim   2
conditions. As many as 60 percent of all married women are beaten at
least once by their husbands.[3] One in every hundred children is beaten,
sexually molested, or severely neglected by parents.[4] And between 500,000
and one million elderly parents are abused each year by the adult offspring
they live with.[5] Whatever the family in the United States is, it isn't
Father Knows Best.[6]

[1] Susan Dworkin, "Carter Wants to Save the Family, but He Can't Even Save His Family Conference," *Ms.*, September 1987, pp. 62, 98. [Author's note]
[2] Beth B. Hess, *Growing Old in America* (New Brunswick, N.J.: Transaction Books, 1976), p. 26. [Author's note]
[3] Terry Davidson, *Conjugal Crime: Understanding and Changing the Wifebeating Pattern* (New York: Hawthorn, 1978), pp. 6–7. [Author's note]
[4] Naomi Feigelson Chase, *A Child Is Being Beaten* (New York: Holt, Rinehart, & Winston, 1975), p. 185. [Author's note]
[5] Lynn Langway, "Unveiling a Family Secret," *Newsweek*, Feb. 18, 1980, pp. 104–106. [Author's note]
[6] *Father Knows Best:* 1950s TV show featuring a highly idealized family.

There are a lot of people who refuse to believe this, who prefer to attribute both the problems within families and the increasing breakup of families to the "new narcissism" or the evils of the "me generation." This theory, promulgated by many conservatives and liberals, and legitimized by intellectual pseudo-leftists like Christopher Lasch,[7] suggests (Lasch, at least, is shrewd enough never to come out and say it) that if people would only stop worrying about their own personal fulfillment and return to the loving bosom of the patriarchal family, the world would be a happy place. Such apologists for the family tend to ignore the issue of intrafamily abuse, since it paints a somewhat different portrait of "those basic things we used to know." 3

Lasch is totally remarkable in this regard: In neither his massively popular *The Culture of Narcissism* nor his earlier and even more reactionary *Haven in a Heartless World*[8] does he discuss wife abuse or child abuse. Indeed, to perpetuate the myth of the new narcissism, he can't *afford* to acknowledge family violence. The myth of the new narcissism is more than a myth. It's also a lie. And it's important to remember that, although we often confuse the two, "myth" and "lie" are not by definition synonyms. Myth, as the dictionary tells us, is "a traditional story of ostensible historical events that serves to unfold part of the world view of a people or explain a practice, belief, or natural phenomenon." Or, as the introduction to *World Mythology* says, it is "the spontaneous defense of the human mind faced with an unintelligible or hostile world."[9] 4

Objective reality neither affirms nor negates a myth. Athena and Zeus never existed; Jesus existed but little is known about his life; George Washington, Florence Nightingale, and Bo Derek are real people about whom a great deal is known. But all exist mythically, apart from their objective existence or nonexistence. 5

What is true of mythical people is true of mythical concepts. Heaven and hell, the nuclear family, the Russian Revolution: All are myths, though clearly two are also historical facts. They are myths because, apart from whatever reality they have, the way in which we view them helps clarify, even shape, our vision of the world. It is in this sense that I speak of the myth of the family. 6

The myth of the new narcissism bases itself on the myth of the family. As Lasch and others conceptualize it, the theory of the new narcissism 7

---

[7]Christopher Lasch: See p. 533.

[8]Christopher Lasch, *The Culture of Narcissism* (New York: Warner Books, 1979), and *Haven in a Heartless World* (New York: Basic Books, 1977). [Author's note]

[9]Pierre Grimal, ed., *Larousse World Mythology* (London: The Hamlin Publishing Group, 1965), p. 9. [Author's note]

is that nobody cares about social causes any more, nobody cares about anybody else, and everyone is single-mindedly devoted to self-fulfillment. People of the '70s took the liberation ideologies of the '60s and individualized them, creating a selfish and decadent society concerned only with material or psychological gain. This was symbolized most strongly by the breakdown of the family. The agenda of the '80s is thus clear: Return to the good old days, before the breakdown of the nuclear family.

According to this new myth, the world is now divided into *Cosmopolitan* 8 or *Redbook*:[10] You can have a life of sex clubs and high-powered careers or a life of Mommy staying home and cooking, Daddy going to work all day and spending the evening at home, and 2.4 happy and obedient kids. There is nothing else. The acceptance of these alternatives as the parameters of human experience leaves us little real choice. If we wish to retain our humanity — to be caring, nurturing people and, by the same token, cared-for and nurtured people — we must opt for the traditional family. Whatever evils we perceive in the nuclear family, the freedom to live without human relationships is ultimately no freedom, but hell. And so the acceptance of the myth as truth has the very real possibility of turning us — at least women — into collaborators in our own oppression.

The myth of the new narcissism is a perfect example of what Mary 9 Daly calls "false naming." False naming, Daly argues, creates a concept of reality which is a tool of oppression: It invents a definition of reality and forces us to live under the terms of that definition. Speaking specifically of the oppression of women, Daly writes: "Women have had the power of naming stolen from us. We have not been free to use our own power to name ourselves, the world, or god . . . women are now realizing that the universal imposing of names by men has been false because partial. That is, inadequate words have been taken as adequate."[11]

And so it is essential to our survival to name the lie, to look beyond 10 the words to the reality they obscure. To do this, we must start with the base of the myth — the notion that there was once an ideally happy family which has only recently been destroyed by the forces of organized selfishness. Whether that ideal family is supposed to have occurred in the confines of the historically recent nuclear family, or in the older extended family, it exists as a vision of that which has been destroyed,

---

[10] *Cosmopolitan* or *Redbook:* two popular magazines for women, with two very different audiences, as Lindsey indicates.

[11] Mary Daly, *Beyond God the Father: Toward a Philosophy of Women's Liberation* (Boston: Beacon Press, 1973), p. 8. [Author's note]

that to which we must return. As Will Rogers[12] said, things ain't the way they used to be, and maybe they never were.

When *was* the Golden Age of the happy family? Mythmakers vary on   11
this question, but their most common image suggests it was sometime during the nineteenth century that the world was a Norman Rockwell[13] painting. (Lasch, perhaps the shrewdest of the Golden Age mythologizers, never places it in any historical period, though he repeatedly implies that it did indeed exist.) Was it in 1869, when John Stuart Mill wrote *The Subjugation of Women*, decrying the fact that thousands of husbands routinely "indulge in the utmost habitual excesses of bodily violence towards the unhappy wife"?[14] Was it in 1878, when Frances Power Cobbe wrote of the area of Liverpool known as the "kicking district" because so many of its residents kicked their wives' faces with hobnailed boots?[15] Was it in 1890, when the *Encyclopaedia Britannica* noted that the "modern crime of infanticide shows no symptoms of diminishing in the leading nations of Europe"?[16] Was it a little earlier — in the 1830s or '40s, when thousands of temperance societies sprang up throughout the United States in response to the growing number of abusive drunken men? "The drunken spouse could (and did) spend the family money as he chose, sell off his and his wife's property, apprentice their children, and assault wife and children alike."[17]

Perhaps, then, the nineteenth century is too late in history — perhaps   12
the evils of industrialism had taken hold and destroyed the Golden Age. Perhaps we need to look back further to find our happy family — maybe to the Middle Ages, before the forces of industry had torn the family apart, when husband, wife, and children all worked the farm together in domestic harmony. The only problem is that during this period, "men were exhorted from the pulpit to beat their wives and their wives to kiss the rod that beat them. The deliberate teaching of domestic violence, combined with the doctrine that women and children by nature could have no human rights, had taken such hold by the late Middle Ages

[12]*Will Rogers:* U.S. humorist and actor (1879–1935).

[13]*Norman Rockwell:* U.S. painter and illustrator (1894–1978), famous for idealized portraits of American life.

[14]Davidson, p. 108. [Author's note]

[15]Davidson, p. 110. [Author's note]

[16]Chase, p. 17. Infanticide itself seems to have occurred chiefly among the poor — though as always there is reason to suspect its occurrence, discreetly covered up, in more affluent families as well. [Author's note]

[17]Judith Papachristou, *Women Together* (New York: Knopf, 1976), p. 19. [Author's note]

that men had come to treat their wives and children worse than their beasts."[18]

Well, there's always the Renaissance,[19] bringing light to the primitive 13 mentality bred by the Middle Ages. The Spanish scholar Vives, so influential in the court of England under Henry VIII and his first wife, Katharine of Aragón, is usually viewed as one of the more enlightened intellects of the era: He was influential in spreading the theory that girls, as well as boys, should be well educated. He, like dozens of other scholars in the Tudor[20] era, published tracts on childrearing and domestic harmony. Vives wrote approvingly that he knew "many fathers to cut the throats of their daughters, bretheren of their sisters, and kinsmen of their kins-women" when these unfortunate women were discovered to be unchaste.[21] He explained that his own mother had never "lightly laughed upon me, she never cockered me . . . Therefore there was nobody that I did more flee, or was more loath to come nigh, than my mother, when I was a child." Showing affection, or "cherishing," he said, "marreth sons, but it utterly destroyeth daughters."[22]

It was perhaps fortunate for both daughters and sons that they *didn't* 14 feel too comfortable at home, since they were likely to be betrothed at infancy and married off in adolescence — often, in the case of upper-class offspring, never to see their families again. Margaret Beaufort, grandmother of Henry VIII, was married off at 12, gave birth to Henry Tudor,[23] and never had another child — probably as a result of early childbirth. Her granddaughter, Margaret of Scotland, was also forced to marry at 12, and left her home to live with her husband, the King of Scotland; her letters home are filled with misery and homesickness.[24]

Wifebeating and childbeating were approved by most of the tractwriters 15 of the time, though often the husband was advised to use physical abuse only as a last resort. Needless to say many husbands *didn't* obey these pious exhortations. On at least one occasion, the Duke of Norfolk (Anne

---

[18] Davidson, p. 98. [Author's note]

[19] *Renaissance:* the intellectual and artistic movement which spread from 14th-century Italy to the rest of Europe by the 17th century.

[20] *Tudor:* the royal dynasty in England from 1485 to 1603.

[21] Lu Emily Pearson, *Elizabethans at Home* (Stanford, Calif.: Stanford University Press, 1957), p. 248. [Author's note]

[22] H. F. M. Prescott, *Mary Tudor* (New York: Macmillan, 1953), p. 26. [Author's note]

[23] Alison Plowden, *Tudor Women* (New York: Atheneum, 1979), p. 8. [Author's note]

[24] Alison Plowden, *The House of Tudor* (New York: Stein & Day, 1976), p. 47. [Author's note]

Boleyn's uncle) had his servants help him beat his wife; they stopped only when blood began pouring out of her mouth.[25]

The statistics on physical abuse in various historical periods tell us 16 something about family violence in the past. But they don't tell us about the nonviolent forms of misery in people's lives. We can make assumptions about the viability of marriage and family life today because divorce is permissible: People who leave their families are presumably unhappy in them. But how do we know what human misery (as well as human happiness) existed among people who had no option but to live together? How many parents despised the children they had no choice but to raise? How many wives loathed their husbands; how many husbands hated their wives? How many people lived together in a helpless toleration that later ages would call contentment? Such records as we have are usually diaries and letters written by members of privileged classes — people who could read and write, people who had the luxury of privacy in which to record their thoughts.

The story of Anne Askew, the sixteenth-century Protestant martyr who 17 wrote about her life and religion as she awaited execution, and whose maid was able to smuggle the document to the exiled Bishop Bale, provides a terse but poignant picture of miserable cohabitation between a brilliant young woman and a cloddish, conservative husband.[26] How many other Anne Askews were there whose stories were never told, even to their closest friends? We have the words of Lady Jane Grey, the doomed child who was to briefly become England's queen in the same era, complaining to the scholar Roger Ascham of her parents' abuses and coldness. How many such children never voiced their complaints, or voiced them to less-concerned listeners than hers?[27] We are told by Martin Luther, the leading light of the Protestant Reformation, that his parents were severe and abusive, and his childhood miserable.[28] We have a chilling vision of intra-family hatred in the story of the 350 Lollard heretics discovered in Lincoln County in 1521. The reason so many were caught is that parents and children, husbands and wives, eagerly informed against each other.[29] How many people in how many eras would have

[25] Lacey Baldwin Smith, *A Tudor Tragedy: The Life and Times of Catherine Howard* (New York: Pantheon, 1961), p. 28. [Author's note]

[26] John Bale, *Select Works* (London: Parker Society, 1849), pp. 140–240. [Author's note]

[27] Mary M. Luke, *A Crown for Elizabeth* (New York: Coward-McCann, 1970), p. 191. [Author's note]

[28] Philip Hughes, *A Popular History of the Reformation* (Garden City, N.Y.: Hanover House, 1957), p. 98. [Author's note]

[29] A. G. Dickens, *The English Reformation* (New York: Schocken, p. 27). [Author's note]

left their husbands, wives, and parents if there had been any possibility of their doing so?

There is another aspect of family which the proponents of the Golden   18
Age like to ignore: The family has always been a very different reality for each of its members. The father had absolute power over all the other members; the mother had some power over her sons and very much power over her daughters; the son was under his parents' control, but knew that one day he would probably be able to rule his own family and perhaps even the mother who now ruled him; the daughter had no power and could anticipate little. The family may well have been — and may well still be — a "haven from the heartless world" for many men. But for women and children, it has always been the very *center* of the heartless world, from which no haven existed. For man, the limits of the family have been tacitly recognized, and legitimate or quasi-legitimate institutions have been established to supplement their needs. Men have always been permitted mistresses, even if official morality has shaken its head; women have rarely been able to get by with taking lovers. The very existence of prostitution, which has always coexisted with the family, offers implicit approval of men's search for extrafamilial fulfillment. Both Saint Augustine and Saint Thomas Aquinas recognized this, when they likened prostitution to a sewer, ugly but necessary to keep the palace functioning.[30] Monogamous marriage, which the Golden Agers celebrate, has usually meant only monogamous wifehood.

I'm not trying to suggest that families have always been devoid of   19
love, or caring, of the "cherishing" that Vives found so destructive. There are records of happy families, as there are records of unhappy ones. And in any event the human need for communication, for sharing, for love would certainly find a way to be satisfied in almost any situation. The very quality of shared experience, shared history can build strong bonds of love and affection among people. In a family, in a commune, in a prison, people can make deep and indissoluble connections with one another. But if it isn't recognized that the family, historically, *was* a prison, which people entered not by choice but by necessity, the real happiness as well as the real misery becomes mythologized into something quite distinct from the reality. The family becomes, in Daly's words, a creation of false naming.

The false naming that creates the myth of the happy traditional family   20
has its corollary in the false naming that says life outside the family is miserable and empty, that people who choose childlessness have no real

[30] Simone de Beauvoir, *The Second Sex* (New York: Bantam, 1961), p. 95. [Author's note]

relationships with children or with the future, and that friends are never as fulfilling as family. In our culture, there is family, and there are friends. Sometimes friendship is deep, even heroic — especially, perhaps exclusively, among men. Damon and Pythias,[31] Jonathan and David.[32] But mostly, friendship is secondary: Friends are who you pass pleasant time with, who you like but don't love, to whom you make minimal if any commitment. Above all, *friends are not family*. Blood is thicker than water. Your friends are always "other"; your family is who you are. Friends, in that most demeaning of phrases, are "just friends." And we have believed it; we have mystified it and mythologized it. We have taken the lie for the truth, and in doing so we have almost made it true.

But people are larger than the myths they try to live by. And the 21 truth hidden by the myth is that people have always created larger families than the biological family — larger, and infinitely more diverse. It has been there for many of us, perhaps for most of us, and we have always said to ourselves, this is different, this is me and my life, this has nothing to do with the way things are.

Side by side with the language of our oppression, other phrases have 22 evolved and been assimilated into our vocabulary without our understanding their importance: "She's been a second mother to me." "He's just like a brother." "You are the daughter I've never had." "We're all one big happy family." Why have we never suspected that these innocuous phrases contain as much revolutionary potential as anything Karl Marx[33] or Emma Goldman[34] or Mary Wollstonecraft[35] ever said? Such phrases suggest that the family is something more than your husband or wife and the offspring of you and your spouse and the people who are related to you because somebody somewhere has the same blood parent, that someone totally outside the limits of that kinship definition can be your family. The family isn't what we've been taught it is. Thus we are not trapped between the Scylla and Charybdis[36] that the lie of the new

[31] *Damon and Pythias:* in classical mythology, Damon pledged his life to help his friend Pythias.

[32] *Jonathan and David:* in the Old Testament, Jonathan was the son of King Saul of Israel. He saved David from Saul's jealous attack on David's life. See 1 Samuel.

[33] *Karl Marx:* German social and political theorist (1818–83), founder of communism.

[34] *Emma Goldman:* Russian-born American anarchist, speaker, and publisher (1869–1940). She was imprisoned for obstructing the draft and for advocating birth control and was deported in 1919.

[35] *Mary Wollstonecraft:* English writer (1759–1797), one of the first to advocate equal rights for women and men.

[36] *Scylla and Charybdis:* a deadly pair of threats; in classical mythology, they were sea monsters identified with a rock and a whirlpool.

narcissism offers; we do not need to choose between living without human bondings, or with bondings not of our choice. We can create our own bondings, choose them as they meet our needs; we can define, with others we have chosen and who have chosen us, what the nature of our bondings will be.

I think that some of the power that marriage has had for us — at least 23 for women, although possibly for men as well — lies in this concept of choice. In an era when half of all marriages end in divorce, when couples openly live together, when the taint of "illegitimacy" is fading, marriage still has a powerful hold on women. And the power isn't only over women of the mainstream. Radical and socialist feminists marry; women who have lived with their lovers marry; women who have lived with *many* lovers marry. Even women who eschew monogamy marry. Sometimes they marry to placate parents, sometimes to make life easier for the children they plan to have. But I suspect that often these are simply the surface explanations for far more fundamental, more mythic, reasons.

The mythic power of marriage is threefold. To begin with, it offers a 24 feeling of protection, of economic security. Historically, this has been accurate. A woman without a husband to protect her was at the mercy of her relatives and of strangers. The only other economically viable option was the convent, and even here a woman might find herself the "poor relation" of nuns from more affluent or prestigious families. Even today in the United States, women earn 59 percent of what men earn, and the poor are largely made up of women and their children.[37]

The second, and related, mythic power of marriage rests in its promise 25 of permanence. The myth of true-love-forever may be comparatively recent, but a few centuries is long enough to embed a myth into a culture. Further, the permanence of marriage predates romantic love. A man might abuse his wife, he might take on mistresses, he might functionally desert her. But he — or his kin, when he fails to meet his obligations — must support her and their children, and abandonment of one's wife carries strong social censure. Henry VIII's fame as an historic ogre rests not on his dissolution of the monasteries and consequent impoverishment of thousands of monks, nuns, and the beggars who relied on them for charity, not on his arbitrary executions of hundreds of "papists" and "heretics," but on his open willingness to discard, through divorce and execution, four wives. Especially when a woman has children, she is given the right to expect that her husband, whose bloodline she has preserved, will continue to provide for her needs.

[37] Judy Foreman, "9 to 5 grows, so does its clout," *The Boston Globe*, Sept. 28, 1979. [Author's note]

The third myth, and the one that is the concern of this book, is that   26
of the spouse as chosen relative. It is true that only in very recent history
has a woman had any actual choice in whom she marries, that it has
historically been assumed that a spouse will be chosen by the parents
of both men and women. But alongside this reality has always existed
the story of the woman who defies the rule — who chooses, or attempts
to choose, her mate. Cleopatra[38] chose Marc Anthony, Dido[39] chose
Aeneas, and in so doing they destroyed both their empires and their
lives.

This is a negative image of choice, and in any case most women don't   27
have the options available to women who rule nations. But the stories
of royalty have always provided the mythology of the lower classes, and
at the very least these stories introduce the *concept* of choice into the
selection of a mate. In recent centuries, the concept has significantly
changed. The choice has been transmuted into a good one; it is worth
losing everything to maintain the integrity of that choice, select one's
true love, and reject the choice of others, even when that choice seems
more sensible. Indeed, in contemporary mythology, that choice often
guarantees happiness — marry Mr. Right and your troubles are over.

But however the myth varies, its power rests in the fact that except   28
in the atypical instance of adoption, your spouse is the only relative you
are ever permitted to choose. You are born to your parents and, by
extension, to their kin, and you raise the children you give birth to.
The young, modern woman who chooses her mate has behind her a
string of spiritual ancestors as long as Banquo's ghost,[40] ancestors to
whom, at least once, however briefly, the thought of choosing their own
mates must have occurred. It is a thought so monumental that its very
existence must have changed something in the mind of its thinker. Few
women could have voiced this change, and even fewer could have acted
on it. But we are the heirs of that change nonetheless.

Now an even greater concept has entered into our minds. We can   29
choose most of our family. We can choose *all* of our family. In some
ways, recognition of this possibility has begun to surface in popular

---

[38] *Cleopatra:* Queen of Egypt (69–30 B.C.) After two marriages in Egypt and an affair
with Caesar, Cleopatra married Mark Anthony, a potential rival from Rome who fell in
love with her. They eventually committed suicide after military defeats by Roman forces.

[39] *Dido:* in Roman mythology, the Queen of Carthage. Virgil's *Aeneid* describes her love
for Aeneas, a shipwrecked Trojan. When he continued his journey, she threw herself on
a burning pyre.

[40] *Banquo's ghost:* a reference to Shakespeare's *Macbeth* (IV.i); Macbeth, who has murdered
Banquo, sees an apparition of eight kings of Banquo's lineage.

culture. Recently, several magazines published articles about the need to create new, familial ways to celebrate holidays, and described festive scenes shared by former and current spouses, in-laws from both marriages, and offspring from the divorced parents' current and former marriages.

As far as it goes, this represents an important step in breaking through the oppressive definitions of family. For people who have shared history, who have loved each other and lived through major parts of each other's lives together, the concept of "family" should apply, in much the same way as it applied to parents and grown siblings who no longer live together or share the same interests but who are indelibly part of one another's lives.

But it isn't only spouses who share or have shared each other's lives, who have created a common past with each other. Friends, neighbors, co-workers have often lived through as many experiences together as husbands and wives — have created, perhaps unconsciously, equally strong bonds. And slowly these bonds too are seeping into popular mythology.

A good barometer of the change is television, which is probably the most potent force in mid-twentieth-century American mythmaking. In the '50s, the model of the family was clear-cut. Mommy, Daddy, and the kids. *Father Knows Best. I Remember Mama. Ozzie and Harriet. Make Room for Daddy. I Love Lucy. Life of Riley.* Even *Burns and Allen*, miles ahead of the others in wit and sophistication, showed two nuclear families, and the Burns' had a son (though he never appeared till the later episodes). Only *My Little Margie*, saccharine sweet as it was, dared to veer from the accepted family norm: Daddy was a widower who lived with his grown daughter.

In the '60s, things began to change. Divorce was a social reality, but a fantasy taboo, so TV compromised. The mortality rate among television spouses soared: Suddenly widows and widowers with kids were the norm. *The Diahann Carroll Show. The Doris Day Show. The Andy Griffith Show. The Partridge Family.* And then the crème de la crème, *The Brady Bunch*: Widow with cute large brood marries widower with cute large brood, re-creating the two-parent family with a vengeance. It was an interesting attempt to cover up by half admitting what was happening to the family. Viewers who were divorced or separated could identify with the one-parent (or re-created two-parent) family, but could not have the validity of their own experience confirmed. Death is a tragedy, not a choice: The family still works until something more cosmic than human need disrupts it.

By the '70s even that wasn't enough, and the workplace family began to achieve some recognition. It started with *The Mary Tyler Moore*

Show. Mary Richards, the character Moore played, had just broken off with her boyfriend and had come to Minneapolis to seek a job. Her co-workers and her best friend, Rhoda, became her family. This was no accident: The characters on the show *talked* about being a family. In one episode, Rhoda refused a job in New York because it would separate her from Mary. With little fanfare, *The Mary Tyler Moore Show* tastefully broke a taboo.

Then there was *Mod Squad,* the story of three stereotypically alienated 35
kids who become cops, and in the process also become each other's family. Corny as that show was (and reactionary in its basic theme — three dropouts become narcs), a caring and commitment among the three came through as it never did in any other cop show. The relationship, in fact, may have scared some of its creators. A year or two ago, they aired a two-hour special, *Return of the Mod Squad,* in which the three, now living separate lives, are reunited essentially to establish that the old "family" was an adolescent phase and they have now outgrown each other.

But the model of on-the-job families continues — perhaps to reassure 36
all the divorced people, the not-yet-married people, the not-in-romantic-relationship people, that they aren't totally alone. Good shows and bad, serious and silly, they are astoundingly numerous. The cops on *Barney Miller,* the soldiers on *M*A*S*H,* the radio personnel on *WKRP in Cincinnati.* Even on as vacuous a show as *Love Boat,* the workmates in more than one episode are described as a family. Last season, in fact, the *Love Boat* family was solidified by its adoption of a child — Captain Stuebing's illegitimate, ten-year-old daughter, Vicki. In the episode introducing Vicki's residence on board the ship, a social worker at first is reluctant to permit the girl to live in such an unstable environment, with no family but the captain. But she is soon persuaded that Vicki does indeed have a family on the ship. Vicki, she says, is "one lucky lady . . . You have not one parent but five, all of them loving, caring people."[41]

In *M*A*S*H,* too, the family has been verbalized. At one point, 37
fatherly Colonel Potter says, "The 4077 is not just a roster of people; it's my family. Not only that, but a loyal family." In another episode, Corporal Klinger, shattered by the news that his wife is divorcing him, comes to realize that "I may not have a family anymore in Toledo, but I sure have one here." In yet another, Margaret describes the unit as

[41]The quotes from television shows came from the diligent research of Lisa Leghorn, one of my chosen-family members, who selflessly spent hours watching *M*A*S*H* and *Love Boat* to cull them for me. [Author's note]

"like a family," and then corrects herself. "No," she says firmly, "it *is* a family." Sometimes the familial relationship among the characters is mirrored in the relationship of the actors. An interview with the cast of *M*A*S*H* brings up familial references. Gary Burghoff, who played the boyish Radar O'Reilly, told one writer that since the death of his own father, "I think of Harry [Morgan] as my new father."[42]

Some of TV's workplace families are more believable than others: The   38
warmth of the *M*A*S*H* personnel comes through beautifully; the poke-in-the-ribs camaraderie of the *Love Boat* crew evokes little feeling of connection or commitment. But, however successful each is, TV has come to recognize, and institutionalize, the workplace family.

In 1978 a brief-lived show called *The Apple Family* attempted a truly   39
radical idea — the story of a group of unrelated people who came together with the idea of forming a consciously chosen family, not an office family or a thrown-together family. The show didn't last. It wasn't very good, and in any event lots of shows don't last, so maybe that doesn't mean anything. On the other hand, maybe it does. Maybe it means that television, which influences so much of our thinking, can't afford to tell us we can choose our own families. It is, after all, a very dangerous message. It will be interesting to see the fate of a fall 1981 program, *Love, Sidney*, in which a gay man lives with a heterosexual woman and her daughter, forming, in the producer's words, a "surrogate family."[43]

In writing this book, I've had to make choices about terminology. This   40
is always sticky, since words inevitably attempt to pin down human experience, and human experience always exists in countless variations. What do we call the family as we know it? The nuclear family is only a recent phenomenon, springing out of the older extended family. "Family of origin" is inaccurate if it attempts to include grandparents, aunts, uncles, and cousins whom we may not even meet until we are five, ten, or thirty, but who are still part of that concept called family. "Biological family" comes closest, and I have chosen to use it, but not without trepidation, since both marriage and adoption are integral parts of it. I've chosen it because it seems to me to encompass not the whole reality, but the whole *myth*: Blood is thicker than water. Much of the power of the patriarchy rests on the concept of biological kinship: A man needs a son to carry on his genes and his name; hence woman is forced into

[42] David S. Reiss, *M*A*S*H: The Exclusive Inside Story of TV's Most Popular Show* (New York: Bobbs-Merrill, 1980), p. 35. [Author's note]
[43] Frank Swertlow, "TV Update," *TV Guide*, June 6, 1981, p. A–1. [Author's note] (*Love Sidney* was cancelled after two seasons on NBC.)

marriage and monogamy. Marriage historically is the integration of two bloodlines, and it is this, not the more recent myth of romance, that is the central mythical commitment of marriage: "She is the mother of my children." The stepmother in the fairy tale *must* be wicked, because her natural alliance is to the children of her own body, not those of her husband's body. Adoption of children not of one's own bloodline is always an adaptation. When one can't have children of "one's own," one creates a substitute, in effect pretending that the child is blood kin. The reality has changed; the myth remains untouched. Hence, I am using "biological family" to encompass the myth in all its facets, since it is the myth rather than the fact of genetical inheritance that governs our lives.

The same problem of terminology arises when I find myself defining 41 the kinds of contemporary nonbiological family. Definition, the creation of categories — these are useful and necessary, but they are also dangerous. They are useful if, like clothing, they can be worn when they're comfortable and can stretch to fit whatever they cover, allowing themselves to be discarded when they no longer fit properly. If they become straitjackets, restricting and confining, they are destructive; they have become false naming. True naming is a process of infinite growth, infinite flexibility. And so I have drawn up categories of nonbiological family. I think they are useful categories, helping to put into focus a reality we've been taught not to see. But they are loose categories. A given relationship may fall into one, or two, or three categories. There may be — there must be — other categories. I've chosen mine because they fit my experience and my observations.

The three kinds of nonbiological family I've seen are the "honorary 42 relative" family — the family friend who is your "uncle" or "aunt" as you grow up; the workplace family; and, finally, the chosen family — the friends who, with no outside force throwing you together, you have consciously or unconsciously chosen to be your family. . . .

The chosen family isn't always an unmitigated good: I'm not attempting 43 to erase *Father Knows Best* and replace it with an equally silly picture of happy little chosen families creating heaven on earth. Sometimes the chosen family mirrors the worst of biological families — the patriarchal power, the crippling dependency, the negation of the individual selves that can exist in a secure framework. Charles Manson[44] was the leader of a chosen family; so was Jim Jones.[45] Armies create families of men

[44]*Charles Manson:* leader of the "family" that murdered actress Sharon Tate and six of her friends in 1969.

[45]*Jim Jones:* American-born head of the fanatical religious sect, some nine hundred members of which committed mass suicide in 1978 in Guyana.

who are permitted and encouraged through their bonding to rape and kill. To expand definitions, to create choice, doesn't guarantee that the choices will be either wise or moral. But choice itself *is* good, and with it comes a greater potential for good than exists in its absence.

This book, then, is about that choice — how it's been exercised in   44 the past, how it's being exercised in the present, and how we might expand its parameters in the future.

Engaging the Text

1. Is it possible to *choose* one's own family? Are the kinds of chosen families Lindsey describes really families, or just groups of friends?

2. Explain the concept of the "new narcissism." How, according to Lindsey, has it affected the American family?

3. Early in this selection, Lindsey draws a distinction between a MYTH and a lie. Explain and illustrate the difference between these two terms.

4. What, according to Lindsey, is the relationship between patriarchy and the traditional nuclear family?

5. Analyze the structure of Lindsey's argument. How persuasive is the evidence she provides in its defense?

Exploring Connections

1. Drawing on the readings by Lindsey, Elkind, Tocqueville, White, and Skolnick in this chapter, write a composite history of the American family.

2. Analyze the couple in Gloria Naylor's "The Two" (Chapter Four, "Women") as an example of a chosen family. Would Lindsey say they meet her criteria of a functional family? Would you?

Extending the Critical Context

1. At the end of this selection, Lindsey suggests that chosen families may have some negative as well as positive aspects. What, in your opinion, might be the negative implications of a society composed primarily of voluntary families?

2. Do you know any examples of nonbiological families or chosen families? How do they differ from the biological families you know? Are there purposes each serves that the other cannot?

The Gay Family

Richard Goldstein

During the last two decades, gay and lesbian rights have become prominent social issues. Openly gay citizens have sought and won high public office, claimed and rejuvenated urban communities, and challenged traditional ideas and institutions like marriage and the family. In this piece, Richard Goldstein reports on the obstacles faced by homosexuals who choose to marry or raise children. A senior editor and writer for the Village Voice, *Goldstein (b. 1944) writes frequently about popular culture and sexual politics.*

Paul wore white. Scott wore white. They stood under the *chupah*[1] while parents and siblings, *zaydehs* and *bubbas*, looked on. Old friends teared up as the rabbi recited a benediction in Hebrew and English. There were readings from the Song of Songs ("Come, my beloved, let us go into the field . . .") and from *Leaves of Grass*[2] ("To be surrounded by beautiful, curious, breathing, laughing flesh is enough"). Paul and Scott raised a glass to each other's lips and pronounced a benediction of their own: "With this wine, I declare my love for you before this assembly of family and friends and in accord with the traditions of the Jewish people and the spirit of human liberation." Then they stepped on the glass and shattered it. Together.

"We don't call it a wedding," Scott says. "We don't call it a marriage. I correct people. We call it our Ceremony."

Their Ceremony was not so different from many June weddings I've attended: a beautiful site (the Prospect Park picnic house), a groaning buffet, the usual utopian rhetoric. If anything, it smacked of those hippie weddings where the bride and groom wrote their own service, accompanied by a guitarist who sang of world peace and spiritual harmony. But this ceremony was different, of course, for being shorn of any legal significance; and, because of who Paul Horowitz and Scott Klein are, it took on a

---

[1]*chupah:* the canopy at a Jewish wedding ceremony. *Zaydehs* are grandfathers and *bubbas* are grandmothers.

[2]*Leaves of Grass:* 1855 poem by Walt Whitman (1819–1892), revolutionary in its form and frank sexuality.

resonance that made even the song they'd chosen by Sade[3] ("Everybody wants to live together/Why can't we live together?") seem urgent, personal.

Despite my muffled snickers, I cried a bit, in part because I remembered 4 my own wedding to a woman, in part because, sitting next to my male lover, watching Paul and Scott, I yearned for the day when we felt safe enough to laugh at them exchanging vows.

The idea of staging such a ceremony has always intrigued them, but 5 Paul and Scott were spurred to act by a succession of weddings among their college friends. "Here I'm recognizing their relationships in a very public way," says Scott, "and I began to feel we deserve the same kind of recognition. We've been together four years now. We don't talk about forever, but we're very committed to each other, and I think it's important for people to see that there's a depth between us."

A depth, when it must be confined or confided to a few sympathetic 6 friends, can seem like an illusion. A commitment that may never be commemorated in ritual can feel fleeting, fragile. Any relationship is vulnerable to change — many of us prefer it that way — but a gay relationship is a Sisyphean[4] journey: You walk out of your house on a brilliant afternoon and, overcome with limerance,[5] you tousle your lover's hair, only to be plummeted by a passerby's scowl — or worse. No ceremony can prevent such occurrences; the world we will always have with us. But an exchange of vows before parents and peers can offer some protection against worldlessness — that feeling of being out of time and place.

There's a ready remedy for heterosexuals who experience that feeling: 7 marriage. For those who choose to live without the trappings of a sexist institution, there is still the possibility that a man and woman living together or caring for a child could be married. An unmarried couple who take advantage of that assumption can benefit from it; the point is, they have a choice. An unmarried couple is as unlike a gay couple as a bohemian who has chosen poverty is unlike the poor. And because of the particular oppression it addresses, a gay Ceremony, unlike a wedding, is a radical act.

So is having children, if you're gay. Lesbian motherhood and gay 8 fatherhood raise terrors so primal that they make orgies and sexual

[3]*Sade:* contemporary female vocalist.

[4]*Sisyphean:* suggestive of the labors of Sisyphus, who was ruler of Corinth in classical mythology. He offended the gods and was made to roll a stone up a hill endlessly, with the stone always escaping near the top and rolling down again.

[5]*limerance:* word coined by Ursula LeGuin in her sci-fi novel *Left Hand of Darkness;* it refers to a transitional stage between sexes, characterized by aroused sexual feelings.

devices pale as emblems of deviance. If sexual excess connotes a life beyond the pale (and safety net), having kids expresses a commitment not just to a community of peers but to the march of generations. It threatens the stereotype that enables heterosexuals to think of themselves as distinct — and superior. It suggests that, just as Jews are complete without Jesus, homosexuals are whole without the "salvation" of heterosexuality.

How much more comforting to think of gay people as narcissists who consciously reject fertility. Norman Podhoretz[6] has often availed himself of this stereotype; he milked it vigorously in a recent column honoring Father's Day. "A man who decides to live as a homosexual is abdicating his place as a father," he observed. "Indeed, it is entirely possible that this represents, either consciously or unconsciously, one of the main attractions of homosexuality." Podhoretz did not bother to report that many gay people *do* have children: The Kinsey Institute estimated recently that a third of all lesbians and a fifth of all gay men have been married. Half are parents.   9

When they break the covenant of marriage and heterosexuality, much more often than not, gay parents leave their children behind. Judges commonly restrict even visitation rights when a gay parent has a live-in lover; gay friends are often barred from the house while the child is visiting. A judge's order not to "flaunt sexuality" may require withdrawing from a gay church or political organization. Gay parents petitioning for even partial custody often must choose between a child and a lover, friends, and community. A judge in Chicago recently added a new wrinkle when he ordered a gay father to take the HTLV-III antibody test before he could have any contact with his child at all.   10

It's the exception that proves the rule when gay parents are granted custody. But the proportion of lesbian mothers who win such cases has risen from less than one percent in 1970 to 15 percent today. The stereotype of women as natural custodians of children may have more to do with this shift than any tolerance of homosexuality. As for a gay father winning custody over a straight mother, no matter what their respective parental capacities, *Psychology Today* observes: "That would be news."   11

For Rosemary Dempsey and Maggie Wales, raising five children in the home they share has been a struggle whose rewards are barely hinted at by the plate that sits above their mantel: A gift from all their children, it reads, "Happy 10th Anniversary."   12

[6]*Norman Podhoretz:* outspoken editor (b. 1930) of the conservative magazine, *Commentary*.

They can vividly recall the day in 1979 when their vacation in Florida 13
was interrupted by a phone call from the friend they'd left the kids with:
Maggie's cat had died, and not only that; five years after he relinquished
custody, Rosemary's husband had suddenly appeared and taken his children. They drove all night, arrived at her husband's home the next
afternoon, and found her son "hiding in a closet in his pajamas" and her
daughter "crying hysterically." They brought the kids back, only to be
confronted by two policemen who sheepishly arrested Dempsey. A first
year law student (now a prominent attorney in custody law), she spent
that day and night in jail.

It's the nightmare every gay parent lives with: the specter of the state 14
stepping in. "You ask yourself," Rosemary says, "should we just stop
and let them have the kids? Because it sure is painful for them. But
then, the message you give is that they're not worth fighting for." So
they went to trial, assembling a parade of neighbors to testify on their
behalf and rallying feminist groups to their defense, with signs that read
"Save Rosemary's Babies." The judge handed down a landmark ruling:
Though these children were being raised in "an unconventional household,"
there was not "a scintilla of evidence from which the court could infer
that Dempsey's sexual orientation was adversely affecting them." She
was not to be denied custody on the sole basis of her sexuality.

All's well that ends well, except this ordeal did not. Two weeks later, 15
a new set of court papers arrived; this time, Maggie's husband was suing
for custody of *his* kids on similar grounds. And this time, another judge
ruled differently: Maggie could see her three children for a month every
summer, on three weekends out of four, and on alternate holidays. But
for the rest of the year, it was in the best interest of the children to
live with their heterosexual dad.

Maggie and Rosemary are still very much a family, with scrapbooks 16
full of pictures and the usual braggadocio: "Two kids from this household
have won the mayor's award for academic excellence; one is president
of his class and too popular for his own good." Their relationship, which
began shortly after both women left their husbands, has the flinty, tempered
quality of a boulder. "The kids have always known that we loved each
other," Maggie says. "Their main concern was whether we were each
gonna be there for them." They have been through a lot together, and
it has sealed not just their union but their politics. "What often comes
up in these trials is that it's wrong to expose kids to values that are
different from the dominant society's," Rosemary insists. "When they
saw that they couldn't get us on lesbian sexuality, the main thrust was
our involvement in the feminist movement. They won't put you in jail
for fighting to change society — but they might take your kids."

Despite the cultivated image of homosexuals as emotional nomads, 17
most gay people, at some point in their lives, establish a stable, central
relationship. And, despite all that Oscar Wilde[7] has said about marriage
("It's as demoralizing as cigarettes and far more expensive"), there is
nothing new about gay people holding Ceremonies of Union, holy or
otherwise. Historians have uncovered ample evidence of homosexual
marriage rites, performed in private, sometimes by renegade clergy and
occasionally with one party in drag. Half-camp, half-yearning, and all
fantasy, these elaborate fetes were part of the high romanticism of gay
life before Stonewall,[8] when, as diarist Donald Vining recalls with some
disdain, "we thought pairing up was what homosexuals *did*." ("Monogamy,"
he hastens to add, "was seldom part of the deal.")

What is new is the public nature of these ceremonies, and the active 18
participation of family and clergy. Not since the year 342, when homosexual
marriage was outlawed in Europe (it had flourished in the Roman Empire,
largely among the aristocracy; Nero married two men, one of whom was
accorded the status of an empress), has an established religion performed
such ceremonies. But in 1984, the Unitarian/Universalist Association
voted overwhelmingly to permit its ministers to marry congregants of
the same sex. Reverend Robert Wheatly has married many homosexual
couples, especially of the Catholic faith, at his Unitarian church in Boston.
To "sanctify a relationship satisfies a very human need," he says. "It
adds a dimension of integrity and longevity." Individual Quaker meetings
will perform such ceremonies, and so will individual rabbis. "If a gay
couple have, despite all the prejudices, managed to build an enduring
relationship, it deserves to be recognized," says Yoel Kahn of San Francisco,
who presided over Paul and Scott's union. And the Metropolitan Community Church, an openly gay denomination with over 200 congregations
worldwide, will conduct "a ceremony of holy union" for lesbians and
gay men who have lived together for at least a year.

Despite his antipathy to gay marriage, Vining put me in touch with 19
two friends who, as he described it, "wear the ring." One of the pair,
a professor at City College, describes a ceremony performed for him
and his lover in 1969, by a Presbyterian minister who had been arrested
in Selma, Alabama several years earlier. "The civil rights movement was

[7]*Oscar Wilde:* Irish poet, dramatist, novelist, and social critic (1854–1900).
[8]*Stonewall:* the Stonewall or Christopher Street riots of June 1969 in Greenwich Village,
New York City, a watershed event in gay activism. After police closed the Stonewall Inn,
a dance bar frequented by flamboyant and unconventional homosexuals, the crowd attacked
the police with cobblestones and bottles. Several nights of disorder and demonstrations
followed.

the coattail we were riding on," he recalls, "not the Stonewall riot." Their ceremony — along with a full communion service — was held in the chapel, before the entire congregation. As a guitarist played and sang "The Impossible Dream," the pair were pronounced "mate and spouse." "We gave our rings to the minister, who blessed them and put them on our hands. Then we went to his home for a reception with his wife and kids."

"Were you embarrassed?" I asked.   20

"Judging from the photos, we were scared to death. After the exchange   21
of rings, it was clear we could kiss, and *that* was embarrassing. We *did*
kiss, but gingerly, and when the service was over, we dashed into the
back room and kissed good."

Times have changed. Last year, two male stockbrokers planning to   22
marry registered a china pattern in their names at Bloomingdale's. They
were reflecting the three A's of gay life in the '80s: aging, assimilation,
and AIDS. As the Stonewall generation enters midlife, along with the
rest of the baby boom, the entire culture is pushing couplehood. The
gay response, in less tragic times, might be to combine the stability of
a spouse with the serendipity of sexual adventures; but AIDS has ushered
in monogamy, and the bond which suddenly carries with it obligations
of denial and restraint makes gay male couplehood more like traditional
marriage than it ever was. The energy that gay culture once poured into
erotic enterprise — as well as the elaborate chains of "kinship" sex can
forge — all must be redirected. If the predictions are correct, and 180,000
people, most of them gay men, perish from AIDS over the next five
years, the survivors will be very different people, with values antithetical
to those associated with the disease. The urge for couplehood is only
the most visible component of that change: The real reconstitution going
on in gay culture today involves the broader, trickier terrain of family.

The change is hardly limited to gay men. Among lesbians, "couplism,"   23
a heresy second only to "looksism" in some circles, is definitely making
a comeback; but, as with gay male pairings, the return to a discarded
tradition often has a radical edge. The lesbian couple of the '80s may
well "choose children," often through artificial insemination. Heterosexual
women have had to struggle for the right *not* to have children, but dykes
are supposed to be sterile. They must defend their choice to bear children
against social and legal pressures as binding as the system that tracks
straight women toward motherhood.

No one knows how many of the 20,000 women inseminated each year   24
are unmarried, but "turkey baster babies" have become a staple of what's
being referred to as the "lesbian baby boom." The apotheosis of self-

directed motherhood, A.I., confers on women an extraordinary degree of autonomy. As Joy Schulenberg writes in *Gay Parenting*, all that's required is "an ovulating woman, 1 cc. of viable sperm, a cheap piece of equipment, and some very basic knowledge of female anatomy." In the hands of lesbians, A.I. can become an instrument for appropriating the act of conception itself. "I inseminated LeAnn myself," one woman told Schulenberg, "and it was the most beautiful act of love I have ever done."

The contours of gay family, in this setting, have very little to do with the conventional heterosexual paradigm: there may be one or two mommies, sometimes a daddy or uncle, and sometimes, a profusion of parents who have no blood relation to the child. The collectivism of the '60s and '70s, when groups of women marshalled their meager assets and ample resources to care for each other, is being adapted to the tasks of parenting. In the lesbian enclave of Park Slope, a "mommies group" meets monthly, with nine women, two of whom have already borne children. They exchange information and energy, bolstering each other against reservations about raising a child in an unorthodox setting, and all the burdens that come of being out on the edge. 25

Not everyone is happy about the lesbian baby boom. "I'm horrified by it," says one woman whose lover is six months pregnant. "For me, part of being a lesbian is not being baby centered, and it seems to me that the lesbian world is becoming more baby centered every hour." At this rate, the Michigan Womyn's Music Festival, a sort of lesbian Woodstock, will soon have to drop its rule prohibiting males over the age of seven from mingling with women and girls. 26

All these changes are occurring at a time when the gay rights movement is having its most tangible success — at least in cities where homosexuals have translated their ample presence into political clout. Among urban professionals, at any rate, there is probably less onus attached to being openly gay than at any time in American history; Paul and Scott, for example, were able to get a "marriage discount" on their joint mortgage from the bank where Paul works because it has a nondiscrimination hiring policy. 27

In the face of such relative equity, gay life is becoming increasingly demystified and, in the process, it is losing its compensatory — if colorful — edge. As distinctions become more subtle (among the young it sometimes seems that lesbians and gay men are Yuppies with brighter eyes), much of what used to seem inherent about homosexuality — its argot, costumes, inflection, and gait — is slipping away, leaving men who love men and women who love women but who are fundamentally different from heterosexuals in no other respect. 28

So much in gay tradition mocks the institutions of heterosexuality that 29
what often goes unnoticed is the yearning to lead an ordinary life — to
play a role in society without hiding one's sexuality. As the stereotypes
drop away and new options open up, gay people are discovering a more
authentically individual relationship to social conventions. "'We're strong
enough as a movement to support people's real life choices," says one
lesbian mother-to-be.

The gay family is shorthand for a new institution; one that bears little 30
resemblance to the patriarchal structure most of us were raised in.
Homosexuals are, by definition, outside that structure, and given our
status, when we try to appropriate the tradition of forming families, we
end up creating something new.

Do gay families subvert the family? A more salient question might 31
be, is the family subverting itself? By now, the statistics have been
drummed into our fornicating brains: The average American marriage
lasts 9.4 years; nearly 20 percent of all children are born to unwed
mothers; four out of 10 children born in the '70s will spend some time
in single-parent households. Depending on whether you like what you
see, these figures epitomize either the crisis of family life or its evolution.
In any case, the change has created a new class of single parents and
their lovers — millions of people, most of them straight. The battle
being waged on this cutting edge of gay liberation has implications for
all unmarried people, since, when it comes to employee benefits, at
least, gay couples are usually treated like heterosexuals "living in sin."

For most gay couples, the struggle has less to do with subverting the 32
patriarchy than with getting a lover's children covered on your health
plan. But symbolism is never far from the surface. As Nan Hunter, newly
appointed director of the ACLU's[9] Lesbian and Gay Rights Project,
observes: "The idea that other kinds of relationships would be accorded
some of the economic breaks of marriage, or that other kinds of relationships
can provide a loving atmosphere for the raising of children, is deeply
frightening for society."

So far, activists have had their greatest success in the private sector. 33
In 1982, the *Village Voice*'s union won health coverage for live-in "spouse
equivalents" of its rank and file. Similar plans have been adopted by
several small companies, and some progressive unions are considering
raising the issue in collective bargaining. But when San Francisco's Board
of Supervisors passed a bill in 1982 that would have extended benefits
to the "domestic partners" of city workers and authorized a municipal

[9]*ACLU:* the American Civil Liberties Union.

registry for them, it was as if a line had been crossed. Gay rights, yes; gay power, reluctantly; but subsidizing relationships out of wedlock, never! Mayor Dianne Feinstein vetoed the bill.

But similar measures have passed in Berkeley and West Hollywood, 34 a newly constituted city whose politics are dominated by homosexuals and retirees. For both groups, the benefits of domestic partnership legislation are more than financial: Hospitals and convalescent homes must extend full visitation rights to live-in lovers. The AIDS crisis has heightened the urgency of these issues for gay male couples: Suddenly, the power to make life-and-death decisions about a lover's medical treatment seems worth fighting for.

So does the right to grieve. In California, a railroad worker denied 35 funeral leave to mourn his male lover, who had died of AIDS, sued and won time off. Retaining shared assets after a lover's death is another point of contention, especially when those possessions include a rent-controlled or stabilized apartment. A judge in New York recently ruled that a man who had lived with and cared for his male lover through a terminal struggle with AIDS was, in effect, a relative, and could continue to reside in their apartment, though his name is not on the lease. The case is currently being appealed.

. . . In California, where court decisions affirming the validity of re- 36 lationships outside marriage date back to 1921, gay adoptive parents meet relatively little resistance. In New York, the governor's executive order prohibiting discrimination in state services has been interpreted to apply to foster care and adoption. Gay people can and do adopt children here, but their road is seldom an easy one.

It's difficult, in any case, for a single male to adopt; the old wisdom 37 is that men make poor care providers, so agencies are especially loath to place infants with "bachelors." But Rubén is an exception: a physician who has lived with his lover, an executive, for 19 years, he's the kind of adoptive parent any agency would relish — except for the fact that he's gay. But in New York, the subject of sexuality rarely comes up in adoption proceedings; officially, gay couples are treated like other unmarried couples: Only one member can qualify as the legal parent. Even though the agency knew Rubén was a single male in his mid forties who lived with a male roommate, it had no immediate reservations about placing a three-week-old boy in his care — the procedure took all of four days.

Then the trouble began. When Rubén went to Family Court to have 38 the adoption certified, the judge noticed the reference to a roommate and drew her own conclusions; she asked for a second home study. A probation officer visited Rubén and popped the question: Was he gay? His heart stopped. "I decided to be honest. I had heard that this was not supposed to be a deterrent to adoption, so I swallowed hard and said yes."

What followed was a two-year ordeal, during which the probation 39 officer, the original agency, and the judge wavered over whether to certify the adoption. The court ordered two more home studies, called in a child psychologist, appointed an attorney to represent the child. "Through all those proceedings," Rubén remembers, "nobody said this shouldn't happen; but one thing or another kept standing in the way. And I began to sense that they were looking for a reason to say no."

Meanwhile, the child was bonding with his new family — calling 40 Rubén "daddy" and the lover "father." Rubén's mother, who took to the child immediately, began to feel as if her grandson were only temporary. On more than one occasion, Rubén says, he was tempted "to take my kid and run away to Canada." But he stuck it out, in part because he understood that the longer a child lives in its adoptive home, the harder for a court to take it away. "It would have been devastating for him to be removed," Rubén says.

Finally, two weeks after the boy's second birthday, the adoption was 41 finalized. "In retrospect, it seems they all wanted to see that every i was dotted, in case a problem came up afterward," he says. The final hearing in Family Court took all of five minutes, at the end of which, the judge looked up at Rubén's son and said, "Take good care of your father."

What about the children. Will they be insecure? Enraged? Gay? The 42 latter question is often thrust at gay parents in the form of an accusation, but the evidence, scanty as it is, says otherwise. "At this stage, I tentatively suggest that children being raised by . . . homosexual parents do not differ appreciably from children raised in more conventional family settings," says Richard Greene, a professor of psychiatry and psychology at Stony Brook. All the children in his study were able to "comprehend and verbalize the atypical nature of their parents' lifestyles and to view that atypicality in the broader perspective of the cultural norm." Greene thinks that the formation of a sexual identity has more do with interactions outside the home than with a parent's personal choice of a mate.

But that doesn't mean the children of gay people are *never* gay. The 43 director of a camp for children of "alternative families" (mostly the daughters of lesbians), says: "My sense is that most of these kids will probably end up heterosexual — but not strictly so. They're more open-minded. A lot of them say they're bisexual, or that they don't know yet." There are anxieties peculiar to the situation: "Most kids go through a particularly homophobic period in junior high school. They're very judgmental. The girls are very into makeup and badly want to have boyfriends." The sons of gay men are even more likely than other adolescent boys to experience profound anxieties about their sexual identity. The best adjustment, a University of Alberta study suggests, is made by children whose parents are candid about sexuality and live in a stable relationship.

One gay father, interviewed in *Psychology Today*, remembers telling 44
his sons when they were both 15. "I told them bluntly and then explained what it was all about," he said. "They wept — then they coped."

Gay families face a situation that is, in many ways, analogous to what 45
interracial families confronted a generation ago. The children are typically more circumspect, especially about confiding in their peers. But the bonds they form are strong and their sense of social justice keen. "What he assimilates at this point is that anyone can love anyone — and it's not just a right but a fact," says one lesbian mother about her nine-year-old son. "He also knows that some people try to prevent it from happening, and that we're struggling for freedom just as they're struggling for freedom in South Africa."

All the gay parents interviewed for this article describe their children 46
as self-directed and unafraid to speak out. It's a trait many gay parents cultivate from their own tribulations — a determination to make your own decisions and a drive to remake the world in your own terms. Even Rubén notices that, at three, his son has "a strong will. He's not a follower. So I'm hoping that, if he sees my situation is right for me, then he'll be able to deal with what the world thinks of it."

Tommy is not Dee's biological child, but neither was he formally 47
adopted. Dee just happened to be in the right place at the right time; within a few hours of hearing that an infant was available, she became a mother.

Raised by a divorced woman at a time when that was, in many eyes, 48
as problematic as being raised by a lesbian is today, Dee says, "I'd always been attracted to the idea that you don't have to be married to have a child. While I was living with a guy, I deliberately became pregnant, but miscarried. I tried again with a second guy; I proposed becoming pregnant, but it was clear that I would be the parent, and *I* would decide what his relationship to the child could be." They broke up before Dee conceived.

Then something unexpected happened: She fell in love with another 49
woman. While they were vacationing in the Caribbean, Dee heard the maids talking about an abandoned baby at the hospital. "They were asking each other, does anybody want this child, because by three that afternoon, when its mother checked out of the hospital, he would be going to the orphanage." Her lover chimed in: "I know someone who

wants a baby, don't you, Dee?" A thought flashed through her mind: "If I don't do this now, I may never [get] a chance again."

She raced to the hospital, got the mother's permission, put her name 50 on the birth certificate, and paid the bill. Then she went to the baby room and asked for infant number three. "They handed me this piss-smelling baby wrapped in blankets. All I could see was his face and hairy head." Back at the hotel, the maids showed her how to diaper the baby. She slept on the floor that night, terrified when he began to hiccup. The next day she called her mother in New York: "Sit down," Dee said. "You're a grandmother. I want you to pick the middle name."

An "informal custodial arrangement" like Dee's is fraught with un- 51 certainty. Has the child been abducted? Will the "coyote" hired to transport the baby across the border prove reliable? Will the mother, or her surrogate, suddenly appear with blackmail in mind? Such risks notwithstanding, once a child has reached its destination, its actual status is hard to discern; after several years, even if the truth is discovered, the courts are reluctant to separate a child from caring parents — even if they are gay. And given the immensely bureaucratic procedures gay people face when they try to adopt legally, the immediate availability of an abandoned baby is an offer difficult to refuse.

"I think most human beings want to be parents," Dee says, "and I 52 don't think there's any reason to negate those desires just because you're not married or not heterosexual or even not in a couple." She bristles at the recollection of encounters with "separatist lesbians and radical feminists who think I'm not to be taken seriously because I've sold out." For Dee, becoming a mother and living as a lesbian intersected: "The strength I gained from single motherhood — both in terms of my identity as a woman and in terms of dealing with society — gave me the courage I needed to come out. I remember sitting on a couch and thinking, 'My God, I have done something very few people have the privilege to do. I can take my life and turn it in a different direction and say, This is good! And it will work.' "

If there's one thing gay parents have in common, it's a design for 53 living. They are deliberate and determined, almost to a fault — it comes with the territory.

Julie Greenberg, 29, is a rabbinical student and a lesbian. In about 54 a month, she intends to become pregnant with her first child. The semen, donated by a close friend, is waiting in the sperm bank for her. She calls it "alternate conception."

"I have 100 percent custody," she says. "I will do all the work and 55 take the responsibility. But I would like the child to have a relationship with a father figure, and I intend to foster it." So the child will call the donor "daddy," and Julie will call him "Sam." A contract between them will enumerate his rights and responsibilities, which include some financial support.

Though some women insist on an anonymous donor — it avoids the 56 prospect of a custody battle by the biological father — there's an evident risk to that approach: There's no way to evaluate an unknown donor's health. More often, the donor is known — a dear friend — and though he will never become "the man of the house," he will play a role in the child's life. Sam is heterosexual, but for many lesbians, the dear friend who is willing to be present but not dominant is a gay man who has tested negative for HTLV-III antibodies. (The odds of passing AIDS on to a woman and child via A.I. are not to be ignored.) The baby signifies not just a bond between its lesbian coparents, but between male and female homosexuals, one of the least acknowledged and most abiding relationships in gay life.

If the formation of families ever does become significant for homosexuals, 57 A.I. will be one reason why. It requires neither medical intervention nor approval by the state, nor the capacity to function heterosexually. I know two gay men among my circle of friends who have entered into contractual relationships with women, intending to be the primary parent of the child that evolves. More commonly, lesbians enter into contractual relationships with men for a child who will be raised by the mother and her female lover. Julie intends to be "a single mother living in a feminist community. They'll contribute bits and pieces. And we'll be poor."

It remains to be seen how a congregation, even one willing to break 58 with Jewish tradition, will react when it becomes apparent that its rabbi is pregnant and unmarried. But Julie is optimistic: "They don't necessarily have to deal with the fact that I'm a lesbian," she says, "but I'm hoping they'll be receptive to another form of Jewish family. We're saying there's no such thing as *the* family; there are various forms of family — single parents by choice, single parents not by choice, shared custody arrangements, collective networks. . . ."

Can a family be formulated by contract? In a sense, the point is moot: 59 There's no more binding way for a mother and "father-figure" to declare their intentions; there aren't even words to describe such a relationship. Gay families are always coming up against the boundaries of language, which affirm their position on the edge of social change. And being on that edge carries a special burden: With no models or precedents, you don't know how to prepare for what the future may hold. So contracts and rituals take on an almost mystical significance. (Julie plans to appropriate an ancient fertility rite; she will stand among her friends and call forth a *neshuma*, or soul, into the world.)

Reba is six months pregnant now. When the baby arrives, by the 60 terms of a 12-page contract, she will be the parent who makes all the decisions about its care. Ray will have custody of the child on weekends, alternate Wednesdays, and for three weeks every summer. "I'm still uncertain about what to call myself," he says. "I'm the daddy/uncle." Reba's lover Katy has taken to calling herself the "sometime-mommy," although she's tempted by the term "daddy" because, she says, "I want the privilege. I haven't had a biological desire to be a mother. I've always felt the family system as I know it is overwhelming, too nuclear. So the idea of sharing is all that makes this appealing to me."

Katy's parents have been drumming their fears into her head: What 61 if Reba runs off and sticks her with a kid that isn't even "your own"? And Reba's parents resent the presence of another woman whose rights vis-à-vis their grandchild are uncodified. "I mean, they hung up the phone when they heard the baby was going to carry Katy's father's name," Reba recalls. "They asked me *not* to name it after *tanta Mascha*.[10] I realize my family's been bargaining with me about what to tell people. At best, they're gonna have to concoct a story about their daughter having an illegitimate child. At worst, they'll have to admit that their daughter is a lesbian mother."

Spend some time with the gay family and you may feel transported 62 to the summer of love. But these "hippies" are a lot less innocent. They understand that progress is not inevitable, and they've learned to watch their backs. This counterculture is emerging at a time of mixed signals. Courts and agencies are distinctly more tolerant of unorthodox parenting arrangements, but the culture is lurching rightward; judges can be replaced.

Given the uncertainties, gay families are easier to imagine than to 63 maintain. Under stress, some will fall apart. Father-figures will breach their contracts. Children will suffer. Priests will proclaim, "They tampered with God's will." Friends will mutter, "I told you so."

And the world will change. 64

[10]*tanta Mascha:* Aunt Mascha.

Engaging the Text

1. Traditional wedding ceremonies are public statements of personal commitment. In what ways does the "radical act" of a gay marriage take on meanings beyond those of a traditional wedding?

2. What evidence does Goldstein offer of the active oppression of gays?

3. Gays and lesbians, like many MARGINALIZED groups, are concerned with the issue of ASSIMILATION into MAINSTREAM American culture and the attendant loss of personal and group identity. Where does Goldstein seem to stand on the issue of gay assimilation?

4. In your view, does the fact that Goldstein is gay weaken or strengthen his credibility as a journalist in writing this article?

Exploring Connections

1. Drawing on the pieces by Goldstein, Elkind, Skolnick, and Lindsey in this chapter, debate whether or not a couple like Maggie Wales and Rosemary Dempsey should be given custody of their children.

Extending the Critical Context

1. Using your library or information provided by community interest groups, research the ways in which your state regulates child custody. You may want to focus either on recent legislation or on the history of this issue.

6

Grading American Education

Americans have always been ambivalent about education. Our frontier practicality tells us that formal book learning is a waste of time. But as a nation, we have also been peculiarly obsessed with the nature of schooling. We argue incessantly about the quality of our students and the shortcomings of our schools, and we may have done more than any other country to promote the ideal of universal public education. As a means of self-improvement and as the source of an enlightened citizenry, education lies at the heart of the American Dream and the conception of democratic self-government.

The first section of this chapter, The Hidden Curriculum, considers the ways contemporary education covertly shapes our values and attitudes. Theodore Sizer's "What High School Is" looks critically at a typical day in an American high school. Next, two cartoons by Matt Groening offer a student's perspective on classroom coercion. Jules Henry then explores some of the ways schools "fetter" the mind and instill values. The section ends with a brief selection by Jeannie Oakes suggesting that schools themselves may promote inequality in American society.

The second section, Challenging the Traditional Classroom, examines the complexities of education in a diverse society. The excerpts by Richard Rodriguez and Malcolm X offer contrasting personal reflections on the power of education and its meaning for those who stand outside the mainstream. In the third selection, Frances Maher argues that traditional schools unfairly favor male interests, values, and ways of thinking. The chapter concludes with a frank discussion of how "rumors of inferiority" have affected black students in America's colleges and universities.

Before Reading . . .

Write short descriptions of your best and worst educational experiences. Working in small groups, compare notes to see if you can reach any consensus about how formal schooling helps or hinders learning.

THE HIDDEN CURRICULUM

What High School Is
THEODORE SIZER

For better or for worse, high school is the one institution that nearly every U.S. citizen must participate in; in a sense, it is our one shared cultural experience. But what is the experience of an American high school like? Theodore Sizer's answer to this question, Horace's Compromise: The Dilemma of the American High School, *offers a comprehensive and insightful analysis of the public school system. The following excerpt describes a day in the life of a typical high school student, actually a fictional composite of many students interviewed during Sizer's research. Sizer (b. 1932) is chair of the Education Department at Brown University.*

Mark, sixteen and a genial eleventh-grader, rides a bus to Franklin   1
High School, arriving at 7:25. It is an Assembly Day, so the schedule
is adapted to allow for a meeting of the entire school. He hangs out

with his friends, first outside school and then inside, by his locker. He carries a pile of textbooks and notebooks; in all, it weighs eight and a half pounds.

From 7:30 to 8:19, with nineteen other students, he is in Room 304 2 for English class. The Shakespeare play being read this year by the eleventh grade is *Romeo and Juliet*. The teacher, Ms. Viola, has various students in turn take parts and read out loud. Periodically, she interrupts the (usually halting) recitations to ask whether the thread of the conversation in the play is clear. Mark is entertained by the stumbling readings of some of his classmates. He hopes he will not be asked to be Romeo, particularly if his current steady, Sally, is Juliet. There is a good deal of giggling in class, and much attention paid to who may be called on next. Ms. Viola reminds the class of a test on this part of the play to be given next week.

The bell rings at 8:19. Mark goes to the boys' room, where he sees 3 a classmate who he thinks is a wimp but who constantly tries to be a buddy. Mark avoids the leech by rushing off. On the way, he notices two boys engaged in some sort of transaction, probably over marijuana. He pays them no attention. 8:24. Typing class. The rows of desks that embrace big office machines are almost filled before the bell. Mark is uncomfortable here: Typing class is girl country. The teacher constantly threatens what to Mark is a humiliatingly female future: "Your employer won't like these erasures." The minutes during the period are spent copying a letter from a handbook onto business stationery. Mark struggles to keep from looking at his work; the teacher wants him to watch only the material from which he is copying. Mark is frustrated, uncomfortable, and scared that he will not complete his letter by the class's end, which would be embarrassing.

Nine tenths of the students present at school that day are assembled 4 in the auditorium by the 9:18 bell. The dilatory[1] tenth still stumble in, running down aisles. Annoyed class deans try to get the mob settled. The curtains part; the program is a concert by a student rock group. Their electronic gear flashes under the lights, and the five boys and one girl in the group work hard at being casual. Their movements on stage are studiously at three-quarter time, and they chat with one another as though the tumultuous screaming of their schoolmates were totally inaudible. The girl balances on a stool; the boys crank up the music. It is very soft rock, the sanitized lyrics surely cleared with the assistant principal. The girl sings, holding the mike close to her mouth, but can scarcely be heard. Her light voice is tentative, and the lyrics indecipherable.

[1]*dilatory:* tending to delay or procrastinate.

The guitars, amplified, are tuneful, however, and the drums are played with energy.

The students around Mark — all juniors, since they are seated by 5 class — alternately slouch in their upholstered, hinged seats, talking to one another, or sit forward, leaning on the chair backs in front of them, watching the band. A boy near Mark shouts noisily at the microphone-fondling singer, "Bite it . . . ohhh," and the area around Mark explodes in vulgar male laughter, but quickly subsides. A teacher walks down the aisle. Songs continue, to great applause. Assembly is over at 9:46, two minutes early.

9:53 and biology class. Mark was at a different high school last year 6 and did not take this course there as a tenth-grader. He is in it now, and all but one of his classmates are a year younger than he. He sits on the side, not taking part in the chatter that goes on after the bell. At 9:57, the public address system goes on, with the announcements of the day. After a few words from the principal ("Here's today's cheers and jeers . . ." with a cheer for the winning basketball team and a jeer for the spectators who made a ruckus at the gymnasium), the task is taken over by officers of ASB (Associated Student Bodies). There is an appeal for "bat bunnies." Carnations are for sale by the Girls' League. Miss Indian American is coming. Students are auctioning off their services (background catcalls are heard) to earn money for the prom. Nominees are needed for the ballot for school bachelor and school bachelorette. The announcements end with a "thought for the day. When you throw a little mud, you lose a little ground."

At 10:04 the biology class finally turns to science. The teacher, Mr. 7 Robbins, has placed one of several labeled laboratory specimens — some are pinned in frames, others swim in formaldehyde — on each of the classroom's eight laboratory tables. The three or so students whose chairs circle each of these benches are to study the specimen and make notes about it or drawings of it. After a few minutes each group of three will move to another table. The teacher points out that these specimens are of organisms already studied in previous classes. He says that the period-long test set for the following day will involve observing some of these specimens — then to be without labels — and writing an identifying paragraph on each. Mr. Robbins points out that some of the printed labels ascribe the specimens names different from those given in the textbook. He explains that biologists often give several names to the same organism.

The class now falls to peering, writing, and quiet talking. Mr. Robbins 8 comes over to Mark, and in whispered words asks him to carry a requisition form for science department materials to the business office. Mark, because of his "older" status, is usually chosen by Robbins for this kind of errand. Robbins gives Mark the form and a green hall pass to show to any teacher who might challenge him, on his way to the office, for being out of a classroom. The errand takes Mark four minutes. Meanwhile Mark's group is hard at work but gets to only three of the specimens before the bell rings at 10:42. As the students surge out, Robbins shouts a reminder about a "double" laboratory period on Thursday.

Between classes one of the seniors asks Mark whether he plans to be 9
a candidate for schoolwide office next year. Mark says no. He starts to explain. The 10:47 bell rings, meaning that he is late for French class.

There are fifteen students in Monsieur Bates's language class. He 10
hands out tests taken the day before: "*C'est bien fait, Etienne . . . c'est mieux, Marie . . . Tch, tch, Robert . . .*" Mark notes his C + and peeks at the A − in front of Susanna, next to him. The class has been assigned seats by M. Bates; Mark resents sitting next to prissy, brainy Susanna. Bates starts by asking a student to read a question and give the correct answer. "*James, question un.*" James haltingly reads the question and gives an answer that Bates, now speaking English, says is incomplete. In due course: "*Mark, question cinq.*" Mark does his bit, and the sequence goes on, the eight quiz questions and answers filling about twenty minutes of time.

"Turn to page forty-nine. *Maintenant, lisez après moi . . .*" and Bates 11
reads a sentence and has the class echo it. Mark is embarrassed by this and mumbles with a barely audible sound. Others, like Susanna, keep the decibel count up, so Mark can hide. This I-say-you-repeat drill is interrupted once by the public address system, with an announcement about a meeting for the cheerleaders. Bates finishes the class, almost precisely at the bell, with a homework assignment. The students are to review these sentences for a brief quiz the following day. Mark takes note of the assignment, because he knows that tomorrow will be a day of busy-work in French class. Much though he dislikes oral drills, they are better than the workbook stuff that Bates hands out. Write, write, write, for Bates to throw away, Mark thinks.

11:36. Down to the cafeteria, talking noisily, hanging out, munching. 12
Getting to Room 104 by 12:17: U.S. history. The teacher is sitting cross-legged on his desk when Mark comes in, heatedly arguing with three students over the fracas that had followed the previous night's basketball game. The teacher, Mr. Suslovic, while agreeing that the spectators from their school certainly were provoked, argues that they should neither have been so obviously obscene in yelling at the opposing cheerleaders nor have allowed Coke cans to be rolled out on the floor. The three students keep saying that "it isn't fair." Apparently they and some others

had been assigned "Saturday mornings" (detentions) by the principal for the ruckus.

At 12:34, the argument appears to subside. The uninvolved students, including Mark, are in their seats, chatting amiably. Mr. Suslovic climbs off his desk and starts talking: "We've almost finished this unit, chapters nine and ten . . ." The students stop chattering among themselves and turn toward Suslovic. Several slouch down in their chairs. Some open notebooks. Most have the five-pound textbook on their desks. 13

Suslovic lectures on the cattle drives, from north Texas to railroads west of St. Louis. He breaks up this narrative with questions ("Why were the railroad lines laid largely east to west?"), directed at nobody in particular and eventually answered by Suslovic himself. Some students take notes. Mark doesn't. A student walks in the open door, hands Mr. Suslovic a list, and starts whispering with him. Suslovic turns from the class and hears out this messenger. He then asks, "Does anyone know where Maggie Sharp is?" Some one answers, "Sick at home"; someone else says, "I thought I saw her at lunch." Genial consternation.[2] Finally Suslovic tells the messenger, "Sorry, we can't help you," and returns to the class: "Now, where were we?" He goes on for some minutes. The bell rings. Suslovic forgets to give the homework assignment. 14

1:11 and Algebra II. There is a commotion in the hallway: Someone's locker is rumored to have been opened by the assistant principal and a narcotics agent. In the five-minute passing time, Mark hears the story three times and three ways. A locker had been broken into by another student. It was Mr. Gregory and a narc. It was the cops, and they did it without Gregory's knowing. Mrs. Ames, the mathematics teacher, has not heard anything about it. Several of the nineteen students try to tell her and start arguing among themselves. "O.K., that's enough." She hands out the day's problem, one sheet to each student. Mark sees with dismay that it is a single, complicated "word" problem about some train that, while traveling at 84 mph, due west, passes a car that was going due east at 55 mph. Mark struggles: Is it $d = rt$ or $t = rd$? The class becomes quiet, writing, while Mrs. Ames writes some additional, short problems on the blackboard. "Time's up." A sigh; most students still writing. A muffled "Shit." Mrs. Ames frowns. "Come on, now." She collects papers, but it takes four minutes for her to corral them all. 15

"Copy down the problems from the board." A minute passes. "William, try number one." William suggests an approach. Mrs. Ames corrects and cajoles, and William finally gets it right. Mark watches two kids to his right passing notes; he tries to read them, but the handwriting is 16

[2]*genial consternation:* good-humored confusion or bewilderment.

illegible from his distance. He hopes he is not called on, and he isn't. Only three students are asked to puzzle out an answer. The bell rings at 2:00. Mrs. Ames shouts a homework assignment over the resulting hubbub.

Mark leaves his books in his locker. He remembers that he has home- 17 work, but figures that he can do it during English class the next day. He knows that there will be an in-class presentation of one of the *Romeo and Juliet* scenes and that he will not be in it. The teacher will not notice his homework writing, or won't do anything about it if she does.

Mark passes various friends heading toward the gym, members of the 18 basketball teams. Like most students, Mark isn't an active school athlete. However, he is associated with the yearbook staff. Although he is not taking "Yearbook" for credit as an English course, he is contributing photographs. Mark takes twenty minutes checking into the yearbook staff's headquarters (the classroom of its faculty adviser) and getting some assignments of pictures from his boss, the senior who is the photography editor. Mark knows that if he pleases his boss and the faculty adviser, he'll take that editor's post for the next year. He'll get English credit for his work then.

After gossiping a bit with the yearbook staff, Mark will leave school 19 by 2:35 and go home. His grocery market bagger's job is from 4:45 to 8:00, the rush hour for the store. He'll have a snack at 4:30, and his mother will save him some supper to eat at 8:30. She will ask whether he has any homework, and he'll tell her no. Tomorrow, and virtually every other tomorrow, will be the same for Mark, save for the lack of the assembly: Each period then will be five minutes longer.

Most Americans have an uncomplicated vision of what secondary ed- 20 ucation should be. Their conception of high school is remarkably uniform across the country, a striking fact, given the size and diversity of the United States and the politically decentralized character of the schools. This uniformity is of several generations' standing. It has, however, two appearances, each quite different from the other, one of words and the other of practice, a world of political rhetoric and Mark's world.

A California high school's general goals, set out in 1979, could serve 21 equally well most of America's high schools, public and private. This school had as its ends:

- Fundamental scholastic achievement . . . to acquire knowledge and share in the traditionally accepted academic fundamentals . . . to develop the ability to make decisions, to solve problems, to reason independently, and to accept responsibility for self-evaluation and continuing self-improvement.

- Career and economic competence . . .
- Citizenship and civil responsibility . . .
- Competence in human and social relations . . .
- Moral and ethical values . . .
- Self-realization and mental and physical health . . .
- Aesthetic awareness . . .
- Cultural diversity . . .[3]

In addition to its optimistic rhetoric, what distinguishes this list is its 22
comprehensiveness. The high school is to touch most aspects of an
adolescent's existence — mind, body, morals, values, career. No one of
these areas is given especial prominence. School people arrogate to
themselves an obligation to all.

An example of the wide acceptability of these goals is found in the 23
courts. Forced to present a detailed definition of "thorough and efficient
education," elementary as well as secondary, a West Virginia judge
sampled the best of conventional wisdom and concluded that

> there are eight general elements of a thorough and efficient system of
> education: (a) Literacy, (b) The ability to add, subtract, multiply, and
> divide numbers, (c) Knowledge of government to the extent the child
> will be equipped as a citizen to make informed choices among persons
> and issues that affect his own governance, (d) Self-knowledge and knowl-
> edge of his or her total environment to allow the child to intelligently
> choose life work — to know his or her options, (e) Work-training and
> advanced academic training as the child may intelligently choose, (f)
> Recreational pursuits, (g) Interests in all creative arts such as music,
> theater, literature, and the visual arts, and (h) Social ethics, both behavioral
> and abstract, to facilitate compatibility with others in this society.[4]

That these eight — now powerfully part of the debate over the purpose 24
and practice of education in West Virginia — are reminiscent of the
influential list, "The Seven Cardinal Principles of Secondary Education,"

[3]Shasta High School, Redding, California. An eloquent and analogous statement, "The
Essentials of Education," one stressing explicitly the "interdependence of skills and content"
that is implicit in the Shasta High School statement, was issued in 1980 by a coalition of
education associations. Organizations for the Essentials of Education (Urbana, Illinois).
[Author's note]

[4]Judge Arthur M. Recht, in his order resulting from *Pauley v. Kelly*, 1979, as reprinted
in *Education Week*, May 26, 1982, p. 10. See also, in *Education Week*, January 16, 1983,
pp. 21, 24, Jonathan P. Sher, "The Struggle to Fulfill at Judicial Mandate: How Not to
'Reconstruct' Education in W. Va." [Author's note]

promulgated in 1918 by the National Education Association, is no surprise.[5] The rhetoric of high school purpose has been uniform and consistent for decades. Americans agree on the goals for their high schools.

That agreement is convenient, but it masks the fact that virtually all 25 the words in these goal statements beg definition. Some schools have labored long to identify specific criteria beyond them; the result has been lists of daunting pseudospecificity and numbing earnestness. However, most leave the words undefined and let the momentum of traditional practice speak for itself. That is why analyzing how Mark spends his time is important: From watching him one uncovers the important purposes of education, the ones that shape practice. Mark's day is similar to that of other high school students across the country, as similar as the rhetoric of one goal statement to others'. Of course, there are variations, but the extent of consistency in the shape of school routine for a large and diverse adolescent population is extraordinary, indicating more graphically than any rhetoric the measure of agreement in America about what one does in high school, and, by implication, what it is for.

The basic organizing structures in schools are familiar. Above all, 26 students are grouped by age (that is, freshman, sophomore, junior, senior), and all are expected to take precisely the same time — around 720 school days over four years, to be precise — to meet the requirements for a diploma. When one is out of his grade level, he can feel odd, as Mark did in his biology class. The goals are the same for all, and the means to achieve them are also similar.

Young males and females are treated remarkably alike; the schools' 27 goals are the same for each gender. In execution, there are differences, as those pressing sex discrimination suits have made educators intensely aware. The students in metalworking classes are mostly male; those in home economics, mostly female. But it is revealing how much less sex discrimination there is in high schools than in other American institutions. For many young women, the most liberated hours of their week are in school.

School is to be like a job: You start in the morning and end in the 28 afternoon, five days a week. You don't get much of a lunch hour, so you go home early, unless you are an athlete or are involved in some special school or extracurricular activity. School is conceived of as the children's workplace, and it takes young people off parents' hands and out of the

---

[5] Bureau of Education, Department of the Interior, "Cardinal Principles of Secondary Education: A Report of the Commission on the Reorganization of Secondary Education, appointed by the National Education Association," *Bulletin*, no. 35 (Washington: U.S. Government Printing Office, 1918). [Author's note]

labor market during prime-time work hours. Not surprisingly, many students see going to school as little more than a dogged necessity. They perceive the day-to-day routine, a Minnesota study reports, as one of "boredom and lethargy." One of the students summarizes: School is "boring, restless, tiresome, puts ya to sleep, tedious, monotonous, pain in the neck."[6]

The school schedule is a series of units of time: The clock is king.   29
The base time block is about fifty minutes in length. Some schools, on what they call modular scheduling, split that fifty-minute block into two or even three pieces. Most schools have double periods for laboratory work, especially in the sciences, or four-hour units for the small numbers of students involved in intensive vocational or other work-study programs. The flow of all school activity arises from or is blocked by these time units. "How much time do I have with my kids" is the teacher's key question.

Because there are many claims for those fifty-minute blocks, there is   30
little time set aside for rest between them, usually no more than three to ten minutes, depending on how big the school is and, consequently, how far students and teachers have to walk from class to class. As a result, there is a frenetic[7] quality to the school day, a sense of sustained restlessness. For the adolescents, there are frequent changes of room and fellow students, each change giving tempting opportunities for distraction, which are stoutly resisted by teachers. Some schools play soft music during these "passing times," to quiet the multitude, one principal told me.

Many teachers have a chance for a coffee break. Few students do. In   31
some city schools where security is a problem, students must be in class for seven consecutive periods, interrupted by a heavily monitored twenty-minute lunch period for small groups, starting as early as 10:30 A.M. and running to after 1:00 P.M. A high premium is placed on punctuality and on "being where you're supposed to be." Obviously, a low premium is placed on reflection and repose. The student rushes from class to class to collect knowledge. Savoring it, it is implied, is not to be done much in school, nor is such meditation really much admired. The picture that these familiar patterns yield is that of an academic supermarket. The purpose of going to school is to pick things up, in an organized and predictable way, the faster the better.

[6]Diane Hedin, Paula Simon, and Michael Robin, *Minnesota Youth Poll: Youth's Views on School and School Discipline*, Minnesota Report 184 (1983), Agricultural Experiment Station, University of Minnesota, p. 13. [Author's note]
[7]*frenetic:* frantic; frenzied.

What is supposed to be picked up is remarkably consistent among all sorts of high schools. Most schools specifically mandate three out of every five courses a student selects. Nearly all of these mandates fall into five areas — English, social studies, mathematics, science, and physical education. On the average, English is required to be taken each year, social studies and physical education three out of the four high school years, and mathematics and science one or two years. Trends indicate that in the mid-eighties there is likely to be an increase in the time allocated to these last two subjects. Most students take classes in these four major academic areas beyond the minimum requirements, sometimes in such special areas as journalism and "yearbook," offshoots of English departments.[8]

Press most adults about what high school is for, and you hear these subjects listed. *High school? That's where you learn English and math and that sort of thing.* Ask students, and you get the same answer. High school is to "teach" these "subjects."

What is often absent is any definition of these subjects or any rationale for them. They are just there, labels. Under those labels lie a multitude of things. A great deal of material is supposed to be "covered"; most of these courses are surveys, great sweeps of the stuff of their parent disciplines.

While there is often a sequence *within* subjects — algebra before trigonometry, "first-year" French before "second-year" French — there is rarely a coherent relationship or sequence *across* subjects. Even the most logically related matters — reading ability as a precondition for the reading of history books, and certain mathematical concepts or skills before the study of some of physics — are only loosely coordinated, if at all. There is little demand for a synthesis of it all; English, mathematics, and the rest are discrete items, to be picked up individually. The incentive for picking them up is largely through tests and, with success at these, in credits earned.

Coverage within subjects is the key priority. If some imaginative teacher makes a proposal to force the marriage of, say, mathematics and physics or to require some culminating challenges to students to use several subjects in the solution of a complex problem, and if this proposal will take "time" away from other things, opposition is usually phrased in terms of what may be thus forgone. If we do that, we'll have to give up colonial history. We won't be able to get to programming. We'll not

32

33

34

35

36

[8]I am indebted to Harold F. Sizer and Lyde E. Sizer for a survey of the diploma requirements of fifty representative secondary schools, completed for A Study of High Schools. [Author's note]

be able to read *Death of a Salesman*.[9] There isn't time. The protesters usually win out.

The subjects come at a student like Mark in random order, a kaleidoscope 37 of worlds: algebraic formulae to poetry to French verbs to Ping-Pong to the War of the Spanish Succession, all before lunch. Pupils are to pick up these things. Tests measure whether the picking up has been successful.

The lack of connection between stated goals, such as those of the 38 California high school cited earlier, and the goals inherent in school practice is obvious and, curiously, tolerated. Most striking is the gap between statements about "self-realization and mental and physical growth" or "moral and ethical values" — common rhetoric in school documents — and practice. Most physical education programs have neither the time nor the focus really to ensure fitness. Mental health is rarely defined. Neither are ethical values, save at the negative extremes, such as opposition to assault or dishonesty. Nothing in the regimen of a day like Mark's signals direct or implicit teaching in this area. The "schoolboy code" (not ratting on a fellow student) protects the marijuana pusher, and a leechlike associate is shrugged off without concern. The issue of the locker search was pushed aside, as not appropriate for class time.

Most students, like Mark, go to class in groups of twenty to twenty- 39 seven students. The expected attendance in some schools, particularly those in low-income areas, is usually higher, often thirty-five students per class, but high absentee rates push the actual numbers down. About twenty-five per class is an average figure for expected attendance, and the actual numbers are somewhat lower. There are remarkably few students who go to class in groups much larger or smaller than twenty-five.[10]

A student such as Mark sees five or six teachers per day; their differing 40 styles and expectations are part of his kaleidoscope. High school staffs are highly specialized: Guidance counselors rarely teach mathematics, mathematics teachers rarely teach English, principals rarely do any class-room instruction. Mark, then, is known a little bit by a number of people, each of whom sees him in one specialized situation. No one may know him as a "whole person" — unless he becomes a special problem or has special needs.

Save in extracurricular or coaching situations, such as in athletics, 41 drama, or shop classes, there is little opportunity for sustained conversation

[9]*Death of a Salesman:* 1957 award-winning drama by American playwright Arthur Miller.
[10]Education Research Service, Inc. *Class Size: A Summary of Research* (Arlington, Virginia, 1978); and *Class Size Research: A Critique of Recent Meta-Analyses* (Arlington, Virginia, 1980). [Author's note]

between student and teacher. The mode is a one-sentence or two-sentence exchange: *Mark, when was Grover Cleveland president?* Let's see, was 1890 . . . or something . . . wasn't he the one . . . he was elected twice, wasn't he? . . . *Yes . . . Gloria, can you get the dates right?* Dialogue is strikingly absent, and as a result the opportunity of teachers to challenge students' ideas in a systematic and logical way is limited. Given the rushed, full quality of the school day, it can seldom happen. One must infer that careful probing of students' thinking is not a high priority. How one gains (to quote the California school's statement of goals again) "the ability to make decisions, to solve problems, to reason independently, and to accept responsibility for self-evaluation and continuing self-improvement" without being challenged is difficult to imagine. One certainly doesn't learn these things merely from lectures and textbooks.

Most schools are nice places. Mark and his friends enjoy being in theirs. The adults who work in schools generally like adolescents. The academic pressures are limited, and the accommodations to students are substantial. For example, if many members of an English class have jobs after school, the English teacher's expectations for them are adjusted, downward. In a word, school is sensitively accommodating, as long as students are punctual, where they are supposed to be, and minimally dutiful about picking things up from the clutch of courses in which they enroll. 42

This characterization is not pretty, but it is accurate, and it serves to describe the vast majority of American secondary schools. "Taking subjects" in a systematized, conveyor-belt way is what one does in high school. That this process is, in substantial respects, not related to the rhetorical purposes of education is tolerated by most people, perhaps because they do not really either believe in those ill-defined goals or, in their heart of hearts, believe that schools can or should even try to achieve them. The students are happy taking subjects. The parents are happy, because that's what they did in high school. The rituals, the most important of which is graduation, remain intact. The adolescents are supervised, safely and constructively most of the time, during the morning and afternoon hours, and they are off the labor market. That is what high school is all about. 43

Engaging the Text

1. Sizer uses METAPHORS describing Mark's classes as a "kaleidoscope of worlds" and comparing his school to an "academic supermarket" or a "conveyor belt" from which students "pick up" ideas. What does Sizer mean by these metaphors? What do they suggest about the problems of high school education in the United States?

2. What kind of student is Mark? Imagine his background and home life. Why do you think Sizer chose him to illustrate his view of high school?

3. Would you say that Sizer's depiction of American high schools is accurate? How does it compare with your high school experience?

4. Debate Sizer's claim that "for most young women, the most liberated hours of their week are in school."

Exploring Connections

1. Compare and contrast Sizer's analysis of institutionalized education with that offered by David Elkind in Chapter Five, "The Changing Family."

2. Look ahead to Erich Fromm's selection, "Work in an Alienated Society," (p. 529). What connections can you see between Sizer's depiction of the high school routine and the kind of working situations described by Fromm?

Extending the Critical Context

1. Work in groups to design a high school that would make a "supermarket" or "kaleidoscope" approach to education impossible. What can students do within the structure of a traditional school to lessen the fragmentation of intellectual experience that Sizer describes?

2. Working in groups, write an educational "Bill of Wrongs" — a MANIFESTO detailing the shortcomings of education at the high school you attended and calling for specific reforms.

Life in School
MATT GROENING

The following two cartoons from Matt Groening's enormously popular collections, Life is Hell *and* School is Hell, *capture some of the rage, hopelessness, and humor that many students associate with the classroom. They're meant to make you laugh, but they may also help you examine some of the reservations you may have about your own school experience. Groening (b. 1954), a writer and syndicated cartoonist, has been nominated for an Emmy award for his work on* The Tracey Ullman Show.

© 1988 *School Is Hell* by Matt Groening. Reprinted by permission of Pantheon Books.

© 1988 *Love Is Hell* by Matt Groening. Reprinted by permission of Pantheon Books.

Engaging the Text

1. What attitude toward teachers and schools do these cartoons portray? How do they portray students? How accurate are these depictions?
2. What role does silence play in Groening's view of education?
3. Why does the "student" have only one ear?

Exploring Connections

1. How would Theodore Sizer, author of the previous selection, explain the humor in Groening's cartoons?

Extending the Critical Context

1. Try writing your own captions for Groening's cartoon balloons, or try your hand at drawing your own cartoon strip about school life.
2. Cite a few examples from your own school experience when you were just killing time in the way Groening's second cartoon suggests. Also cite examples of occasions when you believe you learned something truly beneficial. Compare notes with classmates.

Golden Rule Days: American Schoolrooms
JULES HENRY

This anthropological analysis of American education challenges conventional views of teaching and learning. Henry attempts to examine the effects of education as objectively as possible: He is interested in explaining what school actually does to the individual, not what we think it ought to do. Jules Henry (1904–1969) taught at Washington University for more than twenty years. His highly acclaimed Culture Against Man *(1963), from which this passage is taken, is considered a classic study of American culture.*

Introduction

School is an institution for drilling children in cultural orientations. 1 Educationists have attempted to free the school from drill, but have failed because they have gotten lost among a multitude of phantasms — always choosing the most obvious "enemy" to attack. Furthermore, with every enemy destroyed, new ones are installed among the old fortifications — the enduring contradictory maze of the culture. Educators think that when they have made arithmetic or spelling into a game; made it unnecessary for children to "sit up straight"; defined the relation between teacher and children as democratic; and introduced plants, fish, and hamsters into schoolrooms, they have settled the problem of drill. They are mistaken.

Education and the Human Condition

Learning to Learn. The paradox of the human condition is expressed   2
more in education than elsewhere in human culture, because learning to learn has been and continues to be *Homo sapiens'* most formidable evolutionary task. Although it is true that mammals, as compared to birds and fishes, have to learn so much that it is difficult to say by the time we get to chimpanzees what behavior is inborn and what is learned, the learning task has become so enormous for man that today learning — education — along with survival, constitutes a major preoccupation. In all the fighting over education we are simply saying that we are not yet satisfied — after about a million years of struggling to become human — that we have mastered the fundamental human task, learning. It must also be clear that we will never quite learn how to learn, for since *Homo sapiens* is self-changing, and since the *more* culture changes the *faster* it changes, man's methods and rate of learning will never quite keep pace with his need to learn. This is the heart of the problem of "cultural lag," for each fundamental scientific discovery presents man with an incalculable number of problems which he cannot foresee. Who, for example, would have anticipated that the discoveries of Einstein would have presented us with the social problems of the nuclear age, or that information theory would have produced unemployment and displacement in world markets?

Fettering and Freeing. Another learning problem inherent in the human   3
condition is the fact that we must conserve culture while changing it; that we must always be *more* sure of surviving than of adapting — *as we see it.* Whenever a new idea appears, our first concern as *animals* must be that it does not kill us; then, and only then, can we look at it from other points of view. While it is true that we are often mistaken, either because we become enchanted with certain modes of thought or because we cannot anticipate their consequences, this tendency to look first at survival has resulted in fettering the capacity to learn new things. In general, primitive people solved this problem simply by walling their

children off from new possibilities by educational methods that, largely through fear (including ridicule, beating, and mutilation) so narrowed the perceptual sphere that other than traditional ways of viewing the world became unthinkable. Thus throughout history the cultural pattern has been a device for binding the intellect. Today, when we think we wish to free the mind so it will soar, we are still, nevertheless, bound by the ancient paradox, for we must hold our culture together through clinging to old ideas lest, in adopting new ones, we literally cease to exist.

In searching the literature on the educational practices of other civ-   4
ilizations I have found nothing that better expresses the need to teach and to fetter than the following, from an account by a traveler along the Niger River in Africa in the fourteenth century:

> . . . their zeal for learning the Koran[1] by heart [is so great that] they
> put their children in chains if they show any backwardness in memorizing
> it, and they are not set free until they have it by heart. I visited the
> qadi[2] in his house on the day of the festival. His children were chained
> up, so I said to him, "Will you not let them loose?" He replied, "I
> shall not do so until they learn the Koran by heart."[3]

Perhaps the closest material parallel we have to this from our own   5
cultural tradition is the stocks in which ordinary English upper-class children were forced to stand in the eighteenth century while they pored over their lessons at home. The fettering of the mind while we "set the spirit free" or the fettering of the spirit as we free the mind is an abiding paradox of "civilization" in its more refined dimensions. It is obvious that chimpanzees are incapable of this paradox. It is this capacity to pass from the jungles of the animal world into the jungle of paradox of the human condition that, more than anything else, marks off human from animal learning. It is this jungle that confronts the child in his early days at school, and that seals his destiny — if it has not previously been determined by poverty — as an eager mind or as a faceless learner.

Since education is always against some things and for others, it bears   6
the burden of the cultural obsessions. While the Old Testament extols without cease the glory of the One God, it speaks with equal emphasis

---

[1]*Koran:* the sacred text of the Islamic religion; the foundation of Islamic law, culture, and politics.

[2]*qadi:* a judge in an Islamic community.

[3]Ibn Battuta, *Travels in Asia and Africa,* London: Broadway House, Carter Lane, 1957, p. 330. (Translated and selected by H.A.R. Gibb, from the original written in 1325–54.) [Author's note]

against the gods of the Philistines,[4] while the children of the Dakota Indians learned loyalty to their own tribe, they learned to hate the Crow; and while our children are taught to love our American democracy, they are taught contempt for totalitarian regimes. It thus comes about that most educational systems are imbued with anxiety and hostility, that they are against as many things as they are for. Because, therefore, so much anxiety inheres in any human educational system — anxiety that it may free when it should fetter; anxiety that it may fetter when it should free; anxiety that it may teach sympathy when it should teach anger; anxiety that it may disarm where it should arm — our contemporary education system is constantly under attack. When, in anxiety about the present state of our world, we turn upon the schools with even more venom than we turn on our government, we are "right" in the sense that it is in the schools that the basic binding and freeing processes that will "save" us will be established. But being "right" derives not so much from the faults of our schools but from the fact that the schools are the central conserving force of the culture. The Great Fear thus turns our hostility unerringly in the direction of the focus of survival and change, in the direction of education.

Creativity and Absurdity. The function of education has never been 7 to free the mind and the spirit of man, but to bind them; and to the end that the mind and spirit of his children should never escape, *Homo sapiens* has employed praise, ridicule, admonition, accusation, mutilation, and even torture to chain them to the culture pattern. Throughout most of his historic course *Homo sapiens* has wanted from his children acquiescence, not originality. It is natural that this should be so, for where every man is unique there is no society, and where there is no society there can be no man. Contemporary American educators think they want creative children, yet it is an open question as to what they expect these children to create. And certainly the classrooms — from kindergarten to graduate school — in which they expect it to happen are not crucibles of creative activity and thought. It stands to reason that were young people truly creative the culture would fall apart, for originality, by definition, is different from what is given, and what is given is the culture itself. From the endless, pathetic, "creative hours" of kindergarten to the most abstruse problems in sociology and anthropology, the function of education is to prevent the truly creative intellect from getting out of hand. Only in the exact and the biological sciences do we permit

---

[4]*Philistines:* inhabitants of ancient Philistia on the eastern Mediterranean and the antagonists of the early Israelites.

unlimited freedom, for we have (but only since the Renaissance, since Galileo[5] and Bruno[6] underwent the Inquisition[7]) found a way — or *thought* we had found a way — to bind the explosive powers of science in the containing vessel of the social system.

American classrooms, like educational institutions anywhere, express   8
the values, preoccupations, and fears found in the culture as a whole. School has no choice; it must train the children to fit the culture as it is. School can give training in skills; it cannot teach creativity. All the American school can conceivably do is nurture creativity when it appears. And who has the eyes to see it? Since the creativity that is conserved and encouraged will always be that which seems to do the most for culture, which seems at the moment to do the most for the obsessions and the brutal preoccupations and anxieties from which we all suffer, schools nowadays encourage the child with gifts in mathematics and the exact sciences. But the child who has the intellectual strength to see through social shams is of no consequence to the educational system.

Creative intellect is mysterious, devious, and irritating. An intellectually   9
creative child may fail, for example, in social studies, simply because he cannot understand the stupidities he is taught to believe as "fact." He may even end up agreeing with his teachers that he is "stupid" in social studies. Learning social studies is, to no small extent, whether in elementary school or the university, learning to be stupid. Most of us accomplish this task before we enter high school. But the child with a socially creative imagination will not be encouraged to play among new social systems, values, and relationships; nor is there much likelihood of it, if for no other reason than that the social studies teachers will perceive such a child as a poor student. Furthermore, such a child will simply be unable to fathom the absurdities that seem transparent *truth* to the teacher. What idiot believes in the "law of supply and demand," for example? But the children who do tend to *become* idiots, and learning to be an idiot is part of growing up! Or, as Camus[8] put it, learning to be *absurd*. Thus the child who finds it impossible to learn to think the absurd the truth, who finds it difficult to accept absurdity as a way of life, the intellectually creative child whose mind makes him flounder

[5]*Galileo:* Galileo Galilei, Italian physicist and astronomer (1564–1642), who was forced by the Roman Catholic Church to recant his revolutionary scientific ideas.

[6]*Bruno:* Giordano Bruno, Italian philosopher (1548–1600), burnt at the stake because of his unorthodox religious ideas.

[7]*Inquisition:* a religious tribunal established by the Roman Catholic Church in the fourteenth century that combated and punished individuals who held unorthodox ideas.

[8]*Camus:* Albert Camus, French-Algerian novelist, essayist, and dramatist (1913–1960), recipient of the Nobel Prize for literature in 1957.

like a poor fish in the net of absurdities flung around him in school, usually comes to think himself stupid.

The schools have therefore never been places for the stimulation of 10 young minds. If all through school the young were provoked to question the Ten Commandments, the sanctity of revealed religion, the foundations of patriotism, the profit motive, the two-party system, monogamy, the laws of incest, and so on, we would have more creativity than we could handle. In teaching our children to accept fundamentals of social relationships and religious beliefs without question we follow the ancient highways of the human race, which extend backward into the dawn of the species, and indefinitely into the future. There must therefore be more of the caveman than of the spaceman about our teachers.

Up to this point I have argued that learning to learn is man's foremost 11 evolutionary task, that the primary aim of education has been to fetter the mind and the spirit of man rather than to free them, and that nowadays we confront this problem in our effort to stimulate thought while preventing the mind of the child from going too far. I have also urged that since education, as the central institution for the training of the young in the ways of the culture, is thus burdened with its obsessive fears and hates, contemporary attacks upon our schools are the reflection of a nervousness inherent in the school as a part of the central obsession. Finally, I argued that creativity is the last thing wanted in any culture because of its potentialities for disruptive thinking; that the primordial dilemma of all education derives from the necessity of training the mighty brain of *Homo sapiens* to be stupid; and that creativity, when it is encouraged (as in science in our culture), occurs only after the creative thrust of an idea has been tamed and directed toward socially approved ends. In this sense, then, creativity can become the most obvious conformity. In this sense we can expect scientists — our cultural maximizers — to be socially no *more* creative than the most humble elementary school teacher, and probably less creative socially than a bright second-grader.

Communication

Much of what I have to say in the following pages pivots on the 12 inordinate capacity of a human being to learn more than one thing at a time. Although it is true that all the higher orders of animals can learn several things at a time, this capacity for polyphasic learning reaches unparalleled development in man. A child writing the word "August" on the board, for example, is not only learning the word "August" but also how to hold the chalk without making it squeak, how to write clearly, how to keep going even though the class is tittering at his slowness, how to appraise the glances of the children in order to know whether he is doing it right or wrong, et cetera. If the spelling, arithmetic, or music lesson were only what it appeared to be, the education of the American child would be much simpler; but it is all the things the child learns *along with* his subject matter that really constitute the drag on the educational process as it applies to the curriculum.

A classroom can be compared to a communications system, for certainly   13
there is a flow of messages between teacher (transmitter) and pupils (receivers) and among the pupils; contacts are made and broken, messages can be sent at a certain rate of speed only, and so on. But there is also another interesting characteristic of communications systems that is applicable to classrooms, and that is their inherent tendency to generate *noise*. *Noise*, in communications theory, applies to all those random fluctuations of the system that cannot be controlled. They are the sounds that are not part of the message: the peculiar quality communicated to the voice by the composition of the telephone circuit, the static on the radio, and so forth. In a classroom lesson on arithmetic, for example, such *noise* would range all the way from the competitiveness of the students, the quality of the teacher's voice ("I remember exactly how she sounded when she told me to sit down"), to the shuffling of the children's feet. The striking thing about the child is that along with his arithmetic — his "messages about arithmetic" — he learns all the noise in the system also. It is this inability to avoid *learning the noise with the subject matter* that constitutes one of the greatest hazards for an organism so prone to polyphasic learning as man. It is this that brings it about that an objective observer cannot tell which is being learned in any lesson, the *noise* or the formal subject matter. But — and mark this well — it is *not* primarily the message (let us say, the arithmetic or the spelling) that constitutes the most important subject matter to be learned, but the noise! The most significant cultural learnings — primarily the cultural drives — are communicated as *noise*.

Let us take up these points by studying selected incidents in some   14
of the suburban classrooms my students and I studied over a period of six years.

The Realm of Song

It is March 17 and the children are singing songs from Ireland and her neighbors. The teacher plays on the piano, while the children sing. While some children sing, a number of them hunt in the index, find a song belonging to one of Ireland's neighbors, and raise their hands in order that they may be called on to name the next song. The singing is of that pitchless quality always heard in elementary school classrooms.

The teacher sometimes sings through a song first, in her off key, weakishly husky voice.

The usual reason for having this kind of a song period is that the children are broadened, while they learn something about music and singing. 15

It is true that the children learn something about singing, but what they learn is to sing like everybody else, in the standard, elementary school pitchlessness of the English-speaking world — a phenomenon impressive enough for D. H. Lawrence[9] to have mentioned it in *Lady Chatterley's Lover*. The difficulty in achieving true pitch is so pervasive among us that missionaries carry it with them to distant jungles, teaching the natives to sing hymns off key. Hence on Sundays we would hear our Pilagá Indian friends, all of them excellent musicians in the Pilagá scale, carefully copy the missionaries by singing Anglican hymns, translated into Pilagá, off key exactly as sharp or as flat as the missionaries sang. Thus one of the first things a child with a good ear learns in elementary school is to be musically stupid; he learns to doubt or to scorn his innate musical capacities. 16

But possibly more important than this is the use to which teacher and pupils put the lesson in ways not related at all to singing or to Ireland and her neighbors. To the teacher this was an opportunity to let the children somehow share the social aspects of the lesson with her, to democratically participate in the selection of the songs. The consequence was distraction from singing as the children hunted in the index and raised their hands to have their song chosen. The net result was to activate the competitive, achievement, and dominance drives of the children, as they strove with one another for the teacher's attention, and through her, to get the class to do what they wanted it to do. In this way the song period on Ireland and her neighbors was scarcely a lesson in singing but rather one in extorting the maximal benefit for the Self from *any* situation. The first lesson a child has to learn when he comes to school is that lessons are not what they seem. He must then forget this and act as if they were. This is the first step toward "school mental health"; it is also the first step in becoming absurd. In the first and second grades teachers constantly scold children because they do not raise their hands enough — the prime symbol of having learned what school is all about. After that, it is no longer necessary; the kids have "tumbled" to the idea. 17

[9]*D. H. Lawrence:* English author and poet (1885–1930), best known for his controversial novel *Lady Chatterley's Lover*.

The second lesson is to put the teachers' and students' criteria in place   18
of his own. He must learn that the proper way to sing is tunelessly and
not the way *he* hears the music; that the proper way to paint is the way
the teacher says, not the way he sees it; that the proper attitude is not
pleasure but competitive horror at the success of his classmates, and so
on. And these lessons must be so internalized that he will fight his
parents if they object. The early schooling process is not successful unless
it has accomplished in the child an acquiescence in its criteria, unless
the child *wants* to think the way school has taught him to think. He
must have accepted alienation as a rule of life. What we see in the
kindergarten and the early years of school is the pathetic surrender of
babies. How could it be otherwise?

Now, if children are taught to adopt alienation as a way of life, it   19
follows that they must have feelings of inadequacy, for nothing so saps
self-confidence as alienation from the Self. It would follow that school,
the chief agent in the process, must try to provide the children with
"ego support," for culture tries to remedy the ills it creates.

Hence the effort to give recognition; and hence the conversion of the   20
songfest into an exercise in Self-realization. That anything essential was
nurtured in this way is an open question, for the kind of individuality
that was recognized as the children picked titles out of the index was
mechanical, without a creative dimension, and under the strict control
of the teacher. Let us conclude this discussion by saying that *school
metamorphoses the child, giving it the kind of Self the school can manage,
and then proceeds to minister to the Self it has made*.

Perhaps I have put the matter grossly, appearing to credit the school   21
with too much formative power. So let us say this: let us grant that
American children, being American, come to school on the first day with
certain potentialities for experiencing success and failure, for enjoying
the success of their mates or taking pleasure in their failure, for competitiveness, for cooperation, for driving to achieve or for coasting along,
et cetera. But school cannot handle variety, for as an institution dealing
with masses of children it can manage only on the assumption of a
homogeneous mass. Homogeneity is therefore accomplished by defining
the children in a certain way and by handling all situations uniformly.
In this way no child is directly coerced. It is simply that the child must
react in terms of the institutional definitions or he fails. The first two
years of school are spent not so much in learning the rudiments of the
three Rs, as in learning definitions.

It would be foolish to imagine that school, as a chief molder of character,   22
could do much more than homogenize the children, but it does do more
— it sharpens to a cutting edge the drives the culture needs.

If you bind or prune an organism so it can move only in limited ways, 23
it will move rather excessively in that way. If you lace a man into a
strait jacket so he can only wiggle his toes, he will wiggle them *hard*.
Since in school children are necessarily constrained to limited human
expression, under the direction of the teacher, they will have a natural
tendency to do with exaggerated enthusiasm what they are permitted
to do. They are like the man in the strait jacket. In class children are
usually not permitted to talk much, to walk around much, to put their
arms around each other during lessons, to whistle or sing. But they are
permitted to raise their hands and go to the pencil sharpener almost at
will. Thus hand-raising, going to the pencil sharpener, or hunting in the
back of a song book for a song for the class to sing are not so much
activities stemming from the requirements of an immediate situation as
expressions of the intensified need of the organism for relief from the
five-hour-a-day pruning and confining process. This goes under the pedagogical title of "release of tension"; but in our view the issue is that
what the children are at length permitted — and invited — to do, and
what they therefore often throw themselves into with the enthusiasm of
multiple pent-up feelings, are cultural drive-activities narrowly construed
by the school.

At the Blackboard

> Boris had trouble reducing "12/16" to the lowest terms, and could
> only get as far as "6/8". The teacher asked him quietly if that was as
> far as he could reduce it. She suggested he "think." Much heaving up
> and down and waving of hands by the other children, all frantic to
> correct him. Boris pretty unhappy, probably mentally paralyzed. The
> teacher, quiet, patient, ignores the others and concentrates with look
> and voice on Boris. She says, "Is there a bigger number than two you
> can divide into the two parts of the fraction?" After a minute or two,
> she becomes more urgent, but there is no response from Boris. She
> then turns to the class and says, "Well, who can tell Boris what the
> number is?" A forest of hands appears, and the teacher calls Peggy.
> Peggy says that four may be divided into the numerator and the
> denominator.

Thus Boris's failure has made it possible for Peggy to succeed; his 24
depression is the price of her exhilaration; his misery the occasion for
her rejoicing. This is the standard condition of the American elementary
school, and is why so many of us feel a contraction of the heart even if
someone we never knew succeeds merely at garnering plankton in the
Thames:[10] because so often somebody's success has been bought at the

[10]*Thames:* a river in southern England flowing through London.

cost of our failure. To a Zuni, Hopi, or Dakota Indian, Peggy's performance would seem cruel beyond belief. . . . Yet Peggy's action seems natural to us; and so it is. How else would you run our world! And since all but the brightest children have the constant experience that others succeed at their expense they cannot but develop an inherent tendency to hate — to hate the success of others, to hate others who are successful, and to be determined to prevent it. Along with this, naturally, goes the hope that others will fail. This hatred masquerades under the euphemistic name of "envy."

Looked at from Boris's point of view, the nightmare at the blackboard was, perhaps, a lesson in controlling himself so that he would not fly shrieking from the room under the enormous public pressure. Such experiences imprint on the mind of every man in our culture the *Dream of Failure,* so that over and over again, night in, night out, even at the pinnacle of success, a man will dream not of success, but of failure. *The external nightmare is internalized for life.* It is this dream that, above all other things, provides the fierce human energy required by technological drivenness. It was not so much that Boris was learning arithmetic, but that he was learning the *essential nightmare. To be successful in our culture one must learn to dream of failure.*

From the point of view of the other children, of course, they were learning to yap at the heels of a failure. And why not? Have they not dreamed the dream of flight themselves? If the culture does not teach us to fly from failure or to rush in, hungry for success where others have failed, who will try again where others have gone broke? Nowadays, as misguided teachers try to soften the blow of classroom failure, they inadvertently sap the energies of success. The result will be a nation of chickens unwilling to take a chance.

When we say that "culture teaches drives and values" we do not state the case quite precisely. One should say, rather, that culture (and especially the school) provides the occasions in which drives and values are *experienced in events* that strike us with *overwhelming and constant force.* To say that culture "teaches" puts the matter too mildly. Actually culture invades and infests the mind as an obsession. If it does not, culture will not "work," for only an obsession has the power to withstand the impact of critical differences; to fly in the face of contradiction; to engulf the mind so that it will see the world only as the culture decrees that it shall be seen; to compel a person to be absurd. The central emotion in obsession is fear, and the central obsession in education is fear of failure. In order not to fail most students are willing to believe anything and to care not whether what they are told is true or false. Thus one becomes absurd

25

26

27

through being afraid; but paradoxically, *only by remaining absurd can one feel free from fear*. Hence the immovableness of the absurd.

In examining education as a process of teaching the culture pattern, 28 I have discussed a singing lesson [and] an arithmetic lesson. . . . Now let us consider a spelling lesson in a fourth-grade class.

"Spelling Baseball"

> The children form a line along the back of the room. They are to play "spelling baseball," and they have lined up to be chosen for the two teams. There is much noise, but the teacher quiets it. She has selected a boy and a girl and sent them to the front of the room as team captains to choose their teams. As the boy and girl pick the children to form their teams, each child chosen takes a seat in orderly succession around the room. Apparently they know the game well. Now Tom, who has not yet been chosen, tries to call attention to himself in order to be chosen. Dick shifts his position to be more in the direct line of vision of the choosers, so that he may not be overlooked. He seems quite anxious. Jane, Tom, Dick, and one girl whose name the observer does not know, are the last to be chosen. The teacher even has to remind the choosers that Dick and Jane have not been chosen. . . .
>
> The teacher now gives out words for the children to spell, and they write them on the board. Each word is a pitched ball, and each correctly spelled word is a base hit. The children move around the room from base to base as their teammates spell the words correctly. With some of the words the teacher gives a little phrase: "Tongue: watch your tongue; don't let it say things that aren't kind." Butcher: the butcher is a good friend to have." "Dozen: twelve of many things." "Knee: get down on your knee." "Pocket: keep your hand out of your pocket, and anybody else's." "No talking! Three out!" The children say, "Oh, oh!"
>
> The outs seem to increase in frequency as each side gets near the children chosen last. The children have great difficulty spelling "August." As they make mistakes, those in the seats say, "No!" The teacher says, "Man on third." As a child at the board stops and thinks, the teacher says, "There's a time limit; you can't take too long, honey." At last, after many children fail on "August" one child gets it right and returns, grinning with pleasure, to her seat. . . . The motivation level in this game seems terrific. All the children seem to watch the board, to know what's right and wrong, and seem quite keyed up. There is no lagging in moving from base to base. The child who is now writing "Thursday" stops to think after the first letter, and the children snicker. He stops after another letter. More snickers. He gets the word wrong. There are frequent signs of joy from the children when their side is right.

Since English is not pronounced as it is spelled, "language skills" are 29 a disaster for educators as well as for students. We start the problem of "spelling baseball" with the fact that the spelling of English is so mixed up and contradictory and makes such enormous demands on the capacity for being absurd that nowadays most people cannot spell. "Spelling baseball" is an effort to take the "weariness, the fever, and the fret" out of spelling by absurdly transforming it into a competitive game. Over and over again it has seemed to our psychologist designers of curriculum scenery that the best way to relieve boredom is to transmute it into competition. Since children are usually good competitors, though they may never become good spellers, and although they may never learn to *spell* "success" (which really should be written sukses), they know what it *is*, how to go after it, and how it feels not to have it. A competitive game is indicated when children are failing, because the drive to succeed in the *game* may carry them to victory over the *subject matter*. At any rate it makes spelling less boring for the teacher and the students, for it provides the former with a drama of excited children, and the latter with a motivation that transports them out of the secular dreariness of classroom routine. "Spelling baseball" is thus a major effort in the direction of making things seem not as they are. But once a spelling lesson is cast in the form of a game of baseball a great variety of *noise* enters the system, because the sounds of *baseball* (the baseball "message") cannot but be *noise* in a system intended to communicate *spelling*. Let us therefore analyze some of the baseball noise that has entered this spelling system from the sandlots and the bleachers.

We see first that a teacher has set up a choosing-rejecting system 30 directly adopted from kid baseball. I played ball just that way in New York. The two best players took turns picking out teammates from the bunch, coldly selecting the best hitters and fielders first; as we went down the line it did not make much difference who got the chronic muffers (the kids who couldn't catch a ball) and fanners (the kids who couldn't hit a ball). I recall that the kids who were not good players danced around and called out to the captains, "How about me, Slim? How about me?" Or they called attention to themselves with gestures and intense grimaces, as they pointed to their chests. It was pretty noisy. Of course, it didn't make any difference because the captains knew whom they were going to try to get, and there was not much of an issue after the best players had been sorted out to one or the other team. It was an honest jungle and there was nothing in it that did not belong to the high tension of kid baseball. But nobody was ever left out; and even the worst were never permitted to sit on the sidelines.

"Spelling baseball" is thus sandlot baseball dragged into the schoolroom 31 and bent to the uses of spelling. If we reflect that one could not settle a baseball game by converting it into a spelling lesson, we see that baseball is bizarrely *irrelevant* to spelling. If we reflect further that a kid who is a poor speller might yet be a magnificent ballplayer, we are even further impressed that learning spelling through baseball is learning by absurd association. In "spelling baseball" words become detached from their real significance and become assimilated to baseballs. Thus a spelling game that promotes absurd associations provides an indispensable bridge between the larger culture, where doubletalk is supreme, and the primordial meaningfulness of language. It provides also an introduction to those associations of mutually irrelevant ideas so well known to us from advertising — girls and vodka gimlets, people and billiard balls, lipstick and tree-houses, et cetera.

In making spelling into a baseball game one drags into the classroom 32 whatever associations a child may have to the impersonal sorting process of kid baseball, and in this way some of the *noise* from the baseball system enters spelling. But there are differences between the baseball world and the "spelling baseball" world also. Having participated in competitive athletics all through my youth, I seem to remember that we sorted ourselves by skills, and we recognized that some of us were worse than others. In baseball I also seem to remember that if we struck out or muffed a ball we hated ourselves and turned flips of rage, while our teammates sympathized with our suffering. In "spelling baseball" one experiences the sickening sensation of being left out as others are picked — to such a degree that the teachers even have to remind team captains that some are unchosen. One's failure is paraded before the class minute upon minute, until, when the worst spellers are the only ones left, the conspicuousness of the failures has been enormously increased: Thus the *noise* from baseball is amplified by a *noise* factor specific to the classroom.

It should not be imagined that I "object" to all of this, for in the first 33 place I am aware of the indispensable social functions of the spelling game, and in the second place, I can see that the rendering of failure conspicuous, the forcing of it on the mind of the unchosen child by a process of creeping extrusion from the group, cannot but intensify the quality of the essential nightmare, and thus render an important service to the culture. Without nightmares human culture has never been possible. Without hatred competition cannot take place.

One can see from the description of the game that drive is heightened 34 in a complex competitive interlock: Each child competes with every other to get the words right; each child competes with all for status and approval among his peers; each child competes with the other children for the approval of the teacher; and finally, each competes as a member of a team. Here failure will be felt doubly because although in an ordinary spelling lesson one fails alone, in "spelling baseball" one lets down the children on one's team. Thus though in the game the motivation toward spelling is heightened so that success becomes triumph, so does failure become disaster. The greater the excitement the more intense the feeling of success and failure, and the importance of spelling or failing to spell "August" becomes exaggerated. But it is in the nature of an obsession to exaggerate the significance of events.

We come now to the *noise* introduced by the teacher. In order to make the words clear she puts each one in a sentence: "Tongue: watch your tongue; don't let it say things that aren't kind." "Butcher: the butcher is a good friend to have." "Dozen: twelve of many things." "Knee: get down on your knee." "Pocket: keep your hand out of your pocket, and anybody else's." More relevant associations to the words would be, "The leg bends at the knee." "A butcher cuts up meat." "I carry something in my pocket," etc. What the teacher's sentences do is introduce a number of her idiosyncratic cultural preoccupations, without clarifying anything; for there is no *necessary* relation between butcher and friend, between floor and knee, between pocket and improperly intrusive hands, and so on. In her way, therefore, the teacher establishes the same irrelevance between words and associations as the game does between spelling and baseball. She amplifies the *noise* by introducing ruminations from her own inner communication system.

The unremitting effort by the system to bring the cultural drives to a fierce pitch must ultimately turn the children against one another; and though they cannot punch one another in the nose or pull each other's hair in class, they can vent some of their hostility in carping criticism of one another's work . . .

It stands to reason that a competitive system must do this; and adults, since they are always tearing each other to pieces, should understand that children will be no different. School is indeed a training for later life not because it teaches the 3 Rs (more or less), but because it instills the essential cultural nightmare fear of failure, envy of success, and absurdity.

Engaging the Text

1. What does Henry mean when he speaks of "culture lag," the role of "anxiety" in education, "polyphasic learning," and "noise"? Try to illustrate each concept with CONCRETE examples as you explain them.

2. According to Henry, culture both fetters and frees the individual. How does

education assist this process? What is Henry's attitude regarding the fettering aspects of education?

3. What does Henry mean when he says that the end of schooling is learning to be absurd?

4. Offer your own counterinterpretations of the classroom interactions Henry describes here. Ask yourself, for example, if competition has any value beyond its ability to instill fear of failure. Are there important aspects of education and the school experience that he overlooks?

Exploring Connections

1. To what extent does Sizer's appraisal of the American high school (p. 429) support or refute Henry's analysis of education?

2. How might Henry interpret Groening's cartoons (pp. 441, 442)? Is Groening's lone student "absurd" by Henry's definition?

Extending the Critical Context

1. Describe in detail a habitual activity you performed in elementary school, including the behavior of teachers and students, the stated purpose of the activity, and so on. Work in small groups to interpret these rituals as Henry might.

2. Do you agree with Henry that "education is always against some things and for others"? From your PERSPECTIVE, what things has your education been for and against?

3. Assuming you are the principal of a school founded on a frank acknowledgment of Henry's view of education, draw up a list of the qualities you would look for in a good teacher. Draw up another list describing your educational goals and the criteria you would use to measure academic success.

4. One form of the competition that Henry describes is competition for grades. Stage a debate in your class on the utility of testing and grading.

Keeping Track

JEANNIE OAKES

Most students in the United States have experienced "tracking" — the practice of placing students in a special sequence of courses according to measurements of their achievement, ability, or motivation. The following selection presents some of the arguments used to justify academic tracking.

It also presents a collection of revealing statements by students and teachers in vocational and college preparatory tracks. Jeannie Oakes (b. 1943) works for RAND, a company specializing in social research, and is co-author of the book Critical Perspective on the Organization and Improvement of Schooling: 1986.

. . . Tracking is the process whereby students are divided into categories 1 so that they can be assigned in groups to various kinds of classes. Sometimes students are classified as fast, average, or slow learners and placed into fast, average, or slow classes on the basis of their scores on achievement or ability tests. Often teachers' estimates of what students have already learned or their potential for learning more determine how students are identified and placed. Sometimes students are classified according to what seems most appropriate to their future lives. Sometimes, but rarely in any genuine sense, students themselves choose to be in "vocational," "general," or "academic" programs. In some schools students are classified and placed separately for each academic subject they take — fast in math, average in science; in other schools a single decision determines a student's program of classes for the entire day, semester, year, and perhaps even six years of secondary schooling. However it's done, tracking, in essence, is sorting — a sorting of students that has certain predictable characteristics.

First, students are identified in a rather public way as to their intellectual 2 capabilities and accomplishments and separated into a hierarchical system of groups for instruction. Second, these groups are labeled quite openly and characterized in the minds of teachers and others as being of a certain type — high ability, low achieving, slow, average, and so on. Clearly these groups are not equally valued in the school; occasional defensive responses and appearances of special privilege — i.e., small classes, programmed learning, and the like for slower students — rarely mask the essential fact that they are less preferred. Third, individual students in these groups come to be defined by others — both adults and their peers — in terms of these group types. In other words, a student in a high-achieving group is seen as a high-achieving *person,* bright, smart, quick, and in the eyes of many, *good.* And those in the low-achieving groups come to be called slow, below average, and — often when people are being less careful — dummies, sweathogs, or yahoos. Fourth, on the basis of these sorting decisions, the groupings of students that result, and the way educators see the students in these groups, teenagers are treated by and experience schools very differently.

Tracking is [a] taken-for-granted school practice. It is so much a part 3 of how instruction is organized in secondary schools — and has been for as long as most of us can remember — that we seldom question it. We *assume* that it is best for students. But we don't very often look behind this assumption to the evidence and beliefs on which it rests.

I don't mean to imply by this that no one is concerned about grouping 4 students. I think, in fact, that the contrary is true. School people usually spend a great deal of thought deciding what group students should be placed in. They want to make sure that placements are appropriate and fair. And further, what appear to be incorrect placements are often brought to the attention of teachers and counselors, usually with a great deal of concern. Adjustments sometimes need to be made. This is something we seem to want to be very responsible about. But this very concern over correct and fair placements underscores my point. In some way, we all know that what group or track a student is in makes a very real difference in his education. So at some level, we know that grouping is a very serious business. What we don't seem to question very much, however, is whether the practice of grouping students itself helps us achieve what we intend in schools.

Learning Beyond Content

QUESTION:
What are the five most critical things you want the students in your class to learn this year? By learn, we mean everything that the student should have upon leaving the class that (s)he did not have upon entering.

We asked this question of each of the teachers during our interviews 5 with them. Among their responses, teachers of high-track classes typically included the following kinds of answers.

RESPONSES:
Interpreting and identifying.
Evaluation, investigating power

High-track Science — junior high

Deal with thinking activities — Think for basic answers — essay-type questions.

High-track English — junior high

Ability to reason logically in all subject areas.

High-track math — senior high

The art of research.

High-track English — senior high

Learn how to test and prove ideas. Use and work with scientific equipment. Learning basic scientific facts and principles.

High-track Science — junior high

Scientific reasoning and logic.

High-track Science — senior high

Investigating technology, investigating values.

High-track Social Science — junior high

Self-reliance, taking on responsibilities themselves.

High-track Science — junior high

To learn values and morals — to make own personal decisions.

High-track English — junior high

To think critically — to analyze, *ask* questions.

High-track Social Science — junior high

Individual interpretation of materials covered.

High-track English — senior high

Logical thought processes. Analysis of given information. Ability to understand exactly what is asked in a question. Ability to perceive the relationship between information that is given in a problem or a statement and what is asked.

High-track Science — senior high

Love and respect for math — want them to stay curious, excited and to keep believing they can do it.

High-track Math — junior high

To realize that all people are entitled to certain inalienable rights.

High-track Social Science — junior high

To think critically (analyzing).

High-track English — senior high

How to think critically — analyze data, convert word problems into numerical order.

High-track Math — senior high

To be creative — able to express oneself.

High-track English — senior high

The most important thing — think more logically when they leave.

High-track Math — senior high

Ability to think and use information. Concept development.

High-track Science — senior high

Ability to think for themselves.

High-track Science — senior high

How to evaluate — think objectively. To think logically and with clarity and to put it on paper. To be able to appreciate a variety of authors' works and opinions without judging them by their own personal standards.

High-track English — senior high

Confidence in their own thoughts.

High-track English — senior high

Able to collect and organize information. Able to think critically.

High-track Social Science — junior high

Determine best approach to problem solving. Recognize different approaches.

> High-track Math — senior high

That their own talents and thoughts are important. Development of imagination. Critical thinking.

> High-track English — senior high

Problem-solving situations — made to think for themselves. Realizing importance of their education and use of time. Easy way is not always the best way.

> High-track Science — senior high

Better feeling for their own abilities and sense of what it's like in a college course.

> High-track Math — senior high

To gain some interpretive skills.

> High-track English — senior high

Teachers of low-track classes said the following kinds of learning were 6
essential for their students:

Develop more self-discipline — better use of time.

> Low-track English — junior high

Respect for each other.

> Low-track Math — junior high

I want them to respect my position — if they'll get this, I'll be happy.

> Low-track Math — junior high

That they know that their paychecks will be correct when they receive them. Punctuality, self-discipline and honesty will make them successful in their job. They must begin and end each day with a smile. To be able to figure their own income tax (at the) end of the year. Properly planning to insure favorable performances.

> Low-track Math — senior high

Self-discipline, cooperativeness, and responsibility.

> Low-track Science — junior high

I teach personal hygiene — to try to get the students to at least be aware of how to keep themselves clean.

> Low-track Vocational Education — junior high

Independence — start and complete a task on their own.

> Low-track English — senior high

Responsibility of working with people without standing over them.

> Low-track Science — senior high

Ability to use reading as a tool — e.g., how to fill out forms, write a check, get a job.

> Low-track English — junior high

How to fill out insurance forms. Income tax returns.

> Low-track Math — senior high

Understanding the basic words to survive in a job. Being able to take care of their own finances — e.g., banking, income tax, etc. Being able to prepare for, seek, and maintain a job. To associate words with a particular job.

Low-track English — senior high

To be able to work with other students. To be able to work alone. To be able to follow directions.

Low-track English — junior high

Socialization — retarded in social skills.

Low-track English — junior high

How to cope with frustration.

Low-track English — junior high

Business-oriented skills — how to fill out a job application.

Low-track English — junior high

More mature behavior (less outspoken).

Low-track Science — junior high

Respect for their fellow man (students and teachers).

Low-track Science — junior high

Learn to work independently — use a sense of responsibility.

Low-track Science — senior high

Content — minimal. Realistic about goals. Develop ones they *can* achieve.

Low-track Science — senior high

Practical math skills for everyday living. A sense of responsibility.

Low-track Math — senior high

To learn how to follow one set of directions at a time, take a directive order and act upon it.

Low-track Social Science — junior high

Life skills. Work with checking account.

Low-track Math — junior high

Good work habits.

Low-track Math — junior high

Respect. Growth in maturity.

Low-track Math — junior high

QUESTION:
What is the most important thing you have learned or done so far in this class?

High-track students named the following kinds of things: 7

RESPONSES:
I have learned to form my own opinions on situations. I have also learned to not be swayed so much by another person's opinion but to look at both opinions with an open mind. I know now that to have a

good solid opinion on a subject I must have facts to support my opinion. Decisions in later life will probably be made easier because of this.

High-track English — senior high

I've learned to study completely, and to know everything there is to know.

High-track English — senior high

I have learned to speak in front of a group of people, and not be scared to death of everyone.

High-track English — senior high

To know how to communicate with my teachers like friends and as teachers at the same time. To have confidence in myself other than my skills and class work.

High-track English — junior high

I have learned to be creative and free in doing things.

High-track English — senior high

I have learned how to make hard problems easier to solve.

High-track Math — senior high

The most important thing I have learned in this class this quarter is how to express my feelings.

High-track English — senior high

How to organize myself and present an argument.

High-track English — senior high

I'm learning how to communicate with large groups of people.

High-track English — senior high

The most important thing I have learned or done in this class is I now have the ability to be able to speak in front of a crowd without being petrified, as I was before taking this class.

High-track English — senior high

I want to be a lawyer and debate has taught me to dig for answers and get involved. I can express myself.

High-track English — senior high

The most important thing I have learned is how to speak in front of a group of people with confidence.

High-track English — senior high

I have learned how to argue in a calm and collected way.

High-track English — senior high

How to express myself through writing and being able to compose the different thoughts in a logical manner; this is also a class where I may express my creativity.

High-track English — senior high

Learned to think things out. Like in a book I learned to try and understand what the author is really saying to find the author's true thoughts.

High-track English — senior high

I've learned to look into depth of certain things and express my thoughts on paper.

High-track English — senior high

The most important thing I have learned in this class is to loosen up my mind when it comes to writing. I have learned to be more imaginative.

High-track English — senior high

How to present myself orally and how to listen and to think quick.

High-track English — senior high

To understand concepts and ideas and experiment with them. Also, to work independently.

High-track Science — senior high

My instructor has opened a whole new world for me in this class, I truly enjoy this class. He has given me the drive to search and find out answers to questions. If there is one thing that I have learned from this class it would have to be the want for learning.

High-track Social Studies — senior high

It taught us how to think in a logical way to work things out with a process of elimination.

High-track Math — senior high

I have learned that in high school the English classes treat you more like an adult.

High-track English — senior high

I have proved to myself that I have the discipline to take a difficult class just for the knowledge, even though it has nothing to do with my career plans.

High-track Math — senior high

I have learned that I have a wider span of imagination than I thought. I have also learned to put how I feel and what I feel into words and explain them better.

High-track English — senior high

Many times in this class I get wrong answers, but in this class you learn to learn from your mistakes, also that even if you do have a wrong answer you should keep trying and striving for that correct answer. This, along with the subject I have learned from this class, and I think it's very important.

High-track Math — senior high

How to think and reason logically and scientifically.

High-track Math — senior high

I think the most important thing I've done in this class is exercise my brain. To work out problems logically so I can learn to work out problems later in life logically.

High-track Math — senior high

Brains work faster and faster.

High-track Math — senior high

Learning about how others respond and act — what makes them do the things they do — talking about relations, and how happenings in earlier life can affect children when they are growing up. The class discussions make it really interesting and the teacher startles us sometimes because he can really understand things from our point of view.

High-track Social Science — senior high

The most important thing that I have learned in this class is the benefit of logical and organized thinking, learning is made much easier when the simple processes of organizing thoughts have been grasped.

High-track Math — senior high

Low-track students were more likely to give answers like these: 8

Behave in class.

Low-track English — junior high

I have learned that I should do my questions for the book when he asks me to.

Low-track Science — senior high

Self-control.

Low-track Social Studies — junior high

Manners.

Low-track English — junior high

How to shut up.

Low-track Vocational Education — junior high

The most important thing I have learned in this class is to always have your homework in and have materials ready whenever she is ready.

Low-track Vocational Education — senior high

Write and getting my homework done.

Low-track English — junior high

Working on my Ps and Qs.

Low-track English — junior high

I think the most important is coming into class and getting our folders and going to work.

Low-track Math — junior high

I have learned about many things like having good manners, respecting other people, not talking when the teacher is talking.

Low-track English — junior high

Learned to work myself.

Low-track Math — junior high

I learned about being quiet when the teacher is talking.

Low-track Social Studies — junior high

To learn how to listen and follow the directions of the teacher.

Low-track Math — senior high

I learn to respect the teacher.

> Low-track Vocational Education — junior high

Learn to get along with the students and the teacher.

> Low-track English — junior high

How to go through a cart and find a folder by myself.

> Low-track Math — junior high

To be a better listener in class.

> Low-track English — senior high

In this class, I have learned manners.

> Low-track English — junior high

Engaging the Text

1. Using the quotations provided by Oakes, what conclusions can you draw about the educational goals of high-track instructors and about their attitudes toward their students? How do their goals and attitudes compare with those of instructors in low-track classes? What assumptions do these instructors make about their students? Are they justified?

2. Again using the information provided by Oakes, compare the attitudes of high- and low-track students toward education.

3. Overall, what kind of role in society does a high-track education prepare students for? A low-track education?

Exploring Connections

1. How might Gordon Allport (Chapter Two, "Justice for All") analyze the impact of educational tracking on the social world of the school and on the individual attitudes of those who are tracked?

2. Which track are the students in Groening's cartoons on? Would the cartoons look different for students in high and low tracks?

Extending the Critical Context

1. How were students tracked in your high school? What specific courses did high- and low-track students take? How were students routed into them?

2. Interview teachers and students who have had experience in tracked classes in order to find out whether tracking does, in fact, help all students learn more effectively than they would in mixed classrooms.

Challenging the Traditional Classroom

The Achievement of Desire

Richard Rodriguez

*Hunger of Memory, the autobiography of Richard Rodriguez and the
source of the following selection, set off a storm of controversy in the
Chicano community when it appeared. Some hailed it as an uncompromising
portrayal of the difficulties of growing up between two cultures; others
condemned it because it seemed to blame Mexican-Americans for the
difficulties they encountered in assimilating into mainstream American
culture. Rodriguez was born in 1944 into an immigrant family outside
San Francisco. Though he was unable to speak English when he entered
school, his educational career could only be described as brilliant: undergraduate work at Stanford University, graduate study at Berkeley
and Columbia, a Fulbright fellowship to study English literature in
London, a subsequent grant from the National Endowment for the Hu-
manities. In this selection, Rodriguez analyzes the motives that led him
to abandon his study of Renaissance literature and return to live with
his parents.*

I stand in the ghetto classroom — "the guest speaker" — attempting 1
to lecture on the mystery of the sounds of our words to rows of diffident
students. "Don't you hear it? Listen! The music of our words. '*Sumer
is i-cumen in. . . .*' And songs on the car radio. We need Aretha Franklin's
voice to fill plain words with music — her life." In the face of their
empty stares, I try to create an enthusiasm. But the girls in the back
row turn to watch some boy passing outside. There are flutters of smiles,
waves. And someone's mouth elongates heavy, silent words through the
barrier of glass. Silent words — the lips straining to shape each voiceless
syllable: "*Meet meee late errr.*" By the door, the instructor smiles at
me, apparently hoping that I will be able to spark some enthusiasm in

the class. But only one student seems to be listening. A girl, maybe fourteen. In this gray room her eyes shine with ambition. She keeps nodding and nodding at all that I say; she even takes notes. And each time I ask a question, she jerks up and down in her desk like a marionette, while her hand waves over the bowed heads of her classmates. It is myself (as a boy) I see as she faces me now (a man in my thirties).

The boy who first entered a classroom barely able to speak English, 2 twenty years later concluded his studies in the stately quiet of the reading room in the British Museum. Thus with one sentence I can summarize my academic career. It will be harder to summarize what sort of life connects the boy to the man.

With every award, each graduation from one level of education to the 3 next, people I'd meet would congratulate me. Their refrain always the same: "Your parents must be very proud." Sometimes then they'd ask me how I managed it — my "success." (How?) After a while, I had several quick answers to give in reply. I'd admit, for one thing, that I went to an excellent grammar school. (My earliest teachers, the nuns, made my success their ambition.) And my brother and both my sisters were very good students. (They often brought home the shiny school trophies I came to want.) And my mother and father always encouraged me. (At every graduation they were behind the stunning flash of the camera when I turned to look at the crowd.)

As important as these factors were, however, they account inadequately 4 for my academic advance. Nor do they suggest what an odd success I managed. For although I was a very good student, I was also a very bad student. I was a "scholarship boy," a certain kind of scholarship boy. Always successful, I was always unconfident. Exhilarated by my progress. Sad. I became the prized student — anxious and eager to learn. Too eager, too anxious — an imitative and unoriginal pupil. My brother and two sisters enjoyed the advantages I did, and they grew to be as successful as I, but none of them ever seemed so anxious about their schooling. A second-grade student, I was the one who came home and corrected the "simple" grammatical mistakes of our parents. ("Two negatives make a positive.") Proudly I announced — to my family's startled silence — that a teacher had said I was losing all trace of a Spanish accent. I was oddly annoyed when I was unable to get parental help with a homework assignment. The night my father tried to help me with an arithmetic exercise, he kept reading the instructions, each time more deliberately, until I pried the textbook out of his hands, saying, "I'll try to figure it out some more by myself."

When I reached the third grade, I outgrew such behavior. I became 5 more tactful, careful to keep separate the two very different worlds of my day. But then, with ever-increasing intensity, I devoted myself to my studies. I became bookish, puzzling to all my family. Ambition set me apart. When my brother saw me struggling home with stacks of library books, he would laugh, shouting: "Hey, Four Eyes!" My father opened a closet one day and was startled to find me inside, reading a novel. My mother would find me reading when I was supposed to be asleep or helping around the house or playing outside. In a voice angry or worried or just curious, she'd ask: "What do you see in your books?" It became the family's joke. When I was called and wouldn't reply, someone would say I must be hiding under my bed with a book.

(How did I manage my success?) 6

What I am about to say to you has taken me more than twenty years 7 to admit: *A primary reason for my success in the classroom was that I couldn't forget that schooling was changing me and separating me from the life I enjoyed before becoming a student.* That simple realization! For years I never spoke to anyone about it. Never mentioned a thing to my family or my teachers or classmates. From a very early age, I understood enough, just enough about my classroom experiences to keep what I knew repressed, hidden beneath layers of embarrassment. Not until my last months as a graduate student, nearly thirty years old, was it possible for me to think much about the reasons for my academic success. Only then. At the end of my schooling, I needed to determine how far I had moved from my past. The adult finally confronted, and now must publicly say, what the child shuddered from knowing and could never admit to himself or to those many faces that smiled at his every success. ("Your parents must be very proud. . . .")

At the end, in the British Museum (too distracted to finish my dis- 8 sertation) for weeks I read, speed-read, books by modern educational theorists, only to find infrequent and slight mention of students like me. (Much more is written about the more typical case, the lower-class student who barely is helped by his schooling.) Then one day, leafing through Richard Hoggart's *The Uses of Literacy*, I found, in his description of the scholarship boy, myself. For the first time I realized that there were other students like me, and so I was able to frame the meaning of my academic success, its consequent price — the loss.

Hoggart's description is distinguished, at least initially, by deep un- 9 derstanding. What he grasps very well is that the scholarship boy must move between environments, his home and the classroom, which are at cultural extremes, opposed. With his family, the boy has the intense pleasure of intimacy, the family's consolation in feeling public alienation.

Lavish emotions texture home life. *Then,* at school, the instruction bids him to trust lonely reason primarily. Immediate needs set the pace of his parents' lives. From his mother and father the boy learns to trust spontaneity and nonrational ways of knowing. *Then,* at school, there is mental calm. Teachers emphasize the value of a reflectiveness that opens a space between thinking and immediate action.

Years of schooling must pass before the boy will be able to sketch the 10 cultural differences in his day as abstractly as this. But he senses those differences early. Perhaps as early as the night he brings home an assignment from school and finds the house too noisy for study.

> He has to be more and more alone, if he is going to "get on." He will have, probably unconsciously, to oppose the ethos[1] of the hearth, the intense gregariousness of the working-class family group. Since everything centres upon the living-room, there is unlikely to be a room of his own; the bedrooms are cold and inhospitable, and to warm them or the front room, if there is one, would not only be expensive, but would require an imaginative leap — out of the tradition — which most families are not capable of making. There is a corner of the living-room table. On the other side Mother is ironing, the wireless is on, someone is singing a snatch of song or Father says intermittently whatever comes into his head. The boy has to cut himself off mentally, so as to do his homework, as well as he can.[2]

The next day, the lesson is as apparent at school. There are even rows 11 of desks. Discussion is ordered. The boy must rehearse his thoughts and raise his hand before speaking out in a loud voice to an audience of classmates. And there is time enough, and silence, to think about ideas (big ideas) never considered at home by his parents.

Not for the working-class child alone is adjustment to the classroom 12 difficult. Good schooling requires that any student alter early childhood habits. But the working-class child is usually least prepared for the change. And, unlike many middle-class children, he goes home and sees in his parents a way of life not only different but starkly opposed to that of the classroom. (He enters the house and hears his parents talking in ways his teachers discourage.)

Without extraordinary determination and the great assistance of others 13 — at home and at school — there is little chance for success. Typically most working-class children are barely changed by the classroom. The exception succeeds. The relative few become scholarship students. Of

[1] *ethos:* the fundamental spirit or character of a thing.
[2] All quotations are from Richard Hoggart, *The Uses of Literacy* (London: Chatto and Windus, 1957), chapter 10. [Author's note]

these, Richard Hoggart estimates, most manage a fairly graceful transition. Somehow they learn to live in the two very different worlds of their day. There are some others, however, those Hoggart pejoratively terms "scholarship boys," for whom success comes with special anxiety. Scholarship boy: good student, troubled son. The child is "moderately endowed," intellectually mediocre, Hoggart supposes — though it may be more pertinent to note the special qualities of temperament in the child. High-strung child. Brooding. Sensitive. Haunted by the knowledge that one *chooses* to become a student. (Education is not an inevitable or natural step in growing up.) Here is a child who cannot forget that his academic success distances him from a life he loved, even from his own memory of himself.

Initially, he wavers, balances allegiance. ("The boy is himself [until 14 he reaches, say, the upper forms[3]] very much of *both* the worlds of home and school. He is enormously obedient to the dictates of the world of school, but emotionally still strongly wants to continue as part of the family circle.") Gradually, necessarily, the balance is lost. The boy needs to spend more and more time studying, each night enclosing himself in the silence permitted and required by intense concentration. He takes his first step toward academic success, away from his family.

From the very first days, through the years following, it will be with 15 his parents — the figures of lost authority, the persons toward whom he feels deepest love — that the change will be most powerfully measured. A separation will unravel between them. Advancing in his studies, the boy notices that his mother and father have not changed as much as he. Rather, when he sees them, they often remind him of the person he once was and the life he earlier shared with them. He realizes what some Romantics[4] also know when they praise the working class for the capacity for human closeness, qualities of passion and spontaneity, that the rest of us experience in like measure only in the earliest part of our youth. For the Romantic, this doesn't make working-class life childish. Working-class life challenges precisely because it is an *adult* way of life.

The scholarship boy reaches a different conclusion. He cannot afford 16 to admire his parents. (How could he and still pursue such a contrary life?) He permits himself embarrassment at their lack of education. And to evade nostalgia for the life he has lost, he concentrates on the benefits education will bestow upon him. He becomes especially ambitious. Without

[3]*upper forms:* upper grades or classes in British secondary schools.
[4]*Romantics:* adherents of the principles of romanticism — a literary and philosophical movement that emphasized the imagination, freedom, nature, the return to a simple life, and the ordinary individual.

the support of old certainties and consolations, almost mechanically, he assumes the procedures and doctrines of the classroom. The kind of allegiance the young student might have given his mother and father only days earlier, he transfers to the teacher, the new figure of authority. "[The scholarship boy] tends to make a father-figure of his form-master,"[5] Hoggart observes.

But Hoggart's calm prose only makes me recall the urgency with which   17
I came to idolize my grammar school teachers. I began by imitating their accents, using their diction, trusting their every direction. The very first facts they dispensed, I grasped with awe. Any book they told me to read, I read — then waited for them to tell me which books I enjoyed. Their every casual opinion I came to adopt and to trumpet when I returned home. I stayed after school "to help" — to get my teacher's undivided attention. It was the nun's encouragement that mattered most to me. (She understood exactly what — my parents never seemed to appraise so well — all my achievements entailed.) Memory gently caressed each word of praise bestowed in the classroom so that compliments teachers paid me years ago come quickly to mind even today.

The enthusiasm I felt in second-grade classes I flaunted before both   18
my parents. The docile, obedient student came home a shrill and precocious son who insisted on correcting and teaching his parents with the remark: "My teacher told us. . . ."

I intended to hurt my mother and father. I was still angry at them   19
for having encouraged me toward classroom English. But gradually this anger was exhausted, replaced by guilt as school grew more and more attractive to me. I grew increasingly successful, a talkative student. My hand was raised in the classroom; I yearned to answer any question. At home, life was less noisy than it had been. (I spoke to classmates and teachers more often each day than to family members.) Quiet at home, I sat with my papers for hours each night. I never forgot that schooling had irretrievably changed my family's life. That knowledge, however, did not weaken ambition. Instead, it strengthened resolve. Those times I remembered the loss of my past with regret, I quickly reminded myself of all the things my teachers could give me. (They could make me an educated man.) I tightened my grip on pencil and books. I evaded nostalgia. Tried hard to forget. But one does not forget by trying to forget. One only remembers. I remembered too well that education had changed my family's life. I would not have become a scholarship boy had I not so often remembered.

Once she was sure that her children knew English, my mother would   20

---

[5]*form-master:* a teacher in a British secondary school.

tell us, "You should keep up your Spanish." Voices playfully groaned in response. "¡*Pochos*!"[6] my mother would tease. I listened silently.

After a while, I grew more calm at home. I developed tact. A fourth-grade student, I was no longer the show-off in front of my parents. I became a conventionally dutiful son, politely affectionate, cheerful enough, even — for reasons beyond choosing — my father's favorite. And much about my family life was easy then, comfortable, happy in the rhythm of our living together: hearing my father getting ready for work; eating the breakfast my mother had made me; looking up from a novel to hear my brother or one of my sisters playing with friends in the backyard; in winter, coming upon the house all lighted up after dark.

But withheld from my mother and father was any mention of what most mattered to me: the extraordinary experience of first-learning. Late afternoon: In the midst of preparing dinner, my mother would come up behind me while I was trying to read. Her head just over mine, her breath warmly scented with food. "What are you reading?" Or, "Tell me all about your new courses." I would barely respond, "Just the usual things, nothing special." (A half smile, then silence. Her head moving back in the silence. Silence! Instead of the flood of intimate sounds that had once flowed smoothly between us, there was this silence.) After dinner, I would rush to a bedroom with papers and books. As often as possible, I resisted parental pleas to "save lights" by coming to the kitchen to work. I kept so much, so often, to myself. Sad. Enthusiastic. Troubled by the excitement of coming upon new ideas. Eager. Fascinated by the promising texture of a brand-new book. I hoarded the pleasures of learning. Alone for hours. Enthralled. Nervous. I rarely looked away from my books — or back on my memories. Nights when relatives visited and the front rooms were warmed by Spanish sounds, I slipped quietly out of the house.

It mattered that education was changing me. It never ceased to matter. My brother and sisters would giggle at our mother's mispronounced words. They'd correct her gently. My mother laughed girlishly one night, trying not to pronounce *sheep* as *ship*. From a distance I listened sullenly. From that distance, pretending not to notice on another occasion, I saw my father looking at the title pages of my library books. That was the scene on my mind when I walked home with a fourth-grade companion and heard him say that his parents read to him every night. (A strange-sounding book — *Winnie the Pooh*.) Immediately, I wanted to know, "What is it like?" My companion, however, thought I wanted to know

[6]*pocho:* a derogatory Spanish word for a Mexican-American who has adopted the attitudes, values, and lifestyle of Anglo culture.

about the plot of the book. Another day, my mother surprised me by asking for a "nice" book to read. "Something not too hard you think I might like." Carefully I chose one, Willa Cather's[7] *My Ántonia*. But when, several weeks later, I happened to see it next to her bed unread except for the first few pages, I was furious and suddenly wanted to cry. I grabbed up the book and took it back to my room and placed it in its place, alphabetically on my shelf.

"Your parents must be very proud of you." People began to say that   24
to me about the time I was in sixth grade. To answer affirmatively, I'd smile. Shyly I'd smile, never betraying my sense of the irony: I was not proud of my mother and father. I was embarrassed by their lack of education. It was not that I ever thought they were stupid, though stupidly I took for granted their enormous native intelligence. Simply, what mattered to me was that they were not like my teachers.

But, "Why didn't you tell us about the award?" my mother demanded,   25
her frown weakened by pride. At the grammar school ceremony several weeks after, her eyes were brighter than the trophy I'd won. Pushing back the hair from my forehead, she whispered that I had "shown" the *gringos*. A few minutes later, I heard my father speak to my teacher and felt ashamed of his labored, accented words. Then guilty for the shame. I felt such contrary feelings. (There is no simple roadmap through the heart of the scholarship boy.) My teacher was so soft-spoken and her words were edged sharp and clean. I admired her until it seemed to me that she spoke too carefully. Sensing that she was condescending to them, I became nervous. Resentful. Protective. I tried to move my parents away. "You both must be very proud of Richard," the nun said. They responded quickly. (They were proud.) "We are proud of all our children." Then this afterthought: "They sure didn't get their brains from us." They all laughed. I smiled.

In fourth grade I embarked upon a grandiose reading program. "Give   26
me the names of important books," I would say to startled teachers. They soon found out that I had in mind "adult books." I ignored their suggestion of anything I suspected was written for children. (Not until I was in college, as a result, did I read *Huckleberry Finn* or *Alice's Adventures in Wonderland*.) Instead, I read *The Scarlet Letter* and Franklin's *Autobiography*. And whatever I read I read for extra credit. Each time I finished a book, I reported the achievement to a teacher and basked in the praise my effort earned. Despite my best efforts, however, there seemed to be more and more books I needed to read.

[7]*Willa Cather:* U.S. novelist (1876–1947).

At the library I would literally tremble as I came upon whole shelves of books I hadn't read. So I read and I read and I read: *Great Expectations*; all the short stories of Kipling; *The Babe Ruth Story*; the entire first volume of the *Encyclopaedia Britannica* (A-ANSTEY); the *Iliad*; *Moby Dick*; *Gone with the Wind*; *The Good Earth*; *Ramona*; *Forever Amber*; *The Lives of the Saints*; *Crime and Punishment*; *The Pearl*. . . . Librarians who initially frowned when I checked out the maximum ten books at a time started saving books they thought I might like. Teachers would say to the rest of the class, "I only wish the rest of you took reading as seriously as Richard obviously does."

But at home I would hear my mother wondering, "What do you see 27 in your books?" (Was reading a hobby like her knitting? Was so much reading even healthy for a boy? Was it the sign of "brains"? Or was it just a convenient excuse for not helping around the house on Saturday mornings?) Always, "What do you see . . . ?"

What *did* I see in my books? I had the idea that they were crucial 28 for my academic success, though I couldn't have said exactly how or why. In the sixth grade I simply concluded that what gave a book its value was some major idea or theme it contained. If that core essence could be mined and memorized, I would become learned like my teachers. I decided to record in a notebook the themes of the books that I read. After reading *Robinson Crusoe*, I wrote that its theme was "the value of learning to live by oneself." When I completed *Wuthering Heights*, I noted the danger of "letting emotions get out of control." Rereading these brief moralistic appraisals usually left me disheartened. I couldn't believe that they were really the source of reading's value. But for many more years, they constituted the only means I had of describing to myself the educational value of books.

I entered high school having read hundreds of books. My habit of 29 reading made me a confident speaker and writer of English. Reading also enabled me to sense something of the shape, the major concerns, of Western thought. (I was able to say something about Dante[8] and Descartes[9] and Engels[10] and James Baldwin[11] in my high school term papers.) In these various ways, books brought me academic success as I hoped that they would. But I was not a good reader. Merely bookish, I lacked a point of view when I read. Rather, I read in order to acquire

[8]*Dante:* Dante Alighieri, Italian poet (1265–1321); author of the *Divine Comedy*.

[9]*Descartes:* René Descartes, French philosopher and mathematician (1596–1650).

[10]*Engels:* Friedrich Engels, German socialist (1820–1895); co-author with Karl Marx of the *Communist Manifesto* in 1848.

[11]*James Baldwin:* American author (1924–1987).

a point of view. I vacuumed books for epigrams, scraps of information, ideas, themes — anything to fill the hollow within me and make me feel educated. When one of my teachers suggested to his drowsy tenth-grade English class that a person could not have a "complicated idea" until he had read at least two thousand books, I heard the remark without detecting either its irony or its very complicated truth. I merely determined to compile a list of all the books I had ever read. Harsh with myself, I included only once a title I might have read several times. (How, after all, could one read a book more than once?) And I included only those books over a hundred pages in length. (Could anything shorter be a book?)

There was yet another high school list I compiled. One day I came 30 across a newspaper article about the retirement of an English professor at a nearby state college. The article was accompanied by a list of the "hundred most important books of Western Civilization." "More than anything else in my life," the professor told the reporter with finality, "these books have made me all that I am." That was the kind of remark I couldn't ignore. I clipped out the list and kept it for the several months it took me to read all of the titles. Most books, of course, I barely understood. While reading Plato's *Republic*, for instance, I needed to keep looking at the book jacket comments to remind myself what the text was about. Nevertheless, with the special patience and superstition of a scholarship boy, I looked at every word of the text. And by the time I reached the last word, relieved, I convinced myself that I had read *The Republic*. In a ceremony of great pride, I solemnly crossed Plato off my list.

. . . The scholarship boy does not straddle, cannot reconcile, the two 31 great opposing cultures of his life. His success is unromantic and plain. He sits in the classroom and offers those sitting beside him no calming reassurance about their own lives. He sits in the seminar room — a man with brown skin, the son of working-class Mexican immigrant parents. (Addressing the professor at the head of the table, his voice catches with nervousness.) There is no trace of his parents' accent in his speech. Instead he approximates the accents of teachers and classmates. Coming from *him* those sounds seem suddenly odd. Odd too is the effect produced when *he* uses academic jargon — bubbles at the tip of his tongue: "*Topos* . . . negative capability . . . vegetation imagery in Shakespearean comedy."[12] He lifts an opinion from Coleridge, takes something else from

---

[12] *topos . . . negative capability . . . etc.*: technical terms associated with the study of literary criticism.

Frye or Empson or Leavis.[13] He even repeats exactly his professor's earlier comment. All his ideas are clearly borrowed. He seems to have no thought of his own. He chatters while his listeners smile — their look one of disdain.

When he is older and thus when so little of the person he was survives, 32 the scholarship boy makes only too apparent his profound lack of *self-confidence*. This is the conventional assessment that even Richard Hoggart repeats:

> [The scholarship boy] tends to over-stress the importance of examinations, of the piling-up of knowledge and of received opinions. He discovers a technique of apparent learning, of the acquiring of facts rather than of the handling and use of facts. He learns how to receive a purely literate education, one using only a small part of the personality and challenging only a limited area of his being. He begins to see life as a ladder, as a permanent examination with some praise and some further exhortation at each stage. He becomes an expert imbiber and doler-out; his competence will vary, but will rarely be accompanied by genuine enthusiasms. He rarely feels the reality of knowledge, of other men's thoughts and imaginings, on his own pulses . . . He has something of the blinkered pony about him. . . .

But this is criticism more accurate than fair. The scholarship boy is a 33 very bad student. He is the great mimic; a collector of thoughts, not a thinker; the very last person in class who ever feels obliged to have an opinion of his own. In large part, however, the reason he is such a bad student is because he realizes more often and more acutely than most other students — than Hoggart himself — that education requires radical self-reformation. As a very young boy, regarding his parents, as he struggles with an early homework assignment, he knows this too well. That is why he lacks self-assurance. He does not forget that the classroom is responsible for remaking him. He relies on his teacher, depends on all that he hears in the classroom and reads in his books. He becomes in every obvious way the worst student, a dummy mouthing the opinions of others. But he would not be so bad — nor would he become so successful, a *scholarship* boy — if he did not accurately perceive that the best synonym for primary "education" is "imitation."

Like me, Hoggart's imagined scholarship boy spends most of his years 34 in the classroom afraid to long for his past. Only at the very end of his schooling does the boy-man become nostalgic. In this sudden change of heart, Richard Hoggart notes:

[13]*Coleridge . . . Frye . . . Empson . . . Leavis:* important literary critics.

He longs for the membership he lost, "he pines for some Nameless Eden where he never was." The nostalgia is the stronger and the more ambiguous because he is really "in quest of his own absconded self yet scared to find it." He both wants to go back and yet thinks he has gone beyond his class, feels himself weighted with knowledge of his own and their situation, which hereafter forbids him the simpler pleasures of his father and mother. . . .

According to Hoggart, the scholarship boy grows nostalgic because he 35 remains the uncertain scholar, bright enough to have moved from his past, yet unable to feel easy, a part of a community of academics.

This analysis, however, only partially suggests what happened to me 36 in my last years as a graduate student. When I traveled to London to write a dissertation on English Renaissance literature, I was finally confident of membership in a "community of scholars." But the pleasure that confidence gave me faded rapidly. After only two or three months in the reading room of the British Museum, it became clear that I had joined a lonely community. Around me each day were dour faces eclipsed by large piles of books. There were the regulars, like the old couple who arrived every morning, each holding a loop of the shopping bag which contained all their notes. And there was the historian who chattered madly to herself. ("Oh dear! Oh! Now, what's this? What? Oh, my!") There were also the faces of young men and women worn by long study. And everywhere eyes turned away the moment our glance accidentally met. Some persons I sat beside day after day, yet we passed silently at the end of the day, strangers. Still, we were united by a common respect for the written word and for scholarship. We did form a union, though one in which we remained distant from one another.

More profound and unsettling was the bond I recognized with those 37 writers whose books I consulted. Whenever I opened a text that hadn't been used for years, I realized that my special interests and skills united me to a mere handful of academics. We formed an exclusive — eccentric! — society, separated from others who would never care or be able to share our concerns. (The pages I turned were stiff like layers of dead skin.) I began to wonder: Who, beside my dissertation director and a few faculty members, would ever read what I wrote? And: Was my dissertation much more than an act of social withdrawal? These questions went unanswered in the silence of the Museum reading room. They remained to trouble me after I'd leave the library each afternoon and feel myself shy — unsteady, speaking simple sentences at the grocer's or the butcher's on my way back to my bed-sitter.

Meanwhile my file cards accumulated. A professional, I knew exactly 38 how to search a book for pertinent information. I could quickly assess and summarize the usability of the many books I consulted. But whenever

I started to write, I knew too much (and not enough) to be able to write anything but sentences that were overly cautious, timid, strained brittle under the heavy weight of footnotes and qualifications. I seemed unable to dare a passionate statement. I felt drawn by professionalism to the edge of sterility, capable of no more than pedantic, lifeless, unassailable prose.

Then nostalgia began. 39

After years spent unwilling to admit its attractions, I gestured nostalgically 40 toward the past. I yearned for that time when I had not been so alone. I became impatient with books. I wanted experience more immediate. I feared the library's silence. I silently scorned the gray, timid faces around me. I grew to hate the growing pages of my dissertation on genre[14] and Renaissance literature. (In my mind I heard relatives laughing as they tried to make sense of its title.) I wanted something — I couldn't say exactly what. I told myself that I wanted a more passionate life. And a life less thoughtful. And above all, I wanted to be less alone. One day I heard some Spanish academics whispering back and forth to each other, and their sounds seemed ghostly voices recalling my life. Yearning became preoccupation then. Boyhood memories beckoned, flooded my mind. (Laughing intimate voices. Bounding up the front steps of the porch. A sudden embrace inside the door.)

For weeks after, I turned to books by educational experts. I needed 41 to learn how far I had moved from my past — to determine how fast I would be able to recover something of it once again. But I found little. Only a chapter in a book by Richard Hoggart . . . I left the reading room and the circle of faces.

I came home. After the year in England, I spent three summer months 42 living with my mother and father, relieved by how easy it was to be home. It no longer seemed very important to me that we had little to say. I felt easy sitting and eating and walking with them. I watched them, nevertheless, looking for evidence of those elastic, sturdy strands that bind generations in a web of inheritance. I thought as I watched my mother one night: Of course a friend had been right when she told me that I gestured and laughed just like my mother. Another time I saw for myself: My father's eyes were much like my own, constantly watchful.

But after the early relief, this return, came suspicion, nagging until 43 I realized that I had not neatly sidestepped the impact of schooling. My desire to do so was precisely the measure of how much I remained an

---

[14]*genre:* a class or category of artistic work; e.g., the genre of poetry.

academic. *Negatively* (for that is how this idea first occurred to me): My need to think so much and so abstractly about my parents and our relationship was in itself an indication of my long education. My father and mother did not pass their time thinking about the cultural meanings of their experience. It was I who described their daily lives with airy ideas. And yet, *positively:* The ability to consider experience so abstractly allowed me to shape into desire what would otherwise have remained indefinite, meaningless longing in the British Museum. If, because of my schooling, I had grown culturally separated from my parents, my education finally had given me ways of speaking and caring about that fact.

My best teachers in college and graduate school, years before, had 44 tried to prepare me for this conclusion, I think, when they discussed texts of aristocratic pastoral literature. Faithfully, I wrote down all that they said. I memorized it: "The praise of the unlettered by the highly educated is one of the primary themes of "elitist" literature." But, "the importance of the praise given the unsolitary, richly passionate and spontaneous life is that it simultaneously reflects the value of a reflective life." I heard it all. But there was no way for any of it to mean very much to me. I was a scholarship boy at the time, busily laddering my way up the rungs of education. To pass an examination, I copied down exactly what my teachers told me. It would require many more years of schooling (an inevitable miseducation) in which I came to trust the silence of reading and the habit of abstracting from immediate experience — moving away from a life of closeness and immediacy I remembered with my parents, growing older — before I turned unafraid to desire the past, and thereby achieved what had eluded me for so long — the end of education.

Engaging the Text

1. What is a "scholarship boy"? Why does Rodriguez consider himself to be a "bad" student despite his obvious academic success?

2. What drives Rodriguez to succeed? Why does he ultimately abandon his studies at Oxford?

3. What does education represent to Rodriguez, to his father and mother? What role does cultural ASSIMILATION play in Rodriguez's AMBIVALENCE toward education?

4. Rodriguez uses parentheses heavily in this autobiographical essay. What is the effect of this frequent embedding of thoughts? What is he trying to achieve?

Exploring Connections

1. Compare Rodriguez, Stephen Cruz (p. 77), and Jane Ellen Wilson (p. 569) in terms of their attitudes toward success within MAINSTREAM American culture.

Extending the Critical Context

1. What are your personal motives for academic success? How do they compare with those of Rodriguez?

2. One generation after the first great influx of immigrant and working-class people into American higher education, many college students find that they are following in the footsteps of family members — and not breaking ground as Rodriguez did. What special difficulties do such second- or third-generation college students face?

Learning to Read

MALCOLM X

Born Malcolm Little on May 19, 1925, Malcolm X was one of the most articulate and powerful leaders of black America during the 1960s. A street hustler convicted of robbery in 1946, he spent seven years in prison, where he educated himself and became a disciple of Elijah Muhammad, founder of the Black Muslim religion. In the days of the civil rights movement, Malcolm X emerged as the leading spokesman for black separatism, a philosophy that urged black Americans to cut political, social, and economic ties with the white community. After a pilgrimage to Mecca, the capital of the Muslim world, in 1964, he became an orthodox Muslim, adopted the Muslim name of El Hajj Malik El-Shabazz, and distanced himself from the teachings of the Black Muslims. He was assassinated in 1965. In the following excerpt from his autobiography co-authored with Alex Haley, Malcolm X describes his self-education.

It was because of my letters that I happened to stumble upon starting   1
to acquire some kind of a homemade education.

I became increasingly frustrated at not being able to express what I   2
wanted to convey in letters that I wrote, especially those to Mr. Elijah
Muhammad.[1] In the street, I had been the most articulate hustler out
there — I had commanded attention when I said something. But now,
trying to write simple English, I not only wasn't articulate, I wasn't even
functional. How would I sound writing in slang, the way I would *say*
it, something such as, "Look, daddy, let me pull your coat about a cat,
Elijah Muhammad —"

Many who today hear me somewhere in person, or on television, or   3
those who read something I've said, will think I went to school far beyond
the eighth grade. This impression is due entirely to my prison studies.

It had really begun back in the Charlestown Prison, when Bimbi[2] first   4
made me feel envy of his stock of knowledge. Bimbi had always taken
charge of any conversations he was in, and I had tried to emulate him.
But every book I picked up had few sentences which didn't contain
anywhere from one to nearly all of the words that might as well have
been in Chinese. When I just skipped those words, of course, I really
ended up with little idea of what the book said. So I had come to the
Norfolk Prison Colony still going through only book-reading motions.
Pretty soon, I would have quit even these motions, unless I had received
the motivation that I did.

I saw that the best thing I could do was get hold of a dictionary —   5
to study, to learn some words. I was lucky enough to reason also that
I should try to improve my penmanship. It was sad. I couldn't even
write in a straight line. It was both ideas together that moved me to
request a dictionary along with some tablets and pencils from the Norfolk
Prison Colony school.

I spent two days just riffling uncertainly through the dictionary's pages.   6
I'd never realized so many words existed! I didn't know *which* words I
needed to learn. Finally, just to start some kind of action, I began
copying.

In my slow, painstaking, ragged handwriting, I copied into my tablet   7
everything printed on that first page, down to the punctuation marks.

I believe it took me a day. Then, aloud, I read back, to myself,   8
everything I'd written on the tablet. Over and over, aloud, to myself,
I read my own handwriting.

I woke up the next morning, thinking about those words — immensely   9

---

[1]*Elijah Muhammad:* U.S. clergyman (1897–1975); leader of the Black Muslims 1935–
1975.
    [2]*Bimbi:* a fellow inmate whose encyclopedic learning and verbal facility greatly impressed
Malcolm X.

proud to realize that not only had I written so much at one time, but I'd written words that I never knew were in the world. Moreover, with a little effort, I also could remember what many of these words meant. I reviewed the words whose meanings I didn't remember. Funny thing, from the dictionary first page right now, that "aardvark" springs to my mind. The dictionary had a picture of it, a long-tailed, long-eared, burrowing African mammal, which lives off termites caught by sticking out its tongue as an anteater does for ants.

I was so fascinated that I went on — I copied the dictionary's next 10 page. And the same experience came when I studied that. With every succeeding page, I also learned of people and places and events from history. Actually the dictionary is like a miniature encyclopedia. Finally the dictionary's A section had filled a whole tablet — and I went on into the B's. That was the way I started copying what eventually became the entire dictionary. It went a lot faster after so much practice helped me to pick up handwriting speed. Between what I wrote in my tablet, and writing letters, during the rest of my time in prison I would guess I wrote a million words.

I suppose it was inevitable that as my word-base broadened, I could 11 for the first time pick up a book and read and now begin to understand what the book was saying. Anyone who has read a great deal can imagine the new world that opened. Let me tell you something: From then until I left that prison, in every free moment I had, if I was not reading in the library, I was reading on my bunk. You couldn't have gotten me out of books with a wedge. Between Mr. Muhammad's teachings, my correspondence, my visitors — usually Ella and Reginald — and my reading of books, months passed without my even thinking about being imprisoned. In fact, up to then, I never had been so truly free in my life.

The Norfolk Prison Colony's library was in the school building. A 12 variety of classes was taught there by instructors who came from such places as Harvard and Boston universities. The weekly debates between inmate teams were also held in the school building. You would be astonished to know how worked up convict debaters and audiences would get over subjects like "Should Babies Be Fed Milk?"

Available on the prison library's shelves were books on just about 13 every general subject. Much of the big private collection that Parkhurst had willed to the prison was still in crates and boxes in the back of the library — thousands of old books. Some of them looked ancient: covers faded, old-time parchment-looking binding. Parkhurst, I've mentioned, seemed to have been principally interested in history and religion. He had the money and the special interest to have a lot of books that you wouldn't have in general circulation. Any college library would have been lucky to get that collection.

As you can imagine, especially in a prison where there was heavy 14 emphasis on rehabilitation, an inmate was smiled upon if he demonstrated an unusually intense interest in books. There was a sizable number of well-read inmates, especially the popular debaters. Some were said by many to be practically walking encyclopedias. They were almost celebrities. No university would ask any student to devour literature as I did when this new world opened to me, of being able to read and *understand*.

I read more in my room than in the library itself. An inmate who was 15 known to read a lot could check out more than the permitted maximum number of books. I preferred reading in the total isolation of my own room.

When I had progressed to really serious reading, every night at about 16 ten P.M. I would be outraged with the "lights out." It always seemed to catch me right in the middle of something engrossing.

Fortunately, right outside my door was a corridor light that cast a 17 glow into my room. The glow was enough to read by, once my eyes adjusted to it. So when "lights out" came, I would sit on the floor where I could continue reading in that glow.

At one-hour intervals the night guards paced past every room. Each 18 time I heard the approaching footsteps, I jumped into bed and feigned sleep. And as soon as the guard passed, I got back out of bed onto the floor area of that light-glow, where I would read for another fifty-eight minutes — until the guard approached again. That went on until three or four every morning. Three or four hours of sleep a night was enough for me. Often in the years in the streets I had slept less than that.

The teachings of Mr. Muhammad stressed how history had been "whit- 19 ened" — when white men had written history books, the black man simply had been left out. Mr. Muhammad couldn't have said anything that would have struck me much harder. I had never forgotten how when my class, me and all of those whites, had studied seventh-grade United States history back in Mason, the history of the Negro had been covered in one paragraph, and the teacher had gotten a big laugh with his joke, "Negroes' feet are so big that when they walk, they leave a hole in the ground."

This is one reason why Mr. Muhammad's teachings spread so swiftly 20 all over the United States, among *all* Negroes, whether or not they became followers of Mr. Muhammad. The teachings ring true — to every Negro. You can hardly show me a black adult in America — or a white one, for that matter — who knows from the history books anything like the truth about the black man's role. In my own case, once I heard of the "glorious history of the black man," I took special pains to hunt in the library for books that would inform me on details about black history.

I can remember accurately the very first set of books that really 21
impressed me. I have since bought that set of books and I have it at home for my children to read as they grow up. It's called *Wonders of the World*. It's full of pictures of archeological finds, statues that depict, usually, non-European people.

I found books like Will Durant's[3] *Story of Civilization*. I read H. G. 22
Wells'[4] *Outline of History*. *Souls of Black Folk* by W. E. B. Du Bois[5] gave me a glimpse into the black people's history before they came to this country. Carter G. Woodson's *Negro History* opened my eyes about black empires before the black slave was brought to the United States, and the early Negro struggles for freedom.

J. A. Rogers' three volumes of *Sex and Race* told about race-mixing 23
before Christ's time; about Aesop being a black man who told fables; about Egypt's Pharaohs; about the great Coptic Christian Empires;[6] about Ethiopia, the earth's oldest continuous black civilization, as China is the oldest continuous civilization.

Mr. Muhammad's teaching about how the white man had been created 24
led me to *Findings In Genetics* by Gregor Mendel.[7] (The dictionary's G section was where I had learned what "genetics" meant.) I really studied this book by the Austrian monk. Reading it over and over, especially certain sections, helped me to understand that if you started with a black man, a white man could be produced; but starting with a white man, you never could produce a black man — because the white chromosome is recessive. And since no one disputes that there was but one Original Man, the conclusion is clear.

During the last year or so, in the *New York Times*, Arnold Toynbee[8] 25
used the word "bleached" in describing the white man. (His words were: "White (i.e., bleached) human beings of North European origin. . . ."

[3]*Will Durant:* U.S. author and historian (1885–1981).
[4]*H. G. Wells:* English novelist and historian (1866–1946).
[5]*W. E. B. Du Bois:* William Edward Burghardt Du Bois, distinguished black scholar, author, and activist, (1868–1963). Du Bois was the first director of the NAACP and was an important figure in the Harlem Renaissance; his best-known book is *Souls of Black Folk*.
[6]*Coptic Christian Empire:* the domain of the Coptic Church, a native Egyptian Christian church that retains elements of its African origins.
[7]*Gregor Mendel:* Austrian monk, botanist, and pioneer in genetic research (1822–1884).
[8]*Arnold Toynbee:* English historian (1889–1975).

Toynbee also referred to the European geographic area as only a peninsula of Asia. He said there is no such thing as Europe. And if you look at the globe, you will see for yourself that America is only an extension of Asia. (But at the same time Toynbee is among those who have helped to bleach history. He has written that Africa was the only continent that produced no history. He won't write that again. Every day now, the truth is coming to light.)

I never will forget how shocked I was when I began reading about 26
slavery's total horror. It made such an impact upon me that it later became one of my favorite subjects when I became a minister of Mr. Muhammad's. The world's most monstrous crime, the sin and the blood on the white man's hands, are almost impossible to believe. Books like the one by Frederick Olmstead[9] opened my eyes to the horrors suffered when the slave was landed in the United States. The European woman, Fanny Kemble,[10] who had married a Southern white slaveowner, described how human beings were degraded. Of course I read *Uncle Tom's Cabin*.[11] In fact, I believe that's the only novel I have ever read since I started serious reading.

Parkhurst's collection also contained some bound pamphlets of the 27
Abolitionist[12] Anti-Slavery Society of New England. I read descriptions of atrocities, saw those illustrations of black slave women tied up and flogged with whips; of black mothers watching their babies being dragged off, never to be seen by their mothers again; of dogs after slaves, and of the fugitive slave catchers, evil white men with whips and clubs and chains and guns. I read about the slave preacher Nat Turner, who put the fear of God into the white slavemaster. Nat Turner wasn't going around preaching pie-in-the-sky and "non-violent" freedom for the black man. There in Virginia one night in 1831, Nat and seven other slaves started out at his master's home and through the night they went from one plantation "big house" to the next, killing, until by the next morning 57 white people were dead and Nat had about 70 slaves following him. White people, terrified for their lives, fled from their homes, locked themselves up in public buildings, hid in the woods, and some even left the state. A small army of soldiers took two months to catch and

[9]*Frederick Olmstead:* Frederick Law Olmstead, U.S. landscape architect, city planner, and abolitionist, (1822–1903).
[10]*Fanny Kemble:* Frances Anne Kemble, English actress and author (1809–1893); best known for her autobiographical *Journal of a Residence on a Georgia Plantation*, published in 1863 to win support in Britain for the abolitionist cause.
[11]*Uncle Tom's Cabin:* Harriet Beecher Stowe's 1852 antislavery novel.
[12]*abolitionist:* advocating the prohibition of slavery.

hang Nat Turner. Somewhere I have read where Nat Turner's example is said to have inspired John Brown[13] to invade Virginia and attack Harpers Ferry nearly thirty years later, with thirteen white men and five Negroes.

I read Herodotus,[14] "the father of History," or, rather, I read about   28
him. And I read the histories of various nations, which opened my eyes gradually, then wider and wider, to how the whole world's white men had indeed acted like devils, pillaging and raping and bleeding and draining the whole world's non-white people. I remember, for instance, books such as Will Durant's *The Story of Oriental Civilization*, and Mahatma Gandhi's[15] accounts of the struggle to drive the British out of India.

Book after book showed me how the white man had brought upon   29
the world's black, brown, red, and yellow peoples every variety of the sufferings of exploitation. I saw how since the sixteenth century, the so-called "Christian trader" white man began to ply the seas in his lust for Asian and African empires, and plunder, and power. I read, I saw, how the white man never has gone among the non-white peoples bearing the Cross in the true manner and spirit of Christ's teachings — meek, humble, and Christlike.

I perceived, as I read, how the collective white man had been actually   30
nothing but a piratical opportunist who used Faustian[16] machinations to make his own Christianity his initial wedge in criminal conquests. First, always "religiously," he branded "heathen" and "pagan" labels upon ancient non-white cultures and civilizations. The stage thus set, he then turned upon his non-white victims his weapons of war.

I read how, entering India — half a *billion* deeply religious brown   31
people — the British white man, by 1759, through promises, trickery and manipulations, controlled much of India through Great Britain's East India Company. The parasitical British administration kept tentacling out to half of the sub-continent. In 1857, some of the desperate people of India finally mutinied — and, excepting the African slave trade, nowhere has history recorded any more unnecessary bestial and ruthless human carnage than the British suppression of the non-white Indian people.

[13]*John Brown:* U.S. abolitionist (1800–1859); leader of an attack on Harpers Ferry, West Virginia in 1859.

[14]*Herodotus:* early Greek historian (484?–425? B.C.).

[15]*Mahatma Gandhi:* Hindu religious leader, social reformer, and advocate of nonviolence (1869–1948).

[16]*Faustian:* relating to or resembling Faust, a legendary character who sold his soul to the devil for knowledge and power; hence, someone who sacrifices spiritual values or principles for personal gain.

Over 115 million African blacks — close to the 1930's population of   32
the United States — were murdered or enslaved during the slave trade.
And I read how when the slave market was glutted, the cannibalistic
white powers of Europe next carved up, as their colonies, the richest
areas of the black continent. And Europe's chancelleries for the next
century played a chess game of naked exploitation and power from Cape
Horn to Cairo.

Ten guards and the warden couldn't have torn me out of those books.   33
Not even Elijah Muhammad could have been more eloquent than those
books were in providing indisputable proof that the collective white man
had acted like a devil in virtually every contact he had with the world's
collective non-white man. I listen today to the radio, and watch television,
and read the headlines about the collective white man's fear and tension
concerning China. When the white man professes ignorance about why
the Chinese hate him so, my mind can't help flashing back to what I
read, there in prison, about how the blood forebears of this same white
man raped China at a time when China was trusting and helpless. Those
original white "Christian traders" sent into China millions of pounds of
opium. By 1839, so many of the Chinese were addicts that China's
desperate government destroyed twenty thousand chests of opium. The
first Opium War[17] was promptly declared by the white man. Imagine!
Declaring *war* upon someone who objects to being narcotized! The
Chinese were severely beaten, with Chinese-invented gunpowder.

The Treaty of Nanking made China pay the British white man for the   34
destroyed opium: forced open China's major ports to British trade; forced
China to abandon Hong Kong; fixed China's import tariffs so low that
cheap British articles soon flooded in, maiming China's industrial
development.

After a second Opium War, the Tientsin Treaties legalized the ravaging   35
opium trade, legalized a British-French-American control of China's customs. China tried delaying that Treaty's ratification; Peking was looted
and burned.

"Kill the foreign white devils!" was the 1901 Chinese war cry in the   36
Boxer Rebellion.[18] Losing again, this time the Chinese were driven from
Peking's choicest areas. The vicious, arrogant white man put up the
famous signs, "Chinese and dogs not allowed."

Red China after World War II closed its doors to the Western white   37

---

[17] *Opium War:* 1839–1842 war between Britain and China that ended with China's cession
of Hong Kong to British rule.
[18] *Boxer Rebellion:* the 1898–1900 uprising by members of a secret Chinese society who
opposed foreign influence in Chinese affairs.

world. Massive Chinese agricultural, scientific, and industrial efforts are described in a book that *Life* magazine recently published. Some observers inside Red China have reported that the world never has known such a hate-white campaign as is now going on in this non-white country where, present birth-rates continuing, in fifty more years Chinese will be half the earth's population. And it seems that some Chinese chickens will soon come home to roost, with China's recent successful nuclear tests.

Let us face reality. We can see in the United Nations a new world 38 order being shaped, along color lines — an alliance among the non-white nations. America's U.N. Ambassador Adlai Stevenson[19] complained not long ago that in the United Nations "a skin game" was being played. He was right. He was facing reality. A "skin game" *is* being played. But Ambassador Stevenson sounded like Jesse James accusing the marshal of carrying a gun. Because who in the world's history ever has played a worse "skin game" than the white man?

Mr. Muhammad, to whom I was writing daily, had no idea of what 39 a new world had opened up to me through my efforts to document his teachings in books.

When I discovered philosophy, I tried to touch all the landmarks of 40 philosophical development. Gradually, I read most of the old philosophers, Occidental and Oriental. The Oriental philosophers were the ones I came to prefer; finally, my impression was that most Occidental philosophy had largely been borrowed from the Oriental thinkers. Socrates, for instance, traveled in Egypt. Some sources even say that Socrates was initiated into some of the Egyptian mysteries. Obviously Socrates got some of his wisdom among the East's wise men.

I have often reflected upon the new vistas that reading opened to me. 41 I knew right there in prison that reading had changed forever the course of my life. As I see it today, the ability to read awoke inside me some long dormant craving to be mentally alive. I certainly wasn't seeking any degree, the way a college confers a status symbol upon its students. My homemade education gave me, with every additional book that I read, a little bit more sensitivity to the deafness, dumbness, and blindness that was afflicting the black race in America. Not long ago, an English writer telephoned me from London, asking questions. One was, "What's your alma mater?" I told him, "Books." You will never catch me with a free fifteen minutes in which I'm not studying something I feel might be able to help the black man.

Yesterday I spoke in London, and both ways on the plane across the 42

---

[19]*Adlai Stevenson:* U.S. politician (1900–1965); Democratic candidate for the presidency in 1952 and 1956.

Atlantic I was studying a document about how the United Nations proposes to insure the human rights of the oppressed minorities of the world. The American black man is the world's most shameful case of minority oppression. What makes the black man think of himself as only an internal United States issue is just a catch-phrase, two words, "civil rights." How is the black man going to get "civil rights" before first he wins his *human* rights? If the American black man will start thinking about his *human* rights, and then start thinking of himself as part of one of the world's great peoples, he will see he has a case for the United Nations.

I can't think of a better case! Four hundred years of black blood and 43
sweat invested here in America, and the white man still has the black man begging for what every immigrant fresh off the ship can take for granted the minute he walks down the gangplank.

But I'm digressing. I told the Englishman that my alma mater was 44
books, a good library. Every time I catch a plane, I have with me a book that I want to read — and that's a lot of books these days. If I weren't out here every day battling the white man, I could spend the rest of my life reading, just satisfying my curiosity — because you can hardly mention anything I'm not curious about. I don't think anybody ever got more out of going to prison than I did. In fact, prison enabled me to study far more intensively than I would have if my life had gone differently and I had attended some college. I imagine that one of the biggest troubles with colleges is there are too many distractions, too much panty-raiding, fraternities, and boola-boola and all of that. Where else but in a prison could I have attacked my ignorance by being able to study intensely sometimes as much as fifteen hours a day?

Engaging the Text

1. What motivates Malcolm X to educate himself?

2. In what ways does learning to read free or empower Malcolm X?

3. Some readers are offended by the strength of Malcolm X's accusations and by his grouping of all members of a given race into "collectives." Given the history of racial injustice he recounts here, do you feel he is justified in taking such a position?

Exploring Connections

1. Compare and contrast Malcolm X's views on the meaning and purpose of education — or on the value and nature of reading — with those of Rodriguez (p. 469). How can you account for the differences in their attitudes?

2. How well does Jules Henry's analysis of institutionalized education earlier in

the chapter account for the differences between Richard Rodriguez's and Malcolm X's views on learning?

Extending the Critical Context

1. Survey some typical elementary or secondary school textbooks to test Malcolm X's charge that the educational establishment presents a "whitened" view of America. What view of America is currently being projected in public school history and social science texts?

2. Discuss the benefits and drawbacks of an unsystematic self-education like Malcolm X's.

Women Students in the Classroom

FRANCES MAHER

In this essay Frances Maher explores the challenges that women face in an educational system dominated by men and traditionally male values. While her point of view is expressly feminist, her critique of American education draws heavily on the pedagogical philosophy of Paulo Freire, a well-known Brazilian social activist and teacher, who insists that learning and teaching always recognize the historical, political, and economic dimensions of the student's experience. Maher's call for a student-centered classroom has implications for all students — male as well as female. Maher (b. 1942) is chair of the Education Department at Wheaton College.

Women by now are over half the undergraduate population (Perun, 1982). Presumably they receive the same education and have the same college experience as men, including access to all college facilities, courses, and activities. Outside and inside the classroom, however, their experiences are very different from those of their male counterparts. College is a male-dominated hierarchy in which male professors hold social and intellectual sway over other males (their students and disciples) and females in many subordinate roles (their wives, secretaries and female students and disciples). Female professors are fewer in number (even in all-women's colleges they are seldom a majority), usually lower in status, and do not command a similar "retinue" (see Rich, 1979, p. 137). In this regard, of course, college life reflects accurately many aspects of life in the society at large. Thus women students not only lack enough role models of women as scholars, but are faced with women in a variety of traditional, subordinate, and demeaning roles even as they are presumably enjoying equal educational opportunities and status.

We are most concerned here, however, with the classroom setting. 2
How are women, and women's experiences, devalued *inside* the classroom? Paulo Freire and others have described oppressed peoples in traditional and authoritarian societies as being denied their own voices and experiences by the imposition of the single dominant worldview of "the oppressor" as the only reality. In the traditional model of education that Freire portrays, the teacher (representing the oppressor) is the sole authority and the "Subject" (capitalization as original) of the learning process; he chooses the content which the oppressed students passively accept. In essence, he makes deposits of predetermined information into the empty vaults of the students' minds (see Freire, 1970, p. 59). The application of this concept of "banking education" to women in modern American society is striking.[1] Men in general have often been described as the "subject" for which women are the "object." More importantly, women are silenced, objectified and made passive through both the course content and the pedagogical style of most college classrooms.

First, academic disciplines ignore and distort the experience of women 3
as a group by structuring their concepts and subject-matter around male-derived norms. Second, however, the dominant pedagogical style of most classrooms discriminates against women's experience and participation in a variety of ways, all of which reinforce female passivity. Professors — male and, sometimes, female — tend to call on women students less in discussion, to ask them less probing questions, and to interrupt them more often. They make more frequent eye-contact with men and are more attentive to male questions or comments (see Thorne, 1975, quoted in Hale and Sandler, 1982, pp. 7–9). On a deeper level, classroom discussions (as well as lectures) are usually conducted so as to reward "assertive speech," competitive "devil's advocate" interchanges, and impersonal and abstract styles — often incorporating the generic "he" (*ibid.*,

---

[1]The relevance of Freire's work for women is ironic because Freire never mentions women. He uses "people," sometimes, but usually discusses men: "It is not surprising that the banking concept of education regards men as adaptable, manageable beings" (Freire, 1970, p. 60). [Author's note]

pp. 9, 10). These modes of speech, while perhaps not inherently "masculine," seem more natural to men in this culture; women tend to be more tentative, polite, and hesitant in their comments and thus are taken less seriously by teachers. Women who try to be more assertive face a double bind, for they are perceived as "hostile" females rather than as "forceful" men. Perhaps as a result of this treatment, as well as the subject-matter, women college students as a group are simply more silent than men. Like Freire's "oppressed," they do not speak up; their experiences, their interpretations, their questions are not heard as often.

What are the implications of this analysis for interpreting and changing 4 current classroom practices? At the root of the problem of awakening women students is a recognition of the central validity of their own perceptions in choosing and interpreting their education. In order for the oppressed to be liberated, according to Freire, their experiences under the oppressors must be raised to the level of personal consciousness, recognized and affirmed. Then teachers and students can be equals in a cooperative search for understanding about the experiences of people in their world (Freire, 1970, p. 67).

In this light we can begin to see the primary importance of the inclusion 5 of women's perspectives in the subject-matter disciplines. But we can also reexamine women's patterns of classroom participation and see them as cooperative and constructive, rather than non-assertive and hesitant. Common patterns of competition and argument in discussion came not only from "masculine" modes of speech, but from traditional notions of learning, wherein we search for objective truth and the single "right answer" rather than for shared and comparative conclusions about multiple experiences. In fact, Hale and Sandler, in their research on college women's classroom experiences, intimate that "feminine" styles might be more conducive to a notion of discussion as a "cooperative development of ideas" rather than as "competition from the floor." They describe women's tendency to end questions with a questioning intonation, encouraging the next speaker to elaborate. They quote findings to show more class participation by both sexes in courses taught by women, although women teachers are not immune to the discriminatory practices we have been describing (Hale and Sandler, 1982, p. 10).

Simply in terms of classroom interactions, then, we can suggest that 6 teaching practices which stress cooperative rather than competitive participation may encourage more women students (and more students) actively to question and examine the implications of the material they are learning for their own experience and their own lives, thus better addressing their educational needs and priorities.

Components of Interactive Pedagogy

The needs of the students, of the research process, and of the disciplines 7
themselves thus all require an interactive pedagogy for the treatment
of women's experiences. While women students (and many men) have
been silenced in college classrooms, a new process of relating subject-
matter to student needs and interests depends upon the active participation
of all students, particularly women, whose experiences (and voices) have
until recently been considered illegitimate. Such a process also draws
on the "female" modes of collaborative, rather than competitive, interaction.
Researchers have turned away from a competitive search for the one
best theory or explanation of phenomena (which can then be "taught"
to students) towards a collaborative, evolutionary and complementary
approach (which can be opened up to include student views). In addition,
the content of major disciplines is being reshaped to accept multiple
viewpoints as equally valid, particularly those which have been unexpressed
and suppressed before. Therefore, student contributions can enrich interpretations in the discipline as well as in their own learning.

What are some concrete and practical aspects of this "interactive" 8
pedagogy? How does subject-matter presentation change? What are some
roles and activities of the teacher and student? How can classes be
structured? What issues and problems need further discussion?

Subject-matter Presentation

A subject-matter that denies or contradicts a student's own experience 9
can still be absorbed in several ways. Students may "learn" it on its own
terms, without expecting the content to have any personal relevance or
meaning. For instance, many have memorized historical facts and dates,
and even used them appropriately in essays, without ever having ex-
periential reference-points for these facts. A second mode of reception
is that of misunderstanding. A teacher may describe a law as "progressive,"
a certain family as "middle class," or a person as "depressed." In each
of these cases, students may "understand" these words in a different
sense from the one the teacher intends, and thus perhaps misinterpret
course assignments and presentations. In either of the above examples,
the traditional lecture approach leaves no room for clarification. Obviously,
the more distant the students' own experience from the subject-matter
as defined by the teacher, the more difficult and alienating this lack of
understanding will be (as in women's exclusion from male-derived norms
and concepts).

However, training in all disciplines involves the study of unfamiliar 10
terms or terms used in discipline-specific ways. Thus, if we want our

students to construct both an accurate and personally meaningful version of our subject-matter — one that can be discussed and built on with the teacher and each other — we must begin with the construction of a common vocabulary and language among teacher and students. Too often we assume that students attach the same attributes to key concepts as we do. In our formulation, we often use one term which is unfamiliar to students to describe another unfamiliar term — leaving them confused and reduced to rote memorization and passive learning (see Maher and Lyman, 1982). Teachers can begin classes by asking students for their *own* meanings for key terms, and then using these in the definitions of new ones. For example, students in an educational psychology class are asked to evaluate the concept of "intelligence" as it relates to IQ testing. To prepare for this discussion, they write an essay entitled "How Smart I Am" to express their own experience of this loaded and controversial concept.

For Paulo Freire, this act of naming our experiences is a crucial step 11 in the awakening of the consciousness of the oppressed. The essence of dialogue is the "word." By constructing common names and meanings for their realities, people describe and activate the world for each other — and, in so doing, may change it. Once armed with the concept of "exploitation," for example, they can begin to define its features and interpret them: "Dialogue is the encounter between men, mediated by the world, in order to name the world" (Freire, 1970, p. 76). In our terms, *women* need to name and describe our world, to differentiate its terms and meanings from those of male experience, if only to see our commonalities as well. (For example, is "depression" different for women than for men? How can the two forms be described and compared?) Until teachers explicitly work toward constructing a commonly understood language in their classrooms, the subject-matter concepts will be alien to some students' experiences.

A more fundamental change in subject-matter presentation involves 12 making explicit connections in course topics among the three levels of theory, research, and the students' (and teacher's) own observations and experiences. As students explore different explanatory models for data discussed in courses, they learn that the validity of any strong theory comes from its ability to explain aspects of both learned about and personally experienced reality. They also learn some ways in which different perspectives, including their own, help to determine what data is used and considered important. Thus Bunch (1979) has students compare personal solutions to set discrimination issues with those of feminist theorists. In my educational psychology course the students (all female) contrast a new model of female moral development (Gilligan, 1982) to the more traditional approaches of Kohlberg, Piaget and others. They analyze their own thinking in relation to these theories through class discussions of moral dilemmas. In so doing, they are able not only to challenge a previously held norm, but also to reassess the universal applicability of all such stage theories to explain human development.

In another course, students examine sexism in schools — the controversy over girls and math, discriminatory tracking and counseling practices, and classroom interaction patterns that favor boys. They compare research findings to classroom observations and to their own experiences as females in school. They look at explanatory models for this discrimination from feminist and non-feminist schools of thought. (For example, are girls' minds genetically different, or socially programmed for different interests?) Relating theory, research, and experience in this way, they can begin to think of ways schools might serve not only girls, but a wide variety of students perhaps previously ignored or demeaned by the imposition of a single academic norm.

The Roles of Teacher and Student
Beyond such new treatment of subject-matter topics described above, there are several related ways of transforming our pedagogy to reflect the collaborative and interactive nature of the new scholarship on women. If this work has legitimized the study of ordinary lives from multiple perspectives, and made explicit the connection between the framework of the knower and what is known, then students and teachers can use their own experience in the creation, as well as the illustration, of course topics. One way to do this is by the use of the "self as subject." Student educational autobiographies in education courses and family trees and family history in history courses are examples of this approach. In one education course, students analyze the significance for both women's roles and the education profession of the fact that most teachers in America have been women. (See, for example, Grumet, 1981.) In a related discussion of their educational family trees, students in one class found that *every* grandmother who worked was at one time a teacher. This common background, besides giving these education students a strong sense of historical identification and persisting societal norms, also encouraged them to reevaluate their own possible choice of teaching as a career. Central to this inclusion of the self as subject, however, is the teacher's acknowledgment of his or her perspective as, of necessity, a partial one as well. Instead of presenting all course topics and materials as objective truth, the teacher must be explicit about his or her rationale behind the choice of readings, issues and so on.

There is here, as we have said above, an admitted "intersubjectivity of meaning of subject and object . . . the questions that the investigator asks of the object of knowledge grow out of her own concerns and experiences" (Westcott, 1979, p. 426). Westcott and others see this dialectical relationship between self and material as particularly powerful for women studying women, because "knowledge of the other and knowledge of the self are mutually informing . . . self and other share a common condition of being women." However, this paradigm[2] may illustrate any exploration in which aspects of personal identity illuminate the subject-matter — whether workers studying workers, Italians studying Italians, and so on. The interpretation of particular masculine experiences as generalized truths has denied such insights to many groups. Students and teachers using the "self as subject" can call up and legitimize a variety of hitherto unexplored experiences and themes. (The validity and power of self-examination, and explicit subjectivity, in contributing to a personally meaningful education has also been recently explicated by many modern curriculum theorists. See, for example, Freire, 1970; Greene, 1975; and Mitrano, 1981.)

A second way of empowering students as experts is to use the notion   16
of the "self as inquirer." Here, more than in other modes of teaching, we are asking our students not only to answer questions, but to pose them; to become creators and constructors, as well as learners, of knowledge. We can assign them topics to pursue in which they take a particular interest (once again being explicit about the connection between knowledge and knower); their research can then be challenged and enriched by each other's contributions and perspectives. Such assignments can make individuals or groups responsible for constructing components of the course: in a government course, for example, students can research and present the policies of a particular party, country, or pressure group. Or assignments can illustrate or examine course theories: as mentioned above, student field observations in elementary schools can test presumed differences in boy/girl behavior raised in education and psychology classes. Thus, student research into the experiences of particular groups can build on and/or transform theories or hypotheses introduced in class. Such research gives the material personal importance for students, as well as enriching the discipline itself.

The Structure of Classes and Courses

This consideration of students as "subjects" and "inquirers" involves,   17
however, the serious inclusion of their contributions in both the presentation and the structuring of our courses. Thus, in interactive and democratic

[2]*paradigm:* an example serving as a model; a pattern.

teaching modes the most common form of communication is discussion, not lecture. The teacher (or student) raises a problem from the readings; students explore its meaning and ramifications, relate it to their own experiences, consider solutions and so on. The teacher may have been responsible for the selection of the reading and the framing of the problem, but the discussion legitimizes the experience of all in analyzing it. Hence, both teacher and students can play the role of both experts and learners.

In conducting discussions, teachers need to encourage students to 18 listen and react to each other's statements, and to put student comments on the board for emphasis. To gain maximum participation, discussion on specific topics can be arranged in small groups, with results reported to the class as a whole and emphasized by the teacher. In general, habits of inferiority and passivity, of looking to the teacher for the answer, have to be deliberately challenged to be broken. We can be explicit that a course relies on student contributions and formulations, but we must also arrange classroom discussion so that this reliance is genuine. With women students (especially silenced) and Women's Studies (until recently not considered a legitimate field of inquiry) such new patterns should be particularly emphasized.

Differences among students are often an issue in ongoing class dis- 19 cussions. Some students are more vocal than others: for example, males tend to volunteer more answers than females. Females, and quieter students, need to be explicitly encouraged; to be called on when not volunteering and to be placed in small groups where participation may be easier. Students with differing perspectives may also actively disagree. They may not see each other's perspectives as mutually reinforcing, but as conflicting — which is sometimes the case. For example, in a recent Women's Studies case, working-class white women and upper-middle-class black women argued extensively over the relative weight of class and race in female oppression. Each group had both personal experience and evidence to support their position. More specifically, as Davis points out, "feminist" students whose consciousness has already been raised may feel uncomfortable with their more traditional sisters. "However 'advanced' their intellectual and emotional grasp of feminist issues, [they] often lack empathy with or respect for the hard choices and important conflicts of traditional women" (Davis, 1981, p. 8).

For differences and divisions like these (and again such differences 20 can come up in any classroom where multiple perspectives are discussed), the teacher can function as a "simultaneous translator . . . hearing and giving back in other words what another person has just said, and presenting an explanation in another language which will illuminate the issue for a second group without alienating the first" (ibid., p. 9). In such discussions, the prior creation of common definitions for terms and a common language for the group is particularly important. If all agree on what "social class" means, then unnecessary misunderstanding can be avoided. Furthermore, the teacher can both model and explain the rationale for her translating activities. A more complete view of the world does not come from dichotomizing views into "good" or "bad," "right" or "wrong," but rather using them to build a more complex picture of the problem. This stance does not, and should not, minimize conflict or disagreement: it clarifies it and seeks to put it in a larger context. In addition, students can also be taught to listen to, and to translate, each other's languages and concerns. In this way, they may replace their own search for "right answers" with a critical understanding and evaluation of their own and others' perspectives.

Second, courses can be structured so as to depend on, and draw from,   21 student research as an integral part of the course work itself (rather than scheduling "oral reports" at the end). Several students can read and comment on each other's papers before they are presented in class, so that the students can lead a discussion of the paper. Students can research topics that illuminate and build on course themes; such topics can become an integral part of the course syllabus (as in history via family trees, or psychology via biography and autobiography.) A related teacher responsibility may be to train students in the appropriate research and writing skills for successfully completing such assignments. Depending on the level of the students, teachers may hand out guidelines for research papers, for the use of the library and so on. Teachers can also encourage students to help each other on projects. Students may be put in cooperative groups for research as well as discussion purposes (see the work of David and Roger Johnson, 1975).

Related Issues

Classes and courses can thus be deliberately structured to build on,   22 and encourage, active student (and teacher) involvement in a collaborative learning enterprise. Other issues and considerations arise, however. There are differences *among* students, to which we assign relative value in the form of grades. Grading policies vary and are controversial. An interactive pedagogy may imply that students grade themselves, or are involved in the process by which criteria for grades are set. However, teachers who wish to retain these powers of grading can be explicit about the criteria they themselves use. Written guidelines for conducting discussions, for research papers and for projects, as mentioned above, can function as checklists of evaluative criteria which are actually applied to student work. Many teachers also allow rewrites of papers after comments are discussed.

Finally, a word about large classes. This essay has assumed group 23 sizes appropriate for discussions. In classes of forty, eighty, or more, can we use interactive pedagogics? Outside of lectures, students can be divided into reading and discussion groups, or task forces for particular assignments and projects. The teacher can occasionally take class time to meet with these groups, and can schedule student-led presentations and discussions, as well. However, the structure of the university, in which large lecture courses are a dominant mode, is a paradigm for the traditional concept of knowledge as a fixed store of information and expertise to be pumped into passive student minds. The content of this knowledge has been masculine experiences, standards, and worldviews; its form is oppressive and exclusive. Even were the content of lectures in this mode to be replaced with a "Women's Studies" content, it has been the thrust of this essay that such *forms* of both research and teaching must be changed to reflect the existence of multiple experiences of the world.

Works Cited

Davis, Barbara Hillyer (1981), "Teaching the Feminist Minority," *Women's Studies Quarterly*, vol. 9, no. 4, winter, pp. 7–9. Reprinted as ch. 22 in the present work.

Freire, Paulo (1970), *Pedagogy of the Oppressed*, New York: Continuum, 17th printing, 1981.

Gilligan, Carol (1982), *In a Different Voice: Psychological Theory and Women's Development*, Cambridge, Mass.: Harvard University Press.

Greene, Maxine (1975), "Curriculum and Cultural Transformation," *Cross Currents*, vol. 25, no. 2, summer, pp. 175–86.

Grumet, Madeleine (1981), "Pedagogy for Patriarchy: The Feminization of Teaching," *Interchange on Educational Policy*, vol. 12, nos 2/3, pp. 165–84.

Hale, Roberta, and Bernice Sandler (1982), *The Classroom Climate: A Chilly One for Women?* Project on the Status and Education of Women, Washington, DC: American Association of Colleges.

Johnson, David, and Roger Johnson (1975), *Learning Together and Alone*, Englewood Cliffs, New Jersey: Prentice-Hall.

Maher, Frances, and Kathleen Lyman (1982), "Definitions of Social Studies Concepts: A Precondition for Inquiry," unpublished paper, December.

Mitrano, Barbara (1981), "Feminism and Curriculum Theory, Implications for Teacher Education," *Journal of Curriculum Theorizing*, vol. 3, no. 2, summer, pp. 5–85.

Rich, Adrienne (1979), *On Lies, Secrets and Silence*, New York: Norton.

Thorne, Barrie, and Nancy Henley (1975), *Language and Sex, Difference and Dominance*, Rowley, Mass.: Newbury House Publishers.

Westcott, Marcia (1979), "Feminist Criticism of the Social Sciences," *Harvard Educational Review*, vol. 49, no. 4, November, pp. 422–30.

Engaging the Text

1. What are the implications of the Freirean "banking" METAPHOR that Maher uses to describe the student-teacher relationship in a traditional classroom? Is this an accurate picture of what happens in most classes? What other metaphors might you use to describe teaching and learning?

2. What changes does Maher recommend to "feminize" the classroom? Would such changes enhance your education?

3. How does Maher feel about grades? What effects do grades have on your attitude as a student?

Exploring Connections

1. How would Jules Henry (p. 444) respond to Maher's call for a democratized classroom? How do his views of teachers, students, and education differ from Maher's?

2. Use Marilyn French's and Carol Gilligan's selections in Chapter Four, "Women," to expand upon Maher's contention that traditional classrooms neglect women's values and ways of knowing.

Extending the Critical Context

1. Survey the courses you are currently enrolled in for evidence of gender bias. You may want to compare, for example, how often female and male students speak in class, the kinds of contributions they make, and the way that their teachers respond to them. You may also want to note how often personal experience and personal interactions enter into classroom experience.

2. Research the percentages of men and women at various ranks of faculty, administrative, and clerical staff at your institution. How well represented are women in each of these areas? To extend the research, study a selection of college texts. Who are the authors, and whose experiences do the texts discuss? Report on your findings to the class, drawing any conclusions you feel are justified about male-female equality at your school.

3. Maher talks about ways teachers can make education more student-centered. What can students do on their own to promote collaboration over competition, to integrate personal experience with academic learning, and to play a more active role in their education?

Rumors of Inferiority

JEFF HOWARD AND RAY HAMMOND

Twenty years after Affirmative Action admission policies increased the minority enrollment at most colleges, critics have charged that minority students in general cannot compete intellectually with their peers and that, as a result, the quality of American higher education has been eroded. In the following essay, two Afro-American scholars consider the implications of these "rumors of inferiority." Although they consider only black students in this selection, their conclusions may extend to students from any marginalized group. Jeff Howard (b. 1948) is a psychologist; Ray Hammond (b. 1951) is a physician and an ordained minister.

Today's black Americans are the beneficiaries of great historical 1
achievements. Our ancestors managed to survive the brutality of slavery and the long history of oppression that followed emancipation. Early in this century they began dismantling the legal structure of segregation that had kept us out of the institutions of American society. In the 1960s they launched the civil rights movement, one of the most effective mass movements for social justice in history. Not all of the battles have been won, but there is no denying the magnitude of our predecessors' achievement.

Nevertheless, black Americans today face deteriorating conditions in 2
sharp contrast to other American groups. The black poverty rate is triple that of whites, and the unemployment rate is double. Black infant mortality not only is double that of whites, but may be rising for the first time in a decade. We have reached the point where more than half of the black children born in this country are born out of wedlock — most to teenage parents. Blacks account for more than 40 percent of the inmates in federal and state prisons, and in 1982 the probability of being murdered was six times greater for blacks than for whites. The officially acknowledged high school dropout rate in many metropolitan areas is more than 30 percent. Some knowledgeable observers say it is over 50 percent in several major cities. These problems not only reflect the current depressed state of black America, but also impose obstacles to future advancement.

The racism, discrimination, and oppression that black people have 3
suffered and continue to suffer are clearly at the root of many of today's

problems. Nevertheless, our analysis takes off from a forward-looking, and we believe optimistic, note: We are convinced that black people today, because of the gains in education, economic status, and political leverage that we have won as a result of the civil rights movement, are in a position to substantially improve the conditions of our communities using the resources already at our disposal. Our thesis is simple: The progress of any group is affected not only by public policy and by the racial attitudes of society as a whole, but by that group's capacity to exploit its own strengths. Our concern is about factors that prevent black Americans from using those strengths.

It's important to distinguish between the specific circumstances a group   4
faces and its capacity to marshal its own resources to change those circumstances. Solving the problems of black communities requires a focus on the factors that hinder black people from more effectively managing their own circumstances. What are some of these factors?

Intellectual Development. Intellectual development is the primary focus   5
of this article because it is the key to success in American society. Black people traditionally have understood this. Previous generations decided that segregation had to go because it relegated blacks to the backwater of American society, effectively denying us the opportunities, exposure, and competition that form the basis of intellectual development. Black intellectual development was one of the major benefits expected from newly won access to American institutions. That development, in turn, was expected to be a foundation for future advancement.

Yet now, three decades after *Brown v. Board of Education,*[1] there is   6
pervasive evidence of real problems in the intellectual performance of many black people. From astronomical high school dropout rates among the poor to substandard academic and professional performance among those most privileged, there is a disturbing consistency in reports of lagging development. While some black people perform at the highest levels in every field of endeavor, the percentages who do so are small. Deficiencies in the process of intellectual development are one effect of the long-term suppression of a people; they are also, we believe, one of the chief causes of continued social and economic underdevelopment. Intellectual underdevelopment is one of the most pernicious effects of racism, because it limits the people's ability to solve problems over which they are capable of exercising substantial control.

[1] *Brown v. Board of Education:* the landmark 1954 Supreme Court decision that mandated the end of "separate but equal" segregationist policies common since the late 19th century.

Black Americans are understandably sensitive about discussions of the   7
data on our performance, since this kind of information has been used
too often to justify attacks on affirmative action and other government
efforts to improve the position of blacks and other minorities. Nevertheless,
the importance of this issue demands that black people and all others
interested in social justice overcome our sensitivities, analyze the problem,
and search for solutions.

The Performance Gap. Measuring intellectual performance requires   8
making a comparison. The comparison may be with the performance of
others in the same situation, or with some established standard of excellence, or both. It is typically measured by grades, job performance
ratings, and scores on standardized and professional tests. In recent years
a flood of articles, scholarly papers, and books have documented an
intellectual performance gap between blacks and the population as a
whole.

- In 1982 the College Board,[2] for the first time in its history, published
  data on the performance of various groups on the Scholastic Aptitude
  Test (SAT). The difference between the combined median scores of
  blacks and whites on the verbal and math portions of the SAT was
  slightly more than 200 points. Differences in family income don't
  explain the gap. Even at incomes over $50,000, there remained a
  120-point difference. These differences persisted in the next two years.
- In 1983 the NCAA[3] proposed a requirement that all college athletic
  recruits have a high school grade-point average of at least 2.0 (out of
  a maximum of 4.0) and a minimum combined SAT score of 700. This
  rule, intended to prevent the exploitation of young athletes, was
  strongly opposed by black college presidents and civil rights leaders.
  They were painfully aware that in recent years less than half of all
  black students have achieved a combined score of 700 on the SAT.
- Asian-Americans consistently produce a median SAT score 140 to 150
  points higher than blacks with the same family income.
- The pass rate for black police officers on New York City's sergeant's
  exam is 1.6 percent. For Hispanics, it's 4.4 percent. For whites, it's
  10.6 percent. These are the results *after* $500,000 was spent, by court
  order, to produce a test that was job-related and nondiscriminatory.
  No one, even those alleging discrimination, could explain how the
  revised test was biased.
- Florida gives a test to all candidates for teaching positions. The pass

[2]*College Board:* a not-for-profit corporation that prepares and administers college entrance
examinations.
[3]*NCAA:* the National Collegiate Athletic Association.

rate for whites is more than 80 percent. For blacks, it's 35 percent to 40 percent.

This is just a sampling. All these reports demonstrate a real difference between the performance of blacks and other groups. Many of the results cannot be easily explained by socioeconomic differences or minority status per se.

What is the explanation? Clear thinking about this is inhibited by the 10 tendency to equate performance with ability. Acknowledging the performance gap is, in many minds, tantamount to inferring that blacks are intellectually inferior. But inferior performance and inferior ability are not the same thing. Rather, the performance gap is largely a behavioral problem. It is the result of a remediable tendency to avoid intellectual engagement and competition. Avoidance is rooted in the fears and self-doubt engendered by a major legacy of American racism: the strong negative stereotypes about black intellectual capabilities. Avoidance of intellectual competition is manifested most obviously in the attitudes of many black youths toward academic work, but it is not limited to children. It affects the intellectual performance of black people of all ages and feeds public doubts about black intellectual ability.

I. Intellectual Development

The performance gap damages the self-confidence of many black people. 11 Black students and professional people cannot help but be bothered by poor showings in competitive academic and professional situations. Black leaders too often have tried to explain away these problems by blaming racism or cultural bias in the tests themselves. These factors haven't disappeared. But for many middle-class black Americans who have had access to educational and economic opportunities for nearly 20 years, the traditional protestations of cultural deprivation and educational disadvantage ring hollow. Given the cultural and educational advantages that many black people now enjoy, the claim that all blacks should be exempt from the performance standards applied to others is interpreted as a tacit admission of inferiority. This admission adds further weight to the questions, in our own minds and in the minds of others, about black intelligence.

The traditional explanations — laziness or inferiority on the one hand; 12 racism, discrimination, and biased tests on the other — are inaccurate and unhelpful. What is required is an explanation that accounts for the subtle influences people exert over the behavior and self-confidence of other people.

Developing an explanation that might serve as a basis for corrective 13
action is important. The record of the last 20 years suggests that waiting
for grand initiatives from the outside to save the black community is
futile. Blacks will have to rely on our own ingenuity and resources. We
need local and national political leaders. We need skilled administrators
and creative business executives. We need a broad base of well-educated
volunteers and successful people in all fields as role models for black
youths. In short, we need a large number of sophisticated, intellectually
developed people who are confident of their ability to operate on an
equal level with anyone. Chronic mediocre intellectual performance is
deeply troubling because it suggests that we are not developing enough
such people.

The Competitive Process. Intellectual development is not a fixed asset 14
that you either have or don't have. Nor is it based on magic. It is a
process of expanding mental strength and reach. The development process
is demanding. It requires time, discipline, and intense effort. It almost
always involves competition as well. Successful groups place high value
on intellectual performance. They encourage the drive to excel and use
competition to sharpen skills and stimulate development in each succeeding
generation. The developed people that result from this competitive process
become the pool from which leadership of all kinds is drawn. Competition,
in other words, is an essential spur to development.

Competition is clearly not the whole story. Cooperation and solitary 15
study are valuable, too. But of the various keys to intellectual development,
competition seems to fare worst in the estimation of many blacks. Black
young people, in particular, seem to place a strong negative value on
intellectual competition.

Black people have proved to be very competitive at some activities, 16
particularly sports and entertainment. It is our sense, however, that
many blacks consider intellectual competition to be inappropriate. It
appears to inspire little interest or respect among many youthful peer
groups. Often, in fact, it is labeled "grade grubbing," and gives way to
sports and social activity as a basis for peer acceptance. The intellectual
performance gap is one result of this retreat from competition.

II. The Psychology of Performance

Rumors of Inferiority. The need to avoid intellectual competition is 17
a psychological reaction to an image of black intellectual inferiority that
has been projected by the larger society, and to a less than conscious
process of internalization of that image by black people over the generations.

The rumor of black intellectual inferiority has been around for a long 18
time. It has been based on grounds as diverse as twisted biblical citations,
dubious philosophical arguments, and unscientific measurements of skull

capacity. The latest emergence of this old theme has been in the controversy over race and IQ. For 15 years newsmagazines and television talk shows have enthusiastically taken up the topic of black intellectual endowment. We have watched authors and critics debate the proposition that blacks are genetically inferior to whites in intellectual capability.

Genetic explanations have a chilling finality. The ignorant can be educated, the lazy can be motivated, but what can be done for the individual thought to have been born without the basic equipment necessary to compete or develop? Of course the allegation of genetic inferiority has been hotly disputed. But the debate has touched the consciousness of most Americans. We are convinced that this spectacle has negatively affected the way both blacks and whites think about the intellectual capabilities of black people. It also has affected the way blacks behave in intellectually competitive situations. The general expectation of black intellectual inferiority, and the fear this expectation generates, cause many black people to avoid intellectual competition. 19

Our hypothesis, in short, is this. (1) Black performance problems are caused in large part by a tendency to avoid intellectual competition. (2) This tendency is a psychological phenomenon that arises when the larger society projects an image of black intellectual inferiority and when that image is internalized by black people. (3) Imputing intellectual inferiority to genetic causes, especially in the face of data confirming poorer performance, intensifies the fears and doubts that surround this issue. 20

Clearly the image of inferiority continues to be projected. The internalization of this image by black people is harder to prove empirically. But there is abundant evidence in the expressed attitudes of many black youths toward intellectual competition; in the inability of most black communities to inspire the same commitment to intellectual excellence that is routinely accorded athletics and entertainment; and in the fact of the performance gap itself — especially when that gap persists among the children of economically and educationally privileged households. 21

Expectancies and Performance. The problem of black intellectual performance is rooted in human sensitivity to a particular kind of social interaction known as "expectancy communications." These are expressions of belief — verbal or nonverbal — from one person to another about the kind of performance to be expected. "Mary, you're one of the best workers we have, so I know that you won't have any trouble with this assignment." Or, "Joe, since everyone else is busy with other work, do as much as you can on this. When you run into trouble, call Mary." The first is a positive expectancy; the second, a negative expectancy. 22

Years of research have clearly demonstrated the powerful impact of 23 expectancies on performance. The expectations of teachers for their students have a large effect on academic achievement. Psychological studies under a variety of circumstances demonstrate that communicated expectations induce people to believe that they will do well or poorly at a task, and that such beliefs very often trigger responses that result in performance consistent with the expectation. There is also evidence that "reference group expectancies" — directed at an entire category of people rather than a particular individual — have a similar impact on the performance of members of the group.

Expectancies do not always work. If they come from a questionable 24 source or if they predict an outcome that is too inconsistent with previous experience, they won't have much effect. Only credible expectancies — those that come from a source considered reliable and that address a belief or doubt the performer is sensitive to — will have a self-fulfilling impact.

The widespread expectation of black intellectual inferiority — com- 25 municated constantly through the projection of stereotyped images, verbal and nonverbal exchanges in daily interaction, and the incessant debate about genetics and intelligence — represents a credible reference-group expectancy. The message of the race/IQ controversy is: "We have scientific evidence that blacks, because of genetic inadequacies, can't be expected to do well at tasks that require great intelligence." As an explanation for past black intellectual performance, the notion of genetic inferiority is absolutely incorrect. As an expectancy communication exerting control over our present intellectual strivings, it has been powerfully effective. These expectancies raise fear and self-doubt in the minds of many blacks, especially when they are young and vulnerable. This has resulted in avoidance of intellectual activity and chronic underperformance by many of our most talented people. Let us explore this process in more detail.

The Expectancy/Performance Model. The powerful effect of expectancies 26 on performance has been proved, but the way the process works is less well understood. Expectancies affect behavior, we think, in two ways. They affect performance behavior: the capacity to marshal the sharpness and intensity required for competitive success. And they influence cognition: the mental processes by which people make sense of everyday life.

Behavior. As anyone who has experienced an "off day" knows, effort 27 is variable; it is subject to biological cycles, emotional states, motivation. Most important for our discussion, it depends on levels of confidence going into a task. Credible expectancies influence performance behavior. They affect the intensity of effort, the level of concentration or distractibility, and the willingness to take reasonable risks — a key factor in the development of self-confidence and new skills.

Cognition. Expectations also influence the way people think about or 28
explain their performance outcomes. These explanations are called "attributions." Research in social psychology has demonstrated that the causes to which people attribute their successes and failures have an important impact on subsequent performance.

All of us encounter failure. But a failure we have been led to expect 29
affects us differently from an unexpected failure. When people who are confident of doing well at a task are confronted with unexpected failure, they tend to attribute the failure to inadequate effort. The likely response to another encounter with the same or a similar task is to work harder. People who come into a task expecting to fail, on the other hand, attribute their failure to lack of ability. Once you admit to yourself, in effect, that "I don't have what it takes," you are not likely to approach that task again with great vigor.

Indeed, those who attribute their failures to inadequate effort are 30
likely to conclude that more effort will produce a better outcome. This triggers an adaptive response to failure. In contrast, those who have been led to expect failure will attribute their failures to lack of ability, and will find it difficult to rationalize the investment of greater effort. They will often hesitate to continue "banging my head against the wall." They often, in fact, feel depressed when they attempt to work, since each attempt represents a confrontation with their own feared inadequacy.

This combined effect on behavior and cognition is what makes expectancy 31
so powerful. The negative expectancy first tends to generate failure through its impact on behavior, and then induces the individual to blame the failure on lack of ability, rather than the actual (and correctable) problem of inadequate effort. This misattribution in turn becomes the basis for a new negative expectancy. By this process the individual, in effect, internalizes the low estimation originally held by others. This internalized negative expectancy powerfully affects future competitive behavior and future results.

The process we describe is not limited to black people. It goes on all 32
the time, with individuals from all groups. It helps to explain the superiority of some groups at some areas of endeavor, and the mediocrity of those same groups in other areas. What makes black people unique is that they are singled out for the stigma of genetic intellectual inferiority.

The expectation of intellectual inferiority accompanies a black person 33
into each new intellectual situation. Since each of us enters these tests under the cloud of predicted failure, and since each failure reinforces

doubts about our capabilities, all intellectual competition raises the specter of having to admit a lack of intellectual capacity. But this particular expectancy goes beyond simply predicting and inducing failure. The expectancy message explicitly ascribes the expected failure to genes, and amounts to an open suggestion to black people to understand any failure in intellectual activity as confirmation of genetic inferiority. Each engagement in intellectual competition carries the weight of a test of one's own genetic endowment and that of black people as a whole. Facing such a terrible prospect, many black people recoil from any situation where the rumor of inferiority might be proved true.

For many black students this avoidance manifests itself in a concentration 34 on athletics and socializing, at the expense of more challenging (and anxiety-provoking) academic work. For black professionals, it may involve a tendency to shy away from competitive situations or projects, or an inability to muster the intensity — or commit the time — necessary to excel. This sort of thinking and behavior certainly does not characterize all black people in competitive settings. But it is characteristic of enough to be a serious problem. When it happens, it should be understood as a less than conscious reaction to the psychological burden of the terrible rumor.

The Intellectual Inferiority Game. There always have been constraints 35 on the intellectual exposure and development of black people in the United States, from laws prohibiting the education of blacks during slavery to the Jim Crow laws[4] and "separate but equal" educational arrangements that persisted until very recently. In dismantling these legal barriers to development, the civil rights movement fundamentally transformed the possibilities for black people. Now, to realize those possibilities, we must address the mental barriers to competition and performance.

The doctrine of intellectual inferiority acts on many black Americans 36 the way that a "con" or a "hustle" like three-card monte[5] acts on its victim. It is a subtle psychological input that interacts with characteristics of the human cognitive apparatus — in this case, the extreme sensitivity to expectancies — to generate self-defeating behavior and thought processes. It has reduced the intellectual performance of millions of black people.

Intellectual inferiority, like segregation, is a destructive idea whose 37 time has passed. Like segregation, it must be removed as an influence

[4]*Jim Crow laws:* laws that made it possible to segregate and discriminate against blacks by mandating "separate but equal" public institutions and accommodations.
[5]*three-card monte:* a game that involves identifying one of three shuffled cards.

in our lives. Among its other negative effects, fear of the terrible rumor has restricted discussion by all parties, and has limited our capacity to understand and improve our situation. But the intellectual inferiority game withers in the light of discussion and analysis. We must begin now to talk about intellectual performance, work through our expectations and fears of intellectual inferiority, consciously define more adaptive attitudes toward intellectual development, and build our confidence in the capabilities of all people.

The expectancy/performance process works both ways. Credible positive 38
expectancies can generate self-confidence and result in success. An important part of the solution to black performance problems is converting the negative expectancies that work against black development into positive expectancies that nurture it. We must overcome our fears, encourage competition, and support the kind of performance that will dispel the notion of black intellectual inferiority.

III. The Commitment to Development

In our work with black high school and college students and with 39
black professionals, we have shown that education in the psychology of performance can produce strong performance improvement very quickly. Black America needs a nationwide effort, now, to ensure that all black people — but especially black youths — are free to express their intellectual gifts. That effort should be built on three basic elements:

- Deliberate control of expectancy communications. We must begin with the way we talk to one another: the messages we give and the expectations we set. This includes the verbal and nonverbal messages we communicate in day-to-day social intercourse, as well as the expectancies communicated through the educational process and media images.
- Definition of an "intellectual work ethic." Black communities must develop strong positive attitudes toward intellectual competition. We must teach our people, young and mature, the efficacy of intense, committed effort in the arena of intellectual activity and the techniques to develop discipline in study and work habits.
- Influencing thought processes. Teachers, parents, and other authority figures must encourage young blacks to attribute their intellectual successes to ability (thereby boosting confidence) and their failures to lack of effort. Failures must no longer destroy black children's confidence in their intelligence or in the efficacy of hard work. Failures should be seen instead as feedback indicating the need for more intense effort or for a different approach to the task.

The task that confronts us is no less challenging than the task that   40
faced those Americans who dismantled segregation. To realize the possibilities presented by their achievement, we must silence, once and for
all, the rumors of inferiority.

Who's Responsible? Expectations of black inferiority are communicated,   41
consciously or unconsciously, by many whites, including teachers, managers, and those responsible for the often demeaning representations of
blacks in the media. These expectations have sad consequences for many
blacks, and those whose actions lead to such consequences may be held
accountable for them. If the people who shape policy in the United
States, from the White House to the local elementary school, do not
address the problems of performance and development of blacks and
other minorities, all Americans will face the consequences: instability,
disharmony, and a national loss of the potential productivity of more
than a quarter of the population.

However, when economic necessity and the demands of social justice   42
compel us toward social change, those who have the most to gain from
change — or the most to lose from its absence — should be responsible
for pointing the way.

It is time that blacks recognize our own responsibility. When we react   43
to the rumor of inferiority by avoiding intellectual engagement, and
when we allow our children to do so, black people forfeit the opportunity
for intellectual development that could extinguish the debate about our
capacities, and set the stage for group progress. Blacks must hold ourselves
accountable for the resulting waste of talent — and valuable time. Black
people have everything to gain — in stature, self-esteem, and problem-
solving capability — from a more aggressive and confident approach to
intellectual competition. We must assume responsibility for our own
performance and development.

Engaging the Text

1. What explanation for the "performance gap" between black and white students
are Howard and Hammond rebutting in this selection? Why do they reject this
position?

2. How do Howard and Hammond view the role of competition in schools?

3. Explain the concept of "expectancy communications," using illustrations drawn
from your own experience.

4. What suggestions do the authors propose for closing the performance gap?
What changes would we have to make in schools and in society at large to put
their suggestions into practice? In your view, would these changes make a
difference?

Exploring Connections

1. Drawing on the quotations from teachers and students offered by Jeannie Oakes earlier in this chapter (p. 459), what expectancy communications are conveyed to students in the tracking system?

2. Stage a forum involving Howard and Hammond, Jules Henry, Frances Maher (in this chapter), Joseph L. White (Chapter Five, "The Changing Family"), Carol Gilligan and Marilyn French (Chapter Four, "Women") on the proper role of competition in education.

Extending the Critical Context

1. Apply the concept of expectancy communications in education to different groups. How, for example, do consciously and unconsciously conveyed expectations affect female, Asian-American, or physically challenged students?

2. Keep a log documenting how expectancy communications are conveyed in your current classes. Compare your observations with those made by other students in your class.

7

Making a Living
How Work Shapes the Worker

Whether considered a pleasure, a virtue, or a curse, work has always played a central role in the American Dream. In our national mythology, Horatio Alger heroes rise from rags to riches through honesty, purity, and hard work. In school, children learn how Benjamin Franklin set out to make his fortune with little more than a willingness to labor honestly and plan wisely. In the daily news, we read about recent immigrants working their way up the ladder of success. Work permeates our national consciousness: It tells us who we are and what we're worth.

In the first half of this chapter, The Meaning of Work, we examine how work affects values, attitudes, and sense of self. The two short poems that open the chapter, "Short-order Cook" and "Waitresses," address work experiences familiar to many students. The next two selections, "Mike LeFevre" and "Work in an Alienated Society," explore the dehumanization that accompanies many blue-collar jobs. Christopher Lasch provides a historical context for our attitudes toward work in "The Original Meaning of the Work Ethic." The section ends with Douglas Harper's description of "Willie," a self-employed mechanic who finds satisfaction and significance in his job.

The rest of the chapter, Occupation and Social Status, studies the relationship between work, social class, and identity. In "Gender, Status, and Feeling," Arlie Russell Hochschild addresses the "emotional labor" that many women are called upon to perform in their jobs. Next, Richard

Sennett and Jonathan Cobb discuss the "hidden injuries" — the feelings of inadequacy, contempt, and anger — that can result from upward mobility. Finally, Jane Ellen Wilson describes her struggle to balance her academic career with her working-class farming background.

Before Reading . . .

Assume for a moment that all jobs pay the same salary. What job would you choose, and why?

THE MEANING OF WORK

Short-order Cook
JIM DANIELS

This poem describing a brief episode in the day of a short-order cook questions easy assumptions about work and success. Jim Daniels (b. 1956) has worked as a Dairy Queen clerk, a liquor store cashier, a bookkeeper, a factory worker, and a college professor. He's also been a short order cook. His poetry, including Factory Poems *(1979) and* Places, Everyone *(1985), has won several national awards. He currently teaches writing at Carnegie Mellon University.*

An average joe comes in
and orders thirty cheeseburgers and thirty fries.

I wait for him to pay before I start cooking.
He pays.
He ain't no average joe.   5

The grill is just big enough for ten rows of three.
I slap the burgers down
throw two buckets of fries in the deep frier

and they pop pop spit spit . . .
psss . . .   10
The counter girls laugh.
I concentrate.
It is the crucial point —
they are ready for the cheese:
my fingers shake as I tear off slices   15
toss them on the burgers/fries done/dump/
refill buckets/burgers ready/flip into buns/
beat that melting cheese/wrap burgers in plastic/
into paper bags/fries done/dump/fill thirty bags/
bring them to the counter/wipe sweat on sleeve   20
and smile at the counter girls.
I puff my chest out and bellow:
"Thirty cheeseburgers, thirty fries!"
They look at me funny.
I grab a handful of ice, toss it in my mouth   25
do a little dance and walk back to the grill.
Pressure, responsibility, success,
thirty cheeseburgers, thirty fries.

Engaging the Text

1. Who is the "average joe" mentioned in the poem's first line?

2. What role do the waitresses play in the poem? How do their reactions add to its meaning?

3. What is Daniels's attitude toward the cook? What details reveal this attitude?

4. Debate whether cooking hamburgers is a proper subject for poetry.

5. What precisely is "poetic" about this piece of writing?

Exploring Connections

1. Compare the view of success presented here to that of Andrew Carnegie or Stephen Cruz in Chapter One, "American Dreams."

Extending the Critical Context

1. Break into groups and discuss your own experiences of work in fast-food restaurants, retail stores, or other settings. How varied are your experiences as a class? What similarities can you find between them? What was your own attitude toward the work that you did? What were the attitudes of those you worked for or with?

Waitresses

RANICE HENDERSON CROSBY

Jobs that look simple often involve unexpected complexities and demands, as this short poem attests. Ranice Henderson Crosby (b. 1952), a former waitress, considers the psychological cost of "service with a smile." Crosby quit her waitressing job shortly after writing this poem to work for The Feminist Press.

I think they give us uniforms
so we remember who we are
that's what I think.

our faces are
one gigantic grin.   5
I don't think they even notice
when we show our teeth
and raise our hackles.
we're always smiling
and nodding   10
and pleasing.

as for me
my uniform feels like skin.

Engaging the Text

1. What do you think the SPEAKER of the poem means when she says that "they give us uniforms/so we remember who we are"? Who are "they"?

2. How do you interpret the poem's concluding lines?

3. What is the speaker's attitude toward work?

Exploring Connections

1. Compare this poem to Daniels's poem (p. 517). How do the demands of their work differ? Is it harder for the speaker here to gain the feeling of accomplishment felt by the cook? Do they simply have different attitudes?

Extending the Critical Context

1. Break into groups and discuss the roles that you have been asked to play in work situations. What differences, if any, do you find between the roles that men and women are expected to perform?
2. Loosely imitating either Daniels or Crosby, write a poem drawing on your own work experience.

Mike LeFevre

STUDS TERKEL

This interview with Chicago steel worker Mike LeFevre first appeared in Working, *Studs Terkel's acclaimed collection of oral history. (More information on Studs Terkel can be found on page 77.) LeFevre represents a long tradition of industrial, or blue-collar, laborers — a "dying breed,"· as he puts it, who built America with the strength of their backs and the determination to carve a better future for their children. He also speaks for many others who have felt dehumanized by their work.*

It is a two-flat dwelling, somewhere in Cicero, on the outskirts of 1 *Chicago. He is thirty-seven. He works in a steel mill. On occasion, his wife Carol works as a waitress in a neighborhood restaurant; otherwise, she is at home, caring for their two small children, a girl and a boy.*

At the time of my first visit, a sculpted statuette of Mother and Child 2 *was on the floor, head severed from body. He laughed softly as he indicated his three-year-old daughter: "She Doctor Spock'd it."[1]*

I'm a dying breed. A laborer. Strictly muscle work . . . pick it up, 3 put it down, pick it up, put it down. We handle between forty and fifty thousand pounds of steel a day. (Laughs.) I know this is hard to believe — from four hundred pounds to three- and four-pound pieces. It's dying.

You can't take pride any more. You remember when a guy could point 4 to a house he built, how many logs he stacked. He built it and he was

---
[1]*Doctor Spock:* Dr. Benjamin Spock, prominent U.S. child-care expert (b. 1903).

proud of it. I don't really think I could be proud if a contractor built a home for me. I would be tempted to get in there and kick the carpenter in the ass (laughs), and take the saw away from him. 'Cause I would have to be part of it, you know.

It's hard to take pride in a bridge you're never gonna cross, in a door 5 you're never gonna open. You're mass-producing things and you never see the end result of it. (Muses.) I worked for a trucker one time. And I got this tiny satisfaction when I loaded a truck. At least I could see the truck depart loaded. In a steel mill, forget it. You don't see where nothing goes.

I got chewed out by my foreman once. He said, "Mike, you're a good 6 worker but you have a bad attitude." My attitude is that I don't get excited about my job. I do my work but I don't say whoopee-doo. The day I get excited about my job is the day I go to a head shrinker. How are you gonna get excited about pullin' steel? How are you gonna get excited when you're tired and want to sit down?

It's not just the work. Somebody built the pyramids. Somebody's going 7 to build something. Pyramids, Empire State Building — these things just don't happen. There's hard work behind it. I would like to see a building, say, the Empire State, I would like to see on one side of it a foot-wide strip from top to bottom with the name of every bricklayer, the name of every electrician, with all the names. So when a guy walked by, he could take his son and say, "See, that's me over there on the forty-fifth floor. I put the steel beam in." Picasso can point to a painting. What can I point to? A writer can point to a book. Everybody should have something to point to.

It's the not-recognition by other people. To say a woman is *just* a 8 housewife is degrading, right? Okay. *Just* a housewife. It's also degrading to say *just* a laborer. The difference is that a man goes out and maybe gets smashed.

When I was single, I could quit, just split. I wandered all over the 9 country. You worked just enough to get a poke, money in your pocket. Now I'm married and I got two kids . . . (trails off). I worked on a truck dock one time and I was single. The foreman came over and he grabbed my shoulder, kind of gave me a shove. I punched him and knocked him off the dock. I said, "Leave me alone. I'm doing my work, just stay away from me, just don't give me the with-the-hands business."

Hell, if you whip a damn mule he might kick you. Stay out of my 10 way, that's all. Working is bad enough, don't bug me. I would rather work my ass off for eight hours a day with nobody watching me than five minutes with a guy watching me. Who you gonna sock? You can't sock General Motors, you can't sock anybody in Washington, you can't sock a system.

A mule, an old mule, that's the way I feel. Oh yeah. See. (Shows   11
black and blue marks on arms and legs, burns.) You know what I heard from more than one guy at work? "If my kid wants to work in a factory, I am going to kick the hell out of him." I want my kid to be an effete snob. Yeah, mm-hmm. (Laughs.) I want him to be able to quote Walt Whitman,[2] to be proud of it.

If you can't improve yourself, you improve your posterity. Otherwise   12
life isn't worth nothing. You might as well go back to the cave and stay there. I'm sure the first caveman who went over the hill to see what was on the other side — I don't think he went there wholly out of curiosity. He went there because he wanted to get his son out of the cave. Just the same way I want to send my kid to college.

I work so damn hard and want to come home and sit down and lay   13
around. *But I gotta get it out.* I want to be able to turn around to somebody and say, "Hey, fuck you." You know? (Laughs.) The guy sitting next to me on the bus too. 'Cause all day I wanted to tell my foreman to go fuck himself, but I can't.

So I find a guy in a tavern. To tell him that. And he tells me too.   14
I've been in brawls. He's punching me and I'm punching him, because we actually want to punch somebody else. The most that'll happen is the bartender will bar us from the tavern. But at work, you lose your job.

This one foreman I've got, he's a kid. He's a college graduate. He   15
thinks he's better than everybody else. He was chewing me out and I was saying, "Yeah, yeah, yeah." He said, "What do you mean, yeah, yeah, yeah. Yes, *sir.*" I told him, "Who the hell are you, Hitler? What is this "*Yes, sir*" bullshit? I came here to work, I didn't come here to crawl. There's a fuckin' difference." One word led to another and I lost.

I got broke down to a lower grade and lost twenty-five cents an hour,   16
which is a hell of a lot. It amounts to about ten dollars a week. He came over — after breaking me down. The guy comes over and smiles at me. I blew up. He didn't know it, but he was about two seconds and two feet away from a hospital. I said, "Stay the fuck away from me." He was just about to say something and was pointing his finger. I just reached my hand up and just grabbed his finger and I just put it back in his pocket. He walked away. I grabbed his finger because I'm married. If I'd a been single, I'd a grabbed his head. That's the difference.

[2]*Walt Whitman:* influential U.S. poet (1819–92); best known for *Leaves of Grass* (1855).

You're doing this manual labor and you know that technology can do 17 it. (Laughs.) Let's face it, a machine can do the work of a man; otherwise they wouldn't have space probes. Why can we send a rocket ship that's unmanned and yet send a man in a steel mill to do a mule's work?

Automation? Depends how it's applied. It frightens me if it puts me 18 out on the street. It doesn't frighten me if it shortens my work week. You read that little thing: What are you going to do when this computer replaces you? Blow up computers. (Laughs.) Really. Blow up computers. I'll be goddamned if a computer is gonna eat before I do! I want milk for my kids and beer for me. Machines can either liberate man or enslave 'im, because they're pretty neutral. It's man who has the bias to put the thing one place or another.

If I had a twenty-hour workweek, I'd get to know my kids better, my 19 wife better. Some kid invited me to go on a college campus. On a Saturday. It was summertime. Hell, if I had a choice of taking my wife and kids to a picnic or going to a college campus, it's gonna be the picnic. But if I worked a twenty-hour week, I could go do both. Don't you think with that extra twenty hours people could really expand? Who's to say? There are some people in factories just by force of circumstance. I'm just like the colored people. Potential Einsteins don't have to be white. They could be in cotton fields, they could be in factories.

The twenty-hour week is a possibility today. The intellectuals, they 20 always say there are potential Lord Byrons, Walt Whitmans, Roosevelts, Picassos working in construction or steel mills or factories. But I don't think they believe it. I think what they're afraid of is the potential Hitlers and Stalins that are there too. The people in power fear the leisure man. Not just the United States. Russia's the same way.

What do you think would happen in this country if, for one year, they 21 experimented and gave everybody a twenty-hour week? How do they know that the guy who digs Wallace[3] today doesn't try to resurrect Hitler tomorrow? Or the guy who is mildly disturbed at pollution doesn't decide to go to General Motors and shit on the guy's desk? You can become a fanatic if you had the time. The whole thing is time. That is, I think, one reason rich kids tend to be fanatic about politics: They have time. Time, that's the important thing.

It isn't that the average working guy is dumb. He's tired, that's all. 22 I picked up a book on chess one time. That thing laid in the drawer for two or three weeks, you're too tired. During the weekends you want

[3]*Wallace:* George C. Wallace (b. 1919), governor of Alabama in three separate terms spanning three decades. Wallace was a key opponent of school desegregation in 1963, but recanted and won significant black support in the 1982 election.

to take your kids out. You don't want to sit there and the kid comes up: "Daddy, can I go to the park?" You got your nose in a book? Forget it.

I know a guy fifty-seven years old. Know what he tells me? "Mike, 23 I'm old and tired *all* the time." The first thing happens at work: When the arms start moving, the brain stops. I punch in about ten minutes to seven in the morning. I say hello to a couple of guys I like, I kid around with them. One guy says good morning to you and you say good morning. To another guy you say fuck you. The guy you say fuck you to is your friend.

I put on my hard hat, change into my safety shoes, put on my safety 24 glasses, go to the bonderizer. It's the thing I work on. They rake the metal, they wash it, they dip it in a paint solution, and we take it off. Put it on, take it off, put it on, take it off, put it on, take it off . . .

I say hello to everybody but my boss. At seven it starts. My arms get 25 tired about the first half-hour. After that, they don't get tired any more until maybe the last half-hour at the end of the day. I work from seven to three thirty. My arms are tired at seven thirty and they're tired at three o'clock. I hope to God I never get broke in, because I always want my arms to be tired at seven thirty and three o'clock. (Laughs.) 'Cause that's when I know that there's a beginning and there's an end. That I'm not brainwashed. In between, I don't even try to think.

If I were to put you in front of a dock and I pulled up a skid in front 26 of you with fifty hundred-pound sacks of potatoes and there are fifty more skids just like it, and this is what you're gonna do all day, what would you think about — potatoes? Unless a guy's a nut, he never thinks about work or talks about it. Maybe about baseball or about getting drunk the other night or he got laid or he didn't get laid. I'd say one out of a hundred will actually get excited about work.

Why is it that the communists always say they're for the workingman, 27 and as soon as they set up a country, you got guys singing to tractors? They're singing about how they love the factory. That's where I couldn't buy communism. It's the intellectuals' utopia, not mine. I cannot picture myself singing to a tractor, I just can't. (Laughs.) Or singing to steel. (Singsongs.) Oh whoop-dee-doo, I'm at the bonderizer, oh how I love this heavy steel. No thanks. Never hoppen.

Oh yeah, I daydream. I fantasize about a sexy blonde in Miami who's 28 got my union dues. (Laughs.) I think of the head of the union the way I think of the head of my company. Living it up. I think of February in Miami. Warm weather, a place to lay in. When I hear a college kid say, "I'm oppressed," I don't believe him. You know what I'd like to do for one year? Live like a college kid. Just for one year. I'd love to.

Wow! (Whispers.) Wow! Sports car! Marijuana! (Laughs.) Wild, sexy broads. I'd love that, hell yes, I would.

Somebody has to do this work. If my kid ever goes to college, I just want him to have a little respect, to realize that his dad is one of those somebodies. This is why even on — (muses) yeah, I guess, sure — on the black thing . . . (Sighs heavily.) I can't really hate the colored fella that's working with me all day. The black intellectual I got no respect for. The white intellectual I got no use for. I got no use for the black militant who's gonna scream three hundred years of slavery to me while I'm busting my ass. You know what I mean? (Laughs.) I have one answer for that guy: Go see Rockefeller. See Harriman.[4] Don't bother me. We're in the same cotton field. So just don't bug me. (Laughs.) 29

After work I usually stop off at a tavern. Cold beer. Cold beer right away. When I was single, I used to go into hillbilly bars, get in a lot of brawls. Just to explode. I got a thing on my arm here (indicates scar). I got slapped with a bicycle chain. Oh, wow! (Softly.) Mmm. I'm getting older. (Laughs.) I don't explode as much. You might say I'm broken in. (Quickly.) No, I'll never be broken in. (Sighs.) When you get a little older, you exchange the words. When you're younger, you exchange the blows. 30

When I get home, I argue with my wife a little bit. Turn on TV, get mad at the news. (Laughs.) I don't even watch the news that much. I watch Jackie Gleason. I look for any alternative to the ten o'clock news. I don't want to go to bed angry. Don't hit a man with anything heavy at five o'clock. He just can't be bothered. This is his time to relax. The heaviest thing he wants is what his wife has to tell him. 31

When I come home, know what I do for the first twenty minutes? Fake it. I put on a smile. I got a kid three years old. Sometimes she says, "Daddy, where've you been?" I say, "Work." I could have told her I'd been in Disneyland. What's work to a three-year-old kid? If I feel bad, I can't take it out on the kids. Kids are born innocent of everything but birth. You can't take it out on your wife either. This is why you go to a tavern. You want to release it there rather than do it at home. What does an actor do when he's got a bad movie? I got a bad movie every day. 32

I don't even need the alarm clock to get up in the morning. I can go out drinking all night, fall asleep at four, and bam! I'm up at six — no matter what I do. (Laughs.) It's a pseudo-death, more or less. Your whole system is paralyzed and you give all the appearance of death. It's 33

[4]*Harriman:* Edward Harriman, railroad tycoon (1848–1909) and father of New York governor W. Averell Harriman. Like Rockefeller, a rich, powerful man.

an ingrown clock. It's a thing you just get used to. The hours differ. It depends. Sometimes my wife wants to do something crazy like play five hundred rummy or put a puzzle together. It could be midnight, could be ten o'clock, could be nine thirty.

What do you do weekends? 34

Drink beer, read a book. See that one? *Violence in America.* It's one 35
of them studies from Washington. One of them committees they're always appointing. A thing like that I read on a weekend. But during the weekdays, gee . . . I just thought about it. I don't do that much reading from Monday through Friday. Unless it's a horny book. I'll read it at work and go home and do my homework. (Laughs.) That's what the guys at the plant call it — homework. (Laughs.) Sometimes my wife works on Saturday and I drink beer at the tavern.

I went out drinking with one guy, oh, a long time ago. A college boy. 36
He was working where I work now. Always preaching to me about how you need violence to change the system and all that garbage. We went into a hillbilly joint. Some guy there, I didn't know him from Adam, he said, "You think you're smart," I said, "What's your pleasure?" (Laughs.) He said, "My pleasure's to kick your ass." I told him I really can't be bothered. He said, "What're you, chicken?" I said, "No, I just don't want to be bothered." He came over and said something to me again. I said, "I don't beat women, drunks, or fools. Now leave me alone."

The guy called his brother over. This college boy that was with me, 37
he came nudging my arm, "Mike, let's get out of here." I said, "What are you worried about?" (Laughs.) This isn't unusual. People will bug you. You fend it off as much as you can with your mouth and when you can't, you punch the guy out.

It was close to closing time and we stayed. We could have left, but 38
when you go into a place to have a beer and a guy challenges you — if you expect to go in that place again, you don't leave. If you have to fight the guy, you fight.

I got just outside the door and one of these guys jumped on me and 39
grabbed me around the neck. I grabbed his arm and flung him against the wall. I grabbed him here (indicates throat), and jiggled his head against the wall quite a few times. He kind of slid down a little bit. This guy who said he was his brother took a swing at me with a garrison belt.[5] He just missed and hit the wall. I'm looking around for my junior Stalin (laughs), who loves violence and everything. He's gone. Split.

---

[5] *garrison belt:* the wide, heavy belt worn by soldiers, with metal clasps at each end.

(Laughs.) Next day I see him at work. I couldn't get mad at him, he's a baby.

He saw a book in my back pocket one time and he was amazed. He 40 walked up to me and he said, "You read?" I said, "What do you mean, I read?" He said, "All these dummies read the sports pages around here. What are you doing with a book?" I got pissed off at the kid right away. I said, "What do you mean, all these dummies? Don't knock a man who's paying somebody else's way through college." He was a nineteen-year-old effete snob.

Yet you want your kid to be an effete snob? 41

Yes. I want my kid to look at me and say, "Dad, you're a nice guy, 42 but you're a fuckin' dummy." Hell yes, I want my kid to tell me that he's not gonna be like me . . .

If I were hiring people to work, I'd try naturally to pay them a decent 43 wage. I'd try to find out their first names, their last names, keep the company as small as possible, so I could personalize the whole thing. All I would ask a man is a handshake, see you in the morning. No applications, nothing. I wouldn't be interested in the guy's past. Nobody ever checks the pedigree on a mule, do they? But they do on a man. Can you picture walking up to a mule and saying, "I'd like to know who his granddaddy was?"

I'd like to run a combination bookstore and tavern. (Laughs.) I would 44 like to have a place where college kids came and a steelworker could sit down and talk. Where a workingman could not be ashamed of Walt Whitman and where a college professor could not be ashamed that he painted his house over the weekend.

If a carpenter built a cabin for poets, I think the least the poets owe 45 the carpenter is just three or four one-liners on the wall. A little plaque: Though we labor with our minds, this place we can relax in was built by someone who can work with his hands. And his work is as noble as ours. I think the poet owes something to the guy who builds the cabin for him.

I don't think of Monday. You know what I'm thinking about on Sunday 46 night? Next Sunday. If you work real hard, you think of a perpetual vacation. Not perpetual sleep . . . What do I think of on a Sunday night? Lord, I wish the fuck I could do something else for a living.

I don't know who the guy is who said there is nothing sweeter than 47 an unfinished symphony. Like an unfinished painting and an unfinished poem. If he creates this thing one day — let's say, Michelangelo's Sistine Chapel. It took him a long time to do this, this beautiful work of art. But what if he had to create this Sistine Chapel a thousand times a year?

Don't you think that would even dull Michelangelo's mind? Or if da Vinci had to draw his anatomical charts thirty, forty, fifty, sixty, eighty, ninety, a hundred times a day? Don't you think that would even bore da Vinci?

Way back, you spoke of the guys who built the pyramids, not the pharaohs, 48 *the unknowns. You put yourself in their category?*

Yes. I want my signature on 'em, too. Sometimes, out of pure meanness, 49 when I make something, I put a little dent in it. I like to do something to make it really unique.

Engaging the Text

1. Why does LeFevre feel that people can't "take pride any more" in their work? Do you agree with him? Is this true for everyone?
2. From your reading of this interview, what kind of worker do you think LeFevre is? How would you characterize his attitudes toward work?
3. Why does LeFevre resent "college kids"? Is he too harsh on them?
4. In what ways does LeFevre's interview confirm or challenge common STE-REOTYPES about blue-collar workers?

Exploring Connections

1. Contrast LeFevre's attitudes toward work with those of Nora Quealey (Chapter Four, "Women"). To what extent does gender appear to shape their responses to their respective job situations?
2. What does the American Dream mean to LeFevre? What aspects of it are reflected in his thinking?
3. To what extent does LeFevre illustrate Marilyn French's assertion (Chapter Four, "Women,") that males view relationships only in terms of power exchanges? How might he respond to her analysis of power?

Extending the Critical Context

1. Working in small groups, design a list of questions to be used in interviewing people about their attitudes toward work. Using these questions as a guide, have each member of the group conduct interviews with several people from a particular occupational group (e.g., manual, skilled, white-collar, or professional workers). Write up the results of your interviews and compare notes with the rest of your group. Draft a group report summarizing your findings and drawing conclusions about how occupation affects perceptions of and attitudes toward work.

Work in an Alienated Society

ERICH FROMM

Born in 1900 in Frankfurt, Germany, Erich Fromm became a naturalized U.S. citizen in 1940. A psychiatrist primarily concerned with the condition of the human spirit, Fromm has had enormous influence on scholars and practitioners in psychology, sociology, history, economics, anthropology, and theology. In his best known work, Escape from Freedom *(1941), he analyzed the character of modern humanity and the problems we face in a highly industrialized society. In the following excerpt from* The Sane Society *(1955), Fromm suggests that industrial workers, like Mike LeFevre in the previous reading, have been "alienated" from themselves and their society by their work. Fromm died in 1980.*

What becomes the meaning of *work* in an alienated society?   1

. . . Since this problem is of utmost importance, not only for the   2
understanding of present-day society, but also for any attempt to create
a saner society, I want to deal with the nature of work separately and
more extensively in the following pages.

Unless man exploits others, he has to work in order to live. However   3
primitive and simple his method of work may be, by the very fact of
production, he has risen above the animal kingdom; rightly has he been
defined as "the animal that produces." But work is not only an inescapable
necessity for man. Work is also his liberator from nature, his creator as
a social and independent being. *In the process of work, that is, the
molding and changing of nature outside of himself, man molds and
changes himself.* He emerges from nature by mastering her; he develops
his powers of co-operation, of reason, his sense of beauty. He separates
himself from nature, from the original unity with her, but at the same
time unites himself with her again as her master and builder. The more
his work develops, the more his individuality develops. In molding
nature and re-creating her, he learns to make use of his powers, increasing
his skill and creativeness. Whether we think of the beautiful paintings
in the caves of Southern France, the ornaments on weapons among
primitive people, the statues and temples of Greece, the cathedrals of
the Middle Ages, the chairs and tables made by skilled craftsmen, or
the cultivation of flowers, trees or corn by peasants — all are expressions
of the creative transformation of nature by man's reason and skill.

In Western history, craftsmanship, especially as it developed in the 4
thirteenth and fourteenth centuries, constitutes one of the peaks in the
evolution of creative work. Work was not only a useful activity, but one
which carried with it a profound satisfaction. The main features of craftsmanship have been very lucidly expressed by C. W. Mills. "There is
no ulterior motive in work other than the product being made and the
processes of its creation. The details of daily work are meaningful because
they are not detached in the worker's mind from the product of the
work. The worker is free to control his own working action. The craftsman
is thus able to learn from his work; and to use and develop his capacities
and skills in its prosecution. There is no split of work and play, or work
and culture. The craftsman's way of livelihood determines and infuses
his entire mode of living."[1]

With the collapse of the medieval structure, and the beginning of the 5
modern mode of production, the meaning and function of work changed
fundamentally, especially in the Protestant countries. Man, being afraid
of his newly won freedom, was obsessed by the need to subdue his
doubts and fears by developing a feverish activity. The outcome of this
activity, success or failure, decided his salvation, indicating whether he
was among the saved or the lost souls. *Work, instead of being an activity
satisfying in itself and pleasurable, became a duty and an obsession.*
The more it was possible to gain riches by work, the more it became a
pure means to the aim of wealth and success. Work became, in Max
Weber's[2] terms, the chief factor in a system of "inner-worldly asceticism,"
an answer to man's sense of aloneness and isolation.

However, work in this sense existed only for the upper and middle 6
classes, those who could amass some capital and employ the work of
others. For the vast majority of those who had only their physical energy
to sell, work became nothing but forced labor. The worker in the eighteenth
or nineteenth century who had to work sixteen hours if he did not want
to starve was not doing it because he served the Lord in this way, nor
because his success would show that he was among the "chosen" ones,
but because he was forced to sell his energy to those who had the means
of exploiting it. The first centuries of the modern era find the meaning
of work divided into that of *duty* among the middle class, and that of
forced labor among those without property.

The religious attitude toward work as a duty, which was still so prevalent 7
in the nineteenth century, has been changing considerably in the last

[1]C. W. Mills, *White Collar*, Oxford University Press, New York, 1951, p. 220. [Author's
note]
[2]*Max Weber:* German sociologist and political theorist (1864–1920).

decades. Modern man does not know what to do with himself, how to spend his lifetime meaningfully, and he is driven to work in order to avoid an unbearable boredom. But work has ceased to be a moral and religious obligation in the sense of the middle-class attitude of the eighteenth and nineteenth centuries. Something new has emerged. Ever-increasing production, the drive to make bigger and better things, have become aims in themselves, new ideals. Work has become alienated from the working person.

What happens to the industrial worker? He spends his best energy 8 for seven or eight hours a day in producing "something." He needs his work in order to make a living, but his role is essentially a passive one. He fulfills a small isolated function in a complicated and highly organized process of production, and is never confronted with "his" product as a whole, at least not as a producer, but only as a consumer, provided he has the money to buy "his" product in a store. He is concerned neither with the whole product in its physical aspects nor with its wider economic and social aspects. He is put in a certain place, has to carry out a certain task, but does not participate in the organization or management of the work. He is not interested, nor does he know why one produces this, instead of another commodity — what relation it has to the needs of society as a whole. The shoes, the cars, the electric bulbs, are produced by "the enterprise," using the machines. He is a part of the machine, rather than its master as an active agent. The machine, instead of being in his service to do work for him which once had to be performed by sheer physical energy, has become his master. Instead of the machine being the substitute for human energy, man has become a substitute for the machine. *His work can be defined as the performance of acts which cannot yet be performed by machines.*

Work is a means of getting money, not in itself a meaningful human 9 activity. P. Drucker, observing workers in the automobile industry, expresses this idea very succinctly: "For the great majority of automobile workers, the only meaning of the job is in the pay check, not in anything connected with the work or the product. Work appears as something unnatural, a disagreeable, meaningless, and stultifying condition of getting the pay check, devoid of dignity as well as of importance. No wonder that this puts a premium on slovenly work, on slowdowns, and on other tricks to get the same pay check with less work. No wonder that this results in an unhappy and discontented worker — because a pay check is not enough to base one's self-respect on."[3]

[3]cf. Peter F. Drucker, *Concept of the Corporation*, The John Day Company, New York, 1946, p. 179. [Author's note]

This relationship of the worker to his work is an outcome of the whole   10
social organization of which he is a part. Being "employed,"[4] he is not
an active agent, has no responsibility except the proper performance of
the isolated piece of work he is doing, and has little interest except the
one of bringing home enough money to support himself and his family.
Nothing more is expected of him, or wanted from him. He is part of
the equipment hired by capital, and his role and function are determined
by this quality of being a piece of equipment. In recent decades, increasing
attention has been paid to the psychology of the worker, and to his
attitude toward his work, to the "human problem of industry"; but this
very formulation is indicative of the underlying attitude; there is a human
being spending most of his lifetime at work, and what should be discussed
is the *industrial problem of human beings*," rather than "*the human
problem of industry*."

Most investigations in the field of industrial psychology are concerned   11
with the question of how the productivity of the individual worker can
be increased, and how he can be made to work with less friction; psychology
has lent its services to "human engineering," an attempt to treat the
worker and employee like a machine which runs better when it is well
oiled. While Taylor was primarily concerned with a better organization
of the technical use of the worker's physical powers, most industrial
psychologists are mainly concerned with the manipulation of the worker's
psyche. The underlying idea can be formulated like this: If he works
better when he is happy, then let us make him happy, secure, satisfied,
or anything else, provided it raises his output and diminishes friction.
In the name of "human relations," the worker is treated with all devices
which suit a completely alienated person; even happiness and human
values are recommended in the interest of better relations with the
public. Thus, for instance, according to *Time* magazine, one of the best-
known American psychiatrists said to a group of fifteen hundred Supermarket executives: "It's going to be an increased satisfaction to our
customers if we are happy. . . . It is going to pay off in cold dollars and
cents to management, if we could put some of these general principles
of values, human relationships, really into practice." One speaks of "human
relations" and one means the most in-human relations, those between
alienated automatons; one speaks of happiness and means the perfect
routinization which has driven out the last doubt and all spontaneity.

The alienated and profoundly unsatisfactory character of work results   12

---

[4]The English "employed" and the German *angestellt* are terms which refer to things
rather than to human beings. [Author's note]

in two reactions: one, the ideal of complete *laziness;* the other a deep-seated, though often unconscious *hostility* toward work and everything and everybody connected with it.

It is not difficult to recognize the widespread longing for the state of complete laziness and passivity. Our advertising appeals to it even more than to sex. There are, of course, many useful and labor saving gadgets. But this usefulness often serves only as a rationalization for the appeal to complete passivity and receptivity. A package of breakfast cereal is being advertised as *"new — easier to eat."* An electric toaster is advertised with these words: ". . . the most distinctly different toaster in the world! Everything is done *for* you with this new toaster. You need not even bother to lower the bread. Power-action, through a unique electric motor, *gently takes the bread right out of your fingers!"* How many courses in languages, or other subjects are announced with the slogan "effortless learning, no more of the old drudgery." Everybody knows the picture of the elderly couple in the advertisement of a life-insurance company, who have retired at the age of sixty, and spend their life in the complete bliss of having nothing to do except just travel.   13

Radio and television exhibit another element of this yearning for laziness: the idea of "push-button power"; by pushing a button, or turning a knob on my machine, I have the power to produce music, speeches, ball games, and on the television set, to command events of the world to appear before my eyes. The pleasure of driving cars certainly rests partly upon this same satisfaction of the wish for push-button power. By the effortless pushing of a button, a powerful machine is set in motion; little skill or effort is needed to make the driver feel that he is the ruler of space.   14

But there is far more serious and deep-seated reaction to the meaninglessness and boredom of work. It is a hostility toward work which is much less conscious than our craving for laziness and inactivity. Many a businessman feels himself the prisoner of his business and the commodities he sells; he has a feeling of fraudulency about his product and a secret contempt for it. He hates his customers, who force him to put up a show in order to sell. He hates his competitors because they are a threat; his employees as well as his superiors, because he is in a constant competitive fight with them. Most important of all, he hates himself, because he sees his life passing by, without making any sense beyond the momentary intoxication of success. Of course, this hate and contempt for others and for oneself, and for the very things one produces, is mainly unconscious, and only occasionally comes up to awareness in a fleeting thought, which is sufficiently disturbing to be set aside as quickly as possible.   15

Engaging the Text

1. What is the meaning of work for Fromm? What special qualities does he attribute to what he calls "craftsmanship"?
2. What does Fromm mean by "asceticism"?
3. How, according to Fromm, does class position affect one's attitudes toward work?
4. Why does Fromm question attempts to humanize the workplace?

Exploring Connections

1. Analyze Mike LeFevre (p. 520) as an example of Fromm's notion of the alienated industrial worker.
2. How does Fromm's alienated worker compare to the typical high school student as portrayed in Theodore Sizer's "What High School Is" (Chapter Six, "Grading American Education")? How would either Sizer or Fromm explain this connection?
3. The definition of work that Fromm offers in this selection might be seen as being particularly male-centered. Based on your reading of Carol Gilligan (p. 281) and Marilyn French (p. 290), offer a counterdefinition of the meaning of work, this time from the PERSPECTIVE of what they regard as women's values.

Extending the Critical Context

1. In small groups, discuss whether or not Fromm's notion of alienated labor fits your own work experience.
2. Toward the end of this selection, Fromm suggests that Americans are being seduced by what he calls "the ideal of laziness" and that we display a greater hostility toward work than ever before. Examine representations of work in contemporary culture (TV shows, movies, etc.) to find evidence of this change in attitude. Does your research support Fromm's THESIS?

The Original Meaning of the Work Ethic
CHRISTOPHER LASCH

In the past twenty years, Christopher Lasch has built a reputation as an outspoken critic of contemporary American culture. In books like Haven in a Heartless World: The Family Besieged *(1977) and* The Culture of Narcissism *(1979), Lasch has dissected the national psyche, offering provocative interpretations of our desires, values, and obsessions. In the following passage from* The Culture of Narcissism, *Lasch examines the evolution of America's "work ethic" — the belief in the inherent value of hard work — from its origin among the colonial Puritans to its most recent manifestation in the entrepreneur. Lasch (b. 1932) is chair of the History Department at the University of Rochester in New York. His most recent book on contemporary American culture is* The Minimal Self *(1984).*

Until recently, the Protestant work ethic stood as one of the most 1 important underpinnings of American culture. According to the myth of capitalist enterprise, thrift and industry held the key to material success and spiritual fulfillment. America's reputation as a land of opportunity rested on its claim that the destruction of hereditary obstacles to advancement had created conditions in which social mobility depended on individual initiative alone. The self-made man, archetypical embodiment of the American dream, owed his advancement to habits of industry, sobriety, moderation, self-discipline, and avoidance of debt. He lived for the future, shunning self-indulgence in favor of patient, painstaking accumulation; and as long as the collective prospect looked on the whole so bright, he found in the deferral of gratification not only his principal gratification but an abundant source of profits. In an expanding economy, the value of investments could be expected to multiply with time, as the spokesmen for self-help, for all their celebration of work as its own reward, seldom neglected to point out.

In an age of diminishing expectations, the Protestant virtues no longer 2 excite enthusiasm. Inflation erodes investments and savings. Advertising undermines the horror of indebtedness, exhorting the consumer to buy now and pay later. As the future becomes menacing and uncertain, only fools put off until tomorrow the fun they can have today. A profound shift in our sense of time has transformed work habits, values, and the definition of success. Self-preservation has replaced self-improvement as the goal of earthly existence. In a lawless, violent, and unpredictable society, in which the normal conditions of everyday life come to resemble those formerly confined to the underworld, men live by their wits. They hope not so much to prosper as simply to survive, although survival itself increasingly demands a large income. In earlier times, the self-made man took pride in his judgment of character and probity; today he anxiously scans the faces of his fellows not so as to evaluate their credit but in order to gauge their susceptibility to his own blandishments. He practices the classic arts of seduction and with the same indifference to moral niceties, hoping to win your heart while picking your pocket. The happy hooker stands in place of Horatio Alger[1] as the prototype of personal success. If Robinson Crusoe embodied the ideal type of economic man, the hero of bourgeois society in its ascendancy, the spirit of Moll Flanders[2] presides over its dotage.

The new ethic of self-preservation has been a long time taking shape; 3 it did not emerge overnight. In the first three centuries of our history, the work ethic constantly changed its meaning; these vicissitudes, often imperceptible at the time, foreshadowed its eventual transformation into an ethic of personal survival. For the Puritans, a godly man worked diligently at his calling not so much in order to accumulate personal wealth as to add to the comfort and convenience of the community. Every Christian had a "general calling" to serve God and a "personal calling," in the words of Cotton Mather,[3] "by which his Usefulness, in his Neighborhood, is distinguished." This personal calling arose from the circumstance that "God hath made man a Sociable Creature." The Puritans recognized that a man might get rich at his calling, but they saw personal aggrandizement as incidental to social labor — the collective transformation of nature and the progress of useful arts and useful knowledge. They instructed men who prospered not to lord it over their neighbors. The true Christian, according to Calvinist conceptions of an honorable and godly existence, bore both good fortune and bad with equanimity, contenting himself with what came to his lot. "This he had learned to doe," said John Cotton, "if God prosper him, he had learned not to be puffed up, and if he should be exposed to want, he could do it without murmuring. It is the same act of unbeleefe, that makes a man murmure in crosses, which puffes him up in prosperity."

Whatever the moral reservations with which Calvinism surrounded 4 the pursuit of wealth, many of its practitioners, especially in New England, waxed fat and prosperous on the trade in rum and slaves. As the Puritan gave way to the Yankee, a secularized version of the Protestant ethic emerged. Whereas Cotton Mather advised against going into debt on the grounds that it injured the creditor ("Let it be uneasy unto you, at

---

[1]*Horatio Alger:* U.S. author (1834–1899) of books for boys, now synonymous with the rags-to-riches dream.

[2]*Robinson Crusoe . . . Moll Flanders:* hero and heroine of novels by Daniel Defoe (1659?–1731). Whereas the shipwrecked Robinson Crusoe was industrious and self-sufficient, Moll Flanders was a pickpocket.

[3]*Cotton Mather:* U.S. clergyman and author (1663–1728). John Cotton, quoted later in this paragraph, was his grandfather.

any time to think, *I have so much of another mans Estate in my Hands, and I to his damage detain it from him"*), Benjamin Franklin argued that indebtedness injured the debtor himself, putting him into his creditors' hands. Puritan sermons on the calling quoted copiously from the Bible; Franklin codified popular common sense in the sayings of Poor Richard.[4] *God helps them that help themselves. Lost time is never found again. Never leave that till to-morrow which you can do today. If you would know the value of money, go and try to borrow some; for he that goes a borrowing goes a sorrowing.*

The Puritans urged the importance of socially useful work; the Yankee 5 stressed self-improvement. Yet he understood self-improvement to consist of more than money-making. This important concept also implied self-discipline, the training and cultivation of God-given talents, above all the cultivation of reason. The eighteenth-century ideal of prosperity included not only material comfort but good health, good temper, wisdom, usefulness, and the satisfaction of knowing that you had earned the good opinion of others. In the section of his *Autobiography* devoted to "The Art of Virtue," Franklin summed up the results of a lifelong program of moral self-improvement:

> To Temperance he ascribes his long-continu'd Health, and what is still left to him of a good Constitution. To Industry and Frugality, the early Easiness of his Circumstances, and Acquisition of his Fortune, with all that Knowledge which enabled him to be an useful Citizen, and obtain'd for him some Degree of Reputation among the Learned. To Sincerity and Justice the Confidence of his Country, and the honourable Employs it conferr'd upon him. And to the joint influence of the whole Mass of the Virtues, evenness of Temper, and that Cheerfulness in Conversation which makes his Company still sought for, and agreeable even to his younger Acquaintance.

Virtue pays, in the eighteenth-century version of the work ethic; but 6 what it pays cannot be measured simply in money. The real reward of virtue is to have little to apologize for or to repent of at the end of your life. Wealth is to be valued, but chiefly because it serves as one of the necessary preconditions of moral and intellectual cultivation.

---

[4] *Poor Richard:* a fictitious character, unschooled but wise, in Benjamin Franklin's annual *Poor Richard's Almanack*, 1732–1757. He is the speaker of many famous aphorisms on the value of thrift and hard work.

From "Self-Culture" to Self-Promotion
through "Winning Images"

In the nineteenth century, the ideal of self-improvement degenerated 7
into a cult of compulsive industry. P. T. Barnum,[5] who made a fortune
in a calling the very nature of which the Puritans would have condemned
("Every calling, whereby God will be Dishonored; every Calling whereby
none but the Lusts of men are Nourished: . . . every such Calling is to
be Rejected"), delivered many times a lecture frankly entitled "The Art
of Money-Getting," which epitomized the nineteenth-century conception
of worldly success. Barnum quoted freely from Franklin but without
Franklin's concern for the attainment of wisdom or the promotion of
useful knowledge. "Information" interested Barnum merely as a means
of mastering the market. Thus he condemned the "false economy" of
the farm wife who douses her candle at dusk rather than lighting another
for reading, not realizing that the "information" gained through reading
is worth far more than the price of the candles. "Always take a trustworthy
newspaper," Barnum advised young men on the make, "and thus keep
thoroughly posted in regard to the transactions of the world. He who
is without a newspaper is cut off from his species."

Barnum valued the good opinion of others not as a sign of one's 8
usefulness but as a means of getting credit. "Uncompromising integrity
of character is invaluable." The nineteenth century attempted to express
all values in monetary terms. Everything had its price. Charity was
a moral duty because "the liberal man will command patronage, while
the sordid, uncharitable miser will be avoided." The sin of pride was
not that it offended God but that it led to extravagant expenditures. "A
spirit of pride and vanity, when permitted to have full sway, is the
undying cankerworm which gnaws the very vitals of a man's worldly possessions."

The eighteenth century made a virtue of temperance but did not 9
condemn moderate indulgence in the service of sociability. "Rational
conversation," on the contrary, appeared to Franklin and his contemporaries
to represent an important value in its own right. The nineteenth century
condemned sociability itself, on the grounds that it might interfere with
business. "How many good opportunities have passed, never to return,
while a man was sipping a 'social glass' with his friend!" Preachments
on self-help now breathed the spirit of compulsive enterprise. Henry

---

[5]*P. T. Barnum:* U.S. showman and circus owner (1810–1891), reputed to have said,
"There's a sucker born every minute."

Ward Beecher[6] defined "the *beau ideal*[7] of happiness" as a state of mind in which "a man [is] so busy that he does not know whether he is or is not happy." Russell Sage[8] remarked that "work has been the chief, and, you might say, the only source of pleasure in my life."

Even at the height of the Gilded Age,[9] however, the Protestant ethic   10
did not completely lose its original meaning. In the success manuals, the McGuffey readers, the Peter Parley Books, and the hortatory writings of the great capitalists themselves, the Protestant virtues — industry, thrift, temperance — still appeared not merely as stepping-stones to success but as their own reward.

The spirit of self-improvement lived on, in debased form, in the cult   11
of "self-culture" — proper care and training of mind and body, nurture of the mind through "great books," development of "character." The social contribution of individual accumulation still survived as an undercurrent in the celebration of success, and the social conditions of early industrial capitalism, in which the pursuit of wealth undeniably increased the supply of useful objects, gave some substance to the claim that "accumulated capital means progress." In condemning speculation and extravagance, in upholding the importance of patient industry, in urging young men to start at the bottom and submit to "the discipline of daily life," even the most unabashed exponents of self-enrichment clung to the notion that wealth derives its value from its contribution to the general good and to the happiness of future generations.

The nineteenth-century cult of success placed surprisingly little emphasis   12
on competition. It measured achievement not against the achievements of others but against an abstract ideal of discipline and self-denial. At the turn of the century, however, preachments on success began to stress the will to win. The bureaucratization of the corporate career changed the conditions of self-advancement; ambitious young men now had to compete with their peers for the attention and approval of their superiors. The struggle to surpass the previous generation and to provide for the next gave way to a form of sibling rivalry, in which men of approximately equal abilities jostled against each other in competition for a limited number of places. Advancement now depended on "will-

[6] *Henry Ward Beecher:* U.S. preacher and writer (1813–1887), brother of Harriet Beecher Stowe.

[7] *beau ideal:* the perfect type or highest embodiment of something (based on a mistranslation of this French phrase for "ideal beauty").

[8] *Russell Sage:* U.S. financier and politician (1816–1906).

[9] *Gilded Age:* the late 1870s in the United States, named after Mark Twain and Charles D. Warner's *The Gilded Age,* a satirical novel unveiling government corruption and rampant materialism.

power, self-confidence, energy, and initiative" — the qualities celebrated in such exemplary writings as George Lorimer's[10] *Letters from a Self-Made Merchant to His Son.* "By the end of the nineteenth century," writes John Cawelti in his study of the success myth, "self-help books were dominated by the ethos of salesmanship and boosterism. Personal magnetism, a quality which supposedly enabled a man to influence and dominate others, became one of the major keys to success." In 1907, both Lorimer's *Saturday Evening Post* and Orison Swett Marden's *Success* magazine inaugurated departments of instruction in the "art of conversation," fashion, and "culture." The management of interpersonal relations came to be seen as the essence of self-advancement. The captain of industry gave way to the confidence man, the master of impressions. Young men were told that they had to sell themselves in order to succeed.

At first, self-testing through competition remained almost indistinguishable from moral self-discipline and self-culture, but the difference became unmistakable when Dale Carnegie[11] and then Norman Vincent Peale[12] restated and transformed the tradition of Mather, Franklin, Barnum, and Lorimer. As a formula for success, winning friends and influencing people had little in common with industry and thrift. The prophets of positive thinking disparaged "the old adage that hard work alone is the magic key that will unlock the door to our desires." They praised the love of money, officially condemned even by the crudest of Gilded Age materialists, as a useful incentive. "You can never have riches in great quantities," wrote Napoleon Hill in his *Think and Grow Rich,* "unless you can work yourself into a white heat of *desire* for money." The pursuit of wealth lost the few shreds of moral meaning that still clung to it. Formerly the Protestant virtues appeared to have an independent value of their own. Even when they became purely instrumental, in the second half of the nineteenth century, success itself retained moral and social overtones, by virtue of its contribution to the sum of human comfort and progress. Now success appeared as an end in its own right, the victory over your competitors that alone retained the capacity to instill a sense of self-approval. The latest success manuals differ from earlier ones — even surpassing the cynicism of Dale Carnegie and Peale — in

13

---

[10]*George Lorimer:* editor of *The Saturday Evening Post* from 1899 to 1937, during which time he published works by key American writers.

[11]*Dale Carnegie:* U.S. lecturer (1888–1955) and author of *How to Win Friends and Influence People* (1936) and other books on presenting a successful personality.

[12]*Norman Vincent Peale:* U.S. pastor, religious writer, and radio and television preacher (b. 1898). Peale's *The Power of Positive Thinking* (1952) set a record by being a best-seller for three years.

their frank acceptance of the need to exploit and intimidate others, in their lack of interest in the substance of success, and in the candor with which they insist that appearances — "winning images" — count for more than performance, ascription for more than achievement. One author seems to imply that the self consists of little more than its "image" reflected in others' eyes. "Although I'm not being original when I say it, I'm sure you'll agree that the way you see yourself will reflect the image you portray to others." Nothing succeeds like the appearance of success.

The Eclipse of Achievement

In a society in which the dream of success has been drained of any meaning beyond itself, men have nothing against which to measure their achievements except the achievements of others. Self-approval depends on public recognition and acclaim, and the quality of this approval has undergone important changes in its own right. The good opinion of friends and neighbors, which formerly informed a man that he had lived a useful life, rested on appreciation of his accomplishments. Today men seek the kind of approval that applauds not their actions but their personal attributes. They wish to be not so much esteemed as admired. They crave not fame but the glamour and excitement of celebrity. They want to be envied rather than respected. Pride and acquisitiveness, the sins of an ascendant capitalism, have given way to vanity. Most Americans would still define success as riches, fame, and power, but their actions show that they have little interest in the substance of these attainments. What a man does matters less than the fact that he has "made it." Whereas fame depends on the performance of notable deeds acclaimed in biography and works of history, celebrity — the reward of those who project a vivid or pleasing exterior or have otherwise attracted attention to themselves — is acclaimed in the news media, in gossip columns, on talk shows, in magazines devoted to "personalities." Accordingly it is evanescent, like news itself, which loses its interest when it loses its novelty. Worldly success has always carried with it a certain poignancy, an awareness that "you can't take it with you"; but in our time, when success is so largely a function of youth, glamour, and novelty, glory is more fleeting than ever, and those who win the attention of the public worry incessantly about losing it. 14

Success in our society has to be ratified by publicity. The tycoon who lives in personal obscurity, the empire builder who controls the destinies of nations from behind the scenes, are vanishing types. Even nonelective officials, ostensibly preoccupied with questions of high policy, have to keep themselves constantly on view; all politics becomes a form of spectacle. 15

It is well known that Madison Avenue packages politicians and markets them as if they were cereals or deodorants; but the art of public relations penetrates even more deeply into political life, transforming policy making itself. The modern prince does not much care that "there's a job to be done" — the slogan of American capitalism at an earlier and more enterprising stage of its development; what interests him is that "relevant audiences," in the language of the Pentagon Papers,[13] have to be cajoled, won over, seduced. He confuses successful completion of the task at hand with the impression he makes or hopes to make on others. Thus American officials blundered into the war in Vietnam because they could not distinguish the country's military and strategic interests from "our reputation as a guarantor," as one of them put it. More concerned with the trappings than with the reality of power, they convinced themselves that failure to intervene would damage American "credibility." They borrowed the rhetoric of games theory to dignify their obsession with appearances, arguing that American policy in Vietnam had to address itself to "the relevant 'audiences' of U.S. actions" — the communists, the South Vietnamese, "our allies (who must trust us as 'underwriters')," and the American public.

When policy making, the search for power, and the pursuit of wealth 16 have no other objects than to excite admiration or envy, men lose the sense of objectivity, always precarious under the best of circumstances. Impressions overshadow achievements. Public men fret about their ability to rise to crisis, to project an image of decisiveness, to give a convincing performance of executive power. Their critics resort to the same standards: when doubts began to be raised about the leadership of the Johnson administration, they focused on the "credibility gap." Public relations and propaganda have exalted the image and the pseudo-event. People "talk constantly," Daniel Boorstin has written, "not of things themselves, but of their images."

In the corporate structure as in government, the rhetoric of achievement, 17 of single-minded devotion to the task at hand — the rhetoric of performance, efficiency, and productivity — no longer provides an accurate description of the struggle for personal survival. "Hard work," according to Eugene Emerson Jennings, ". . . constitutes a necessary but not sufficient cause of upward mobility. It is not a route to the top." A newspaper man with experience both in journalism and in the Southern Regional Council has

[13]*Pentagon Papers:* the popular name given to a secret 1967–1969 Department of Defense study that criticized United States involvement in Southeast Asia and suggested that the government had misrepresented its role in the Vietnam War.

reported that "in neither, I realized, did it matter to the people in charge how well or how badly I performed. . . . Not the goals, but keeping the organization going, became the important thing." Even the welfare of the organization, however, no longer excites the enthusiasm it generated in the fifties. The "self-sacrificing company man," writes Jennings, has become "an obvious anachronism."[14] The upwardly mobile corporate executive "does not view himself as an organization man." His "anti-organizational posture," in fact, has emerged as his "chief characteristic." He advances through the corporate ranks not by serving the organization but by convincing his associates that he possesses the attributes of a "winner."

[14]In the 1950s, the organization man thought of an attractive, socially gifted wife as an important asset to his career. Today executives are warned of the "apparent serious conflict between marriage and a management career." A recent report compares the "elite corps of professional managers" to the Janissaries, elite soldiers of the Ottoman empire who were taken from their parents as children, raised by the state, and never allowed to marry. "A young man considering [a managerial] career might well think of himself as a modern-day Janissary — and consider very, very carefully whether marriage in any way conforms to his chosen life." [Author's note]

Engaging the Text

1. Discuss Lasch's assertion that today we work simply to survive and not to "prosper" in the original sense of the word.

2. Explain the Puritan concept of a "calling." How does it differ from the contemporary view of a job or career?

3. What differences in values does Lasch see between the Puritan, the Yankee, and the nineteenth-century captain of industry?

4. According to Lasch, what type of person is the modern American entrepreneur? What is the difference between being "esteemed" and "admired"?

Exploring Connections

1. How would Lasch analyze Andrew Carnegie's attitudes toward work and success in Chapter One, "American Dreams"?

2. In your view, does the IMAGE of the "new organization man" still reflect the values that Robert Bellah et al. associate with American individualism (Chapter One, "American Dreams")?

Extending the Critical Context

1. As a class, reach a consensus on five living Americans you deem successful. What qualities do they share? Do they illustrate Lasch's view of what it means to be a success in modern America?

2. To what extent do you think that the appearance of success dominates American culture today? What evidence do you find in contemporary culture that appearances are valued more highly than other, more traditional measures of success or fulfillment?

Willie

DOUGLAS HARPER

In the fall of 1975, Douglas Harper began teaching sociology at State University College of New York at Potsdam, a small town near the U.S.-Canadian border. When the old Saab he was driving at the time broke down, he met Willie, the backwoods mechanic whose life and attitudes Harper recorded in Working Knowledge, *source of the following selection. In this passage, Harper explains how work contributes to Willie's identity and to his position in his immediate community of friends, family, and neighbors. Douglas Harper (b. 1948) has also written* Good Company *(1982), a first-hand view of the life, thinking, and values of the tramps who ride America's railroads.*

A person is many things — mate, parent, worker, entertainer, community 1 member. Self-consciousness, and sometimes self-deception, integrates the often contradictory demands of different roles. In traditional or preindustrial societies there are relatively few of these personal role contradictions. Willie's community, though tied to industrial society, is in this way a great deal like the traditional world. Work is the well from which the other components of self are drawn. The single source makes the different roles minor variations rather than entirely different personae. In the following I study Willie's sense of himself both in the immediate sphere of his work and in the context of his community.

Willie finds himself in his work. To study Willie's attitude toward 2 work, then, is to study his attitudes toward his own being. This is best done in the family and community contexts in which the work exists.

Willie's children have grown up knowing their father, in large part, 3 by helping him work. As I have watched Willie showing one of his children how to do a job, a sequence from *Nanook of the North*, a 1922 documentary of Eskimo life, has often come to mind. As Nanook teaches his young son to shoot his miniature bow and arrow at a tiny snow polar bear — patient, ever attentive, warming his son's hands with his own — the viewer is shown that the Eskimo experiences the world directly and that the skills needed to manage it are known by the father and taught to the children. Willie's children recognize his skill and understand its value because they see and participate in the work of the shop and overhear the conversations and stories that are always going on. Willie's skill is also relevant to their personal worlds — it is not only their bikes, their motor scooters, and eventually their automobiles and houses that Willie helps them assemble or maintain. One day I was a bit startled to find Willie bent over white lace fabric spread on the floor of his house, making a dress (without a pattern) for the confirmation ceremony of one of his daughters. The idea that his children know their father through his work seems simple. But it is unusual in a society where most fathers work away from home, doing things their children do not really know about and that are in any case probably irrelevant to the children's own needs or problems. Willie's authority as a parent, then, is related to his children's recognition of his skills and the frequent relevance of those skills to their own lives.[1]

His relationship with his wife is also strongly rooted in his work. In 4 a number of ways the shop represents the collective work of a family. Pauline often helps with jobs, shares the paperwork or the hassles that go with collecting on bad checks, and feeds people who are in her house because of their business with Willie. Although the work is collective, the division of labor is based on traditional male and female roles. Willie often makes it clear that though many people participate in the work of the shop, he is — at the center — the provider.

Finally, Willie's self-image exists in the context of the community. 5 His status, born in his work world, extends into such varied roles as

---

[1] The idea that parental authority is traditionally rooted in family work systems, and that it has been largely displaced by industrial capitalism — that is, the creation of wage labor and the subsequent removal of the father from productive activity in the house — is a central theme in modern sociology. In *Middletown* (1924), Robert and Helen Lynd described the effect of these industrial processes one generation after they had taken place. [Author's note]

candidate for the office of highway supervisor, president of his bowling league, organizer of citizens band radio activities, and leader in public hearings over zoning legislation.

Willie's self-image comes, then, from the various human contexts he lives in. It also comes from the self-consciousness that arises from his working experience. This self-recognition has several elements. Overall, Willie's accounts reflect an understanding of the effect good work has upon a person. He typically discounts, with no false modesty, the specialness of his talents, yet he also identifies his work as unique and important to the community. Finally, he recognizes and uses the social power that comes from having knowledge and skill needed by others. 6

Willie discounts his skill by suggesting that the key to his method is patience and the willingness to do jobs others will not take on. Many mechanics do not accept the jobs Willie does because they are too ill defined, too time consuming, and even, one can say, too difficult. [A] blower repair . . . for example, came to Willie because "nobody else would fix it." Willie discounted the particular difficulties of the job with the statement that all the job required was patience. This is a common theme Willie sometimes plays with. Recently, for example, a new customer brought him a water-pump casing with three bolts broken off even with the surface. Willie began with a frown: "*Oh-oh — cast* and steel — *that's* trouble!" The man told Willie he'd been to a machine shop in town, but they couldn't fix his pump. I envisioned a long process of drilling out the studs, extracting the pieces, and rethreading the holes. Willie clamped the casing in his vise, brought out a small punch he had sharpened on one side, and picked up a tiny ball peen hammer. He carefully turned the broken pieces out of the casing by hammering ever so delicately with the beveled punch on the uneven surface of the broken studs. But when the customer hailed his accomplishment, Willie replied that the other machinist could easily have done the job; he just didn't want to be bothered with such stuff. It may or may not have been true, but in any case it was a characteristic disclaimer. 7

Willie does, however, understand that his patience is unusual and important to his own working method. "Oh, yes," Willie once replied, "you get stumped. But you've got to be a little calm, a little patient, and figure out *why*." 8

To succeed at repairs other mechanics either haven't wanted to attempt or could not manage certainly fosters a positive self-image. Part of Willie's satisfaction comes from his capacity to focus on each step of a task as equally important. And part of the satisfaction, one can assume, comes from the simple problem solving in his daily work. Willie put it this way: 9

A lot of them that come in here are pretty impatient. If you rush through things, you can't enjoy them. And it's a challenge — no job's the same. If you had a thousand jobs in a year, not two of those thousand jobs would be the same. Even the ones that are supposed to be the same aren't. Things are broken or worn in different ways — they each have their own characteristics.

Although Willie often discounts his skill, he also recognizes its quality. 10
He tells some stories over and over, such as how he established his reputation with the owner of the local Saab dealership by fixing the first Saab transmission he'd ever seen in three hours less than shop time[2] for the job. But usually when Willie tells these stories it is because he cannot believe others could not easily do as well. At times a story tells how he put an unusual material to use, such as when he made a head gasket for a tractor from a sheet of copper ("that was twenty years ago, and that tractor is still running — it's owned by the town of Louisville"), or relates his ability to save his customers money by solving their problems more simply than other mechanics thought possible.

Willie also sees himself as something of a visionary. He patiently 11
explains his designs and their logic to customers and friends. It might be an electrical system, a solar heating design, or a novel approach to a mundane repair. If the listener cannot fully grasp what he is talking about, Willie approaches his subject from several directions until the listener is at least convinced that *Willie* knows what he is talking about. I once asked Willie when he had begun the designing and engineering that is now such an important part of his work. He told me about making a violin out of a cigar box as a school project for the county fair, winning twelve dollars and a blue ribbon. Then he pointed to a small wooden airplane that hung up by the ceiling, nearly hidden between the beams.

> That airplane was made back before many people thought airplanes should look that way. Everyone laughed at me when I was making it. A few years after that was made, airplanes started to look like that. They were all double wingers before that. I made that in 1936. . . . That took first prize in the fair, too. I whittled it out with a knife — every bit of it. I was just a boy. I used shoe nails — cobbler nails they call it — to put it together with. My father used to do all our shoe work.

We take the airplane down to examine it more closely. I comment 12
that the joints are still tight.

> Lost the wheels off it — the landing gear — that got broke off. . . .

[2] *shop time:* the average time expected to be required for a given repair.

My idea for that was out of Buck Rogers.[3] I called it a Buck Rogers plane at the time. Your five-passenger planes came out looking like that. . . . I figured that was the safest place to hang it — up there out of sight! You start looking at that and you start reminiscing, though, about school days. I was about eleven years old when I carved that out — ten or eleven, something like that. And I was fifteen or sixteen when we made our first glider. Our gliders were built on the same principle as this. But we rode in those.

The engineering, embedded as it is in the daily work of the shop,   13
cannot be separated from the continuing work of repair. Willie summed up his attitude toward his whole range of mechanical skills:

It's like when I was taking aviation mechanics. The guy who taught us says, "Some of you boys will go out of here mechanics, and some of you will go out of here as parts exchangers — you'll never be a mechanic." It's a type of knowledge that you can pick up and store in your mind. Quite a difference between the two. And we've got more parts exchangers around here than we've got mechanics. Fewer people find out the reason something has broken and solve the problem as well as maybe changing the part.

Willie is, in his own eyes, a mechanic. That identity is reconfirmed   14
every time a job is completed.

Willie also recognizes the importance of his work to the community,   15
and this recognition contributes a significant part of his overall self-image. He knows he is good at what he does and that his work is often crucial to his neighbors. Although some of this work gets neighbors out of mechanical jams, the primary responsibility Willie expresses is to the farmers he works for. This responsibility is expressed indirectly toward the farmers and more directly toward their work. During the peak periods in the farmers' schedules Willie works long hours. It is not uncommon on a rainy day in the summer to find five or six farmers at the shop, waiting their turns as Willie fixes and mends others' equipment. This is one way he put his attitude toward this work:

I've worked for the farmers around here for so long I can't turn them away. Their work comes ahead of anything else. A guy's broke down in the field — they've got to get fixed and get back working. Because weather has a lot to do with their work. I've been with these farmers twenty-seven years.

Perhaps the most telling example of his attitude toward work, and   16

[3]*Buck Rogers:* 1930s hero of space adventure films, novels by Philip Francis Nowlan, and comic strips by Nowlan and Dick Calkins.

thus self, is his view of those his own age who live on disability payments. When I first began spending time at the shop I found the number of these men who stopped by or hung around to be surprisingly large. It appears to be a form of early retirement for many working-class men, some of whom look quite healthy. Many of the real health problems are the result of industrial accidents. Others are caused by diseases like arthritis, hypoglycemia,[4] or, quite commonly, diabetes (called "sugar"). Willie himself suffers, often severely, from the effects of his industrial accident and from hypoglycemia, but he continues working. He spoke about the issue:

> You know the thing that gets me, though, on something like that — he's [a man who often came to the shop] more able to work than I am, and he's drawing disability. He claims he can't use his arms. I can't raise my one arm up and use it the way I'm supposed to, either. See, even when I scratch my head I use my other hand! [Scratches head.] Some of the ones on disability have lost it because they got sent to a different doctor when they went back to be reclassified, and the doctors found out there was nothing wrong with them. Some guys have artificial legs, or partial artificial legs — several of those. Some are wearing braces. I know guys that have worked every day of their lives who are that way.

I ask Willie why he didn't go on disability after his accident: 17

> They put me on [classified me as] full disability. I refused it, because I'd have to close the shop if I took it. With compensation disability — you don't work. You can't work at all, unless they give you percentage disability. If they'd given me percentage disability I'd be all right. But they gave me full disability.
>
> "In the ten years I've known you," I say, "you've had a lot of illness that seems to be connected with that old injury."
>
> Oh, yeah. Like right now I'm hurting in my shoulder. And this arm is just like a toothache. I didn't take my pain pills like I'm supposed to. Which I forget quite often. Intentionally, most of the time.

The decision not to stop working to gain disability payments is perhaps 18
most important because it signals Willie's view of the proper role of work in a person's life. It is true that the net of social services, because of his low income and frequent illness owing to his old injury, has extended to Willie and his family in the form of assistance for medical bills, occasional surplus food, and so forth. These are seen by Willie,

---

[4]*hypoglycemia:* excess of sugar in the blood.

and others in his environment, as legitimate claims from a working person temporarily in need of help.

Engaging the Text

1. According to Willie, what is the difference between a mechanic and a "parts exchanger"? Why is this distinction important?
2. What qualities, values, and abilities does Willie associate with his working identity?
3. How does work inform Willie's relationship with his family and his community?
4. Is Willie a reasonable model for workers to aspire to, or is there something too unusual about his circumstances or personality for him to serve as a role model?

Exploring Connections

1. Compare and contrast the meaning of work for Willie with its meaning for one of the following: Stephen Cruz (p. 77), Anzia Yezierska's narrator (p. 208), Nora Quealey (p. 267), and Jane Ellen Wilson (p. 569).
2. How might Erich Fromm (p. 529) explain Willie's satisfaction with his work?
3. Where would Christopher Lasch (p. 534) place Willie in relation to the Protestant work ethic?

Extending the Critical Context

1. Working in groups, list jobs that seem to offer the kind of satisfaction and fulfillment that Willie finds as a self-employed mechanic. What features do such jobs have in common? How do they differ from less satisfying types of employment? How and to what extent could some of the less desirable jobs be improved? Are there jobs that could never be personally rewarding?

OCCUPATION AND SOCIAL STATUS

Gender, Status, and Feeling

ARLIE RUSSELL HOCHSCHILD

As newspapers and popular magazines never tire of telling us, we are entering a new economic era, one that emphasizes services and information over the industrial production that has dominated the American workplace for the past century. Instead of "making" things, workers may now discover that the "raw material" of their labor can be their own personality, emotion, and physical appearance. In this selection from The Managed Heart *(1983), Arlie Russell Hochschild addresses the personal costs of selling one's "emotional labor" for a wage. Hochschild (b. 1940) is a professor of sociology at the University of California, Berkeley.*

> *Emotional.* 2. *subject to or easily affected by emotion:* **She** is an emotional woman, easily upset by any disturbance.
> *Cogitation.* 1. *meditation, contemplation:* After hours of cogitation **he** came up with a new proposal.
> 2. *the faculty of thinking:* **She** was not a serious student and seemed to lack the power of cogitation.
> — *Random House Dictionary of the English Language*

More emotion management goes on in the families and jobs of the upper classes than in those of the lower classes. That is, in the class system, social conditions conspire to make it more prevalent at the top. In the gender system, on the other hand, the reverse is true: social conditions make it more prevalent, and prevalent in different ways, for those at the bottom — women. In what sense is this so? And why?

Both men and women do emotion work, in private life and at work. In all kinds of ways, men as well as women get into the spirit of the party, try to escape the grip of hopeless love, try to pull themselves out of depression, try to allow grief. But in the whole realm of emotional experience, is emotion work as important for men as it is for women? And is it important in the same ways? I believe that the answer to both questions is No. The reason, at bottom, is the fact that women in general have far less independent access to money, power, authority, or status in society. They are a subordinate social stratum, and this has four consequences.

First, lacking other resources, women make a resource out of feeling 3 and offer it to men as a gift in return for the more material resources they lack. (For example, in 1980 only 6 percent of women but 50 percent of men earned over $15,000 a year.) Thus their capacity to manage feeling and to do "relational" work is for them a more important resource.

Second, emotion work is important in different ways for men and for 4 women. This is because each gender tends to be called on to do different kinds of this work. On the whole, women tend to specialize in the flight attendant side of emotional labor, men in the bill collection side of it. This specialization of emotional labor in the marketplace rests on the different childhood training of the heart that is given to girls and to boys. ("What are little girls made of? Sugar and spice and everything nice. What are little boys made of? Snips and snails and puppy dog tails.") Moreover, each specialization presents men and women with different emotional tasks. Women are more likely to be presented with the task of mastering anger and aggression in the service of "being nice." To men, the socially assigned task of aggressing against those that break rules of various sorts creates the private task of mastering fear and vulnerability.

Third, and less noticed, the general subordination of women leaves 5 every individual woman with a weaker "status shield" against the displaced feelings of others. For example, female flight attendants found themselves easier targets for verbal abuse from passengers so that male attendants often found themselves called upon to handle unwarranted aggression against them.

The fourth consequence of the power difference between the sexes is 6 that for each gender a different portion of the managed heart is enlisted for commercial use. Women more often react to subordination by making defensive use of sexual beauty, charm, and relational skills. For them, it is these capacities that become most vulnerable to commercial exploitation, and so it is these capacities that they are most likely to become estranged from. For male workers in "male" jobs, it is more often the capacity to wield anger and make threats that is delivered over to the company, and so it is this sort of capacity that they are more likely to feel estranged from.

Women as Emotion Managers

Middle-class American women, tradition suggests, feel emotion more 7
than men do. The definitions of "emotional" and "cogitation" in the
Random House Dictionary of the English Language reflect a deeply
rooted cultural idea. Yet women are also thought to command "feminine
wiles," to have the capacity to premeditate a sigh, an outburst of tears,
or a flight of joy. In general, they are thought to *manage* expression and
feeling not only better but more often than men do. How much the
conscious feelings of women and men may differ is an issue I leave aside
here. However, the evidence seems clear that women do *more* emotion
managing than men. And because the well-managed feeling has an outside
resemblance to spontaneous feeling, it is possible to confuse the condition
of being more "easily affected by emotion" with the action of willfully
managing emotion when the occasion calls for it.

Especially in the American middle class, women tend to manage feeling 8
more because in general they depend on men for money, and one of
the various ways of repaying their debt is to do extra emotion work —
*especially emotion work that affirms, enhances, and celebrates the well-
being and status of others*. When the emotional skills that children learn
and practice at home move into the marketplace, the emotional labor
of women becomes more prominent because men in general have not
been trained to make their emotions a resource and are therefore less
likely to develop their capacity for managing feeling.

There is also a difference in the kind of emotion work that men and 9
women tend to do. Many studies have told us that women adapt more
to the needs of others and cooperate more than men do. These studies
often imply the existence of gender-specific characteristics that are inevitable if not innate. But do these characteristics simply exist passively
in women? Or are they signs of a social work that women *do* — the
work of affirming, enhancing, and celebrating the well-being and status
of others? I believe that much of the time, the adaptive, cooperative
woman is actively working at showing deference. This deference requires
her to make an outward display of what Leslie Fiedler has called the
"seriously" good girl in her and to support this effort by evoking feelings
that make the "nice" display seem natural. Women who want to put
their own feelings less at the service of others must still confront the
idea that if they do so, they will be considered less "feminine."

What it takes to be more "adaptive" is suggested in a study of college 10
students by William Kephart (1967). Students were asked: "If a boy or
girl had all the other qualities you desire, would you marry this person
if you were not in love with him/her?" In response, 64 percent of the
men but only 24 percent of the women said No. Most of the women

answered that they "did not know." As one put it: "I don't know, if he were that good, maybe I could *bring myself around* to loving him." In my own study (1975), women more often than men described themselves as "trying to make myself love," "talking myself into not caring," or "trying to convince myself." A content analysis of 260 protocols[1] showed that more women than men (33 percent versus 18 percent) spontaneously used the language of emotion work to describe their emotions. The image of women as "more emotional," more subject to uncontrolled feelings, has also been challenged by a study of 250 students at UCLA, in which only 20 percent of the men but 45 percent of the women said that they deliberately show emotion to get their way. As one woman put it: "I pout, frown, and say something to make the other person feel bad, such as 'You don't love me, you don't care what happens to me.' I'm not the type to come right out with what I want; I'll usually hint around. It's all hope and a lot of beating around the bush" (Johnson and Goodchilds, 1976, p. 69).

The emotional arts that women have cultivated are analogous to the 11 art of feigning that Lionel Trilling has noted among those whose wishes outdistance their opportunities for class advancement. As for many others of lower status, it has been in the woman's interest to be the better actor. As the psychologists would say, the techniques of deep acting have unusually high "secondary gains." Yet these skills have long been mislabeled "natural," a part of woman's "being" rather than something of her own making.

Sensitivity to nonverbal communication and to the micro-political sig- 12 nificance of feeling gives women something like an ethnic language, which men can speak too, but on the whole less well. It is a language women share offstage in their talk "about feelings." This talk is not, as it is for men offstage, the score-keeping of conquistadors. It is the talk of the artful prey, the language of tips on how to make him want her, how to psyche him out, how to put him on or turn him off. Within the traditional female subculture, subordination at close quarters is understood, especially in adolescence, as a "fact of life." Women accommodate, then, but not passively. They actively adapt feeling to a need or a purpose at hand, and they do it so that it *seems* to express a passive state of agreement, the chance occurrence of coinciding needs. Being becomes a way of doing. Acting is the needed art, and emotion work is the tool.

The emotion work of enhancing the status and well-being of others is 13

---

[1]*protocol:* in research studies that use interviews, the conversation between interviewer and subject (usually transcribed for detailed analysis). Some of the quotations in this selection come from such protocols.

a form of what Ivan Illich has called "shadow labor," an unseen effort, which, like housework, does not quite count as labor but is nevertheless crucial to getting other things done. As with doing housework well, the trick is to erase any evidence of effort, to offer only the clean house and the welcoming smile.

We have a simple word for the product of this shadow labor: "nice." 14 Niceness is a necessary and important lubricant to any civil exchange, and men make themselves nice, too. It keeps the social wheels turning. As one flight attendant said, "I'll make comments like 'Nice jacket you have on' — that sort of thing, something to make them feel good. Or I'll laugh at their jokes. It makes them feel relaxed and amusing." Beyond the smaller niceties are the larger ones of doing a favor, offering a service. Finally, there is the moral or spiritual sense of being seriously nice, in which we embrace the needs of another person as more important than our own.

Each way of being "nice" adds a dimension to deference. Deference 15 is more than the offering of cold respect, the formal bow of submission, the distant smile of politeness; it can also have a warm face and offer gestures small and large that show support for the well-being and status of others.

Almost everyone does the emotion work that produces what we might, 16 broadly speaking, call deference. But women are expected to do more of it. A study by Wikler (1976) comparing male with female university professors found that students expected women professors to be warmer and more supportive than male professors; given these expectations, proportionally more women professors were perceived as cold. In another study, Broverman, Broverman, and Clarkson (1970) asked clinically trained psychologists, psychiatrists, and social workers to match various characteristics with "normal adult men" and "normal adult women"; they more often associated "very tactful, very gentle, and very aware of feelings of others" with their ideas of the normal adult woman. In being adaptive, cooperative, and helpful, the woman is on a private stage behind the public stage, and as a consequence she is often seen as less good at arguing, telling jokes, and teaching than she is at expressing appreciation of these activities. She is the conversational cheerleader. She actively enhances other people — usually men, but also other women to whom she plays woman. The more she seems natural at it, the more her labor does not show as labor, the more successfully it is disguised as the *absence* of other, more prized qualities. As a *woman* she may be praised for out-enhancing the best enhancer, but as a *person* in comparison with comics, teachers, and argument-builders, she usually lives outside the climate of enhancement that men tend to inhabit. Men, of course, pay court to certain other men and women and thus also do the emotion work that keeps deference sincere. The difference between men and women is a difference in the psychological effects of having or not having power.

Racism and sexism share this general pattern, but the two systems differ in the avenues available for the translation of economic inequality into private terms. The white manager and the black factory worker leave work and go home, one to a generally white neighborhood and family and the other to a generally black neighborhood and family. But in the case of women and men, the larger economic inequality is filtered into the intimate daily exchanges between wife and husband. Unlike other subordinates, women seek *primary* ties with a supplier. In marriage, the principle of reciprocity applies to wider arenas of each self: there is more to choose from in how we pay and are paid, and the paying between economically unequal parties goes on morning, noon, and night. The larger inequities find intimate expression. 17

Women at Work

With the growth of large organizations calling for skills in personal relations, the womanly art of status enhancement and the emotion work that it requires has been made more public, more systematized, and more standardized. It is performed by largely middle-class women in largely public-contact jobs. . . . Jobs involving emotional labor comprise over a third of all jobs. But they form only a *quarter* of all jobs that men do, and over *half* of all jobs that women do. 18

Many of the jobs that call for public contact also call for giving service to the public. Richard Sennett and Jonathan Cobb,[2] in *The Hidden Injuries of Class*, comment on how people tend to rank service jobs in relation to other kinds of jobs: "At the bottom end of the scale are found not factory jobs but service jobs where the individual has to perform personally for someone else. A bartender is listed below a coal miner, a taxi driver below a truck driver; we believe this occurs because their functions *are felt to be more dependent on and more at the mercy of others*" (Sennett and Cobb, 1973, p. 236; my emphasis). Because there are more women than men in service jobs (21 percent compared with 9 percent), there are "hidden injuries" of gender attached to those of class. 19

Once women are at work in public-contact jobs, a new pattern unfolds: They receive less basic deference. That is, although some women are still elbow-guided through doors, chauffeured in cars, and protected from 20

[2]*Richard Sennett and Jonathan Cobb:* See the headnote for the next essay.

rain puddles, they are not shielded from one fundamental consequence of their lower status: Their feelings are accorded less weight than the feelings of men.

The feelings of the lower-status party may be discounted in two ways: 21 by considering them rational but unimportant or by considering them irrational and hence dismissable. An article entitled "On Aggression in Politics: Are Women Judged by a Double Standard?" presented the results of a survey of female politicians. All those surveyed said they believed there was an affective[3] double standard. As Frances Farenthold, the president of Wells College in Aurora, New York, put it: "You certainly see to it that you don't throw any tantrums. Henry Kissinger can have his scenes — remember the way he acted in Salzburg? But for women, we're still in the stage that if you don't hold in your emotions, you're pegged as emotional, unstable, and all those terms that have always been used to describe women" (*New York Times*, Feb. 12, 1979). These women in public life were agreed on the following points. When a man expresses anger, it is deemed "rational" or understandable anger, anger that indicates not weakness of character but deeply held conviction. When women express an equivalent degree of anger, it is more likely to be interpreted as a sign of personal instability. It is believed that women are more emotional, and this very belief is used to invalidate their feelings. That is, the women's feelings are seen not as a response to real events but as reflections of themselves as "emotional" women.

Here we discover a corollary of the "doctrine of feelings":[4] the lower 22 our status, the more our manner of seeing and feeling is subject to being discredited, and the less believable it becomes. An "irrational" feeling is the twin of an invalidated perception. A person of lower status has a weaker claim to the right to define what is going on; less trust is placed in her judgments; and less respect is accorded to what she feels. Relatively speaking, it more often becomes the burden of women, as with other lower-status persons, to uphold a minority viewpoint, a discredited opinion.

Medical responses to male and female illness provide a case in point. 23 One study of how doctors respond to the physical complaints of back pain, headache, dizziness, chest pain, and fatigue — symptoms for which a doctor must take the patient's word — showed that among fifty-two married couples, the complaints of the husbands elicited more medical response than those of the wives. The authors conclude: "The data may bear out . . . that the physicians . . . tend to take illness more seriously in men than in women." Another study of physician interactions with

[3]*affective*: relating to the emotions.
[4]*"doctrine of feelings"*: the idea that the feelings of high-status employees deserve consideration, while the feelings of low-status workers do not.

184 male and 130 female patients concluded that "doctors were more likely to consider the psychological component of the patient's illness important when the patient was a woman" (Wallens et al., 1979, p. 143). The female's assertion that she was physically sick was more likely to be invalidated as something "she just imagined," something "subjective," not a response to anything real.

To make up for either way of weighing the feelings of the two sexes 24 unequally, many women urge their feelings forward, trying to express them with more force, so as to get them treated with seriousness. But from there the spiral moves down. For the harder women try to oppose the "doctrine of feeling" by expressing their feelings more, the more they come to fit the image awaiting them as "emotional." Their efforts are discounted as one more example of emotionalism. The only way to counter the doctrine of feelings is to eliminate the more fundamental tie between gender and status.

The Status Shield at Work

Given this relation between status and the treatment of feeling, it 25 follows that persons in low-status categories — women, people of color, children — lack a status shield against poorer treatment of their feelings. This simple fact has the power to utterly transform the content of a job. The job of flight attendant, for example, is not the *same job* for a woman as it is for a man. A day's accumulation of passenger abuse for a woman differs from a day's accumulation of it for a man. Women tend to be more exposed than men to rude or surly speech, to tirades against the service, the airline, and airplanes in general. As the company's main shock absorbers against "mishandled" passengers, their own feelings are more frequently subjected to rough treatment. In addition, a day's exposure to people who resist authority in women is a different experience for a woman than it is for a man. Because her gender is accorded lower status, a woman's shield against abuse is weaker, and the importance of what she herself might be feeling — when faced with blame for an airline delay, for example — is correspondingly reduced. Thus the job for a man differs in essential ways from the same job for a woman.

In this respect, it is a disadvantage to be a woman — as 85 percent 26 of all flight attendants are. And in this case, they are not simply women in the biological sense. They are also a highly visible distillation of middle-class American notions of femininity. They symbolize Woman. Insofar as the category "female" is mentally associated with having less status and authority, female flight attendants are more readily classified as "really" female than other females are. And as a result their emotional lives are even less protected by the status shield.

More than female accountants, bus drivers, or gardeners, female flight 27 attendants mingle with people who expect them to *enact* two leading roles of Womanhood: the loving wife and mother (serving food, tending the needs of others) and the glamorous "career woman" (dressed to be seen, in contact with strange men, professional and controlled in manner, and literally very far from home). They do the job of symbolizing the transfer of homespun femininity into the impersonal marketplace, announcing, in effect, "I work in the public eye, but I'm still a woman at heart."

Passengers borrow their expectations about gender biographies from home and from the wider culture and then base their demands on this borrowing. The different fictive biographies they attribute to male and female workers make sense out of what they expect to receive in the currency of caretaking and authority. One male flight attendant noted: 28

> They always ask about my work plans. "Why are you doing this?" That's one question we get all the time from passengers. "Are you planning to go into management?" Most guys come in expecting to do it for a year or so and see how they like it, but we keep getting asked about the management training program. I don't know any guy that's gone into management from here.

In contrast, a female flight attendant said: 29

> Men ask me why I'm not married. They don't ask the guys that. Or else passengers will say, "Oh, when you have kids, you'll quit this job. I know you will." And I say, "Well, no, I'm not going to have kids." "Oh yes you will," they say. "No I'm not," I say, and I don't want to get more personal than that. They may expect me to have kids because of my gender, but I'm not, no matter what they say.

If a female flight attendant is seen as a protomother, then it is natural that the work of nurturing should fall to her. As one female attendant said: "The guys bow out of it more and we pick up the slack. I mean the handling of babies, the handling of children, the coddling of the old folks. The guys don't get involved in that quite as much." Confirming this, one male flight attendant noted casually, "Nine times out of ten, when I go out of my way to talk, it will be to attractive gal passengers." In this regard, females generally appreciated gay male flight attendants who, while trying deftly to sidestep the biography test, still gravitate more toward nurturing work than straight males are reputed to do. 30

Estrangement from Sexual Identity

Regardless of gender, the job poses problems of identity. What is my work role and what is "me"? How can I do deep acting without "feeling phony" and losing self-esteem? . . . 31

But there are other psychological issues a flight attendant faces if she 32 is a woman. In response to her relative lack of power and her exposure to the "doctrine of feelings," she may seek to improve her position by making use of two traditionally "feminine" qualities — those of the supportive mother and those of the sexually desirable mate. Thus, some women *are* motherly; they support and enhance the well-being and status of others. But in *being* motherly, they may also *act* motherly and may sometimes experience themselves using the motherly act to win regard from others. In the same way, some women are sexually attractive and may act in ways that are sexually alluring. For example, one flight attendant who played the sexual queen — swaying slowly down the aisle with exquisitely understated suggestiveness — described herself as using her sexual attractiveness to secure interest and favors from male passengers. In each case, the woman is using a feminine quality for private purposes. But it is also true, for the flight attendant, that both "motherly" behavior and a "sexy" look and manner are partly an achievement of corporate engineering — a result of the company's emphasis on the weight and (former) age requirements, grooming classes, and letters from passengers regarding the looks and demeanor of flight attendants. In its training and supervisory roles, the company may play the part of the protective duenna.[5] But in its commercial role as an advertiser of sexy and glamorous service, it acts more like a backstage matchmaker. Some early United Airlines ads said, "And she might even make a good wife." The company, of course, has always maintained that it does not meddle in personal affairs.

Thus the two ways in which women traditionally try to improve their 33 lot — by using their motherly capacity to enhance the status and well-being of others, and by using their sexual attractiveness — have come under company management. Most flight attendants I spoke with agreed that companies used and attached profit to these qualities.

What is the result? On the status-enhancement side, some women 34 feel estranged from the role of woman they play for the company. On the sexual side, Melanie Matthews, a sex therapist who had treated some fifty flight attendants for "loss of sexual interest" and "preorgasmic problems," had this to say:

> The patients I have treated who have been flight attendants tend to fit a certain pattern. They tend to have been "good" girls when they were young — nurturing and considerate to others. Then the company gets them while they are young and uses those qualities further. These women don't ever get the chance to decide who they are, and this shows up in their sexual life. They play the part of the ultra-female,

---

[5]*duenna:* chaperone or governess.

of someone who takes an interest in others, and they don't get the chance to explore the other sides of their character and to discover their own needs, sexual or otherwise. Some of them have been so fixed on pleasing others that while they don't dislike men, they don't actively like them either. It's not so much that they are preorgasmic as that they are prerelational in this one sense. They hold onto their orgasmic potential as one of the few parts of themselves that someone else doesn't possess.

Freud generally found sexual stories beneath social ones, but there are also social stories beneath sexual ones. The social story here concerns young women who want to please (and who work for companies that capitalize on this characteristic) while they also want to keep a part of themselves independent of this desire. Their sexual problems could be considered a prepolitical form of protest against the overextension and overuse of their traditional femininity. This form of protest, this holding onto something so intimate as "mine," suggests that vast territories of the self may have been relinquished as "not mine." The self we define as "real" is pushed further and further into a corner as more and more of its expressions are sensed as artifice. 35

Estrangement from aspects of oneself are, in one light, a means of defense. On the job, the acceptance of a division between the "real" self and the self in a company uniform is often a way to avoid stress, a wise realization, a saving grace. But this solution also poses serious problems. For in dividing up our sense of self, in order to save the "real" self from unwelcome intrusions, we necessarily relinquish a healthy sense of wholeness. We come to accept as normal the tension we feel between our "real" and our "on-stage" selves. 36

More women than men go into public-contact work and especially into work in which status enhancement is the essential social-psychological task. In some jobs, such as that of the flight attendant, women may perform this task by playing the Woman. Such women are more vulnerable, on this account, to feeling estranged from their capacity to perform and enjoy two traditional feminine roles — offering status enhancement and sexual attractiveness to others. These capacities are now under corporate as well as personal management. 37

Perhaps this realization accounts for the laughter at a joke I heard surreptitiously passed around the Delta Training Office, as if for an audience of insiders. It went like this: A male passenger came across a woman flight attendant seated in the galley, legs apart, elbows on knees, her chin resting in one hand and a lighted cigarette in the other — held between thumb and forefinger. "Why are you holding your cigarette like that?" the man asked. Without looking up or smiling, the woman took another puff and said, "If I had balls, I'd be driving this plane." Inside 38 the feminine uniform and feminine "act" was a would-be man. It was an estrangement joke, a poignant behind-the-scenes protest at a commercial logic that standardizes and trivializes the dignity of women.

Works Cited

Broverman, Inge K., Donald M. Broverman, and Frank E. Clarkson, "Sex role stereotypes and clinical judgments of mental health." *Journal of Consulting and Clinical Psychology* 34 (1970):1–7.

Hochschild, Arlie, "The sociology of feeling and emotion: selected possibilities." Pp. 280–307. In Marcia Millman and Rosabeth Kanter (eds.), *Another Voice*. Garden City, N.Y.: Anchor, 1975.

Johnson, Paula B., and Jacqueline D. Goodchilds, "How women get their way." *Psychology Today* 10 (1976):69–70.

Kephart, William, "Some correlates of romantic love." *Journal of Marriage and the Family* 29 (1967):470–474.

Sennett, Richard, and Jonathan Cobb, *Hidden Injuries of Class*. New York: Vintage, 1973.

Wallens, Jacqueline, Howard Waitzkin, and John Stoeckle, "Physician stereotypes about female health and illness: a study of patient's sex and the informative process during medical interviews." *Women and Health* 4 (1979):125–146.

Wikler, Norma, "Sexism in the classroom." Paper presented at the annual meeting of the American Sociological Association, New York, 1976.

Engaging the Text

1. Explain what Hochschild means by the concept of "emotional work." Do you agree that the control or use of feelings is a kind of labor?

2. What is a "status shield"? How does status protect men — or anyone in a position of power — from the stress that accompanies working with the public?

3. What, according to Hochschild, do corporations do to promote the management of their employees' emotional lives?

Exploring Connections

1. Use the concept of emotional management to interpret Ranice Crosby's poem "Waitresses," which appears earlier in this chapter.

2. Compare Hochschild's view of alienation on the job with that offered by Fromm earlier in this chapter. What is lost by the worker according to these two analyses? How would you explain the difference in their PERSPECTIVES?

3. Analyze the classroom incidents Jules Henry describes (Chapter Six, "Grading American Education") as instances of emotional management. In what other ways are students emotionally managed in the typical classroom? Does this process change as students progress from elementary school to college?

1. The notion of emotional engineering, the deliberate manipulation of feelings, can be seen at work in many contexts in American society — not only in the workplace. What other situations involve emotional management?
2. Hochschild mentions that workers often engage in "behind-the-scenes protests" against the emotional management they labor under. What kinds of informal protests have you seen workers engage in behind the scenes? With what results?

From *The Hidden Injuries of Class*

RICHARD SENNETT AND JONATHAN COBB

What you do for a living is intimately linked with where you stand in society; in America your job, to a large extent, determines your class position. According to sociologists Richard Sennett (b. 1943) and Jonathan Cobb (b. 1946), work and class position have tremendous impact on our images of ourselves, particularly because our culture promises the chance of "upward mobility." In this selection from The Hidden Injuries of Class *(1973), they explain how class position undermines the confidence of two typical working-class individuals: Frank Rissarro, a man who has worked his way up to become a loan officer in a bank, and James, a college student from a blue-collar family.*

Frank Rissarro,[1] a third-generation Italian-American, forty-four years old when we talked with him, had worked his way up from being a shoeshine boy at the age of nine to classifying loan applications in a bank. He makes $10,000 a year, owns a suburban home, and every August rents a small cottage in the country. He is a man who at first glance appears satisfied — "I know I did a good job in my life" — and yet he is also a man who feels defensive about his honor, fearing that people secretly do not respect him; he feels threatened by his children, who are "turning out just the way I want them to be," and he runs his home in a dictatorial manner.

[1]This is not his real name, nor are the details that follow about his job, age, and income precisely accurate. [Author's note]

Rissarro was born in 1925, the second-eldest child and only son of   2
parents who lived in a predominantly Italian section of Boston. His father,
an uneducated day laborer, worked hard, drank hard, and beat his wife
and children often. As a young boy, Rissarro was not interested in school
— his life was passed in constant fear of his father's violence. He was
regarded by his family as a spoiled brat, with no brains and no common
sense. His sisters and cousins did better than he scholastically, all finishing
high school. Yet even as a child, Rissarro worked nights and weekends
helping to support his family. At sixteen he quit school, feeling incapable
of doing the work and out of place. After two years in the military, he
worked as a meat-cutter for nearly twenty years.

Rissarro was and is a man of ambition. The affluence spreading across   3
America in the decades following the Second World War made him
restless — he wanted to either get a butcher shop of his own or get
out. The capital for a small business being beyond his reach, he had a
friend introduce him to the branch manager of a bank setting up a new
office in his neighborhood. He won a job processing loans for people
who come in off the street; he helps them fill out the forms, though he
is still too low-level to have the power to approve or disapprove the
loans themselves.

A success story: From chaos in the Depression, from twenty years of   4
hacking away at sides of beef, Rissarro now wears a suit to work and
has a stable home in respectable surroundings. Yes, it is a success story
— except that *he* does not read it that way.

As we explored with Rissarro the reasons why these good things have   5
come to him, we found the declarations of self-satisfaction almost instantly
giving way to a view of himself as a passive agent in his own life, a man
who has been on the receiving end of events rather than their cause:
"I was just at the right place at the right time," he says again and again.
"I was lucky," he claims, in describing how he emotionally withstood
the terrors of his father's home.

Is this modesty? Not for him. He feels passive in the midst of his   6
success because he feels illegitimate, a pushy intruder, in his entrance
to the middle-class world of neat suburban lawns, peaceable families,
happy friendships. Despite the fact that he has gained entrée, he doesn't
believe he deserves to be respected. In discussing, for instance, his
marriage — to a woman somewhat more educated than he, from an
Italian background equivalent to "lace-curtain Irish"[2] — Rissarro told us
something impossible to believe, considering his ungrammatical speech,
his obsession with his childhood, his mannerisms and gestures: "My wife
didn't know that I had no background to speak of, or else she would

[2]*lace-curtain Irish:* a mildly derogatory term for relatively prosperous Irish-Americans.

never have married me." The possibility that she accepted him for himself, and never made an issue of where he came from, he simply cannot accept.

Sociologists have a neat formula to explain the discontent caused by upward mobility; they call Frank's malaise a product of "status incongruity": Because Frank does not yet know the rules of his new position, because he is caught between two worlds, he feels something is wrong with him. This formula falls back on an image of the antithesis between working-class struggle and educated, "higher" culture. 7

The trouble here, however, is that Frank *doesn't* feel caught between two worlds. He knows what the rules of middle-class life are, he has played at them now for some years; furthermore, he is not in any way ashamed of his working-class past. Indeed, he is proud of it, he thinks it makes him a more honest person at work: 8

> I'm working, like I said, with fellows that are educated, college boys, in that office. I'm about the only one in there in any straits to say I'm educated. I'm enjoying this job, I'm going in with the big shots. I go in at nine, I come out at five. *The other fellows, because they got an education, sneaks out early and comes in late.* The boss knows I'm there, a reliable worker. 'Cause I've had the factory life, I know what it is. I mean, a man deserves — the least you can do is put your hours in and do your job. I'm a good employee. I know I am because I see others who are educated.

In fact, toward educated white-collar work itself, beyond all its symbolic connotations of success, Frank Rissarro harbors an innate disrespect: "These jobs aren't real work where you make something — it's just pushing papers." 9

The word "educated" as used by Rissarro, and by other men and women we talked to, is what psychologists call a "cover term"; that is, it stands for a whole range of experiences and feelings that may in fact have little to do with formal schooling. Education covers, at the most abstract level, the development of capacities within a human being. At the most concrete level, education meant to the people we interviewed getting certificates for social mobility and job choice, and they felt that American society parcels out the certificates very unequally and unfairly, so that middle-class people have more of a chance to become educated than themselves. But if the abstract is connected to the concrete, this means middle-class people have more of a chance than workers to escape from becoming creatures of circumstance, more chance to develop the defenses, the tools of personal, rational control that "education" gives. Why should one class of human beings get a chance to develop the weapons of self more than another? And yet, if that class difference is 10 a *fait accompli,* what has a man without education got inside himself to defend against this superior power?

Rissarro believes people of a higher class have a power to judge him 11 because they seem internally more developed human beings; and he is afraid, because they are better armed, that they will not respect him. He feels compelled to justify his own position, and in his life he has felt compelled to put himself up on their level in order to earn respect. All of this, in turn — when he thinks just of himself and *is not comparing himself* to his image of people in a higher class — all of this is set against a revulsion against the work of educated people in the bank, and a feeling that manual labor has more dignity.

What does he make of this contradiction in his life? That he is an 12 impostor — but more, that the sheer fact that he is troubled must prove he really is inadequate. After all, he has played by the rules, he has gained the outward signs of material respectability; if, then, he still feels defenseless, something must be wrong with *him:* His unhappiness seems to him a sign that he simply cannot become the kind of person other people can respect.

This tangle of feelings appeared again and again as we talked to people 13 who started life as poor, ethnically isolated laboring families, and have been successful in making the sort of material gains that are supposed to "melt" people into the American middle class.

The children who get formal education are no more exempt than 14 parents like Rissarro from a feeling of inadequate defenses in the very midst of success. Nationally, about half the children from white, blue-collar homes get started in the kind of schooling their parents want — that is, about half go beyond high school. There is a large difference between girls and boys in this; depending on whose figures you use, between ten and twenty-five percent of boys from blue-collar homes receive some further schooling, while between forty and fifty percent of the girls do. A much smaller percentage of boys gets through four years of college or technical school (three to five percent); a slightly higher, though still small, percentage of girls do.

As with blue-collar workers who have moved into offices, we are 15 dealing with a minority — a minority, however, on whom much hope is pinned. Observers of the college scene like John McDermott have suggested that this may be a more desperately unhappy group of students than the disaffected young from suburban homes.[3] McDermott and, in

[3]See John McDermott, "The Laying On of Culture," *The Nation,* vol. 208, no. 10 (March 10, 1969). [Author's note]

another context, David Riesman believe these working-class boys and girls are made to feel inadequate by a "laying-on of culture" practiced in college by their teachers and the more privileged students — a process that causes people to feel inadequate in the same way "status incongruity" does, by subjecting them to an unfamiliar set of rules in a game where respect is the prize.

Yet here is James, in his third year at a local college accessible to 16
sons and daughters from blue-collar homes. James's father works as a clerk for the city by day and mends rugs at night and on the weekend. James knows the rules for making it in college, and he has survived the weeding-out process of the first years with good grades. But James disrespects school in the same way Frank disrespects pushing papers around at the bank; the status of "educated man" is greater than that of a craftsman, but the intrinsic satisfaction seems less. James feels, however, that he must stay in school, above all for his father's sake:

> The American Dream for my father is to see his kids get a college education, something he never had. If it had to kill them, they were gonna get a college education. He never really forced it on us, but we knew that this was really gonna make him happy — that we could get a college degree.

James also knows what leaving school would mean materially: a loss 17
of security, status jobs, money. He is going to stay in school, because he feels compelled by these material considerations even as he disrespects them on their own.

How does he deal with the conflict success in school has set up in 18
his life? Like Frank Rissarro, he blames himself for feeling so ambivalent. On the one hand he says, "I still don't have the balls to go out into the world," i.e., to quit school; on the other hand, "If I really had what it takes, I could make this school thing worthwhile." He takes personal responsibility for his social position, and the result is that he makes himself feel inadequate no matter which way he turns in attempting to deal with success.

James has gone through a profound dislocation in his life, and his 19
discontent is pronounced. His problem, however, is shared in more muted form by others who have made more modest gains. These are kids who have had a little schooling beyond high school and then gone into such jobs as sales-work or management traineeships. They feel they have had more opportunity open to them than their manual-laboring parents. At the same time, they see the parents' work as intrinsically more interesting and worthwhile, and they suffer, therefore, from a feeling of not having made use of their opportunities. When all the

discipline of sticking it out in school yields an occupation they feel little engagement in, they hold themselves to blame, for not feeling more self-confidence, for having failed to develop. "If only I had what it takes," says a young shoe salesman, son of a factory laborer, "things would have been different."

One way to make sense of these confusing metaphors of self-worth is to recast them as issues of *freedom* and *dignity*. Class is a system for limiting freedom: It limits the freedom of the powerful in dealing with other people, because the strong are constricted within the circle of action that maintains their power; class constricts the weak more obviously in that they must obey commands. What happens to the dignity men see in themselves and in each other, when their freedom is checked by class?

Engaging the Text

1. What is Frank Rissarro's attitude toward work and success? How do you explain his feelings about white-collar work?

2. Explain the concept of status incongruity. How does it differ from nostalgia? Why doesn't it capture the full complexity of Rissarro's relationship to his own upward mobility?

Exploring Connections

1. How might Erich Fromm (p. 529) explain Rissarro's AMBIVALENCE towards success?

2. Analyze Stephen Cruz's attitudes toward his career (p. 77) using the notion of status incongruity.

3. Apply Gordon Allport's theory of reference groups (p. 85) to Rissarro's situation.

Extending the Critical Context

1. Sennett and Cobb suggest that higher education creates "hidden injuries" in many students because it confronts them with values and behaviors that seem threatening or foreign. Have you ever experienced this kind of ambivalence about your own education? What specific values and behaviors have troubled you the most in college?

Jane Ellen Wilson

JAKE RYAN AND CHARLES SACKREY

Upward mobility, moving from a lower to a higher job status and class position, has been a central feature of the American dream. But, as Richard Sennett and Jonathan Cobb point out in the preceding reading, upward mobility has its costs. In this reminiscence, Jane Ellen Wilson describes her difficulty negotiating between the farming background of her family and the elite intellectual world of the university. Jane Ellen Wilson's story was originally published in Jake Ryan and Charles Sackrey's Strangers in Paradise: Academics from the Working Class *(1984), an oral history of professional academicians who come from marginalized social groups. Charles Sackrey (b. 1936) has published both as an economist and as an editor of stories and poems, which he says remind him "that the people that lie just the other side of all the statistical data have very individual tales to tell." Sackrey is associate professor of economics at Bucknell University; Jake Ryan (b. 1933) is associate professor of politics at Ithaca College.*

I was born in a hospital, and I grew up on my family's farm three 1 miles east of the Susquehanna River in a fertile valley of central Pennsylvania. My great-grandfather was a druggist in a small town for most of his life, but when his health demanded it he bought this farm and moved his family upriver twenty miles. My grandfather and father were actually born here, as well as my great aunt, great uncle, and uncle. My sister grew up here with me.

My father's family, of their generation in this country, boasts a few 2 ministers, some schoolteachers, and a lawyer ("Uncle George"). They also farmed and worked in factories. When I got my Ph.D., I became the most educated person in the family — a subject much and proudly discussed at the recent family reunions. My mother's family holds farmers, loggers, laborers, and many nameless women.

I grew up close to all four of my grandparents. My father's father 3 farmed all his life, raising bumper crops and building up a Holstein dairy herd. Towards the end of his life he wrote poetry: about the land, the animals, the weather. He showed me plants and trees and taught me some of their names and uses. His wife farmed, cooked, milked cows, and taught me to read at the age of four. I learned to play piano using her old upright and the pump organ in the parlor.

My mother's father was a cheerful man with a strong sense of justice. 4 He smoked Camels, tickled me with his whiskers, and let me play with his wooden leg (I liked to put things in the holes in it.) He left his real leg in the Argonne during the first World War. Even with his wooden one he farmed, worked in the limestone quarry, and, as he got older, began sharpening saws for a living. My grandmother grew up on farms and in logging camps, helping her mother cook for the loggers. In spite of her irregular education she was valedictorian of her high school class. She married and quickly had three children, going on to work as a cook, a nurse's aide, and finally an LPN.[1] In her fifties she began to paint, and now paints wonderful pictures of the activities of her early life in the woods and farmland of Pennsylvania.

My father graduated from high school and wanted to go to college, 5 but was prevailed upon by his family to stay and help with the farm. In addition to farming, he was interested in music, and learned to play guitar and call square dances. After he and my mother married they put together a country and western band (she played bass and sang) and played for local festivals, at square dances, and on the local radio station. They still do this, taking off very little time from their work. When his father died, my father went on to become a carpenter and local contractor, farming in the evenings and on weekends, trying to make ends meet. Besides helping with all the farm work, my mother has worked as a cook, housekeeper, and companion to elderly ladies.

The people I come from get up at dawn, work hard all day, go to the 6 Lutheran church on Sunday, abstain from liquor, get married, stay married and have children (there are a few old maids), and live close to their family and close to the earth. We had little cash but lots of food and a beautiful piece of land to live on.

Among these people farms pass to sons, not daughters. Although my 7 parents had no sons — only two daughters — it was expected that we would marry and leave. It was never expected that we would become farmers and stay there. This bothered me; I felt dispossessed by default. My family decided that I had a gift for music, so they brought me up to play in their band. They had me sing as soon as I could talk, and taught me to play guitar as soon as my hands were big enough. They decided I had a gift for schooling, too. I read everything I could find and was "smart." Like everyone else on the farm, I did all I could to help in

---

[1] *LPN:* Licensed Practical Nurse.

the fields, at the barn, and in the house: making hay, butchering, doing daily chores, sewing, cooking, gardening. They imagined futures for me: I could be a nurse or a teacher; I could marry a farmer or a factory worker and stay near home; I could marry a rich man (that future came highly recommended and in fact my mother still mentions it); I could go to Nashville and become a country music star. They had no better idea than I did how to reconcile my abilities (which they wanted me to develop) with traditional women's roles (which they wanted me to follow).

By the time I was twelve I had opinions about everything, most of them different from my parents'. Country music: didn't like it; Christianity: thought it was hypocritical; country living: I wanted to go to the city, hear "folk music" (i.e., Bob Dylan), and visit Europe; government: I was generally against it; war: didn't like it in general and in particular was concerned about Vietnam (this was 1965). My folks were appalled; a revolutionary ancestor was ok, but a revolutionary teenager was another story. My voracious reading and musical taste had given me ideas. I was stuck with these ideas, however, three miles out of town in a household with strict parents. I was sure the exciting, real world was going on elsewhere and I was missing it. By the time I graduated from high school I had built up a tremendous head of steam and was out to find what I had been missing. 8

I went to college. Getting married or going to school were the two acceptable ways to leave my family and I bet on education. However, I was still only sixteen, and my parents wanted me to stay close to home; of the nearby colleges I chose the most intellectual and radical and moved to the dorm to enter another world. What I found was more middle and upper class people than I knew existed; and for the first time I met people who didn't know that trees had names. 9

I expected to find intellectual stimulation and community; fun and companionship; new ideas and political concern; and all the things I had been missing just ten miles away in Rural Delivery Route 2. I also strongly expected academia not to discriminate against women. I knew that if I married someone who worked at Chef Boyardee or AC & F that I'd be expected to conform to traditional women's roles. I also knew that physically I couldn't work the way that men did; I didn't like baling hay when I had my period, for example. And though I had a lot of endurance for physical work, that didn't seem like strength to me; strength meant picking up a hundred pound sack of grain. (Little did I realize how hard that was for men, too.) But clearly (I thought), being an academic didn't involve physical labor or childbearing, so I trustingly assumed that the academic world did not discriminate against women. 10

What I found at college was disillusioning; but I had invested heavily 11
in my bet on education, and I lasted two years the first time. I found
some intellectual stimulation; and I found lots of people making themselves
miserable with their intellect: agonizing over Hegel and Nietzsche[2] and
talking in (I thought) circles. I found a great deal of personal freedom:
to come and go, talk and dress as I pleased. I found some companionship;
my first boyfriend was from upper class suburbia. While I had no expectations about women's roles there, I did believe (for years) that the
long-haired pacifist men of the late sixties extended their gentleness and
egalitarianism to women as well as to the Vietnamese.

I had a scholarship and I borrowed money; I worked in the library. 12
I found people who shared my taste in music and I played with them
and by myself in college coffeehouses. I tried to be a music major, since
I was more interested in music than anything, but found that I didn't
have enough of the right kind of training — classical — to do much,
instrumentally. My music instructors were very authoritarian, I thought,
demanding class attendance and sign-in sheets at concerts; although I
breezed through music theory, I couldn't bring myself to abide by the
letter of their law. Finally the chairman politely told me I wasn't suited
to being a music major, and suggested if I couldn't get up in the mornings
for his class, I should see a psychiatrist. This was my first major disappointment with academia.

I dropped out and spent the summer on the farm. Eventually I got 13
a job as a waitress at a local Pancake House. In a few months, I had
saved money and wanted to go to England, although I couldn't quite
figure out how to go about it; in the meantime, two of my former
professors convinced me to return to college as an English major, saying
that the campus needed "creative people" like me, and that they had
designed a new program with more freedom. I believed (I was nineteen)
and signed up again only to be told by the dean that I was, as a junior,
too old to be part of this new program. I slogged through English courses,
writing poems and songs instead of term papers.

Because academic reality seemed reductive, flat, lifeless to me, I kept 14
seeking other realities. I worked occasionally as a musician (coffeehouses)
and as a music instructor for children, in summer arts programs and in
a hospital. I also worked at a small, local hotel as an all night desk clerk.
Although just downtown — seven blocks — this was a world away from
the college. I had begun to realize — through my high-class, crazy
boyfriend — that most people at the college came from a middle class
suburban world, with its own trappings, values, customs — most of

---

[2]*Hegel and Nietzsche:* nineteenth-century German philosophers Georg Wilhelm Friedrich
Hegel (1770–1831) and Friedrich Wilhelm Nietzsche (1844–1900).

which I did not find congenial, even though I was supposed to be aspiring to them (by virtue of betting on education). At the Hotel I dealt with truck drivers and their girlfriends, with women from New York and Philadelphia come to visit their husbands and lovers in the nearby federal penitentiary, with small town dramas and informal prostitution. In a way I felt at home with this — country music on the juke box, drinking, adultery, high drama in a small pond. I did not feel at home with truck driver machismo, but started to learn to deal with it. When I became friends with a driver from Cincinnatti, I was shocked to learn that his wife wrote poetry and he thought it was great. Mostly I was shocked by my own arrogance in assuming that this class of people wouldn't know or care about art. After I realized that my own assumptions had been cutting me off from people, I started to feel a little more at home in the world.

I graduated from college and moved to my boyfriend's hometown. He lived in the high class Philadelphia suburbs, and I lived in a house in town, as did some students, and all the black people. For many reasons, I wasn't very happy there. Thus, having discovered that there wasn't much room for my voice in the working world, and seeing little room for my voice in a suburban lifestyles (sic), I bet again on education. Well, maybe I couldn't get an interesting job because I wasn't educated enough. (The extent to which this was also influenced by my being a woman and by my class background was just beginning to dawn on me.) And maybe, I thought, I just hadn't found the right subject to study in academia. 15

I had always felt there was something missing in academia's view of the world. In literature, for example, they studied Englishmen writing literature; I knew that people exercised verbal creativity in many more ways than that. My grandfather told stories, my father told stories, every truck driver that walked into the hotel had a story to tell. In music, academics studied classical (mostly European) music; I knew that people exercised musical creativity in more ways than that. My political concerns had led me from the first to an interest in folk music (and vice versa). From somewhere, it occurred to me that people in the academy might actually study these things. Maybe one of my professors told me how I could look that up — maybe it was a librarian that showed me the index where universities were listed according to the majors they offered; I don't remember. But in any case, I started applying to graduate school in folklore; I also applied to my alma mater to study for an M.A. in English. My experience in the working world had upped the ante on my bet on education. 16

Another reason to keep betting on education was that I had rejected my family's way of life and values. More accurately, I couldn't see any 17 place for myself in it. Laboring from dawn to dark was not my idea of a good time, even if I had been a man. Still, I love living in the country and growing food. But what farmer wanted a "smart" wife? That was not part of my family's imagined future for me.

My family didn't always see much sense in my ongoing education. 18 When my friends from suburbia wanted to drop out of school and become carpenters, farmers, musicians, their families were horrified. The family of one woman I knew threatened to have her committed to an asylum when she persisted in her desire to do physical labor and live in the country. My family, on the other hand, often said they thought I should go to Nashville and become a country music star. While they saw some sense in going to college for four years, they hoped I would become a teacher at the end of that (one of their few models of educated people, I guess). When I found only menial jobs and then went back to school, they were mystified. To their credit, they were fairly supportive. But, even when I was an undergraduate, they had little money to spare for education, and when I persisted in this system, they told me I was on my own.

Two schools accepted me as a graduate student in folklore; neither 19 could offer any financial assistance. My alma mater offered me a scholarship to get an M.A. in English. It seemed easy to do. I had also figured out a way to deal with their system, I thought, and I was already living in that town. So I deferred folklore for a year and went back to my first school.

Taking four courses a semester didn't daunt me; in fact, I was quite 20 nonchalant about the experience at the time. Nights, I worked at the hotel again, taught some music, and lived cheap (the garden vegetables helped). In twelve months I had an M.A., and it was on to grad schooling folklore in the big city . . . and, at a famous Ivy League school.

Again with some nonchalance, I borrowed money to finance the first 21 year. I was very excited about having found a field that, I thought, expressed my innermost concerns and would provide me with the socially, intellectually acceptable means to bring forth those concerns into the world. The second year, I got a scholarship which paid my tuition; I still had to meet my living expenses. By this time I felt comfortable enough in the city to begin playing music for money. I did this with the new man I had taken up with, a good talker and interesting character, a high school dropout from the Jewish suburban middle class. The rigors of being straight academically were compensated for by the fieldwork I was doing as part of that — I had begun to interview people in my home county about folk medicine.

Active as I was as a graduate student, the methods of academia still 22 seemed alien to me. Although I conceived of my discipline as subversive within the larger intellectual reality of our culture (as did a number of my colleagues, explicitly), on a day-to-day basis, we felt as oppressed by our own discipline as by those disciplines we had come from. The hierarchies and game playing which seemed essential for survival in the system were offensive to me. It also made me sad to see my fellow students so cowed by authority.

I was disillusioned when my discipline (committed at least intellectually   23
to the views of the "folk," the peasants, the poor, the disenfranchised) had to debate whether or not to become involved in political issues. Many folklorists said that an academic group should not have political views. It seemed so obvious to me that we were living in the same world as Phyllis Schlafly, Gloria Steinem[3] and millions of women and should recognize the fact (that mysterious, physical, universal world which we were all part of — although my faith in this had become hazy). *The Journal of American Folklore* published a scholarly article on the involvement of folklorists in the Third Reich. A number of women and I planned a conference on Women and Folklore and boycotted the larger meetings in Utah, which had not ratified the ERA.[4]

During these years I was also playing music three or four nights a   24
week in city and suburban bars. Being in the city was stimulating musically as well as intellectually. I felt that I had finally learned to use my mind, to stretch my abilities. I felt I had finally met large numbers of people who were just as smart and smarter than me, just as talented and more talented musically than me, as crazy, radical, poetic, visionary, anything! In the city I was no longer the eccentric I was at my rural High School. I had finally been to the place where everything was happening and had measured myself against it, had jumped in with both feet and found the water fine. I got comfortable with my abilities and felt less disenfranchised than I ever had. However, at the same time, living in the city and being a graduate student was strenuous and downright dangerous.

The whole process of becoming highly educated was for me a process   25
of losing faith. I was taught not to trust my perceptions, but to refer to the bibliography and the traditions of my field; my original reasons for taking up folklore had been translated into the particulars of twenty courses and many conferences, parties, guest speakers, administrative

[3]*Phyllis Schlafly . . . Gloria Steinem:* Respectively, a prominent opponent of the women's movement and one of its leaders.

[4]*ERA:* the proposed Equal Rights Amendment to the U.S. Constitution, which would formally give women equal legal rights. It has not yet been ratified by enough states to become law.

wranglings, by the interdepartmental feuds and machinations, by papers and newsletters and meetings, by the anger I felt at my discipline's shortcomings and its treatment of women, by the cultivating of professors, by the hairsplitting which is essential in European intellectual culture.

As I did my studies, I also began working by myself in the city. It 26 was an educational and terrifying experience. Fortunately for my financial situation, I was hired to play three nights a week in a little bar/restaurant near the waterfront, near a newly hip section of the city. What I liked most about the place was its mixed clientele: longshoremen, businessmen, beautiful people on dates from center city, gay men and women, artists and craftspeople of every ilk, Catholic Italians from south Philly, and occasionally some of my fellow graduate students. Because I played mostly for tips, I had to learn to communicate musically and verbally with all these people. I enjoyed that challenge and its contrast to the academic world across the river. Crazy as the Left Bank was, I felt at home with the folks there and gained a lot more poise. I also learned how to deal with obnoxious drunks of all ages and classes; and noticed that the whole scene got crazier when the moon was full.

The main drawback to working at the Left Bank and elsewhere as a 27 musician was that I was no longer under a man's protection. Aside from the expected barroom hassles, I often went home alone, and had to park far from my house and walk there — four, five blocks, in the middle of the night. In order to survive, I had to think defensively. That sounds sensible enough, but what that meant was walking home from work every night considering how I might or might not be jumped, robbed or raped. That made me very angry.

Finally, after a few minor street incidents, I tangled with serious crime. 28 I found that my house had been broken into, robbed, and set on fire. I lost cash, instruments, all my clothes, personal belongings, stereo, everything valuable. Most of my papers and all my notes for my dissertation were o.k. The police thought it was the work of a psychopath, but had no clues. My friends and neighbors were freaked out, and so was I. I pulled myself together enough to finish writing a paper and delivered it at the folklore society meetings that month, and then I left the city and my close association with the academic world.

What living in the city and living in the academy have in common, 29 for me, are two things: Both took me closer to the realities of mainstream American culture than I had ever been (you know what I mean: official culture, high culture, the majority consensus of reality; the trappings of the American dream, or depending on your point of view, the "heart of the dragon."); and both were the opposite of what I grew up with, the farthest poles, that I had to explore in seeking what was missing from what I knew. Well, what I discovered (as many people before me) was that what I was searching for didn't exist "out there." Only by coming to terms with my own past, my own background, and seeing that in context of the world at large, have I begun to find my true voice and to understand that, since it is my own voice, that no pre-cut niche exists for it; that part of the work to be done is making a place, with others, where my and our voices can stand clear of the background noise and voice our concerns as part of a larger song.

As I have come to realize this, to come full circle to where I started, I have found more and more people who share some part of my vision. This makes me very hopeful and also makes confronting the realities of America somewhat less grim. I have also come to believe that most people feel like strangers in the world. 30

Specifically, my sense of community comes from both inside and outside the academy. Recently I have found a number of people my age who now have Ph.D.s and are functioning inside universities — often we share some past in the 1960s, some transformation of those concerns and times; and recently I have come to realize that many folklorists come from working class backgrounds. Last year at our annual meetings (which have the character of a festival, family reunion, academic racetrack, business luncheon, and singles bar) I had several conversations with people about coming from "the folk" and how strange academia was, how strange the assumptions of the middle class, and how strange our families found our bet on education (though not necessarily in principle: A number of our families espoused onward and upward). What they found strange was either that we were women doing it, or that the realities of it — years of study, poverty, academic power trips — did not match their image of the dream. One of my fellow graduate students, from a working class English background, had difficulty explaining the ins and outs of academic life to his family until he compared interdepartmental politics to the cutthroat business practices with which his family was familiar. And then they were appalled to realize how similar academics were to the rest of the people. 31

A more positive connection for me, comes from the subject of my field, and my own interests in that field. It's no accident that I've studied the people that I came from. It's their reality I'm trying to describe, to affirm, to give voice to. Doing this gives me great satisfaction, because I can put my intellect (whose restlessness forced me to leave what I knew) and my academic experience (for better or for worse, it's part of me now) to use for the people and the place where my heart lies. 32

When writing my dissertation I lived on my family's farm. Instead of paying rent, I worked in the fields and garden. What I resented as a 33 child, I then enjoyed as a choice that I made; I came to see the positive values in my family's way of life as well as all the negative ones which I had rebelled against. I came to see that those values have been part of me even while I thought I was doing something very different. My folks, too, while they couldn't understand the purpose of my education while I was going through it, enjoyed reading my dissertation (which is about a kind of folk medicine they both know and is written in a style meant to be useful to both academics and the people whom it's about).

I feel the same way about academia; it's like an eccentric member of 34 my family whose company I enjoy at annual reunions and family dinners. My intellect, as well as my background, is a part of me that I can't deny. I would rather give a lecture on mythology for an honorarium than work as a waitress for the same amount of money. (I would also rather play music in smokey bars than work as a factory supervisor for the same amount of money.) I'd rather spend the day writing than driving a tractor, five days a week. I would rather do any of the above than be wife to someone whose support bought my subservience.

What I value and begin to find, even in the academy, is: cooperation, 35 a sense of community, a concern for the disenfranchised, an attempt to lead a balanced life. My first job teaching was at a community college where most of the students majored in forestry, nursery management, horticulture, welding, wood products technology, graphic arts, nursing, etc. I taught freshman composition; a required course, though there were no English majors there. I liked this job because these people were "down to earth." That's how I find myself putting it. What I mean is they came from the same class background as I did. This made me comfortable. I tell myself that I enjoyed these people more than students with pretensions about themselves and their backgrounds, and with illusions about the class value of education. I felt silly, sometimes, teaching them English grammar (I call myself the grammar police) and I felt ambivalent about the fact that it might have enabled them to get on in the system that values education; but I liked to talk to them about writing, about communication, about ideas, about how to write resumes and letters to the editor.

I found it significant that some of my former professors considered 36 this a low class job. But it's all the same to me whether I correct grammar or whether I try to impose some standard of writing style. While I might rather have been talking about some fine points of folklore, still, it was a job; and one way or another, my working class background makes me want to keep working in my second job. It makes me want to survive in this cash economy, and to work to bring forth in the world a voice that speaks for my vision and for the vision of the people and place that

I come from. Those people and that place gave me life, beauty, dreams, and purpose, and to speak for them is the least I can do.

Engaging the Text

1. How would you characterize Wilson's attitudes toward education, work, and family? What role does each play in her life, and how does she keep them in balance?
2. To what extent does her gender enter into or limit her aspirations?
3. What is Wilson "searching for"?

Exploring Connections

1. How accurately does Sennett and Cobb's notion of "hidden injuries" (p. 563) describe the attitudes of Jane Ellen Wilson? What enables Wilson to cope better than Frank Rissarro with the pressures of upward mobility?
2. Compare and contrast the conflicts faced by Richard Rodriguez (Chapter Six, "Grading American Education") and Jane Ellen Wilson in their attempts to balance the demands of home and school. How does each resolve or try to resolve these conflicts?
3. Analyze the ways Malcolm X (Chapter Six, "Grading American Education") and Jane Ellen Wilson shape and are shaped by their educational experiences.

Extending the Critical Context

1. Jane Ellen Wilson says that her family imagined various "futures" for her. What "futures" has your family imagined for you, and how consistent are these expectations with your own goals?

8

Television and the Consumption of Images

In placing this chapter after those on family, education, and work, we have taken the hopeful view that those other institutions influence people more deeply than television does. Yet if you consider that millions of Americans watch TV more than six hours daily, you must acknowledge its enormous potential to affect society. Unlike much of what is written about television, the pieces reprinted here go far beyond a simplistic condemnation of sex and violence. In the first section, they investigate TV's magnetic power; in the second, they examine the interplay of entertainment, artistry, commercialism, and American values.

The first section, The Power of Television, opens with Maurine Doerken's broad overview of the state of American TV and its implications for minorities, children, women, and the population as a whole. Next, Jerry Mander offers a highly unorthodox explanation for the lure of television, suggesting that it has a biological base. The rock lyric "Television Man" and the poem "Homesick in Los Angeles" are markedly different personal responses to the power of television.

"*The Cosby Show*" leads off the second section, Consumerism and TV Culture, and touches on most of its themes: the connections between advertising and programming, the importance or unimportance of race, and the cultural messages communicated to the viewer. In a complementary essay on "post-racism," Martha Bayles warns of misinterpreting the success of comedians like Bill Cosby, Richard Pryor, and Eddie Murphy. "Advertising as Art" presents a complex and intriguing view of commercials

as sophisticated and meaningful art, and Jay Rosen'
same vein interprets the metaphorical messages pr
ments. The chapter and book end with Pat Aufden.
these ideas to a distinct TV culture: music videos.

Before Reading . . .

Write an informal self-analysis of your own TV viewing, covering such
topics as how much, when, and why you watch, how you react to commercials, what kinds of shows you like best, and what problems (if any)
you see in America's TV habits. Compare notes with your classmates.

THE POWER OF TELEVISION

What's Left After Violence and Advertising?
MAURINE DOERKEN

In this selection from the provocatively titled Classroom Combat:
Teaching and Television, *Maurine Doerken (b. 1950) makes a case for
the powerful and dangerous influence television exerts over children.
Pushing beyond the usual debates about violence and advertising, she
argues that TV's escapist fare diminishes social awareness and fosters
passivity and personal isolation. Doerken is currently studying for a
Ph.D. at the University of Southern California.*

Attitudes Toward Entertainment

If the average person on the street were stopped and asked what the   1
three most frequent offerings on American television are (excluding commercials), he would probably answer action/adventure, situation comedy,
and musical/variety talk shows. This same person then most likely would
turn around and classify these all under the rubric "entertainment."

But Shakespearean plays and grand opera are also "entertainment," 2 yet they are hardly the same kind as is usually offered on our TV screens. This is a problem we Americans face when discussing television programming, . . . because we have grown so accustomed to think of TV material as general entertainment when it is, in fact, light fare of a very specific kind. The vast majority of TV offerings in this country have been and continue to be fantasy/escapist entertainment, *not* the entertainment we get from Othello or Beethoven. Some entertainment, to be sure, can be very engaging and very moving without being escapist, but those who organize TV material in America usually give the broad name "entertainment" to what is only a narrow section of the whole. This is not *always* the case, but generally it is.

Consequently, over the past thirty years, viewers have been exposed 3 with great consistency to fantasy/escapist entertainment and a narrowing of tastes to fit "the average," not entertainment of a more serious, thought-provoking kind or one based predominantly on real life. So when we discuss the impact of television on young people, we are talking about the impact of three decades of fantasy/escapist fare. Even during the mid-fifties, light entertainment constituted approximately seventy-five percent of total TV time, and a brief glance at *TV Guide* today hardly reveals much of a change. Escapist entertainment still dominates the screen. In this sense, TV material has become what one broadcast historian calls a strategy word, for it minimizes the importance of what is presented.[1] Rather, entertainment is there to lull our critical faculties by sending us into the domain of low-involvement learning. It has no meaning, essentially, other than diverting and filling time between commercials.

This brings to mind several questions. With such a heavy diet of fantasy 4 material, where are viewers, especially children and adolescents, to receive a comparable amount of reality presentations? Is it better to get a solid footing in reality or fantasy? Or at least an equal grounding in both? These questions are particularly relevant to preliterate youngsters who cannot read to counterbalance what they see and hear, for they are even more susceptible to informal television influence.

The effect of this fantasy/escapist entertainment has to be different 5 in character and kind than if we had had three decades of plays and dramas from renowned writers; a spectrum of musical offerings; fewer commercials; or more quality programming geared specifically toward children. This is self-evident. TV has been promoted as a window to the world, and in many cases, this has been true. But, in many other

[1]Erik Barnouw, *The Sponsor: Notes on a Modern Potentate*, Oxford University Press, New York, 1978, pp. 100–102. [Author's note]

ways, it most certainly has not been so, due to the fantasy material which has dominated the screen. One need only look at American TV entertainment over the past three decades to see what a distorted view has been presented as life.

The Sexes and Racial Groups

As far as men, women, and various racial groups are concerned, television 6 in this country has generally shown the following picture:

1. The most powerful group is the white American male. He usually is young, middle class, and unmarried — and is likely to be involved in violence.
2. Women make up a smaller proportion of all TV characters, regardless of ethnic background. They usually appear in a sexual context or in romantic roles. Two out of three are married or engaged, though this is now changing.
3. Women participate less in violence but are victimized more, and if a woman engages in aggression, she is not as likely to succeed as a man.
4. Women are also cast more frequently in domestic/comedic roles.
5. Married women are less likely to be victims of aggression. Housewives are not portrayed as villains as much as single women or those who are employed.[2]

It was not until 1968 that the first black series was offered over the 7 TV airwaves. A young child growing up with TV during the fifties might have thought that blacks and other minorities did not exist. Not only were many people and races virtually ignored at TV's inception, but when they did appear, they often were presented as unfavorable stereotypes (i.e., Indians as bloodthirsty drunks or Chinese as cooks, servants, and laundry owners). For nearly three decades, television has concentrated on showing the twenty- to fifty-year-olds, thereby ignoring the very young and the elderly. There has been a constant push in the informal learning domain to telescope all age groups into a young adult market, focusing intently on the NOW.

Themes and Format of Programs

Not only has our escapist TV entertainment centered on specific races 8 and ages, implicitly denying the existence of many other people and life styles, but recurring themes and ideas emerge as well. As indicated previously, violence has been a staple on the American TV screen, but

---

[2]Liebert et al., *The Early Window*, pp. 18–19. [Author's note]

Table 1 Comparison of Television Crimes and Real-Life Crimes[3]

FREQUENCY RANKING OF FBI CRIME INDEX FROM 1970	FREQUENCY RANKING OF TV CRIMES FROM 1972
1. Burglary	1. Murder
2. Larceny	2. Assault
3. Auto Theft	3. Robbery
4. Robbery	4. Auto Theft
5. Assault	5. Burglary
6. Rape	6. Larceny
7. Murder	7. Rape

even though it has occurred with mind-boggling regularity as "true-to-life action drama," it still follows the same pattern of unreality. Street crime, for example, has not been as important in the world of TV as it is in real life. Murder and assault have accounted for about fifty percent of all TV crime, yet this is not true of life on the outside. As one can see [in Table 1], almost a complete inversion has taken place.

Generally, crime on American TV has: 9

1. overrepresented violent crimes directed against individuals; real-life crime is usually nonviolent and directed at property;
2. underrepresented blacks, young people, and lower-class individuals involved in crime;
3. reinforced the moral that crime does not pay; the main intent is to reassure society that right will prevail; in the real world, however, this obviously is not so, for crime often pays quite well;
4. concentrated on "the hunt" as being all-important rather than the legal processes involved after apprehension;
5. underrepresented nonwhites as murder victims;
6. underrepresented violent crimes between family members; and
7. made crime motives appear simple and easily understood; in real life, this often is not the case at all.[4]

Quite clearly, this picture has little to do with reality, even though   10
it has been presented as "true" life. Yet, how much misinformation is being assimilated incidentally by children who watch a moderate to heavy amount? How much do they accept at face value? A very false image of

[3]Chart from Joseph R. Dominick, "Crime and Law Enforcement on Prime-Time Television," *Public Opinion Quarterly*, 1973, Vol. 37, pp. 245–246. [Author's note]
[4]Same as above, p. 249. [Author's note]

the world could be in the making, which might be difficult to untangle later on.

TV Employment

Aside from these misrepresentations of various groups and crime in 11 our society, another important aspect of television distortion concerns employment. Not surprisingly, the most frequent form of TV work is law enforcement. Nearly one-third of the American TV labor force at one time or another has been concerned with the pursuit of law and order. In reality, however, only about one percent of the population is so involved. . . . Jobs associated with entertainment rank second in the world of TV, which is hardly true to life either. Professional workers have been overrepresented, and there has always been that push for a higher socioeconomic status — informal messages consistent with the consuming world of TV. A corresponding underrepresentation of worker roles has been evident, though this is changing. As a source of incidental learning for young people about jobs and work, television provides a very slanted view of what is considered important, which could have serious ramifications in children's attitudes regarding employment later on.

A case in point: When a group of children was questioned about work, 12 they overwhelmingly chose *power* as the most important factor to consider when thinking about employment. Money, prestige, and travel came next; helping others was last. The interesting point here is that these results held for both rich and poor children; urban and rural; male and female; dull and bright.[5] Television's influence was pervasive in all areas of society. The fantasy/escapist material had been successful in changing their attitudes and aspirations toward a career.

Is this a form of programmed discontent? Does television teach un- 13 happiness about work in general by presenting a false picture of the way life really *is?* If a child consistently sees powerful or dangerous jobs cast in glamorous settings, what kinds of ideas will he form about what he wants to be? His informal learning from television may be a source of disappointment and conflict when he finally starts to work, for it is not easy to become rich and powerful. In effect, such portrayals take the child away from the ordinary, which is a very real part of living, a part which needs to be met and dealt with often. How might all this influence his evaluation of work or his choice of job opportunities after leaving high school or college?

[5]Melvin DeFleur, "Occupational Roles as Portrayed on Television," *Public Opinion Quarterly*, 1964, Vol. 28, p. 68. [Author's note]

These instances of misrepresentation are but a few examples of how   14
television escapist fare has twisted and turned images of life. All this
may be obvious to the adult viewer, but how the past thirty years have
affected children growing up under TV's powerful, informal gaze is another
matter entirely. We are talking about analyzing human reactions and
emotions in the area of incidental, deferred learning, which certainly is
not an easy task. Yet, the impact of all this may be profound and go
much deeper than many of us suspect. . . .

Personal Isolation and Television

Another important aspect in the conflict of television and children is   15
the personal and emotional isolation fostered by TV. How does this affect
individual growth and development? It must be remembered that when
a child accepts the box as a form of leisure activity or comfort, he turns
away from *people* and all the direct stimulation they provide. His learning
becomes vicarious rather than first-hand; he substitutes something in-
animate for live, direct interaction. TV allows him to escape from personal
involvement by substituting something that *seems* like close contact but
which in fact is not. Some people believe television is the perfect refuge
for those who are unable to cope with life because it acts as solace to
the individual who cannot deal with the outside world. Rather than
encouraging him to face his problems and learn from other people, TV
offers him a place to hide or becomes a way to kill time so he will not
have to cope with reality.

The following case study is a good example of this type of influence   16
and how it can directly alter a child's behavior in school. A little girl
named "Susie" exhibited marked antisocial tendencies in class. She would
not participate in group activities and refused to become involved with
other children. When her teacher discovered that Susie was a heavy TV
viewer, she suggested to the mother that she put her daughter on a TV
diet.

During the first week without TV, Susie was very upset over not being   17
allowed to watch. Her teacher reported that she was moodier than usual
and would sit and stare at the ground. After only one week, however,
changes began to appear. Susie started to ask her mother to invite
playmates over to the house after school. This was something she had
never wanted before, and her teacher also noticed her playing more
with the other children during classtime. By the end of the four weeks,
the youngster no longer was just an outsider but a participant. She played
by herself and with other children, and both mother and teacher thought
her a much happier child. Several weeks later, however, when the girl's
mother allowed her to resume watching television, Susie's previous

Table 2 Amount of Viewing and Personality Characteristics[6]

CHARACTERISTIC	WATCH A GREAT DEAL OF TV	WATCH TV FREQUENTLY	WATCH TV SELDOM
Lonely	95%	5%	0%
Shy	70%	22%	7%
Listless	51%	22%	27%
Pampered	49%	25%	28%
Emotional	39%	39%	22%
Obedient	4%	79%	17%
Has Friends	4%	29%	68%
Active	1%	34%	65%

symptoms returned. She simply refused to interact with other people. There appeared to be a direct relationship between the little girl's social maladjustment and her TV-watching behavior.[7] . . .

There is also the possibility that those who consume large amounts   18 of television may possess certain introverted personality traits which are only reinforced by the medium's tendency to isolate and remove. As one can see [in Table 2], there is evidence to support this claim.

Though television by no means warrants universally adverse effects,   19 among heavy viewers certain patterns do begin to emerge. Like the little girl just mentioned, the heavy user is lonelier, more listless, and shy. On the other hand, children who watch little TV, according to the above figures, are almost the opposite. Nor is it merely the only child or the child whose parents work who is the heavy viewer, but more importantly, the insecure child who has trouble making friends or who feels safer alone than in a group.

Whether television stimulates these personality/emotional tendencies   20 or draws individuals to it who are already predisposed to such traits does not really matter, because the net result is a negative influence on personal development. TV can prevent a child from being lonely, but this is not necessarily good, especially if that child is inclined to shyness in the first place. He should, on the contrary, be encouraged to participate with those around him. In other cases, television may keep children from learning how to be alone and cope with aloneness, both of which

[6]Chart compiled from information in Robert D. Hess and Harriet Goldman, "Parents' Views of the Effects of Television on Their Children," *Child Development*, 1962, Vol. 33, p. 415. [Author's note]
[7]Safran, "How TV Changes Children," p. 17. [Author's note]

represent vital aspects of growth. As psychologist Bruno Bettelheim[8] suggests:

> Children who have been taught, or conditioned, to listen passively most of the day to the warm verbal communication coming from the TV screen . . . are often unable to respond to real persons because they arouse so much *less* feeling than the skilled actor. Worse, they lose the ability to learn from reality because life experiences are more complicated than the ones they see on the screen, and there is no one who comes in at the end to explain it all . . . If this block of solid inertia is not removed, the emotional isolation from others that starts in front of the TV may continue. This . . . is one of the real dangers of TV.[9]

This isolation and lack of personal involvement may lead to an increase in all dependent behaviors and may hamper the development of individuals into people capable of forming their own decisions. . . .

It must be remembered, too, that television's isolating effect has been   21 going on for several decades now. It is not a question of a few random individuals like little Susie holing up with the box, but if the Nielsens[10] are correct, almost an entire nation! This fourteen-year-old's comment states the case well:

> Television is perfect to tune out to the rest of the world. But I don't relate with my family much because we're all too busy watching TV.[11]

Narcotic Dysfunction of Television

This tendency of television to isolate individuals may have further   22 educational and social ramifications. As people substitute watching TV for *doing*, and as they interact less with one another, they cease in a sense being social creatures. They decrease their actual involvement and learning from others and the world around them, though they may vicariously see a great deal. In this way, television acts as a narcotic or drug, as some people have claimed, for it removes people from people by taking real life away. At the flick of the switch, seas of fantasy/escapist material are readily available to pass the time of day.

But by providing the individual, especially the growing child, with so   23

---

[8] *Bruno Bettelheim:* American psychologist and educationist (b. 1903) best known for his work on children and the nature of prejudice.

[9] Martin Mayer, *About Television*, Harper & Row, New York, 1972, p. 128. [Author's note]

[10] *the Nielsens:* the Nielsen rating system — a marketing research service used to measure and rank the popularity of television shows.

[11] "What TV Does to Kids," p. 67. [Author's note]

many escape valves from outside pressures, television may simultaneously stunt the growth of personal and group responsibility. It may provide steady relief from daily life and all the tensions that go along with it; but if used to hide from anxiety or duties, it can also reduce the likelihood of involvement and genuine concern. Using the medium to run away from problems or to put them off indefinitely makes the viewer less aware of troubles that do in fact exist. Continually accepting a dream world or confusing reality with fantasy is not conducive to the development of social consciousness. It is quite possible that gradual changes could result in attitudes and behavior, *away* from individual awareness and public commitment.

The term narcotisizing dysfunction has been coined by psychologists 24
to describe this particular effect of television.[12] Even though the medium exposes us to vast amounts of information, it still may evoke only minimal interest in real social problems, and this could develop into mass apathy. Excessive TV exposure may actually deaden rather than enliven the emotions of the average viewer, because the more time he spends with television, the less time he has for action and work. Similar to the case of excessive violence viewing, a general habituation or desensitization to life's problems may take place. A person might have enormous amounts of material available to him but still fail to make any decisions regarding that information or to act upon his own feelings and instincts.

TV will not necessarily reinforce apathy among those already committed, 25
but it will tend to do so with those who are poor self-starters in the first place. The problem here is that the apathetic generally make up a far larger number of the whole. There are always more people who do not wish to act or who have trouble overcoming their own inertia. Teachers and educators have always been confronted with the problem of student motivation. Yet, however difficult genuine social concern may be to achieve, it does not change the fact that we need a critical, perceptive, and caring citizenry, particularly among the young growing to adulthood. In an age of global politics, social awareness and responsibility toward the whole are crucial to all.

Television certainly has great capacity to foster the development of 26
such attitudes, but something seems to have gone amiss along the way. There can be no doubt, for example, that TV helped to encourage some of the awareness and concern which manifested themselves during the sixties. Some very real and disturbing events found their way onto the

---

[12]See Paul Lazarsfeld and Robert Merton, "Mass Communication, Popular Taste, and Organized Social Action," in *The Process and Effect of Mass Communication*, Schramm and Roberts (Editors), pp. 565ff. [Author's note]

screen, events which have left a deep impression on an entire generation. But perhaps the habit of escaping into fantasy and materialism — also promoted by television — was stronger in the long run than the effort required for continual commitment to social activism. In the short term, TV can inspire concern among people because immediate events are exciting or disturbing. But over longer periods of time, a different pattern may emerge. The preponderance of escapist fare, which allows the viewer to avoid real life or which places material above ideological concerns, may contravene both social and political action. . . .

American Schizophrenia

There are other points to consider in relationship to this narcotisizing 27 aspect of the medium's power. In conjunction with TV's tendency to isolate and its potential for, in effect, drugging people not to care, there is also the real danger of much personal, internal conflict resulting from heavy exposure. Constantly shifting between what is and what is not; between shows, ideas, images, and channels literally is enough to push some people over the "deep end" or to make them nervous temperamentally. So much TV is based upon illusion and fantasy that it becomes very difficult at times to know what is truth and what is not. This is especially true of young children, who have not yet accumulated a vast catalogue of personal experiences against which to evaluate TV content.

One wonders: Is there something inherently jarring and debilitating 28 about the American television experience? The National Institute of Mental Health Report actually cites a study comparing American and foreign TV which suggests this may be so. Foreigners who are accustomed to a much slower pace of television say they find American TV unnerving and experience a kind of physical pain when they first see commercial television in this country. The Report declares:

> The rapid form of presentation characterizing American television in which novelty piles upon novelty in short sequences may well be counterproductive for organized and effective learning sequences. The young child who has not yet developed strategies for tuning out irrelevancies may be especially vulnerable in this respect; even programs that seek to be informative as well as entertaining may miss the mark because they allow too little time for reflection. . . . Extremely rapid-pace material, presenting novelty along with high levels of sound and fast movement, may generate surprise and confusion in a viewer whose anticipatory strategies . . . are not yet prepared for coping with this material.[13]

[13] National Institute of Mental Health Report, p. 20. [Author's note]

All this points to the fact that a very disturbing element of schizophrenia 29
lies at the very heart of American television. On the one hand is a vast
display of random bits of life; on the other is the constant psychic irritation
of rampant consumerism. If mental breakdown is the common result of
endless new patterns of information, then TV in this country certainly
provides agitation in abundance. All the contradictory input could very
well create a widespread state of subconscious confusion. This is most
true for the young, because they generally need reassurance, structure,
and freedom within reason in order to grow and learn at their best.

Yet, how can youngsters possibly analyze and catalogue all that they 30
view on television — especially if their parents do not take the time to
discuss with them what they see? Is television somehow grooming us
for mass nervous disorder and resentment? A pervasive malaise existing
just below the surface of our lives? There is evidence that this is indeed
likely. A survey of fifth- and sixth-grade students, for example, reveals
that many emotional and personal problems suffered by these children,
such as worries about looks, being fat, having bad complexions, and
being accepted by others, all related to the kinds of television they
watched.[14] Moreover, this country's mental hospitals are now overloaded
with young patients, and many children today currently undergo some
form of counseling or private therapy because they seem so unable to
cope with life. There is also growing evidence that many children in the
United States suffer from clinical depression and suicidal tendencies even
though very young.[15]

. . . If we were to construct a picture of the average TV consumer 31
based upon the data presented thus far, the image we come up with is
rather disheartening. The moderate to heavy viewer is somewhat duller,
more materialistic, and less knowledgeable about life. He reads less and
may lack a certain amount of spontaneity and creativity. He is less
interested in the real world and people than in an edited, fantasy version
of life. He may be somewhat shy and introverted; and though he may
crave human contact, he has not had the practice to know how to go
about being a friend. He may even be a personality type bordering at
times on the mildly neurotic and mentally unstable. Or, he simply may
be an inert mass which does not care and is willing to watch life go by.

[14]Schramm *et al.*, *Television in the Lives of Our Children*, p. 119. [Author's note]
[15]*Los Angeles Times*, July 25, 1978, part 1, pp. 1, 17, 18. [Author's note]

Engaging the Text

1. According to Doerken, what general IMAGE of American life does TV convey? Do you agree with this assessment?

2. How, according to Doerken, does TV "program" discontent in viewers?

3. Explain Doerken's claim that TV acts as a narcotic or a drug. What evidence, if any, have you seen that "heavy users" tend to be shy, lonely, and listless?

4. What, according to Doerken, are the social consequences of the escapism promoted by TV? Discuss whether or not she attributes too much influence to TV. How consistent are her statements about the influence of TV?

Exploring Connections

1. How might Doerken explain the role that movies play in Henry Blanton's unhappiness (Chapter One, "American Dreams")?

2. Using Doerken as a point of departure, analyze how TV enters into the mother-child relationship in "A Kid's Guide to Divorce" (Chapter Five, "The Changing Family").

Extending the Critical Context

1. Working in groups, test Doerken's conclusions about what television programs teach us about race, gender, crime, and work. Are the STEREOTYPES she describes still common on TV? What new images, if any, have taken their place?

2. Doerken mentions that what TV *omits* can influence viewers as powerfully as what it presents. Working in groups, survey several evenings of prime-time programming to determine what groups, situations, and values are omitted. Why do you suppose these omissions occur? What message is conveyed by the specific omissions you note?

Artificial Unusualness
JERRY MANDER

In this excerpt, Jerry Mander points out that despite its amazing popular appeal, television is actually an inherently boring medium. According to Mander, TV's limitations — two-dimensionality, fuzzy picture, minimal sensual appeal — cannot compete with the fullness and vividness of real life. TV must make up for this deficit by creating excitement artificially. Mander (b. 1936) has worked for over a decade as an advertising and public relations executive; this passage comes from his book, Four Arguments for the Elimination of Television *(1978).*

Technical limitations . . . conspire to create a . . . deep and . . . 1
serious problem for television: It is inherently boring.

With information confined to only two sensory modes, with sensory 2
synesthesia shifted,[1] with low-definition imagery, with the total loss of context (aura and time), and with viewers whose thought processes are dulled, the producers of television programs begin with a difficult task. How to create interest through a medium that is predisposed to turn people off?

My friend Jack Edelson has put it this way: "It's the most curious 3
thing; when I watch television I'm bored and yet fixated at the same time. I hate what I'm watching and I feel deeply disinterested but I keep watching anyway." His statement was echoed by dozens of letters I have received, and children describe their TV experience in similar terms.

The hypnotic-addictive quality of the medium goes a long way to keep 4
the bored viewer fixated before the screen. So does the fact that our mediated environments don't offer much by way of stimulation. TV is the only action. However, there is much more to this bored fixation than that. Television producers and directors, deeply aware of the inherent limitations of the medium, have developed a vast technology of tricks — a technology of attachment, actually — that can succeed in keeping a viewer engaged despite the lack of any real desire to be watching. Most of the techniques were originally developed by advertising people, who have always had vast amounts of money available for experiments and whose *raison d'être*[2] is to develop technologies to fixate the viewer.

Most of the techniques are rooted in an exploitation and inversion of 5
a single emotionally based human tendency: interest in "highlighted moments."

---

[1] *sensory synesthesia shifted:* Mander is noting that when we watch TV, our senses become "desynchronized" — we see and hear events in the broadcast, but we smell, feel, and taste unrelated stimuli.
[2] *raison d'être:* [French] reason for being; justification for existence.

Instinct to the Extraordinary

I described [earlier in the book excerpted here] the Amazon Indians' 6
means of discovering, understanding, and interacting with their forest
environment. The events that caused them the greatest alarm were the
unique, the out of the ordinary: a broken twig that could not be explained,
or a distant sound that had not been heard before. It is the unusual that
stimulates heightened attention.

You can experience this yourself the next time you're out walking. 7
Whether in a city or in a country meadow, the field of images, sounds,
smells proceeds into you without your particularly noticing them. Then,
an extraordinary event will occur. A bird will dive nearby, a boulder
will roll across the path, a car will screech to a halt. You snap into a
more alert condition, a decision may be required. A thought results.

Obviously being alert to the unusual moment is useful for survival. 8
But aside from survival, the sensory interest in the unusual is a means
toward gaining knowledge and pleasure.

Knowledge is gained by discerning change, by noting the event that 9
is different from all others, by making distinctions and establishing patterns.
The fiftieth time you watch a field of daisies you can still learn something
new about natural form since no two observations are alike. Then there
is the clearly special event: the single ten-foot daisy or the hole appearing
where none had been the day before.

In both cases, the extraordinary induces notation, study, and eventually 10
knowledge. "Sometimes in a field of daisies," one might say, "one daisy
will grow abnormally large." That is knowledge. "It is the same with
bears and foxes." This is a second level of knowledge. "Perhaps animals
are like plants; I must watch for further examples of this." A process of
self-education about planetary patterns has begun. The observation of
differences is at the heart of the knowledge.

The senses are just as attuned to differentiation as the mind. We 11
notice water or someone else's skin against our own because the moment
of the touch is different from the moment before the touch. As the same
touch is repeated over and over, we slowly sink back into automatic pilot. Although there can be comfort and security in the routine and the
repetitive, the most stimulating event is the creative one, the new one.

Television is an exceedingly odd phenomenon. On the one hand it 12
offers non-unique, totally repetitive experience. No matter what is on
television, the viewer is sitting in a darkened room, almost all systems
shut down, looking at light.

But within this deprived, repetitive, inherently boring environment, 13
television producers create the fiction that something unusual is going

on, thereby fixing attention. They do this in two ways: first, by outrageously fooling around with the imagery; second, by choosing content outside of ordinary life, thereby fitting the test of unusualness.

These two tactics combine to create a hierarchy of production standards 14 that in the trade are lumped together as "good television." As we shall see, the term applies more to a quality of manipulation than a quality of content. I shall take these one at a time.

The Bias toward Technique as Replacement of Content

When you are watching television, you are seeing images that are 15 utterly impossible in nature. This in itself qualifies the imagery for your attention, even when the content within the image is nothing you'd otherwise care about. For example, the camera can circle the subject. It can rise above it or go below it. It can zoom in or back away from it. The image can be changed in size or made to fade and reappear. Editors make it possible for a scene in one room to be followed instantly by a scene in another room, or at another time, or another place. Words appear over images. Music rises and falls in the background. Two images or three can appear simultaneously. One image can be superimposed on another on the screen. Motion can be slowed down or sped up.

None of these effects is possible in unmediated imagery. When you 16 lift your eyes from this paper and look around your room, it doesn't become some other room or some other time. It could not possibly do that. Nor does your room circle around you or zoom back away from you. If it did do that, you would certainly pay one hell of a lot of attention to it, just as you would to anything new and unexplained that appeared in your field of vision.

Through these technical events, television images alter the usual, 17 natural imagery possibilities, taking on the quality of a naturally highlighted event. They make it seem that what you are looking at is unique, unusual, and extraordinary.

Attention is stimulated as though something new or important was 18 going on, such as landslides, gigantic boulders, or ten-foot daisies. But nothing unusual is going on. All that's happening is that the viewer is watching television, which is the same thing that happened an hour ago, or yesterday. A trick has been played. The viewer is fixated by a conspiracy of dimmed-out environments combined with artificial, impossible, fictitious unusualness.

To get an idea of the extent to which television is dependent upon 19 technical tricks to maintain your interest, I suggest you try the following experiment, which I call the Technical Events Test.

Put on your television set and simply count the number of times there 20
is a cut, a zoom, a superimposition, a voice-over, the appearance of words on the screen — a technical event of some kind.

You will find it goes something like this. 21

You are looking at a face speaking. Just as you are becoming accustomed 22
to it, there's a cut to another face. (*technical event*) Then there might be an edit back to the first face. (*technical event*) Then the camera might slowly draw back to take in some aspect of a wider scene. (*technical event*) Then the action suddenly shifts outdoors to the street. (*technical event*) Intercut with these scenes might be some other parallel line of the story. It may be a series of images of someone in a car racing to meet the people on that street we have just visited. (*technical event*) The music rises. (*technical event*) And so on.

Each technical event — each alteration of what would be natural 23
imagery — is intended to keep your attention from waning as it might otherwise. The effect is to lure your attention forward like a mechanical rabbit teasing a greyhound. Each time you are about to relax your attention, another technical event keeps you attached.

The luring forward never ceases for very long. If it did, you might 24
become aware of the vacuousness of the content that can get through the inherent limitations of the medium. Then you would be aware of the boredom. If, for example, the camera made no movements and there was no cutting in time and place; if one camera merely sat in one place and recorded the entire length of a conversation, including all the pauses, redundancies, diversions, inaction — the way conversations happen in real life and real time — you would be disinclined to watch for very long. The program would have to be hours long before much of anything happened. Television can't wait for this, so it stimulates your interest technically.

Once you actually try the Technical Events Test you will probably 25
find that in the average commercial television program, there are eight or ten technical events for every sixty-second period. That is, the flow of natural imagery is interrupted eight or ten times every minute, sometimes much more often than that.

You may also find that there is rarely a period of twenty seconds 26
without any sort of technical event at all. That may give you an idea of the extent to which producers worry about whether the content itself can carry your interest.

One can only guess at the effect upon viewers of these hyperactive 27
images, aside from fixating attention on the television set. Dr. Matthew

Dumont,[3] . . . says these technical effects help cause hyperactivity among children. They must surely also contribute to the decline of attention span and the inability to absorb information that comes muddling along at natural, real-life speed.

To be constantly buffeted by bizarre and impossible imagery cannot help but produce stress in viewers. To have one's attention interrupted every ten seconds must jar mental processes that were otherwise attuned to natural, personal informational rhythms in which such interruptions would be literally maddening. 28

Leaving the television set to go outdoors, or to have an ordinary conversation, becomes unsatisfying. One wants action! Life becomes boring, and television interesting, all as a result of a system of technical hypes. 29

Meanwhile, the speed and activity of commercial programming are further exaggerated in advertising. 30

When you try the Technical Events Test on a few thirty- or sixty-second television commercials you will find that advertising has roughly twice the technical action of the already hyped-up programs that the ads interrupt. On the average, a thirty-second commercial will have from ten to fifteen technical events. There is almost never a six-second period without a technical event. What's more, the technical events in advertising have much more dimension than those in the programming. In addition to the camera zooms, pans, rolls, and cuts, they are far more likely to have words flashing on and off the screen, songs going on and off, cartoon characters doing bizarre things, voice-overs, shots from helicopters, and so on. 31

If regular television programming is hard-pressed to maintain your attention without tricks, advertisers have the problem many times over. In regular programming at least there are stories or news, *something* of interest. Within television's limits, regular programming has the option to present relevant content. Advertising content has no inherent interest at all. The content is always the same. The image may be a seascape and the product is beer. Or it may be a landscape and the product is cars. Or it may be a home and the product is coffee. Whatever the setting, the content of advertising is always a sales pitch. There is nothing inherently interesting in this. It is worse than boring; it is annoying. So tricks *must* be used in every advertisement. Maxwell Arnold, a San Francisco advertising man who is one of the industry's few outspoken critics, once told a radio interviewer: "Who the hell would choose to 32

---

[3]*Dr. Matthew Dumont:* a psychiatrist, quoted earlier by Mander, who has studied the connection between TV viewing and hyperactivity.

watch ads if there wasn't something going on aside from the content?" In the absence of interesting content, technical style is the name of the game.

Advertisers spend staggering amounts of money to achieve their technical 33 successes. The average production budget for a minute of advertising is roughly ten times the cost of the average minute of programming. It is not at all unusual for a thirty-second commercial to have a production budget of fifty thousand to one hundred thousand dollars, enough to cover the total costs of many half-hour programs. This money is spent in techniques, and research upon techniques, to obtain your interest where there would otherwise be none. The frequently heard comment, "You know, I sometimes think advertising is the most interesting thing on television," is a testament to the success of these expenditures.

The fact that advertising contains many more technical events per 34 minute than commercial programming is significant from another, more subtle perspective. Advertising starts with a disadvantage with respect to the programming. It must be *more* technically interesting than the program or it will fail. That is, advertising must itself become a highlighted moment compared with what surrounds it.

If advertising failed to work on television, then advertisers would cease 35 to sponsor the programs, leading, at least as things are presently structured, to the immediate collapse of television's economic base. If the programs ever become too interesting, that will be the end of television. The ideal relationship between program and commercial is that the program should be just interesting enough to keep you interested but not so interesting as to actually dominate the ads.

This applies to technique as well as content. On the rare occasion 36 when something real or gripping appears on television — the SLA shoot-out,[4] President Kennedy's funeral, an emergency presidential address — and the viewer is awakened from lethargy by the emergence of *real* highlighted content, as opposed to technique, advertisers make every attempt to cancel their spots. They will say they are doing this because it is in "bad taste" to advertise in such moments.

But when is advertising *not* in bad taste? Do they mean that interrupting 37 people's lives to start hawking products is not rude and offensive behavior at any time? If someone came to your door every night to do that, you would soon call the police. Advertising is always in bad taste. What

---

[4]*SLA shootout:* refers to the 1974 gun battle between Los Angeles police and members of the Symbionese Liberation Army — a self-styled terrorist group that had abducted newspaper heiress Patricia Hearst earlier the same year.

advertisers mean when they use the "bad taste" excuse is that when something really real happens on television, it may affect how well the ad works. In the context of concrete reality, advertising can be understood as vacuous, absurd, rude, outrageous. Advertising can succeed only in an environment in which the real merges with the fictional, and all become semireal with equal tone and undifferentiated meaning. In that context advertising can use its technical tricks to jump forward out of the medium, creating its artificial unusualness. The best environment for advertising is a dull and even one, where *it* can become the highlighted event.

This explains the tendency to sponsor programs that have that quality of even tone, from Walter Cronkite[5] to Archie Bunker[6] to Kojak.[7] They all merge with each other, making an appropriate backdrop for the advertising. In probably the most brilliant article that has ever been written on television ("Sixteen Notes on Television," reprinted in *Literature in Revolution*), Todd Gitlin said: "The commercial is the purpose, the essence; the program is the package." 38

The program is only the excuse to get you to watch the advertising. Without the ads there would be no programs. Advertising is the true content of television and if it does not remain so, then advertisers will cease to support the medium, and television will cease to exist as the popular entertainment it presently is. 39

In Favor of "Alienated" Viewing

The Technical Events Test is extremely subversive to television. This is one reason I have asked you to do it. As people become aware of the degree to which technique, rather than anything intrinsically interesting, keeps them fixed to the screen, withdrawal from addiction and immersion can begin. I have seen this happen with my own children. Once I had put them to the task of counting and timing these technical events, their absorption was never the same. 40

When viewers become alert to the technology being used upon them, they can separate technique from content. With the effects of technique stripped away, the true content of the program has to stand on its own. In the case of advertising, it falls apart. Regular programming also assumes its true worth and it is often even less than you may have imagined was possible. 41

[5]*Walter Cronkite:* (b. 1916), anchorman of *The CBS Evening News* from 1962 to 1981, once voted the "most trusted" man in America.

[6]*Archie Bunker:* bigoted and outspoken central character of *All in the Family*, a popular 1970s situation comedy.

[7]*Kojak:* a popular 1970s TV detective series.

As you become able to pull back out of the immersion in the TV set, 42
you can widen your perceptual environment to again include the room
you are in. Your feelings and personal awareness are rekindled. With
self-awareness emerging you can perceive the quality of sensory deadness
television induces, the one-dimensionality of its narrowed information
field, and arrive at an awareness of boredom. This leads to channel
switching at first and eventually to turning off the set.

Any act that breaks immersion in the fantastic world of television is 43
subversive to the medium, because without the immersion and addiction,
its power is gone. Brainwashing ceases. As you watch advertising, you
become enraged.

The great German dramatist Bertolt Brecht used the term "alienation" 44
to describe this process of breaking immersion. Writing during the early
thirties, Brecht used the term to mean the shattering of theatrical illusion.
By breaking immersion in the fantasy the theater-goer becomes *self-
aware* and attains a mental attitude that allows discernment, criticism,
thought, and political understanding of the material on display. Without
"alienation," involvement is at an unconscious level, the theater-goer
absorbing rather than reflecting and reacting. Brecht argued that becoming
lost or immersed in the words, fantasies, and entertainments of theater
was preparation for similar immersion in words and fantasies of theatrical
leadership: Hitler.

Brecht developed his concept of "alienation" in order to break the 45
form of the theatrical relationship. To accomplish this, he would interrupt
the line of the theatrical action; or have the actors step out of their parts
to speak directly to the audience personally or politically; or add such
elements as placards. In films, he would put words on the screen to
explain the meaning of a scene that might otherwise have been received
as "entertainment," thereby shattering unconscious absorption.

In Brechtian terms, if an actor developed a character in such a way 46
that the audience became absorbed in the character rather than the
meaning of the character, then the actor would have failed. The goal
was that each member of the audience become aware that he or she
is in a theater, that actors are performing, that the characters are created on purpose to convey a message, and that the message applies directly to each person in the audience. In this way, theater had the
capacity to become educational in a revolutionary way, capable of moving
people to action. Without this shattering of illusion, Brecht felt, theater
remains an example of mindless immersion within an autocratic format.
And yet, because theater involves a live public performance, the possi-

bilities for technically created illusion are far fewer than in film or tele-vision.

It is this very quality of "alienation" from the illusion, the experience 47 of self-awareness, that advertisers and program producers go to such lengths to avoid. They may not actually be thinking to themselves: "I have got to keep these viewers hyped and away from boredom or I'll lose them." Instead, they define some production values as "good television" and others as "bad television." They will do anything they can to develop and keep your fixed gaze and total involvement. They've found that technical tricks do better than content because, as we have seen, the content loses too much in the translation through the medium to be engrossing on its own.

However, they *do* also choose content for its immersive and hyperactive 48 value. In addition to shattering your normal perceptual patterns by artificially unusual imagery, dragging your mind and awareness forward, never allowing stasis or calm or a return to self-awareness, producers must also make program choices that fit the process.

The Bias to Highlighted Content: Toward the Peaks, Away from the Troughs

At one end of what we might think of as the spectrum of personal 49 experience, there is the occasional momentous event. Emotionally en-gulfing. Intellectually overpowering. These experiences happen to every-one, but they are relatively rare. Between these "highs," life moves along from routine experience to routine experience, flowing one into the next, developing the overall pattern that is life's true content.

When you sit down in a café with a friend, you don't need to have 50 an orgasm for the experience to be worthwhile. Perhaps nothing will happen in that hour or two. No exclamations of passion. No news of dire events. No shoot-outs at the next table or in the street. Perhaps you will merely converse or watch the passing parade. Perhaps you will explore some obscure detail in your friend's feelings or personal history. Perhaps you will muse about fashion. Most coffeehouse conversations, like the rest of life, will go more or less that way.

Ordinary life contains peaks and valleys of experience, highs and lows, 51 long periods of dormancy, many periods of quiet, indecision, ambiguity, resolution, failed resolution. All of these fit into a wide pattern that is the way life is actually lived. Included within this pattern are occasional highlighted events: great shocks, unexpected eruptions, sudden achieve-ments. Life would be frustrating without such catharsis and excitement, but life would be bizarre and maddening if it had too many of these peak events.

Much of the nervousness in the world today in both individual and 52
national life may be attributable to the density and power of the experiences
that are prearranged for our consumption. Too much happens too fast
to be absorbed and integrated into an overall pattern of experience.

It is no accident that the world outside television has concentrated 53
increasingly on large and cathartic events. All artificial environments and
the consumer life encourage focus on peak events. When nature is
absent, so is natural subtlety. Personal attunement to slower, nature-
based rhythms is obscured. We focus on the "hits" that are provided,
and these reduce more and more to commodities. Every commodity is
advertised as offering a bigger and better and more powerful experience
than the one that preceded it. Since life's experiences have been reduced
to packaged commodities, like the chimpanzee in the lab, that is what
we seek.

Television, in addition to being the prime exponent of the commodity 54
life,[8] makes a direct contribution to distorting life in the direction of
highlighted experiences by choosing its contents to fit this pattern. It is
a technological necessity that it do so.

Since television is such a vague and limited medium, so unlikely to 55
produce much of any response in a viewer, producers must necessarily
divide all content into two distinct categories: peaks and troughs, the
highlighted and the routine, always choosing the former and not the
latter. In this way, the choices in content match the technical bias toward
artificial unusualness and also the tendencies of the wider commodity-
based, artificial environment.

The programming bias is always toward the more vivid, more powerful, 56
more cathartic, more definite, "clean" peaks of content. The result, not
the process. The bizarre, rather than the usual.

[8]*the commodity life:* commercialism or commercial culture, in which all values and
relations have been reduced to economic terms.

Engaging the Text

1. Explain Mander's concept of "highlighted moments." How does he link this
notion to the way we know or recognize something?

2. What relationship does Mander perceive between regular television programming and commercials? Do you agree with his analysis?

3. What, according to Mander, is the value of channel switching? Propose other
possible explanations for this habit.

4. Debate Mander's assertion that, largely because of modern media, we live
in a "hyperactive" culture.

Exploring Connections

1. Compare Mander's analysis of the effects of TV to that offered by Doerken in the previous reading. Are they compatible? Do you find one more persuasive than the other?

Extending the Critical Context

1. Try Mander's "technical events test" yourself on several different kinds of television offerings. Does your experiment support his claims?

2. Examine several popular TV shows to test Mander's theory of highlighted moments and "peaks and troughs." Does the nature of highlighted moments — their intensity and frequency — vary with the general type of show in question (e.g., prime-time drama, "dramedy," soap opera, sitcom, etc.)?

3. Can you find other examples of what Mander calls "hyperactivity" in American culture? To what extent do they seem to be the direct result of TV's influence?

Television Man

DAVID BYRNE

It's not fair to present a rock lyric divorced from its music, so we hope you will be able to find the Talking Heads' Little Creatures *album and listen to "Television Man." Even on their own, though, the lyrics convey a sense of the dreamlike world of the narrator's mind. Songwriter David Byrne (b. 1953) was dubbed "Rock's Renaissance Man" by* Time *magazine in recognition of his innovative work in music videos, New Wave songwriting, modern dance scores, and film.*

I'm looking and I'm dreaming for the first time
I'm inside and I'm outside at the same time
And everything is real
Do I like the way I feel?

When the world crashes in, into my living room   5
Television made me what I am

People like to put the television down
But we are just good friends
(I'm a) television man

I knew a girl, she was a macho man   10
But it's alright, I wasn't fooled for long
This is the place for me
I'm the king and you're the queen

When the world crashes in, into my living room
Television made me what I am   15
People like to put the television down
But we are just good friends
(I'm a) television man

Take a walk in the beautiful garden
Everyone would like to say hello   20
It doesn't matter what you say
Come and take us away

The world crashes in, into my living room
The world crashes in, into my living room
The world crashes in, into my living room   25
The world crashes in, into my living room

And we are still good friends . . . (Television man)
I'm watching everything . . . (Television man)
Television man . . . (Television man)
I'm watching everything . . . (Television man)   30
Television man . . . and I'm gonna say
We are still good friends . . . and I'm trying to be
Watchin' everything . . . and I gotta say
We are still good friends . . . You know the way it is
Television man . . . I've got what you need   35
We are still good friends . . . I know the way you are
Television man . . . I know you're trying to be
Watchin' everything . . . and I gotta say
That's how the story ends.

Engaging the Text

1. These lyrics do not make sense in the way a story does. To help generate responses to this text, break into groups and tackle one STANZA at a time: How might it be connected to television? Start with the following questions:

- What is the mood or TONE of the stanza? Is the SPEAKER apparently calm, excited, happy, amused?
- What IMAGES or language in the stanza might come from television itself. What images or language might describe someone watching TV?

Compare notes with other groups.

2. In the first line the speaker mentions dreaming. In what ways, if any, are the lyrics dreamlike? How might the idea of dreaming help you interpret the song?

3. The Talking Heads' concert film is called *Stop Making Sense*. Is it misguided to try to unravel a rock-and-roll song in the way the above questions suggest?

Exploring Connections

1. Compare the attitudes toward TV expressed in "Television Man" and the poem "Homesick in Los Angeles" (see below).

Extending the Critical Context

1. Write your own poem or song about TV using TV images that in your view capture the essence of the medium.

Homesick in Los Angeles
LAURENCE GOLDSTEIN

Center of the television industry, Los Angeles is an appropriate setting for this reflective poem. The "homesick" of the title gains meaning as Goldstein evokes his sense of loss in a world dominated by reruns, talk shows, and chase scenes. Goldstein (b. 1943), a native Angeleno, is an English professor at the University of Michigan, where he edits the Michigan Quarterly Review.

Overnight storms have unsmogged the mountains.
I can see their half-million-dollar homes

rising like pantheons[1] from the greener scrub.
Here in the basin[2] iceplant gleams under eucalyptus
and bird of paradise[3] so vibrant it seems to take wing.   5
For this twilight the city should become a single eye
observing its own lucent, lost perfection.

Cyclops[4] waits indoors. My parents sleepwatch
as I tiptoe through the fluent chatter
of some latest Zsa Zsa,[5] avoid her emerald eyes,   10
the dizzying abyss of her decolletage.[6]
Everyone must see her new picture, she says,
a high-speed chase and numerous fornications.
Unnoticed, I begin to eavesdrop,
and how can the gaze not rest on her smile?   15

Use has more force than reason.
A Super Chief[7] carried them from Iowa to these shores,
journey I reenacted with toy engines
while they called the stations from Boone to L.A.
Every mile swallowed into this cave of light,   20
gone with orange groves they tasted of in January
and the facade of Tara[8] pointing toward the sea.

Moistened by rain, pink blossoms glisten
between fingers of the jade tree they planted.
It is brighter inside than the glow of any tree.   25
News briefs, reruns that kill an hour or two,
then game shows, a movie, and later news.
Every four minutes merchandise bullies them.
Mother and father, how shall I wield my love
against the raucous cannibal of this house?   30

---

[1]*pantheons:* originally, Greek temples for the gods; here referring to buildings designed
to imitate Greek architecture.
[2]*basin:* the natural geographical basin formed by the intersection of several mountain
ranges surrounding Los Angeles.
[3]*bird of paradise:* a waxy, extremely colorful tropical plant common in Los Angeles.
[4]*cyclops:* a man-eating, one-eyed giant in Greek mythology.
[5]*Zsa Zsa:* Zsa Zsa Gabor, a glamorous Hollywood and TV celebrity.
[6]*decolletage:* the low-cut neckline of a dress.
[7]*Super Chief:* a passenger train.
[8]*Tara:* the O'Hara family plantation in Margaret Mitchell's novel, *Gone with the Wind.*

Engaging the Text

1. State in one or two sentences the main idea of each STANZA, even if some details remain puzzling.

2. What is the SPEAKER's attitude toward TV, and how does it differ from his parents' attitude? What details in the poem support your conclusions?

3. The speaker seems to have grown up in Los Angeles. If that is true, how can you explain the title?

4. Goldstein refers to many southern Californian plants and trees: iceplant, eucalyptus, bird of paradise, orange, and jade trees. What is the effect of these references? How do they relate to the idea of television?

5. Analyze the IMAGE of the "raucous cannibal" in the last line. Why is each of these words appropriate?

Exploring Connections

1. To what extent would Goldstein agree with Doerken's analysis of TV's impact on the viewer earlier in this chapter?

2. Use Mander's idea of "artificial unusualness" to analyze this poem. Does the term apply to more than TV itself here?

CONSUMERISM AND TV CULTURE

The Cosby Show
MARK CRISPIN MILLER

One of the most popular sitcoms in television history, The Cosby Show *has been praised for bringing a new realism to TV comedy, reaffirming family values, showcasing black talent, promoting black culture, while still attracting a large mainstream white audience. Mark Crispin Miller sees another picture: In this selection from a much longer essay, he castigates* Cosby *for promoting shallow consumerism, authoritarian family structures, and black stereotypes. Is there a real* Cosby Show *or does it just reflect what you want to see? Miller (b. 1949) directs the Film Studies Program at Johns Hopkins University and has published many articles on TV and popular culture. His latest book is* Boxed In: The Culture of TV.

Cosby is today's quintessential[1] TV Dad — at once the nation's best-   1
liked sitcom character and the most successful and ubiquitous of celebrity pitchmen. Indeed, Cosby himself ascribes his huge following to his appearances in the ads: "I think my popularity came from doing solid 30-second commercials. They can cause people to love you and see more of you than in a full 30-minute show." Like its star, *The Cosby Show* must owe much of its immense success to advertising, for this sitcom is especially well attuned to the commercials, offering a full-scale confirmation of their vision. The show has its charms, which seem to set it well apart from TV's usual crudeness; yet even these must be considered in the context of TV's new integrity.

On the face of it, the Huxtables' milieu is as upbeat and well stocked   2
as a window display at Bloomingdale's,[2] or any of those visions of domestic happiness that graced the billboards during the Great Depression. Everything within this spacious brownstone[3] is luminously clean and new, as if it had all been set up by the state to make a good impression on a group of visiting foreign dignitaries. Here are all the right commodities — lots of bright sportswear, plants and paintings, gorgeous bedding, plenty of copperware, portable tape players, thick carpeting, innumerable knickknacks, and, throughout the house, big, burnished dressers, tables, couches, chairs, and cabinets (Early American yet looking factory-new). Each week, the happy Huxtables nearly vanish amid the porcelain, stainless steel, mahogany, and fabric of their lives. In every scene, each character appears in some fresh designer outfit that positively glows with newness, never to be seen a second time. And, like all this pricey clutter, the plots and subplots, the dialogue and even many of the individual shots reflect in some way on consumption as a way of life: Cliff's new juicer is the subject of an entire episode; Cliff does a monologue on his son Theo's costly sweatshirt; Cliff kids daughter Rudy for wearing a dozen

[1]*quintessential:* the most perfect embodiment of something; the purest form of something.
[2]*Bloomingdale's:* an exclusive New York-based department store.
[3]*brownstone:* a multistory row house, typically built of reddish-brown stone.

wooden necklaces. Each Huxtable, in fact, is hardly more than a mobile display case for his/her momentary possessions. In the show's first year, the credit sequence was a series of vivid stills presenting Cliff alongside a shiny Dodge Caravan, out of which the lesser Huxtables then emerged in shining playclothes, as if the van were their true parent, with Cliff serving as the genial midwife to this antiseptic birth. Each is routinely upstaged by what he/she eats or wears or lugs around: In a billowing blouse imprinted with gigantic blossoms, daughter Denise appears, carrying a tape player as big as a suitcase; Theo enters to get himself a can of Coke from the refrigerator, and we notice that he's wearing both a smart beige belt *and* a pair of lavender suspenders; Rudy munches cutely on a piece of pizza roughly twice the size of her own head.

As in the advertising vision, life among the Huxtables is not only well 3 supplied, but remarkable for its surface harmony. Relations between these five pretty kids and their cute parents are rarely complicated by the slightest serious discord. Here affluence is magically undisturbed by the pressures that ordinarily enable it. Cliff and Clair, although both employed, somehow enjoy the leisure to devote themselves full-time to the trivial and comfortable concerns that loosely determine each episode: a funeral for Rudy's goldfish, a birthday surprise for Cliff, the kids' preparations for their first day of school. And daily life in this bright house is just as easy on the viewer as it is (apparently) for Cliff's dependents: *The Cosby Show* is devoid of any dramatic tension whatsoever. Nothing happens, nothing changes, there is no suspense or ambiguity or disappointment. In one episode, Cliff accepts a challenge to race once more against a runner who, years before, had beaten him at a major track meet. At the end, the race is run, and — it's a tie!

Of course, *The Cosby Show* is by no means the first sitcom to present 4 us with a big, blissful family whose members never collide with one another, or with anything else; *Eight Is Enough*, *The Brady Bunch*, and *The Partridge Family* are just a few examples of earlier prime-time idylls.[4] Here are, however, some crucial differences between those older shows and this one. First of all, *The Cosby Show* is far more popular than any of its predecessors. It is (as of this writing) the top-rated show in the United States and elsewhere, attracting an audience that is not only vast, but often near fanatical in its devotion. Second, and stranger still, this show and its immense success are universally applauded as an exhilarating sign of progress. Newspaper columnists and telejournalists routinely deem *The Cosby Show* a "breakthrough" into an unprecedented

---

[4]*idylls:* short poems or prose works depicting the pleasant simplicity of rural life; in general terms, an ideal situation.

realism because it uses none of the broad plot devices or rapid-fire gags that define the standard sitcom. Despite its fantastic ambience of calm and plenty, *The Cosby Show* is widely regarded as a rare glimpse of truth, whereas *The Brady Bunch* et al., though just as cheery, were never extolled in this way. And there is a third difference between this show and its predecessors that may help explain the new show's greater popularity and peculiar reputation for progressivism: Cliff Huxtable and his dependents are not only fabulously comfortable and mild, but also noticeably black.

Cliff's blackness serves an affirmative purpose within the ad that is 5 *The Cosby Show*. At the center of this ample tableau, Cliff is himself an ad, implicitly proclaiming the fairness of the American system: "Look!" he shows us. "Even *I* can have all this!" Cliff is clearly meant to stand for Cosby himself, whose name appears in the opening credits as "Dr. William E. Cosby, Jr., Ed.D." — a testament both to Cosby's lifelong effort at self-improvement, and to his sense of brotherhood with Cliff. And, indeed, Dr. Huxtable is merely the latest version of the same statement that Dr. Cosby has been making for years as a talk show guest and stand-up comic: "I got mine!" The comic has always been quick to raise the subject of his own success. "What do I care what some ten-thousand-dollar-a-year writer says about me?" he once asked Dick Cavett. And on *The Tonight Show* a few years ago, Cosby told of how his father, years before, had warned him that he'd never make a dime in show business, "and then he walked slowly back to the projects. . . . Well, I just lent him forty thousand dollars!"

That anecdote got a big hand, just like *The Cosby Show*, but despite 6 the many plaudits for Cosby's continuing tale of self-help, it is not quite convincing. Cliff's brownstone is too crammed, its contents too lustrous, to seem like his — or anyone's — own personal achievement. It suggests instead the corporate showcase which, in fact, it is. *The Cosby Show* attests to the power, not of Dr. Cosby/Huxtable, but of a consumer society that has produced such a tantalizing vision of reality. As Cosby himself admits, it was not his own Algeresque[5] efforts that "caused people to love" him, but those ads put out by Coca-Cola, Ford, and General Foods — those ads in which he looks and acts precisely as he looks and acts in his own show.

Cosby's image is divided in a way that both facilitates the corporate 7 project and conceals its true character. On the face of it, the Cosby style is pure impishness. Forever mugging and cavorting, throwing mock tantrums or beaming hugely to himself or doing funny little dances with

[5]*Algeresque:* reminiscent of the writings of Horatio Alger (1834–1899), a U.S. novelist whose rags-to-riches tales of success were popular at the turn of the century.

his stomach pushed out, Cosby carries on a ceaseless parody of some euphoric eight-year-old. His delivery suggests the same childish spontaneity, for in the high, coy gabble of his harangues and monologues there is a disarming quality of baby talk. And yet all this artful goofiness barely conceals an intimidating hardness — the same uncompromising willfulness that we learn to tolerate in actual children (however cute they may be), but which can seem a little threatening in a grown-up. And Cosby is indeed a most imposing figure, in spite of all his antics: a big man boasting of his wealth, and often handling an immense cigar.

It is a disorienting blend of affects, but it works perfectly whenever 8 he confronts us on behalf of Ford or Coca-Cola. With a massive car or Coke machine behind him, or with a calculator at his fingertips, he hunches toward us, wearing a bright sweater and an insinuating grin, and makes his playful pitch, cajoling us to buy whichever thing he's selling, his face and words, his voice and posture all suggesting this implicit and familiar come-on: "Kitchy-koo!" It is not so much that Cosby makes his mammoth bureaucratic masters seem as nice and cuddly as himself (although such a strategy is typical of corporate advertising); rather, he implicitly assures us that *we* are nice and cuddly, like little children. At once solicitous and overbearing, he personifies the corporate force that owns him. Like it, he comes across as an easygoing parent, and yet, also like it, he cannot help but betray the impulse to coerce. We see that he is bigger than we are, better known, better off, and far more powerfully sponsored. Thus, we find ourselves ambiguously courted, just like those tots who eat up lots of Jell-O pudding under his playful supervision.

Dr. Huxtable controls his family with the same enlightened deviousness. 9 As widely lauded for its "warmth" as for its "realism," *The Cosby Show* has frequently been dubbed "the *Father Knows Best* of the eighties." Here again (the columnists agree) is a good strong Dad maintaining the old "family values." This equation, however, blurs a crucial difference between Cliff and the early fathers. Like them, Cliff always wins; but this modern Dad subverts his kids not by evincing the sort of calm power that once made Jim Anderson[6] so daunting, but by seeming to subvert himself at the same time. His is the executive style, in other words, not of the small businessman as evoked in the fifties, but of the corporate manager, skilled at keeping his subordinates in line while half concealing his authority through various disarming moves: Cliff rules the roost through teasing put-downs, clever mockery, and amiable shows of helpless bafflement. This Dad is no straightforward tyrant, then, but the playful

[6]*Jim Anderson:* father's name in the early TV series *Father Knows Best*.

type who strikes his children as a peach, until they realize, years later, and after lots of psychotherapy, what a subtle thug he really was.

An intrusive kidder, Cliff never fails to get his way; and yet there is 10
more to his manipulativeness than simple egomania. Obsessively, Cliff sees to it, through his takes and teasing, that his children always keep things light. As in the corporate culture and on TV generally, so on this show there is no negativity allowed. Cliff's function is therefore to police the corporate playground, always on the lookout for any downbeat tendencies.

In one episode, for instance, Denise sets herself up by reading Cliff 11
some somber verses that she's written for the school choir. The mood is despairing; the refrain, "I walk alone . . . I walk alone." It is clear that the girl does not take the effort very seriously, and yet Cliff merrily overreacts against this slight and artificial plaint as if it were a crime. First, while she recites, he wears a clownish look of deadpan bewilderment, then laughs out loud as soon as she has finished, and finally snidely moos the refrain in outright parody. The studio audience roars, and Denise takes the hint. At the end of the episode, she reappears with a new version, which she reads sweetly, blushingly, while Cliff and Clair, sitting side by side in their high-priced pajamas, beam with tenderness and pride on her act of self-correction:

> My mother and my father are my best friends.
> When I'm all alone, I don't have to be.
> It's because of me that I'm all alone, you see.
> Their love is real. . . .
>
> Never have they lied to me, never connived me,
> talked behind my back.
> Never have they cheated me.
> Their love is real, their love is real.

Clair, choked up, gives the girl a big warm hug, and Cliff then takes 12
her little face between his hands and kisses it, as the studio audience bursts into applause.

Thus, this episode ends with a paean[7] to the show itself (for "their 13
love" is *not* "real," but a feature of the fiction), a moment that, for all its mawkishness, attests to Cliff's managerial adeptness. Yet Cliff is hardly a mere enforcer. He is himself also an underling, even as he seems to run things. This subservient status is manifest in his blackness. Cosby's blackness is indeed a major reason for the show's popularity, despite his frequent claims, and the journalistic consensus, that *The Cosby Show*

[7]*paean:* a poem or song of praise.

is somehow "colorblind," simply appealing in some general "human" way. Although whitened by their status and commodities, the Huxtables are still unmistakably black. However, it would be quite inaccurate to hail their popularity as evidence of a new and rising amity between the races in America. On the contrary, *The Cosby Show* is such a hit with whites in part because whites are just as worried about blacks as they have always been — not blacks like Bill Cosby, or Lena Horne, or Eddie Murphy, but poor blacks, and the poor in general, whose existence is a well-kept secret on prime-time TV.

And yet TV betrays the very fears that it denies. In thousands of high-security buildings, and in suburbs reassuringly remote from the cities' "bad neighborhoods," whites may, unconsciously, be further reassured by watching not just Cosby, but a whole set of TV shows that negate the possibility of black violence with lunatic fantasies of containment: *Diff'rent Strokes* and *Webster*, starring Gary Coleman and Emmanuel Lewis, respectively, each an overcute, miniaturized black person, each playing the adopted son of good white parents. Even the oversized and growling Mr. T, complete with Mohawk, bangles, and other primitivizing touches, is a mere comforting joke, the dangerous ex-slave turned comic and therefore innocuous by campy excess; and this behemoth too is kept in line by a casual white father, Hannibal Smith, the commander of the A-Team, who employs Mr. T exclusively for his brawn. 14

As a willing advertisement for the system that pays him well, Cliff Huxtable also represents a threat contained. Although dark-skinned and physically imposing, he ingratiates us with his childlike mien and enviable life-style, a surrender that must offer some deep solace to a white public terrified that one day blacks might come with guns to steal the copperware, the juicer, the microwave, the VCR, even the TV itself. On *The Cosby Show*, it appears as if blacks in general can have, or do have, what many whites enjoy, and that such material equality need not entail a single break-in. And there are no hard feelings, none at all, now that the old injustice has been so easily rectified. Cosby's definitive funny face, flashed at the show's opening credits and reproduced on countless magazine covers, is a strained denial of all animosity. With its little smile, the lips pursed tight, eyes opened wide, eyebrows raised high, that dark face shines toward us like the white flag of surrender — a desperate look that no suburban TV Dad of yesteryear would ever have put on, and one that millions of Americans today find indispensable. 15

By and large, American whites need such reassurance because they are now further removed than ever, both spatially and psychologically, from the masses of the black poor. And yet the show's appeal cannot be explained merely as a symptom of class and racial uneasiness, because 16 there are, in our consumer culture, anxieties still more complicated and pervasive. Thus, Cliff is not just an image of the dark Other capitulating to the white establishment, but also the reflection of any constant viewer, who, whatever his/her race, must also feel like an outsider, lucky to be tolerated by the distant powers that be. There is no negativity allowed, not anywhere; and so Cliff serves both as our guide and as our double. His look of tense playfulness is more than just a sign that blacks won't hurt us; it is an expression that we too would each be wise to adopt, lest we betray some devastating sign of anger or dissatisfaction. If we stay cool and cheerful, white like him,[8] and learn to get by with his sort of managerial acumen, we too, perhaps, can be protected from the world by a barrier of new appliances, and learn to put down others as each of us has, somehow, been put down.

Such rampant putting-down, the ridicule of all by all, is the very essence of the modern sitcom. Cliff, at once the joker and a joke, infantilizing others and yet infantile himself, is exemplary of everybody's status in the sitcoms, in the ads, and in most other kinds of TV spectacle (as well as in the movies). No one, finally, is immune. 17

[8]*white like him:* an allusion to *Black Like Me*, the 1961 account by John H. Griffin, a white reporter who underwent surgical treatment so that he could pass for black and document racial segregation in the South.

Engaging the Text

1. Briefly summarize Miller's thoughts about Cosby's IMAGE, the corporate culture he represents, and his observations about the show and race relations. How persuasive do you find his arguments?

2. Find all the comparisons and ANALOGIES in paragraph 2. How fair and accurate are these comparisons? To what extent does the argument here depend on our accepting these analogies at the outset?

3. Is Miller attacking Cosby? Explain. How might Cosby respond to Miller's observations?

4. Pinpoint Miller's assumptions about the nature of U.S. society today. What evidence does he cite to support his view? Do you think his assumptions are accurate? Cite more examples to support his point of view, or find counterexamples.

Exploring Connections

1. Read or review the selections by Gordon Allport (Chapter Two, "Justice for All") and Kwame Toure (Chapter Three, "One Nation or Many?"). Where do the Huxtables stand on the spectrum from "Anglo conformity" to SEPARATISM?

Support your answer with specific evidence from one or more episodes of *The Cosby Show.*

2. To what extent does the Huxtable family reflect the values and tensions Arlene Skolnick (p. 347) associates with contemporary families?

3. Compare and contrast Dr. Huxtable and "Willie" (Chapter Seven, "Making a Living") in terms of how their work is related to their identities, their roles in their families, and their connection to a wider community.

Extending the Critical Context

1. Watch one episode of *The Cosby Show* and use it to test Miller's claims. It will help to write out Miller's main points on an "observation sheet" before starting to watch. Compare observations with classmates and then write an essay based on your analysis.

2. Miller disagrees with critics who praise *The Cosby Show* for being more realistic than most TV comedies. Watch an episode and write a short analysis of what elements of the show seem true to life and which seem unrealistic. To get a better perspective on the show, you might compare it to another family sitcom like *Family Ties.*

The Problem with Post-Racism

Martha Bayles

Martha Bayles reminds us that the phenomenal success of The Cosby Show *is, in one sense, nothing new. Her discussion of "crossover" entertainers — black musicians and comedians who attract large numbers of white fans — points to some very early historical precedents. She is skeptical of the argument that modern crossovers herald a color-blind era of "post-racism," and critiques the idea that mass appeal necessarily compromises the ethnic identities of the performers themselves. Bayles (b. 1948) serves as TV critic for the* Wall Street Journal.

Many years ago, before Eddie Murphy, Richard Pryor, or even Bill   1
Cosby were born, there were black comedians who made a splash with the white folks. One of these, Bert Williams, got top billing in the

Ziegfeld Follies,[1] made movies and records, and appeared before the king of England. Williams died in 1922, but if TV had been invented in his lifetime, who knows? He and his partner, George Walker, might have shuffled their way into America's living rooms, wearing blackface and calling themselves "Two Real Coons."

Williams and Walker added the word "real" to emphasize that their 2 "coon show" was being performed by black men, not white. Without it, the audience might not have been able to tell, because both black and white minstrel performers[2] were expected to apply the same burnt cork and engage in the same outlandish burlesque[3] of black life. Needless to say, in such a context the word "real" takes on ironic reverberations — which only increase when we recall that it was Bert Williams's stated desire "to stop doing piffle and interpret the *real* Negro on stage." Of course, in those days it was fairly simple to distinguish between the piffle and the real. Or so it must have seemed to Williams when his only appearance without burnt cork — as a song-and-dance man in the 1914 movie *Darktown Jubilee* — provoked whites into starting a race riot.

Nowadays the distinction is a lot muddier, because wave after wave 3 of black performers has broken through the barriers that once separated black taste from white. Not only that, but since the 1920s there have been countless "crossover" black musicians and comedians whose popularity among whites has been facilitated by the technology of private consumption. (It's one thing for whites to absorb the forms of black culture through records and TV, quite another for them to go out and rub elbows with real blacks.) Cinema occupies an interesting middle ground; most objections to blacks in film have been raised by distributors and theater owners concerned about attracting the wrong racial mix to their theaters.

It's hardly surprising, given this divergence between the private-cultural 4 and the public-social experiences of white Americans, that their racial attitudes would diverge as well. I first noticed this back in the 1960s, when an acquaintance insisted that the Temptations[4] were the best musical group of all time. When asked if she'd ever seen them live, she replied that I must be kidding. She went to one concert, she said, but left right away, because she felt uncomfortable in a crowd that was predominantly black.

---

[1]*Ziegfeld Follies:* an enormously popular theatrical variety show early in this century famous for its "Ziegfeld Girls."

[2]*minstrel performers:* performers in minstrel shows — musical comedy shows that featured white performers in black makeup.

[3]*burlesque:* parody; a comically exaggerated imitation.

[4]*Temptations:* a Motown group that reached stardom in the 1960s with recordings of "My Girl" and "The Way You Do the Things You Do."

Such paradoxical reactions are quite common, but it is rare to see   5
critics acknowledge them. Perhaps to make themselves feel important,
pop-cultural pundits of all stripes claim a direct causal relation between
the screen and the street. They forget that white America has been
grooving on its black entertainers since Day One; and that since Day
Two, some critics have declared this to be proof that white racism has
gone the way of the dodo bird, while others (including most blacks) have
looked, in ever more sophisticated ways, for those telltale signs of burnt
cork. Neither side wants to give up the high ground of social-cultural
analysis and admit the simple fact that whites can genuinely appreciate
black cultural styles without necessarily acquiring new sympathy or liking
for their black fellow citizens.

Now a new wave of black superstars is enthralling white America   6
through its VCRs and laser disk players, and the pundits are carrying
on the same old debate about what it all means. From the optimistic
right, Richard Grenier proclaims (in *Commentary* and the *New York
Times*) that "God created Eddie Murphy" to tickle the funny bone of
mass white audiences who are tired of being made to feel guilty about
a "racist America," which "has not existed for many years now, and is,
indeed, a piece of liberal mythology." A similar optimism radiates from
the *Washington Post* film critic Paul Attanasio, who watches a slew of
black-oriented movies (*Purple Rain, Beverly Hills Cop, A Soldier's Story,*
and *The Last Dragon*) and deduces that race is no longer fate, but fashion.
"Racial flair," he rhapsodizes, is now "a species of attire attractively
displayed in the great Bloomingdale's[5] of the soul . . . you can, on any
given day, be black or Chinese or Italian, regardless of birthright. Race
isn't indelible, but it isn't flattened, either; it's freed from genes and
made available to the will, as the rootedness of racial style evanesces[6]
in absurdity."
I can just picture young Mr. Attanasio evanescing his way into Wash-   7
ington's countercultural Adams-Morgan neighborhood,[7] where his racial
flair can blend with that of his exotic black brethren. Too bad he doesn't
admit the continuing hothouse nature of the experiment — the fact that
evanescing is a whole lot easier in a trendy Ethiopian restaurant than
among the unemployed men drinking paper-sack cocktails three blocks
east of the *Post*. By these lights, the Motion Picture Academy needs a
new rating: not PG or R but PR, for "post-racist."

[5]*Bloomingdale's:* an exclusive New York-based department store.
[6]*evanesces:* fades from sight like mist; vanishes.
[7]*Adams-Morgan neighborhood:* an inner-city area in Washington, D.C.

Meanwhile, back on the left, the phenomenon of black "crossover" 8
appeal is interpreted more gloomily. A recent *Village Voice* article lambastes
Eddie Murphy for being a "Reagan Court Jester" who "drifts right into
homophobia and racism." Unlike Richard Pryor, whose authentically
black humor is described as coming out of "memories of a wretched
childhood" that put him "nose-to-nose with the system," Murphy is a
"defiantly shallow . . . suburban kid" whose chief motivation is to be
loved and accepted by whites. What Grenier admires — Murphy's ability
to distance himself from the clichés of black protest humor — the *Voice*
abhors as craven cultural oreoism.[8]

None of this would matter if the public could just go on enjoying the 9
superstars' latest super-games: Murphy as Jesse Jackson crooning a de-
wop version of "Good Old Hymietown"; Bill Cosby making gentle fun
of the only white tot at a slumber party; Prince and Michael Jackson
pumping out their music while dressing like extras from *Amadeus*.[9] But
the critics' worldview is not just the critics'. It is a powerful myth, shared
by many performers, which decrees that widespread white acceptance
of a black act can mean only one of two things: either the act is a coon
show, or another breakthrough has occurred in American race relations.

Stuck with this dilemma, black performers can react in just a few 10
ways. Those who live a sheltered life, like Jackson and his sweetness-
and-light predecessor, Stevie Wonder, talk a lot about "love." Obviously
they don't see themselves as cultural oreos (nor should they), so they
harp on the post-racist theme. As Jackson gushed recently to *Ebony*:
"an artist can be built up so big in his career that this could change the
whole world. . . . That's why it's so important to give off love vibes."

Stars more in touch with reality, like Richard Pryor, go for the other 11
horn of the dilemma and torment themselves about losing their blackness
and becoming old-fashioned clowns for the white folks. Before his recent
burning accident,[10] Pryor had a tendency (no doubt exacerbated by drugs
and alcohol) toward bursts of violent temper over real or imagined racial
slurs. And unlike Murphy, he rarely made allowances in his comedy
routines for the presence of hip white fans who appreciate even his
saltiest life-in-the-ghetto vignettes. Instead he won the hearts of the
Village Voice crowd by hammering away at the twin stereotypes of the

[8]*oreoism:* Oreo cookies are black outside, white inside; hence, a derogatory term for
the adoption by blacks of white values and attitudes. (See also "cultural oreo" in paragraph
10.)

[9]*Amadeus:* Peter Shaffer's 1981 play based on the life of celebrated composer Wolfgang
Amadeus Mozart (1756–1791).

[10]*recent burning accident:* refers to the 1980 drug-related accident that hospitalized
comedian Richard Pryor.

brutish redneck and the prissy white liberal. Since his injury, he has been producing a Saturday morning children's TV program, which suggests that he may be switching over to the "love" mode. Still, I wonder if he will ever get rid of that deep-seated black performer's instinct to prove he's not wearing blackface by expressing hostility toward whites.

The other way of proving authentic blackness is obscenity. If the quip is true about the British army, that within its ranks the word "fucking" signifies nothing more than the approach of a noun, then Pryor could teach the soldiers a few things about verbs, adjectives, adverbs, and prepositions. And it's not just parts of speech; he makes long, graphic speeches about parts. Eddie Murphy does the same thing, although Grenier tries to minimize this aspect of his humor when claiming him for "post-racist America." Grenier misquotes Murphy's parting shot at last year's concert at Washington's Constitution Hall, which he delivered after reminding the audience that Marian Anderson[11] had not been allowed to perform there 30 years before: "Here we are, not even 50 years later, a 22-year-old black man on stage. . . . God bless America!" Fill in Grenier's decorous ellipsis, and you have Murphy's actual comment: "Here we are, not even 50 years later, a black man on stage holding his dick. God bless America!"

They may not affect the patriotism, but those three words, "holding his dick," turn Murphy from an Eagle Scout back into a raunchy comedian. They also restore a certain edge to his blackness, placing him in a tradition dating back through Redd Foxx[12] to the Apollo Theater's[13] legendary "Pigmeat" Markham.[14] Whites have their own bawdy traditions, but there was a time when blacks and whites did not enjoy sexual humor in each other's company. This is still true to the extent that whites feel uncomfortable with immoderate blue humor delivered by blacks, especially when it is tinged with braggadocit. Black performers know this perfectly well, and increase the dose of obscenity — along with hostility — whenever they wish to appear more "black."

Unfortunately, self-definition in these terms has the potential of leaving black performers with little to call their own except sex and anger. I don't care how expertly these topics are handled; it's pathetic to see the

[11]*Marian Anderson:* American opera star (b. 1902); first black singer to perform at the Metropolitan Opera in New York.
[12]*Redd Foxx:* black American comedian (b. 1922); star of the 1970s television series *Sanford and Son.*
[13]*Apollo Theater:* famed Harlem theater, a showcase for black American entertainers since 1934.
[14]*"Pigmeat" Markham:* black comic actor and pantomime artist who performed regularly at the Apollo in the 1930s.

culture of black Americans reduced to obscenity and hostility, as if these constituted its pure essence or core. Yet there are a great many pundits and performers who take precisely this view, for the simple reason that obscenity and hostility have become isolated, over the years, as those ingredients of black expression most likely to offend whites.

Of course, thanks to increasing levels of private consumption, this   15
offense has been rapidly lessening. Today's MTV-addicted young whites feel perfectly comfortable when Prince licks the microphone, or Murphy boasts about his "dick." As for the hostility, I will grant that the angle of attack has narrowed. These young black performers make a generous allowance for sophisticated whites who know how to dig this riff or that routine. But they are just as merciless as ever toward the unhip, the uptight — the *honky*. Just look at the incredible arrogance Murphy displays in his movies.

Which brings us to Bill Cosby, who reigns over the largest white   16
audience of all — watchers of prime-time network television. Perhaps because Cosby has never gotten stuck on a dilemma about the social or artistic implications of his enormous popularity, he has been able to lift an entire network (NBC) into second place over ABC, which is still (along with CBS) gnashing its teeth over having rejected the pitch that became *The Cosby Show*. Last fall, when the series premiered, the critics came out with the usual suspicions. "Cosby," the *Village Voice* hissed, "no longer qualifies as black enough to be an Uncle Tom." *Newsweek* quoted other critics who called the show, about an upper-middle-class black family, "a racial neuter" and "*Father Knows Best* in blackface." Some of these objections are still floated, although they are mere sticks on the flood of adulation that has followed the show's amazing success in the ratings. TV columnists nationwide proclaim that America has had (guess what?) another racial breakthrough.

When Cosby pooh-poohs both interpretations, he gets called "defensive."   17
He isn't defensive, he just doesn't buy the myth that nothing authentically black can be accepted by whites as long as prejudice prowls the land. Unlike the all-black sitcoms of the 1970s (*Sanford and Son*, *The Jeffersons*, *Good Times*), *The Cosby Show* does not rely upon the Norman Lear[15] formula of jive-talking, poor-mouthing, and liberal speech-making to convey a sense of blackness. Lear and his followers knew they couldn't put obscenity and hostility on the national airwaves, so they substituted their Hollywood-derived notion of black people as happy-go-lucky good

[15]*Norman Lear:* American television producer (b. 1922); noted for situation comedies like *All in the Family* and *The Jeffersons*.

guys with a self-righteous gripe. The talents of cast members like Redd Foxx kept this genre alive for a while, but the combination of tasteless jokes and solemn preaching eventually turned viewers off. It became an industry axiom that the audience was sick of blacks, except one at a time in bizarre aberrations like *Diff'rent Strokes, Webster, Gimme a Break,* and *Benson* — four shows on the air now that feature one black face in an affluent all-white setting.

But the audience isn't sick of blacks. It's sick of Hollywood blacks. 18
Those who say that Cosby's sitcom family isn't "black" betray their own disturbingly narrow assumption that blacks are what Norman Lear says they are: a collection of poverties, problems, and pathologies about which we can only laugh or lecture. Why else would anyone deny this one ethnic group a privilege accorded all others — namely the chance to combine mobility with identity? Cosby's sitcom family is equally as black as any well-to-do Jewish, Italian, or Greek family is Jewish, Italian, or Greek — provided they have not lost their taste for their grandparents' values, art, music, food, and banter.

The most salient thing about *The Cosby Show,* however, is not its 19
blackness but its portrayal of a human type rarely seen on TV: parents who are wiser than their kids. Like every other aspect of popular culture, TV has succumbed to the cult of youth, as children are invariably smarter, hipper, and more enlightened than well-meaning but backward Mom and Dad. Not so Cosby's Huxtables. Never mind his genius for entertaining children, as the father in this family he does something far more significant and attractive to contemporary viewers: He wields authority. On this program the kids do not have all the lines, and their rebellious, self-centered excuses don't stand a chance against Cosby's old-fashioned zingers: "Because I told you so," and "Because I'm your father, I brought you into this world, and I can take you out."

More than anything, this affirmation of adult authority eliminates that 20
hard core of hostility that has come to dominate the youth culture, sex and anger being the adolescent's favorite weapons against the adult world. The secret of Cosby's success is deceptively simple: He has suggested, in this seemingly innocuous television show, that there is more to black life in America than those habits of the underclass that appeal most to screaming white teenagers.

Engaging the Text

1. What does Bayles mean by the term "post-racism," and why does she feel that we have not transcended racism? What evidence can you find to support or refute her position?

2. Bayles argues that "whites can genuinely appreciate black cultural styles without necessarily acquiring new sympathy or liking for their black fellow citizens." Do you agree or disagree? Could the same claim be made about other ETHNIC cultural styles?

3. Bayles criticizes the views of several critics, both liberal and conservative, as oversimplified. Look closely at her language in this portion of the essay: How do her quotations and PARAPHRASES of these critics' articles indicate her disagreement? How does she characterize those she disagrees with, and what TONE does she use? Evaluate the effectiveness of her strategy.

4. Why does Bayles suggest that Bill Cosby's attitude toward being a black entertainer in a white society is healthier — or more productive — than Richard Pryor's? Do you agree or disagree?

Exploring Connections

1. Compare and contrast Bayles's treatment of *The Cosby Show* with the view offered by Miller in the preceding selection.

2. How does Bayles's analysis of the imitation of ethnic styles complicate Gordon Allport's analysis of in-groups and out-groups in Chapter Two, "Justice For All"?

3. Use Boggs's theory of economic EXPLOITATION in Chapter Two to explain such phenomena as the commercialization of ethnic fashion and entertainment. What limits, if any, do you see to this approach?

4. How would Karen Lindsey and David Elkind (Chapter Five, "The Changing Family") respond to Bayles's claim that the best thing about *The Cosby Show* is its "affirmation of adult authority"?

Extending the Critical Context

1. According to Bayles, many white fans of black performers keep a "safe" distance from live shows in order to avoid mixing with a predominantly black audience. Upon what evidence does she base this conclusion? Does your own experience with audiences at live events tend to confirm or disprove her assertion?

2. Have you noticed as much "crossover" by white fans for Latino or Asian performers as for black entertainers? If not, how do you account for the difference?

3. Watch one or more episodes of *227* or *Amen* and analyze what you see in terms of race and "post-racism." For example, is it good or bad to have characters speak in nonstandard English?

Advertising as Art

MICHAEL SCHUDSON

TV exists to sell things. From the very start, it has been a commercial medium, one whose development is intimately associated with modern advertising. In this selection from Advertising, the Uneasy Persuasion, *Michael Schudson (b. 1946) challenges us to take an unusual view of ads and their role: He asks us to consider advertising as a — perhaps even the — central art form of our age. A professor of sociology and chair of the Communication Department at the University of California, San Diego, Schudson has written extensively on the media.*

The Functions of a Pervasive Art Form

If advertising is not an official or state art, it is nonetheless clearly 1
art. The development of painting, photography, and prints in the fine arts has been intimately intertwined with the development of commercial art for a century. While few American writers have joined Malcolm Cowley[1] in exclaiming that literature "should borrow a little punch and confidence from American business,"[2] artists and photographers from Toulouse-Lautrec[3] on have frequently done commercial art or been influenced by it. The difference between fashion photography and photography as art is subtle, if it exists at all, and certainly the techniques and innovations in fashion photography influence photography as fine art as often as the other way around. In recent years, television commercial techniques have influenced film and commercial directors have become makers of feature films.[4]

Needless to say, most advertising is dull and conventional, as creative 2
workers in the business are the first to point out. But there is no question that advertising shapes aesthetic tastes, and at least occasionally educates the eye in ways serious artists can applaud. Critics quick to attack the "desires" advertising promotes are apt not to notice, or having noticed,

[1]*Malcolm Cowley:* American writer, editor, and lecturer (b. 1898).
[2]Cowley is cited in David E. Shi, "Advertising and the Literary Imagination During the Jazz Age," *Journal of American Culture* 2 (Summer 1979): 172. [Author's note]
[3]*Toulouse-Lautrec:* Henri Toulouse-Lautrec, French painter and lithographer (1864–1901).
[4]See John Barnicoat, *A Concise History of Posters* (New York: Oxford University Press), on the intertwining of art history and advertising history. [Author's note]

to reject, the visual tastes advertising shapes. One can gaze, as literary historian Leo Spitzer observed, "with disinterested enjoyment" at an advertisement whose claims for its product do not seem the least bit credible. Advertising "may offer a fulfillment of the *aesthetic* desires of modern humanity."[5] In a study of children's attitudes toward television commercials, Thomas Robertson and John Rossiter found a sharp decline in the extent to which children trust commercials, from first grade to third grade to fifth. But when asked if they *liked* commercials, the decline was less severe.[6] Even cultivated and critical adults, if honest, will acknowledge very often a certain "liking" or aesthetic appeal in ads they may in other respects find offensive.

It is important to acknowledge, then, that advertising is art — and is often more successful aesthetically than commercially. (In a 1981 survey of what television commercials people find the "most outstanding," a third of the people who selected Kodak ads praised James Garner and Mariette Hartley for their roles. In fact, Garner and Hartley appeared in Polaroid commercials — aesthetically successful without leaving as strong a commercial impression as the sponsor might have wished.)[7] We collect it. Old candy and coffee tins, old Coke signs, old tourist brochures, these are our antiques, our collected unconscious. But if advertising is art, the question remains: What does art do? What does art that is intended to do something do? What does art do, especially art as pervasive and penetrating as advertising in the contemporary United States? 3

As obvious as this question seems to be, its formulation is not yet satisfactory. Does advertising turn people into consumers? Does it create needs and desires? Or does it rest for its minimal plausibility on exactly the world its critics (and some of its proponents) claim it is creating? Take, for instance, James Duesenberry's theory of consumer behavior, which he derives from the simple assumptions that (1) people see goods around them superior to what they own and (2) that people believe high-quality goods are desirable and important. Surely advertising reinforces the belief that high-quality goods are desirable and important and surely it leads people to see representations of superior goods around them but it does not seem reasonable to imagine that advertising had much 4

---

[5] Leo Spitzer, "American Advertising Explained as Popular Art," *Essays on English and American Literature* (Princeton: Princeton University Press, 1962), p. 265n22 and p. 249n2. [Author's note]

[6] Thomas Robertson and John Rossiter, "Children and Commercial Persuasion: An Attribution Theory Analysis," *Journal of Consumer Research* 1 (June 1974): 17. [Author's note]

[7] Bill Abrams, "The 1981 TV Advertisements That People Remember Most," *Wall Street Journal*, February 25, 1982, p. 29. [Author's note]

to do with creating these conditions in the first place. Duesenberry takes the belief in the worth of superior goods to lie deep in American culture:

> In a fundamental sense the basic source of the drive toward higher consumption is to be found in the character of our culture. A rising standard of living is one of the major goals of our society. Much of our public policy is directed toward this end. Societies are compared with one another on the basis of the size of their incomes. In the individual sphere people do not expect to live as their parents did, but more comfortably and conveniently. The consumption pattern of the moment is conceived of not as part of a way of life, but only as a temporary adjustment to circumstances. We expect to take the first available chance to change the pattern.[8]

That sounds like a world advertising would love to create, if it could. 5 But it also sounds like the world Tocqueville[9] described in 1830, well before advertising was much more than long gray lists of patent medicine notices in the newspapers. It sounds as much like a world likely to invent modern advertising as a world that modern advertising would like to invent.

Then what does advertising do? 6

Advertising might be said to lead people to a belief in something. 7 Advertising may make people believe they are inadequate without Product X and that Product X will satisfactorily manage their inadequacies. More likely, it may remind them of inadequacies they have already felt and may lead them, once at least, to try a new product that just might help, even though they are well aware that it probably will not. Alternatively, advertising may lead people to believe generally in the efficacy of manufactured consumer goods for handling all sorts of ills, medical or social or political, even if a given ad fails to persuade that a given product is efficacious. There is the question of belief in a small sense — do people put faith in the explicit claims of advertisements, change their attitudes toward advertised goods, and go out and buy them? And there is the question of belief in a larger sense — do the assumptions and attitudes implicit in advertising become the assumptions and attitudes of the people surrounded by ads, whether or not they actually buy the advertised goods?

Social critics have argued that the greatest danger of advertising may 8 be that it creates belief in the larger sense. It has been common coin

---

[8]James S. Duesenberry, *Income, Saving, and the Theory of Consumer Behavior* (Cambridge: Harvard Economic Study No. 87, 1949; New York: Oxford University Press, 1967), p. 26. [Author's note]

[9]*Tocqueville:* Alexis de Tocqueville; see headnote, p. 341.

of advertising critics that advertising is a kind of religion. This goes back at least to James Rorty[10] who wrote of the religious power of advertising, holding that "advertising . . . becomes a body of doctrine."[11] Ann Douglas[12] has written that advertising is "the only faith of a secularized consumer society."[13] In more measured tones, Leo Spitzer relates advertising to the "preaching mentality" in Protestantism and says that advertising "has taken over the role of the teacher of morals." The advertiser, "like the preacher" must constantly remind the backslider of "his real advantage" and "must 'create the demand' for the better."[14]

Others have observed that many leading advertisers were the children 9 of ministers or grew up in strict, religious households.[15] The trouble with these remarks, and others like them, is that they fail to establish what kind of belief, if any, people actually have in advertisements. And they fail to observe that advertising is quintessentially part of the profane, not the sacred, world. Marghanita Laski[16] has observed of British television that neither religious programs nor royal occasions are interrupted or closely juxtaposed to commercial messages. This is true, though to a lesser degree, with American television — the more sacred the subject, the less the profanity of advertising is allowed to intrude. If it does intrude, the advertiser takes special pains to provide unusually dignified and restrained commercials. If the advertiser fails to make such an adjustment, as in the commercial sponsorship of a docudrama on the Holocaust in 1980, public outrage follows.[17]

So I am not persuaded by the "advertising is religion" metaphor, on 10 the face of it. But the problem with seeing advertising as religion goes still deeper: Advertising may be more powerful the *less* people believe in it, the less it is an acknowledged creed. This idea can be formulated in several ways. Northrop Frye[18] has argued that advertisements, like other propaganda, "stun and demoralize the critical consciousness with

[10]*James Rorty:* American editor, poet, journalist, and author (1891–1973).
[11]James Rorty, *Our Master's Voice* (New York: John Day, 1934, Arno Press, reprint, 1976), p. 16. [Author's note]
[12]*Ann Douglas:* American scholar and author (b. 1942), who has published widely in the fields of American studies and women's studies.
[13]Ann Douglas, *The Feminization of American Culture* (New York: Alfred A. Knopf, 1977), p. 80. [Author's note]
[14]Spitzer, "American Advertising," p. 273. [Author's note]
[15]Daniel Pope, "The Development of National Advertising, 1865–1920" (Ph.D. diss., Columbia University, 1973), p. 320. [Author's note]
[16]*Marghanita Laski:* English journalist, critic, and author (1915–1988).
[17]Marghanita Laski, "Advertising: Sacred and Profane," *Twentieth Century* 165 (February 1959): 118–29. [Author's note]
[18]*Northrop Frye:* Canadian literary critic and theoretician (b. 1912).

statements too absurd or extreme to be dealt with seriously by it." Advertisements thus wrest from people "not necessarily acceptance, but dependence on their versions of reality." Frye continues:

> Advertising implies an economy which has some independence from the political structure, and as long as this independence exists, advertising can be taken as a kind of ironic game. Like other forms of irony, it says what it does not wholly mean, but nobody is obliged to believe its statements literally. Hence it creates an illusion of detachment and mental superiority even when one is obeying its exhortations.[19]

Literary critics have been more sensitive than social scientists to the possibility that communications do not mean what they say — and that this may be the very center of their power. There has rarely been room for the study of irony in social science but irony is a key element in literary studies. Leo Spitzer, like Frye, observes that ads do not ask to be taken literally. In a Sunkist oranges ad he analyzed, he found that the ad "transports the listener into a world of Arcadian beauty,[20] but with no insistence that this world really exists." The ad pictures "an Arcady of material prosperity," but Spitzer holds that the spectator "is equipped with his own criteria, and subtracts automatically from the pictures of felicity and luxury which smile at him from the billboards."[21]   11

According to Spitzer, people are detached in relation to advertising. They feel detached, disillusioned, and forcibly reminded of the tension between life as it is lived and life as it is pictured. This is a characteristic attitude toward precious or baroque art.[22] In this attitude, no condemnation of the excess of the art is necessary because one is so firmly anchored in the matter-of-fact reality that contradicts it.   12

For Spitzer, people are genuinely detached in relation to advertising. They view it from an aesthetic distance. For Frye, in contrast, people have only "an illusion of detachment." For Frye, it is precisely the belief people have that they *are* detached that makes the power of advertising all the more insidious.[23] Advertising may create attitudes and inclinations even when it does not inspire belief; it succeeds in creating attitudes because it does not make the mistake of *asking* for belief.   13

This corresponds to the argument of a leading market researcher, Herbert Krugman, of General Electric Co. research. He holds that the   14

---

[19] Northrop Frye, *The Modern Century* (Toronto: Oxford University Press, 1967), p. 26. [Author's note]

[20] *Arcadian beauty:* natural, unspoiled beauty.

[21] Spitzer, "American Advertising," p. 264 and p. 265n22. [Author's note]

[22] *baroque art:* a highly ornamental style of art.

[23] *insidious:* characterized by treachery; more dangerous than seems evident.

special power of television advertising is that the ads interest us so little, not that they appeal to us so much. Television engages the audience in "low-involvement learning." Krugman's argument is that the evidence in psychology on the learning and memorization of nonsense syllables or other trivial items is very much like the results in market research on the recall of television commercials. He draws from this the suggestion that the two kinds of learning may be psychologically the same, a "learning without involvement." In such learning, people are not "persuaded" of something. Nor do their attitudes change. But there is a kind of "sleeper" effect. While viewers are not persuaded, they do alter the structure of their perceptions about a product, shifting "the relative salience[24] of attributes" in the advertised brand. Nothing follows from this until the consumer arrives at the supermarket, ready to make a purchase. Here, at the behavioral level, the real change occurs:

> . . . the purchase situation is the catalyst that reassembles or brings out all the potentials for shifts in salience that have accumulated up to that point. The product or package is then suddenly seen in a new, "somehow different" light although nothing verbalizable may have changed *up to that point.*[25]

Consumers in front of the television screen are relatively unwary. 15 They take ads to be trivial or transparent or both. What Krugman suggests is that precisely this attitude enables the ad to be successful. Were consumers convinced of the importance of ads, they would bring into play an array of "perceptual defenses" as they do in situations of persuasion regarding important matters.

Any understanding of advertising in American culture must come to 16 grips with the ironic game it plays with us and we play with it. If there are signs that Americans bow to the gods of advertising, there are equally indications that people find the gods ridiculous. It is part of the popular culture that advertisements are silly. Taking potshots at commercials has been a mainstay of *Mad* magazine and of stand-up comedians for decades. When Lonesome Rhodes meets Marsha Coulihan, station manager for a country radio station, in Budd Schulberg's story, "Your Arkansas Traveler," he says to her: "You must be a mighty smart little gal to be handlin' this here raddio station all by yourself." She replies: "My good man, I am able to read without laughing out loud any commercial that is placed before me. I am able to pick out a group of records and point

---

[24]*salience:* prominence, conspicuousness.
[25]Herbert E. Krugman, "The Impact of Television Advertising: Learning Without Involvement," *Public Opinion Quarterly* 29 (1965): 161. [Author's note]

to the guy in the control room each time I want him to play one. And that is how you run a rural radio station."[26]

If advertising is the faith of a secular society, it is a faith that inspires 17 remarkably little professed devotion. If it is a body of doctrine, it is odd that so few followers would affirm the doctrine to be true, let alone inspired. Christopher Lasch[27] has seen this problem. He argues that the trouble with the mass media is not that they purvey untruths but that "the rise of mass media makes the categories of truth and falsehood irrelevant to an evaluation of their influence. Truth has given way to credibility, facts to statements that sound authoritative without conveying any authoritative information."[28] But this analysis will not do for the problem of advertising. People are not confused about the importance of truth and falsity in their daily lives. It is just that they do not regularly apply judgments of truth to advertisements. Their relationship to advertisements is not a matter of evidence, truth, belief, or even credibility.

Then what is it? Whether Krugman's formulation is right or wrong, 18 his view at least leads us to ask more pointedly what kind of belief or nonbelief people have in relation to advertising. Again, this is in some sense a question about religion. The form of the question of whether or not people believe advertising messages is like the question of whether or not people believe in and are affected by religious teachings. On the latter question, anthropologist Melford Spiro has distinguished five levels at which people may "learn" an ideology:[29]

1. Most weakly, they may *learn about* an ideological concept.
2. They may learn about and *understand* the concept.
3. They may *believe* the concept to be true or right.
4. The concept may become salient to them and inform their "behavioral environment" — that is, they may not only believe the concept but organize their lives contingent on that belief.
5. They may internalize the belief so that it is not only cognitively salient but motivationally important. It not only guides but instigates action.[30]

---

[26] Budd Schulberg, *Some Faces in the Crowd* (New York: Random House, 1953). [Author's note]

[27] *Christopher Lasch:* see headnote, p. 534.

[28] Christopher Lasch, *The Culture of Narcissism* (New York: W. W. Norton, 1978), p. 74. [Author's note]

[29] *ideology:* the doctrines, ideas, values, and beliefs of a particular group.

[30] Melford Spiro, "Buddhism and Economic Action in Burma," *American Anthropologist* 68 (October 1966): 1163. [Author's note]

Tests of the effectiveness of advertising are most often tests of "recall"; 19
ads are judged by the market researchers to be "effective" if they have
established Level 1 belief, learning about a concept. Advertisers, of
course, are more interested in Levels 4 and 5, although their ability to
measure success at these levels is modest. Most theories of advertising
assume that the stages of belief are successive, that consumers must go
through Level 1 before Level 2, Level 2 before Level 3, and so on.
What Krugman argues and what Northrop Frye can be taken to be
saying, is that one can reach Level 4 without ever passing through Level
3. The voices of advertising may inform a person's "behavioral environment"
without inspiring belief at any time or at any fundamental level. The
stages are not sequential. One is independent from the next.

"What characterizes the so-called advanced societies," Roland Barthes[31] 20
wrote, "is that they today consume images and no longer, like those of
the past, beliefs; they are therefore more liberal, less fanatical, but also
more 'false' (less 'authentic') . . ."[32] Barthes is right about the present
but very likely exaggerates the break from the past. A few years ago I
saw a wonderful exhibit at the Museum of Traditional and Popular Arts
in Paris, dealing with religion in rural France in the nineteenth century.
The exhibit demonstrated that religious imagery was omnipresent in the
French countryside. There were paintings, crucifixes, saints, and Bible
verses adorning the most humble objects — plates, spoons, cabinets,
religious articles of all sorts, especially holiday objects, lithographs for
the living room wall, greeting cards, illustrated books, board games for
children, pillowcases, marriage contracts, painted furniture for children,
paper dolls, carved and painted signs for religious processions, and so
forth. Of course, the largest architectural monuments in most towns
were the churches, presiding over life crises and the visual landscape
alike. And, as French historian Georges Duby has argued, the grandeur
of church architecture was intended as a form of "visual propaganda."[33]

None of this necessarily made the ordinary French peasant a believing 21
Christian. There were pagan rites in nineteenth-century rural France,
as there are still today. Nor, I expect, did this mass-mediated reinforcement
of Christian culture make the peasant ignore the venality of the church
as an institution or the sins of its local representatives.

---

[31] *Roland Barthes:* French literary critic and philosopher (1915–1980).
[32] Roland Barthes, *Camera Lucida* (New York: Hill and Wang, 1981), p. 119. [Author's
note]
[33] Georges Duby, *The Age of the Cathedrals: Art and Society, 980–1420* (Chicago:
University of Chicago Press, 1981), p. 135. [Author's note]

Still, the Church self-consciously used imagery to uplift its followers 22 and potential followers, and there was no comparable suffusion of the countryside by other systems of ideas, ideals, dreams, and images. When one thought of salvation or, more modestly, searched for meanings for making sense of life, there was primarily the materials of the Church to work with. It has been said that languages do not differ in what they can express but in what they can express *easily*.[34] It is the same with pervasive or official art: It brings some images and expressions quickly to mind and makes others relatively unavailable. However blatant the content of the art, its consequences remain more subtle. Works of art, in general, anthropologist Clifford Geertz has written, do not in the first instance "celebrate social structure or forward useful doctrine. They materialize a way of experiencing; bring a particular cast of mind into the world of objects, where men can look at it."[35] Art, he says, does not create the material culture nor serve as a primary force shaping experience. The experience is already there. The art is a commentary on it. The public does not require the experience it already has but a statement or reflection on it: "What it needs is an object rich enough to see it in; rich enough, even, to, in seeing it, deepen it."[36]

Capitalist realist art, like socialist realism,[37] more often flattens than 23 deepens experience. Here I judge the art and not the way of life it promotes. Jack Kerouac[38] may deepen our experience of the road and the automobile, but the advertising agencies for General Motors and Ford typically flatten and thin our experience of the same objects. This need not be so. The AT&T "Reach Out and Touch Someone" commercials for long-distance telephone calling sentimentalize an experience that genuinely has or can have a sentimental element. If these ads do not deepen the experience they at least articulate it in satisfying ways.

There is another side to the coin: If an ad successfully romanticizes 24 a moment, it provides a model of sentiment that one's own more varied and complicated experience cannot live up to. Most of our phone calls, even with loved ones, are boring or routine. When art romanticizes the

---

[34]"Languages differ not so much as to what *can* be said in them, but rather as to what it is *relatively easy* to say in them." Charles Hockett, "Chinese vs. English: An Exploration of the Whorfian Hypothesis," in *Language in Culture*, ed. H. Hoijer (Chicago: University of Chicago Press, 1954), p. 122. [Author's note]

[35]Clifford Geertz, "Art as a Cultural System," *MLN* 91 (1976): 1478. [Author's note]

[36]Ibid., p. 1483. [Author's note]

[37]*socialist realism:* the officially endorsed artistic style of the Soviet Union until the 1980s, promoting doctrinaire communist values and themes.

[38]*Jack Kerouac:* American author (1922–1969) whose 1957 novel *On the Road* is credited with the birth of the "beat" generation.

exotic or the exalted, it does not call our own experience into question, but when it begins to take everyday life as the subject of its idealization, it creates for the audience a new relationship to art. The audience can judge the art against its own experience and can thereby know that the art idealizes and falsifies. At the same time, the art enchants and tantalizes the audience with the possibility that it is *not* false. If it can play on this ambiguity, art becomes less an imitation of life and turns life into a disappointing approximation of art.

The issue is not that advertising art materializes or "images" certain 25 *experiences* but, as Geertz says, a *way of experiencing*. The concern with advertising is that this way of experiencing — a consumer way of life — does not do justice to the best that the human being has to offer and, indeed, entraps people in exploitative and self-defeating activity. But what can it really mean to say that art materializes a way of experience? What does that *do?* Why should a social system *care* to materialize its way of experiencing? The individual artists, writers, and actors who put the ads together do not feel this need. They frequently have a hard time taking their work seriously or finding it expressive of anything at all they care about.

Think of a smaller social system, a two-person social system, a marriage. 26 Imagine it to be a good marriage, where love is expressed daily in a vast array of shared experiences, shared dreams, shared tasks and moments. In this ideal marriage, the couple continually make and remake their love. Then why, in this marriage, would anything be amiss if the two people did not say to each other, "I love you"? Why, in a relationship of such obviously enacted love, should it seem necessary to say out loud, "I love you"?

Because, I think, making the present audible and making the implicit 27 explicit is necessary to engage and renew a whole train of commitments, responsibilities, and possibilities. "I love you" does not create what is not present. Nor does it seal what is present. But it must be spoken and respoken. It is necessary speech because people need to see in pictures or hear in words even what they already know as deeply as they know anything, *especially* what they know as deeply as they know anything. Words are actions.

This is also true in large social systems. Advertising is capitalism's way 28 of saying "I love you" to itself.

The analogy, of course, is not perfect and I do not mean to jump from 29 marriage to market with unqualified abandon. But in social systems writ large — and not just capitalism but all social systems — there are efforts both individual and collective to turn experience into words, pictures, and doctrines. Once created, these manifestations have consequences.

They become molds for thought and feeling, if one takes a deterministic metaphor, or they become "equipment for living" if one prefers a more voluntaristic model or — to borrow from Max Weber[39] and choose a metaphor somewhere in the middle, they serve as switchmen on the tracks of history. In the case of advertising, people do not necessarily "believe" in the values that advertisements present. Nor need they believe for a market economy to survive and prosper. People need simply get used to, or get used to not getting used to, the institutional structures that govern their lives. Advertising does not make people believe in capitalist institutions or even in consumer values, but so long as alternative articulations of values are relatively hard to locate in the culture, capitalist realist art will have some power.

Of course, alternative values *are* available in American culture. In some artistic, intellectual, and ethnic enclaves, one can encounter premises and principles that directly challenge capitalism and the expansion of the market to all phases of life. In contrast, the mainstream news and entertainment media operate within a relatively circumscribed range of values. But even in this narrower discourse, there is often criticism of consumer values or of the excesses of a consumer society. I came upon attacks on materialism, suburbia, conformity, and advertising in the 1950s as a student in social studies classes in a public junior high school and high school. Only a few years ago, people spoke contemptuously of the "me generation" and President Jimmy Carter diagnosed a national "crisis of confidence," opining that "we've discovered that owning things and consuming things does not satisfy our longing for meaning."[40] Recent lampooning of "Preppies" and "Yuppies" (young, upwardly-mobile professionals) betrays anxiety about, if also accommodation to, consumption as a way of life. So I do not suggest that advertisements have a monopoly in the symbolic marketplace. Still, no other cultural form is as accessible to children; no other form confronts visitors and immigrants to our society (and migrants from one part of society to another) so forcefully; and probably only professional sports surpasses advertising as a source of visual and verbal clichés, aphorisms, and proverbs. Advertising has a special cultural power.

The pictures of life that ads parade before consumers are familiar, scenes of life as in some sense we know it or would like to know it. Advertisements pick up and represent values already in the culture. But these values, however deep or widespread, are not the only ones people

[39]*Max Weber:* German sociologist and political economist (1864–1920).
[40]"Transcript of President's Address to Country on Energy Problems," *New York Times,* July 16, 1979, p. A–10. [Author's note]

have or aspire to, and the pervasiveness of advertising makes us forget this. Advertising picks up some of the things that people hold dear and re-presents them to people as *all* of what they value, assuring them that the sponsor is the patron of common ideals. That is what capitalist realist art, like other pervasive symbolic systems, does. Recall again that languages differ not in what they can express but in what they can express *easily*. This is also true in the languages of art, ideology, and propaganda. It is the kind of small difference that makes a world of difference and helps construct and maintain different worlds.

Engaging the Text

1. Working in groups, select one or two of the authorities on the "art of TV" that Schudson cites. To what extent does he agree or disagree with them? How does he use their ideas to construct his own argument? Share your conclusions with those of other groups.

2. Explain what Schudson means when he says that TV advertising "flattens" experience.

3. Evaluate the claim that advertising itself has become a form of modern art.

4. Explain Schudson's claim that TV commercials can be highly effective even if people feel distanced from them and do not take them seriously.

5. In Schudson's view, what does advertising have in common with religion, and how does it differ?

Exploring Connections

1. According to Schudson, how important is the *form* of TV programming and advertising as opposed to their *content*? Compare Schudson's views with those expressed by Jerry Mander earlier in this chapter.

2. Look ahead to Pat Aufderheide's "The Look of the Sound" later in this chapter. What connections do you see between Schudson's analysis of the meaning of advertising and the imaginary worlds projected in music videos?

Extending the Critical Context

1. Watch several TV ads closely and examine how they "flatten" experience. What values, experiences, etc. do they omit or suppress?

2. Working in small groups, outline an anti-advertisement — one that would make viewers conscious of the limitations and implications of traditional advertisements.

3. If ads are art, watch some TV ads (or reflect on some you already know well)

and select a small number of artistic ads for an "exhibition." Be sure your show has a theme (for example, family or patriotism). What messages does your exhibit convey?

The Presence of the Word in TV Advertising

Jay Rosen

Have you ever watched TV with the sound turned off? In the following selection, Jay Rosen suggests that silent viewing is the best way to find out what TV commercials are really telling us. Rosen (b. 1956) is an assistant professor of journalism and mass communications at New York University and a contributing editor of Channels *magazine.*

It is safe to say that most inquiries into the language of television [1] advertising would look at the sort of language actually used in the ads. I could imagine, for example, a rather interesting article on how an advertising slogan like "Where's the Beef?" became almost instantly part of the American language in the summer of 1984. Indeed, in a journal like *Et cetera*[1] there could easily be an entire issue devoted to "Where's the Beef?" For cultural observers, then, there is quite a lot of material in the language employed by television advertising. But that is not the direction I want to take in this article.

I would like to begin by observing the following fact. All over America [2] there are people who have discovered a new way of watching television. The advertising industry calls them "flippers," people who drift restlessly around the dial by remote control, changing the channel at the slightest provocation — the appearance on screen of Angie Dickinson,[2] for example. I know one man — not an academic, as it turns out — who says he hits the button as soon as he feels the smallest hint of content coming on. My own habits are not quite so severe, but I am, I confess, a flipper. (By the way, most flippers are male, something no one has thought to

[1]*Et cetera:* a periodical dedicated to the role of words and symbols in human behavior.
[2]*Angie Dickinson:* star of the 1970s series *Policewoman.*

study yet.) If the advertising industry is concerned about flippers, it would be doubly concerned about me. For I am not only a flipper, but I often flip with the sound off. I find it easier to recognize patterns that way, and pattern recognition is, so to speak, my profession.

Now, flipping with the sound off is a good way of investigating television   3
ads. Frequently I find myself asking, "what is this ad about?" as I watch the images float by. "What is this ad about?" is a different question, of course, from, "what *product* is this an ad for?" To ask what an ad is "about" is to inquire into the underlying message of the ad. . . . Deodorant ads, as almost everyone knows, are about shame and the body, no matter what they may seem to be saying. The art of flipping makes it easier to recognize such things, and I recommend it to everyone as an inexpensive research tool.

You don't have to be a flipper to recognize that one trend in television   4
advertising is toward increasing visualization — more images, arriving at a faster clip, and packing more of a punch. Often they are accompanied by music, and frequently this music is borrowed or adapted from hit songs on the radio. MTV is thus an obvious influence on this sort of advertising, but there's an important difference. A certain vagueness or incoherence is possible, even desirable, in a music video. As a result, it is often impossible to say what music videos are really about, despite the presence of a lot of striking images. In advertising there is not as much license. The images must succeed, not only in grabbing attention, but in communicating a single concept or theme which can then be linked to the product. This is what I mean by "deep structure" in TV advertising.

A good example is a new series of ads for Michelob beer. You may   5
recall that Michelob's slogan used to be "Weekends Were Made For Michelob." In the new campaign the line is, "The Night Belongs to Michelob," suggesting that by the 1990s, Michelob will have colonized the entire week. In any event, the ads now feature a series of images, very well shot, all of which vivify life in the big city at night. Well dressed women step out of cabs, skylines twinkle and glow, performers take the stage in smoky nightclubs, couples kiss on the street, backlit by the headlights of cars. These are not only images *of* the night; they are *about* the night as an idea or myth. Their goal is to create a swirl of associations around the word "night," which is actually heard in the ad if you have the sound on. Phil Collins of the rock band Genesis sings a song in which the word "tonight" is repeated over and over.

But what's interesting about the ads is that neither the lyrics of Phil   6
Collins nor the slogan, "The Night Belongs to Michelob" are necessary to get the message. The word "night" comes through in the very texture

of the images. It's there even when the sound is off and no language is being heard. What Walter Ong[3] once called "the presence of the word" does not, in this case, depend on the presence of language. For example, a singer is shown silhouetted in a spotlight on stage at a nightclub. This is not merely a picture *taken* at night, in a place associated *with* the night. It is almost an abstract diagram of the concept of night. The beam of the spotlight, because it is visible, demonstrates the presence of darkness all around. The singer appears as a silhouette, a black shape who is in, of, and surrounded by the night. The spotlight, then, is the very principle of intelligibility at work: It lights up the night, not in order to obliterate it, but to give it form, to demonstrate what "night" is, almost like a Sesame Street vocabulary lesson. This giving of form to an abstract concept is the logic behind a number of ads on television.

Levi's, for example, has created a series of ads about the idea of "blue." 7 Naturally they are shot in blue tones on city streets. They also feature blues songs being strummed in the background. And, of course, the actors are all wearing blue jeans. But blue is communicated on a deeper level, as well. The feeling of blue — the meaning blue has taken on in popular culture — is brought out in the way a girl walks wistfully down the street, blowing soap bubbles into the air. In these ads, blue would come through without the sound of blues songs or the product name — Levi's 501 blues. Indeed, I am tempted to say that blue would come through even on a black and white set. Why? Because the director has found images which "mean" blue at the deepest cultural level. It is not the surfaced presence of the *color* blue that matters, but a kind of inner architecture of blue, on top of which blue scenes, blue jeans and blues songs have been placed.

This may seem easy enough with a concept, like blue, that is primarily 8 visual. But what about notions that are essentially verbal? The Hewlett-Packard company[4] has attempted something along these lines. It is now running a series of ads whose slogan is "What if . . . ?" In these ads, Hewlett-Packard people are seen pondering difficult problems, hitting upon a possible answer, and rushing to their colleagues to announce, "I've got it: What if . . ." and the sound fades out.

Of course, if you turn the sound off, there is no "what if" to be heard 9 and no fade out. And yet the idea of "what if" is not necessarily gone. Picture this: An intelligent-looking woman in glasses is shown alone in her office, tapping a pencil and sort of looking skyward, as if contemplating a majestic possibility. Here the attempt is to produce a visual image of

[3]*Walter Ong:* American literary critic and student of literacy (b. 1912).
[4]*Hewlett-Packard company:* American electronics firm.

"what-if ness," a notion ordinarily expressed in words or mathematical symbols. It has often been said that pictures have no tense. But Hewlett-Packard is attempting to prove that a tense — in this case, the conditional — can in fact be a visual idea — borrowed from language, but expressed in images. Perhaps we will soon see ads visualizing a host of ideas we ordinarily think of as linguistic. How about a series of pictures about the concept of "nevertheless" or "because"?

What I am trying to point out is a certain irony in the trend toward   10
increased visualization. As TV ads become shorter, they become more visual, as a way of saying more in a smaller amount of time. But as they become more visual, the ads seem to be about concepts which are inescapably verbal. Advertising may appear to be relying less on language, but language is simply functioning on a deeper level. It has not, in any sense, gone away. And a final irony is this: In order to discover this deeper level of language it is necessary to ignore the language on the surface. In a strange way, turning the sound off allows you to hear what's really being said.

Engaging the Text

1. What does Rosen mean by the "deep structure" of ads?

2. In what sense can the IMAGES in an advertisement have "texture"?

3. Working in groups, discuss Rosen's special uses of the words "verbal" and "language."

4. Evaluate Rosen's claim that as TV commercials rely increasingly on visual effects, the messages they convey become increasingly ABSTRACT and "verbal."

Exploring Connections

1. Compare and contrast Rosen's views of what advertisements express with those of Michael Schudson in the previous selection.

Extending the Critical Context

1. Watch several TV commercials with the sound turned off as Rosen suggests and try to describe what they are "about" — what abstract ideas they attempt to convey. Does your experiment confirm or challenge Rosen's theory?

2. Working in groups, design your own thirty-second silent commercial meant to convey or evoke an abstract, verbal concept like "nevertheless," "on the other hand," "never again," "why not?", or one of your own invention.

The Look of the Sound
PAT AUFDERHEIDE

Some of the most exotic images Americans consume are served up by music videos, and if MTV hardly rivals the networks in terms of audience, its images can nevertheless attain the status of cultural icons: Who hasn't seen Michael Jackson's moonwalk? According to Aufderheide, there's more to MTV than meets the eye, or the ear. Music videos create a self-contained fantasy world, a subculture with its own ideas about authority, freedom, and identity. They also sell a lot of clothes. Pat Aufderheide (b. 1948) is an associate professor of communications at American University and senior editor of In These Times, *a weekly alternative newspaper.*

Music videos are more than a fad, or fodder for spare hours and dollars 1 of young consumers. They are pioneers in video expression, and the results of their reshaping of the form extend far beyond the TV set.

Music videos have broken through TV's most hallowed boundaries. 2 As commercials in themselves, they have erased the very distinction between the commercial and the program. As nonstop sequences of discontinuous episodes, they have erased the boundaries between programs.

Music videos have also set themselves free from the television set, 3 inserting themselves into movie theaters, popping up in shopping malls and department store windows, becoming actors in both live performances and the club scene. As omnivorous as they are pervasive, they draw on and influence the traditional image-shaping fields of fashion and advertising. Even political campaigning is borrowing from these new bite-sized packages of desire.

With nary a reference to cash or commodities, music videos cross the 4 consumer's gaze as a series of mood states. They trigger moods such as nostalgia, regret, anxiety, confusion, dread, envy, admiration, pity, titillation — attitudes at one remove from primal expression such as passion, ecstasy, and rage. The moods often express a lack, an incompletion, an instability, a searching for location. In music videos, those feelings are carried on flights of whimsy, extended journeys into the arbitrary.

In appealing to and playing on these sensations, music videos have 5 animated and set to music a tension basic to American youth culture. It is that feeling of instability that fuels the search to buy-and-belong, to possess a tangible anchor in a mutable universe while preserving the essence of that universe — its mutability. It allows the viewer to become a piece of the action in a continuous performance.

Music videos did not discover the commercial application of anxiety, 6 of course. The manufacturer of Listerine was selling mouthwash on anxiety sixty years ago. Nor did music videos succeed in making themselves widely appealing by somehow duping passive audiences into an addiction to commercial dreams. Music videos are authentic expressions of a populist industrial society. For young people struggling to find a place in communities dotted with shopping malls but with few community centers, in an economy whose major product is information, music videos play to the adolescent's search for identity and an improvised community.

The success of MTV has been based on understanding that the channel 7 offers not videos but environment, a context that creates mood. The goal of MTV executive Bob Pittman, the man who designed the channel, is simple: His job, he says, is to "amplify the mood and include MTV in the mood." Young Americans, he argues, are "television babies," particularly attracted to appeals to heart rather than head. "If you can get their emotions going," he says, "forget their logic, you've got 'em." Other executives describe MTV as "pure environment," in which not performers but music is the star of the perpetual show.

MTV's "pure environment" is expertly crafted. The pace is relentless, 8 set by the music videos, which offer, in the words of one producer, "short bursts of sensual energy." But the image of the program service is casual and carefree. The channel's VJs are chosen for their fresh, offhand delivery and look. They are "themselves," celebrities whose only claim to fame is their projection of a friendly image to youthful viewers. The sets are designed to look like a basement hideaway a fifteen-year-old might dream of, with rock memorabilia and videocassettes adorning walls and shelves. Lighting is intentionally "shitty," instead of the classic no-shadow bright lighting of most TV productions. MTV intends to offer viewers not just a room of their own, but a room that is an alternate world.

MTV promotes itself as the populist, even democratic expression of 9 its viewers. Rock stars in promo spots call on viewers to say, "I want my Em Tee Vee!," as if someone were threatening to take it away from them. "Their" MTV, as its own ads portray it, is the insouciant,[1] irreverent rejection of a tedious other world — not the real-life one of work and family, but the world as network news reports it. One commercial spoofs network news promos. Flashing the familiar "Coming at 11" slogan, the

[1]*insouciant:* carefree, indifferent, unbothered.

ad promises, "MTV provides *reason to live*, despite news of *botched world!*" On a miniature TV set, a logo reads, "Botched World." MTV superimposes its own version of reality on television's historic moments as well. Space flights — which made history not least for television's live coverage of them — are a favorite subject for MTV's own commercials. One shows astronauts planting an MTV flag on the moon. Another asks, "What if time had never been invented!," showing a space launch count-down without numbers. MTV's promise to remove the viewer from history is succinctly put into the slogan "24 hours every day . . . so you'll be able to live forever!"

Wherever they appear, music videos are distinctive because they imitate 10 dreams rather than the plot or event structure of bounded programs. Even the usually thin narrative threads in song lyrics rarely provide the basis for a video's look and action. ("If you can hear them, the words help a bit," says video producer Zelda Barron wryly; her videos for Culture Club feature the bizarre, supernatural, and exotic, and use hectic montage[2] rather than narrative logic. Her explanation for her style — that the budgets aren't big enough to produce a coherent story — fails to explain why the features have the heady dream elements they do.) In *Film Quarterly*, Marsha Kinder has noted strong parallels between dreams and music videos. She cites five elements: unlimited access (MTV's continuous format and people's ability to both sleep and daydream); structural discontinuity (for instance, abrupt scene shifts); decentering (a loosely connected flow of action around a theme); structural reliance on memory retrieval (both videos and dreams trigger blocks of associations with pungent images); and the omnipresence of the spectator. In *Fabula*, Margaret Morse notes many of the same features, particularly the absence of reliance on narrative; she focuses on the magical quality of the word, as lip-synched by the performer who can appear anywhere in the video without being linked with the images or events, as if a dreamer who could create a world.

Many videos in fact begin with someone dreaming or daydreaming. 11 For instance, Kool and the Gang's "Misled" begins with a band member in his bedroom, launching into a dream-adventure in which he is both himself and a small Third World boy, threatened by a glamorous white female ghost and engaged in an adventure that imitates *Raiders of the Lost Ark*[3] — significantly, another commercial fantasy. The dream never really ends, since after his band members wake him up, they all turn

---

[2] *montage:* a composite picture; a rapid sequence of images in motion pictures or TV.
[3] *Raiders of the Lost Ark:* a popular action/adventure movie by American director Steven Spielberg.

into ghosts. Thelma Houston's "Heat Medley" shows the performer day-dreaming to escape an unpleasant morning conflict with her husband. She daydreams a central role for herself on a *Love Boat*-like episode that turns into a nightmare of disastrous romance.

While the fantasies of music videos are open-ended, they do play on   12
classic story lines, such as boy-meets-loses-wins-girl and child-is-menaced-by-monster-and-conquers-it. Some weave fairy tale themes — in which the protagonist is either a preschooler or is infantilized — into the dream. But performers easily switch identities, magical transportations occur, and sets are expressionistically large or small. In Midnight Star's "Operator," giant telephones dwarf performers, and a telephone booth magically pops up and disappears on highways. In Billy Joel's "Keeping the Faith," a judge's bench becomes a giant jukebox on a set featuring commercial talismans of the 1950s. In ABC's "The Look of Love," Central Park becomes a cartoon set (commercial kiddie culture), and Nolan Thomas' "Yo' Little Brother" looks like a Saturday morning cartoon version of *The Cabinet of Dr. Caligari*.[4]

Kinder believes that manufactured fantasy may have a much more far-   13
reaching effect on people's subconscious attitudes and expectations than we now imagine, perhaps conditioning not only our expectations today but our dreams tomorrow. Her fears are far-reaching — and unprovable — but her careful analysis of parallels between dream structure and music video structure have fascinating implications for the form. Music videos offer a ready-made alternative to social life. With no beginnings or endings — no history — there may be nightmarish instability, even horror, but not tragedy. Tragedy is rooted in the tension between an individual and society. Likewise, there is no comedy, which provokes laughter with sharp, unexpected shifts of context, making solemnity slip on a banana peel. Dreams by contrast create gestalts,[5] in which sensations build and dissolve. And so they nicely match the promise and threat of consumer-constructed identity, endlessly flexible, depending on your income and taste. Obsolescence[6] is built in. Like fashion, identity can change with a switch of scene, with a change in the beat. The good news is: You can be anything, anywhere. That is also the bad news — which whets the appetite for more "news," more dreams.

Music video's lack of a clear subject carries into its constant play with   14

[4]*The Cabinet of Dr. Caligari:* Fritz Lang's 1919 silent film, noted for its bizarre lighting and distorted sets.
[5]*gestalts:* in Gestalt psychology, the integrated patterns that make up experience; forms or patterns.
[6]*obsolescence:* the process of becoming obsolete, out of date, or outmoded.

the outward trappings of sex roles. Male images include sailors, thugs, gang members, and gangsters. Female images include prostitutes, nightclub performers, goddesses, temptresses, and servants. Most often, these images are drawn not from life or even myth, but from old movies, ads, and other pop culture clichés.

Social critics, especially feminists, have denounced sadomasochistic   15
trappings and stereotypes of exotic women (especially East Asians) in videos. This may indeed be evidence of entrenched prejudice in the culture. For instance, women are often portrayed in videos as outsiders and agents of trouble, which reflects in part the macho traditions of rock. The fetishistic[7] female costumery of many videos probably reflects the role of artifice in shaping feminine sex roles in the culture; there is a fuller cultural grab bag for feminine than for masculine sexual objects.

Male or female, grotesquerie is the norm. Combine grotesquerie with   16
shifting identities and you get androgyny,[8] as with Culture Club's flamboyant Boy George. Androgyny may be the most daring statement that an entire range of sex roles is fair game for projecting one's own statement of the moment. Gender is no longer fixed; male and female are fractured into a kaleidoscope of images.

Fashion's unstable icons also exist in a spooky universe. The landscape   17
on which transient images take shape participates in the self-dramatizing style of the performer-icons. Ordinary sunlight is uncommon; night colors — especially blue and silver — are typical; and neon light, light that designs itself and comes in brilliantly artificial colors, is everywhere. Natural settings are extreme — desert sands, deep tropical forests, oceans. Weather often becomes an actor, buffeting performers and evoking moods. The settings are hermetic and global at the same time, locked into color schemes in which colors complement each other but no longer refer to a natural universe.

It can be a lonely world, but even the loneliness is hypnotically en-   18
grossing. One music video visual cliché that provides continuity in the absence of plot is the shot of the performer simply gazing, often at himself or herself in the previous shot. In Roxy Music's "The Main Thing," Bryan Ferry gazes from an armchair at his own just projected image. In Chicago's "You're the Inspiration," members of the group pretend to practice in a nostalgically lit loft. Intercut are scenes of couples

---

[7]*fetishistic:* relating to any object that commands unusual or unreasonable admiration or devotion.
[8]*androgyny:* the state of being both male and female or of having attributes of both sexes.

in wistful moods and shots of performers brooding individually. It is images like these that provoke Marsha Kinder to call videos solipsistic.[9]

Their world, however, is also one of cosmic threat and magical power. The self-transforming figures are menaced by conglomerate figures of authority, which often trigger all-powerful fantasy acts of destruction and salvation. Parents, school principals, teachers, police, and judges provide a cultural iconography of repression. In Heaven's "Rock School," a principal wears a stocking mask, and a school guard menaces students with a Doberman. Bon Jovi's "Runaway" features a girl in miniskirted rebellion against her parents (harking back nostalgically to an era when miniskirts could express rebellion). In retaliation against restrictions, she incinerates them with powers reminiscent of those used in the films *Carrie* and *Firestarter*; we're seeing word magic, the power of dream-song, at work. Sammy Hagar, in "I Can't Drive 55," exercises his "right" to drive as fast as he wants to (desire being asserted as a right); he ends up before a judge whose name is Julius Hangman, from whom he escapes by waking up. Videos often play on the overlapping sexual and political iconography of power in Naziesque sadomasochistic fetishes, with symbols connoting total power without moral or social context. In Billy Idol's "Flesh for Fantasy," as he sings "Face to face and back to back/You see and feel my sex attack," the video shows Idol strutting, preening, performing Nazi-like salutes. Cutting into this one-man parade is a sequence of body parts and geometric forms, some of them drawn from the starkly abstract set. Idol's "sex attack" is not directed; while he sometimes looks directly at the camera, the video's "story" is the construction of a movie-picture portrait of Idol in his stormtrooper/S & M outfit.

The National Coalition on Television Violence, among other groups, has criticized the violence, "especially senseless violence and violence between men and women," in music videos. The criticisms are grounded in a history of objections to violence in TV programs. These violent actions are seen by NCTV analysts (and the middle-class consumers who support the pressure group) as virtual prescriptions to violence in life. But it is hard to assign a prescriptive meaning to random violence that is used not as action but as atmosphere and aestheticizer. Even Central American conflict has been retailed in videos by Don Henley and Mick Jagger, as a backdrop for the dislocated performers making a stand amid rubble and military action in which no side stands for anything. George Gerbner, dean of the Annenberg School of Communications at the University of Pennsylvania, has reassessed the implications of violence in music video, saying, "Many videos express a sense of defiance and basic

[9]*solipsistic:* concerned with the self in an exaggerated or extreme way.

insensitivity, an unemotional excitement." The sensations evoked by video imagery are disconnected from the realm of social responsibility altogether.

. . . But music video's fulcrum position may best be revealed in the   21
way it has traveled beyond television, especially in its use by fashion designers. There, the construction of identity through fashion is at the center of the business. Since 1977, when Pierre Cardin began making video recordings of his fashion shows, designers have been incorporating video into their presentations. Videos now run continuously in retail store windows and on floor displays. For many designers, what sells records already sells fashion, and some foresee a fashion channel. The Cooperative Video Network, a television news service, already offers a half-hour program, *Video Fashion News*, with three-minute segments on current designer models. Some designers regard video as a primary mode of expression. Norma Kamali now shows her work only on video, both in stores and on programs. One of her best-known works is a video called "The Shoulder Pad Song." Another designer, Lloyd Allen, makes videos that sensually evoke his own fashion career. Designer Bill Tice demands that his contracts for personal appearances include showings of his fashion videos. Kamali, saying that her tapes allow her to approach customers "without interpretation," also thinks that video adds a dimension to her work, because it "extends my fantasy," which of course is the reality of her business.

The marketing crossover is becoming global, a kind of perpetual feedback   22
system. Michael Jackson has begun to sell fashion licenses for his look, and Christie Brinkley, a supermodel who starred in Billy Joel's "Uptown Girl," recently started her own fashion line. The videos undertaken at Perkins Productions are seen as prospective vehicles for extensive cross-promotion, in which a performer may use a prominently featured soap and a designer fragrance. The video may then circulate freely — in hotel lobbies, stores, and on airplane flights as well as on television programs. Video thrills are moving into all aspects of daily life. McDonald's has installed TV monitors at many cash registers, offering tempting images of food and giving shoppers the sense that fast food is part of a high-tech media world, a piece of the fashion action. "Video wallpaper" is being produced for bars and discos, with commercial products deliberately inserted into the montages in a style called by one producer "bordering on subliminal advertising."[10] In general, the boundary between commercial

[10] *subliminal advertising:* advertising that appeals directly to the unconscious through the suggestiveness of hidden or deliberately obscured words and images.

and noncommercial images is eroding. One Manhattan boutique asked General Electric for a copy of a music videoesque commercial to use in its floor display, "for atmosphere," not for any message but simply for its style.

As media image-making comes to dominate electoral politics, music 23 video has invaded that domain too. Consultants to both the Democratic and Republican parties have used music video to explore the mind-set of younger generations. "You can see the tensions among kids rising in their music," said pollster Patrick Caddell, "as they struggle to figure out what they will become." Or, he might have added, what they are. Republican strategist Lee Atwater decided, "We've got a bunch of very confused kids out there." That hasn't stopped politicians from using music videos as ads; videos were also enlisted (without marked results) in voter registration campaigns in 1984. The collision of music video with traditional political mobilizing brings one world — that of the consumer, concerned with individual choice — smack up against another — that of the citizen, charged with responsibility for public decisions. It is this collision that led fashion analyst Gerri Hirshey, noting the passionate investment of the young in their "look," to write: "If one's strongest commitment is to a pair of red stiletto heel pumps, style has a higher price tag than we'd imagine." In one sense, politics is fully ready for music video, if the success of Ronald Reagan — whose popularity rests on a pleasant media image to which "nothing sticks" while critics search in vain for a corresponding reality — is any guide.

The enormous popularity and rapid evolution of music videos give the 24 lie to conspiracy theorists who think commodity culture is force-fed into the gullets of unwilling spectators being fattened for the cultural kill. But it should also chasten free-market apologists who trust that whatever sells is willy-nilly an instrument of democracy. Music videos are powerful, if playful, postmodern art. Their raw materials are aspects of commercial popular culture; their structures those of dreams; their premise the constant permutation of identity in a world without social relationships. These are fascinating and disturbing elements of a form that becomes not only a way of seeing and of hearing but of being. Music videos invent the world they represent. And people whose "natural" universe is that of shopping malls are eager to participate in the process. Watching music videos may be diverting, but the process that music videos embody, echo, and encourage — the constant re-creation of an unstable self — is a full-time job.

Engaging the Text

1. Use Aufderheide's article to generate several claims about MTV. To give yourself room for notes, spread these claims out on two pages and watch a half hour or more of MTV, writing down specific observations that support or contradict Aufderheide's claims. Write a brief essay supporting, modifying, or attacking her view, using your observations as evidence.

2. Examine an hour or more of MTV for its portrayal of women. Write up your findings using specific examples. Are women "outsiders and agents of trouble"? Are they "prostitutes, nightclub performers, goddesses, temptresses, and servants"? Do you find STEREOTYPES of exotic women, or sadomasochistic suggestions?

3. Do you agree that music videos are a powerful force in shaping the identities of youth? Explain and defend your position.

Exploring Connections

1. Drawing on the selections by Schudson, Rosen, and Mander earlier in this chapter, discuss the contribution that advertising has made to the form and content of music videos. What, if anything, do current TV ads seem to borrow from music videos? Do ads on MTV differ from those on network TV?

2. Explain Aufderheide's argument that MTV helps create an "unstable" or changeable identity. To extend the discussion, analyze the speaker of Byrne's "Television Man" (p. 603) as an unstable self.

3. Compare Pat Aufderheide's views on the impact of television on community and social responsibility with those of Doerken (p. 581). Do you agree with their analyses?

Extending the Critical Context

1. Watch a half hour or more of network TV. Do you see any evidence of music video influence? Describe and explain it. Be sure to watch commercials as well as regular programming.

2. If you have attended rock concerts, write an Aufderheidean analysis of rock concert dynamics (audience, message, environment). Describe particular rock concerts only to provide supporting detail; concentrate on the general phenomenon.

Further Connections

The following questions ask you to draw upon selections throughout *Rereading America* to address complex, wide-ranging issues. Because they ask you to consider several readings at once, the questions call for longer, more involved responses than do the questions which appear after individual readings.

1. In Chapter One, "American Dreams," Charlie Sabatier says that "we are a nation of dissenters." Write an essay connecting Sabatier's ideas and experience to other readings in this anthology that address oppression and resistance. What similarities and differences can you discern in the histories and thoughts of various dissenters? Does your analysis support Sabatier's conclusion? To what extent do resistance and dissent enter into the American Dream, into American history, or into the popular images that you encounter in the media? Among the selections you may wish to consider for this assignment are those by:

Maya Angelou p. 312
Ralph Ellison p. 122
Matt Groening p. 441
Inés Hernández p. 247
Thomas Jefferson p. 3
Maxine Hong Kingston p. 241
Janice Mirikitani p. 188

Wendy Rose p. 166
Studs Terkel ("C. P. Ellis")
  p. 143
Kwame Toure p. 250
Luis M. Valdez p. 154
Ida B. Wells p. 168
Malcolm X p. 483

2. The excerpt from Gordon Allport's book which opens Chapter Two, "Justice for All," defines "out-groups" but does not investigate the consequences of being excluded or "marginalized." Drawing on four or five of the readings below, discuss the costs of membership in a marginalized group:

Ralph Ellison p. 122
Carol Gilligan p. 281
Richard Goldstein p. 413
Shirley Ann Grau p. 388
Bell Hooks p. 303
Howard and Hammond p. 504
Langston Hughes p. 17
Enrique "Hank" López p. 232
Gloria Naylor p. 330
Adrienne Rich p. 101

Richard Rodriguez p. 469
Jean Reith Schroedel ("Nora
  Quealey") p. 267
Sennett and Cobb p. 563
John Tateishi p. 175
Studs Terkel ("Mike LeFevre")
  p. 520
Anzia Yezierska p. 208
Rose Weitz p. 317

3.   Synthesizing information from David Elkind's selection on growing up too fast in American culture (Chapter Five, "The Changing Family"), Theodore Sizer's description of the modern American high school (Chapter Six, "Grading American Education"), Erich Fromm's theory of alienation and work (Chapter Seven, "Making a Living"), and Doerken's and Mander's analyses of the social effects of television (Chapter Eight, "Television and the Consumption of Images"), write an extended essay on fragmentation in American society.

4.   In a society that prizes freedom and individuality, citizens should presumably be comfortable "being themselves" — that is, acting, dressing, speaking, and behaving the way they choose. Yet it's quite clear that many speakers in this book, like many people we see in our daily lives, are consciously or unconsciously concerned with their outward appearance (for example, Henry Blanton wants to look like an authentic Western hero and Stephen Cruz becomes concerned that he is being paraded as a "visible man"). Drawing on several readings in the book and, if possible, on your own experience, write an essay exploring the relationship between personal identity and public image in American culture. Some of the authors who speak to this issue include:

Maya Angelou p. 312	David Elkind p. 360
Pat Aufderheide p. 639	Arlie Russell Hochschild p. 551
Robert Bellah et al. p. 44	Christopher Lasch p. 534
Ranice Henderson Crosby	Mark Crispin Miller p. 607
p. 519	Luis M. Valdez p. 154

5.   To what extent do race, gender, and class shape personal identity, and to what extent does each determine an individual's "life chances" — that is, his or her opportunities for education, success, power, or other goals? Which of these factors seems most important to you, and why? To answer these questions, write an extended essay based on your own experience, on previous reading, on your understanding of American culture in general, and on some of the readings listed here:

Maya Angelou p. 312	Jean Reith Schroedel ("Nora
Bell Hooks p. 303	Quealey") p. 267
Karen Lindsey p. 398	Studs Terkel ("Mike LeFevre")
Enrique "Hank" López p. 232	p. 520
Adrienne Rich p. 101	Studs Terkel ("Stephen Cruz") p.
Richard Rodriguez p. 469	77
Ryan and Sackrey ("Jane Ellen	Anzia Yezierska p. 208
Wilson") p. 569	

6. Several of the readings in this book propose a significantly different world view or argue in favor of a different social order. Pick three or four of the authors listed below and discuss what their ideas have in common. In addition, explain to what extent you share their views:

Paula Gunn Allen p. 273   Karen Lindsey p. 398
Marilyn French p. 290   Frances Maher p. 493
Carol Gilligan p. 281   Joseph L. White p. 379

Glossary

ABSTRACT: Not perceptible to the physical senses (for example, an idea or emotion). When writing is abstract, it relies more on generalizations than on specific examples or concrete facts. For example, the following sentence uses abstract wording: The Supreme Court's 1954 *Brown* decision rectified a grave injustice.

The following much more informative sentence uses concrete wording: The Supreme Court's 1954 *Brown* decision outlawed racially segregated schools.

Critical thinkers are wary of arguments that depend heavily on abstract language because it can conceal the writer's or speaker's specific intentions. For instance, all U.S. politicians would say that they favored "defending democracy," but their specific interpretations of this abstraction could lead to anything from supporting legal protection of political dissent to advocating military intervention in a foreign country. [See *concrete*.]

ALLUSION: A direct or indirect reference made in passing. For example, in "We, the Dangerous," Janice Mirikitani alludes to the internment of Japanese-Americans during World War II in the following lines: "And they commanded we dwell in the desert/Our children be spawn of barbed wire and barracks." Mirikitani uses a number of such allusions to evoke stereotypes of Asian-Americans and to recall the oppression that Asians and Asian-Americans have suffered throughout history. Experienced writers use allusions as a kind of shorthand, but heavily allusive writing can alienate readers who don't share the writer's knowledge and thus fail to understand the references.

AMBIVALENCE: Uncertainty caused by the desire to say or do two opposite things. For example, in "The Achievement of Desire" (p. 469), Richard Rodriguez describes the scholarship boy as "a child who cannot forget that his academic success distances himself from a life he loved, even from his own memory of himself." This boy is ambivalent toward school because he cannot succeed there without turning away from his family.

ANALOGY: A comparison between two things based on similar features. For example, in the excerpt from *The Hurried Child* (p. 360), David Elkind argues that "if we ignore the special needs of children, we are behaving just as if we denied Hispanic or Indian children bilingual programs, or denied the handicapped their ramps and guideposts." Writers use analogies to bolster an argument, enliven their prose, or clarify difficult concepts by comparing them to more familiar things. In the example above, Elkind advances his argument by comparing what he proposes for children to what he knows people accept for other groups.

However, when used as the primary basis of an argument, analogies can distort the issue or limit analysis. For example, when Jules Henry ("Golden Rule Days," p. 444) describes the teacher-student relationship in terms of an electronic communications system, like a telephone or radio, he may present only a limited view of what happens in the classroom. Perhaps not all teacher-student relationships are as mechanical and manipulative as Henry's analogy suggests. Similarly, there might be more accurate analogies for the classroom.

ANGLO-AMERICAN: Technically, an American of English descent or something characteristic of English and American culture; used more generally to refer to any English-speaking U.S. citizen of northern European ancestry or to something characteristic of the dominant culture in the United States. *Example:* Poet Wendy Rose often writes about the conflict between Anglo-American and Native American values.

ASSIMILATION: The process of adjusting to life in a different culture, which typically involves adapting to new customs, learning a new language or dialect, learning new values, and suppressing some attitudes and behavior associated with one's original culture. *Example:* Assimilation is generally more difficult for refugees who were driven from their native country than it is for those who emigrate voluntarily.

CHARACTER: Any fictional or historical person represented in a story, novel, play, or film. *Example:* López points out that the character of Pancho Villa in the film *Viva Villa!* is a grossly distorted portrait — not at all like the real man.

Because characters are the products of a writer's imagination, they may serve any number of functions: some may appear to behave like real people, but others may defy the laws of nature (and live for five hundred years, for example); they may also represent some abstract idea like truth, or be used to prove a point the writer wants to make. Even characters based on historical figures may or may not bear much resemblance to the original, as the Villa example suggests.

CHARACTERISTIC: Distinctive; a distinguishing feature or quality. For example, Joseph L. White claims that the close-knit extended family is characteristic of black American life. Or: The close-knit extended family is an important characteristic of black American life.

CONCRETE: Perceptible to the senses, tangible. Concrete writing refers to what's real, solid, and particular. For example, in "Split at the Root (p. 101), Adrienne Rich writes: "But this begins, for me, in Baltimore, where I was born in my father's workplace, a hospital in the Black ghetto, whose lobby contained an immense white marble statue of Christ."

Abstractions can conceal specific realities. Concrete facts can be deceptive in a different way, leading readers to forget to examine underlying causes and assumptions. For example, popular writers produce book-length analyses, full of concrete examples and details concerning how to "get the winning edge," but they seldom (if ever) question the value or cost of competition. Critical thinkers look at facts, but also look *beyond* them, asking not only "What?" but "Why?" and "Is there another way of seeing this?" [See *abstract*.]

CONFORMIST: A person who adopts, usually without question, the customs, behavior, and appearance of the majority. *Example:* The conformist's goal is not to stand out but to blend in with the crowd.

CONNOTATION: The implicit or understood meaning of a word or phrase (as opposed to its explicit definition, or denotation). *Example:* In practical terms, "home" simply refers to where you live, but it also has connotations of warmth, comfort, love, and privacy.

Synonyms — words with the same denotation (explicit meaning) — can have very different connotations. Consider the attitudes and assumptions implied by these synonyms: "females," "women," "ladies," and "babes"; "friendly nation," "ally," and "satellite"; "leader," "president," "strongman," and "head of state"; "revolutionary," "terrorist," and "freedom fighter." Because of sometimes subtle differences in connotation, even writing that appears objective can actually convey opinion. [See *denotation*.]

CONSUMERISM: The endless buying or consumption of products, motivated not by need but by a desire for novelty or status. *Example:* One sign of our society's consumerism is that, whether we're shopping for soap or stereos, we encounter a dizzying variety of brands and styles.

CRITIQUE: A critical evaluation of a work, subject, or idea; the practice of making such an evaluation. *Examples:* Boggs offers a critique of theories that explain racism as a matter of individual psychology. Or: Boggs critiques all theories of racism that are based on individual psychology.

DENOTATION: The explicit meaning or definition of a word. [See *connotation*.]

DICTION: The style of speaking or writing that comes from word choice; diction determines how formal or informal the prose sounds. *Examples:* My history prof's really tough — she's been calling on us a lot this week. [informal diction]. My history professor is extremely rigorous — recently she has demanded constant attention and participation in class. [formal diction.]

Generally, informal diction makes a writer sound more conversational and relaxed, while formal diction makes her sound more reserved and scholarly. An experienced writer can use either style (or even mix them) effectively; in making this choice she thinks carefully about the image she wants to project and the effect that image is likely to have on her readers.

DISCOURSE: Communication through speech or writing. *Example:* Many groups adopt a distinctive style of discourse that distinguishes members from nonmembers.

"Level of discourse" refers to the relative difficulty or formality of a writer's style; "discourse community" refers to a group of people who share a particular vocabulary or style of expression (like gang members, computer programmers, or weightlifters).

EPIGRAPH: A quotation at the beginning of a book, essay, or chapter; writers may use epigraphs to capture the reader's interest, set up their own argument, preview an important point to be discussed, set the tone of the work, or appropriate some of the glamour and credibility of a better-known writer. For example, Wendy Rose turns this telling entry from a museum's records into the epigraph that introduces her poem, "Three Thousand Dollar Death Song" (p. 166): "Nineteen American Indian Skeletons from Nevada . . . valued at $3,000. . . . — MUSEUM INVOICE, 1975."

ETHNIC: Belonging to or characteristic of a particular cultural tradition. *Example:*

The ethnic makeup of the United States is constantly changing as immigrants arrive from different parts of the world.

ETHNICITY: Affiliation with a particular ethnic group. *Example:* Since the 1960s, many Americans, including Afro-Americans, Italians, and Puerto Ricans, have asserted pride in their ethnicity, learning or relearning the history and customs of their ancestors.

EXPLOITATION: The use and abuse of people, natural resources, or cherished values for personal or financial profit. *Example:* Advertisements often rely on the sexual exploitation of women to sell products: The most obvious of these ads feature scantily clad models, suggestive language, or close-ups of female lips, legs, and breasts.

FEMINISM: The assertion of any or all of the following principles: (1) the social and political equality of women; (2) the absolute worth of women, and the qualities and values associated with them; (3) the need to reshape culture around such "feminine" values as cooperation, nurturance, and nonviolence. Also, the social and political movement that advocates these principles.

FIGURATIVE LANGUAGE: Language characterized by figures of speech, such as metaphors. *Example:* In "Dear John Wayne" (p. 41), Louise Erdrich's figurative language dramatizes the contrast between Hollywood's view of Indians and the Native Americans' own perspective. [See *analogy, metaphor, simile*.]

HERITAGE: Something that is transmitted or acquired from an ancestor or predecessor. Heritage usually refers to the cultural traditions, values, and customs that are passed down from generation to generation. It's important to remember that there are many different cultural heritages in a pluralistic society like the United States. Although we share a common political heritage — a democratic government based on respect for individual rights — our cultural heritages differ according to race, region, religion, economic background, and other factors.

HYPOTHESIZE: To offer a tentative explanation of a particular phenomenon. A scientific researcher, for example, forms a hypothesis to explain a natural event she has observed, and then designs and conducts an experiment to test this hypothesis. To hypothesize, then, means to draw on all of one's prior knowledge, experience, and common sense to offer the best possible "educated guess" about the outcome or cause of a particular event or situation.

HIERARCHY: An arrangement of objects, values, or people into a ranking according to some variable like size, wealth, or power. For example, within the hierarchy of political power in the United States, the president occupies a higher position than a state senator or an environmental activist. When you think about social or political hierarchies, it's important to keep in mind the historical and ideological forces that underlie them and make them possible.

IDEOLOGY: In the formal sense, a systematic body of ideas about life, politics, and culture. Used in this traditional way, ideology is almost identifiable with philosophy — a self-conscious and rational account of one's ideas and beliefs about the world. The word is also typically used to denote the total of one's beliefs, ideas, and values — unconscious as well as conscious. In this sense, when we refer to the ideology of a historical era — or of an entire nation —

we mean the ideas, values, and beliefs that appear to dominate the events associated with it. The term is often also used to disparage the ideas and views of a political or philosophical opponent. In this sense, the word carries the implication of false or extreme ideas.

IMAGE: Impression, representation, or picture. In literary studies, this word is used to refer to both the sensory experiences produced in the mind by the verbal description of perceptual events (appearances, sounds, smells, physical sensations, .etc.) and to the verbal descriptions that themselves produce these mental impressions. *Example:* "And they would have us strange scented women,/Round shouldered/strong and yellow/like the moon/to pull the thread to the cloth/to loosen their backs massaged in myth." This excerpt from Mirikitani's poem "We, the Dangerous" (p. 188) contains images that help readers see and feel what the speaker of the poem experiences: the simultaneous feelings of isolation and strength, of rejection and power. Writers use such images to lend immediacy and vividness to their descriptions. Images may be classified by the type of sensory experience they evoke; thus, we can talk about images of sight, sound, smell, touch, and taste.

INEQUITIES: Instances of injustice or unfairness. For example, lower pay for equivalent work is one of the inequities women suffer in a sexist society. In the United States, the fundamental idea of equality and fairness on which the notion of "inequity" depends has its roots in *The Declaration of Independence*. It is common to speak of inequities in relation to any social group that has suffered because of its powerlessness or minority status.

INTEGRATION: As used in this anthology, the goal of extending equal civil rights and equal access to resources and goods to all members of society. Since the 1960s, integration has been the primary goal of governmental policies and programs to remedy past racial discrimination in the United States. As a tool of public policy, it has been faulted by conservative critics because, they say, laws aimed at integration attempt to "legislate behavior." Some liberal critics of integration feel that, as a goal, it encourages minority group members to conform to the standards and values of the dominant Anglo-American culture; therefore, it suggests that the dominant culture is itself in need of no change or improvement.

IRONY: In literature, the use of language or situations in order to indicate an attitude or intention opposite to that which is stated. Irony generally implies a critical or mocking attitude toward the actions, characters, or ideas presented in a text. Unlike outright sarcasm, however, irony is always indirect and implied; irony thus relies on subtle interpretive reading and sensitivity to tone and appropriateness. It has played an important role in the work of minority group writers because it offers a powerful yet indirect means of self-expression and social critique. In Ralph Ellison's *Invisible Man*, for instance, the narrator, a young black man, is publicly abused and humiliated, and then delivers a speech on "equality" and "social responsibility." Ironically, he fails to understand the absurdity of preaching about social responsibility to racists.

LEGACY: Anything handed down from an ancestor or a predecessor [See *heritage*.]

MAINSTREAM: As used in this anthology, mainstream refers to the group that politically and culturally dominates life in the United States — the white, Anglo-

Saxon Protestant middle and upper classes. *Example:* College administrators often worry today about how best to integrate minority students into the mainstream student population.

The notion of a "mainstream" is obviously open to challenge. It implies numerical superiority — the sheer mass of the "main" stream compared to which all other groups are merely adjuncts. Yet, in many areas of the United States today, populations identified as typically mainstream are in the minority. The term also implies that the culture of the politically dominant group is more central than — or preferable to — nonmainstream cultures.

MANIFESTO: A public declaration of intentions, opinions, goals, and motives. *The Declaration of Independence* was a political manifesto intended to publicize the colonies' reasons for revolting against British rule.

MARGINAL: As used in this book, marginal refers to those people, usually minority group members, who do not belong to society's politically and culturally dominant groups. Such groups are thought of as marginal because they exist on the margins, or fringes, of society — they generally do not have easy access to political influence, economic power, and cultural resources. *Example:* Members of minority groups often feel as if they are marginal people in a society still influenced by racism, sexism, and other forms of prejudice.

For many social theorists, the concept of marginality implies the active oppression of minority groups by those in positions of power; marginal groups do not occupy positions on the fringes of society by chance, but because they have been historically excluded by socially dominant groups.

METAPHOR: In literature, a figure of speech in which two apparently unlike things are equated. Metaphors work through direct suggestion of resemblance. A metaphor differs from a simile in that it suggests, or implies, an equation of generally dissimilar objects or people while a simile relies on comparative expressions like "as" and "like" to make an explicit connection between things. *Example of a metaphor:* "A riot is the language of the unheard." (Martin Luther King, Jr.) *Example of a simile:* "as for me/my uniform feels like skin." (Ranice Henderson Crosby)

MOTIVATION: In literary studies, the psychological factors that underlie and explain a character's actions. A character's motivation for a given action generally includes unconscious or unacknowledged motives as well as conscious reasons and desires.

MYTH: A story that depicts, in a richly symbolic or imaginative way, the basic values and structures of a particular culture or civilization. Myths often address themes like the creation of life, the founding of civilization, the birth and rebirth of a god or of nature. They also frequently employ bizarre or fantastic events and characters. Unlike legends and sagas, myths cannot be easily traced to remembered historical events. In this text, when we speak of our common cultural myths we mean those familiar stories — like the innumerable tales of rags-to-riches success that accompany the American dream — that embody the ideals and values we have come to identify with our national character.

MYTHOLOGY: A coherent system or body of individual myths that express the fundamental values and meanings central to a particular civilization. The myth of "Leda and the Swan," for example, is part of a collection of stories that we identify as Greek mythology. The readings in Chapter One, "American Dreams," reveal that our national mythology is based on such values as freedom, individualism, and success.

NARRATIVE: An account in prose or verse of actual or fictional events — a story. While the term narrative is generally applied only to fictional works of literature, it may also be used to describe historical or journalistic works depicting factual events.

NARRATOR: The speaker of a narrative. The narrator of a fictional work should be carefully distinguished from the author, since the narrator can be considered another fictional character whose point of view and personal values may influence — or may perhaps even be the focus of — the story he or she relates.

ORAL HISTORY: A collection of tape-recorded first-hand accounts focusing on a particular aspect of contemporary life or on a particular historical event. Oral histories are often transcribed, edited, and published in anthologies. For examples, see the selections by Studs Terkel (pp. 77, 143, 520) and Ryan and Sackrey (p. 569).

PARADOX: A statement, situation, or idea that seems to contradict itself but may actually contain a truth. For example, consider the saying: "The more things change, the more they stay the same." "Paradox" is also used informally to describe ideas which seem obvious or true from one point of view but false from another. For example, there is a notion that the more terrible the threat of nuclear war, the safer the world becomes.

PARAPHRASE: A rewording of a text or statement, usually to achieve greater clarity or brevity. ("Paraphrase" can also be used as a verb.) Note that paraphrasing — at least in college — does not mean simply changing a few key words in a passage taken from a book. A paraphrase should be a fresh, clear restating of something heard or read.

PERSPECTIVE: As used most often in this anthology, one's point of view — that is, one's mental view of facts or ideas and their relationships. (This meaning of the word is derived from its use to describe a viewer's perception of depth and relationships in a picture.) *Example:* From the perspective of an Iroquois Indian, European settlement of America was a serious threat, while from the perspective of the Europeans it seemed an exciting advancement of civilization.

PLURALISM (*adj.* PLURALISTIC): A social and political stance that welcomes variety in the makeup of society. A pluralistic attitude accepts and indeed celebrates a mix of traditions, languages, beliefs, and values. Americans have argued constantly about how much diversity is acceptable: some see too much variety as a threat to the unity of the nation, while others believe that variety renews and strengthens democracy.

POINT OF VIEW: In most speech and writing, "point of view" is interchangeable with "perspective" as defined just above. In the discussion of literature, point of view refers to how and from what vantage point a story is told. For example, does the narrator of the story use "I" and place herself in the action, as Anzia Yezierska does in *America and I* (p. 208)? This is called first-person narration. Or does the narrator stand above the characters and reveal their thoughts, as in the first part of Gloria Naylor's story, "The Two" (p. 330)? This is omniscient third-person narration.

PROSE: Any speech or writing that is not poetry (or "verse"). That is, prose does not rhyme, and it is not arranged into controlled rhythmical units. Novels, stories, newspaper articles, speeches, letters, and ads are all examples of prose.

PROSE POEM: A prose passage that takes on some of the qualities of poetry, such as artful repetition, rhythmic constructions, richly figurative language, or compact expression of ideas.

RATIONALE: A system of reasons or fundamental principles. A rationale may be convincing or unconvincing, depending on whether or not one shares the principles and beliefs in question. *Example:* The rationale behind the death penalty is the belief that capital punishment will deter people from committing serious crimes.

REFRAIN: Lines of a song or poem repeated at the end of each verse. For example, David Byrne's "Television Man" (p. 603) repeats: *When the world crashes in, into my living room/Television made me what I am/People like to put the television down/But we are just good friends/(I'm a) television man.*

SEPARATISM: The political (or sometimes religious) position that a particular group must maintain its identity by consciously resisting integration into mainstream culture. Black leaders in particular have at various times in U.S. history called for an independent, self-supporting black community or even for a "back-to-Africa" movement. For an extended example of a separatist argument, see the essay by Kwame Toure in Chapter Three, "One Nation or Many?"

SETTING: The time and place of a novel, story, poem, or play. Luis M. Valdez's play, *Los Vendidos* (p. 154), for example, is set in California in 1969. Note that the setting, and especially an author's description of it, can have a symbolic meaning: consider the dark, gloomy, isolated motel in the film *Psycho*.

SIMILE: A comparison of two otherwise unlike things indicated by the words "like" or "as." For example, in Erdrich's "Dear John Wayne" (p. 41), Wayne's face is "pitted/like the land that was once flesh." [See *metaphor*.]

SOCIAL STATUS: One's standing in society, based on such factors as wealth, influence, education, and occupation. A wealthy politician with a law degree and a famous family would enjoy extremely high social status. It is important to consider whether gender and ethnicity also affect social status; do female surgeons or black executives command the same respect as their white male colleagues?

SOCIOECONOMIC: "Pertaining to a combination of social and economic factors." Child care is a socioeconomic issue, because it involves not only economic policy but also social concerns, such as the education of children and the role of women in society.

SPEAKER: Used most often in discussions of poetry, this term refers to the narrator or "voice" of the poem. Like the word "narrator," this term is useful because it lets readers distinguish between the author or poet — a living, breathing person — and the character the author has created in a given story or poem.

STANZA: A group of lines or verses in a poem, separated by a space on the page. Stanzas may be of any length; in some poems each stanza is identically structured — that is, the number of lines and the pattern of rhyme are the same.

STEREOTYPE: A standardized, preconceived view of something or someone that fails to acknowledge individual differences. In this book, the term refers most often to stereotypes of ethnic groups — prejudged or prejudiced expectations that Asian students will be good in math, that Latinos are hot-tempered, and so on. Many groups battle stereotypes, including women, gays, and the elderly.

STIGMATIZE: Derived from the Greek word for "tattoo," this word means to mark with disgrace (symbolically, not physically). For example, U.S. society has generally stigmatized illegitimate children, divorced parents, citizens on welfare, and unwed mothers. The term often implies that someone has been disgraced unfairly due to social prejudices.

STYLE: A distinctive or characteristic way of doing something — usually, in this book, *writing* in a particular manner. An author's style reflects her characteristic choices in many areas, including the type of words used, the length and complexity of sentences, and the rhythms developed in her prose or poetry.

SYMBOL: A word, phrase, or object that represents or stands for something else. We all recognize numerous symbols in ordinary life: a badge is a symbol of authority; a handshake symbolizes friendliness. In literature, an author may develop symbols that have special meaning within the particular story being told. For example, in Rose's "Three Thousand Dollar Death Song" (p. 166), the American Indian bones symbolize all that whites have taken from Native Americans and have tried to put a price on.

THEME: The subject of a composition or, in the discussion of literature, an important, recurring idea. For example, the theme of *The Declaration of Independence* (p. 3) is stated clearly in the first line: "We hold these truths to be self-evident, that all men are created equal. . . ."

THESIS: The central focus of a composition; in argumentative writing, the thesis is the point the author is trying to prove. For example, Frederick Jackson Turner's thesis in our opening chapter (p. 20) is that American life and culture were shaped in crucial ways by conditions on the American frontier.

TONE: The attitude or emotional stance expressed by an author. The tone of an essay or story could be angry, bitter, amused, gently critical, or smug. Tone results from a complex interplay of the subject matter or topic, the ideas expressed, and especially the author's choice of words.

TREATISE: A formal and systematic essay on a single subject, especially one that addresses basic principles. For example, Darwin's *Origin of Species* is a treatise on evolution.

UTOPIAN: Describing a perfect society. Sir Thomas More coined the word — which mixes Greek words for "good place" and "no place" — for his *Utopia* (1516), a description of an island with an ideal social and political system. The word is often used critically to ridicule the ideas of dreamers who ignore practical problems.

VALIDATE: To give approval, respect, or credit to. A teacher can validate a student's opinions by truly listening to them and responding thoughtfully and honestly.

VOICE: In informal usage, the distinctive style of an author or a particular piece of writing.

Acknowledgments (continued from p. iv)

Gordon W. Allport, "Formation of In-Groups." From *The Nature of Prejudice*, by Gordon W. Allport. Copyright © 1954 by Addison-Wesley. Reprinted by permission of Addison-Wesley Publishing Co.

Maya Angelou, from *I Know Why the Caged Bird Sings*, by Maya Angelou. Copyright © 1969 by Maya Angelou. Reprinted by permission of Random House, Inc.

Pat Aufderheide, "The Look of the Sound." From *Watching Television*, edited by Todd Gitlin. Copyright © 1986 by Pat Aufderheide. Reprinted by permission of Pantheon Books, a division of Random House, Inc.

Martha Bayles, "The Problem with Post-Racism." Copyright © 1985 by the author. Reprinted by permission of Martha Bayles.

Robert Bellah, et al., "The Paradox of Individualism." From *Habits of the Heart: Individualism and Commitment in American Life*. Copyright © 1985 by the Regents of the University of California. Reprinted by permission of University of California Press.

James Boggs, "Uprooting Racism and Racists in the United States." From *Racism and the Class Struggle: Further Pages from a Black Worker's Notebook*, by James Boggs. Copyright © 1970 by James Boggs. Reprinted by permission of the Monthly Foundation.

Joseph Bruchac, "Ellis Island." Copyright © 1978 by Joseph Bruchac. First appeared in *Entering Onondaga*, Cold Mountain Press. Reprinted by permission of the author.

David Byrne, "Television Man." © 1985 Index Music Inc. and Bleu Disque Music Co. Inc. Administered by WB Music Corp. All rights reserved. Used by permission.

Janet Saltzman Chafetz, "Some Individual Costs of Gender Role Conformity." From *Masculine, Feminine, or Human? An Overview of the Sociology of Gender Roles*, pp. 47–55. Copyright © 1974 by F. E. Peacock, Publishers. Reproduced by permission of the publisher, F. E. Peacock Publishers, Itasca, Ill.

Alistair Cooke, "The Huddled Masses." From *Alistair Cooke's America*, by Alistair Cooke. Copyright © 1973 by Alistair Cooke. Reprinted by permission of Alfred A. Knopf, Inc.

Lorenza Calvillo Craig, "Men." From *Hispanics in the United States*, edited by Gary D. Keller and Francisco Jimenez. Copyright © 1980 by Bilingual Press, Arizona State University, Tempe, Ariz. Reprinted by permission of Bilingual Press.

Ranice Henderson Crosby, "Waitresses," a poem by Ranice Henderson Crosby. Copyright © 1975 by Ranice Henderson Crosby. Reprinted by permission of Ranice Henderson Crosby.

Jim Daniels, "Short-order Cook." From *Places/Everyone*, by Jim Daniels. Copyright © 1985 by the Board of Regents of University of Wisconsin System. Reprinted by permission of the University of Wisconsin Press.

Maurine Doerkin, "What's Left After Violence and Advertising?" From *Classroom Combat: Teaching and Television*. Copyright © 1983 by Educational Technology Publications. Reprinted by permission of Educational Technology Publications.

David Elkind, from *The Hurried Child*. © 1981, Addison-Wesley Publishing Co., Inc., Reading, Massachusetts. Pp. 3–4, 6–15, and 17–22. Reprinted with permission.

Ralph Ellison, from *Invisible Man*. Copyright © 1947, 1948, 1952 by Ralph Ellison. Reprinted by permission of Random House, Inc.

Louise Erdrich, "Dear John Wayne." From *Jacklight: Poems*, by Louise Erdrich. Copyright © 1984 by Louise Erdrich. Reprinted by permission of Henry Holt and Co., Inc.

Marilyn French, "The Ideal of Equality." From *Beyond Power*. Copyright © 1985 by Belles-Lettres, Inc. Reprinted by permission of Summit Books, a division of Simon & Schuster, Inc.

Erich Fromm, "Work in an Alienated Society." From *The Sane Society* by Erich Fromm. Copyright © 1955 and renewed 1983 by Erich Fromm. Reprinted by permission of Henry Holt and Co., Inc.

Carol Gilligan, "Images of Relationships." From *In a Different Voice: Psychological Theory and Women's Development*, by Carol Gilligan. Copyright © 1982 by Carol Gilligan. Reprinted by permission of Harvard University Press, Cambridge, Mass.

Laurence Goldstein, "Homesick in Los Angeles." From *The Tree Gardens*, Copper Beech Press, Providence, R.I., 1987. Reprinted by permission of the author.

Richard Goldstein, "The Gay Family." Copyright © 1986 by Richard Goldstein. First appeared in *The Village Voice*, July 1, 1986. Reprinted by permission of the author.

Milton M. Gordon, "Assimilation in America." Copyright © 1961 by *Daedalus*. Reprinted by permission of *Daedalus*, Journal of the American Academy of Arts and Sciences, Ethnic Groups in American Life, vol. 90, no. 2, Spring 1961, Cambridge, Mass.

Shirley Ann Grau, "The Beginning." From *Nine Women*, by Shirley Ann Grau. Copyright © 1985 by Shirley Ann Grau. Reprinted by permission of Alfred A. Knopf, Inc.

John Langston Gwaltney, "Charlie Sabatier." From *The Dissenters: Voices From Contemporary America*, by John Gwaltney. Copyright © 1986 by John Langston Gwaltney. Reprinted by permission of Random House, Inc.

Douglas Harper, "Willie." From *Working Knowledge*, by Douglas Harper. Copyright © 1987 by the University of Chicago Press. Reprinted by permission of the University of Chicago Press.

Jules Henry, "Golden Rule Days: American Schoolrooms." From *Culture Against Man* by Jules Henry. Copyright © 1963 by Random House, Inc. Reprinted by permission of Random House, Inc.

Inés Hernández, "Para Teresa." From *Con Razon, Corazón: Poetry*. Copyright © 1987 by Inés Hernández. Reprinted by permission of the author.

Adam Hochschild, from *Half the Way Home: A Memoir of Father and Son*, by

Adam Hochschild. Copyright © 1986 by Adam Hochschild. Reprinted by permission of Viking Penguin, Inc.

Arlie Russell Hochschild, "Gender, Status, and Feeling." From *The Managed Heart: The Commercialization of Human Feelings* by Arlie Russell Hochschild. Copyright © 1983 by the Regents of the University of California. Reprinted by permission of the University of California Press.

Bell Hooks, "Racism and Feminism." From *Ain't I a Woman? Black Women and Feminism*, by Bell Hooks. Copyright © 1981 by Bell Hooks. Reprinted by permission of the author and of the publisher, South End Press, 116 St. Botolph St., Boston, Mass. 02115.

Jeff Howard and Ray Hammond, "Rumors of Inferiority." © 1985 The New Republic, Inc. Reprinted by permission of *The New Republic*.

Langston Hughes, "Let America Be America Again." From *International Workers Order*. Copyright © 1938, 1965 by Langston Hughes. Reprinted by permission of Harold Ober Associates, Inc.

Maxine Hong Kingston, from *The Woman Warrior: Memoirs of A Girlhood Among Ghosts*, by Maxine Hong Kingston. Copyright © 1975, 1976 by Maxine Hong Kingston. Reprinted by permission of Alfred A. Knopf, Inc.

Jane Kramer, from *The Last Cowboy*, by Jane Kramer. Reprinted by permission of Georges Borchardt Inc. for the author. Copyright © 1977 by Jane Kramer.

Christopher Lasch, "The Original Meaning of the Work Ethic." From *The Culture of Narcissism: American Life in an Age of Diminishing Expectations*, by Christopher Lasch. Copyright © 1979 by W. W. Norton & Company. Reprinted by permission of W. W. Norton & Company, Inc.

Karen Lindsey, from *Friends as Family*. Copyright © 1981 by Karen Lindsey. Reprinted by permission of Beacon Press.

Peter Loewenberg, "The Psychology of Racism." From *The Great Fear: Race in the Mind of America*, edited by Gary B. Nash and Richard Weiss. Copyright © 1970 Gary B. Nash and Richard Weiss. Reprinted by permission of Holt, Rinehart and Winston, Inc.

Enrique "Hank" López, "Back to Bachimba." Used by permission from *Horizon* Magazine, Vol. IX, no. 1. Copyright © 1967 by American Heritage Publishing Co. a division of Forbes, Inc.

Frances Maher, "Women Students in the Classroom." From "Classroom Pedagogy and the New Scholarship on Women," in *Gendered Subjects*, edited by Margo Culley and Catherine Portuges. Copyright © 1985 by Routledge & Kegan Paul. Reprinted by permission of Routledge & Kegan Paul.

Jerry Mander, "Artificial Unusualness." From *Four Arguments for the Elimination of Television*, by Jerry Mander. Copyright © 1978 by Jerry Mander. Reprinted by permission of Jerry Mander.

Mark Crispin Miller, "The Cosby Show." From *Watching Television*, edited by Todd Gitlin. Copyright © 1986 by Mark Crispin Miller. Reprinted by permission of Random House, Inc.

Janice Mirikitani, "We, the Dangerous." Reprinted from *Awake in the River, Poetry and Prose*, by Janice Mirikitani, Isthmus Press, 1978, San Francisco, Calif. Copyright © 1978 by Janice Mirikitani.

Index of Authors and Titles

To the Student

We regularly revise the books we publish in order to make them better. To do this well we need to know what instructors and students think of the previous edition. At some point your instructor will be asked to comment on *Rereading America*; now we would like to hear from you.

Please take a few minutes to rate the selections and complete this questionnaire. Send it to Bedford Books of St. Martin's Press, 29 Winchester Street, Boston, Massachusetts 02116. We promise to listen to what you have to say. Thanks.

School _____

School location (city, state) _____

Course title _____

Instructor's name _____

Please rate the selections.

	Liked a lot	Okay	Didn't like	Didn't read
1. American Dreams				
Jefferson, *The Declaration of Independence*	____	____	____	____
Crèvecoeur, *What Is an American?*	____	____	____	____
Hughes, *Let America Be America Again*	____	____	____	____
Turner, *The Significance of the Frontier*	____	____	____	____
Kramer, *Cowboy*	____	____	____	____
Erdrich, *Dear John Wayne*	____	____	____	____
Bellah et al, *The Paradox of Individualism*	____	____	____	____
Gwaltney, *Charlie Sabatier*	____	____	____	____
Carnegie, *The Gospel of Wealth*	____	____	____	____
Terkel, *Stephen Cruz*	____	____	____	____
2. Justice for All				
Allport, *Formation of In-Groups*	____	____	____	____
Rich, *Split at the Root*	____	____	____	____
Loewenberg, *The Psychology of Racism*	____	____	____	____
Ellison, From *Invisible Man*	____	____	____	____
Boggs, *Uprooting Racism and Racists in the United States*	____	____	____	____

	Liked a lot	Okay	Didn't like	Didn't read
Terkel, *C.P. Ellis*	——	——	——	——
Valdez, *Los Vendidos*	——	——	——	——
Rose, *Three Thousand Dollar Death Song*	——	——	——	——
Wells, *Lynching at the Curve*	——	——	——	——
Tateishi, *Mary Tsukamoto*	——	——	——	——
Mirikitani, *We, the Dangerous*	——	——	——	——

3. One Nation or Many?

Cooke, *The Huddled Masses*	——	——	——	——
Yezierska, *America and I*	——	——	——	——
Bruchac, *Ellis Island*	——	——	——	——
Piñero, *Puerto Rico's Reply*	——	——	——	——
Gordon, *Assimilation in America*	——	——	——	——
Tran, *Letter to My Mother*	——	——	——	——
López, *Back to Bachimba*	——	——	——	——
Kingston, From *The Woman Warrior*	——	——	——	——
Hernández, *Para Teresa*	——	——	——	——
Toure, *What We Want*	——	——	——	——

4. Women: The Emerging Majority

Chafetz, *Some Individual Costs of Gender Role Conformity*	——	——	——	——
Schroedel, *Nora Quealey*	——	——	——	——
Allen, *Where I Come from Is Like This*	——	——	——	——
Gilligan, *Images of Relationships*	——	——	——	——
Craig, *Men*	——	——	——	——
French, *The Ideal of Equality*	——	——	——	——
Hooks, *Racism and Feminism*	——	——	——	——
Angelou, From *I Know Why the Caged Bird Sings*	——	——	——	——
Weitz, *What Price Independence?*	——	——	——	——
Naylor, *The Two*	——	——	——	——

5. The Changing Family

Tocqueville, *Influence of Democracy on the Family*	——	——	——	——
Skolnick, *The Paradox of Perfection*	——	——	——	——
Hochschild, From *Half the Way Home*	——	——	——	——
Elkind, From *The Hurried Child*	——	——	——	——

	Liked a lot	Okay	Didn't like	Didn't read
Moore, *The Kid's Guide to Divorce*	——	——	——	——
White, *Black Family Life*	——	——	——	——
Grau, *The Beginning*	——	——	——	——
Lindsey, *Friends as Family*	——	——	——	——
Goldstein, *The Gay Family*	——	——	——	——

6. Grading American Education

Sizer, *What High School Is*	——	——	——	——
Groening, *Life in School*	——	——	——	——
Henry, *Golden Rule Days*	——	——	——	——
Oakes, *Keeping Track*	——	——	——	——
Rodriguez, *The Achievement of Desire*	——	——	——	——
Malcolm X, *Learning to Read*	——	——	——	——
Maher, *Women Students in the Classroom*	——	——	——	——
Howard and Hammond, *Rumors of Inferiority*	——	——	——	——

7. Making a Living

Daniels, *Short-order Cook*	——	——	——	——
Crosby, *Waitresses*	——	——	——	——
Terkel, *Mike LeFevre*	——	——	——	——
Fromm, *Work in an Alienated Society*	——	——	——	——
Lasch, *The Original Meaning of the Work Ethic*	——	——	——	——
Harper, *Willie*	——	——	——	——
Hochschild, *Gender, Status, and Feeling*	——	——	——	——
Sennett and Cobb, From *The Hidden Injuries of Class*	——	——	——	——
Ryan and Sackrey, *Jane Ellen Wilson*	——	——	——	——

8. Television and the Consumption of Images

Doerken, *What's Left After Violence and Advertising?*	——	——	——	——
Mander, *Artificial Unusualness*	——	——	——	——
Byrne, *Television Man*	——	——	——	——
Goldstein, *Homesick in Los Angeles*	——	——	——	——
Miller, *The Cosby Show*	——	——	——	——
Bayles, *The Problem with Post-Racism*	——	——	——	——
Schudson, *Advertising as Art*	——	——	——	——

	Liked a lot	Okay	Didn't like	Didn't read
Rosen, *The Presence of the Word in TV Advertising*	——	——	——	——
Aufderheide, *The Look of the Sound*	——	——	——	——

Any general comments or suggestions? _____

_____

_____

_____

_____

_____

_____

_____

_____

Name _____

Mailing Address _____

_____

Date _____